This modern text is designed to prepare you for your future professional career. While theories, ideas, techniques, and data are dynamic, the information contained in this volume will provide you a quick and useful reference as well as a guide for future learning for many years to come. Your familiarity with the contents of this book will make it an important volume in your professional library.

EX LIBRIS

MANAGERIAL ACCOUNTING
Concepts for Planning, Control, Decision Making

Managerial Accounting

Concepts for Planning, Control, Decision Making

RAY H. GARRISON, D.B.A., CPA

School of Accountancy
Brigham Young University

Fourth Edition • 1985

BUSINESS PUBLICATIONS, INC. Plano, Texas 75075

To
Mildred Olsen Norman
Vernal Obray Norman

For their lives of service and example

Material from Uniform CPA Examination Questions
and Unofficial Answers, copyright © 1968
through 1977 by the American Institute of
Certified Public Accountants, Inc., is
reprinted (or adapted) with permission.

Material from the Certificate in Management Accounting
Examinations, copyright © 1972 through 1981 by the
National Association of Accountants, is reprinted
(or adapted) with permission.

Material from the SMA Examination, copyright
© 1974 by the Society of Management Accountants
of Canada, is reprinted (or adapted) with
permission.

ISBN 0-256-03261-0

Library of Congress Catalog Card No. 84–71560

Printed in the United States of America

1 2 3 4 5 6 7 8 9 0 K 2 1 0 9 8 7 6 5

This textbook is accompanied by a Student Workbook/Study Guide,
published by Business Publications, Inc. and available through
your college bookstore. The Study Guide is designed to enhance
your learning experience in this course by offering additional
supplementary material and review questions for self-examination
or extra credit work. If the bookstore does not have the Study
Guide in stock, please ask your bookstore manager to order a
copy for you.

Preface

This text is designed for a one-term course in managerial accounting for use by students who have already completed one or two terms of basic financial accounting. The emphasis of *Managerial Accounting* is on uses of accounting data internally by managers in directing the affairs of business and nonbusiness organizations.

Managers need information in order to carry out three essential functions in an organization: (1) to plan operations; (2) to control activities; and (3) to make decisions. The purpose of *Managerial Accounting* is to show *what kinds* of information the manager needs, *where* this information can be obtained, and *how* this information is used in carrying out these essential functions. The book has a "top-down" focus in that it looks at accounting data through the eyes of those who must use the data in the management of an enterprise. Looking at accounting data from this perspective allows several things to be accomplished with the book. First, it helps students to realize that accounting data are a *means* rather than an *end*. Second, it provides a unifying base on which to build concepts. And third, it permits the instructor to portray the internal accountant in his or her true role—that of a key participant in the basic functions of management.

Although the emphasis of the book is on uses of accounting data, care has been taken to not sacrifice the student's need for basic technical understanding. To this end, topics are covered in enough depth to ensure full comprehension of basic concepts. The student is then able to proceed with confidence and understanding in the application of these concepts to organizational problems.

A paramount objective in writing this book has been to make a clear and balanced presentation of relevant subject material. Effort has been made to draw examples and homework problems, where appropriate, from service-oriented as well as from profit-oriented situations, and from nonmanufacturing as well as from manufacturing situations.

In the revision process, care has been taken to retain all of the strengths cited by users of the first three editions. The book has been updated where needed, however, with the following changes or additions:

1. Special emphasis has been given to writing new exercise and problem material. As a result of this special emphasis, a majority of the exercises and problems in the book are either completely revised or new to this edition. As in prior editions, users will find a wide range of problems in terms of level of difficulty.

2. Written definitions have been provided for all "key terms" at the end of each chapter. In addition, thcsc tcrms are now shown in bold-face type where they first appear in the chapter. In all, nearly 300 managerial accounting terms are thus highlighted and defined for the student.

3. Several new exhibits have been added to Chapter 2 ("Cost Terms, Concepts, and Classifications") to assist the student in digesting new cost terms. Also, a comprehensive review problem on cost terms has been added to the chapter.

4. Chapter 4 ("Systems Design: Process Costing") has been completely rewritten. The chapter now includes a bridge between Chapters 3 and 4 so that the student can see the similarities and differences between job-order and process costing more clearly. Many illustrations and exhibits are included in the new chapter to clarify the more complex parts of process costing. Also, the production report has been restructured to simplify its preparation and to show a more logical flow of data.

5. A discussion of independent and dependent variables has been added to Chapter 5 ("Cost Behavior: Analysis and Use") to assist the student in better understanding cost analysis.

6. Some of the material in Chapter 7 ("Segmented Reporting, and the Contribution Approach to Costing") dealing with direct and absorption costing has been rewritten. An effort has been made to simplify the discussion somewhat, and a review problem on direct and absorption costing has been added to the chapter.

7. A new section dealing with inflation and capital budgeting has been added as an appendix to Chapter 14 ("Capital Budgeting Decisions").

8. Much of the material in Chapter 15 ("Further Aspects of Investment Decisions") dealing with income taxes and capital budgeting has been rewritten. Also, the material dealing with tax effects on payback and simple rate of return has been removed from the chapter and placed in an appendix.

In addition to the above, scores of small "polishing" changes have been made throughout the book in an effort to further improve flow, comprehension, and readability. In no case, however, has change been made simply for the sake of change (other than in the assignment material). Rather, the revision has been completed with a single objective in mind—to make the fourth edition of *Managerial Accounting* the most teachable book of its kind available anywhere.

Using the text

As in the prior editions, flexibility in meeting the needs of courses varying in length, content, and student composition continues to be a prime concern in the organization and content of the book. Sufficient text material is available to permit the instructor to choose topics and depth of coverage as desired. Appendixes, parts of chapters, or even whole chapters can be omitted without adversely affecting the continuity of the course. An instructor's manual is available which gives a number of alternate assignment outlines and suggestions as to the problems to be assigned from various chapters.

The book contains over 750 questions, exercises, and problems for in-class use or for homework assignment. In addition, a study guide is available as is a comprehensive test bank containing over 1,000 objective-type questions. My appreciation is extended to professors Roland Minch, SUNY—Albany; Richard Hodges, University of Nebraska at Omaha; and Ronald B. Pawliczek, Boston College, who prepared the bulk of the test bank materials.

Acknowledgments

Ideas and suggestions have been received from many faculty members who used the prior edition of the book. Each has my thanks, since the book is a better product as a result of their insightful comments.

The following professors spent considerable time providing in-depth reviews of the prior edition: Richard Hodges, University of Nebraska at Omaha; Linda M. Marquis, University of Cincinnati, Leslie R. Loschen, University of Southern California; Sherry K. Moore, University of Texas at San Antonio; John M. Alvis, University of Kentucky; Jesse F. Dillard, The Ohio State University, Columbus; Felix P. Kollaritsch, The Ohio State University, Columbus; and Thomas J. O'Neil, American International College.

Permission has been received from the Institute of Management Accounting of the National Association of Accountants to use questions and/or unofficial answers from past CMA examinations. Also, my appreciation is extended to the American Institute of Certified Public Accounts, and the Society of Management Accountants of Canada for permission to use (or adapt) selected problems from their examinations. These problems bear the notations CMA, CPA, and SMA, respectively.

Ray H. Garrison

Contents

MANAGERIAL ACCOUNTING
Concepts for Planning, Control, Decision Making

1 Managerial Accounting—A Perspective

Learning objectives

After studying Chapter 1, you should be able to:

Explain what an organization is, and describe the work done by management in organizations.

Name the steps in the planning and control cycle, and explain how each step impacts on the work of management.

Prepare an organization chart, and explain its purpose.

Distinguish between the line and staff responsibilities in an organization.

Name the three groups into which organizations can be classified, and discuss the ways in which nearly all organizations are similar.

Describe the three broad purposes for which the manager needs accounting information.

Identify the major differences and similarities between financial and managerial accounting.

Define or explain the key terms listed at the end of the chapter.

Managerial accounting is concerned with providing information to *managers*—that is, those who are *inside* an organization and who are charged with directing and controlling its operations. Managerial accounting can be contrasted with **financial accounting,** which is concerned with providing information to stockholders, creditors, and others who are *outside* an organization.

Because it is manager oriented, any study of managerial accounting must be preceded by some understanding of the management process and of the organizations in which managers work. Accordingly, the purpose of this chapter is to examine briefly the work of the manager and to look at the characteristics, structure, and operation of the organizations in which this work is carried out. The chapter concludes by examining the major differences and similarities between financial and managerial accounting.

ORGANIZATIONS AND THEIR OBJECTIVES

An **organization** can be defined as a group of people united for some common purpose. A bank providing financial services is an organization, as is a university providing educational services, the General Electric Company producing appliances and other products. An organization consists of *people,* not physical assets. Thus, a bank building is not an organization; rather, the organization consists of the people who work in the bank and who are bound together for the common purpose of providing financial services to a community.

The common purpose toward which an organization works is called its *objective.* Not all organizations have the same objective. For some organizations the objective is to produce a product and earn a profit. For other organizations the objective may be to render humanitarian service (the Red Cross), to provide aesthetic enrichment (a symphony orchestra), or to provide government services (a water department). To assist in our discussion, we will focus on a single organization, the Bestway Furniture Company, and look closely at this organization's objectives, structure, and management, and at how these factors influence its need for managerial accounting data.

Setting objectives

The Bestway Furniture Company is a corporation, and its owners have placed their money in the organization with the thought in mind of earning a return, or profit, on their investment. Thus, one objective of the company is to earn a profit on the funds committed to it. The profit objective is tempered by other objectives, however. The company is anxious to acquire and maintain a reputation of integrity, fairness, and dependability. It also wants to be a positive force in the social and ecological environment in which it carries out its activities.

The owners of the Bestway Furniture Company prefer not to be involved in day-to-day operation of the company. Instead, they have outlined the broad objectives of the organization and have selected a president to oversee the implementation of these objectives. Although the president is charged with the central objective of earning a profit on the owners' investment, he[1] must do so with a sensitivity for the other objectives that the organization desires to achieve.

Strategic planning

The implementation of an organization's objectives is known as *strategic planning*. In any organization, **strategic planning** occurs in two phases:

1. Deciding on the products to produce and/or the services to render.
2. Deciding on the marketing and/or manufacturing strategy to follow in getting the intended product or service to the proper audience.

The set of strategies emerging from strategic planning is often referred to as an organization's *policies,* and strategic planning itself is often referred to as *setting policy.*[2]

Phase 1: product strategy   In deciding on the products to produce or the services to render, there are several strategies that the president of the Bestway Furniture Company could follow. The company could specialize in office furniture; it could specialize in appliances; it could be a broad "supermarket" type of furniture outlet; or it could employ any one of a number of other product and/or service strategies.

After careful consideration of the various strategies available, a decision has been made to sell only home furnishings, including appliances. The president, for one reason or another, has rejected several other possible strategies. He has decided, for example, not to service appliances. He has also decided not to sell office furniture or to deal in institutional-type furnishings.

Phase 2: marketing strategy   Having decided to concentrate on home furnishings, the president of the Bestway Furniture Company is now faced with a second strategy decision. Some furniture dealers handle only the highest quality home furnishings, thereby striving to maintain the image of a "quality" dealer. The markups of these dealers is usually quite high, their volume is quite low, and their promotional efforts are directed toward a relatively small segment of the public. Other furniture dealers operate "volume" outlets. They try to keep markups relatively low, with the thought that overall profits will be augmented by a larger number of units sold. Still other dealers may follow different strategies. The selection of a particular strategy is simply a matter of managerial judgment; some companies make a profit by following

---

[1] The English language lacks a generic singular pronoun signifying he *or* she. For this reason the maculine pronouns *he* and *his* are used to some extent in this book for purposes of succinctness and to avoid repetition in wording. As used, these pronouns are intended to refer to both females and males.

[2] For an expanded discussion of strategic planning, see Harold Koontz and Cyril J. O'Donnell, *Management,* 7th ed. (New York: McGraw-Hill, 1980); and William H. Newman and E. Kirby Warren, *Process of Management,* 5th ed. (Englewood Cliffs, N.J.: Prentice-Hall, 1982).

one strategy, while other companies are equally profitable following another. In the case at hand, the Bestway Furniture Company has decided to operate "volume" outlets and to focus on maintaining a "discount" image.

Every organization must make similar strategy decisions. The set of strategies resulting from these decisions may not be written down, but they exist nonetheless and they are a central guiding force in the organization's activities and in its need for accounting information.

The work of management

The work of management centers on what is to be managed—the organization itself. Essentially, the manager carries out four broad functions in an organization:

1. Planning.
2. Organizing and directing.
3. Controlling.
4. Decision making.

These functions are carried on more or less simultaneously and often under considerable stress, urgency, and pressure. Rarely (if ever) will managers stop to examine which function they are engaged in at a particular moment. Perhaps they couldn't tell even if they tried, since a specific action might touch on all four.

Planning In **planning,** managers outline the steps to be taken in moving the organization toward its objectives. We saw the planning function in operation in the Bestway Furniture Company, as the president decided on a set of strategies to be followed. The president's next step will be to develop further, more specific plans, such as store locations, methods of financing customer purchases, hours of operation, and discount policies. As these plans are made, they will be communicated throughout the organization. When implemented, the plans will serve to coordinate, or meld together, the efforts of all parts of the organization toward the company's objectives.

Organizing and directing In **organizing,** managers decide how best to put together the organization's human and other resources in order to carry out established plans. As a customer enters one of the Bestway Furniture Company's stores, the results of the managers' organizational efforts should be obvious in several ways. Certain persons will be performing specific functions, some directly with the customer and some not. Some persons will be overseeing the efforts of other persons. The store's physical assets will be arranged in particular ways, and certain procedures will be followed if a sale is made. These and a host of other things, seen and unseen, will all exist to assure that the customer is assisted in the best way possible and to assure that the company moves toward its profit objectives. In short, the organization that is apparent in most companies doesn't simply happen; it is a result of the efforts of the manager who must visualize and fit together the structure that is needed to get the job done, whatever the job may be.

In **directing,** managers oversee day-to-day activities and keep the organization functioning smoothly. Employees are assigned to tasks; disputes between departments or between employees are arbitrated; questions are answered; on-the-spot problems are solved; and numerous small routine and nonroutine decisions are made involving customers and/or procedures. In effect, directing is that part of the managers' work that deals largely with the routine and with the here and now.

Controlling In carrying out the **control** function, managers take those steps necessary to ensure that each part of the organization is following the plan that was outlined for it at the planning stage. To do this, managers study the accounting and other reports coming to them and compare these reports against the plans set earlier. These comparisons may show where operations are not proceeding effectively or where certain persons need help in carrying out their assigned duties. The accounting and other reports coming to management are called **feedback.** The feedback which management receives may suggest the need to replan, to set new strategies, or to reshape the organizational structure. It is a key to the effective management of any organization. As we shall see in chapters following, the generation of feedback to the manager is one of the central purposes of internal accounting.

Decision making In **decision making,** managers attempt to make rational choices between alternatives. Decision making isn't a separate management function, per se; rather, it is an inseparable part of the *other* functions already discussed. Planning, organizing and directing, and controlling all require that decisions be made. For example, when first establishing its organizational strategies, the Bestway Furniture Company had to make a decision as to which of several available strategies would be followed. Such a decision is often called a *strategic decision* because of its long-term impact on the organization. In organizing and in directing day-to-day operations, as well as in controlling, managers must make scores of lesser decisions, all of which are important to the organization's overall well-being.

All decisions are based on *information.* In large part, the quality of management's decisions will be a reflection of the quality of the accounting and other information which it receives. Simply put, bad information will generally lead to bad decisions—thus the need for a course in managerial accounting in which we deal directly with the informational needs of management in carrying out decision-making responsibilities.

The planning and control cycle

The work of management can be summarized very nicely in a model such as that shown in Exhibit 1–1. This model, which depicts the **planning and control cycle,** illustrates the smooth flow of management activities from planning through organizing, directing, and controlling, and then back to planning again. All of these activities turn on the hub of decision making.

EXHIBIT 1–1
The planning and control cycle

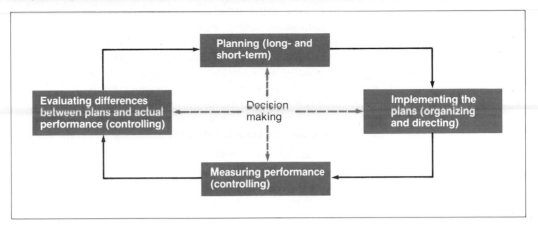

ORGANIZATIONAL STRUCTURE

Just as organizations are made up of people, management accomplishes its objectives by working *through* people. The president of the Bestway Furniture Company could not possibly execute all of the company's strategies alone. The president must rely on other people to carry a large share of the management load. This is done by the creation of an organizational structure that will permit a *decentralization* of management responsibilities.

Decentralization

Decentralization means the delegation of decision-making authority throughout an organization by allowing managers at various operating levels to make key decisions relating to their area of responsibility. In effect, decentralization moves the decision-making point to the lowest managerial level possible for each decision that must be made.

All organizations are decentralized to some extent out of economic necessity. It would be impossible for top management to have the time or to be well-enough informed to make every one of the myriad decisions that arise daily. Thus, top management in virtually all organizations must delegate some decision-making authority to managers at lower levels. The greater the degree of this delegation, the greater is the amount of decentralization that exists. In some companies, top management delegates virtually all decisions to managers at lower levels; these companies are viewed as being strongly decentralized. In other companies, top management delegates only minor or routine decisions to managers at lower levels; these companies are viewed as being strongly centralized. Most companies fall somewhere between these extremes.

Under the presumption that the manager closest to a problem is the one best qualified to solve the problem, the president of the Bestway Furniture Company has delegated broad decision-making authority to the various levels of the organization. These levels are as follows: The company has three stores, each of which has a furnishings department and an appliances department. Each store has a store manager, as well as a separate manager over each department. In addition, the company has a purchasing department and an accounting department. The managers of these stores and departments have broad decision-making authority over matters relating to the activities within their areas of responsibility, so long as their decisions are made within the overall framework of the company's operating strategies. The organizational structure of the firm is depicted in Exhibit 1–2.

The arrangement of boxes shown in Exhibit 1–2 is commonly called an **organization chart.** Each box depicts an area of management responsibility, and the lines between the boxes show the lines of authority between managers. The chart tells us, for example, that the managers of the stores are responsible to the vice president in charge of sales. In turn, the latter is responsible to the company president, who in turn is responsible to the board of directors. The purpose of an organization chart, then, is to show how responsibility has been divided between managers and to show formal lines of reporting

EXHIBIT 1–2
Organization chart, Bestway Furniture Company

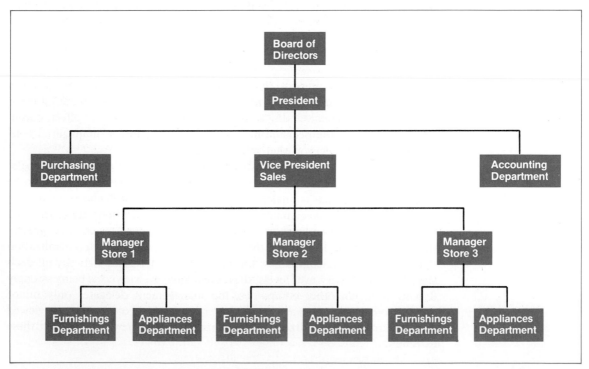

and communication. If the manager of store 3 has a problem, he or she should not go directly to the company president but rather should take the problem to the sales manager, who is the immediate superior.

In very large organizations, *informal* relationships and channels of communication often develop. These informal lines of communication are spontaneous and come about through the personal and social contacts beween managers. The informal structure that may exist in an organization is never depicted on a formal organization chart, but its existence is often very helpful in maintaining a smooth flow of activity. Generally, these informal channels are unstable and subject to frequent change.

Line and staff relationships

An organization chart also depicts *line* and *staff* positions in an organization. A **line** position is one that relates *directly* to the carrying out of the basic objectives of an organization. A **staff** position, by contrast, is one that relates only *indirectly* to the carrying out of basic objectives. Staff positions are *supportive* in nature, in that they provide service or assistance to line positions or to other parts of the organization. Refer again to the organization chart in Exhibit 1–2. Since the basic objective of the Bestway Furniture Company is to sell furnishings and appliances to the public, those managers whose areas of responsibility relate directly to the sales effort occupy line positions. These would include the managers of the separate departments in each store, the store managers, and the vice president in charge of sales.

By contrast, the manager of the purchasing department occupies a staff position, since the only function of the purchasing department is to support and serve the line (sales) departments by doing their purchasing for them. The company has found that better buys can be obtained by having one central unit purchase for the entire organization. Therefore, the purchasing department has been organized as a staff department to perform this service function. It cannot be called a line department, since it is involved only indirectly with the sales effort and since its role is *supportive* in nature. By this line of reasoning, the accounting department is also a staff department, since its purpose is to provide specialized accounting services to other departments.

The Bestway Furniture Company's organization chart shows only two staff departments. In a larger organization, there would be many more staff departments, including perhaps finance, engineering, medical services, cafeteria, personnel, advertising, and research and development.

The distinction we have drawn between line and staff is an important one, since the role of staff persons is basically advisory in nature, and thus they have no authority over line units. Because their role is advisory, in most organizations policy is not formulated by persons occupying staff positions. Rather, policy setting and the making of key operating decisions are done by line managers, with staff persons either providing input or carrying out other duties as directed by top management.

EXHIBIT 1–3
Organization of the controller's office

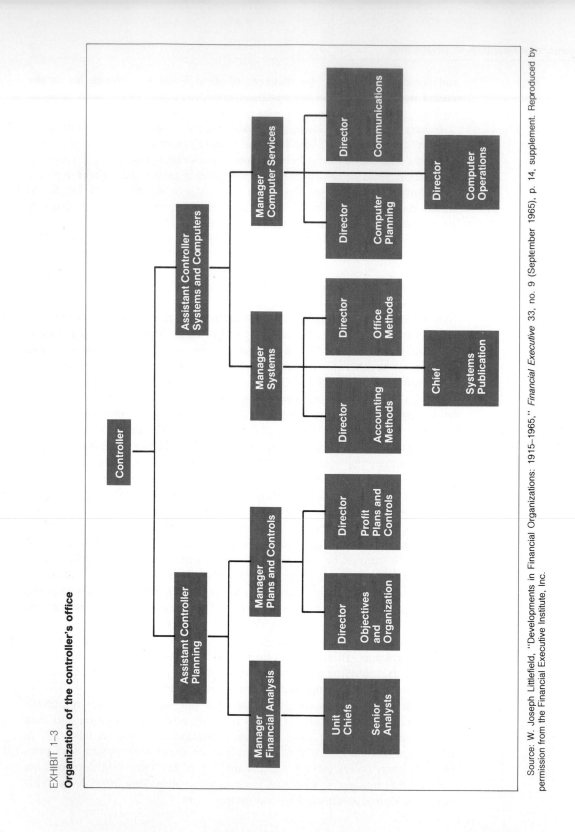

Source: W. Joseph Littlefield, "Developments in Financial Organizations: 1915–1965," *Financial Executive* 33, no. 9 (September 1965), p. 14, supplement. Reproduced by permission from the Financial Executive Institute, Inc.

Since accounting is in a staff position, where does it get the authority to set policy in accounting and financial reporting matters? The answer is simple. Top management *delegates* to the accounting department the right to prescribe uniform accounting procedures and the right to require reports and other information from line units. In carrying out these duties, the accounting department is not exercising line authority over other departments; it is simply acting for top management as its delegated voice.

The controller

The manager in charge of the accounting department is known as the **controller.** He or she is a member of the top-management team and an active participant in the planning, control, and decision-making processes. Although the controller does not "control" in terms of line authority (remember, accounting is a staff function), as chief information officer he or she is in a position to exercise control in a very special way. This is through the reporting and interpreting of data needed in decision making. By supplying and interpreting relevant and timely data, the controller has a significant influence on decisions and thus plays a key part in directing an organization toward its objectives.

Because of the controller's position as a member of the top-management team, his or her time is generally kept free of technical and detailed activities. The controller oversees the work of others, directs the preparation of special reports and studies, and advises top management in special problem situations. The organization of a modern controller's office is shown in Exhibit 1–3.

Since the focus of this book is on managerial accounting, we are particularly interested in the work of the controller and the department he or she manages. The information that the accounting department generates is used throughout an organization in many different ways, as we shall see in chapters following.

Basic similarities among organizations

Organizations can be classified into three basic groups:

1. Profit-oriented business enterprises that are privately owned and operated as corporations, partnerships, and proprietorships.
2. Service-oriented agencies and associations that are either publicly or privately controlled, such as the Red Cross, the YMCA, and the Salvation Army, and that are usually operated as nonprofit corporations.
3. Service-oriented agencies such as the Department of Defense, a state university, and a city water department that are created and controlled by government bodies.

Each of these groups contains thousands of organizations. Each organization may be unique in its own right, but nearly all organizations will share the following basic similarities:

1. Each will have an objective or group of objectives toward which it is working.

2. Each will have a set of strategies designed to assist in achieving the basic objective or objectives.
3. Each will have a manager or managers who plan, organize, direct, and control the organization's activities, and who make numerous decisions of both a long- and short-term nature.
4. Each will have an organizational structure that shows responsibility relationships between various managers and that shows line and staff relationships.
5. Each will have an insatiable need for information to assist in the execution of its strategies.

Because of these basic similarities, much of what we say in this book about managerial accounting and its uses will have almost universal application among organizations. To the extent that organizations differ, some of our topics will of necessity be narrower in their focus. It is our intent, however, to be concerned with the nature and uses of managerial accounting data in all types of organizations; for this reason, the reader will find chapter examples and problems relating to organizations that are service oriented as well as to those that are profit oriented.

THE MANAGER'S NEED FOR INFORMATION

Information is the "motor" that makes management go. In the absence of a steady flow of information, management would be powerless to do anything. Fortunately, a large part of management's information needs are satisfied within the structure of the organization itself. As suggested by the organization chart in Exhibit 1–2, there are channels of communication extending throughout an organization through which the various levels of management can communicate. Through these channels, policies and instructions are submitted to subordinates, problems are discussed, formal and informal contacts are made, reports and memos are transmitted, and so on. Without these channels of communication, it would be impossible for management to function effectively.

The management of an organization also depends on specialists to provide a large part of its information needs. Economists, marketing specialists, organizational behavior specialists, accountants, and others all provide information to management and advise on various phases of the organization's activities. Economists, for example, provide information on contemplated economic conditions; marketing specialists provide information essential to the effective promotion and distribution of goods and services; and organizational behavior specialists assist in the structure and functioning of the organization itself.

Accounting information

The information provided by accounting is essentially financial in nature, helping the manager to do three things:

1. Plan effectively and focus attention on deviations from plans.
2. Direct day-to-day operations.
3. Arrive at the best solutions to the operating problems faced by the organization.

Plan effectively The plans of management are expressed formally as **budgets,** and the term *budgeting* is often applied to management planning generally. Budgets are usually prepared on an annual basis, and they express the desires and goals of management in specific, quantitative terms. For example, the Bestway Furniture Company plans sales by month a full year in advance. These plans are expressed as departmental budgets, which are communicated throughout the organization.

But planning is not enough. Once the budgets have been set, the president and other managers of the Bestway Furniture Company will need information inflows that indicate how well the plans are working out. Accounting assists in meeting this information need by supplying *performance reports* that help the manager focus on problems or opportunities that might otherwise go unnoticed. A **performance report** is a detailed report to management comparing budgeted data against actual data for a specific time period. If the performance report on a particular department indicates that problems exist, then the manager will need to find the cause of the problems and take corrective action. If the performance report indicates that things are going well, then the manager is free to do other work. In sum, performance reports are a form of feedback to the manager, directing his or her attention toward those parts of the organization where managerial time can be used most effectively.

Direct operations The manager has a constant need for accounting information in the routine conduct of day-to-day operations. For example, as departmental managers in the Bestway Furniture Company price new items going onto the display floor, they will rely on information provided by accounting to ensure that cost price relationships are in harmony with the marketing strategies adopted by the firm. The company's store managers will rely on other accounting information such as sales volumes and inventory levels as they attempt to prepare advertising programs. And the purchasing department manager will rely on still other accounting information in evaluating the costs of storage and handling. In these and a score of other ways, the work of the accountant and the manager is inextricably connected in the conduct of day-to-day operations.

Solve problems Accounting information is often a key factor in analyzing alternative methods of solving a problem. The reason is that various alternatives usually have specific costs and benefits that can be measured and used as an input in deciding which alternative is best. Accounting is generally responsible for gathering available cost and benefit data and for communicating it in a usable form to the appropriate manager. For example, the Bestway Furniture Company may discover that competitors are making inroads on the company's business. In deciding among the alternatives of reducing prices, increasing advertising, or doing both in an attempt to maintain its market share, the company will rely heavily on cost-benefit data provided by accounting. It is important to note here that the needed information may not be in readily available form; in fact, accounting may find it necessary to do a large amount of special analytical work, including some forecasting, in order to prepare the needed data.

Information must be in summary form

An essential element of managerial accounting information is that it be in summary form. In your study of financial accounting, you learned that an accounting system handles an enormous amount of detail in recording the results of day-to-day transactions. The availability of this detail is vital to the effective management of an organization. However, a manager's *initial* need is not for detail but rather for *summaries* of detailed information that have been drawn from the accounting records. Using these summaries, the manager can see where problems exist and where time must be spent in order to improve the effectiveness of the organization.

Because of the great value of summarized data to the manager, the bulk of our time in this book is spent on learning the *kinds* of summarized data that the manager needs and on learning how these data are used in directing the affairs of an enterprise.

COMPARISON OF FINANCIAL AND MANAGERIAL ACCOUNTING

In our discussion of managerial accounting, we have noted that it differs in several ways from financial accounting. To assist the reader in making the transition from the study of financial accounting to the study of managerial accounting, it is desirable at this point to summarize these differences, as well as to point out certain similarities between the two fields of study.

Differences between financial and managerial accounting

In all, we can identify eight major differences between financial and managerial accounting:

1. Managerial accounting focuses on providing data for internal uses by the manager.
2. Managerial accounting places much more emphasis on the future.
3. Managerial accounting is not governed by generally accepted accounting principles.
4. Managerial accounting emphasizes the relevance and flexibility of data.
5. Managerial accounting places less emphasis on precision and more emphasis on nonmonetary data.
6. Managerial accounting emphasizes the segments of an organization, rather than just looking at the organization as a whole.
7. Managerial accounting draws heavily from other disciplines.
8. Managerial accounting is not mandatory.

Internal uses by the manager   For internal purposes, the manager does not need the same kinds of information as are needed externally by stockholders and others. The manager must direct day-to-day operations, plan for the future, solve problems, and make numerous routine and non-routine decisions, all of which require their own special information inputs. Much of the information needed by the manager for these purposes would be either confusing or valueless to stockholders and others because of the form in which the information is prepared and used.

Emphasis on the future   Since a large part of the overall responsibilities of the manager have to do with *planning,* the manager's information needs have a strong future orientation. Summaries of past costs and other historical data are useful in planning, but only to a point. The difficulty with summaries of the past is that the manager can't assume that the future will simply be a reflection of what has happened in the past. Changes are constantly taking place in economic conditions, customer needs and desires, competitive conditions, and so on. All of these changes demand that the manager's planning framework be built in large part on estimated data that may or may not be reflective of past experience.

By contrast, financial accounting records the *financial history* of an organization. Financial accounting has little to do with estimates and projections of the future. Rather, entries are made in the accounting records only after transactions have already occurred.

Generally accepted accounting principles   Financial accounting statements must be prepared in accordance with generally accepted accounting principles. The reason is that these statements are relied on by persons outside the organization. These outside persons must have some assurance that the information they are receiving has been prepared in accordance with some common set of ground rules; otherwise, great opportunity could exist for fraud or misrepresentation and confidence in financial statements would be destroyed. The managers of a company, by contrast, are not governed by generally accepted accounting principles in the information that they receive. Managers can set their own ground rules on the form and content of information that is to be used internally. Whether these ground rules conform to generally accepted accounting principles is immaterial. For example, management might direct that for internal uses, financial statements be expressed on a cash basis, depreciation of plant and equipment be based on appraised value, and that fixed production costs be ignored in product costing, even though all of these procedures would be in violation of generally accepted accounting principles. In sum, when information is to be used internally, managers are free to reshape data as they desire in order to obtain information in its most useful form.

Relevance and flexibility of data   Financial accounting data are expected to be objectively determined and to be verifiable. For internal uses, the manager is often more concerned about receiving information that is relevant and flexible than about receiving information that is completely objective or even verifiable. By relevant, we mean *pertinent to the problem at* *hand.* So long as information inflows are relevant to problems that must be solved, the manager may view objectivity and verification as matters of secondary importance. The manager must also have information that is flexible enough to be used in a variety of decision-making situations. For example, the cost information needed for pricing transfers of goods between sister divisions may be far different from the cost information needed for pricing sales to outside customers.

Less emphasis on precision   When information is needed, speed is often more important than precision. The more rapidly information comes to a manager, the more rapidly problems are attended to and resolved. For this reason, the manager is often willing to trade off some accuracy for information that is immediately available. If a decision must be made, waiting a week for information that will be slightly more accurate may be considered less desirable than simply acting on the information that is already available. This means that the manager's need is often for good estimates and good approximations rather than for numbers that are accurate to the last penny. Managerial accounting recognizes this need and therefore tends to place less emphasis on precision than does financial accounting. In addition, managerial accounting places considerable weight on nonmonetary data. For example, time lost due to machine breakdowns, sales representatives' impressions concerning a new product, information on weather conditions, and even rumors could be helpful to the manager, even though some of this information might be difficult to quantify or to even express in a monetary form.

Segments of an organization   Financial accounting is primarily concerned with the reporting of business activities for a company as a whole. By contrast, managerial accounting focuses less on the whole and more on the parts, or **segments,** of a company. These segments may be the product lines, the sales territories, the divisions, the departments, or any other way that a company can be broken down. In financial accounting, it is true that some companies do report some breakdown of revenues and costs, but this tends to be a secondary emphasis. In managerial accounting, segmented reporting is the primary emphasis.

Draws on other disciplines   Managerial accounting extends beyond the boundaries of the traditional accounting system and draws heavily on other disciplines, including economics, finance, statistics, operations research, and organizational behavior. These "outside" sources give managerial accounting a strong interdisciplinary flavor as well as a decidedly pragmatic orientation.

Not mandatory   Financial accounting is mandatory; that is, it must be done. Financial records must be kept so that sufficient information will be available to satisfy the requirements of various outside parties. Often the financial records that are to be kept are specified by regulatory bodies, such as the Securities and Exchange Commission (SEC). Even if a company is not covered by SEC or other regulations, it must meet certain financial accounting requirements if it is to have its statements examined by professional outside accountants. In addition, *all* companies must keep adequate records to meet the requirements of taxing authorities. By contrast, managerial accounting is not mandatory. A company is completely free to do as much or as little as it wishes. There are no regulatory bodies or other outside agencies that specify what is to be done, or for that matter, whether anything is to be done at all. Since managerial accounting is completely optional, the important question is always "Is the information useful?" rather than "Is the information required?"

Similarities between financial and managerial accounting

Although many differences exist between financial and managerial accounting, they are similar in at least two ways. First, both rely on the accounting information system. It would be a total waste of money to have two *different* data-collecting systems existing side by side. For this reason, managerial accounting makes extensive use of routinely generated financial accounting data, although it both expands on and adds to these data, as discussed earlier. Second, both financial and managerial accounting rely heavily on the concept of *responsibility,* or *stewardship.* Financial accounting is concerned with stewardship over the company *as a whole;* managerial accounting is concerned with stewardship over its *parts,* and this concern extends to the last person in the organization who has any responsibility over cost. In effect, financial accounting can be viewed as being the apex, with managerial accounting filling in the bulk of the pyramid underneath, from a responsibility accounting point of view.

THE EXPANDING ROLE OF MANAGERIAL ACCOUNTING

Managerial accounting is in its infancy. Historically, it has played a secondary role to financial accounting, and in many organizations it still is little more than a by-product of the financial reporting process. However, events of the last three decades have spurred the development of managerial accounting, and it is becoming widely recognized as a field of expertise separate from financial accounting.

Increased needs for information

Among the events that have spurred the development of managerial accounting, we can note increased business competition, a severe cost-price squeeze, and rapidly developing technology. The changes brought about by these events have intensified the manager's need for information, and particularly for financial information beyond that contained in the traditional income statement and balance sheet. Consider the following:

Over the last three decades products have become obsolete at accelerating rates. Various scientific breakthroughs have resulted in the development of many new basic components, such as the transistor and the electronic "chip," which have literally revolutionized many industries and their products. Scientific researchers report that this "revolution" is only in its beginnings.

Dramatic changes have taken place in production methods over the last three decades. The term *automation* was coined in the early 1950s to describe a process that was new at the time. Today many products are produced virtually untouched by human hands. Oil refinery operations are controlled by massive computers; machine tools are electronically controlled; and there are even entire manufacturing plants where workers do little more than monitor instrument panels. In many settings, robots are becoming the new "steel collar" workers of industry. These robots can be programmed to "see" and "feel" small objects and can work in virtually any environment.

Modes of management and methods of decision making have been affected by the development of powerful new quantitative tools such as linear programming, probability analysis, and decision theory. These new tools, which have come from the mathematical and statistical sciences, are becoming indispensable in day-to-day decision making.

Whole new industries have emerged as a result of various technological breakthroughs. A few short years ago petrochemicals and laser beams were little more than laboratory novelties and space exploration was little more than a dream. Today the petrochemical industry stands as a powerful competitive force in the business environment, laser beams are used for everything from cutting steel to delicate eye surgery, and students work amazingly complex mathematical computations on tiny electronic calculators that are a direct outgrowth of aerospace exploration.

In some industries, costs have more than doubled over the last 10 years. These cost increases have forced the companies involved to make many adjustments, including modification of products, changes in methods of marketing, and the discovery of new sources and means of financing.

The economic impact of these and other factors has been far-reaching. As managers have grappled with the effects of increased competition, escalating costs, and evolving technology, the role of managerial accounting has expanded manyfold from what was common in earlier years. Looking to the future, we can expect this role to expand even further. As many business writers have observed, the ability of an organization to survive in this time of rocketing change will be directly related to how quickly and how well it responds to new challenges.[3] Certainly the role of managerial accounting in meeting these challenges will be very significant.

The certificate in management accounting (CMA)

Specific recognition is given to the management accountant as a trained professional in the National Association of Accountants' (NAA) *Certificate in Management Accounting* program. The purpose and operation of the program are described in the following excerpts from a brochure issued by the NAA:

---

[3] "Comment," *Management Accounting* 59, no. 3 (September 1977), p. 4.

Significant changes have taken place in accounting and in the role of the accountant in business. The accountant is no longer simply a recorder of business history but now plays a dynamic role in making business decisions, in future planning, and in almost every aspect of business operations. The management accountant who sits with top management has key responsibilities for developing, producing, and analyzing information to help management make sound decisions. Many management accountants and financial managers earn their way into top-management positions.

In response to the needs of business and at the request of many in the academic community, the National Association of Accountants established a program to recognize professional competence and educational attainment in this field—a program leading to the Certificate in Management Accounting.

The CMA program requires candidates to pass a series of uniform examinations and meet specific education and professional standards to qualify for and maintain the Certificate in Management Accounting. NAA has established the Institute of Management Accounting to administer the program, conduct the examinations, and grant certificates to those who qualify. The program is open to all interested persons, whether or not they are members of NAA.

The objectives of the program are threefold:

1. To establish management accounting as a recognized profession by identifying the role of the management accountant and financial manager and the underlying body of knowledge, and by outlining a course of study by which such knowledge can be acquired.
2. To foster higher educational standards in the field of management accounting.
3. To establish an objective measure of an individual's knowledge and competence in the field of management accounting.

SUMMARY

Understanding organizations and the work of those who manage organizations helps us to understand managerial accounting and its functions. All organizations have basic objectives and a set of strategies for achieving those objectives. Both the setting of strategy, sometimes called strategic planning, and planning of a more short-term nature are basic functions of the manager. In addition to planning, the work of the manager centers on organizing and directing day-to-day operations, controlling, and decision making.

The managers of an organization choose an organizational structure that will permit a decentralization of responsibility by placing managers over specific departments and other units. The responsibility relationships between managers are shown by the organization chart. The organization chart also shows which organizational units are performing line functions and which are performing staff functions. Line functions relate to the specific objectives of the organization, whereas staff functions are supportive in nature, their purpose being to provide specialized services of some type.

A large part of the information needs of management is provided within the structure of the organization itself. Channels of communication exist between various levels of management through which information flows. Management also calls on various specialists to provide information, including the economist, the engineer, the operations research specialist, and the accountant. The information provided internally by the accountant is used by management in three ways: (1) to make plans and to monitor how well these plans are working out; (2) to direct day-to-day operations, including the setting of prices and the establishment of advertising policy; and (3) to solve problems confronting the organization.

Since managerial accounting is geared to the needs of the manager rather than to the needs of stockholders and others, it differs substantially from financial accounting. Among other things, it is oriented more toward the future, it is not governed by generally accepted accounting principles, it places less emphasis on precision, it emphasizes segments of an organization (rather than the organization as a whole), it draws heavily on other disciplines, and it is not mandatory. The role of managerial accounting is expanding rapidly, and managerial accounting has become recognized as a field of professional study through which professional certification can be obtained.

KEY TERMS FOR REVIEW

At the end of each chapter, a list of key terms for review is given, along with the definition of each term. (These terms are set in boldface type where they first appear in the chapter.) Each term should be studied with care to be sure you understand its meaning, since these terms are used repeatedly in the chapters that follow. The list for Chapter 1 is:

Budget A detailed plan for the future, usually expressed in formal quantitative terms.

Control The process of instituting procedures and then obtaining feedback as needed to ensure that all parts of the organization are functioning effectively and moving toward overall company goals.

Controller The manager in charge of the accounting department in an organization.

Decentralization The delegation of decision-making authority throughout an organization by allowing managers at various operating levels to make key decisions relating to their area of responsibility.

Decision making The process of making rational choices among alternatives.

Directing The overseeing of day-to-day activities in order to keep an organization functioning smoothly.

Feedback Accounting and other reports coming to management that help the manager to monitor performance and to focus on problems and/or opportunities that might otherwise go unnoticed.

Financial accounting The phase of accounting that is concerned with providing information to stockholders and others who are outside of an organization for use in evaluating operations and current financial condition.

Line A position in an organization that relates directly to the carrying out of the organization's basic objectives.

Managerial accounting The phase of accounting that is concerned with providing information to managers for use in planning and controlling operations and in decision making.

Organization A group of people united for some common purpose.

Organization chart A visual diagram of a firm's organizational structure that depicts formal lines of reporting, communication, and responsibility between managers.

Organizing The process of putting together an organization's human and other resources in such a way as to most effectively carry out established plans.

Performance report A detailed report to management comparing budgeted data against actual data for a specific time period.

Planning The development of objectives in an organization and the preparation of various budgets to achieve these objectives.

Planning and control cycle The flow of management activities through the steps (in sequence) of planning, organizing and directing, controlling, and then back to planning again.

Segment Any part of an organization that can be evaluated independently of other parts and about which the manager seeks cost data. Examples would include a product line, a sales territory, a division, or a department.

Staff A position in an organization that relates only indirectly to the carrying out of the organization's basic objectives. Such positions are supportive in nature, in that they provide service or assistance to line positions or to other parts of the organization.

Strategic planning The planning that leads to the implementation of an organization's objectives. Such planning occurs in two phases: (1) deciding on the products to produce and/or the services to render, and (2) deciding on the marketing and/or manufacturing methods to employ in getting the intended products or services to the proper audience.

QUESTIONS

1-1. Contrast financial and managerial accounting.

1-2. What objectives, other than earning a profit, might be important to the managers of a profit-oriented organization?

1-3. Assume that you are about to go into the retail grocery business. Describe some of the operating strategies that you might follow.

1-4. A labor union is an organization. Describe a labor union in terms of what might be its objectives, its strategies, its organizational structure, the work of its managers, and its need for information.

1-5. Some persons consider strategic planning to be the most important work that a manager does. In what ways might this be true? In what ways might it be false?

1-6. Assume that the central objective of a college basketball team is to win games. What strategies might the team follow to achieve this objective?

1-7. Managerial accounting isn't as important in the government as it is in private industry, since the government doesn't have to worry about earning a profit. Do you agree? Explain.

1-8. What function does *feedback* play in the work of the manager?

1-9. "Essentially, the job of a manager is to make decisions." Do you agree? Explain.

1-10. What is the relationship, if any, between information and decision making?

1-11. Choose an organization with which you are familiar. Prepare an organization chart depicting the structure of the organization you have chosen. (The organization you choose should be sufficiently complex to have at least one staff function.) Be prepared to place your organization chart on the board, if your instructor so directs.

1-12. One of the key responsibilities of an accounting department is to keep records for the entire organization. Why don't line managers keep their own records?

1-13. Managerial accounting information is sometimes described as a means to an end, whereas financial accounting information is described as an end in itself. In what sense is this true?

1-14. A student planning a career in management commented, "Look, I'm going to be a manager, so why don't we just leave the accounting to the accountants?" Do you agree? Explain.

1-15. Accountants are sometimes compared to journalists in that accountants don't just "report" information to the manager; they "editorialize" the information. What implications does this hold for the accountant "managing the news," so to speak?

1-16. Distinguish between line and staff positions in an organization.

1-17. "The term *controller* is a misnomer, because the controller doesn't 'control' anything." Do you agree? Explain.

1-18. A production superintendent once complained, "Accounting is a staff function. Those people have no right to come down here and tell us what to do." Do you agree? Why or why not?

1-19. What are the major differences beween financial and managerial accounting? In what ways are the two fields of study similar?

1-20. "If an organization's managerial accounting system functions properly, it will provide management with all the information needed to operate with maximum effectiveness." Do you agree? Explain.

PROBLEMS

P1-1. **Preparing an organization chart.** Bristow University is a large private school located in the Midwest. The university is headed by a president, who has five vice presidents reporting to him. These vice presidents are responsible for, respectively, auxiliary services, admissions and records, academics, financial services (controller), and physical plant.

In addition, the university has managers over several areas who report to these vice presidents. These include managers over central purchasing, the university press, and the university bookstore, all of whom report to the vice president for auxiliary services; managers over computer services and over accounting and finance, who report to the vice president for financial services; and managers over grounds and custodial services and over plant and maintenance, who report to the vice president for physical plant.

The university has four colleges—business, humanities, fine arts, and engineering and quantitative methods—and a law school. Each of these units has a dean who is responsible to the academic vice president. There are several departments in each college.

Required: 1. Prepare an organization chart for Bristow University.
2. Which of the positions on your chart would be line positions? Why would they be line positions? Which would be staff positions? Why?
3. Which of the positions on your chart would have need for accounting information? Explain.

P1–2. **Setting long-range objectives.**   Successful organizations appear to be those that have clearly defined long-range objectives or goals and a well-planned strategy to reach these objectives. Such organizations understand the markets in which they do business and also understand their own internal strengths and weaknesses. They take advantage of this knowledge in order to grow in a consistent and disciplined manner.

Required: 1. Discuss the need for long-range objectives or goals in business organizations.
2. Discuss how long-range objectives are set.
3. Define the concepts of strategic planning and management control. Discuss how they relate to each other and contribute to the progress toward attainment of long-range objectives.   (CMA, adapted)

P1–3. **Strategic planning**   One element necessary to the life of an organization is strategic planning. Strategic planning establishes an organization's long-range goals or objectives and the means to achieve them. Even before a company can begin operations, its managers must develop the plan or plans necessary to determine its future. Among the questions that must be answered are the following: What products or services will the company provide? How will the company be financed and structured? Where will the company and its distributors be located? How will the company's products or services be marketed?

Line and staff management play specific roles in strategic planning. They have different responsibilities and functions in an organization. In addition, the activities of these two management groups must be coordinated.

Required: 1. In the *formulation* of an organization's strategic plans, describe the contribution to be made by:
    a.   The line managers.
    b.   The staff groups or departments.
    In your answer, identify the types of decisions that these two groups of managers would probably make as they participate in the formulation of strategic plans.
2. In the *implementation* of an organization's strategic plans:
    a.   State how the responsiblities of line management differ from those of staff management.
    b.   Describe how line and staff responsibilities interrelate in the implementation of strategic planning.   (CMA, adapted)

PART 1

Managerial
Accounting
Fundamentals

2 Cost Terms, Concepts, and Classifications

Learning objectives

After studying Chapter 2, you should be able to:

Identify and give examples of each of the three basic cost elements involved in the manufacture of a product.

Distinguish between product costs and period costs and give examples of each.

Explain the difference between the financial statements of a manufacturing firm and those of a merchandising firm.

Prepare a schedule of cost of goods manufactured in good form.

Explain the flow of direct materials cost, direct labor cost, and manufacturing overhead cost from the point of incurrence to sale of the completed product.

Properly classify costs associated with idle time, overtime, and labor fringe benefits in an organization.

Identify and give examples of variable costs and fixed costs and explain the difference in their behavior.

Define or explain the key terms listed at the end of the chapter.

As explained in Chapter 1, the work of management centers on (1) planning, which includes setting objectives and outlining the means of attaining those objectives, and (2) control, which includes the steps taken or the means used to ensure that objectives are realized. In order to discharge planning and control responsibilities, the manager needs *information* about the organization. From an accounting point of view, the manager's information needs most often relate to the *costs* of the organization.

In financial accounting, the term *cost* is defined as the sacrifice made in order to obtain some good or service. The sacrifice may be measured in cash expended, property transferred, service performed, and so on. This definition is easily stated and widely accepted in financial accounting.

In managerial accounting, the term *cost* is used in many different ways. The reason is that there are many different types of costs, and these costs are classified differently according to the immediate needs of management. In this chapter, we look at some of these different types of costs and at some of the ways in which managers classify them for their own use internally.

GENERAL COST CLASSIFICATIONS

Costs are associated with all types of organizations—business, nonbusiness, service, retail, and manufacturing. Generally, the kinds of costs that are incurred and the way in which these costs are classified will depend on the type of organization involved. Cost accounting is as applicable to one type of organization as to another; for this reason, we shall consider the cost characteristics of a variety of organizations—manufacturing, merchandising, and service—in our discussion.

Manufacturing costs

A manufacturing firm is more complex than most other types of organizations. The reason is that the manufacturing firm is broader in its activities, being involved in production as well as in marketing and administration. An understanding of the cost structure of a manufacturing firm therefore provides a broad, general understanding of costing that can be very helpful in understanding the cost structures of other types of organizations.

Manufacturing involves the conversion of raw materials into finished products through the efforts of factory workers and the use of production equipment. By contrast, **merchandising** is the marketing of products that are in a finished form and that have been acquired from a manufacturer or other outside source. The cost of a manufactured product is made up of three basic elements:

1. Direct materials.
2. Direct labor.
3. Manufacturing overhead.

Direct materials A wide variety of materials can go into the manufacture of a product. These are generally termed **raw materials.** The term is somewhat misleading in that raw materials seems to imply basic, natural resources. Actually, raw materials is inclusive of any materials input into a product; and the finished product of one firm can become the raw materials of another firm. For example, the finished lumber products of a sawmill become the raw material of a construction company.

Direct materials are those materials that become an integral part of a company's finished product and that can be conveniently traced into it. This would include, for example, the sheet steel in a file cabinet or the wood in a table. Some items of materials may become an integral part of the finished product but may be traceable into the product only at great cost and inconvenience. Such items might include the glue used to put a table together or the welding materials used to bond the sheet metal in a file cabinet. Glue and welding materials would be called **indirect materials** and would be included as part of manufacturing overhead.

Direct labor The term **direct labor** is reserved for those labor costs that can be physically traced to the creation of products and that can be so traced without undue cost or inconvenience. The labor costs of assembly line workers, for example, would be direct labor costs, as would the labor costs of carpenters, bricklayers, and machine operators.

Labor costs that cannot be physically traced to the creation of products, or that can be traced only at great cost and inconvenience, are termed **indirect labor** and are treated as part of manufacturing overhead, along with indirect materials. Indirect labor would include the labor costs of janitors, supervisors, materials handlers, engineers, and night security guards. Although the efforts of these workers are essential to production, it would be either impractical or impossible to accurately relate the costs to specific units of product. Hence, such labor costs are treated as indirect labor.

Manufacturing overhead **Manufacturing overhead** can be defined very simply as including all costs of manufacturing except direct materials and direct labor. Included within this classification one would expect to find such costs as indirect materials, indirect labor, heat and light, property taxes, insurance, depreciation on factory facilities, repairs, maintenance, and all other costs of operating the manufacturing division of a company. There may also be costs for heat and light, property taxes, insurance, depreciation, and so forth associated with the selling and administrative functions in an organization, but these costs would not be included as part of manufacturing overhead. Only those costs that are associated with *operating the factory* would be included in the manufacturing overhead category.

Manufacturing overhead is known by various names. Sometimes it is called manufacturing expense, factory expense, overhead, factory overhead, or factory burden. All of these terms are synonymous with "manufacturing overhead."

Manufacturing overhead combined with direct labor is known as **conversion cost.** This term stems from the fact that direct labor costs and overhead costs are incurred in the *conversion* of materials into finished products. Direct labor combined with direct materials is known as **prime cost.**

Nonmanufacturing costs

Traditionally, most of the focus of managerial accounting has been on manufacturing costs and activities. The reason is probably traceable to the complexity of manufacturing operations and to the need for carefully developed costs for pricing and other decisions. However, costing techniques are now coming into use in many nonmanufacturing areas, as firms attempt to get better control over their costs and to provide management with more usable cost data.

Generally, nonmanufacturing costs are subclassified into two categories:

1. Marketing or selling costs.
2. Administrative costs.

Marketing or selling costs would include all costs necessary to secure customer orders and get the finished product or service into the hands of the customer. Since marketing costs relate to contacting customers and providing for their needs, these costs are often referred to as **order-getting and order-filling costs.** Examples of marketing costs would include advertising, shipping, sales travel, sales commissions, sales salaries, and costs associated with finished goods warehouses. *All* organizations have marketing costs, regardless of whether the organizations are manufacturing, merchandising, or service in nature.

Administrative costs would include all executive, organizational, and clerical costs that cannot logically be included under either production or marketing. Examples of such costs would include executive compensation, general accounting, secretarial, public relations, and similar costs having to do with the overall, general administration of the organization *as a whole.* As with marketing costs, *all* organizations have administrative costs.

As mentioned earlier, the concepts of cost accounting are as applicable to nonmanufacturing activities as they are to manufacturing activities, although they have not always been viewed as being so. Service organizations in particular are making increased use of cost concepts in analyzing and costing their services. For example, banks make use of cost analysis in determining the cost of offering such services as checking accounts, consumer loans, and credit cards; and insurance companies determine costs of servicing customers by geographic location, age, marital status, and occupation. Cost breakdowns of these types provide data for control over selling and administrative functions in the same way that manufacturing cost breakdowns provide data for control over manufacturing functions.

Period costs

In addition to being placed in manufacturing and nonmanufacturing categories, costs can also be classified as either *period* costs or *product* costs.

Period costs are those costs that are deducted from revenues on a time period basis and that are not involved in the manufacture of a product. Office rent is a good example of a period cost. Assume that office rent is $500 per month. This amount will have to be paid each month without regard to the amount of business activity that occurs during the month. Thus, the office rent is matched against revenues on a *time period* basis, and for this reason it is said to be a period cost.

All selling and administrative costs are treated as period costs and deducted from revenues as incurred. Thus, advertising, executive salaries, secretarial salaries, general accounting, public relations, and other nonmanufacturing costs as discussed in the preceding section would all be period costs, and they will appear on the income statement as expenses in the time period in which they are incurred.

Product costs

Some costs are better matched against products than they are against periods of time. Costs of this type—called **product costs**—consist of the costs that are involved in the manufacture of goods and include direct materials, direct labor, and manufacturing overhead. These costs are viewed as "attaching" to units of product as the units are produced, and they remain attached until sale takes place. At that time, the costs are released as expenses and matched against sales revenue.

We need to emphasize that unlike period costs, product costs are not necessarily treated as expenses in the time period in which they are incurred. Rather, as explained above, they are treated as expenses in the time period in which the related products *are sold*. This means that a product cost such as direct materials or direct labor might be incurred during one time period but not treated as an expense until a following period when sale of the completed product takes place.

Exhibit 2–1 contains a summary of the cost terms that we have introduced so far in our discussion.

COST CLASSIFICATIONS ON FINANCIAL STATEMENTS

In your prior accounting training, you learned that firms prepare periodic reports for creditors, stockholders, and others to show the financial condition of the firm and the firm's earnings performance over some specified interval. The reports you studied were probably those of merchandising firms, such as retail stores, which simply purchase goods from suppliers for resale to customers.

The financial statements prepared by a *manufacturing* firm are more complex than the statements prepared by a merchandising firm. As stated earlier, manufacturing firms are more complex organizations than merchandising firms because the manufacturing firm must produce its goods as well as

EXHIBIT 2–1
Summary of cost terms

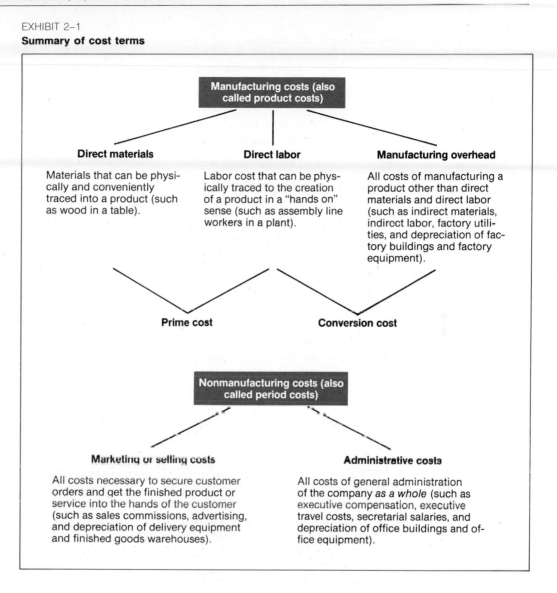

market them. The production process gives rise to many costs that do not exist in a merchandising firm, and somehow these costs must be accounted for on the manufacturing firm's financial statements. In this section, we focus our attention on how this accounting is carried out from a cost classification point of view.

The income statement

Exhibit 2–2 compares the income statement of a merchandising firm with the income statement of a manufacturing firm.

EXHIBIT 2–2
Comparative income statements: Merchandising and manufacturing firms

Merchandising firm

The cost of goods sold to customers comes from the purchased cost of these goods from an outside supplier.	Sales		$1,000,000
	Cost of goods sold:		
	Opening inventory	$100,000	
	Add purchases	650,000	
	Goods available for sale	750,000	
	Ending inventory	150,000	600,000
	Gross margin		400,000
	Less operating expenses:		
	Selling expense	100,000	
	Administrative expense	200,000	300,000
	Net income		$ 100,000

Manufacturing firm

The cost of goods sold to customers comes from the manufacturing costs that have been incurred in the manufacture of the goods. These costs consist of direct materials, direct labor, and manufacturing overhead (see Exhibit 2–3).	Sales		$1,500,000
	Cost of goods sold:		
	Opening finished goods inventory	$125,000	
	Add cost of goods manufactured	850,000	
	Goods available for sale	975,000	
	Ending finished goods inventory	175,000	800,000
	Gross margin		700,000
	Less operating expenses:		
	Selling expense	250,000	
	Administrative expense	300,000	550,000
	Net income		$ 150,000

Notice in the case of a merchandising firm that the cost of goods sold simply consists of the purchase cost of the goods from a supplier. By contrast, the cost of goods sold in a manufacturing firm consists of many different costs that have been incurred in the manufacturing process.

The income statement of a manufacturing firm is supported by a schedule of **cost of goods manufactured,** as illustrated in Exhibit 2–3. This schedule shows the specific costs that have gone into the goods that have been manufactured during the period. Notice that it contains the three elements of cost—direct materials, direct labor, and manufacturing overhead—that we discussed earlier as being the costs that go into any produced item. Also notice at the bottom of the schedule that one must add the beginning work in process inventory to the production costs of a period and then deduct the ending work in process inventory in order to determine the cost of goods manufactured. **Work in process** means goods that are only partially completed at the beginning or at the end of a period.

The balance sheet

The preparation of the balance sheet, or statement of financial condition, is also more complex in a manufacturing firm than in a merchandising firm.

EXHIBIT 2–3
Schedule of cost of goods manufactured

MANUFACTURING FIRM
Schedule of Cost of Goods Manufactured
For the Year Ended May 31, 19xx

Direct materials:		
Beginning raw materials inventory	$ 20,000*	
Add: Purchases of raw materials	165,000	
Raw materials available for use	185,000	
Deduct: Ending raw materials inventory	15,000	
Raw materials used in production		$170,000
Direct labor		300,000
Manufacturing overhead:		
Indirect materials	6,000	
Indirect labor	100,000	
Machine rental	50,000	
Utilities, factory	75,000	
Insurance, factory	21,000	
Depreciation, factory	90,000	
Property taxes, factory	8,000	
Total overhead costs		350,000
Total manufacturing costs		820,000
Add: Beginning work in process inventory		90,000
		910,000
Deduct: Ending work in process inventory		60,000
Cost of goods manufactured (see Exhibit 2–2)		$850,000

* We assume in this example that the Raw Materials inventory account contains only direct materials, and that indirect materials are carried in a separate "supplies" account. This is a common practice among companies. In Chapter 3 we discuss the procedure to be followed if *both* direct and indirect materials are carried in a single account.

A merchandising firm has only one class of inventory—goods purchased from suppliers that are awaiting resale to customers. By contrast, manufacturing firms have three classes of inventory—goods purchased as raw materials to go into manufactured products (known as **raw materials**), goods only partially completed as to manufacturing at the end of a period (known as **work in process**), and goods completed as to manufacturing but not yet sold to customers (known as **finished goods**).

The current asset section of a manufacturing firm's balance sheet is compared to the current asset section of a merchandising firm's balance sheet in Exhibit 2–4. The inventory accounts shown in these current asset sections constitute the *only difference* between the balance sheets of the two types of firms.

Product costs—a closer look

Earlier in the chapter, we defined product costs as being the costs that go into the manufacture of goods, and we stated that these costs consist of direct materials, direct labor, and manufacturing overhead. To understand product costs more fully, it will be helpful at this point to look briefly at

EXHIBIT 2–4
Current asset data: Merchandising firms versus manufacturing firms

Merchandising firm

Current assets:		
Cash		$ 10,000
Accounts receivable		60,000
Merchandise inventory		150,000
Prepaid expenses		5,000
Total current assets		$225,000

A single inventory account, consisting of goods purchased from suppliers.

Manufacturing firm

Current assets:		
Cash		$ 15,000
Accounts receivable		100,000
Inventories:		
Raw materials	$ 15,000	
Work in process	60,000	
Finished goods	175,000	250,000
Prepaid expenses		10,000
Total current assets		$375,000

Three inventory accounts, consisting of materials to be used in production, goods partially manufactured, and goods completely manufactured.

the flow of costs in a manufacturing firm. By doing so, we will be able to see how product costs move through the various accounts, and to see how they affect the balance sheet and the income statement in the course of manufacture and sale of goods.

Exhibit 2–5 illustrates the flow of costs in a manufacturing firm. Notice that direct materials cost, direct labor cost, and manufacturing overhead cost are all added into Work in Process. Work in Process can be viewed most simply as the assembly line in a manufacturing plant, where workers are stationed and where products slowly take shape as they move from one end of the assembly line to the other. The direct materials, direct labor, and manufacturing overhead costs shown in the exhibit as being added into Work in Process are the costs needed to complete these products as they move along this assembly line.

As goods are completed, notice from the exhibit that their cost is transferred from Work in Process into Finished Goods. Here the goods await sale to a customer. As goods are sold, their cost is then transferred from Finished Goods into Cost of Goods Sold. It is at this point that the various material, labor, and overhead costs which have been involved in the manufacture of the units being sold are treated as expenses in determining the net income or loss for the period.

Product costs are often called **inventoriable costs.** The reason, of course, is that these costs go directly into inventory accounts as they are incurred (first into Work in Process and then into Finished Goods), rather than going into expense accounts. Thus, they are termed inventoriable costs. *This is a key concept in managerial accounting, since such costs can end up on the balance sheet as assets if goods are only partially completed or are unsold at*

EXHIBIT 2–5
Cost flows and classifications

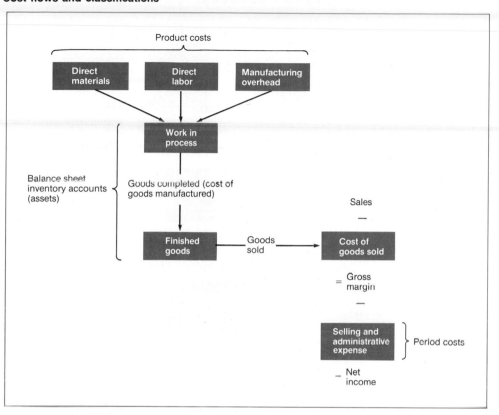

the end of a period. To illustrate this point, refer again to the data in Exhibit 2–5. Whatever materials, labor, and overhead costs which are associated with the units in the Work in Process and Finished Goods inventory accounts at the end of a period will appear on the balance sheet at that time as part of the company's assets. As explained earlier, these costs will not become expenses until later when the goods are completed and sold.

As shown in Exhibit 2–5, selling and administrative expenses have nothing to do with the manufacture of a product. For this reason, they are not treated as product costs, but rather are treated as period costs and go directly into expense accounts as they are incurred.

An example of cost flows   To provide a numerical example of cost flows in a manufacturing company, assume that a company's cost outlay for insurance is $2,000 annually, of which three fourths applies to operation of the factory and one fourth applies to selling and administrative activities. In this case, $1,500 (three fourths) of the $2,000 insurance cost would be a product (inventoriable) cost and would be added to the cost of the goods produced during the year. This concept is illustrated in Exhibit 2–6, where

EXHIBIT 2–6

An example of cost flows in a manufacturing company

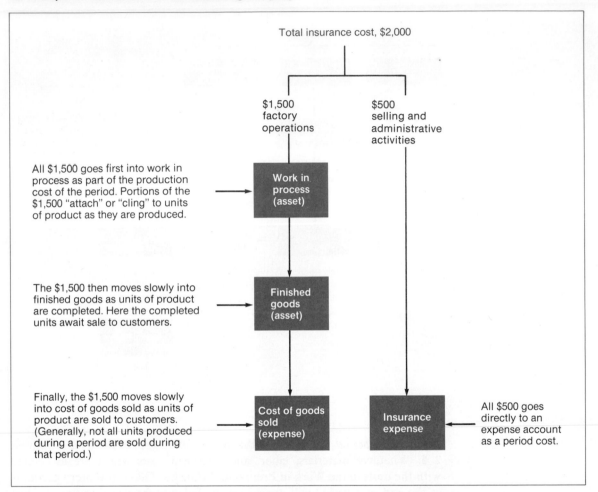

$1,500 of insurance cost is added into Work in Process. As shown in the exhibit, this portion of the year's insurance cost will not become an expense until the goods that are produced during the year are sold (sale may not take place until the following year). Until the goods are sold, the $1,500 will remain as part of the asset, inventory (either as part of Work in Process or as part of Finished Goods), along with the other costs of producing the goods.

By contrast, the $500 of insurance cost that applies to the company's selling and administrative activities will go into an expense account immediately as a charge against the period.

A summary of product and period costs The chart in Exhibit 2–7 contains a summary of product and period costs in both manufacturing and merchandising firms.

EXHIBIT 2–7

A summary of product and period costs

Type of firm	Product costs	Period costs	Treatment
Merchandising firm	Cost of purchased inventory from suppliers		These costs are placed in an inventory account until the goods are sold. When sale takes place, the costs are then taken to expense as cost of goods sold.
Manufacturing firm	Direct materials Direct labor Manufacturing overhead (consists of all costs of production other than direct materials and direct labor)		These costs are placed in inventory accounts until the associated goods are completed and sold. When sale takes place, the costs are then taken (released) to expense as cost of goods sold.

Both merchandising and manufacturing firms		Selling expenses:
		  Salespeople's salaries
		  Depreciation on sales equipment
		  Insurance on sales equipment
		Administration expenses:
		  Secretarial salaries
		  Depreciation on office equipment
		  Insurance on office equipment
			These costs are taken directly to expense accounts. They are classified as operating expenses and deducted from gross margin.

The reader should study this exhibit with care, noting particularly the treatment of each type of cost as shown in the extreme right column.

FURTHER CLASSIFICATION OF LABOR COSTS

Of all the costs of production, labor costs often present the most difficult problems of segregation and classification. Although firms vary considerably in their breakdown of labor costs, the following subdivisions represent the most common approach:

Direct labor	Indirect labor (part of manufacturing overhead)	Other labor costs
(Discussed earlier)	Janitors Supervisors Materials handlers Engineers Night security guards Maintenance workers	Idle time Overtime premium Labor fringe benefits

The costs listed under "Indirect Labor" and under "Other Labor Costs" should not be viewed as being inclusive but rather as being representative of the kinds of costs that one might expect to find under these classifications. Certain of these costs require further comment.

Idle time

Idle time represents the costs of direct labor workers who are unable to perform their assignments due to machine breakdowns, materials shortages, power failures, and the like. Although direct labor workers are involved, the costs of idle time are treated as part of manufacturing overhead cost rather than as part of direct labor cost. The reason is that managers feel that such costs should be spread over *all* the production of a period rather than just over the jobs that happen to be in process when breakdowns and the like occur.

To give an example of how the cost of idle time is computed, assume that a press operator earns $12 per hour. If the press operator works 40 hours during a given week but is idle for 3 hours due to breakdowns, labor cost would be allocated as follows:

Direct labor cost ($12 × 37 hours)	$444
Manufacturing overhead cost (idle time: $12 × 3 hours)	36
Total cost for the week	$480

Overtime premium

The overtime premium paid to *all* factory workers (direct labor as well as indirect labor) is usually considered to be part of manufacturing overhead and not assignable to any particular order or batch of production. At first glance this may seem strange, since overtime is always spent working on some particular order. Why not charge that order for the overtime cost? The reason is that production is usually scheduled on a random basis. If production is randomly scheduled, then it would be unfair to charge an overtime premium against a particular batch of goods simply because the batch *happened* to fall on the tail end of the daily scheduling sheet.

To illustrate, assume that two batches of goods, order A and order B, each take three hours to complete. The production run on order A is scheduled early in the day, but the production run on order B isn't scheduled until late in the afternoon. By the time the run on order B is completed, two hours of overtime have been logged in. The necessity to work overtime was a result of the fact that *total* production exceeded the regular time available. Order B was no more responsible for the overtime than was order A. Therefore, all production should share in the premium charge that resulted. This is a much more equitable way of handling overtime premium in that it doesn't penalize one run simply because it happens to fall late in the day.

Let us again assume that a press operator in a plant earns $12 per hour. He is paid time and a half for overtime (time in excess of 40 hours a week). During a given week he works 45 hours and has no idle time. His labor cost for the week would be allocated as follows:

Direct labor ($12 × 45 hours)	$540
Manufacturing overhead (overtime premium: $6 × 5 hours)	30
Total cost for the week	$570

Notice from this computation that only the overtime premium of $6 per hour is charged to the overhead account—*not* the entire $18 ($12 regular rate × 1.5) earned for each hour of overtime work.

Labor fringe benefits

The proper classification of labor fringe benefits is not so clearly defined as idle time or overtime. Labor fringe benefits are made up of employment-related costs paid by the employer and include the costs of insurance programs, retirement plans, various supplemental unemployment benefits, and hospitalization plans. Many firms treat all such costs as indirect labor by adding them in total to manufacturing overhead. Other firms draw a distinction between those labor fringe benefits relating to direct labor and those relating to indirect labor. These firms treat the cost of benefits relating to direct labor as additional direct labor cost; the cost of benefits relating to indirect labor, on the other hand, is added to manufacturing overhead.

The cost to the employer for fringe benefits is substantial. A recent nationwide survey by the Chamber of Commerce shows that fringe benefits, on the average, cost 37 cents for every dollar of gross wages.

COSTS AND CONTROL

The cost classifications that are used to prepare financial statements may not be the same cost classifications that a manager uses to control operations and to plan for the future. For control purposes, costs are often classified as being variable or fixed, direct or indirect, and controllable or noncontrollable.

Variable and fixed costs

From a planning and control standpoint, perhaps the most useful way to classify costs is by behavior. **Cost behavior** means how a cost will react or respond to changes in the level of business activity. As the activity level rises and falls, a particular cost may rise and fall as well—or it may remain constant. For planning purposes, the manager must be able to anticipate which of these will happen, and if a cost can be expected to change, he or she must know by how much. To provide this information, costs are classified into two categories—variable and fixed.

Variable costs   Variable costs are costs that vary, in total, in direct proportion to changes in the level of activity. A good example of a variable cost is direct materials. The cost of direct materials used during a period will vary, in total, in direct proportion to the number of units that are produced. To illustrate this idea, assume that a company produces automobiles and that each auto produced requires one battery. As the output of autos increases and decreases, the number of batteries used will increase and decrease proportionately. If auto production goes up 10 percent, then the number of batteries used will go up 10 percent as well.

Notice that when we speak of a cost as being variable, we do so in terms of its *total dollar amount*—the total cost rises and falls as the activity level rises and falls. This idea is presented below, assuming that batteries cost $10 each:

Number of autos produced	Cost per battery	Total variable cost— batteries
1	$10	$ 10
10	10	100
100	10	1,000
1,000	10	10,000

Although variable costs, in total, rise and fall in proportion to changes in the activity level, notice from the tabulation above *that they remain constant if expressed on a per unit basis.* That is, the cost of batteries in the tabulation above *remains constant at $10 per battery,* although the total amount of cost involved rises proportionately to the increase in the number of autos produced each period.

There are many examples of variable costs. In a manufacturing firm, they would include direct materials, direct labor, and some items of manufacturing overhead (such as utilities, supplies, and lubricants). In a merchandising firm, they would include cost of goods sold, commissions to salespersons, and billing costs.

Fixed costs   Fixed costs are costs that remain constant, in total, regardless of changes in the level of activity. That is, unlike variable costs, fixed costs are not affected by changes in activity from period to period. Consequently, as the activity level rises and falls, the fixed costs remain constant in total amount unless influenced by some outside force, such as price changes. Rent is a good example of a fixed cost. If a company pays $5,000 rent on a machine each month, that amount of total cost will be sustained regardless of whether 10 units or 1,000 units are produced in a given month.

The fact that fixed costs (in total) are not affected by activity can create difficulties in costing units of product, since the cost computed on a *per unit* basis will depend on the number of units being manufactured. As production increases, the average cost per unit will fall, since the fixed cost is spread over more units; conversely, as production declines, the average cost per unit will rise, since a constant fixed cost figure will be spread over fewer units. This idea is illustrated below, assuming again a monthly rental cost of $5,000 for a piece of equipment that is capable of producing up to 1,000 units of product each month. The cost of the equipment, expressed on a per unit basis, is shown for 10-, 100-, and 1,000-unit levels of output:

Monthly rental cost		Number of units produced	Average cost per unit
$5,000	. . . .	10	$500
5,000	. . . .	100	50
5,000	. . . .	1,000	5

Note that if the company produces only 10 units each month, the rental cost will average $500 per unit. But if 1,000 units are produced each month, the average cost will drop to only $5 per unit. More will be said later on the problems created for both the accountant and the manager by this type of variation in unit costs.

Examples of fixed costs include depreciation, insurance, property taxes, rent, supervisory salaries, and advertising.

Summary of variable and fixed costs   Understanding the behavior of variable and fixed costs is one of the most difficult parts of this chapter. To assist in this understanding, a summary is presented in Exhibit 2–8 of how these costs behave on both a total and a per unit basis. Study this exhibit with care, along with the material in the preceding paragraphs, until you thoroughly understand the concepts involved.

EXHIBIT 2–8
Summary of variable and fixed cost behavior

Cost	Behavior of the cost	
	In total	**Per unit**
Variable cost	Total variable cost increases and decreases in proportion to changes in the activity level.	Variable costs remain constant per unit
Fixed cost	Total fixed cost is not affected by changes in the activity level (i.e., total fixed cost remains constant even if the activity level changes).	Fixed costs decrease per unit as the activity level rises and increase per unit as the activity level falls.

Direct and indirect costs

Costs are often classified as being either direct or indirect. However, these terms have no meaning unless one first identifies some organizational segment to which the costs are to be related. The organizational segment might be a product line, a sales territory, a division, or some other subpart of a company. A **direct cost** is a cost that can be obviously and physically traced to the particular segment under consideration. For example, if the segment under consideration is a product line, then the materials and labor involved in the manufacture of the line would both be direct costs.

An **indirect cost** is a cost that must be allocated in order to be assigned to the segment under consideration. Manufacturing overhead, for example, would be an indirect cost of a product line. The reason is that manufacturing overhead is not directly identifiable with any particular product line but rather is incurred as a consequence of general, overall operating activities. Indirect costs are also known as *common costs.*

In sum, the following guidelines prevail in distinguishing between direct and indirect (common) costs:

1. If a cost can be obviously and physically traced to a unit of product or some other organizational segment, then it is a direct cost with respect to that segment.
2. If a cost must be allocated in order to be assigned to a unit of product or some other organizational segment, then it is an indirect (common) cost with respect to that segment.

Controllable and noncontrollable costs

As with direct and indirect costs, whether a cost is controllable or noncontrollable depends on the point of reference. *All* costs are controllable at some level or another in a company. Only at the lower levels of management can some costs be considered noncontrollable. Top management has the power to expand or contract facilities, hire, fire, set expenditure policies, and generally exercise control over any cost as it desires. At lower levels of management, however, authority may not exist to control the incurrence of some costs, and these costs will therefore be considered noncontrollable *so far as that level of management is concerned.*

A cost is considered to be a **controllable cost** at a particular level of management if that level has power to *authorize* the cost. For example, entertainment expense would be controllable by a sales manager if he or she had power to authorize the amount and type of entertainment for customers. On the other hand, depreciation of warehouse facilities would not be controllable by the sales manager, since he or she would have no power to authorize warehouse construction.

In some situations, there is a time dimension to controllability. Costs that are controllable over the long run may not be controllable over the short run. A good example is advertising. Once an advertising program has been set and a contract signed, management has no power to change the amount of spending. But when the contract expires, advertising costs can be renegotiated, and thus management can exercise control over the long run. Another example is plant acquisition. Management is free to build any size plant it desires, but once a plant has been built, management is largely powerless to change the attendant costs over the short run.

OTHER COST CONCEPTS

There are three other cost concepts with which we should be familiar as we start our study of managerial accounting. These concepts are differential costs, opportunity costs, and sunk costs.

Differential costs

In making decisions, managers compare the alternatives before them. Each alternative will have certain costs associated with it that must be compared to the costs associated with the other alternatives available. Any cost that is present under one alternative but is absent in whole or in part under another alternative is known as a **differential cost.** Differential costs are also known as **incremental costs,** although technically an incremental cost should refer only to an increase in cost from one alternative to another; decreases in cost should be referred to as *decremental costs.* Differential cost is a broader term, encompassing both cost increases (incremental costs) and cost decreases (decremental costs) between alternatives.

The accountant's differential cost concept can be compared to the economist's marginal cost concept. In speaking of changes in cost and revenue, the economist employs the terms *marginal cost* and *marginal revenue.* The revenue that can be obtained from selling one more unit of product is called marginal revenue, and the cost involved in producing one more unit of product is called marginal cost. The economist's marginal concept is basically the same as the accountant's differential concept.

Differential costs can be either fixed or variable. To illustrate, assume that Cosmetics, Inc., is thinking about changing its marketing method from distribution through retailers to distribution by direct sale. Present costs and revenues are compared to projected costs and revenues below:

	Retailer distribution (present)	Direct sale distribution (proposed)	Differential costs and revenues
Revenues (V)	$700,000	$800,000	$100,000
Cost of goods sold (V)	350,000	400,000	50,000
Advertising (F).	80,000	45,000	(35,000)
Commissions (V)	–0–	40,000	40,000
Warehouse depreciation (F)	50,000	80,000	30,000
Other expenses (F)	60,000	60,000	–0–
Total	540,000	625,000	85,000
Net income.	$160,000	$175,000	$ 15,000

V = variable; F = fixed.

The differential revenue is $100,000, and the differential costs total $85,000, leaving a positive differential net income of $15,000 under the proposed marketing plan. As noted earlier, those differential costs representing cost increases could have been referred to more specifically as incremental costs, and those representing cost decreases could have been referred to more specifically as decremental costs. The reader should be acquainted with all of these terms, since they are widely used in day-to-day business practice.

Opportunity costs

An **opportunity cost** can be defined as the potential benefit that is lost or sacrificed when the choice of one course of action requires the giving up of an alternative course of action. To illustrate, consider the following:

Example 1

Vicki has a part-time job that pays her $100 per week. She would like to spend a week at the beach during spring vacation from school, but she has no vacation time available. If she takes the trip anyway, the $100 in lost wages will be an opportunity cost of doing so.

Example 2

A firm is considering the investment of a large sum of money in land that is to be held for future expansion. Rather than being invested in land, the funds could be invested in high-grade securities. If the land is acquired, the opportunity cost will be the investment income that could have been realized if the securities had been purchased instead.

Example 3

Steve is employed with a company that pays him a salary of $20,000 per year. He is thinking about leaving the company in order to return to school. Since returning to school would require that he give up his $20,000 salary, the foregone salary would be an opportunity cost of seeking further education.

Opportunity cost is not usually entered on the books of an organization, but it is a cost that must be explicitly considered in every decision that a manager makes. Virtually every alternative has some opportunity cost attached to it. In example 3 above, for instance, if Steve decides to stay at his job there still is an opportunity cost involved: it is the greater income that could be realized in future years as a result of returning to school.

In short, every alternative course of action facing a manager has a mixture of good and bad features. In rejecting a course of action, the good features must be given up along with the bad. The net good features of a rejected alternative become the opportunity costs of the alternative that is selected.

Sunk costs

A **sunk cost** is a cost *that has already been incurred* and that cannot be changed by any decision made now or in the future. Since sunk costs cannot be changed by any present or future decision, they are not differential costs, and therefore they should not be used in analyzing future courses of action.

To illustrate the notion of a sunk cost, assume that a firm has just paid $50,000 for a special-purpose machine. Since the cost outlay *has been made,* the $50,000 investment in the machine is a sunk cost. Even though by hindsight the purchase may have been unwise, no amount of regret can relieve the company of its decision, nor can any future decision cause the cost to be avoided. In short, the $50,000 is "out the window" from a decision point of view and will have to be reckoned with regardless of what future course of action the company may take. For this reason, such costs are said to be sunk.

SUMMARY

Although the term *cost* has a fairly distinctive meaning in financial accounting, it can be used in many different ways in managerial accounting. In this chapter, we have looked at some of the ways in which it is used by the manager in order to organize and classify data.

We have learned that costs can be classified as being either period costs or product costs. Period costs are incurred as a function of time rather than as a function of goods produced. Product costs relate to goods produced and basically consist of the costs associated with operating the factory. We have found that product costs fall into one of three categories—direct materials, direct labor, and manufacturing overhead. These costs go first into Work in Process. As goods are completed, the costs come out of Work in Process and go into Finished Goods. As goods are shipped to customers, the costs come out of Finished Goods and go into Cost of Goods Sold. The costs of partially completed or unsold goods appear as assets on the balance sheet of a manufacturing company, in the form of work in process inventory or in the form of finished goods inventory.

We have found that costs can also be classified as being either variable or fixed, direct or indirect, and controllable or noncontrollable. In addition, we defined differential costs, opportunity costs, and sunk costs. A differential cost is the difference in cost between two alternatives. An opportunity cost is the benefit that is forgone in rejecting some course of action, and a sunk cost is a cost that has already been incurred.

All of these cost terms and classifications are basic to managerial accounting. We shall use them repeatedly, as well as refine them further, in chapters ahead.

REVIEW PROBLEM ON COST TERMS

Many new cost terms have been introduced in this chapter. It will take you some time to learn what each term means and to learn how to properly classify costs in an organization. To assist in this learning process, consider the following example: Porter Company manufactures a number of furniture

Solution to the review problem

	Variable cost	Fixed cost	Period (selling and administrative) cost	Product cost: Direct materials	Product cost: Direct labor	Product cost: Manufacturing overhead	To units of product: Direct	To units of product: Indirect	Sunk cost	Opportunity cost
1. Wood used in a table (at $100 per table)	X			X			X			
2. Labor cost to assemble a table (at $40 per table)	X				X		X			
3. Salary of the factory supervisor (at $25,000 per year)		X				X		X		
4. Cost of electricity to produce tables (at $2 per labor-hour)	X					X		X		
5. Depreciation of machines used to produce tables (at $10,000 per year)		X				X		X	X*	
6. Salary of the company president (at $100,000 per year)		X	X							
7. Advertising expense (at $250,000 per year)		X	X							
8. Commissions paid to salespersons (at $30 per table sold)	X		X							
9. Rental income forgone on factory space										X†

* This is a sunk cost since the outlay for the equipment was made in some previous period.
† This is an opportunity cost since it represents the potential benefit that is lost or sacrificed as a result of using the factory space to produce tables. Notice that the cost is not classified as a fixed cost or in any other way. Such classifications are of no significance, since opportunity costs are not recorded on the books of an organization.

products, including tables. Selected costs associated with the manufacture of the tables and associated with the general operations of the company are given below:

1. Wood is used in the manufacture of the tables, at a cost of $100 per table.
2. The tables are assembled by workers, at a cost of $40 per table.
3. Workers assembling the tables are supervised by a factory supervisor who is paid $25,000 per year.
4. Electrical costs of $2 per labor-hour are incurred in the factory in the manufacture of the tables. (It requires four labor-hours to produce a table.)
5. The depreciation cost of the machines used in the manufacture of the tables totals $10,000 per year.
6. The salary of the president of Porter Company is $100,000 per year.
7. Porter Company spends $250,000 per year to advertise its products.
8. Salespersons are paid a commission of $30 for each table sold.
9. Instead of producing the tables, Porter Company could rent its factory space out at a rental income of $50,000 per year.

In the table on the preceding page, these costs are classified according to various cost terms used in the chapter. *Carefully study the classification of each cost.* If you don't understand why a particular cost is classified the way it is, turn back and read the section of the chapter dealing with the cost term involved.

KEY TERMS FOR REVIEW

Administrative costs All organizational, executive, and clerical costs associated with the general management of an organization.

Controllable costs A cost is controllable at a particular level of management if that level has power to authorize the cost.

Conversion cost Direct labor cost combined with manufacturing overhead cost.

Cost behavior The way in which a cost will react or respond to changes in the level of business activity.

Cost of goods manufactured The materials, labor, and overhead costs that have gone into the products that have been produced during a period.

Differential cost Any cost that is present under one alternative but is absent in whole or in part under another alternative in a decision-making situation. Also see *Incremental cost.*

Direct cost A cost that can be obviously and physically traced to a unit of product or other organizational segment.

Direct labor Those factory labor costs that can be physically traced to the creation of products in a "hands on" sense.

Direct materials Those materials that become an integral part of a finished product and can be conveniently traced into it.

Finished goods Goods completed as to manufacturing but not yet sold to customers.

Fixed cost A cost that remains constant, in total, regardless of changes in the level of activity. If a fixed cost is expressed on a per unit basis, it varies inversely with the level of activity.

Incremental cost An increase in cost between two alternatives. Also see *Differential cost.*

Indirect cost A cost that must be allocated in order to be assigned to a unit of product or some other organizational segment. Also known as *common cost.*

Indirect labor The factory labor costs of janitors, supervisors, engineers, and others that cannot be traced directly to the creation of products in a "hands on" sense.

Indirect materials Those materials such as glue and nails that may become an integral part of a finished product but are traceable into the product only at great cost or inconvenience.

Inventoriable costs Direct materials, direct labor, and manufacturing overhead costs used in the production process. Also see *Product costs.*

Manufacturing The conversion of raw materials into finished products through the efforts of factory workers and the use of production equipment.

Manufacturing overhead All costs associated with the manufacturing process except direct materials and direct labor.

Marketing or selling costs Those costs necessary to secure customer orders and get the finished product or service into the hands of the customer. This term is synonymous with *order-getting and order-filling costs.*

Merchandising The sale of products that are in finished form and that have been acquired from a manufacturer or other outside source.

Opportunity cost The potential benefit that is lost or sacrificed when the choice of one course of action requires the giving up of an alternative course of action.

Order-getting and order-filling costs Those costs necessary to secure customer orders and get the finished product or service into the hands of the customer. This term is synonymous with *marketing or selling costs.*

Period costs Those costs that are deducted from revenues on a time period basis and that are not involved in the manufacture of a product; such costs consist of selling (marketing) and administrative expenses.

Prime cost Direct materials cost combined with direct labor cost.

Product costs Costs that are involved in the manufacture of goods; such costs consist of direct materials, direct labor, and manufacturing overhead. Also see *Inventoriable costs.*

Raw materials Any materials going into a manufactured product.

Sunk cost Any cost that has already been incurred and that can't be changed by any decision made now or in the future.

Variable cost A cost that varies, in total, in direct proportion to changes in the level of activity. A variable cost is constant per unit.

Work in process Goods that are only partially completed as to manufacturing at the beginning or end of a period and that will need further work before being ready for sale to a customer.

QUESTIONS

2–1. Distinguish between merchandising and manufacturing.

2–2. What are the three major elements in the cost of a manufactured product?

2–3. Distinguish between the following: *(a)* direct materials, *(b)* indirect materials, *(c)* direct labor, *(d)* indirect labor, and *(e)* manufacturing overhead.

2–4. Explain the difference between a product cost and a period cost.

2–5. Describe how the income statement of a manufacturing firm differs from the income statement of a merchandising firm.

2–6. Of what value is the schedule of cost of goods manufactured? How does it tie into the income statement?

2–7. Distinguish between prime cost and conversion cost. What is meant by conversion cost?

2–8. Describe how the balance sheet of a manufacturing firm differs from the balance sheet of a merchandising firm so far as current assets are concerned.

2–9. Why are product costs sometimes called inventoriable costs? Describe the flow of such costs in a manufacturing firm from the point of incurrence until they finally become expenses on the income statement.

2–10. Is it possible for costs such as salaries or depreciation to end up as assets on the balance sheet? Explain.

2–11. Give at least three terms that may be substituted for the term *manufacturing overhead.*

2–12. Mary Adams is employed by Acme Company. Last week she worked 34 hours assembling one of the company's products and was idle 6 hours due to material shortages. Ms. Adams is paid $8 per hour. Allocate her earnings between direct labor cost and manufacturing overhead cost.

2–13. John Olsen operates a stamping machine on the assembly line of the Drake Manufacturing Company. Last week Mr. Olsen worked 45 hours. His basic wage rate is $5 per hour, with time and a half for overtime. How should last week's wage cost be allocated as between direct labor cost and manufacturing overhead cost?

2–14. What is meant by the term *cost behavior?*

2–15. "A variable cost is a cost that varies per unit of product, whereas a fixed cost is constant per unit of product." Do you agree? Explain.

2–16. How do fixed costs create difficulties in costing units of product?

2–17. Why is manufacturing overhead considered an indirect cost of a unit of product?

2–18. Under what conditions is a cost controllable at a particular level of management?

2–19. Define the following terms: differential cost, opportunity cost, and sunk cost.

2–20. Only variable costs can be differential costs. Do you agree? Explain.

EXERCISES

E2–1. Following are a number of cost terms introduced in the chapter:

Prime cost	Fixed cost
Variable cost	Period cost

Opportunity cost   Conversion cost
Product cost   Sunk cost

Choose the cost term or terms above that most appropriately describe the cost identified in each of the following situations. A cost term can be used more than once.

1. The paper going into the manufacture of this book would be called direct materials and classified as a _____ cost. In terms of cost behavior, the paper could also be described as a _____ cost.

2. The paper and other materials used in the manufacture of this book, combined with the direct labor cost involved, would be called _____ cost.

3. Instead of writing this book, the author could have spent many hours consulting with business organizations. The consulting fees forgone would be called _____ cost.

4. Several hundred copies of this book were left over from the prior edition and are stored in a warehouse. The amount invested in these books would be called a _____ cost.

5. Taken together, the direct labor cost and manufacturing overhead cost involved in the manufacture of this book would be called _____ cost.

6. Although depreciation of equipment is a _____ cost in a merchandising organization, it is a _____ cost in a manufacturing organization if the equipment is used in the production process. In terms of cost behavior, depreciation would probably be classified as a _____ cost.

7. The commission paid to the salesperson who sold this book would be classified by the publisher as a _____ cost. In terms of cost behavior, commissions would be classified as a _____ cost.

8. One of the costs listed above is never recorded on the books of an organization. This is _____ cost.

9. A _____ cost is also known as an inventoriable cost, since such costs can appear on the balance sheet at the end of a period as part of either work in process inventory or finished goods inventory.

10. Costs can often be classified in several different ways. For example, we have said that the paper going into the manufacture of this book would be called direct materials; it can also be classified as a _____ cost, a _____ cost, and as part of _____ cost.

E2–2. The following information has been taken from the cost records of Arbor Company for the month of March 19x7:

Raw materials inventory, March 1	$ 20,000
Raw materials inventory, March 31	10,000
Work in process inventory, March 1	30,000
Work in process inventory, March 31	40,000
Finished goods inventory, March 1	56,000
Finished goods inventory, March 31	41,000
Insurance, factory equipment	500
Insurance, office equipment	300
Direct labor cost	90,000
Purchases of raw materials	130,000
Indirect labor cost	29,000
Indirect materials cost	4,000
Depreciation, office equipment	2,000
Rent, factory facilities	17,000
Maintenance, factory equipment	3,000
Depreciation, factory equipment	6,500
Advertising expense	100,000

Required: 1. Prepare a schedule of cost of goods manufactured for March 19x7.

                2. Prepare a schedule of cost of goods sold for March 19x7.

E2–3.   The Devon Motor Company produces automobiles. During April 19x5, the company purchased 8,000 batteries at a cost of $10 per battery. It withdrew 7,600 batteries from the storeroom during the month. Of these, 100 were used to replace batteries in cars being used by the company's traveling sales staff. The remaining 7,500 batteries withdrawn from the storeroom were placed in cars being produced by the company. Of the cars in production during April, 90 percent were completed and transferred from work in process to finished goods. Of the cars completed during the month, 30 percent were unsold at April 30.

          There were no inventories of any type on April 1, 19x5.

Required: 1. Determine the cost of batteries that would appear in each of the following accounts at April 30, 19x5:

                a. Raw Materials.

                b. Work in Process.

                c. Finished Goods.

                d. Cost of Goods Sold.

                e. Selling Expense.

            2. Specify whether each of the above accounts would appear on the balance sheet or on the income statement at April 30.

E2–4.   Below are a number of costs that might be incurred in a manufacturing or service organization. Copy the list of costs down on your answer sheet, and then place an *X* in the appropriate column for each cost to indicate whether the cost involved would be variable or fixed.

		Cost behavior	
Cost		**Variable**	**Fixed**
1.	Steering wheels used in automobile production		
2.	Straight-line depreciation of a building		
3.	Product advertising.		
4.	Electrical costs of running machines		
5.	Top-management salaries		
6.	X rays in a hospital		
7.	Commissions to salespersons		
8.	Property taxes on a factory building		
9.	Direct labor workers in a factory		
10.	Rent on a doctor's office		

E2–5.   Several weeks ago you called the Jiffy Plumbing Company to have some routine repair work done on the plumbing system in your home. The plumber came about two weeks later, at four o'clock in the afternoon, and spent two hours completing your repair work. The bill he handed you at the completion of the work contained a $75 charge for labor—$30 for the first hour and $45 for the second.

          The plumber explained that the higher rate for the second hour contained a charge for an "overtime premium," since the union required that plumbers be paid time and a half for work in excess of eight hours per day. He also explained that the company was working overtime to "catch up a little" on its backlog of work orders.

Required: 1. Do you agree with the plumber's computation of your labor charge? Explain.

            2. Prepare computations to show how the cost of the plumber's time for the day

(nine hours) should be allocated between direct labor cost and general overhead cost on the company's books.

3. Under what circumstances might the company be justified in charging you an overtime premium for the plumber's services?

E2–6. A product cost is also known as an inventoriable cost. Classify the following costs as being either product (inventoriable) costs or period (noninventoriable) costs in a manufacturing company:

1. Depreciation on salespersons' cars.
2. Rent on equipment used in the factory.
3. Lubricants used for maintenance of machines.
4. Salaries of finished goods warehouse personnel.
5. Soap and paper towels used by workers at the end of a shift.
6. Factory supervisors' salaries.
7. Heat, water, and power consumed in the factory.
8. Materials used in boxing units of finished product for shipment overseas. (Units are not normally boxed.)
9. Advertising outlays.
10. Workers' compensation insurance.
11. Depreciation on chairs and tables in the factory lunchroom.
12. The salary of the switchboard operator for the company.
13. Depreciation on a Lear Jet used by the company's executives.
14. Rent on rooms at a Florida resort for holding of the annual sales conference.
15. Replacement of small cutting tools broken on the assembly line.

E2–7. Bill Cameron is employed by the Dahl Company. He works on the company's assembly line and assembles a component part for one of the company's products. Bill is paid $12 per hour for regular time, and he is paid time and a half for all work in excess of 40 hours per week.

Required:
1. Assume that during a given week Bill is idle for two hours due to machine breakdowns and that he is idle for four more hours due to material shortages. No overtime is recorded for the week. Allocate Bill's wages for the week as between direct labor cost and manufacturing overhead cost.
2. Assume that during a following week Bill works a total of 50 hours. He has no idle time for the week. Allocate Bill's wages for the week as between direct labor cost and manufacturing overhead cost.
3. Bill's company provides an attractive package of fringe benefits for its employees. This package includes a retirement program and a health insurance program. So far as direct labor workers are concerned, explain two ways that the company could handle the costs of fringe benefits in its cost records.

E2–8. The following cost and inventory data are taken from the books of the Eccles Company as of June 30, 19x5:

Costs incurred:
Rent, factory	$ 50,000
Direct labor	90,000
Sales salaries	45,000
Purchases of raw materials	120,000
Indirect labor	38,000
Utilities, factory	9,000
Advertising expense	80,000
Indirect materials	3,000

	July 1, 19x4	June 30, 19x5
Inventories;		
Raw materials	$15,000	$ 10,000
Work in process	21,000	26,000
Finished goods	40,000	32,000

Required: 1.   Prepare a schedule of cost of goods manufactured in good form.
2.   Prepare a schedule of cost of goods sold in good form.

PROBLEMS

P2–9.   **Cost classification.**   Various costs associated with the operation of a factory are given below.

1.   Plastic washers used in auto production.
2.   Production superintendent's salary.
3.   Laborers assembling a product.
4.   Electricity for operation of machines.
5.   Janitorial salaries.
6.   Clay used in brick production.
7.   Rent on a factory building.
8.   Wood used in ski production.
9.   Screws used in furniture production.
10.   A supervisor's salary.
11.   Cloth used in suit production.
12.   Depreciation of cafeteria equipment.
13.   Glue used in textbook production.
14.   Lubricants for machines.
15.   Paper used in textbook production.

Required: Classify each cost as being either variable or fixed with respect to volume or level of activity. Also classify each cost as being either direct or indirect with respect to units of product. Prepare your answer sheet as shown below:

	Cost behavior		To units of product	
Cost item	Variable	Fixed	Direct	Indirect
Example: Factory insurance		X		X

If you are unsure whether a cost would be variable or fixed, consider how it would behave over fairly wide ranges of activity.

P2–10.   **Cost identification.**   Several years ago Medex Company purchased a small building adjacent to its manufacturing plant in order to have room for expansion when needed. Since the company had no immediate need for the extra space, the building was rented out to another company for a rental revenue of $40,000 per year. The renter's lease will expire next month, and rather than renewing the lease, Medex Company has decided to use the building itself to manufacture a new product.

Direct materials cost for the new product will total $40 per unit. It will be necessary to hire a supervisor to oversee production. His salary will be $1,500 per month. Workers will be hired to manufacture the new product, with direct labor cost amounting to $18 per unit. Manufacturing operations will occupy all of the building space, so it will be necessary to rent space in a warehouse nearby in order to store finished units of product. The rental cost will be $1,000 per month. In addition, the company will need to rent equipment for use in producing the new product; the rental cost will be $3,000 per month. The company will continue to depreciate the building on a straight-line basis, as in past years. Depreciation on the building is $10,000 per year.

Advertising costs for the new product will total $50,000 per year. Costs of shipping the new product to customers will be $10 per unit. Electrical costs of operating machines and other utility costs will be $2 per unit.

Required: Prepare an answer sheet with the following column headings:

Name of the cost	Variable cost	Fixed cost	Product cost			Period (selling and adminis- trative) cost	Oppor- tunity cost	Sunk cost
			Direct materials	Direct labor	Manufacturing overhead			

List the different costs associated with the new product decision down the extreme left column (under "Name of the cost"). Then place an X under each heading that helps to describe the type of cost involved. There may be X's under several column headings for a single cost. (For example, a cost may be a fixed cost, a period cost, and a sunk cost; you would place an X under each of these column headings opposite the cost.)

P2–11. **Schedule of cost of goods manufactured; cost behavior.** Various cost and sales data for Medco, Inc., for 19x5 are given below:

Purchases of raw materials	$ 80,000
Raw materials inventory, January 1	9,000
Raw materials inventory, December 31	6,000
Depreciation, factory	24,000
Direct labor cost	100,000
Utilities, factory	32,000
Maintenance, factory	7,000
Indirect materials	4,000
Administrative expenses	60,000
Insurance, factory	8,000
Indirect labor	35,000
Work in process inventory, January 1	17,000
Work in process inventory, December 31	20,000
Finished goods inventory, January 1	36,000
Finished goods inventory, December 31	30,000
Sales	500,000
Selling expenses	90,000

Required:
1. Prepare a schedule of cost of goods manufactured for 19x5.
2. Prepare an income statement for 19x5.
3. Assume that the company produced the equivalent of 10,000 units of product during 19x5. What was the per unit cost for direct materials? What was the per unit cost for factory depreciation?
4. Assume that the company expects to produce 15,000 units of product during the coming year. What total cost and what per unit cost would you expect the company to incur for direct materials at this level of activity? For factory depreciation? (In preparing your answer, assume that direct materials is a variable cost and that depreciation is a fixed cost, computed on a straight-line basis.)

5. As the manager responsible for production costs, explain to the president any difference in unit costs between (3) and (4) above.

P2-12. **Classification of salary cost.** You have just been hired by the Ogden Company, which was organized on January 2 of the current year. The company manufactures and sells a single product. It is your responsibility to coordinate shipments of the product from the factory to distribution warehouses located in various parts of the United States so that goods will be available as orders are received from customers.

The company is unsure how to classify your $30,000 annual salary in its cost records. The company's cost analyst says that your salary should be classified as a manufacturing (product) cost; the controller says that it should be classified as a selling expense; and the president says that it doesn't matter which way your salary cost is classified.

Required: 1. Which viewpoint is correct? Why?
2. From the point of view of the reported net income for the year, is the president correct in his statement that it doesn't matter which way your salary cost is classified? Explain, using the data from Exhibit 2–5 and/or Exhibit 2–6 as needed.

P2-13. **Cost identification.** Heritage Company manufactures a beautiful bookcase that enjoys widespread popularity. The company has a backlog of orders that is large enough to keep production going indefinitely at the plant's full capacity of 6,000 bookcases per month. Monthly cost data at full capacity follow:

Materials used (wood and glass)	$130,000
General office salaries	86,000
Factory supervision	40,000
Sales commissions	60,000
Depreciation, factory building	7,600
Depreciation, office equipment	2,000
Indirect materials, factory	15,000
Factory labor (cutting and assembly)	210,000
Advertising	100,000
Insurance, factory	6,000
General office supplies (billing)	4,000
Property taxes, factory	1,500
Utilities, factory	10,000

Required: 1. Prepare an answer sheet with the column headings shown below. Enter each cost item on your answer sheet, placing the dollar amount under the appropriate headings. As examples, this has been done already for the first two items in the list above. Note that each cost item is classified in two ways: first, as being either variable or fixed; and second, as being either a selling and administrative cost or a product cost. (If the item is a product cost, it should be classified as being either direct or indirect as shown.)

	Cost behavior		Selling or administrative cost	Product cost	
Cost item	**Variable**	**Fixed**		**Direct**	**Indirect***
Materials used	$130,000			$130,000	
General office salaries		$86,000	$86,000		

* To units of product.

If you are uncertain whether a cost would be variable or fixed, consider how you would expect it to behave over fairly wide ranges of activity.

2. Total the dollar amounts in each of the columns in (1) above. Compute the cost to produce one bookcase.

3. Due to a recession, assume that production drops to only 3,000 bookcases per month. Would you expect the cost per bookcase to increase, decrease, or remain unchanged? Explain. No computations are necessary.

4. Refer to the original data. The president's next-door neighbor has considered making himself a bookcase and has priced the necessary materials at a building supply store. He has asked the president whether he could purchase a bookcase from the Heritage Company "at cost," and the president has agreed to let him do so.

   a. Would you expect any disagreement between the two men over the price the neighbor should pay? Explain. What price does the president probably have in mind? The neighbor?

   b. Since the company is operating at full capacity, what cost term used in the chapter might be justification for the president to charge the full, regular price to the neighbor and still be selling "at cost"? Explain.

P2–14. **Preparing manufacturing statements.** The Carter Company has just completed operations for September 19x3. The president of the company is very confused by the income statement that she has just received, which shows a large loss for the month. The president is particularly concerned because the income statement was prepared by her brother-in-law, who has little training in accounting work. The company's income statement follows:

CARTER COMPANY
Income Statement
For the Month Ended September 30, 19x3

Sales		$300,000
Less operating expenses:		
Insurance expired during the month	$ 4,000	
Utilities	10,000	
Direct labor cost	60,000	
Selling and administrative salaries	32,000	
Indirect labor cost	12,000	
Depreciation on factory equipment	16,000	
Raw materials purchased during the month	135,000	
Rent on facilities	40,000	309,000
Net loss		$ (9,000)

You have been asked by the company to assist in preparing a corrected income statement for the month. The following additional information is available:

a. The Carter Company is a manufacturing firm that makes a product for sale to outside customers.

b. Some 70 percent of the expired insurance and 90 percent of the utilities cost apply to factory operations; the remaining amounts apply to selling and administrative activities.

c. Inventory balances at the beginning and end of the month were:

	September 1, 19x3	September 30, 19x3
Raw materials	$ 8,000	$38,000
Work in process	42,000	48,000
Finished goods	54,000	40,000

d. Only 80 percent of the rent on facilities applies to factory operations; the remainder applies to selling and administrative activities.

Required: 1. Prepare a schedule of cost of goods manufactured in good form for September 19x3.

2. Prepare a corrected income statement for the month.

P2–15. **Supply missing production and sales data.** Supply the missing data in the cases below. Each case is independent of the others.

	Case 1	Case 2	Case 3	Case 4	Case 5
Direct materials	$ 3,000	$ 1,500	$ 3,000	$ 2,000	$ 5,000
Direct labor.	?	3,000	4,000	4,000	3,000
Manufacturing overhead	4,000	3,500	?	3,000	5,000
Total manufacturing costs	9,000	?	?	?	?
Beginning work in process inventory	2,000	?	2,500	5,000	?
Ending work in process inventory	?	4,000	2,500	2,000	4,000
Cost of goods manufactured	$ 8,000	$ 9,000	$11,000	$?	$?
Sales	$11,500	$15,000	$12,500	$18,000	$20,000
Opening finished goods inventory	2,000	4,000	3,000	?	6,000
Cost of goods manufactured	8,000	?	11,000	?	11,000
Goods available for sale	?	?	?	?	?
Ending finished goods inventory.	?	3,000	?	4,000	7,000
Cost of goods sold	7,000	?	9,000	13,000	?
Gross margin	4,500	5,000	?	5,000	?
Operating expenses	?	1,500	2,000	2,000	6,000
Net Income	$ 2,000	$ 3,500	$ 1,500	$ 3,000	$ 4,000

P2–16. **Cost identification.** Jerry Genius has invented a new type of mousetrap. After giving the matter much thought, Jerry has decided to quit his $2,000 per month job with a computer firm and produce and sell the mousetraps full time. Jerry will rent a garage that will be used as a production plant. The rent will be $150 per month. He has a number of tools and some equipment purchased several years ago at a cost of $4,000 that will be depreciated and used in production. In addition, Jerry will rent other production equipment at a cost of $500 per month.

The cost of materials for each mousetrap will be $0.30. Jerry will hire workers to produce the mousetraps. They will be paid $0.50 for each completed mousetrap. Jerry will rent a room in the house next door for use as his sales office. The rent will be $75 per month. He has arranged for the telephone company to attach a recording device to his home phone to get off-hours messages from customers. The device will increase his monthly phone bill by $20. In addition, he will be charged $0.50 for each message recorded on the device.

Jerry has some money in savings that is earning interest of $1,000 per year. These savings will be withdrawn and used for about a year to get the business going. In order to sell his mousetraps, Jerry will advertise heavily in the local area. Advertising costs will be $400 per month. In addition, Jerry will pay a sales commission of $0.10 for each mousetrap sold.

For the time being, Jerry does not intend to draw any salary from the new company.

Required: Prepare an answer sheet with the following column headings:

Name of the cost	Variable cost	Fixed cost	Product cost			Period (selling and administrative) cost	Opportunity cost	Differential cost*	Sunk cost
			Direct materials	Direct labor	Manufacturing overhead				

* Between the alternatives of producing the mousetraps or staying with the computer firm.

List the different costs associated with the new company down the extreme left column (under "Name of the cost"). Then place an *X* under each heading that helps to describe the type of cost involved. There may be *X*'s under several column headings for a single cost. (That is, a cost may be a fixed cost, a period cost, and a differential cost; you would place an *X* under each of these column headings opposite the cost.)

P2–17. **Schedule of cost of goods manufactured; cost behavior.** Selected account balances for the year ended May 31, 19x1, are provided below for Superior Company:

Raw materials inventory, June 1, 19x0	$ 40,000
Raw materials inventory, May 31, 19x1	30,000
Purchases of raw materials	150,000
Insurance, factory	12,000
Work in process inventory, June 1, 19x0	?
Utilities, factory	45,000
Indirect labor	60,000
Finished goods inventory, June 1, 19x0	85,000
Direct labor	?
Indirect materials	7,000
Work in process inventory, May 31, 19x1	48,000
Rent, factory building	120,000
Finished goods inventory, May 31, 19x1	?
Maintenance, factory	19,000

The goods available for sale for the year totaled $635,000; the total manufacturing costs were $563,000; and the cost of goods sold totaled $560,000 for the year.

Required:
1. Prepare a schedule of cost of goods manufactured in the form illustrated in Exhibit 2–3 in the text and a schedule of cost of goods sold.
2. Assume that the dollar amounts given above are for the equivalent of 40,000 units produced during the year. Compute the unit cost for direct materials. Compute the unit cost for rent on the factory building.
3. Assume that in 19x2 the company produces 50,000 units. What per unit and total cost would you expect to be incurred for direct materials? For rent on the factory building? (In preparing your answer, you may assume that direct materials is a variable cost and that rent is a fixed cost.)
4. As the manager in charge of production costs, explain to the president the reason for any difference in unit costs between (2) and (3) above.

P2–18. **Schedule of cost of goods manufactured; inventory computation.** On January 2, 19x4, Roger Strong organized a company to manufacture and sell a device that he has designed for use as an attachment on small personal computers. Shortly after the end of the first quarter, Roger's accountant had a serious accident and therefore has been unable to prepare financial statements for the quarter. In order to have information on which to base a decision as to whether or not the company should be continued, Roger has prepared the following income statement for the first quarter's activities:

STRONG MANUFACTURING COMPANY
Income Statement
For the Quarter Ended March 31, 19x4

Sales.		$700,000
Less operating expenses:		
Utilities	$ 30,000	
Advertising	100,000	
Direct labor cost.	160,000	
Indirect labor cost	45,000	
Raw materials purchased.	130,000	
Maintenance cost, factory	9,000	
Indirect materials	16,000	
Depreciation, factory equipment	30,000	
Rent on facilities.	60,000	
Sales salaries	50,000	
Other factory overhead costs	35,000	
Administrative salaries.	70,000	
Total operating expenses .		735,000
Net loss		$ (35,000)

Roger is very disappointed in the results of the first quarter and feels that he should discontinue operations and sell his patents to another company. To add to his troubles, just after the quarter had ended, the company's finished goods warehouse was broken into by thieves who took all of the unsold units on hand. The company's insurance policy states that the company will be reimbursed for the "cost" of any finished units destroyed or stolen. Roger figures that this cost is $73.50 per unit, computed as follows:

$$\frac{\text{Total expenses for the quarter, \$735,000}}{\text{Units produced during the quarter, 10,000}} = \$73.50 \text{ per unit}$$

Since the company sold 8,000 of the 10,000 units produced during the quarter, Roger figures that the insurance company owes him $147,000 (10,000 units − 8,000 units = 2,000 units; 2,000 units × $73.50 = $147,000). The insurance company refuses to pay this amount; it has asked you to prepare corrected statements for the quarter and a corrected computation of its liability under the insurance policy. You have obtained the following additional information:

a. Inventories at the beginning and end of the quarter were:

	January 2, 19x4	March 31, 19x4
Raw materials	–0–	$10,000
Work in process	–0–	30,000
Finished goods	–0–	?

b. Ninety percent of the utilities cost and 80 percent of the rent on facilities relate to factory operations. The remaining amounts relate to selling and administrative activities.

Required: 1.   What conceptual errors were made in preparing the income statement above?
2.   Prepare a schedule of cost of goods manufactured for the quarter.
3.   Determine the cost of the 2,000 units in the finished goods inventory at March 31. Using this figure and other data from the problem as needed, prepare a corrected income statement for the quarter. (Note that the finished goods warehouse was broken into *after* the quarter had ended; thus, no loss for this theft should be shown on the income statement.) Based on these data, do you agree that Roger should discontinue operations?
4.   Do you agree that the insurance company owes Roger $147,000 as computed above? Explain your answer.

P2–19.   **Cost classification.**   Listed below are a number of costs that might typically be found in a merchandising, manufacturing, or service company:

1.   Janitorial salaries, factory.
2.   Fire insurance, factory.
3.   Freight-out.
4.   Wood in furniture manufacture.
5.   Sandpaper, furniture manufacture.
6.   Secretary, company president.
7.   Depreciation, finished goods warehouses.
8.   Lubricants for machines.
9.   Freight-in on materials used.
10.   Billing costs.
11.   Aerosol attachment placed on a spray can.
12.   Depreciation, executive jet.
13.   Advertising costs.
14.   Packing supplies for shipment overseas.
15.   Glue for labels on bottles.
16.   Salespersons' commissions.
17.   Fringe benefits, factory labor.
18.   Electricity, machine operation.
19.   Sales manager's salary.
20.   Sand used in concrete manufacture.

Required: Prepare an answer sheet with column headings as shown below. For each cost item, indicate whether it would be variable or fixed in behavior, and then whether it would be a selling cost, an administrative cost, or a manufacturing cost. If it is a manufacturing cost, indicate whether it would be direct or indirect to units of product. Three sample answers are provided for illustration. If you are unsure about whether a cost would be variable or fixed, consider whether it would fluctuate substantially over a fairly wide range of volume.

Cost item	Variable or fixed	Selling cost	Administrative cost	Manufacturing (product) cost	
				Direct	Indirect
Direct labor	V			X	
Executive salaries	F		X		
Factory rent	F				X

P2–20. **Cost behavior; manufacturing statement; unit costs.** Hickey Company, a manufacturing firm, produces a single product. The following information has been taken from the company's production, sales, and cost records for the year 19x6:

Production in units.	30,000
Sales in units	? 26,000
Ending finished goods inventory in units	? 4,000
Sales in dollars.	$650,000
Costs:	
Advertising	$ 90,000
Direct labor	160,000
Indirect labor.	60,000
Raw materials purchased	80,000
Building rent (production uses 80% of the space; administrative and sales offices use the rest)	50,000
Utilities, factory	35,000
Royalty paid for use of production patent, $1 per unit produced	? 30,000
Maintenance, factory	25,000
Rent for special production equipment, $6,000 per year plus $0.10 per unit produced	? 9,000
Selling and administrative salaries	100,000
Other factory overhead costs	11,000
Other selling and administrative expense	20,000

Inventories:	January 1, 19x6	December 31, 19x6
Raw materials	$20,000	$10,000
Work in process	30,000	40,000
Finished goods	–0–	?

The finished goods inventory is being carried at the average unit production cost for the year. The selling price of the product is $25 per unit.

Required:
1. Prepare a schedule of cost of goods manufactured for the year.
2. Compute the following:
    a. The number of units in the finished goods inventory at December 31.
    b. The cost of the units in the finished goods inventory at December 31.
3. Prepare an income statement for the year.

P2–21. **Statements from incomplete data.** Sally Hardluck, the chief accountant of Foremost Enterprises, accidentally tossed the company's cost records into a wastebasket. Realizing her error, she raced to the incinerator, but she was successful in retrieving only a few scraps from the roaring blaze. From these scraps she has been able to determine the following facts about the current year, 19x4:

1. Sales totaled $100,000 during 19x4.
2. The beginning inventories for the year were:

Work in process	$12,000
Finished goods	6,000

3. The company does not carry inventories of raw materials. Materials are purchased as needed for production.
4. Direct labor is equal to 25 percent of conversion cost.
5. The work in process inventory decreased by $2,000 during 19x4.

6. Gross margin during 19x4 was equal to 55 percent of sales.
7. Manufacturing overhead totaled $24,000 for 19x4.
8. Direct labor is equal to 40 percent of prime cost.
9. Administrative expenses for 19x4 were twice as great as net income but only 25 percent of selling expenses.

Ms. Hardluck must have an income statement and a schedule of cost of goods manufactured ready for the board of directors in an hour.

Required:
1. Compute the amount of direct labor cost for the year.
2. Compute the amount of direct materials cost for the year.
3. Prepare a schedule of cost of goods manufactured for the year.
4. Prepare an income statement for the year. (Hint: Remember that selling expenses, adminstrative expenses, and net income added together should equal gross margin.)

3 Systems Design: Job-Order Costing

Learning objectives

After studying Chapter 3, you should be able to:

Distinguish between process costing and job-order costing and identify companies that would use each costing method.

Identify the documents used to control the flow of costs in a job-order costing system.

Prepare journal entries to record the flow of direct materials cost, direct labor cost, and manufacturing overhead cost in a job-order costing system.

Compute predetermined overhead rates and explain why estimated overhead costs (rather than actual overhead costs) are used in the costing process.

Apply overhead cost to Work in Process by use of a predetermined overhead rate.

Compute any balance of under- or overapplied overhead cost for a period and prepare the journal entry needed to close the balance into the appropriate accounts.

Explain why multiple overhead rates are needed in many organizations.

Describe the purpose of normalized overhead rates.

Define or explain the key terms listed at the end of the chapter.

As discussed in Chapter 2, product costing is the process of assigning manufacturing costs to manufactured goods. An understanding of this process is vital to any manager, since the way in which a product is costed can have a substantial impact on reported net income, as well as on the current assets section of the balance sheet.

In this chapter and in Chapter 4, we look at product costing from the **absorption cost** approach. The approach is so named because it provides for the absorption of all manufacturing costs, fixed and variable, into units of product. It is also known as the **full cost** approach. Later, in Chapter 7, we will look at product costing from another point of view (called *direct costing*) and then discuss the strengths and weaknesses of the two approaches.

As we study product costing, we must keep clearly in mind that *the essential purpose of any costing system is to accumulate costs for managerial use.* A costing system is not an end in itself. Rather, it is a managerial tool in that it exists to provide the manager with the cost data needed to direct the affairs of an organization.

THE NEED FOR FACTORY UNIT COST DATA

In studying product costing, we will focus initially on *unit cost of production,* an item of cost data that is generally regarded as being highly useful to managers.

Managers need unit cost data for a variety of reasons. First, unit costs are needed in order to cost inventories on financial statements. The units of product remaining on hand at the end of an operating period must have costs attached to them as the units are carried forward on the balance sheet to the next period.

Second, unit costs are needed for determination of a period's net income. The cost of each unit sold during a period must be placed on the income statement as a deduction from total sales revenue. If unit costs are incorrectly computed, then net income will be equally incorrect.

Finally, managers need unit cost data to assist them in a broad range of decision-making situations. Without unit cost data, managers would find it very difficult to set selling prices for factory output.[1] A knowledge of unit costs is also vital in a number of special decision areas, such as whether to add or drop product lines, whether to make or buy production components, whether to expand or contract operations, and whether to accept special orders at special prices. The particular unit costs that are relevant in this variety of decision-making situations will differ, so we need to learn not only how to derive unit costs but also how to differentiate between those costs that are relevant in a particular situation and those that are not. The matter of relevant costs is reserved until Chapter 13. For the moment, we

---

[1] We should note here that unit cost represents only one of many factors involved in pricing decisions. Pricing is discussed in depth in Chapter 12.

are concerned with gaining an understanding of the concept of unit cost in its broadest sense.

TYPES OF COSTING SYSTEMS

In computing unit costs, the manager is faced with a difficult problem. Many costs are incurred uniformly throughout a year, whereas production may change from month to month, either in terms of the *number of units* or in terms of the *type of goods* being produced. Under these conditions, how is it possible to determine accurate unit costs? The answer is that the computation of unit costs must involve an *averaging* of some type. The way in which this averaging is carried out will depend heavily on the type of manufacturing process involved. Two costing systems have emerged in response to variations in the manufacturing process; these two systems are commonly known as *process costing* and *job-order costing*. Each has its own unique way of averaging costs and thus providing management with unit cost data.

Process costing

A **process costing system** is employed in those situations where manufacturing involves a single product that is produced for long periods at a time. Examples of industries that would use process costing include cement, flour, brick, and various utilities (e.g., natural gas, electricity). All of these industries are characterized by a basically homogeneous product that flows evenly through the production process on a more or less continuous basis.

The basic approach to process costing is to accumulate costs in a particular operation or department for an entire period (month, quarter, year) and then to divide this total by the number of units produced during the period. The basic formula for process costing would be:

$$\frac{\text{Total costs of manufacturing}}{\text{Total units produced (gallons, pounds, bottles)}} = \text{Unit cost per gallon, pound, bottle}$$

Since one unit of product (gallon, pound, bottle) is completely indistinguishable from any other unit of product, each unit bears the same average cost as any other unit produced during the period. This costing technique results in a broad, average unit cost that applies to many thousands of like units flowing in an almost endless stream off the assembly or processing line.

Job-order costing

A **job-order costing system** is used in those manufacturing situations where many *different* products, jobs, or batches of production are being produced each period. Examples of industries that would typically use job-order costing include special-order printing, furniture manufacturing, shipbuilding, and custom equipment manufacturing.

Because the output of firms in these industries is heterogeneous, managers need a costing system in which costs can be accumulated *by job* and in which distinct unit costs can be determined for each job completed. Job-order costing provides such a system. However, it is a more complex system than that provided by process costing. Rather than dividing total costs of production by many thousands of like units, under job-order costing one must somehow divide total costs of production by a few, basically unlike units. Thus, job-order costing entails problems of record keeping that are not present in a process costing system.

Summary of costing methods

To summarize this brief introduction to process and job-order costing, regardless of which system one is dealing with, the problem of determining unit costs involves a need for averaging of some type. The essential difference between the process and job-order methods is the way in which this averaging is carried out. In this chapter, we focus on the design of a job-order costing system. In the following chapter, we focus on process costing and also look more closely at the similarities and differences between the two costing methods.

JOB-ORDER COSTING—AN OVERVIEW

In the preceding chapter, the point was made that there are three broad categories of costs involved in the manufacture of any product:

1. Direct materials.
2. Direct labor.
3. Manufacturing overhead.

As we study the design and operation of a job-order costing system, we will look at each of these costs to see how it is involved in the costing of a unit of product. In doing this, we will also look at the various documents involved in job-order costing and give special emphasis to a key document known as a job cost sheet.

Measuring direct materials cost

The production process begins with the transfer of raw materials from the storeroom to the production line. The bulk of these raw materials will be traceable directly to the goods being produced and will therefore be termed *direct materials*. Other materials, generally termed *indirect materials*, will not be charged to a specific job but rather will be included within the general category of manufacturing overhead. As discussed in Chapter 2, indirect materials would include costs of glue, nails, and miscellaneous supplies.

EXHIBIT 3–1
Materials requisition form

Materials Requisition Number 14873		Date March 2, 19x2	
Job Number to Be Charged 2B47			
Department Milling			

Description	Quantity	Unit Cost	Total Cost
M46 Housing	2	$123	$246
G7 Connector	8	52	416
			$662

Authorized
Signature   Bill White

Raw materials are drawn from the storeroom on presentation of a **materials requisition form.** A materials requisition form is shown in Exhibit 3–1.

As shown in the exhibit, the materials requisition form is a detailed source document that specifies the type and quantity of materials that are to be drawn from the storeroom and that identifies the job to which the materials are to be charged. Thus, the form serves as a means both for controlling the flow of materials into production and for making entries in the accounting records.

If the job being worked on involves a product that is frequently manufactured by a company, then any requisition of materials will typically be based on a **bill of materials** that has been prepared for the product. A bill of materials is simply a control sheet that shows the type and quantity of each item of material going into a completed unit.

The job cost sheet

The cost of direct materials is entered on a job cost sheet similar to the one presented in Exhibit 3–2. A **job cost sheet** is a form prepared for each separate job initiated into production; it serves (1) as a means for accumulating materials, labor, and overhead costs chargeable to a job, and (2) as a means for computing unit costs. Normally, the job cost sheet is prepared by the accounting department after notification by the production department that a production order has been issued for a particular job. The production order is issued only after a firm agreement in terms of quantities, prices, and shipment dates has been reached with the customer.

As materials are issued, the accounting department makes entries directly on the job cost sheet, thereby charging the specific job noted on the sheet

EXHIBIT 3–2
The job cost sheet

JOB COST SHEET

Job Number   2B47   Date Initiated   March 2, 19x2
                                           Date Completed _____

Department   Milling   Units Completed _____
Item   Special order coupling
For Stock _____

Materials		Direct Labor			Manufacturing Overhead		
Req. No.	Amount	Ticket	Hours	Amount	Hours	Rate	Amount
14873	$662						

Cost Summary		Units Shipped		
		Date	Number	Balance
Direct Materials	$			
Direct Labor	$			
Overhead	$			
Total Cost	$			
Unit Cost	$			

with the cost of direct materials used in production. When the job is completed, the total cost of materials used can be summarized in the cost summary section as one element involved in determining the unit cost characteristics of the order.

Measuring direct labor cost

Direct labor cost is accumulated and measured in much the same way as direct materials cost. Direct labor would include those labor charges that are directly traceable to the particular job in process. By contrast, those labor charges that cannot be traced directly to a particular job, or that can be traced only with the expenditure of great effort, are treated as part of manufacturing overhead. As discussed in Chapter 2, this latter category of labor costs is termed *indirect labor* and would include such tasks as maintenance, supervision, and cleanup.

Labor costs are generally accumulated by means of some type of work record prepared each day by each employee. These work records, often termed **time tickets,** constitute an hour-by-hour summary of the activities and assignments completed during the day by the employee. When working on a specific job, the employee enters the job number on the time ticket and notes the number of hours spent on the particular task involved. When not assigned to a particular job, the employee enters the type of indirect labor tasks to which he or she was assigned (such as cleanup and maintenance) and the number of hours spent on each separate task.

An example of an employee time ticket is given below.

Time Ticket No. 843   Date March 3, 19x2
Employee Mary Holden   Station 4

Started	Ended	Time Completed	Rate	Amount	Job Number
7:00	12:00	5.0	$9	$45	2B47
12:30	2:30	2.0	$9	18	2B50
2:30	3:30	1.0	$9	9	Maintenance
Totals		8.0		$72	

Supervisor R. W. Pace

At the end of a day, the time tickets are gathered and the accounting department carefully analyzes each in terms of the number of hours assignable as direct labor to specific jobs and the number of hours assignable to manufacturing overhead as indirect labor. Those hours assignable as direct labor are entered on individual job cost sheets (such as the one shown in Exhibit 3–2), along with the appropriate charges involved. When all direct labor charges associated with a particular job have been accumulated on the job cost sheet, the total can be summarized in the cost summary section. The daily time tickets, in essence, constitute basic source documents used as a basis for labor cost entries into the accounting records.

Application of manufacturing overhead

Manufacturing overhead must be considered along with direct materials and direct labor in determining unit costs of production. However, the assignment of manufacturing overhead to units of product is often a difficult task. There are several reasons why this is so.

First, as explained in Chapter 2, manufacturing overhead is an *indirect* cost to units of product and for this reason can't be traced directly to a particular product or job. Second, manufacturing overhead consists of many unlike items, involving both variable and fixed costs. It ranges from the grease used in machines to the annual salary of the production superintendent. Finally, firms with large seasonal variations in production often find that even though output is fluctuating, manufacturing overhead costs tend to remain relatively constant. The reason is that fixed costs generally constitute a large part of manufacturing overhead.

Given these problems, about the only acceptable way to assign overhead costs to units of product is to do so through an allocation process. This allocation of overhead costs to products is accomplished by having the manager select an *activity base* that is common to all products that the company manufactures or to all services that the company renders. Then by means of this base, an appropriate amount of overhead cost is assigned to each product or service. The trick, of course, is to choose the right base so that the overhead application will be equitable as between jobs. Probably the most widely used bases are direct labor-hours (DLH) and machine-hours (MH), although direct labor cost is also used to some extent. (If a company has only one product, then units of product can also be used.)

Once a base has been chosen, it is divided into the *estimated* total manufacturing overhead cost of the period in order to obtain an *overhead rate.* This rate is then used to apply overhead costs to jobs as the jobs are completed. In sum, the formula for computing the overhead rate is:

$$\frac{\text{Estimated total manufacturing overhead costs}}{\text{Estimated total units in the base (DLH, MH, etc.)}}$$

$$= \text{Predetermined overhead rate}$$

The need for estimated data   Notice from the formula above that estimated data are used in computing the overhead rate. *Actual* overhead costs are rarely, if ever, used in overhead costing. The reason is that actual overhead costs are not available until *after* a period is over. This is too late so far as computing unit costs is concerned, since the manager must have unit cost data available at once in order to set prices on products and make other key marketing and operating decisions. The postponing of such decisions until year-end (in order to have actual overhead cost data available) would destroy an organization's ability to compete effectively. For this reason, rather than using actual overhead costs in developing an overhead application rate, most firms *estimate* total manufacturing overhead costs at the beginning of a year, *estimate* the direct labor-hours (or whatever base is being used) that will be worked during the year, and develop an overhead rate *in advance* based on these estimates. As shown in the formula above, an overhead rate based on estimated data is known as a **predetermined overhead rate.** Such rates are widely used in charging overhead costs to jobs.

Using the predetermined overhead rate   In assigning overhead costs to the job cost sheet (and thereby to units of product), the predetermined overhead rate is multiplied by the number of direct labor-hours (or whatever the base is) worked on the job. The resulting amount of overhead cost is then entered on the job cost sheet as one of the costs involved in the completion of the job. To illustrate, assume that a firm has estimated its total manufacturing overhead costs for the year to be $320,000 and has estimated 40,000 total direct labor-hours for the year. Its predetermined overhead rate for the year would be $8 per direct labor-hour, as shown below:

$$\frac{\$320{,}000}{40{,}000 \text{ direct labor-hours}} = \$8 \text{ per direct labor-hour}$$

If a particular job required 27 direct labor-hours to complete, then that job would be allocated $216 (27 hrs $\times$ $8) of manufacturing overhead cost. This allocation is shown on the job cost sheet in Exhibit 3–3.

Whether the application of overhead in Exhibit 3–3 is made slowly as the job is worked on during the period, or in a single application at the time of completion, is a matter of choice and convenience to the company involved. If a job is not completed at year-end, however, overhead should be applied to the extent needed to properly value the work in process inventory.

Although estimates are involved in the computation of predetermined overhead rates, managers typically become very skilled at making these estimates. As a result, predetermined overhead rates are generally quite accurate, and any difference between the amount of overhead cost that is actually incurred during a period and the amount that is applied to products is usually quite small. This point is discussed further in a following section.

Computation of unit costs

With the application of manufacturing overhead to the job cost sheet, total costs of the job can be summarized in the cost summary section (see Exhibit 3–3 for an example of a completed job cost sheet). The cost of the individual units in the job can then be obtained by dividing the total costs by the number of units produced. The completed job cost sheet is then ready to be transferred to the finished goods inventory file, where it will serve as a basis for either costing unsold units in the ending inventory or charging expense for units sold.

A summary of document flows

The sequence of events just discussed is summarized in Exhibit 3–4. A careful study of the flow of documents in this exhibit will provide an excellent visual review of the overall operation of a job-order costing system.

EXHIBIT 3-3
A completed job cost sheet

JOB COST SHEET

Job Number   2B47   Date Initiated   March 2, 19x2
                                      Date Completed   March 8, 19x2

Department   Milling
Item   Special order coupling   Units Completed   150
For Stock

Materials		Direct Labor			Manufacturing Overhead		
Req. No.	Amount	Ticket	Hours	Amount	Hours	Rate	Amount
14873	$ 662	843	5	$ 45	27	$8/DLH	$216
14875	504	846	8	60			
14912	238	850	4	21			
	$1,404	851	10	54			
			27	$180			

Cost Summary		Units Shipped		
Direct Materials	$1,404	Date	Number	Balance
Direct Labor	$ 180	3/8/x2	—	150
Overhead	$ 216			
Total Cost	$1,800			
Unit Cost	$ 12*			

* $1,800 ÷ 150 units = $12 per unit.

JOB-ORDER COSTING—THE FLOW OF COSTS

Having obtained a broad, conceptual perspective of the operation of a job-order costing system, we are now prepared to take a look at the flow of actual costs through the system itself. We shall consider a single month's activity for a hypothetical company, presenting all data in summary form. As a basis for discussion, let us assume that the Rand Company had two jobs in process during April, the first month of its fiscal year. Job A was

EXHIBIT 3–4

The flow of documents in a job-order costing system

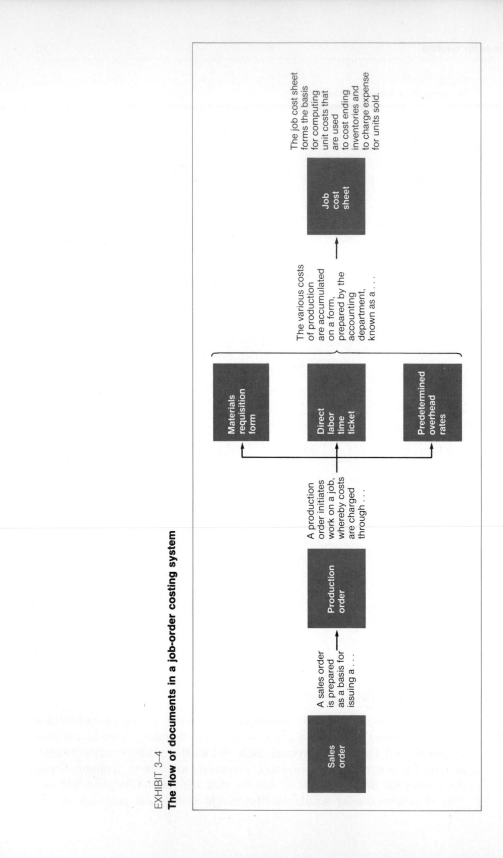

started during March and had $30,000 in manufacturing costs already accumulated on April 1. Job B was started during April.

The purchase and issue of materials

During April, the Rand Company purchased $60,000 in raw materials for use in production. The purchase is recorded in entry (1) below:

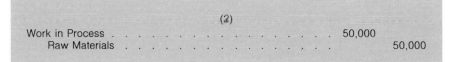

```
                                    (1)
Raw Materials . . . . . . . . . . . . . . . . . . .  60,000
      Accounts Payable . . . . . . . . . . . . . . .          60,000
```

As explained in Chapter 2, Raw Materials is an inventory account. Thus, any materials remaining in the account at the end of a period will appear on the balance sheet under an inventory classification.

Issue of direct materials   During the month, the Rand Company drew $50,000 in raw materials from the storeroom for use in production. Entry (2) records the issue of the materials to the production departments.

```
                                    (2)
Work in Process . . . . . . . . . . . . . . . . . .  50,000
      Raw Materials . . . . . . . . . . . . . . . .           50,000
```

The materials charged to Work in Process represent direct materials assignable to specific jobs on the production line. As these materials are entered into the Work in Process account, they are also recorded on the separate job cost sheets to which they relate. This point is illustrated in Exhibit 3–5.

Notice from the job cost sheets that job A contains $30,000 in manufacturing cost carried forward from the prior month, as does the Work in Process account itself. The reason the $30,000 appears in both places is that the Work in Process account is a control account and the job cost sheets form a subsidiary ledger. Thus, the Work in Process account contains a summarized total of all costs appearing on the individual job cost sheets for all jobs in process at any given point in time. (Since the Rand Company had only job A in process at the beginning of April, its $30,000 balance on that date is equal to the balance in the Work in Process account.) Of the $50,000 in materials added to Work in Process during April, $28,000 was assignable directly to job A and $22,000 was assignable to job B, as shown in Exhibit 3–5.

Issue of both direct and indirect materials   In entry (2) above, we have assumed that all of the materials drawn from the Raw Materials inventory account were assignable to specific jobs as direct materials. If some of the materials drawn are not assignable to specific jobs, then they must be

EXHIBIT 3–5
Raw materials cost flows

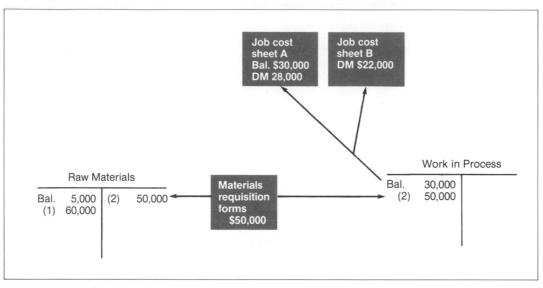

DM = Direct materials.

charged to Manufacturing Overhead as indirect materials. The entry to do this would be:

```
Work in Process (direct materials) . . . . . . . . . . . .   XXX
Manufacturing Overhead (indirect materials) . . . . . . . .   XXX
       Raw Materials . . . . . . . . . . . . . . . . . .           XXX
```

Observe that the Manufacturing Overhead account is separate from Work in Process. The purpose of the Manufacturing Overhead account is to accumulate all manufacturing overhead costs as they are incurred during a period.

Labor cost

As work is performed in various departments of the Rand Company from day to day, employee time tickets are generated, collected, and forwarded to the accounting department. There the tickets are costed according to the various rates paid to the employees, and the resulting costs are classified in terms of being either direct or indirect labor. This costing and classification for the month of April resulted in the following entry:

```
                              (3)
Work in Process . . . . . . . . . . . . . . . . . .   60,000
Manufacturing Overhead . . . . . . . . . . . . . .   15,000
       Salaries and Wages Payable . . . . . . . .            75,000
```

As with raw materials, the amount charged to Work in Process represents the labor costs chargeable directly to specific jobs. It will equal the total of the direct labor charges on the individual job cost sheets. This concept is illustrated in Exhibit 3–6.

The labor costs charged to Manufacturing Overhead represent the indirect labor costs of the period, such as supervision, janitorial work, and maintenance.

Manufacturing overhead costs

As we learned in Chapter 2, all costs of operating the factory other than direct materials and direct labor are classified as manufacturing overhead costs. These costs are entered directly into the Manufacturing Overhead account as they are incurred. To illustrate, assume that the Rand Company incurred the following general factory costs during the month of April:

Utilities (heat, water, and power)	$18,000
Rent on equipment.	12,000
Miscellaneous factory costs.	10,000

EXHIBIT 3–6
Labor cost flows

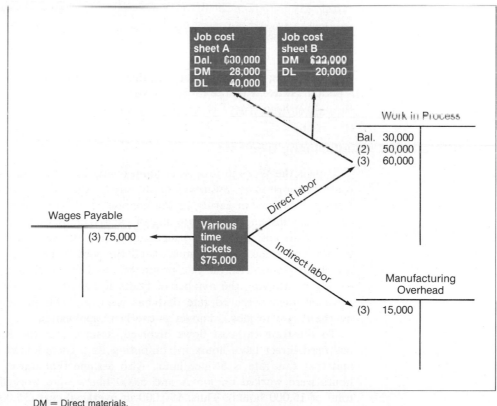

DM = Direct materials.
DL = Direct labor.

The entry to record the incurrence of these costs would be:

```
                              (4)
Manufacturing Overhead  . . . . . . . . . . . .  40,000
    Accounts Payable .  . . . . . . . . . . . .          40,000
```

In addition, let us assume that during April the Rand Company recognized $25,000 in accrued property taxes and $5,000 in insurance expired on factory buildings and equipment. The entry to record these items would be:

```
                              (5)
Manufacturing Overhead  . . . . . . . . . . . .  30,000
    Property Taxes Payable .  . . . . . . . . . .        25,000
    Prepaid Insurance .  . . . . . . . . . . . .          5,000
```

Let us further assume that the company recognized $10,000 in depreciation on factory assets during April. The entry to record the accrual of depreciation would be:

```
                              (6)
Manufacturing Overhead  . . . . . . . . . . . .  10,000
    Accumulated Depreciation .  . . . . . . . . .        10,000
```

In short, *all* manufacturing overhead costs are recorded directly into the Manufacturing Overhead account as they are incurred day by day throughout a period. Notice from the entries above that the recording of *actual* manufacturing overhead costs has no effect on the Work in Process account.

The application of manufacturing overhead

How is the Work in Process account charged for manufacturing overhead cost? The answer is, by means of the predetermined overhead rate. Recall from our discussion earlier in the chapter that a predetermined overhead rate is established at the beginning of each year by estimating the amount of overhead cost that will be incurred during the year, then dividing this estimate by some base common to all the jobs to be worked on, such as direct labor-hours. As the year progresses, overhead is then assigned to each job by multiplying the number of hours it requires for completion by the predetermined overhead rate that has been set. This process of assigning overhead cost to jobs is known as **overhead application.**

To illustrate the cost flows involved, assume that the Rand Company has used direct labor-hours in computing its predetermined overhead rate and that this rate is $6 per hour. Also assume that during April 10,000 hours were worked on job A and 5,000 hours were worked on job B (a total of 15,000 hours). Thus, $90,000 in overhead cost (15,000 hours × $6

= $90,000) would be applied to Work in Process. The entry to record the application would be:

	(7)		
Work in Process		90,000	
Manufacturing Overhead			90,000

The flow of costs through the Manufacturing Overhead account is shown in T-account format in Exhibit 3–7.

The "actual overhead costs" in the Manufacturing Overhead account in Exhibit 3–7 are the costs that were added to the account in entries (3)–(6). Observe that the incurrence of these actual overhead costs [entries (3)–(6)] and the application of overhead to Work in Process [entry (7)] represent two separate and distinct processes.

The concept of a clearing account The Manufacturing Overhead account operates as a clearing account. As we have noted, actual factory overhead costs are charged to it as they are incurred day by day throughout the year. At certain intervals during the year, usually when a job is completed, overhead cost is relieved from the Manufacturing Overhead account and is

EXHIBIT 3–7
The flow of costs in overhead application

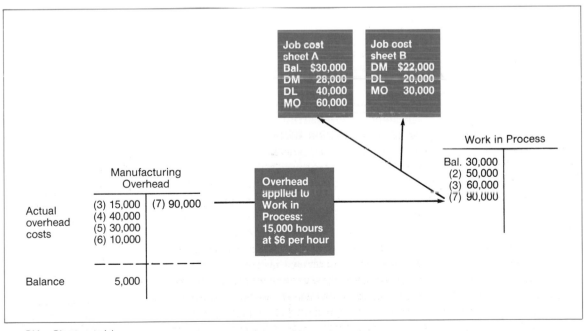

DM = Direct materials.
DL = Direct labor.
MO = Manufacturing overhead.

applied to the Work in Process account by means of the predetermined overhead rate. This sequence of events is illustrated below:

**Manufacturing Overhead
(a clearing account)**

Actual overhead costs are charged to the account as these costs are incurred day by day throughout the period. $\longrightarrow$	$\longrightarrow$ Overhead is applied to Work in Process on a periodic basis by means of the predetermined overhead rate.

As we emphasized earlier, the predetermined overhead rate is based entirely on estimates of what overhead costs are *expected* to be, and it is established before the year begins. As a result, the overhead cost applied during a year may turn out to be more or less than the overhead cost that is actually incurred. For example, notice from Exhibit 3–7 that the Rand Company's actual overhead costs for the period are $5,000 greater than the overhead cost that has been applied to Work in Process, resulting in a $5,000 debit balance in the Manufacturing Overhead account. We will reserve discussion of what to do with this $5,000 balance until a later section, "Problems of overhead application."

For the moment, we can conclude by noting from Exhibit 3–7 that the cost of a completed job consists of the actual materials cost of the job, the actual labor cost of the job, and an *applied* amount of overhead cost to the job. The fact that it is applied overhead cost (not actual overhead cost) that goes into the Work in Process account and onto the job cost sheets is a subtle point that is easy to miss. Thus, this section of the chapter requires special study and consideration.

Nonmanufacturing costs

In addition to incurring costs such as salaries, utilities, and insurance as part of the operation of the factory, manufacturing firms will also incur these same kinds of costs in relation to other parts of their operations. For example, there will be these types of costs arising from activities in the "front office" where secretaries, top management, and others work. There will be identical kinds of costs arising from the operation of the sales staff. *The costs of these nonfactory operations should not go into the Manufacturing Overhead account because the incurrence of these costs is not related to the manufacture of products.* Rather, these costs should be treated as expenses of the period, as explained in Chapter 2, and charged directly to the income statement. To illustrate, assume that the Rand Company incurred the following costs during the month of April:

Top-management salaries	$20,000
Other office salaries	12,000
Total salaries	$32,000

```
Advertising  .   .   .   .   .   .   .   .   .   .   .   .   .   .   .   $30,000
Other selling and administrative expense  .   .   .   .   .   .    15,000
                   Total costs.  .   .   .   .   .   .   .   .   .   .   .   .   $45,000
```

The entries to record the incurrence of these costs would be:

	(8)	
Salaries Expense	32,000	
Salaries and Wages Payable		32,000

	(9)	
Advertising Expense	30,000	
Other Selling and Administrative Expense	15,000	
Accounts Payable		45,000

Since these items go directly into expense accounts, they will have no effect on the costing of the Rand Company's production for the month. The same will be true of all other selling and administrative expenses incurred during the month, including depreciation of salespersons' automobiles, depreciation of office equipment, insurance on office facilities, rent on office facilities, and related costs.

Cost of goods finished

When a job has been completed, the finished output is transferred from the production departments to the finished goods warehouse. By this time, the accounting department will have charged the job with direct materials and direct labor cost, and the job will have absorbed a portion of manufacturing overhead through the application process discussed earlier. A transfer of these costs must be made within the costing system that *parallels* the physical transfer of the goods to the finished goods warehouse. The transfer within the costing system will be to move the costs of the completed job out of the Work in Process account and into the Finished Goods account. The sum of all amounts transferred between these two accounts represents the cost of goods manufactured for the period. (This point was illustrated earlier in Exhibit 2–5 in Chapter 2. The reader may wish to go back to Exhibit 2–5 and refresh this point before reading on.)

In the case of the Rand Company, let us assume that job A was completed during April. The entry to transfer the cost of job A from Work in Process to Finished Goods would be:

	(10)	
Finished Goods	158,000	
Work in Process		158,000

The $158,000 represents the completed cost of job A, as shown on the job cost sheet in Exhibit 3–7. Since job A was the only job completed during the month, the $158,000 also represents the cost of goods manufactured for the month.

Job B was not completed by month-end, so its cost will remain in the Work in Process account and carry over to the next month. If a balance sheet is prepared at the end of April, the cost accumulated thus far on job B will appear under the caption "Work in process inventory" in the assets section.

Cost of goods sold

As units of product in finished goods are shipped to fill customer orders, the unit cost appearing on the job cost sheets is used as a basis for transferring the cost of the sold items from the Finished Goods account into the Cost of Goods Sold account. If a complete job is shipped, as in the case where a job has been done to a customer's specifications, then it is a simple matter to transfer the entire cost appearing on the job cost sheet into the Cost of Goods Sold account. In most cases, however, only a portion of the units involved in a particular job will be sold. In these situations, the unit cost is particularly important in knowing how much product cost should be removed from Finished Goods and charged into Cost of Goods Sold.

For the Rand Company, we will assume that three fourths of the units in job A were shipped to customers on account by month-end. The total selling price of these units was $225,000. The entries needed to record the sale would be (in summary form):

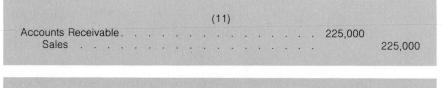

	(11)		
Accounts Receivable .		225,000	
Sales .			225,000

	(12)		
Cost of Goods Sold .		118,500	
Finished Goods .			118,500
($158,000 total cost × ¾ = $118,500)			

With entry (12), the flow of costs through our job-order costing system is completed.

A summary of cost flows

To pull the entire Rand Company example together, a summary of cost flows is presented in T-account form in Exhibit 3–8. The flows of costs through the exhibit are keyed to the numbers (1) through (12). These numbers relate to the numbers of the transactions appearing on the preceding pages.

EXHIBIT 3–8

A summary of cost flows—The Rand Company

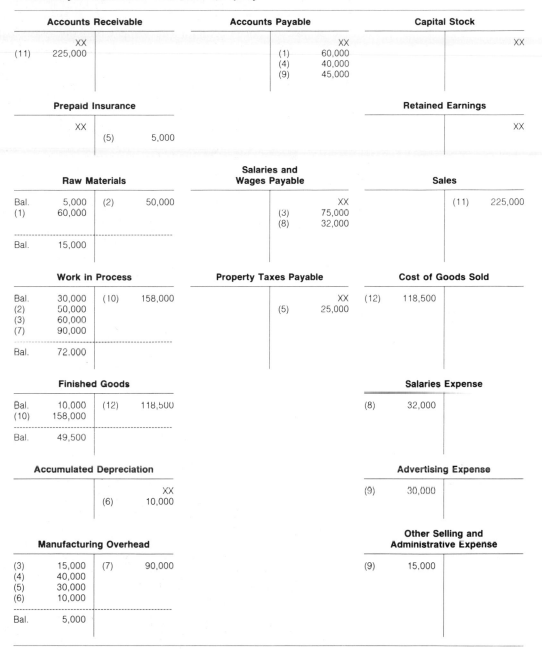

Accounts Receivable				Accounts Payable				Capital Stock		
	XX					XX				XX
(11)	225,000			(1)		60,000				
				(4)		40,000				
				(9)		45,000				

Prepaid Insurance								Retained Earnings		
	XX									XX
(5)		5,000								

Raw Materials				Salaries and Wages Payable				Sales		
Bal.	5,000	(2)	50,000			XX			(11)	225,000
(1)	60,000				(3)	75,000				
					(8)	32,000				
Bal.	15,000									

Work in Process				Property Taxes Payable				Cost of Goods Sold		
Bal.	30,000	(10)	158,000			XX		(12)	118,500	
(2)	50,000				(5)	25,000				
(3)	60,000									
(7)	90,000									
Bal.	72,000									

Finished Goods								Salaries Expense		
Bal.	10,000	(12)	118,500					(8)	32,000	
(10)	158,000									
Bal.	49,500									

Accumulated Depreciation								Advertising Expense		
			XX					(9)	30,000	
		(6)	10,000							

Manufacturing Overhead								Other Selling and Administrative Expense		
(3)	15,000	(7)	90,000					(9)	15,000	
(4)	40,000									
(5)	30,000									
(6)	10,000									
Bal.	5,000									

Note: XX = Normal balance in the account (for example, Accounts Receivable normally carries a debit balance).
Explanation of entries:

(1) The purchase of raw materials.
(2) The issue of raw materials into production.
(3) The recording of labor costs.
(4) The recording of overhead costs.
(5) The recording of overhead costs.
(6) The recording of overhead costs.
(7) The application of overhead costs into Work in Process.
(8) The recording of salaries and commissions expense.
(9) The recording of advertising and other selling and administrative expense.
(10) The transfer of cost of goods manufactured into Finished Goods.
(11) The sale of goods.
(12) The recording of cost of goods sold.

Exhibit 3–9 presents a schedule of cost of goods manufactured and a schedule of cost of goods sold for the Rand Company. Note particularly from Exhibit 3–9 that the cost of goods manufactured for the month ($158,000) agrees with the amount transferred from Work in Process to Finished Goods for the month as recorded earlier in entry (10).

EXHIBIT 3–9
Schedules of cost of goods manufactured and cost of goods sold

Cost of Goods Manufactured

Direct materials:		
Raw materials inventory, April 1	$ 5,000	
Add purchases of raw materials	60,000	
Total raw materials available	65,000	
Deduct raw materials inventory, April 30	15,000	
Raw materials used in production		$ 50,000*
Direct labor		60,000
Manufacturing overhead:		
Indirect labor	15,000	
Utilities	18,000	
Rent	12,000	
Miscellaneous factory costs	10,000	
Property taxes	25,000	
Insurance	5,000	
Depreciation	10,000	
Actual overhead costs	95,000	
Less underapplied overhead	5,000†	
Overhead applied to work in process		90,000
Total manufacturing costs		200,000
Add: Beginning work in process inventory		30,000
		230,000
Deduct: Ending work in process inventory		72,000
Cost of goods manufactured		$158,000

Cost of Goods Sold

Opening finished goods inventory	$ 10,000
Add cost of goods manufactured	158,000
Goods available for sale	168,000
Ending finished goods inventory	49,500
Cost of goods sold	118,500
Add underapplied overhead	5,000
Adjusted cost of goods sold	$123,500

* We assume that this is all direct materials. Any indirect materials included in the $50,000 would have to be deducted out and added to Manufacturing Overhead.

† Note that underapplied overhead must be deducted from actual overhead costs and only the difference ($90,000 above) added to direct materials and direct labor. The reason is that the schedule of cost of goods manufactured represents a summary of costs flowing through the Work in Process account during a period and therefore must exclude any overhead costs that were incurred but never applied to production. If a reverse situation had existed and overhead had been overapplied during the period, then the amount of overapplied overhead would have been added to actual overhead costs on the schedule. This would have brought the actual overhead costs up to the amount that had been applied to production.

Also note that the underapplied overhead deducted on the schedule of cost of goods manufactured is added to cost of goods sold. The reverse would be true if overhead had been overapplied.

PROBLEMS OF OVERHEAD APPLICATION

The concept of underapplied and overapplied overhead

Since the predetermined overhead rate is established before a period begins, and is based entirely on estimated data, there will generally be a difference between the amount of overhead cost that is applied to the Work in Process account and the actual overhead costs that materialize during the period. In the case of the Rand Company, for example, the predetermined overhead rate of $6 per hour resulted in $90,000 of overhead cost being applied to Work in Process, whereas actual overhead costs proved to be $95,000 for the month (see Exhibit 3–7). The difference between the overhead cost applied to Work in Process and the actual overhead costs of a period is termed either **underapplied** or **overapplied overhead.** For the Rand Company, overhead was underapplied because the applied cost ($90,000) was $5,000 less than the actual cost ($95,000). If the tables had been reversed, and the company had applied $95,000 in overhead cost to Work in Process while incurring actual overhead costs of only $90,000, then a situation of overapplied overhead would have existed.

Since the amount of overhead applied to Work in Process is dependent on the predetermined overhead rate, any difference between applied overhead cost and actual overhead cost must be traceable to the estimates going into the overhead rate computation. To illustrate, refer again to the formula used in computing the predetermined overhead rate:

$$\frac{\text{Estimated total manufacturing overhead costs}}{\text{Estimated total units in the base (direct labor-hours, etc.)}}$$

$$-\text{ Predetermined overhead rate}$$

If either the estimated cost or the estimated level of activity used in this formula differs from the actual cost or the actual level of activity for a period, then the predetermined overhead rate will prove to be inaccurate and either under- or overapplied overhead will result. Assume, for example, that two firms have prepared the following estimated data for the year 19x1:

	Company A	Company B
Predetermined overhead rate based on	Machine-hours	Direct labor cost
Estimated manufacturing overhead for 19x1 . . .	$100,000 *(a)*	$120,000 *(a)*
Estimated machine-hours for 19x1	50,000 *(b)*	—
Estimated direct labor cost for 19x1	—	$ 80,000 *(b)*
Predetermined overhead rate, *(a)* ÷ *(b)*.	$2 per machine-hour	150% of direct labor cost

Now assume that the *actual* overhead costs and the *actual* level of activity for 19x1 for each firm are shown as follows:

	Company A	Company B
Actual manufacturing overhead costs.	$99,000	$128,000
Actual machine-hours	48,000	—
Actual direct labor cost	—	88,000

For each company, notice that the actual cost and activity data differ from the estimates used in computing the predetermined overhead rate. The computation of the resulting under- or overapplied overhead for each company is given below:

	Company A	Company B
Actual manufacturing overhead costs.	$99,000	$128,000
Manufacturing overhead cost applied to Work in Process during 19x1:		
48,000 *actual* machine-hours × $2	96,000	
$88,000 *actual* direct labor cost × 150%		132,000
Underapplied (overapplied) overhead.	$ 3,000	$ (4,000)

For Company A, notice that the amount of overhead cost that has been applied to Work in Process ($96,000) is less than the actual overhead cost for the year ($99,000). Therefore, overhead is underapplied. Also notice that the original estimate of overhead in Company A ($100,000) is not directly involved in this computation. Its impact is felt only through the $2 predetermined overhead rate that is used.

EXHIBIT 3–10

Summary of overhead concepts

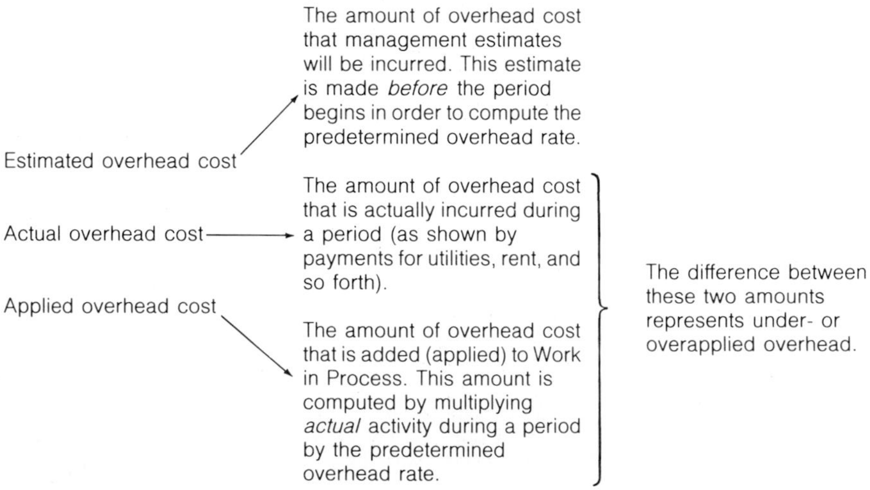

For Company B, the amount of overhead cost that has been applied to Work in Process ($132,000) is greater than the actual overhead cost for the year ($128,000), and so a situation of overapplied overhead exists.

A summary of the concepts discussed in this section is presented in Exhibit 3–10.

Disposition of under- or overapplied overhead balances

What disposition should be made of any under- or overapplied balance remaining in the Manufacturing Overhead account at the end of a period? Generally, any balance in the account is treated in one of two ways:

1. Closed out to Cost of Goods Sold.
2. Allocated between Work in Process, Finished Goods, and Cost of Goods Sold in proportion to the ending balances in these accounts.

Closed out to cost of goods sold   Most firms close out any under- or overapplied overhead to Cost of Goods Sold, since this approach is simpler than allocation. Returning to the example of the Rand Company, the entry to close the underapplied overhead to Cost of Goods Sold would be (see Exhibit 3–8 for the $5,000 cost figure):

	(13)		
Cost of Goods Sold		5,000	
Manufacturing Overhead.			5,000

With this entry, the cost of goods sold for the month increases to $123,500, as shown earlier:

Cost of goods sold (from Exhibit 3–8)	$118,500
Add underapplied overhead [entry (13) above]	5,000
Adjusted cost of goods sold	$123,500

An income statement for the Rand Company for April would therefore appear as shown in Exhibit 3–11.

EXHIBIT 3–11

THE RAND COMPANY
Income Statement
For the Month of April 19xx

Sales		$225,000
Less cost of goods sold ($118,500 + $5,000)		123,500
Gross margin		101,500
Less selling and administrative expenses:		
Salaries expense	$32,000	
Advertising expense	30,000	
Other expense	15,000	77,000
Net income		$ 24,500

Allocated between accounts Allocation of under- or overapplied overhead between Work in Process, Finished Goods, and Cost of Goods Sold is more accurate than closing the entire balance into Cost of Goods Sold. The reason is that allocation assigns overhead costs to where they would have gone in the first place had it not been for the errors in the estimates going into the predetermined overhead rate. Although allocation is more accurate than direct write-off, it is used less often in actual practice because of the time and difficulty involved in the allocation process. Most firms feel that the greater accuracy simply isn't worth the extra effort that allocation requires, particularly when the dollar amounts are small.

Had we chosen to allocate the underapplied overhead in the Rand Company example, the computations and entry would have been:

Work in process inventory, April 30.	$ 72,000	30.0%
Finished goods inventory, April 30 .	49,500	20.6
Cost of goods sold	118,500	49.4
Total cost.	$240,000	100.0%
Work in Process (30.0% × $5,000)	1,500	
Finished Goods (20.6% × $5,000) .	1,030	
Cost of Goods Sold (49.4% × $5,000)	2,470	
Manufacturing Overhead .		5,000

If overhead had been overapplied, the entry above would have been just the reverse, since a credit balance would have existed in the Manufacturing Overhead account.

A general model of product cost flows

The flow of costs in a product costing system can be presented in general model form, as shown in Exhibit 3–12. This model applies as much to a process costing system as it does to a job-order costing system. Visual inspection of the model can be very helpful in gaining a perspective as to how costs enter a system, flow through it, and finally end up as cost of goods sold on the income statement.

Multiple overhead rates

Our discussion in this chapter has assumed that a single overhead rate was being used throughout an entire factory operation. In small companies, and even in some medium-sized companies, a single overhead rate (called a **plantwide overhead rate**) is used and is entirely adequate as a means of allocating overhead costs to production jobs. But in larger companies, **multiple overhead rates** are common, for the reason that a single rate may not be capable of equitably handling the overhead costs of all departments. One department may be labor intensive, for example, and rely almost solely on the efforts of workers in performing needed functions. Allocation of overhead costs in such a department could, perhaps, be done most equitably on a

EXHIBIT 3–12
A general model of cost flows

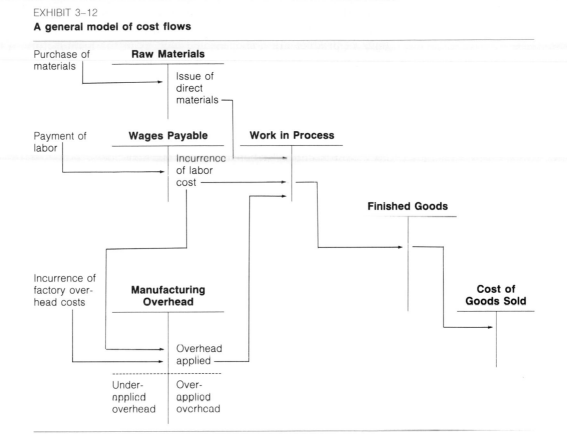

basis of labor-hours or labor cost. Another department in the same factory may be machine intensive, requiring little in the way of worker effort. Allocation of overhead costs in this department could, perhaps, be done most equitably on a basis of machine-hours.

In short, larger organizations often have many predetermined overhead rates—perhaps a different one for each department. As a unit of product moves along the production line, overhead is applied in each department, according to the various overhead rates that have been set. The accumulation of all of these overhead applications represents the total overhead cost of the job.

SUMMARY

Unit cost of production is one of the most useful items of cost data to a manager. There are two methods in widespread use for determining unit costs. These are job-order costing and process costing. Job-order costing is used in those manufacturing situations where units of product differ from each other, such as in the production of special-order machine tools or in shipbuilding. Process costing is used in those manufacturing situations where units of product are homogeneous, such as in the manufacture of cement.

Materials requisition forms and labor time tickets control the assignment of direct materials and direct labor cost to production. Indirect manufacturing costs are assigned to production through use of a predetermined overhead rate, which is developed by estimating the level of manufacturing overhead to be incurred during a period and by dividing this estimate by a base common to all the jobs to be worked on during the period. The most frequently used bases are direct labor-hours and machine-hours.

Since the predetermined overhead rate is based on estimates, the actual overhead cost incurred during a period may be somewhat more or somewhat less than the amount of overhead cost applied to production. Such a difference is referred to as underapplied or overapplied overhead. The underapplied or overapplied overhead of a period can be either (1) closed out to Cost of Goods Sold or (2) allocated between Work in Process, Finished Goods, and Cost of Goods Sold.

KEY TERMS FOR REVIEW

Absorption cost A costing method that includes all manufacturing costs—direct materials, direct labor, and both variable and fixed overhead—as part of the cost of a finished unit of product.

Bill of materials A control sheet that shows the type and quantity of each item of material going into a completed unit of product.

Full cost A term synonymous with *absorption cost.*

Job cost sheet A form prepared for each job initiated into production that serves as a means for accumulating the materials, labor, and overhead costs chargeable to the job and as a means for determining unit costs.

Job-order costing system A costing system used in those manufacturing situations where many different products, jobs, or batches of production are being produced each period.

Materials requisition form A detailed source document that specifies the type and quantity of materials that are to be drawn from the storeroom and identifies the job to which the materials are to be charged.

Multiple overhead rates The setting of a different predetermined overhead rate in each department, rather than having a single predetermined overhead rate for the entire company.

Overapplied overhead A credit balance in the Manufacturing Overhead account that arises when the amount of overhead cost applied to Work in Process is greater than the amount of overhead cost actually incurred during a period.

Overhead application The charging of manufacturing overhead cost to the Work in Process account.

Plantwide overhead rate A single predetermined overhead rate that is used in all departments of a company, rather than each department having its own separate predetermined overhead rate.

Predetermined overhead rate An overhead rate, based on estimated manufacturing overhead cost and estimated production activity, that is established before a period begins.

Process costing system A costing system used in those manufacturing situations where a single, homogeneous product (such as cement or flour) is produced for long periods of time.

Time Ticket A detailed source document that is used to record an employee's hour-by-hour activities during a day.

Underapplied overhead A debit balance in the Manufacturing Overhead account that arises when the amount of overhead cost actually incurred is greater than the amount of overhead cost applied to Work in Process during a period.

APPENDIX: NORMALIZED OVERHEAD RATES

Many firms hesitate to set predetermined overhead rates on the basis of the expected production of a single period if that production is subject to wide variations. The reason is that as production levels fluctuate, the predetermined overhead rate also fluctuates, resulting in high per unit costs in periods when production is low and in low per unit costs in periods when production is high. This problem is traceable to the fact that fixed costs often make up a large part of manufacturing overhead, and, as explained in Chapter 2, these costs go on basically unchanged in total regardless of the level of activity. As a result, when production is low, the fixed overhead costs are spread over a small number of units, resulting in a high cost per unit. When production is high, these costs are spread over a large number of units, resulting in a lower cost per unit.

Fluctuating overhead rate

To illustrate the problems caused by fluctuating overhead rates, let us assume the following production, sales, and cost data for a manufacturing firm:

	Year 1	Year 2
Production and sales data:		
Production in units.	10,000	6,000
Sales in units	8,000	8,000
Estimated manufacturing overhead cost:		
Variable overhead cost ($1 per unit)	$10,000	$ 6,000
Fixed overhead cost	24,000	24,000
Total overhead cost	$34,000	$30,000

If the company sets its overhead rates on the basis of the expected production of each year, the rates will be:

$$\text{Year 1:} \quad \frac{\text{Estimated overhead cost, \$34,000}}{\text{Estimated production, 10,000 units*}} = \$3.40 \text{ per unit}$$

$$\text{Year 2:} \quad \frac{\text{Estimated overhead cost, \$30,000}}{\text{Estimated production, 6,000 units}} = \$5 \text{ per unit}$$

* Rather than setting the overhead rate on a basis of the number of units produced, the company could have set it on a basis of the number of direct labor-hours needed to produce the units; units of product are being used in this example simply for ease of illustration.

If we further assume that each unit of product requires $2 in direct materials cost and $3 in direct labor cost, then the total cost of a unit of product manufactured in each separate year will be:

	Year 1	Year 2
Direct materials	$2.00	$ 2.00
Direct labor	3.00	3.00
Manufacturing overhead	3.40	5.00
Total cost per unit	$8.40	$10.00

Notice the wide variation in unit costs between the two years. Looking at the overhead portion of the cost, we can see that the higher production level in year 1 has caused the overhead to be spread thinner, resulting in a lower cost per unit. Many managers feel that this type of variation in unit costs can lead to distorted financial statements and can cause confusion on the part of statement users. With unit costs jumping up and down, statements become difficult to interpret and can lead to faulty conclusions and unwise decisions.

This point can be seen clearly by preparing a partial income statement for each of the two years from the data above. (Recall from the original data that sales are planned at 8,000 units annually; we will assume a selling price of $10 per unit.)

	Year 1	Year 2	Total
Sales (8,000 units at $10 each).	$80,000	$80,000	$160,000
Cost of goods sold:			
Year 1 (8,000 units at $8.40 each)	67,200		
Year 2 (2,000 units at $8.40 each)		16,800	144,000
(6,000 units at $10 each)		60,000	
Total cost of goods sold.	67,200	76,800	144,000
Gross margin	$12,800	$ 3,200	$ 16,000

Although sales are constant at 8,000 units in each year, the gross margin drops dramatically in year 2. The reason, of course, is that production dropped off in year 2, causing a jump in cost per unit and a drop in gross margin per unit. Yet an uninformed manager seeing these data might be misled into thinking that massive inefficiencies were developing or that a substantial jump in labor or raw materials prices had just taken place. An uninformed stockholder might be led to believe that difficulties were developing in the company that warranted the selling of his or her stock. In reality, we can see that none of these conclusions are correct; the variation in gross margin is simpy a result of a temporary imbalance between production and sales.

The concept of a normalized overhead rate

The company in our illustration may have had good reasons for producing more than it sold in year 1. For example, the company may have been building inventories in anticipation of a strike or a supply interruption in year 2, in order to have goods on hand to meet customer needs. In short, the question isn't whether variations in the level of production are desirable—such variations are often unavoidable. The question is whether these variations should be permitted to influence unit costs—pushing costs up in times of low activity and pulling them down in times of high activity. Many managers would argue that the cost of a unit of product should be the same whether it is produced in year 1, year 2, or any other year, so long as long-run demand for the product is reasonably stable.

How can uniformity in unit cost be attained if a firm's production is fluctuating from year to year? The answer lies in **normalized overhead rates.** A normalized overhead rate is not based on the expected activity of a single period. Rather, a normalized overhead rate is based on an average activity level that spans many periods—past, present, and future. The approach is to determine what level of activity is *normal* over the long run, and then to set predetermined overhead rates on that figure. Such rates are said to be normalized in the sense that they smooth out the hills and valleys in activity that are largely beyond management's control.

An illustration of normalized overhead rates

To show how normalized overhead rates work, let us return to the data used earlier. On a normalized basis, overhead rates would be set on an average production figure of 8,000 units per year rather than on a basis of 10,000 units in year 1 and 6,000 units in year 2. The computations would be.

	Per unit
Fixed overhead cost ($24,000 ÷ 8,000 units)	$3
Variable overhead cost	1
Total predetermined overhead rate	$4

This overhead rate would be used to cost units of product in both years; therefore, the full cost of a unit produced in either year would be:

Direct materials (as before) $2
Direct labor (as before) 3
Manufacturing overhead 4
Total cost per unit $9

With stable unit costs, the erratic behavior that we observed earlier on the company's income statement will be eliminated, as shown below:

	Year 1	Year 2	Total
Sales (8,000 units at $10 each)	$80,000	$80,000	$160,000
Cost of goods sold (8,000 units at $9 each)	72,000	72,000	144,000
Gross margin	$ 8,000	$ 8,000	$ 16,000

Notice that as a result of using normalized overhead rates, the gross margin pattern is even over the two-year period. By contrast, recall from our earlier income statement that when fluctuating overhead rates are used to cost production, the gross margin pattern is erratic, even though the same number of units is sold in each year. In years when production is high, income is also high; in years when production is low, income is also low.

In short, normalized overhead rates largely eliminate from inventories, from cost of goods sold, and from gross margin any unfavorable impact of having production out of balance with the long-run demand for a company's products.

KEY TERM FOR REVIEW (APPENDIX)

Normalized overhead rate An overhead rate that is based on the long-run average (or "normal") level of activity in a company rather than on the expected activity of any given year.

QUESTIONS

3–1. State the purposes for which it is necessary or desirable to compute unit costs.

3–2. Distinguish between job-order costing and process costing.

3–3. What is the essential purpose of any costing system?

3–4. What is the purpose of the job cost sheet in a job-order costing system?

3–5. What is a predetermined overhead rate, and how is it computed?

3–6. Explain how a sales order, a production order, a materials requisition form, and a labor time ticket are involved in the production and costing of products.

3–7. Explain why some production costs must be assigned to products through an allocation process. Name several such costs. Would such costs be classified as *direct* or as *indirect* costs?

3–8. Why do firms use predetermined overhead rates rather than actual manufacturing overhead costs in applying overhead to units of product?

3–9. What factors should be considered in selecting a base to be used in computing the predetermined overhead rate?

3–10. What is meant by the statement that overhead is "absorbed" into units of product? If a company fully absorbs its overhead costs, does this guarantee that a profit will be earned for the period?

3–11. What account is credited when overhead cost is applied to Work in Process? Would you expect the amount applied for a period to equal the actual overhead costs of the period? Why or why not?

3–12. What is underapplied overhead? Overapplied overhead? What disposition is made of these amounts at period end?

3–13. Enumerate several reasons why overhead might be underapplied in a given year.

3–14. What adjustment is made for underapplied overhead on the schedule of cost of goods manufactured, and why is this adjustment necessary? What adjustment is made on the schedule of cost of goods sold?

3–15. What adjustment is made for overapplied overhead on the schedule of cost of goods manufactured, and why is this adjustment necessary? What adjustment is made on the schedule of cost of goods sold?

3–16. Sigma Company applies overhead cost to jobs on a basis of direct labor cost. Job A, which was started and completed during the current period, shows charges of $5,000 for direct materials, $8,000 for direct labor, and $6,000 for overhead on its job cost sheet. Job B, which is still in process at year-end, shows charges of $2,500 for direct materials and $4,000 for direct labor. Should any overhead cost be added to job B at year-end? Explain.

3–17. A company assigns overhead cost to completed jobs on a basis of 125 percent of direct labor cost. The job cost sheet for job 313 shows that $10,000 in direct material has been used on the job and that $12,000 in direct labor cost has been incurred. If 1,000 units were produced in job 313, what is the cost per unit?

3–18. What is a "plantwide" overhead rate? Why are multiple overhead rates, rather than a plantwide rate, used in some companies?

3–19. If overhead rates are set on a basis of each period's activity, then unit costs will rise as the activity level rises, and vice versa. Do you agree? Explain.

3–20. What is the purpose of a normalized overhead rate? Are such rates more or less apt to lead to confusion on the part of statement users than using rates based on the activity of individual periods? Explain.

EXERCISES

E3–1. The Premier Manufacturing Company makes a product that is subject to wide seasonal variations in demand. Unit costs are computed on a quarterly basis by dividing each quarter's manufacturing costs (material, labor, and overhead) by the quarter's production in units. The company's estimated costs, by quarter, for the coming year are given below:

	First quarter	Second quarter	Third quarter	Fourth quarter
Direct materials	$16,000	$ 8,000	$ 4,000	$12,000
Direct labor	30,000	15,000	7,500	22,500
Manufacturing overhead	36,000	33,000	31,500	34,500
Total manufacturing costs	$82,000	$56,000	$43,000	$69,000
Number of units to be produced	20,000	10,000	5,000	15,000
Estimated cost per unit	$4.10	$5.60	$8.60	$4.60

The company is concerned about the variation in unit costs and wonders whether there is a way to more equitably assign the overhead costs to units of product. The company's overhead costs are mostly fixed; therefore, these costs show little sensitivity to changes in production from quarter to quarter, as shown above.

Required: 1. The company uses a job-order cost system. How would you recommend that overhead be assigned to production? Be specific, and show computations.
2. Recompute the company's unit costs in accordance with your recommendations in (1) above.

E3–2. Farnell Company is a manufacturing firm that operates a job-order costing system. Overhead costs are charged to production on a basis of direct labor-hours. At the beginning of 19x6, management estimated that the company would incur $192,000 in manufacturing overhead costs for the year and work 80,000 direct labor-hours.

Required: 1. Compute the company's predetermined overhead rate for 19x6.
2. Assume that during the year the company works only 75,000 direct labor-hours and incurs the following costs in the Manufacturing Overhead and Work in Process accounts:

Manufacturing Overhead		Work in Process	
(Maintenance) 24,000	?	(Direct materials) 200,000	
(Indirect labor) 60,000		(Direct labor) 600,000	
(Utilities) 32,000		(Overhead) ?	
(Insurance) 18,000			
(Depreciation) 50,000			

Copy the data in the T-accounts above onto your answer sheet. Compute the amount of overhead cost that should be applied to Work in Process for the year, and make the entry in your T-accounts.
3. Compute the amount of under- or overapplied overhead for the year, and show the balance in your Manufacturing Overhead T-account. Show the general journal entry that most companies would make to close out the balance in this account.

E3–3. The Foley Company uses a job-order costing system. The following data relate to the month of March 19x9:

a. Raw materials purchased on account, $90,000.
b. Raw materials issued to production, $80,000 (10 percent indirect, 90 percent direct).
c. Direct labor cost incurred, $60,000; indirect labor cost incurred, $25,000.
d. Other manufacturing overhead costs incurred during the month, $48,000 (credit Accounts Payable).

e. The company applies manufacturing overhead cost to production on a basis of $8.50 per direct labor-hour. There were 10,000 direct labor-hours recorded for the month.

f. Production orders costing $200,000 were completed during the month and transferred to Finished Goods.

g. Production orders that had cost $180,000 to complete were shipped to customers during the month. These goods were invoiced at 25 percent above cost. The goods were sold on account.

Required: 1. Prepare journal entries to record the information given above.

2. Prepare T-accounts for Manufacturing Overhead and Work in Process. Post the relevant information above to each account. Assuming that Work in Process has a beginning balance of $3,000, compute the ending balance in each account.

E3–4. Estimated cost and operating data for three companies for 19x6 are given below:

	Company A	Company B	Company C
Direct labor-hours	60,000	30,000	40,000
Machine-hours	25,000	90,000	18,000
Direct labor cost	$300,000	$160,000	$240,000
Manufacturing overhead cost	432,000	270,000	384,000

Predetermined overhead rates are computed on the following bases in the three companies:

Company	Overhead rate based on—
A	Direct labor-hours
B	Machine-hours
C	Direct labor cost

Required: 1. Compute the predetermined overhead rate to be used in each company during 19x6.

2. Assume that three jobs are worked on during 19x6 in Company A. Direct labor-hours recorded by job are:

	Direct labor-hours
Job 318	16,000
Job 319	20,000
Job 320	22,000

How much overhead cost will the company apply to Work in Process? If actual overhead costs total $420,000 for the year, will overhead be over- or underapplied? By how much?

E3–5. The Diewold Company has two departments, milling and assembly. The company uses a job-order cost system and computes a predetermined overhead rate in each department. The milling department bases its rate on machine-hours, and the assembly department bases its rate on direct labor cost. At the beginning of 19x1, the company made the following estimates:

	Milling	Assembly
Direct labor-hours	8,000	40,000
Machine-hours	60,000	3,000
Manufacturing overhead cost	$510,000	$400,000
Direct labor cost	72,000	320,000

Required:
1. Compute the predetermined overhead rate to be used in each department during 19x1.
2. Assume that during June the job cost sheet for job 407 showed the following:

	Milling	Assembly
Direct labor-hours	5	20
Machine-hours	60	4
Materials requisitioned	$300	$120
Direct labor cost	45	160

Compute the total overhead cost of job 407.
3. Would you expect substantially different amounts of overhead cost to be charged to some jobs if the company used a plantwide overhead rate based on direct labor cost instead of using departmental rates? Explain. No computations are necessary.

E3–6. Which method of accumulating product costs, job-order costing or process costing, would be more appropriate in each of the following situations?

a. A textbook publisher.
b. An oil refinery.
c. A manufacturer of powdered milk.
d. A manufacturer of ready-mix cement.
e. A custom home builder.
f. A shop for customizing vans.
g. A chemical manufacturer.
h. An auto repair shop.
i. A tire manufacturing plant.
j. A shipbuilder.

E3–7. The following cost data relate to the manufacturing activities of the Black Company during 19x5:

Manufacturing overhead costs
  incurred during the year:

Insurance, factory	$ 6,000
Indirect labor cost	10,000
Depreciation, factory	24,000
Utilities, factory	8,000
Total actual costs	$48,000

Other costs incurred
  during the year:

Purchases of raw materials	$30,000
Direct labor cost (10,000 hours)	40,000

Inventories:

Raw materials, January 1	7,000
Raw materials, December 31	4,000
Work in process, January 1	6,000
Work in process, December 31	7,500

The company uses a predetermined overhead rate to charge overhead cost to production. The predetermined overhead rate for 19x5 was $5 per direct labor-hour.

Required: 1.   Compute the amount of under- or overapplied overhead for 19x5.
2.   Prepare a schedule of cost of goods manufactured for 19x5.

E3–8.   The Custom Metal Works produces castings and other metal parts to customer specifications, using a job-order cost system. For the year 19x5, the company estimated that it would work 60,000 direct labor-hours and incur $300,000 in manufacturing overhead costs. Overhead is allocated to jobs on a basis of direct labor-hours.

The entire month of March 19x5 was spent on job 382, which called for 8,000 machine parts. Cost data for March are given below.

a.   Materials purchased on account, $48,000.
b.   Materials requisitioned for production, $40,000 (10 percent indirect materials and 90 percent direct materials).
c.   Labor cost incurred, $35,000 (20 percent indirect and 80 percent direct).
d.   Other overhead cost incurred during March, $15,000 (credit Accounts Payable).
e.   Direct labor-hours worked during March, 4,800.
f.   The completed job was moved into the finished goods warehouse on March 31 to await delivery to the customer. (In computing the dollar amount of this entry, remember that the cost of a completed job consists of direct materials, direct labor, and *applied* overhead.)

Required: 1.   Prepare journal entries to record the March activity.
2.   Compute the unit cost that will appear on the job cost sheet.

E3–9.   The Toronto Company began operations on January 2, 19x5. The following activity took place in the Work in Process account for the month of January:

Work in Process

Direct materials	30,000	To finished goods	125,000
Direct labor	60,000		
Manufacturing overhead	45,000		

The Toronto Company uses a job-order costing system and applies manufacturing overhead to work in process on a basis of direct labor cost. At the end of January, only one job was still in process. This job (job 15) has been charged with $4,500 in direct labor cost.

Required: 1.   Compute the overhead rate in use during January.
2.   Complete the following job cost sheet for partially completed job 15:

Job Cost Sheet—Job 15
As of January 31, 19x5

Direct materials . . . . $_____
Direct labor . . . .   _____
Manufacturing overhead . . . .   _____
    Total cost to January 31 . . . . $_____

E3–10.   The following information is taken from the end-of-year account balances of the Sevier Manufacturing Company:

Manufacturing Overhead					Work in Process			
(a)	100,000	(b)	90,000	Bal.	40,000	(c)	250,000
					75,000		
Bal.	10,000				60,000		
				(b)	90,000		
				Bal.	15,000		

Finished Goods					Cost of Goods Sold		
Bal.	35,000	(d)	240,000	(d)	240,000		
(c)	250,000						
Bal.	45,000						

Required:

1. Identify the dollar figures appearing by the letters *(a), (b),* and so forth.
2. Assume that the company closes any balance in the Manufacturing Overhead account directly to Cost of Goods Sold. Prepare the necessary journal entry.
3. Assume that the company allocates any balance in the Manufacturing Overhead account to the other accounts. Prepare the necessary journal entry, with supporting computations.

PROBLEMS

P3–11. **Entries directly into T-accounts; income statement.** Durham Company's trial balance as of January 1, 19x7, is given below:

Cash	$ 9,000	
Accounts Receivable	12,000	
Raw Materials	7,000	
Work in Process	18,000	
Finished Goods	20,000	
Prepaid Insurance	4,000	
Plant and Equipment	230,000	
Accumulated Depreciation		$ 42,000
Accounts Payable		30,000
Capital Stock		150,000
Retained Earnings		78,000
Totals	$300,000	$300,000

Durham Company manufactures items to customers' specifications and employs a job-order cost system. During 19x7, the following transactions took place:

a. Raw materials were purchased on account, $45,000.
b. Raw materials were requisitioned for use in production, $40,000 (80 percent direct and 20 percent indirect).
c. Factory utility costs incurred, $12,000.
d. Depreciation was recorded on plant and equipment, $28,000. Three fourths of the depreciation relates to factory equipment, and the remainder relates to selling and administrative equipment.
e. Costs for salaries and wages were incurred as follows:

Direct labor	$40,000
Indirect labor	18,000
Sales commissions	10,000
Administrative salaries	25,000

f. Insurance expired during the year, $3,000 (80 percent relates to factory operations, and 20 percent relates to selling and administrative activities).

g. Miscellaneous selling and administrative expenses incurred, $18,000.

h. Manufacturing overhead was applied to production. The company applies overhead on a basis of 150 percent of direct labor cost.

i. Goods costing $130,000 to manufacture were transferred to the finished goods warehouse.

j. Goods that had cost $120,000 to manufacture were sold on account for $200,000.

k. Collections from customers during the year totaled $197,000.

l. Payments to suppliers on account during the year, $100,000; payments to employees for salaries and wages, $90,000.

Required:

1. Prepare a T-account for each account in the company's trial balance, and enter the opening balances shown above.

2. Record the transactions above directly into the T-accounts. prepare new T-accounts as needed. Key your entries to the letters *(a)* through *(l)* above. Find the ending balance in each account.

3. Is manufacturing overhead under- or overapplied for the year? Make an entry in the T-accounts to close any balance in the Manufacturing Overhead account to Cost of Goods Sold.

4. Prepare an income statement for the year.

P3–12. **Straightforward journal entries; partial T-accounts; income statement.** Almeda Products, Inc., uses a job-order cost system to accumulate costs in its manufacturing plant. The company's inventory balances on April 1, 19x2 (the start of its fiscal year), were as follows:

Raw Materials	$32,000
Work in process	20,000
Finished goods	48,000

During the year, the following transactions were completed:

a. Raw materials were purchased on account, $170,000.

b. Raw materials were issued from the storeroom for use in production, $180,000 (80 percent direct materials, 20 percent indirect materials).

c. Employee salaries and wages were accrued as follows: direct labor, $200,000; indirect labor, $82,000; and selling and administrative salaries, $90,000.

d. Utility costs were incurred in the factory, $65,000.

e. Advertising costs were incurred, $100,000.

f. Prepaid insurance expired during the year, $20,000 (90 percent related to factory operations, and 10 percent related to selling and administrative activities).

g. Depreciation was recorded, $180,000 (85 percent related to factory assets, and 15 percent related to selling and administrative assets).

h. Overhead cost was applied to production at a rate of 175 percent of direct labor cost.

i. Goods costing $700,000 to complete were transferred to the finished goods warehouse.

j. Sales for the year (all on account) totaled $1,000,000. These goods had cost $720,000 to manufacture.

Required:

1. Prepare journal entries to record the transactions for the year.

2. Prepare T-accounts for Raw Materials, Work in Process, Finished Goods, Manufacturing Overhead, and Cost of Goods Sold. Post the appropriate parts of your

journal entries to these T-accounts. Compute the ending balance in each account. (Don't forget to enter the opening balances in the inventory accounts.)

3. Is Manufacturing Overhead under- or overapplied for the year? Prepare a journal entry to close this balance to Cost of Goods Sold.
4. Prepare an income statement for the year.

P3–13. **Entries directly into T-accounts; overhead balance allocation; income statement.** A balance sheet for Supreme Company as of January 1, 19x1, is given below:

Supreme Company
Balance Sheet
January 1, 19x1
Assets

Current assets:			
Cash			$ 15,000
Accounts receivable			40,000
Inventories:			
Raw materials		$ 25,000	
Work in process		30,000	
Finished goods		45,000	100,000
Prepaid insurance			5,000
Total current assets			160,000
Plant and equipment		500,000	
Less accumulated depreciation		210,000	290,000
Total assets			$450,000

Liabilities and Stockholders' Equity

Accounts payable			$ 75,000
Capital stock		250,000	
Retained earnings		125,000	375,000
Total liabilities and stockholders' equity			$450,000

Supreme Company is a manufacturing firm and uses a job-order cost system. For 19x1, the company estimated that it would incur $80,000 in manufacturing overhead cost and $100,000 in direct labor cost. The following transactions were recorded for the year:

a. Raw materials were purchased on account, $80,000.
b. Raw materials were issued to production, $90,000; $5,000 of this amount was for indirect materials.
c. Payroll costs incurred and paid: direct labor, $120,000; indirect labor, $30,000; and selling and administrative salaries, $75,000.
d. Factory utilities costs incurred, $12,000.
e. Depreciation recorded for the year, $30,000 ($5,000 on selling and administrative assets; $25,000 on factory assets).
f. Insurance expired, $4,800 ($4,000 relates to factory operations, and $800 relates to selling and administrative activities).
g. Advertising expenses incurred, $40,000.
h. Other manufacturing overhead costs incurred, $17,000 (credit Accounts Payable).
i. Manufacturing overhead was applied to production. Overhead is applied on a basis of direct labor cost.
j. Goods costing $310,000 to manufacture were completed during the year.

k. Goods that had cost $300,000 to manufacture were sold on account for $450,000.
l. Collections on account from customers, $445,000.
m. Payments on account to suppliers, $150,000.

Required:
1. Prepare a T-account for each account on the company's balance sheet, and enter the opening balances above.
2. Make entries directly into the T-accounts for the transactions given above. Create new T-accounts as needed. Determine an ending balance for each T-account.
3. Was manufacturing overhead under- or overapplied for the year? Assume that the company allocates any overhead balance between the Work in Process, Finished Goods, and Cost of Goods Sold accounts. Prepare a journal entry to show the allocation for 19x1. (Round allocation percentages to one decimal place.)
4. Prepare an income statement for the year.

P3–14. **Straightforward journal entries; partial T-accounts; income statement.** Fugal company is a manufacturing firm that uses a job-order cost system. On January 1, 19x9, the company's inventory balances were:

Raw materials	$16,000
Work in process	10,000
Finished goods	30,000

The company applies overhead cost to jobs on a basis of direct labor hours. For 19x9, the company estimated that it would work 18,000 direct labor hours and incur $153,000 in manufacturing overhead cost. The following transactions were recorded for the year:

a. Raw materials were purchased on account, $200,000.
b. Raw materials were requisitioned for use in production, $190,000 (80 percent direct and 20 percent indirect).
c. The following costs were incurred for employee services:

Direct labor (20,000 hours)	$160,000
Indirect labor	27,000
Sales commissions	36,000
Administrative salaries	80,000

d. Heat, power, and water costs were incurred in the factory, $42,000.
e. Insurance expired during the year, $10,000 (90 percent relates to factory operations, and 10 percent relates to selling and administrative activities).
f. Advertising costs were incurred, $50,000.
g. Depreciation was recorded for the year, $60,000 (85 percent relates to factory operations, and 15 percent relates to selling and administrative activities).
h. Manufacturing overhead cost was applied to production, ____?____.
i. Goods costing $480,000 to manufacture were completed during the year.
j. Goods were sold on account to customers during the year at a total selling price of $700,000. These goods cost $475,000 to manufacture.

Required:
1. Prepare journal entries to record the transactions given above.
2. Prepare T-accounts for inventories, Manufacturing Overhead, and Cost of Goods Sold. Post relevant data from your journal entries to these T-accounts (don't forget to enter the opening balances in your inventory accounts). Compute an ending balance in each account.

104

3. Is manufacturing overhead under- or overapplied for the year? Prepare a journal entry to close any balance in the Manufacturing Overhead account to Cost of Goods Sold.
4. Prepare an income statement for the year.

P3–15. **Computation of overhead rates; costing units of product.** Clark Engineering, Inc., employs a job-order cost system. The company uses predetermined overhead rates in applying manufacturing overhead to individual jobs. The predetermined overhead rate in Department A is based on machine-hours, and the rate in Department B is based on direct labor cost. At the beginning of 19x3, the company's management made the following estimates for the year:

	Department A	Department B
Direct labor-hours	18,000	40,000
Machine-hours	60,000	9,000
Direct labor cost	$135,000	$320,000
Manufacturing overhead cost	204,000	512,000

Job 127 was initiated into production on April 1 and completed on May 12. The company's cost records show the following information on the job:

	Department A	Department B
Direct labor-hours	36	70
Machine-hours	105	18
Materials placed into production	$412	$230
Direct labor cost	274	590

Required:
1. Compute the predetermined overhead rate that should be used during the year in Department A. Compute the rate that should be used in Department B.
2. Compute the total overhead cost applied to job 127.
3. What would be the total cost of job 127? If the job contained 100 units, what would be the cost per unit?
4. At the end of 19x3, the records of Clark Engineering, Inc., revealed the following *actual* cost and operating data for all jobs worked on during the year:

	Department A	Department B
Direct labor-hours	16,000	42,000
Machine-hours	55,000	9,600
Direct labor cost	$120,000	$328,000
Manufacturing overhead cost	190,000	520,000

What was the amount of underapplied or overapplied overhead in each department at the end of 19x3?

P3–16. **Schedule of cost of goods manufactured; pricing; work in process analysis.** The Pacific Manufacturing Company operates a job-order cost system and applies overhead cost to jobs on a basis of direct labor cost. In computing an overhead rate for 19x6, the company's estimates were: manufacturing overhead cost, $126,000; direct labor cost, $84,000. The company's inventory accounts at the beginning and end of the year were:

	January 1, 19x6	December 31, 19x6
Raw materials	$20,000	$22,000
Work in process	44,000	40,000
Finished goods	68,000	60,000

The following actual costs were incurred during 19x6:

Purchase of raw materials	$140,000
Direct labor cost	80,000
Manufacturing overhead costs:	
Depreciation of equipment	25,000
Indirect labor	42,000
Property taxes	9,000
Maintenance	11,000
Rent, building	36,000

Required:

1. *a.* Compute the predetermined overhead rate for 19x6.
   b. Compute the amount of under- or overapplied overhead for the year.

2. Prepare a schedule of cost of goods manufactured for the year.

3. Compute the cost of goods sold for the year. (Do not include any under- or overapplied overhead in your cost of goods sold figure.) What options are available for disposing of under- or overapplied overhead?

4. Job 137 was started and completed during the year. What price would have been charged to the customer if the job required $3,200 in materials and $4,200 in direct labor cost, and the company priced its jobs at 40 percent above cost to manufacture?

5. Direct labor made up $10,000 of the $32,000 ending Work in Process inventory balance. Supply the information missing below:

Direct materials	$?
Direct labor	10,000
Manufacturing overhead	?
Work in process inventory	$32,000

P3–17. **T-account analysis of job-order cost; periodic inventory method.** Wire Products, Inc., operates under a job-order cost system. At the beginning of 19x1, the company showed inventory balances as follows:

Raw materials	$ 9,500
Work in process	17,900
Finished goods	20,000

During the year, the following transactions were completed:

a. Raw materials were acquired from suppliers on account, $18,500.

b. Raw materials were requisitioned for use in production, $22,000 (80 percent direct and 20 percent indirect).

c. Factory payrolls were accrued, $40,000 (75 percent direct and 25 percent indirect).

d. Cash payments were made:

To suppliers, $18,000.
To employees for payrolls, $40,000.
For factory utilities, $6,000.

For factory rent, $12,000.
For miscellaneous factory costs, $3,660.

e. Overhead was applied to jobs on a basis of 115 percent of direct labor cost.
f. The ending balance in the Work in Process inventory account was determined to be $18,000.
g. The ending balance in the Finished Goods inventory account was determined to be $12,000.

Required: 1. Enter the above transactions directly into T-accounts.
2. As stated in item *(f)* above, the ending balance in Work in Process was $18,000. Factory overhead constituted $5,750 of this balance. The management of Wire Products, Inc., would like to know how much of the balance consisted of direct materials and direct labor. Complete the following schedule:

Direct materials	$?
Direct labor	?
Factory overhead	5,750
Total work in process	$18,000

3. How much was the under- or overapplied factory overhead for the year?
4. What two options does the company have for disposing of its under- or overapplied overhead? Prepare a journal entry under each of these options showing disposition of the under- or overapplied overhead for the year. (It is *not* necessary to post the journal entries to the T-accounts.)

P3–18. **Job cost sheets; overhead rates; journal entries.** The Kenworth Company employs a job-order costing system. Only three jobs were worked on during the months of November and December 19x1—job 105, job 106, and job 107. Job 105 was completed on December 15; the other two jobs were uncompleted at December 31. Job cost sheets on the three jobs are given below:

	Job 105 cost sheet		Job 106 cost sheet		Job 107 cost sheet	
	November costs	**December costs**	**November costs**	**December costs**	**November costs**	**December costs**
Direct materials	$3,500	—	$1,500	$2,500	—	$2,800
Direct labor	6,000	$2,000	2,800	4,000	—	3,000
Manufacturing overhead	4,500	?	2,100	?	—	?

The company assigns overhead costs to production on a basis of direct labor cost. Actual overhead costs for December totaled $7,200. Balances in the inventory accounts at November 30 were: raw materials, $6,000; work in process, ?; and finished goods, $22,500.

Required: 1. Prepare T-accounts for Raw Materials, Work in Process, and Finished Goods. Enter the November 30 balances given above; in the case of Work in Process, compute the November 30 balance and enter it into the Work in Process T-account.
2. Prepare summary journal entries to record the incurrence of direct materials cost, direct labor cost, and manufacturing overhead cost for December, and post these entries to appropriate T-accounts. (It is not necessary to make a separate

entry for each job; make one summary entry for each cost. In the case of manufacturing overhead, credit Accounts Payable.)

3. What apparent overhead rate does the company use to assign overhead costs to jobs? Using this rate, prepare a summary journal entry to record the application of overhead to jobs during December. Post this entry to appropriate T-accounts.

4. Prepare a journal entry to show the completion of job 105 and its transfer off the production line. Post this entry to appropriate T-accounts.

5. Determine the December 31 balance in the Work in Process inventory account. How much of this balance consists of costs traceable to job 106? To job 107?

P3–19. **Job-order cost journal entries; complete T-accounts; income statement.** Dexter Company's trial balance as of January 1, 19x4, is given below:

Cash	$ 9,000	
Accounts Receivable	30,000	
Raw Materials	16,000	
Work in Process	21,000	
Finished Goods	38,000	
Prepaid Insurance	7,000	
Plant and Equipment	300,000	
Accumulated Depreciation		$128,000
Accounts Payable		60,000
Salaries and Wages Payable		3,000
Capital Stock		200,000
Retained Earnings		30,000
	$421,000	$421,000

Dexter Company manufactures products to customers' specifications and uses a job-order cost system. Overhead costs are charged to production on a basis of direct labor-hours. For 19x4, management estimated that the company would incur $135,000 in manufacturing overhead cost and work 18,000 direct labor-hours. The following transactions occurred during the year:

a. Raw materials were purchased on account, $120,000.

b. Raw materials were issued to production, $130,000 (90 percent direct and 10 percent indirect).

c. Factory payrolls were accrued, $200,000 (70 percent direct labor and 30 percent indirect labor). A total of 20,800 direct labor-hours were worked during the year.

d. Sales and administrative salaries were accrued, $150,000.

e. Insurance expired during the year, $4,000 (85 percent relates to factory operations, and 15 percent relates to selling and administrative activities).

f. Factory utilities cost incurred, $36,000.

g. Advertising cost incurred, $100,000.

h. Depreciation recorded for the year, $40,000 (70 percent on factory plant and equipment and 30 percent on selling and administrative equipment).

i. Property taxes accrued on the factory building, $12,600 (credit Accounts Payable).

j. Manufacturing overhead cost was applied to production.

k. Goods were completed at a production cost of $406,000.

l. Sales on account to customers for the year were:

Selling price	$720,000	
Cost of goods sold	?	(Ending finished goods inventory, $24,000)

m. Collections on account from customers during the year, $715,000.

n. Cash payments made during the year: to creditors on account, $270,000; to employees for salaries and wages, $348,000.

Required:
1. Prepare journal entries to record the year's transactions.
2. Prepare a T-account for each account in the company's trial balance, and enter the opening balances given above. Post your journal entries to the T-accounts. Prepare new T-accounts as needed. Compute the ending balance in each account.
3. Is manufacturing overhead under- or overapplied for the year? Prepare the necessary journal entry to close the balance in the Manufacturing Overhead account to Cost of Goods Sold.
4. Prepare an income statement for the year.

P3–20. Alternative methods of disposing of under- or overapplied overhead. Piedmont Company uses a job-order cost system. The company uses predetermined overhead rates, based on direct labor-hours, in applying manufacturing overhead to jobs. Estimated cost and operating data for 19x6 are given below:

Estimated direct labor-hours	45,000
Estimated direct labor cost	$270,000
Estimated manufacturing overhead	180,000

At the end of 19x6, Piedmont Company's cost records revealed the following actual cost and operating data:

Direct labor-hours	40,000
Direct labor cost	$240,000
Manufacturing overhead cost	172,000
Raw materials inventory	8,000
Work in process inventory	25,000
Finished goods inventory	50,000
Cost of goods sold	175,000

Required:
1. Compute the company's predetermined overhead rate for 19x6.
2. Compute the underapplied or overapplied overhead for 19x6.
3. Assume that the company closes any underapplied or overapplied overhead directly to cost of goods sold. Prepare the appropriate journal entry.
4. Assume that the company allocates any underapplied or overapplied overhead to the appropriate accounts. Prepare the journal entry to show this allocation.
5. How much higher or lower will net income be for 19x6 if the underapplied or overapplied balance is allocated rather than closed directly to cost of goods sold?

P3–21. Plantwide and departmental overhead rates. "Blast it!" said David Wilson, president of Teledex Company. "We've just lost the bid on the Koopers job. It seems we're either too high to get the job or too low to make any money on half the jobs we bid."

Teledex Company manufactures products to customers' specifications and operates a job-order cost system. Manufacturing overhead cost is applied to jobs on a basis of direct labor cost. The following estimates were made at the beginning of 19x7, the current year:

	Fabricating department	Machining department	Assembly department	Total plant
Direct labor cost	$200,000	$100,000	$300,000	$600,000
Manufacturing overhead cost	350,000	400,000	90,000	840,000

Jobs require varying amounts of work in the three departments. The Koopers job, for example, would have required manufacturing costs in the three departments as follows:

	Fabricating department	Machining department	Assembly department	Total plant
Direct materials	$3,000	$200	$1,400	$4,600
Direct labor	2,800	500	6,200	9,500
Manufacturing overhead	?	?	?	?

The company uses a plantwide overhead rate to apply manufacturing overhead cost to jobs.

Required: 1. Assuming use of a plantwide overhead rate:

   a. Compute the rate for the current year.
   b. Determine the amount of manufacturing overhead cost that would have been applied to the Koopers job.

2. Suppose that instead of using a plantwide overhead rate, the company had used a separate predetermined overhead rate in each department. Under these conditions:

   a. Compute the rate for each department for the current year.
   b. Determine the amount of manufacturing overhead cost that would have been applied to the Koopers job.

3. Assume that it is customary in the industry to bid jobs at 150 percent of total manufacturing cost (direct materials, direct labor, and applied overhead). What was the company's bid price on the Koopers job? What would the bid price have been if departmental overhead rates had been used to apply overhead cost?

4. At the end of the current year, the company assembled the following *actual* cost data relating to all jobs worked on during the year:

	Fabricating department	Machining department	Assembly department	Total plant
Direct materials	$190,000	$ 16,000	$114,000	$320,000
Direct labor	210,000	108,000	262,000	580,000
Manufacturing overhead . .	360,000	420,000	84,000	864,000

Compute the under- or overapplied overhead for the year *(a)* assuming that a plantwide overhead rate is used and *(b)* assuming that departmental overhead rates are used.

P3–22.   **Schedule of cost of goods manufactured.** The Alberta Company manufactures a single product. The chief accountant has asked your help in preparing a schedule of cost of goods manufactured for the month ended June 30, 19x3. The following information is available:

   a. Ten thousand units were sold at $20 per unit.
   b. Twelve thousand units were produced. (One unit of raw materials is required for each finished unit.)
   c. The finished goods inventory on June 1 was 3,000 units valued at $16 each.
   d. The raw materials inventory on June 1 was 1,000 units valued at $5 each.
   e. During June, two purchases of raw materials were made:

June 6	8,000 units at $6 each
June 22	5,000 units at $5 each

f. The company uses the first-in, first-out method of determining raw materials inventories.

g. The work in process inventories were:

June 1	2,000 units valued at $18,000
June 30	2,000 units valued at $21,000

h. Depreciation is determined on a straight-line basis, at a rate of 10 percent per annum. Depreciable assets include:

Factory machinery.	$240,000 original cost
Office equipment	6,000 original cost

i. Overhead is applied to production on a basis of 70 percent of direct labor cost.

j. Other information provided:

Direct labor	$100,000
Indirect labor	45,000
Salespersons' salaries	10,500
Office salaries	16,000
Sales returns and allowances	5,000
Freight-out	2,500
Heat, light, and power	2,000
Factory rent	8,000
Interest expense	2,000
Miscellaneous factory overhead	10,000

Required: Prepare a schedule of cost of goods manufactured for the month in good form. Show supporting computations. (SMA, adapted)

P3–23. T-account analysis of cost flows. Selected ledger accounts of the Cardin Company are given below for the year 19x2:

Raw Materials

Bal. 1/1	8,000	19x2 credits	?
19x2 debits	60,000		
Bal. 12/31	12,000		

Manufacturing Overhead

19x2 debits	118,000	19x2 credits	?

Work in Process

Bal. 1/1	10,000	19x2 credits	240,000
Direct materials	50,000		
Direct labor	80,000		
Overhead	120,000		
Bal. 12/31	?		

Factory Wages Payable

19x2 debits	91,000	Bal. 1/1	3,000
		19x2 credits	90,000
		Bal. 12/31	2,000

Finished Goods

Bal. 1/1	30,000	19x2 credits	?
19x2 debits	?		
Bal. 12/31	40,000		

Cost of Goods Sold

19x2 debits	?	

Required:
1. What was the cost of raw materials put into production during the year?
2. How much of the materials in part (1) consisted of indirect materials?
3. How much of the factory labor cost for the year consisted of indirect labor?
4. What was the cost of goods manufactured for the year?
5. What was the cost of goods sold for the year (before considering under- or overapplied overhead)?
6. If overhead is applied to production on a basis of direct labor cost, what rate was in effect for 19x2?
7. Was manufacturing overhead under- or overapplied for 19x2? By how much?
8. Compute the ending balance in the Work in Process inventory account. Assume that this balance consists entirely of goods started during the year. If $6,000 of this balance is direct labor cost, how much of it is direct materials cost? Manufacturing overhead cost?

P3–24. **Comprehensive problem: T-accounts; job-order cost flows; statements; pricing.** Top-Products, Inc., produces goods to customers' orders and uses a job-order costing system. A trial balance for the company as of January 1, 19x3, is given below:

Cash.	$ 18,000	
Accounts Receivable	40,000	
Raw Material Inventory	25,000	
Work in Process Inventory	32,000	
Finished Goods Inventory	60,000	
Prepaid Insurance	5,000	
Plant and Equipment	400,000	
Accumulated Depreciation		$148,000
Accounts Payable		90,000
Salaries and Wages Payable		3,000
Capital Stock		250,000
Retained Earnings		89,000
	$580,000	$580,000

The company applies manufacturing overhead cost to jobs on a basis of direct labor cost. The following estimates were made at the beginning of 19x3 for purposes of computing a predetermined overhead rate for the year: manufacturing overhead cost, $228,000; direct labor cost, $190,000. Summarized transactions of the company for 19x3 are given below:

a. Raw materials were purchased on account, $180,000.
b. Raw materials were requisitioned for use in production, $190,000 (all direct materials).
c. Utility costs were incurred in the factory, $57,000.
d. Salary and wage costs were incurred: direct labor, $200,000; indirect labor, $90,000; salaries of selling and administrative employees, $120,000.
e. Insurance expired during the year, $4,000 (75 percent relates to factory operations, and 25 percent relates to selling and administrative activities).
f. Property taxes were incurred on the factory building, $16,000.
g. Advertising costs were incurred, $150,000.
h. Depreciation was recorded for the year, $50,000 (80 percent relates to factory assets, and the remainder relates to selling and administrative assets).
i. Other costs were incurred (credit Accounts Payable): for factory overhead, $30,000; for miscellaneous selling and administrative expenses, $18,000.
j. Manufacturing overhead cost was applied to jobs, _____?_____. 240000
k. Cost of goods manufactured for the year, $635,000.

l. Sales for the year totaled $1,000,000 (all on account); the cost of goods sold was _____?_____. (The ending balance in the Finished Goods inventory account was $45,000.)

m. Cash collections from customers during the year, $950,000.

n. Cash payments during the year: to employees, $412,000; on accounts payable, $478,000.

Required:

1. Enter the company's transactions for the year directly into T-accounts. (Don't forget to enter the opening balances into the T-accounts.) Key your entries to the letters *(a)* through *(n)* above. Create new T-accounts as needed. Find the ending balance in each account.

2. Prepare a schedule of cost of goods manufactured.

3. Prepare a journal entry to close any balance in the Manufacturing Overhead account to Cost of Goods Sold. Prepare a schedule of cost of goods sold.

4. Prepare an income statement for 19x3. Ignore income taxes.

5. Job 316 was one of the many jobs started and completed during the year. The job required $2,400 in materials and $3,000 in direct labor cost. If the job contained 300 units and the company billed the job at 140 percent of the cost to manufacture, what price per unit would have been charged to the customer?

P3–25. **Comprehensive problem: journal entries; T-accounts; statements; pricing.** Southworth Company uses a job-order cost system and applies manufacturing overhead cost to jobs on a basis of direct labor-hours. At the beginning of 19x8, the following estimates were made as a basis for computing a predetermined overhead rate for the year: manufacturing overhead cost, $250,000; direct labor-hours, 20,000. The following transactions took place during the year (all purchases and services were acquired on account):

a. Raw materials were purchased for use in production, $140,000.

b. Raw materials were requisitioned for use in production (all direct materials), $148,000.

c. Utility bills incurred in the factory, $21,000.

d. Salaries and wages costs incurred:

Direct labor (19,200 hours)	$216,000
Indirect labor	90,000
Selling and administrative	140,000

e. Maintenance costs incurred in the factory, $15,000.

f. Advertising costs incurred, $120,000.

g. Depreciation recorded for the year, $50,000 (90 percent relates to factory assets, and the remainder relates to selling and administrative assets).

h. Rental cost incurred on buildings, $90,000 (80 percent of the space is occupied by the factory, and 20 percent is occupied by sales and administration).

i. Miscellaneous selling and administrative costs incurred, $17,000.

j. Manufacturing overhead cost was applied to jobs, _____?_____.

k. Cost of goods manufactured for the year, $590,000.

l. Sales for the year (all on account) totaled $1,000,000. These goods cost $600,000 to manufacture.

The balances in the inventory accounts at the beginning of 19x8 were:

Raw materials	$18,000
Work in process	20,000
Finished goods	35,000

Required: 1. Prepare journal entries to record the above data.
2. Post your entries to T-accounts. (Don't forget to enter the opening inventory balances above.) Determine the ending balances in the inventory accounts and in the Manufacturing Overhead account.
3. Prepare a schedule of cost of goods manufactured.
4. Prepare a journal entry to close any balance in the Manufacturing Overhead account to Cost of Goods Sold. Prepare a schedule of cost of goods sold.
5. Prepare an income statement for the year. Ignore income taxes.
6. Job 218 was one of the many jobs started and completed during the year. The job required $3,600 in materials and 400 hours of direct labor time at a rate of $11 per hour. If the job contained 500 units and the company billed at 60 percent above the cost to manufacture, what price per unit would have been charged to the customer?

P3–26.   **Setting single versus dual overhead rates.**   The Holland Manufacturing Company has recently expanded its plant. The company manufactures metal parts to customer specifications. A job-order costing system is used to accumulate costs by job. After careful study, management has estimated the following activity for 19x5, the coming year:

Direct labor-hours .	100,000
Machine-hours .	500,000
Direct materials cost .	$750,000

In conjunction with this activity, management expects to incur the following overhead costs during 19x5:

Indirect materials .	$185,000
Overtime premium .	80,000
Rent, factory .	175,000
Supervision, factory .	70,000
Utilities, factory .	90,000
Pension and other benefits, factory .	150,000
Depreciation, factory .	325,000
Property taxes, factory .	10,000
Insurance, factory .	40,000

In the past, overtime premium and pension costs have tended to vary closely with direct labor costs, while utilities and indirect materials have tended to vary closely with machine usage. Direct labor rates vary from $4 to $10 per hour and average $8 per hour. All other costs tend to be constant over time.

The company expects to work on about 100 jobs during the year, with about 10 jobs in process at any given time. The proportion of labor time of highly paid workers to that of less highly paid workers is not the same on all jobs.

Required: 1. Name several alternative bases that the company might use to compute its predetermined overhead rate. If a labor base is used, should it be direct labor-hours or direct labor cost? Why?
2. Assume that the company wants to use dual overhead rates and has chosen direct labor cost and machine-hours as the bases to be used. Compute the predetermined overhead rates that would be used for 19x5. (Take care in how you divide overhead costs between these two bases.)
3. Assume that the company wants to use a single, plantwide overhead rate. What activity base would you use in setting the rate? Why? Compute the rate for 19x5.

4. What factors should management consider in deciding between a single rate and dual rates?

P3–27. **Incomplete data; review of cost flows.** After a dispute concerning wages, Orville Arson tossed an incendiary device into the Sparkle Company's record vault. Within moments, only a few charred fragments were readable from the company's factory ledger, as shown below:

Raw Materials		Manufacturing Overhead	
Bal. 4/1 12,000		Actual costs for April 14,800	

Work in Process		Accounts Payable	
Bal. 4/1 4,500			Bal. 4/30 8,000

Finished Goods		Cost of Goods Sold	
Bal. 4/30 16,000			

Sifting through ashes and interviewing selected employees has turned up the following additional information:

a. The controller remembers clearly that the predetermined overhead rate was based on an estimated 60,000 direct labor-hours to be worked over the year and an estimated $180,000 in manufacturing overhead costs.

b. The production superintendent's cost sheets showed only one job in process on April 30. Materials of $2,600 had been added to the job, and 300 direct labor-hours had been expended at $6 per hour.

c. The accounts payable are for raw material purchases only, according to the accounts payable clerk. He clearly remembers that the balance in the account was $6,000 on April 1. An analysis of canceled checks (kept in the treasurer's office) shows that payments of $40,000 were made to suppliers during the month.

d. A charred piece of the payroll ledger shows that 5,200 direct labor-hours were recorded for the month. The employment department has verified that there were no variations in pay rates among employees. (This infuriated Orville, who felt that his services were underpaid.)

e. Records maintained in the finished goods warehouse indicate that the finished goods inventory totaled $11,000 on April 1.

f. From another charred piece in the vault, you are able to discern that the cost of goods manufactured for April was $89,000.

Required: Determine the following amounts:

1. Work in process inventory, April 30.
2. Raw materials purchased during April.
3. Overhead applied to work in process.
4. Cost of goods sold for April.
5. Over- or underapplied overhead for April.
6. Raw materials usage during April.
7. Raw materials inventory, April 30.

(Hint: A good way to proceed is to bring the fragmented T-accounts up to date through April 30 by posting whatever entries can be developed from the information provided.)

4 Systems Design: Process Costing

Learning objectives

After studying Chapter 4, you should be able to:

Enumerate the major similarities and differences between job-order and process costing.

Prepare journal entries to record the flow of materials, labor, and overhead through a process costing system.

Compute equivalent units of production by both the weighted-average and FIFO methods.

Prepare a quantity schedule and explain its significance.

Compute unit costs for a period under both the weighted-average and FIFO methods.

Prepare a cost reconciliation for a period under both the weighted-average and FIFO methods.

Combine the quantity schedule, the unit costs, and the cost reconciliation into a production report.

Define or explain the key terms listed at the end of the chapter.

As explained in the preceding chapter, there are two basic costing systems in use: job-order costing and process costing. We have found that a job-order costing system is used in those situations where many different jobs or batches of production are worked on each period. Examples of industries that would typically use job-order costing include furniture manufacture, special-order printing, shipbuilding, and many types of construction.

By contrast, **process costing** is used in those industries that produce basically homogeneous products such as bricks, flour, cement, screws, bolts, and pharmaceutical items. In addition, process costing is employed in assembly-type operations that manufacture typewriters, automobiles, and small appliances, as well as in utilities producing gas, water, and electricity. As suggested by the length of this list, process costing is in widespread use and warrants study by anyone involved in accounting, management, or systems work.

Our purpose in this chapter is to extend the discussion of product costing that was started in the preceding chapter in order to include a process costing system.

COMPARISON OF JOB-ORDER AND PROCESS COSTING

In some ways process costing is very similar to job-order costing, and in some ways it is very different. In the following two sections, we focus on these similarities and differences in order to provide a foundation for the detailed discussion of process costing that follows.

Similarities between job-order and process costing

It is important to recognize that much of what was learned in the preceding chapter about costing and about cost flows applies equally well to process costing in this chapter. That is, we are not throwing out all that we have learned about costing and starting from "scratch" with a whole new system. The similarities that exist between job-order and process costing can be summarized as follows:

1. The same basic purposes exist in both systems, which are: (*a*) to assign material, labor, and overhead costs to products; (*b*) to provide a mechanism for computing unit costs; and (*c*) to provide data essential for planning, control, and decision making.
2. Both systems maintain and use the same basic manufacturing accounts, including Manufacturing Overhead, Raw Materials, Work in Process, and Finished Goods.
3. Cost flows through the manufacturing accounts in (2) above move in basically the same way in both systems.

As can be seen from this comparison, much of the knowledge that we have already acquired about costing is applicable to a process costing system. Our task now is simply to refine and extend this knowledge to meet special process costing needs.

Differences between job-order and process costing

The differences between job-order and process costing arise from two factors. The first is that the flow of units in a process costing system is more or less continuous, and the second is that these units are indistinguishable from one another. Under process costing, it makes no sense to try to identify materials, labor, and overhead costs with a particular order from a customer (as we did with job-order costing), since each order is just one of many that are filled from a continuous flow of units from the production line. Under process costing, instead of accumulating costs by order, we accumulate costs *by department* and assign these costs equally to all units that pass through the department during a period.

A further difference between the two cost systems is that since we are department oriented rather than job oriented under process costing, the job cost sheet is of no value in a process costing system. In a process costing system, instead of using job cost sheets, a document known as a **production report** is prepared for each department. The production report serves several functions. It provides a summary of the number of units moving through a department during a period, and it also provides a computation of unit costs. In addition, it shows what costs were charged to a department during a period and what disposition was made of these costs. As these comments suggest, the department production report is a key document in a process costing system.

The major differences between job-order and process costing are summarized in Exhibit 4–1.

EXHIBIT 4–1
Differences between job-order and process costing

Job-order costing	Process costing
1. Many different jobs are worked on during each period, with each job having different production requirements.	1. A single product is produced either on a continuous basis or for long periods of time. All units of product are identical.
2. Costs are accumulated by individual job.	2. Costs are accumulated by department.
3. The *job cost sheet* is the key document controlling the accumulation of cost by a job.	3. The *department production report* is the key document showing the accumulation and disposition of cost by a department.
4. Unit costs are computed *by job* on the job cost sheet.	4. Unit costs are computed *by department* on the department production report.

A PERSPECTIVE OF PROCESS COST FLOWS

Before presenting a detailed example of process costing, it will be helpful to gain a visual perspective of how manufacturing costs flow through a process costing system.

Processing departments

A **processing department** is any location in the factory where work is performed on a product and where materials, labor, or overhead costs are added to the product. For example, a brick factory might have two processing departments—one for mixing and molding clay into brick form and one for firing the molded brick. There can be as many or as few processing departments as are needed to complete the manufacture of a product. Some products may go through several processing departments, while others may go through only one or two. Regardless of the number of departments involved, all processing departments have two essential features. First, the activity performed in the processing department must be performed uniformly on all of the units passing through it. And second, the output of the processing department must be homogeneous.

The processing departments involved in the manufacture of a product such as bricks would probably be organized in a *sequential* pattern. By a **sequential processing** pattern, we mean that units simply flow in sequence from one department to another. An example of processing departments arranged in a sequential pattern is given in Exhibit 4–2.

EXHIBIT 4–2
Sequential processing departments

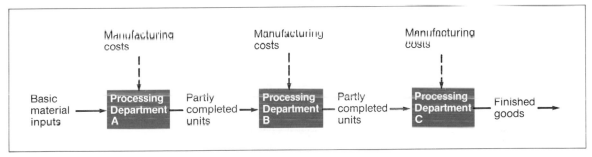

A different type of processing pattern, known as *parallel processing,* is required in the manufacture of some products. **Parallel processing** is used in those situations where not all units go through all processing departments. For example, the petroleum industry may input crude oil into one processing department and then use the refined output for further processing into several end products. Each end product may undergo several steps of further processing after the initial refining, some of which may be shared with other end products and some of which may not. Exhibit 4–3 illustrates one type of parallel processing. The number of possible variations in parallel processing patterns is virtually limitless. The example given in Exhibit 4–3 is intended as just one sample of the many parallel patterns in use today.

EXHIBIT 4–3
Parallel processing departments

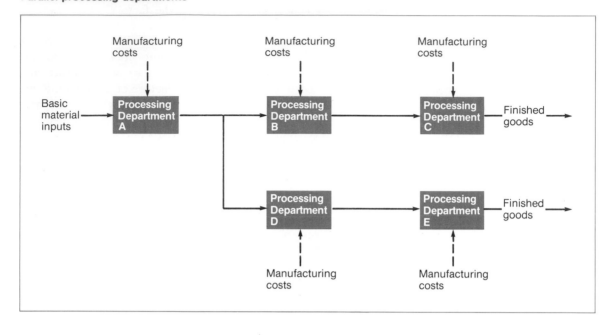

The flow of materials, labor, and overhead costs

Cost accumulation is simpler in a process costing system than in a job-order costing system. The reason is that costs need to be identified only by processing department—not by separate job. Thus, in a process costing system, instead of having to trace costs to hundreds of different jobs, costs are traced to only a few processing departments. This means that costs can be accumulated for longer periods of time and that just one allocation is needed at the end of a period (week, month, and so forth) in order to assign the accumulated costs to the period's output.

A T-account model of materials, labor, and overhead cost flows in a process costing system is given in Exhibit 4–4. Several key points should be noted from this exhibit. First, note that a separate Work in Process account is maintained for *each processing department,* rather than having only a single Work in Process account for the entire company. Second, note that the completed production of the first processing department (Department A in the exhibit) is transferred into the Work in Process account of the second processing department (Department B), where it undergoes further work. After this further work, the completed units are then transferred into Finished Goods. (In this exhibit, we show only two processing departments; there may be several such departments in some companies.)

Finally, note that materials, labor, and overhead costs can be entered

EXHIBIT 4–4

A T-account model of process costing flows

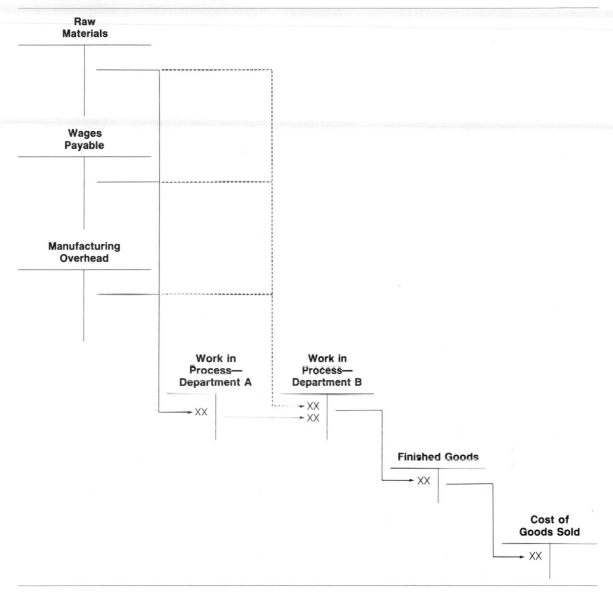

directly into *any* processing department—not just the first. Costs in Department B's Work in Process account would therefore consist of the materials, labor, and overhead costs entered directly into the account plus the costs attached to partially completed units transferred in from Department A (called **transferred-in costs**).

Materials, labor, and overhead cost entries

To complete our discussion of cost flows in a process costing system, in the following sections we show journal entries relating to materials, labor, and overhead costs and also make brief, further comments relating to each of these cost categories.

Materials costs As in job-order costing, materials are drawn from the storeroom by use of a materials requisition form. Charging these materials to departments, rather than to jobs, generally reduces the amount of requisitioning needed, since large amounts of materials can be drawn and put into production at a time. As stated earlier, materials can be added in any processing department, although it is not unusual for materials to be added only in the first processing department, with subsequent departments adding only labor and overhead costs as the partially completed units move along toward completion.

Assuming that the first processing department in a company is Department A, the journal entry for placing materials into process would be:

Work in Process—Department A.	XXX	
Raw Materials		XXX

If other materials are subsequently added in another processing department, the entry would be:

Work in Process—Department B.	XXX	
Raw Materials		XXX

Labor costs Since it is not necessary to identify costs with specific jobs, a time clock is generally adequate for accumulating labor costs and for allocating them to the proper department in a process costing system. Assuming again that a company has two processing departments, A and B, the journal entry to record labor costs for a period would be:

Work in Process—Department A.	XXX	
Work in Process—Department B.	XXX	
Salaries and Wages Payable		XXX

Overhead costs The simplest method of handling overhead costs in a process costing system is to charge products with the actual overhead costs of the period rather than with applied overhead costs. Under this approach, no predetermined overhead rate is computed; overhead costs in each department are simply added directly to that department's Work in Process account either as the costs are incurred or at specified intervals. Since there is no "applied" overhead cost in the sense we talked about in Chapter 3, there is no under- or overapplied overhead balance remaining at the end of a period when this approach is used.

Why is it possible to use actual overhead costs in a process costing system when it is not possible under job-order costing? The answer lies in the nature of the work flowing through the two systems. Under job-order costing, jobs tend to be heterogeneous, requiring different inputs and different times to complete. Also, several jobs will be in process at a given time, each having different output requirements. Thus, the overhead cost chargeable to a job has to be estimated. Under process costing, homogeneous units flow continuously through a department, thus making it possible to charge units with the department's actual overhead costs as the costs are incurred. This approach works well, however, only if production is quite stable from period to period and only if overhead costs are incurred uniformly over the year.

If production levels fluctuate or if overhead costs are not incurred uniformly, then predetermined overhead rates should be used to charge overhead cost to products, the same as in job-order costing. When predetermined overhead rates are used, each department has its own separate rate with the rates being computed in the same way as that discussed on Chapter 3. Overhead cost is then applied to units of product as the units move through the various departments. Since predetermined overhead rates are widely used even in process costing situations, we will assume their use throughout the remainder of this chapter.

If a company has two processing departments, A and B, the journal entry to apply overhead cost to products would be:

Work In Process—Department A.	XXX	
Work in Process—Department B.	XXX	
Manufacturing Overhead.		XXX

As we stated in Chapter 2, direct labor cost combined with manufacturing overhead cost is often referred to as *conversion cost,* since these cost inputs are necessary to convert raw materials into finished products. The term **conversion cost** is widely used in process costing in the preparation of department production reports.

Completing the cost flows   Once processing has been completed in a department, the units are transferred to the next department for further processing, as illustrated earlier in the T-accounts in Exhibit 4–4. The entry to transfer partially completed units from Department A into Department B would be:

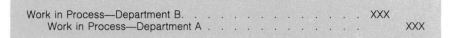

Work in Process—Department B.	XXX	
Work in Process—Department A		XXX

After processing has been completed in department B, the completed units are transferred into the Finished Goods inventory account:

```
Finished Goods  . . . . . . . . . . . . . . . . . . . . .  XXX
        Work in Process—Department B . . . . . . . . . . . .        XXX
```

Finally, when a customer's order is filled and units are sold, the cost of the units is transferred into Cost of Goods Sold:

```
Cost of Goods Sold . . . . . . . . . . . . . . . . . .  XXX
        Finished Goods . . . . . . . . . . . . . . . . . . . .        XXX
```

To summarize, we stated earlier that the cost flows between accounts are basically the same in a process costing system as they are in a job-order costing system. As shown by the entries above, the reader can see that this is indeed correct. The only differences are that in a process costing system *(a)* a separate Work in Process account is maintained for each department, and *(b)* each department can be charged directly for manufacturing costs in addition to those transferred in from the preceding department.

EQUIVALENT UNITS OF PRODUCTION

After materials, labor, and overhead costs have been accumulated in a department, the department's output must be determined so that unit costs can be computed. A department's output is always stated in terms of **equivalent units of production.** Equivalent units can be defined as the number of units that would have been produced during a period if all of a department's efforts had resulted in completed units of product. Equivalent units are computed by taking completed units and adjusting them for partially completed units in the work in process inventory.

The reasoning behind the computation of equivalent units is as follows: Completed units alone will not accurately measure output in a department, since part of the department's efforts during a period will have been expended on units that are only partially complete. To accurately measure output, these partially completed units must also be considered in the output computation. This is done by mathematically converting the partially completed units into fully completed *equivalent units* and then adjusting the output figure accordingly.

To illustrate, assume that a company has 500 units in its ending work in process inventory that are 60 percent complete. Five hundred units 60 percent complete would be equivalent to 300 fully completed units (500 × 60% = 300). Therefore, the ending inventory would be said to contain 300 *equivalent units.* These equivalent units would be added to the fully completed units in determining the period's output.

There are two ways of computing a department's equivalent units, depending on whether the company is accounting for its cost flows by the *weighted-average method* or by the *first-in, first out (FIFO) method.*

Weighted-average method

Under the **weighted-average method,** a department's equivalent units are computed just as described above: Equivalent units of production = Completed units + Equivalent units in the ending work in process inventory.

To provide an extended example, assume the following data:

The Regal Company manufactures a product that goes through two departments— mixing and firing. During 19x1, the following activity took place in the mixing department:

		Percent completed	
	Units	Materials	Conversion
Work in process, beginning.	10,000	100	70
Units started into production during the year	150,000		
Units completed during the year and transferred to the firing department	140,000		
Work in process, ending.	20,000	60	25

Since the work in process inventories are at different stages of completion in terms of the amount of materials and conversion cost that has been added, two equivalent unit figures will have to be computed—one for equivalent units in terms of materials and the other for equivalent units in terms of conversion. The equivalent units computations are given in Exhibit 4–5.

EXHIBIT 4–5
Equivalent units of production: Weighted-average method

	Materials	Conversion
Units completed and transferred to firing	140,000	140,000
Add: Equivalent units, ending work in process:		
20,000 units × 60%	12,000	
20,000 units × 25%		5,000
Equivalent units of production	152,000	145,000

Note from the computations in Exhibit 4–5 that units in the beginning inventory are ignored and that an adjustment is made only for partially completed units in the ending inventory. This is a key point in the computation of equivalent units under the weighted-average method: *Units in the beginning inventory are always treated as if they were started and completed during the current period.* Thus, no adjustment is made for these units, regardless of how much work was done on them before the period started. Although this procedure may seem illogical and inconsistent, it greatly simplifies the preparation of a department production report, as we shall see shortly.

FIFO method

The computation of equivalent units under the **FIFO method** differs from the computation under the weighted-average method in one important way: Under the FIFO method, full consideration is given to the stage of completion of units in the *beginning* work in process inventory as well as in the ending inventory. Thus, units in both inventories are converted to an equivalent units basis. The equivalent units in the ending inventory are added to the completed units of the period (as before), but the equivalent units in the beginning inventory are *deducted* in computing the output figure. The reason they are deducted is that work on these units represents work completed in the prior period; under the FIFO method, this work can't be included in the current period's output.

The computation of equivalent units by the FIFO method (using the Regal Company data), is presented in Exhibit 4–6.

At this point, the reader should stop and compare Exhibit 4–6 with Exhibit 4–5. Note that the only difference between the two exhibits is that the FIFO method carries the computation one step further and considers units in the beginning inventory. A logical question to ask is, why the difference in the handling of beginning inventories? The answer lies in what the two methods are trying to accomplish.

The purpose of the weighted-average method is to *simplify the computation of unit costs.* This is accomplished by treating units in the beginning inventory as if they were started and completed during the current period. By treating units in the beginning inventory in this way, the manager is relieved from having to distinguish between which units were on hand at the start of the year and which were not. Thus, he or she is able to treat all units equally when unit costs are computed. This greatly simplifies the costing process.

By contrast, the purpose of the FIFO method is to distinguish between (*a*) units in the beginning inventory and (*b*) units that were started during the period, so that separate unit costs can be computed for each. Under the FIFO method, units in the beginning inventory are assumed to be com-

EXHIBIT 4–6
Equivalent units of production: FIFO method

	Materials	Conversion
Units completed and transferred to firing	140,000	140,000
Add: Equivalent units, ending work in process:		
20,000 units × 60%	12,000	
20,000 units × 25%		5,000
Total completed units	152,000	145,000
Deduct: Equivalent units, beginning work in process:		
10,000 units × 100%	10,000	
10,000 units × 70%		7,000
Equivalent units of production	142,000	138,000

pleted and transferred out first (thus, a "first-in, first-out" flow) and to carry their own unit costs. Units started during the year are assumed to be completed next and to carry their own unit costs. This is a more complex costing approach than the weighted-average method, although it can be argued that it is also more accurate.

A visual perspective of equivalent units

To assist in your understanding of equivalent units, Exhibit 4–7 contains a visual perspective of the computation of equivalent units (the data are taken from Exhibit 4–6). The exhibit also shows the relationship between equivalent units as computed by the weighted-average method and equivalent units as computed by the FIFO method.

PRODUCTION REPORT—WEIGHTED-AVERAGE METHOD

The purpose of the production report is to summarize for the manager all of the activity that takes place in a department's Work in Process account for a period. This activity includes the units that flow through the Work in Process account as well as the costs that flow through it. A separate production report is prepared for each department, as illustrated in Exhibit 4–8.

EXHIBIT 4–7

A visual perspective of equivalent units

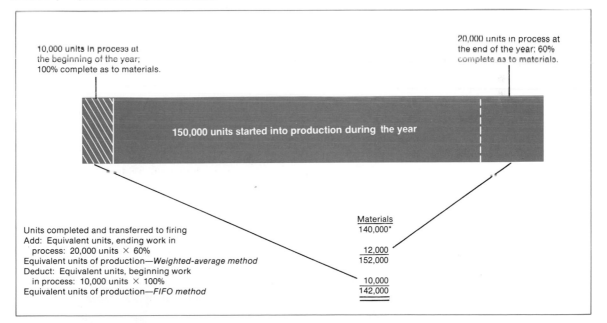

	Materials
Units completed and transferred to firing	140,000*
Add: Equivalent units, ending work in process: 20,000 units × 60%	12,000
Equivalent units of production—*Weighted-average method*	152,000
Deduct: Equivalent units, beginning work in process: 10,000 units × 100%	10,000
Equivalent units of production—*FIFO method*	142,000

* 10,000 units from the beginning inventory + (150,000 − 20,000 = 130,000) units started and completed during the year = 140,000 total units completed.

EXHIBIT 4–8

The production report in a process costing system

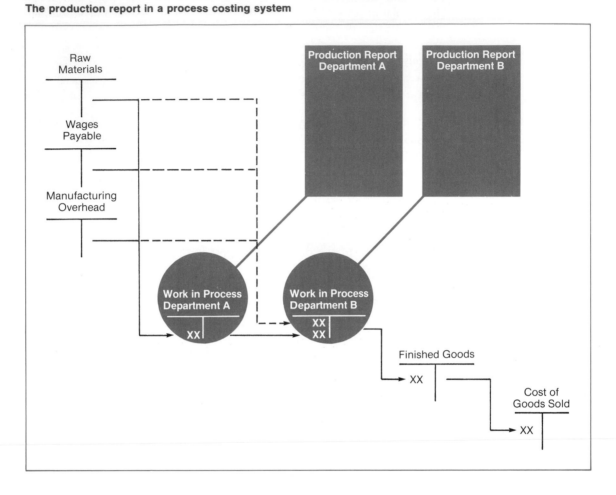

Earlier, when we outlined the differences between job-order costing and process costing, we stated that the production report takes the place of a job cost sheet in a process costing system. Thus, the production report is a key document for the manager and is vital to the proper operation of the system. There are three separate (though highly interrelated) parts to the production report:

1. A quantity schedule (which shows the flow of units through the department).
2. A computation of unit costs.
3. A reconciliation of all cost flows into and out of the department during the period.

We will use the following data to show a numerical example of a production report:

The Stabler Chemical Company has two departments—mixing and cooking. Production activity begins in the mixing department; after mixing, the units are transferred to the cooking department. From cooking, the units are transferred to finished goods.

All of the materials involved in mixing are added at the beginning of work in the mixing department. Labor and overhead costs in that department are incurred uniformly as work progresses. Overhead cost is applied at the rate of 150 percent of direct labor cost.

Cost and other data for May 19x1 include the following for the mixing department:

Work in process, beginning:	
Units in process.	20,000
Stage of completion*	30%
Cost in the beginning inventory:	
Materials cost.	$ 4,000
Labor cost.	5,000
Overhead cost	8,000
Total cost in process	$ 17,000
Units started into production during the month	180,000
Units completed and transferred to cooking	170,000
Costs added to production during the month:	
Materials cost	$ 63,000
Labor cost	88,000
Overhead cost applied	132,000
Work in process, ending:	
Units in process.	30,000
Stage of completion*	40%

* This refers to labor and overhead costs only, since all materials are added at the beginning of work in the mixing department.

In the following sections, we show how a production report is prepared when the weighted-average method is being used to compute unit costs. Later in the chapter, we show how a production report is prepared when the FIFO method is being used.

Step 1: Prepare a quantity schedule

The first section of a production report consists of a **quantity schedule,** which accounts for the physical flow of units through a department. The most widely used format for a quantity schedule shows the number of units worked on during a period and then shows the disposition of those units. To illustrate, a quantity schedule for the Stabler Chemical Company is given below:

Units to be accounted for:	
Units in process, beginning (all materials; 30% labor and overhead).	20,000
Units started into production	180,000
Total units to account for	200,000
Units accounted for as follows:	
Units transferred to cooking.	170,000
Units in process, ending (all materials; 40% labor and overhead).	30,000
Total units accounted for	200,000

The quantity schedule deals with *whole units,* not with equivalent units, although the stage of completion is always shown parenthetically. (The computation of equivalent units comes later.) The quantity schedule permits the manager to see at a glance how many units moved through the department during a period as well as to see the stage of completion of any in-process units. In addition to providing this information for the manager, the quantity schedule serves as an essential guide in preparing and tying together the remaining parts of a production report.

Step 2: Compute unit costs

Earlier in the chapter, we stated that in order to compute unit costs the manager must first compute the equivalent units for the period. The data for computing the equivalent units can be found on the quantity schedule. Notice from the quantity schedule that 170,000 units were completed and transferred to the cooking department during the month, and that another 30,000 units were still in process at the end of the month. The units in process were 100 percent complete as to materials, but they were only 40 percent complete as to labor and overhead.

Using these data and other data from the example, the computation of equivalent units and unit costs would be:

	Materials	Labor	Overhead	Total
Work in process, beginning	$ 4,000	$ 5,000	$ 8,000	$ 17,000
Cost added by the department	63,000	88,000	132,000	283,000
Total cost (*a*)	$67,000	$93,000	$140,000	$300,000
Equivalent units:				
Units transferred out.	170,000	170,000	170,000	
Add: Equivalent units, ending work in process.	30,000	12,000	12,000	
Equivalent units of production (*b*) . . .	200,000	182,000	182,000	
Unit cost, (*a*) ÷ (*b*)	$0.335	$0.511	$0.769	$1.615

As we stated earlier, the weighted-average method treats units in the beginning work in process inventory as if they were started and completed during the current period. Thus, the cost in the beginning work in process inventory has been added in with current period costs above in determining units costs for the month.

The unit costs that we have computed will be used to apply cost to units that are transferred to the next department and will also be used to compute the cost in the ending work in process inventory. A total of all unit costs from both the mixing and cooking departments will represent the final manufactured cost of a unit of product.

Step 3: Prepare a cost reconciliation

The purpose of a **cost reconciliation** is to show (*a*) what costs have been charged to a department during a period and (*b*) how these costs are accounted for. Typically, the costs charged to a department will consist of:

1. Cost in the beginning work in process inventory.
2. Materials, labor, and overhead cost added during the period.
3. Cost (if any) transferred in from the preceding department.

These costs are accounted for by showing:

1. Cost transferred out to the next department (or into Finished Goods).
2. Cost remaining in the ending work in process inventory.

Since this section of the production report is called a cost reconciliation, *the totals of these two groups of cost must always be in agreement.* The content of a cost reconciliation is shown graphically in Exhibit 4–9. Study this exhibit carefully before going on.

In the following section, we give a numerical example of how a cost reconciliation is prepared.

Example of a cost reconciliation

The cost reconciliation depends heavily on the quantity schedule that was developed earlier. In fact, *the simplest way to prepare a cost reconciliation is to follow the quantity schedule line for line and show the cost associated with*

EXHIBIT 4–9

Graphic illustration of the cost reconciliation part of a production report

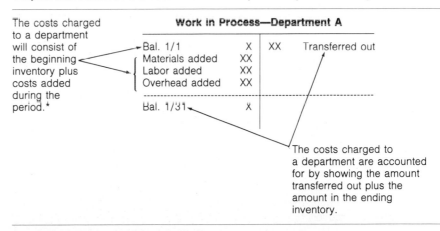

* Departments that follow Department A (Department B and so forth) will also need to show the amount of cost transferred in from the preceding department.

each group of units. This is done in Exhibit 4–10, where we present a completed production report for the Stabler Chemical Company.

Note that the production report has the three sections that we mentioned earlier: (*a*) a quantity schedule; (*b*) a computation of unit costs; and (*c*) a cost reconciliation. As stated, *we follow the quantity schedule line for line in preparing the cost reconciliation.* For example, the quantity schedule shows

EXHIBIT 4–10
Production report—Weighted-average method

Quantity schedule

	Units
Units to be accounted for:	
Units in process, beginning (all materials; 30% labor and overhead)	20,000
Units started into production	180,000
Total units to account for	200,000
Units accounted for as follows:	
Units transferred to cooking	170,000
Units in process, ending (all materials; 40% labor and overhead)	30,000
Total units accounted for	200,000

Computation of unit costs

	Materials	Labor	Overhead	Total
Work in process, beginning	$ 4,000	$ 5,000	$ 8,000	$ 17,000
Cost added by the department	63,000	88,000	132,000	283,000
Total cost (*a*)	$67,000	$93,000	$140,000	$300,000
Equivalent units:				
Units transferred out	170,000	170,000	170,000	
Add: Equivalent units, ending work in process	30,000	12,000	12,000	
Equivalent units of production (*b*)	200,000	182,000	182,000	
Unit cost, (*a*) ÷ (*b*)	$0.335	$0.511	$0.769	$1.615

Cost reconciliation

	Units	Costs
Cost to be accounted for:		
Work in process, beginning	20,000	$ 17,000
Added by the department during the month	180,000	283,000
Total cost to be accounted for	200,000	$300,000
Cost accounted for as follows:		
Transferred to cooking (170,000 × 100% × $1.615)	170,000	$274,590*
Work in process, ending	30,000	
Materials cost (30,000 × 100% × $0.335)		$10,050
Labor cost (30,000 × 40% × $0.511)		6,132
Overhead cost (30,000 × 40% × $0.769)		9,228
Total cost in work in process, ending		25,410
Total cost accounted for	200,000	$300,000

* Rounded upward to avoid a decimal discrepancy in the column totals.

that 20,000 units were in process at the start of the month and that an additional 180,000 units were started into production. Looking at the cost reconciliation part of the report, notice that the 20,000 units in process at the start of the month had $17,000 in cost attached to them and that the department added another $283,000 in cost to production during the month. Thus, the department has $300,000 in cost to account for.

This cost is accounted for in two ways. As shown on the quantity schedule, 170,000 units were transferred to the cooking department during the month and another 30,000 units were still in process at the end of the month. Thus, part of the $300,000 "cost to be accounted for" goes with the 170,000 units to the cooking department, and part of it remains with the 30,000 units in the ending work in process inventory.

Note that the 170,000 units transferred to the cooking department are assigned $1.615 in cost each, or a total of $274,590. The 30,000 units still in process at the end of the month are assigned cost according to their stage of completion. All materials cost has been added to these units, so they are each assigned a full $0.335 in materials cost. These units are only 40 percent complete as to labor and overhead, however, so this partial completion is recognized in assigning labor and overhead cost to them. The amount of labor cost assigned, for example, is computed as follows:

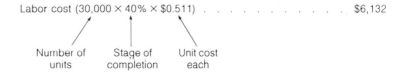

Labor cost (30,000 × 40% × $0.511) $6,132

Number of units   Stage of completion   Unit cost each

Notice that in assigning costs, we have used the unit costs derived in the "computation of unit costs" part of the production report.

After cost has been assigned to the ending work in process inventory, the total cost that we have accounted for ($300,000) agrees with the amount that we had to account for ($300,000). Thus, the cost reconciliation is complete.

PRODUCTION REPORT—FIFO METHOD

When the FIFO method is used to account for cost flows in a process costing system, the steps followed in preparing a production report are the same as those discussed above for the weighted-average method. Those steps are: (1) prepare a quantity schedule; (2) compute unit costs; and (3) prepare a cost reconciliation. However, since the FIFO method makes a distinction between units in the opening inventory and units started during the year, step three above is more complex when the FIFO method is used than it is when the weighted-average method is used. To see how a production report is prepared under the FIFO method, refer again to the data for the Stabler

Chemical Company found on page 129. We will follow these data step by step in the preparation of the report.

Step 1: Prepare a quantity schedule

There is no difference in the quantity schedule between the FIFO and weighted-average methods. This schedule simply shows the flow of units through a department during a period, and the flow is the same regardless of which method is used to account for costs. Just for the sake of completeness of the example, the quantity schedule for the Stabler Chemical Company is reproduced below:

Units to be accounted for:	
Units in process, beginning (all materials;	
30% labor and overhead)	20,000
Units started into production	180,000
Total units to account for	200,000
Units accounted for as follows:	
Units transferred to cooking	170,000
Units in process, ending (all materials;	
40% labor and overhead)	30,000
Total units accounted for	200,000

As with the weighted-average method, once the quantity schedule has been prepared, it becomes a key factor in the preparation of the other two parts of the production report. We have seen that the information it contains is essential in computing equivalent units (and therefore unit costs) and in doing a cost reconciliation.

Step 2: Compute unit costs

In the computation of unit costs, the FIFO method differs from the weighted-average method in two ways. First, costs in the opening inventory are kept separate from current period costs and are not used in unit cost computations. And second, in computing equivalent units, an adjustment is made for work completed in the prior period on any units in the opening work in process inventory. (This difference in computing equivalent units was pointed out in our discussion of equivalent units earlier in the chapter.)

The reason for these differences is simple: *Under the FIFO method, unit costs are intended to relate only to work done during the current period.* Thus, any work done in the prior period on units in the opening inventory must be deducted in computing equivalent units, and any cost incurred in the prior period must be ignored in computing unit costs.

Given these ideas, the computation of equivalent units and unit costs under the FIFO method for the Stabler Chemical Company would be:

	Materials	Labor	Overhead	Total
Cost added by the department (a). . . .	$63,000	$88,000	$132,000	$283,000
Equivalent units:				
Units transferred out.	170,000	170,000	170,000	
Add: Equivalent units, ending work in process.	30,000	12,000	12,000	
Total completed units.	200,000	182,000	182,000	
Deduct: Equivalent units, beginning work in process . . .	20,000	6,000	6,000	
Equivalent units of production (b)	180,000	176,000	176,000	
Unit cost, (a) ÷ (b)	$0.35	$0.50	$0.75	$1.60

As with the weighted-average method, these unit costs are used to cost units as they are transferred to the next department and are also used to cost units in the ending work in process inventory. We illustrate how this is done in the next section.

Step 3: Prepare a cost reconciliation

As stated earlier, the purpose of a cost reconciliation is (a) to show what costs have been charged to a department during a period and (b) to show how these costs are accounted for. In preparing the cost reconciliation, we will again follow the quantity schedule line for line and show the cost associated with each group of units.

The first part of the reconciliation (where we show the "costs to be accounted for") is the same under the FIFO method as it was under the weighted-average method. As before, the Stabler Chemical Company must account for a total of 200,000 units and $300,000 in cost; these amounts are shown in the "cost reconciliation" part of the production report in Exhibit 4–11.

The second part of the cost reconciliation (where we show how these costs are accounted for) is much more complex under the FIFO method than under the weighted-average method. The reason is that in accounting for units transferred out, we must keep units in the opening inventory separate from units that were started and completed during the year.

Cost transferred out   Under the FIFO method, units transferred out of a department are divided into two groups. The first group consists of units from the beginning work in process inventory. The second group consists of units started and completed during the period.

Looking at Exhibit 4–11, notice that 170,000 units were transferred out of the department during the month. Some 20,000 of these units were from the beginning work in process inventory; the remaining 150,000 units (170,000 − 20,000 = 150,000) were started and completed during the month.

EXHIBIT 4–11
Production report—FIFO method

Quantity schedule

	Units
Units to be accounted for:	
Units in process, beginning (all materials; 30% labor and overhead)	20,000
Units started into production	180,000
Total units to account for	200,000
Units accounted for as follows:	
Units transferred to cooking	170,000
Units in process, ending (all materials; 40% labor and overhead)	30,000
Total units accounted for	200,000

Computation of unit costs

	Materials	Labor	Overhead	Total
Cost added by the department (a)	$63,000	$88,000	$132,000	$283,000
Equivalent units:				
Units transferred out	170,000	170,000	170,000	
Add: Equivalent units, ending work in process	30,000	12,000	12,000	
Total completed units	200,000	182,000	182,000	
Deduct: Equivalent units, beginning work in process	20,000	6,000	6,000	
Equivalent units of production (b)	180,000	176,000	176,000	
Unit cost, (a) ÷ (b)	$0.35	$0.50	$0.75	$1.60

Cost reconciliation

	Units	Costs
Cost to be accounted for:		
Work in process, beginning	20,000	$ 17,000
Added by the department during the month	180,000	283,000
Total cost to be accounted for	200,000	$300,000
Cost accounted for as follows:		
(1) Transferred to cooking	170,000	
Units from the beginning inventory:		
Cost in the beginning inventory		$ 17,000
Cost to complete these units:		
Labor cost (20,000 × 70% × $0.50)		7,000
Overhead cost (20,000 × 70% × $0.75)		10,500
Total cost		34,500
Units started and completed during the month (150,000* × 100% × $1.60)		240,000
Total cost transferred to cooking		$274,500
(2) Work in process, ending	30,000	
Materials cost (30,000 × 100% × $0.35)		10,500
Labor cost (30,000 × 40% × $0.50)		6,000
Overhead cost (30,000 × 40% × $0.75)		9,000
Total cost in work in process, ending		25,500
Total cost accounted for	200,000	$300,000

* 170,000 units transferred − 20,000 units in the beginning inventory = 150,000 units.

Note that the 20,000 units from the beginning inventory have been assigned two elements of cost, as follows:

Units from the beginning inventory:
Cost in the beginning inventory $17,000
Cost to complete these units:
Labor cost (20,000 × 70% × $0.50) 7,000
Overhead cost (20,000 × 70% × $0.75) 10,500
Total cost $34,500

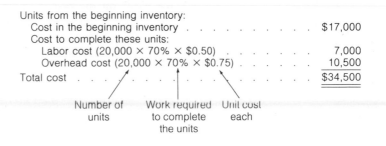

Number of   Work required   Unit cost
units   to complete   each
the units

One element of cost assigned to these units consists of the $17,000 in cost contained in the beginning work in process inventory. The second element consists of the cost required during the current period to complete the units in the beginning inventory. Note from the quantity schedule in Exhibit 4–11 that the units in the beginning inventory were fully complete as to materials when the current month started, but that *they were only 30 percent complete as to labor and overhead*. Thus, 70 percent (100% − 30% = 70%) of the labor and overhead work on these units was done during the current month. We therefore add labor and overhead cost to these units for the current month's efforts as shown above.

The 150,000 units transferred out that were started and completed during the current month are each assigned $1.60 in cost, for a total cost of $240,000. (The $1.60 represents the cost required to complete a unit during the current month, as shown in the unit cost part of the production report in Exhibit 4–11.) This $240,000 in cost plus the $34,500 in cost transferred out with the units from the beginning inventory equals a total of $274,500 in cost transferred out during the month (see Exhibit 4–11).

Cost in the ending work in process inventory Cost assigned to the ending work in process inventory is computed in the same way as under the weighted-average method. As shown in Exhibit 4–11, the units in the ending inventory are multiplied by their stage of completion and then by the current period unit cost. For labor, this is:

Labor cost (30,000 × 40% × $0.50) $6,000

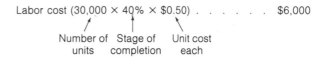

Number of   Stage of   Unit cost
units   completion   each

The total of the materials, labor, and overhead cost assigned to units in the ending inventory ($25,500) is added to the cost assigned to the units transferred out during the month ($274,500) to give the $300,000 in cost that we had to account for. The cost reconciliation is therefore complete.

A comparison of production report content

The production report is the most difficult part of this chapter, and it will require some effort on the reader's part to master the report's content and structure. To assist in this study, Exhibit 4–12 summarizes the major similarities and differences between production reports prepared under the weighted-average and FIFO methods.

EXHIBIT 4–12

A comparison of production report content

Weighted-average method	FIFO method
Quantity schedule	
The quantity schedule is the same under either method.	The quantity schedule is the same under either method.
Computation of unit costs	
1. Costs in the beginning inventory are added in with current period costs in unit cost computations.	1. Only current period costs are included in unit cost computations.
2. Units in the beginning inventory are treated as if they were started and completed during the current period. Therefore, work completed in the prior period is *not* deducted in computing equivalent units.	2. Work completed in the prior period on units in the beginning inventory *is* deducted in computing equivalent units. Therefore, equivalent units represent only work done during the current period.
3. Unit costs will contain some element of cost from the prior period.	3. Unit costs will contain only elements of cost from the current period.
Cost reconciliation	
1. The "cost to be accounted for" section of the report is the same for both methods.	1. The "cost to be accounted for" section of the report is the same for both methods.
2. All units transferred out are treated the same, regardless of whether they were part of the beginning inventory or started and completed during the period.	2. Units transferred out are divided into two groups: *(a)* units in the beginning inventory and *(b)* units started and completed during the period.
3. Units in the ending inventory have cost applied to them in the same way under both methods.	3. Units in the ending inventory have cost applied to them in the same way under both methods.

EVALUATION OF THE WEIGHTED-AVERAGE AND FIFO METHODS

Although the weighted-average and FIFO methods seem to be very different, in most process costing situations they will produce unit costs that are nearly the same. Any major difference in unit costs between the two methods is likely to be traceable to erratic movements in raw materials prices. The reason is that conversion costs (labor and overhead) usually will not fluctuate widely from month to month due to the continuous nature of the flow of goods in process costing situations. In addition, inventory levels in most companies tend to remain quite stable, thereby adding to the general stability of unit costs. Raw materials prices can fluctuate considerably from period to period, however, which can result in a difference in unit costs between the two methods. The reason is that the weighted-average method averages last period's materials costs in with those of the current period.

From the standpoint of cost control, the FIFO method is clearly superior to the weighted-average method. This is because current performance should be measured in relation to costs of the current period only, and the weighted-average method inherently mixes these costs in with costs of the prior period. Thus, under the weighted-average method, the manager's performance is influenced to some extent by what happened in a prior period. This problem does not arise under the FIFO method, since it makes a clear distinction between costs in the beginning inventory and costs incurred during the current period.

On the other hand, some managers feel that the weighted-average method is simpler to apply than the FIFO method. Although this may have been true in the past when much accounting work was done by hand, due to the advent of the computer it is doubtful whether it is still true today. The computer can handle either method with ease. The FIFO method would require a more complex programming effort when a process costing system is first set up, but after that there should be little difference between the two methods so far as difficulty in operating the system is concerned.

SUMMARY

Process costing is used in those manufacturing situations where homogeneous products are produced on a continuous basis. A process costing system is similar to a job-order costing system in that (1) both systems have the same basic purpose of providing data for the manager, (2) both systems use the same manufacturing accounts, and (3) costs flow through the manufacturing accounts in basically the same way in both systems. A process costing system differs from a job-order system in that (1) a single product is involved, (2) costs are accumulated by department (rather than by job), (3) the department production report replaces the job cost sheet, and (4) unit costs are computed by department (rather than by job).

In order to compute unit costs in a department, the department's equivalent units must be determined. Equivalent units can be computed in two ways— by the weighted-average method and by the FIFO method. The weighted-average method treats partially completed units in the beginning work in process inventory as if they were started and completed during the current period. The FIFO method distinguishes between work completed in the prior period and work completed currently, so that equivalent units represent only work completed during the current period.

The activity in a department is summarized on a production report. There are three separate (though highly interrelated) parts to a production report. The first part is a quantity schedule, which shows the flow of units through a department during a period. The second part consists of a computation of unit costs, with unit costs being provided individually for materials, labor, and overhead as well as in total for the period. The third part consists of a cost reconciliation, which summarizes all cost flows through a department for a period.

Although the weighted-average and FIFO methods are somewhat different, in most process costing situations they will produce unit costs that are nearly the same, except perhaps for raw materials. From the viewpoint of cost control, the FIFO method is superior to the weighted-average method because of its focus on current period costs. Although the FIFO method seems more complex in its operation, this complexity is largely overcome today due to the widespread use of the computer.

KEY TERMS FOR REVIEW

Conversion cost Direct labor cost combined with manufacturing overhead cost.

Cost reconciliation The part of a production report that shows what costs a department has to account for during a period and how those costs are accounted for.

Equivalent units of production The number of units that would have been produced during a period if all of a department's efforts had resulted in completed units of product.

FIFO method A method of accounting for cost flows in a process costing system in which equivalent units and unit costs relate only to work done during the current period.

Parallel processing A method of arranging processing departments in which not all units go through all processing departments.

Process costing A costing method used in those industries that produce homogeneous products on a continuous basis.

Processing department Any location in a factory where work is performed on a product and where materials, labor, or overhead costs are added to it.

Production report A report that summarizes all activity in a department's Work in Process account during a period and that contains three sections: a quantity schedule, a computation of unit costs, and a cost reconciliation.

Quantity schedule The part of a production report that shows the flow of units through a department during a period.

Sequential processing A method of arranging processing departments in which all units go through all departments.

Transferred-in cost The amount of cost attached to units of product that have been received from a prior processing department.

Weighted-average method A method of accounting for cost flows in a process costing system in which units in the beginning work in process inventory are treated as if they were started and completed during the current period.

QUESTIONS

4-1. Under what conditions would it be appropriate to use a process costing system?

4-2. What similarities exist between job-order and process costing?

4-3. Costs are accumulated by job in a job-order costing system; how are costs accumulated in a process costing system?

4-4. What two essential features must characterize any processing department?

4-5. Distinguish between departments arranged in a sequential pattern and departments arranged in a parallel pattern.

4-6. Why is cost accumulation easier under a process costing system than it is under a job-order costing system?

4-7. How many Work in Process accounts are maintained in a company using process costing?

4-8. Assume that a company has two processing departments, mixing and firing. Prepare a journal entry to show a transfer of partially completed units from the mixing department to the firing department.

4-9. Assume again that a company has two processing departments, mixing and firing. Explain what costs might be added to the firing department's Work in Process account during a period.

4-10. What is meant by the term *equivalent units of production?*

4-11. Under the weighted-average method, what assumption is made relative to units in the beginning work in process inventory when equivalent units and unit costs are computed?

4-12. How does the computation of equivalent units under the FIFO method differ from the computation of equivalent units under the weighted-average method?

4-13. What is a quantity schedule, and what purpose does it serve?

4-14. On the cost reconciliation part of the production report, the weighted-average method treats all units transferred out in the same way. How does this differ from the FIFO method of handling units transferred out?

4-15. Under process costing, it is often suggested that a product is like a rolling snowball as it moves from department to department. Why is this an apt comparison?

4-16. From the standpoint of cost control, why is the FIFO method superior to the weighted-average method?

EXERCISES

E4-1. Lindex Company manufactures a product that goes through three departments, A, B, and C. Information relating to activity in Department A during October 19x1 is given below:

		Percent completed	
	Units	Materials	Conversion
Work in process, October 1	8,000	100	60
Started into production during October	132,000		
Work in process, October 31	10,000	70	40

Required: Prepare a quantity schedule for Department A for the month.

E4–2. The Northwest Pulp Company processes wood pulp for various manufacturers of paper products. Two departments are involved, Department 1 and Department 2. Data relating to tons of pulp processed in Department 1 during October 19x8 are presented below:

	Tons of pulp	Percent completed*
Beginning inventory, October 1	20,000	30
Started into processing during the month	380,000	—
Ending inventory, October 31	25,000	60

* Labor and overhead only.

All materials are added at the beginning of processing in Department 1. Labor and overhead costs are incurred uniformly throughout processing.

Required: 1. Prepare a quantity schedule for the month in Department 1.
2. Compute the equivalent units of production for the month in Department 1, assuming that the company uses:
   a. The weighted-average method.
   b. The FIFO method.

E4–3. Marcroft Company uses a process costing system. The following data are available for one processing department for April:

		Percent completed	
	Units	Materials	Conversion
Work in process inventory, April 1	20,000	60	30
Work in process inventory, April 30	10,000	80	50

The department started 150,000 units into production during the month and transferred 160,000 completed units to the next department.

Required: 1. Assuming that the company uses the weighted-average method of accounting for units and costs, compute the equivalent units of production for the month.
2. Repeat the computations in (1) above, assuming that the company uses the FIFO method of accounting for units and costs.

E4–4. Malex Company uses a process costing system. The company's single product passes through two processes, cooking and molding. T-accounts showing the flow of costs through the two processes for a recent month follow:

Work in Process—Cooking

Bal. 4/1	8,000	Transferred out	160,000
Direct materials	42,000		
Direct labor	50,000		
Overhead	75,000		

Work in Process—Molding

Bal. 4/1	4,000	Transferred out	240,000
Transferred in	160,000		
Direct labor	36,000		
Overhead	45,000		

Required: Prepare journal entries showing the flow of costs through the two processes during April.

E4–5.   Helox, Inc., manufactures a product that passes through two production processes. A quantity schedule for a recent month for process A follows:

Units to be accounted for:
  Units in process, beginning (all materials;
    40% labor and overhead)   5,000
  Units started into production.   180,000
  Total units to account for   185,000

Units accounted for as follows:
  Units transferred to process B   175,000
  Units in process, ending (all materials;
    30% labor and overhead)   10,000
  Total units accounted for   185,000

Costs in the beginning work in process inventory were: materials, $1,200; labor, $1,800; and overhead, $2,000. Costs added during the month were: materials, $54,000; labor, $140,800; and overhead, $211,200.

Required: Assuming that the company uses the weighted-average cost method, prepare a computation showing equivalent units and unit costs for the month.

E4–6.   (This exercise should be assigned only if Exercise 4–5 is also assigned.) Refer to the data in Exercise 4–5 and to the unit costs that you have computed there.

Required: Complete the following cost reconciliation for process A:

	Units	Costs
Cost to be accounted for:		
Work in process, beginning	?	$?
Added by the department during the month	?	?
Total cost to be accounted for	185,000	$411,000
Cost accounted for as follows:		
Transferred to process B ( )	?	$?
Work in process, ending	?	
Materials cost ( )	$?	
Labor cost ( )	?	
Overhead cost ( )	?	
Total cost in work in process, ending.		?
Total cost accounted for	185,000	$411,000

E4–7.   Refer to the data in Exercise 4–5. Assume that the company uses the FIFO cost method.

Required: Prepare a computation showing equivalent units and unit costs for the month.

E4–8. (This exercise should be assigned only if Exercise 4–7 is also assigned.) Refer to the data in Exercise 4–5 and to the unit costs that you have computed in Exercise 4–7.

Required: Complete the following cost reconciliation for process A:

	Units	Costs
Cost to be accounted for:		
Work in process, beginning	?	$?
Added by the department during the month	?	?
Total cost to be accounted for	185,000	$411,000
Cost accounted for as follows:		
(1) Transferred to process B	?	
Units from the beginning inventory:		
Cost in the beginning inventory		$?
Cost to complete these units:		
Labor cost ( )		?
Overhead cost ( )		?
Total cost		?
Units started and completed during the month ( )		?
Total cost transferred		$?
(2) Work in process, ending	?	
Materials cost ( )		?
Labor cost ( )		?
Overhead cost ( )		?
Total cost in work in process, ending		?
Total cost accounted for	185,000	$411,000

PROBLEMS

P4–9. Quantity schedule and unit cost computation. Starburst Company manufactures a product that goes through three processes. The following information relates to cost and activity in process 1 during March 19x4:

		Percent Completed	
	Units	Materials	Conversion
Beginning work in process	30,000	100	40
Started into production during the month	120,000		
Completed and transferred out during the month	140,000		
Ending work in process	10,000	100	80

The beginning work in process inventory contained $24,000 in materials cost and $14,300 in conversion cost. An additional $108,000 in materials cost and $170,000 in conversion cost was added to production during the month.

Required: 1. Prepare a quantity schedule for process 1 for the month.
2. Assume that the company uses the weighted-average method. Prepare a computation showing equivalent units and unit costs for the month.
3. Assume that the company uses the FIFO method. Prepare a computation showing equivalent units and unit costs for the month.

P4–10. **Partial production report.** Rolex Company uses a process costing system and manufactures a single product. Activity for August 19x6 has just been completed. A partially completed production report for Department A for the month follows:

DEPARTMENT A
Production Report
For the Month Ended August 31, 19x6

Quantity schedule

	Units
Units to be accounted for:	
Units in process, August 1 (all materials;	
80% labor and overhead)	10,000
Units started into production	100,000
Total units to account for.	110,000
Units accounted for as follows:	
Units transferred to department B	95,000
Units in process, August 31 (60% materials;	
20% labor and overhead)	15,000
Total units accounted for	110,000

Computation of unit costs

	Materials	Labor	Overhead	Total
Work in process, August 1	$ 1,500	$ 1,000	$ 5,400	$ 0,700
Cost added during August	154,500	22,700	68,100	245,300
Total cost *(a)*.	$156,000	$24,500	$73,500	$254,000
Equivalent units *(b)*	104,000	98,000	98,000	—
Unit cost, *(a) ÷ (b)*.	$1.50	$0.25	$0.75	$2.50

Cost reconciliation

Cost to be accounted for:
   ?

Cost accounted for as follows:
   ?

Required: 1. Does the company use the weighted-average cost method or the FIFO cost method? Explain. (Hint: Look at the computation of unit costs.)
2. Prepare a schedule showing how the equivalent units above were computed.
3. Complete the "cost reconciliation" part of the production report above.

P4–11. **Step-by-step production report; weighted-average method.** The PVC Company manufactures a high-quality plastic pipe in two departments, cooking and molding. Materials are introduced at the start of work in the cooking department. After cooking, the materials are transferred into the molding department, in which pipe is formed. Materials are accounted for in the cooking department on a pounds basis. Labor and overhead costs are incurred evenly during the cooking process.

Selected data relating to the cooking department during May 19x3 are given below:

Production data:
Pounds in process, May 1; 60% complete
  as to labor and overhead. 15,000
Pounds started into production during May 105,000
Pounds completed and transferred to molding . . . . . . ?
Pounds in process, May 31; 20% complete
  as to labor and overhead. 9,000

Cost data:
Work in process inventory, May 1:
  Materials cost . . . . $ 15,225
  Labor cost 900
  Overhead cost 5,320
Cost added during May:
  Materials cost 110,775
  Labor cost 10,380
  Overhead cost 68,000

The company uses the weighted-average method to account for units and costs.

Required: Prepare a production report for the cooking department. Use the following three steps as a guide in preparing your report:
1. Prepare a quantity schedule.
2. Compute unit costs for the month. (Remember, equivalent units are involved in this computation.)
3. Using the data from (1) and (2), prepare a cost reconciliation.

P4–12. Partial production report. Tumwater, Inc., manufactures a single product that moves through two departments, A and B. A partially completed production report for a recent month in Department A follows:

DEPARTMENT A
Production Report
For the Month Ended March 31, 19x2

Quantity schedule

	Units
Units to be accounted for:	
Units in process, March 1 (all materials; ⅔ labor and overhead)	6,000
Units started into production	40,000
Total units to account for	46,000
Units accounted for as follows:	
Units transferred to Department B	42,000
Units in process, March 31 (all materials; ¼ labor and overhead)	4,000
Total units accounted for	46,000

Computation of unit costs

	Material	Labor	Overhead	Total
Cost added during March *(a)*.	$60,000	$29,250	$48,750	$138,000
Equivalent units *(b)*	40,000	39,000	39,000	—
Unit cost, *(a)* ÷ *(b)*	$1.50	$0.75	$1.25	$3.50

Cost reconciliation

Cost to be accounted for:
  ?

Cost accounted for as follows:
  ?

Required: 1. Does the company use the weighted-average cost method or the FIFO cost method? Explain. (Hint: Look at the computation of unit costs.)
2. Prepare a schedule showing how the equivalent units above were computed.
3. Assume that the cost in the work in process inventory totaled $22,000 at the beginning of the month (March 1). Complete the "cost reconciliation" part of the production report above.

P4–13.   **Step-by-step production report; FIFO method.**   Sarver Company manufactures a single product that goes through two processes, blending and packaging. The following activity was recorded in the blending department during May 19x6:

Production:
Units in process, May 1; 80% complete
   as to conversion costs   10,000
Units started into production   140,000
Units completed and transferred
   to packaging . . . .   ?
Units in process, May 31; 60% complete
   as to conversion costs   30,000

Costs:
Work in process inventory, May 1:
   Materials cost. . . . . $ 21,000
   Conversion cost . . . .   18,000 $ 39,000
Cost added during the month:
   Materials cost.   259,000
   Conversion cost   312,000   571,000
Total cost $610,000

All materials are added at the beginning of work in the blending department. Conversion costs are added uniformly during processing. The company uses the FIFO cost method.

Required: Prepare a production report for the blending department. Use the following three steps as a guide in preparing your report:
1. Prepare a quantity schedule.
2. Compute unit costs for the month. (Remember, equivalent units are involved in this computation.)
3. Using the data from (1) and (2), prepare a cost reconciliation.

P4–14.   **Basic production report; weighted-average method.**   (P4–15 uses these same data with the FIFO method.) Suncrest, Inc., manufactures a product that goes through several departments prior to completion. The following information is available on work in the mixing department during June 19x1:

	Units	Percent completed	
		Materials	Conversion
Work in process, beginning.	20,000	100	75
Started into production	180,000		
Completed and transferred out	160,000		
Work in process, ending.	40,000	100	25

Cost in the beginning work in process inventory and cost added during June were as follows:

	Materials	Conversion
Work in process, beginning	$ 25,200	$ 24,800
Cost added during June	334,800	238,700

The company uses the weighted-average method to compute unit costs. The mixing department is the first department in the production process; after mixing has been completed, the units are transferred to the molding department.

Required: Prepare a production report for the mixing department for the month of June 19x1.

P4–15. Basic production report; FIFO method. Refer to the data in P4–14. Assume that the company uses the FIFO method to compute unit costs rather than the weighted-average method.

Required: Prepare a production report for the mixing department for the month of June 19x1.

P4–16. Straightforward production report; weighted-average method. Home Products, Inc., manufactures a plastering compound that goes through three processing stages prior to completion. Information on work in the first department, cooking, is given below for August 19x2:

	Units	Processing completed	Materials	Labor	Overhead
Work in process, opening	8,000	¾	$ 5,150	$ 660	$ 1,320
Units started in process	45,000	—			
Units transferred out	48,000	—	?	?	?
Work in process, ending.	?	⅖	?	?	?
Cost added during the month			29,300	9,840	19,680

All materials are added at the beginning of work in the cooking department; thus, the "processing completed" above refers to labor and overhead costs. The company uses the weighted-average method to cost units of product.

Required: Prepare a production report for the cooking department for the month.

P4–17. Straightforward production report; FIFO method. Hilox, Inc., produces an antacid product that goes through two departments. Cost and production data for the first department, blending, are given below for May 19x5:

Units:
  In process, May 1: 5,000 units (40% complete as to conversion).
  In process, May 31: 4,000 units (75% complete as to conversion).
  Placed into production: 80,000 units.
  Completed and transferred out: 81,000 units.

Costs:
  In process, May 1: $7,600.
  Added to production during May:
    Material X: $60,000.
    Material Y: $25,500.
    Conversion: $36,900.

Material X is added at the beginning of work in the blending department. Material Y is also added in the blending department, but it is not added until units of product are 60 percent complete as to conversion. Conversion costs are incurred uniformly during work in the blending department. The company uses the FIFO cost method.

Required: Prepare a production report for the blending department for the month.

P4–18.   **Analysis of Work in Process T-account; weighted-average method.**   Weston Products manufactures an industrial cleaning compound that goes through three processing departments: grinding, mixing, and cooking. Raw materials are introduced at the start of work in the grinding department, with conversion costs being incurred evenly throughout the grinding process. The Work in Process T-account for the grinding department for a recent month is given below:

Work in Process—Grinding Department

Inventory, May 1 (18,000 lbs, ⅓ processed)	21,800	Completed and transferred to mixing (? lbs.)	?
May costs added:			
Raw materials (167,000 lbs.)	133,400		
Labor and overhead	226,800		
Inventory, May 31 (15,000 lbs., ⅔ processed)	?		

The May 1 work in process inventory consists of $14,600 in materials cost and $7,200 in labor and overhead cost. The company uses the weighted-average method to account for units and costs.

Required: 1.   Prepare a production report for the grinding department for the month.
        2.   What criticism can be made of the unit costs that you have computed on your production report?

P4–19.   **Analysis of Work in Process T-account; FIFO method.**   Hiko, Inc., manufactures a high-quality pressboard out of wood scraps and sawmill waste. The pressboard goes through two processing departments, shredding and forming. Activity in the shredding department during a recent month is summarized in the department's Work in Process account below:

Work in Process—Shredding Department

Inventory, July 1 (10,000 lbs., 30% processed)	13,400	Completed and transferred to forming (? lbs.)	?
July costs added:			
Wood materials (170,000 lbs.)	139,400		
Labor and overhead	244,200		
Inventory, July 31 (20,000 lbs., 40% processed)	?		

The wood materials are entered into production at the beginning of work in the shredding department. Labor and overhead costs are incurred uniformly throughout the shredding process. The company uses the FIFO cost method.

Required: 1.   Prepare a production report for the shredding department for the month.
        2.   In a process costing system, would you expect per unit materials cost or per

unit labor and overhead cost to show the greater fluctuation from period to period? Why?

P4-20. **Analysis of data; production report; weighted-average method.** Durall Company manufactures a plastic gasket that is used in automobile engines. The gaskets go through three processing departments: mixing, forming, and stamping. The company's accountant (who is very inexperienced) has prepared a summary of production and costs for the mixing department as follows for October 19x5:

Mixing department costs:	
Work in process inventory, October 1, 8,000 units, ⅞ complete as to labor and overhead	$ 22,420*
Material A added during the month (added at the start of work in the mixing department)	81,480
Material B added during the month (added when processing is 50 percent complete in the mixing department)	27,600
Conversion costs added during the month	96,900
Total departmental costs	$228,400
Mixing department costs assigned to:	
Units completed and transferred to the forming department, 100,000 units at $2.284 each	$228,400
Work in process inventory, October 31, 5,000 units, ⅖ complete as to labor and overhead	—
Total departmental costs assigned	$228,400

* Consists of material A: $8,820; material B, $3,400; and labor and overhead, $10,200.

Labor and overhead costs are incurred evenly during processing in the mixing department.

The company's inexperienced accountant assigned no cost to the ending work in process inventory since these units were only partially complete. Durall's president is confused by this report and would like to have a new one prepared. The company uses the weighted-average method.

Required: 1. Prepare a production report for the mixing department for the month.
2. Assume that in order to remain competitive the company has undertaken a major cost-cutting program during the current month. Would the effects of this cost-cutting program tend to show up more under the weighted-average method or under the FIFO method? Explain.

P4-21. **Analysis of data; production report; FIFO method.** Refer to the data for Durall Products in the preceding problem. Assume that the company uses the FIFO method to account for units and costs.

Required: 1. Prepare a production report for the mixing department for the month.
2. Assume as stated in (2) in P4-20 that the company has undertaken a major cost-cutting program during the current month. Would you expect unit costs for the current month to be higher under the FIFO method or under the weighted-average method? Why?

P4–22. **Production report; journal entries; weighted-average method.** Lubricants, Inc., produces a special kind of grease that is widely used by race car drivers. The grease is produced in two processes: refining and blending.

Raw oil products are introduced at the start of work in the refining department; labor and overhead costs are incurred evenly throughout the refining operation. The refined output is then transferred to the blending department.

The following incomplete Work in Process account is available for the refining department for March 19x2:

Work in Process—Refining Department

March 1 inventory (5,000 gal., $\frac{4}{5}$ processed)	6,500	Completed and transferred to blending (? gal.)	?
		29,000	
March costs added:			
Raw oil materials (30,000 gal.)	12,500		
Direct labor	14,500		
Overhead	21,750		
March 31 inventory (6,000 gal., $\frac{2}{3}$ processed)	?		

The March 1 work in process inventory consists of the following cost elements: raw materials, $1,500; direct labor, $2,000; and overhead, $3,000. The company accounts for units and costs by the weighted-average method.

Required:
1. Prepare a production report for the refining department for the month.
2. Assume the following cost and activity in the blending department during March: raw materials used, $4,000; direct labor cost incurred, $8,500; and overhead cost applied to production, $12,750. The blending department completed 25,000 units at a cost of $2.88 per unit. Prepare journal entries to show the flow of costs through the two departments during March.

P4–23. **Production report; journal entries; FIFO method.** ZAB, Inc., produces a very popular low-calorie soft drink. Two processes, blending and bottling, are used to produce the drink.

All materials are added at the start of work in the blending department; labor and overhead costs are incurred evenly during the blending operation. The blended liquid is then transferred to the bottling department, where it is put into bottles for distribution.

The following incomplete Work in Process account for the blending department is available for June 19x8:

Work in Process—Blending Department

June 1 inventory (10,000 gal., 10% processed)	6,500	Completed and transferred to bottling (70,000 gal.)	?
June costs added:			
Materials (? gal.)	32,500		
Direct labor	64,800		
Overhead	97,200		
June 30 inventory (5,000 gal., 60% processed)	?		

The company uses the FIFO method to account for units and costs.

Required: 1. Prepare a production report for the blending department for the month.
2. Assume the following costs and activity in the bottling department for June: raw materials used, $16,000; direct labor cost incurred, $25,200; and overhead cost applied to production, $31,500. The bottling department completed production on 72,000 gallons of the soft drink during June at a cost of $3.60 per gallon. Prepare journal entries to show the flow of costs through the two departments during June.

5 Cost Behavior: Analysis and Use

Learning objectives

After studying Chapter 5, you should be able to:

Identify examples of variable costs and explain the effect of a change in activity on both total variable costs and per unit variable costs.

Identify examples of fixed costs and explain the effect of a change in activity on both total fixed costs and fixed costs expressed on a per unit basis.

Define the relevant range and explain its significance in cost behavior analysis.

Distinguish between committed and discretionary fixed costs.

Analyze a mixed cost by the high-low method and enumerate the strengths and weaknesses of this analytical approach.

Prepare a scattergraph and analyze a mixed cost by visually placing a regression line on the graph.

Perform a least squares analysis of a mixed cost, using either the equation method or the alternative method given in the Appendix.

Prepare an income statement using the contribution format.

Define or explain the key terms listed at the end of the chapter.

In our discussion of cost terms and concepts in Chapter 2, we stated that one way in which costs can be classified is by behavior. We defined cost behavior as meaning how a cost will react or change as changes take place in the level of business activity. An understanding of cost behavior is the key to many decisions in an organization in that by understanding how costs behave, a manager is better able to predict what costs will be under various operating circumstances. Experience has shown that attempts at decision making without a thorough understanding of the costs involved—and how these costs may change with the activity level—can lead to disaster. A decision to double production of a particular product line, for example, might result in the incurrence of far greater costs than could be generated in additional revenues. To avoid such problems, a manager must be able to accurately predict what costs will be at various activity levels. In this chapter, we shall find that the key to effective cost prediction lies in an understanding of cost behavior patterns.

TYPES OF COST BEHAVIOR PATTERNS

In our brief discussion of cost behavior in Chapter 2, we mentioned only variable and fixed costs. There is a third behavior pattern, generally known as a *mixed* or *semivariable* cost. All three cost behavior patterns—variable, fixed, and mixed—are found in most organizations. The *mix* of these three types of costs (that is, the relative proportion of each type of cost) is known as a firm's **cost structure.** For example, a firm might have many fixed costs but few variable costs or mixed costs. Alternatively, it might have many variable costs but few fixed or other costs. A firm's cost structure is very significant from a managerial accounting point of view in that it can have a heavy impact on the decision-making process. We must reserve our discussion of this topic until the next chapter, however, until after we have gained a full understanding of the behavior of each type of cost involved.

In the following sections, we briefly review the definition of variable costs and fixed costs and then discuss the behavior of these costs in greater depth than we were able to do in Chapter 2. After this review and discussion, we turn our attention to the identification and analysis of mixed costs. We conclude the chapter by introducing a new income statement format—called the contribution format—in which costs are organized by behavior rather than by the traditional functions of production, sales, and administration.

Variable costs

We found in Chapter 2 that a variable cost is so named because it varies in total in direct proportion to changes in the activity level. If the activity level doubles, then one would expect the variable costs to also double. If the activity level goes up only 10 percent, then one would expect the variable costs to increase by 10 percent as well.

We also found in Chapter 2 that in order for variable costs to change in total in proportion to changes in the activity level, these costs must be constant on a *per unit* basis. To provide an example, assume that the Premier Motor Company produces trucks. There is one radiator to each truck. The radiators cost $25 each. If we look at the cost of radiators on a *per truck* basis, the cost remains constant at $25 per truck. Because of this constancy in cost per truck, the *total cost* of radiators changes in direct proportion to the number of trucks produced, as shown below:

Number of trucks produced	Radiator cost per truck	Total radiator cost
250.	$25	$ 6,250
500.	25	12,500
750.	25	18,750
1,000.	25	25,000

The idea that a variable cost is constant per unit but varies in total with the activity level is crucial to an understanding of cost behavior patterns. We shall rely on this concept again and again in this chapter and in chapters ahead. Exhibit 5–1 contains a graphical illustration of variable cost behavior.

The activity base For a cost to be variable, it must be variable *with something*. That "something" is the **activity base.** An activity base is a measure of effort that operates as a causal factor in the incurrence of variable cost. Two of the most common activity bases are units produced and units sold. Other activity bases might include the number of miles driven by salespersons,

EXHIBIT 5–1
Variable cost behavior

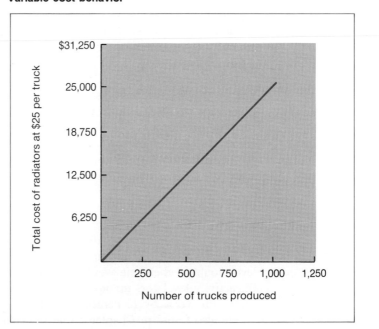

the number of pounds of laundry processed by a hotel, the number of letters typed by a secretary, the number of hours of machine time logged, and the number of occupied beds in a hospital.

In order to plan and control variable costs, a manager must be well acquainted with the various activity bases within the firm. People sometimes get the notion that if a cost doesn't vary with production or with sales, then it is not really a variable cost. This, of course, is not correct. As suggested by the range of bases listed above, costs can be incurred as a function of many different activities within an organization. Whether a cost is variable will depend on whether its incurrence is a function of the activity measure under consideration. For example, if a manager is analyzing the cost of service calls under a product warranty, the relevant activity measure will be the number of service calls made. Those costs that vary in total with the number of service calls made will be variable costs.

Extent of variable costs   The number and type of variable costs present in an organization will depend in large part on the organization's structure and purpose. A highly capital-intensive organization such as a public utility will tend to have few variable costs. The bulk of its costs will be associated with its plant, and these costs will tend to be quite insensitive to changes in levels of service provided. A manufacturing firm, by contrast, will often have many variable costs. It will have variable costs associated both with the manufacture of its products and with their distribution to customers. A service organizaiton or a merchandising firm will tend to fall between these two extremes.

A few of the more frequently encountered variable costs are shown in the tabulation in Exhibit 5–2.

EXHIBIT 5 2

Examples of variable costs

Type of organization	Variable costs
Merchandising firm	Cost of goods (merchandise) sold
Manufacturing firm	Manufacturing costs:
	Prime costs:
	Direct materials
	Direct labor
	Variable portion of manufacturing
	overhead:
	Indirect materials
	Lubricants
	Supplies
	Utilities
	Setup time
	Indirect labor
Both merchandising and manufacturing firms	Selling and administrative costs:
	Commissions to salespersons
	Clerical costs, such as invoicing
	Freight-out
Service organizations	Supplies, travel, clerical

The costs listed under "Variable portion of manufacturing overhead" should not be viewed as being inclusive but rather as being representative of the kinds of variable costs found in this classification.

True variable versus step-variable costs

Not all variable costs have exactly the same behavior pattern. Some variable costs behave in a *true variable* or *proportionately variable* pattern. Other variable costs behave in a *step-variable* pattern.

True variable costs   Direct materials would be a true or proportionately variable cost. Direct materials can be purchased in the exact quantity needed, and quantities used will vary directly with output. In addition, any amounts unused can be stored up and carried forward to the next period as inventory.

Step-variable costs   Indirect labor is also considered to be a variable cost, but it doesn't behave in quite the same way as direct materials. As an example, let us consider the labor cost of maintenance workers, which would be part of indirect labor.

Unlike direct materials, the time of maintenance workers is obtainable only in large chunks, rather than in exact quantities. Moreover, any maintenance time not utilized cannot be stored up as inventory and carried forward to the next period. Either the time is used effectively as it expires hour by hour, or it is gone forever. Furthermore, the utilization of indirect labor time can be quite flexible, whereas the utilization of direct materials is usually quite set. A maintenance crew, for example, can work at a fairly leisurely pace if pressures are light, but then the crew can intensify its efforts if pressures build up. For this reason, somewhat small changes in the level of production

EXHIBIT 5–3
True variable versus step-variable costs

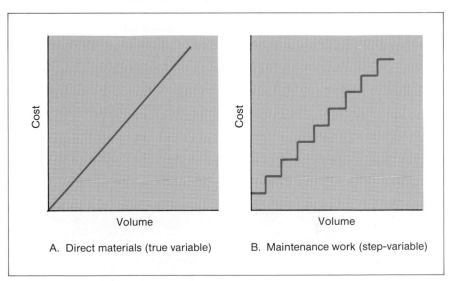

A. Direct materials (true variable)   B. Maintenance work (step-variable)

may have no effect on the number of maintenance people needed to properly carry on maintenance work.

A cost (such as the labor cost of maintenance workers) that is obtainable only in large chunks and that increases or decreases only in response to fairly wide changes in the activity level is known as a **step-variable cost.** The behavior of a step-variable cost, contrasted with the behavior of a true variable cost, is illustrated in Exhibit 5–3.

Notice that the need for maintenance help changes only with fairly wide changes in volume and that when additional maintenance time is obtained, it comes in large, indivisible pieces. The strategy of management in dealing with step-variable costs must be to obtain the fullest use of services possible for each separate step. Great care must be taken in working with these kinds of costs to prevent "fat" from building up in an organization. There is a tendency to employ additional help more quickly than might be needed, and there is generally a reluctance to lay people off when volume declines.

The linearity assumption and the relevant range

In dealing with variable costs, we have assumed a strictly linear relationship between cost and volume, except in the case of step-variable costs. Economists correctly point out that many costs that the accountant classifies as variable actually behave in a *curvilinear* fashion. The behavior of a **curvilinear cost**

EXHIBIT 5–4
Curvilinear costs and the relevant range

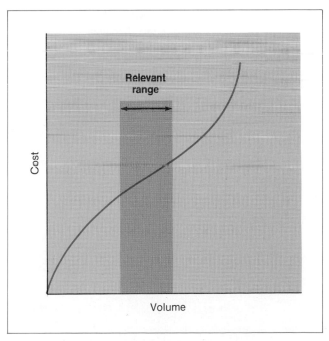

is shown in Exhibit 5–4. Notice that a strictly linear relationship between cost and volume does not exist either at very high or at very low levels of activity.

Although the accountant recognizes that many costs are not linear in their relationship to volume at some points, he or she concentrates on their behavior within narrow bands of activity known as the **relevant range.** The relevant range can be defined as that range of activity within which assumptions relative to cost behavior are valid. Generally, the relationship between variable cost and activity is stable enough within this range that an assumption of strict linearity can be used with insignificant loss of accuracy. The concept of the relevant range is illustrated in Exhibit 5–4.

Fixed costs

In our discussion of cost behavior patterns in Chapter 2, we stated that fixed costs are costs that remain constant in total regardless of changes in the level of activity. To continue the Premier Motor Company example, if the company rents a factory building for $50,000 per year, the *total* amount of rent paid will not change regardless of the number of trucks produced in a year. This concept is shown graphically in Exhibit 5–5.

Since fixed costs remain constant in total, the amount of cost computed on a *per unit* basis will get progressively smaller as the number of units produced becomes greater. If the Premier Motor Company produces only 250 trucks in a year, the $50,000 fixed rental cost would amount to $200

EXHIBIT 5–5
Fixed cost behavior

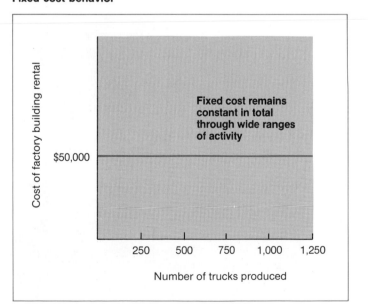

per truck. If 1,000 trucks are produced, it would amount to only $50 per truck. As we noted in Chapter 2, this aspect of fixed costs can be confusing to the manager, although it is necessary in some contexts to express fixed costs on an average per unit basis. We found in Chapter 3, for example, that for purposes of preparing financial statements the manager needs a broad unit cost figure containing both variable and fixed cost elements. For *internal* uses, however, the manager rarely expresses a fixed cost on a per unit basis because of the potential confusion involved. Experience has shown that for internal uses, fixed costs are most easily (and most safely) dealt with on a total basis, rather than on a per unit basis.

The trend toward fixed costs

The trend in many companies today is toward greater fixed costs relative to variable costs. There are at least two factors responsible for this trend. First, automation is becoming increasingly important in all types of organizations. Although automation has played a significant role in factory operations for well over a century, its role continues to increase. In addition, automation is rapidly becoming a significant factor in some traditionally service-oriented industries as well. Increased automation means increased investment in machinery and equipment, with the attendant fixed depreciation or lease charges.

Second, labor unions have been increasingly successful in stabilizing employment through labor contracts. Labor leaders have set guaranteed annual salaries or guaranteed minimum weeks of work high on their list of goals for the future. Although most people would agree that a stabilization of employment is desirable from a social point of view, guaranteed salaries and workweeks do reduce the response of direct labor costs to changes in production.

This shift away from variable costs toward fixed costs has been so significant in some firms that they have become largely "fixed cost" organizations. The textile industry, for example, can be cited as one in which most firms have moved heavily toward automation, with basically inflexible fixed costs replacing flexible, more responsive variable costs to a considerable extent. These shifts are very significant from a managerial accounting point of view, in that planning in many ways becomes much more crucial when one is dealing with large amounts of fixed costs. The reason is that when dealing with fixed costs, the manager is much more "locked in" and generally has fewer options available in day-to-day decisions.

Types of fixed costs

Fixed costs are sometimes referred to as capacity costs, since they result from outlays made for plant facilities, equipment, and other items needed to provide the basic capacity for sustained operations. For planning purposes, fixed costs can be viewed as being either *committed* or *discretionary*.

Committed fixed costs Committed fixed costs are those that relate to the investment in plant, equipment, and the basic organizational structure of a firm. Examples of such costs would include depreciation of plant facilities (buildings and equipment), taxes on real estate, insurance, and salaries of top management and operating personnel.

The two key factors about committed fixed costs are that (1) they are long term in nature, and (2) they can't be reduced to zero even for short periods of time without seriously impairing either the profitability or the long-run goals of a firm. Even if operations are interrupted or cut back, the committed fixed costs will still continue unchanged. During a recessionary period, for example, a firm can't discharge its key executives or sell off part of the plant. Facilities and the basic organizational structure must be kept intact at all times. In terms of long-run goals, the costs of any other course of action would be far greater than any short-run savings that might be realized.

Since committed fixed costs are basic to the long-run goals of a firm, their planning horizon usually encompasses many years. The commitments involved in these costs are made only after careful analysis of long-run sales forecasts and after the relating of these forecasts to future capacity needs. Careful control must be exercised by management in the planning stage to ensure that a firm's long-run needs are properly evaluated. Once a decision is made to build a certain size plant, a firm becomes locked into that decision for many years to come.

After a firm becomes committed to a basic plant and organization, how are the associated costs controlled from year to year? Control of committed fixed costs comes through *utilization*. The strategy of management must be to utilize the plant and organization as effectively as possible in bringing about desired goals.

Discretionary fixed costs Discretionary fixed costs (often referred to as *managed* fixed costs) arise from *annual* decisions by management to spend in certain fixed cost areas. Examples of discretionary fixed costs would include advertising, research, and management development programs.

Basically, two key differences exist between discretionary fixed costs and committed fixed costs. First, the planning horizon for a discretionary fixed cost is fairly short term—usually a single year. By contrast, as we indicated earlier, committed fixed costs have a planning horizon that encompasses many years. Second, under dire circumstances it may be possible to cut certain discretionary fixed costs back for short periods of time with minimal damage to the long-run goals of the organization. For example, a firm that has been spending $50,000 annually on management development programs may be forced because of poor economic conditions to reduce its spending in that area during a given year. Although some unfavorable consequences might result from the cutback, it is doubtful that these consequences would be as great as those that would result if the company decided to economize during the year by disposing of a portion of its plant.

The key factor about discretionary fixed costs is that management is not locked into a decision regarding such costs for any more than a single budget period. Each year a fresh look can be taken at the expenditure level in the various discretionary fixed cost areas. A decision can then be made on whether to continue a particular expenditure, increase it, reduce it, or discontinue it altogether.

Top-management philosophy   In our discussion of fixed costs, we have drawn a sharp line between committed fixed costs and discretionary fixed costs. As a practical matter, the line between these two classes of costs should be viewed as being somewhat flexible. The reason is that whether a cost is committed or discretionary will depend in large part on the philosophy of top management.

Some management groups prefer to exercise discretion as often as possible on as many costs as possible. They prefer to review costs frequently and to adjust costs frequently, as conditions and needs warrant. Managers who are inclined in this direction tend to view fixed costs as being largely discretionary. Other management groups are slow to make adjustments in costs (especially adjustments downward) as conditions and needs change. They prefer to maintain the status quo and to leave programs and personnel largely undisturbed, even though changing conditions and needs might suggest the desirability of adjustments. Managers who are inclined in this direction tend to view virtually all fixed costs as being committed.

To cite an example, during recessionary periods when the level of home building is down, many construction companies lay off their workers and virtually disband operations for a period of time. Other construction companies continue large numbers of employees on the payroll, even though the workers have little or no work to do. In the first instance, management is viewing its fixed costs as being largely discretionary in nature. In the second instance, management is viewing its fixed costs as being largely committed. The philosophy of most management groups will fall somewhere between these two extremes.

Fixed costs and the relevant range

The concept of the relevant range, which was introduced in our discussion of variable costs, also has application in dealing with fixed costs, particularly those of a discretionary nature. At the beginning of a period, programs are set and budgets established. The level of discretionary fixed costs will depend on the support needs of the programs that have been planned, which in turn will depend at least in part on the level of activity envisioned in the organization overall. At very high levels of activity, programs are usually broadened or expanded to include many things that might not be pursued at lower levels of activity. In addition, the support needs at high levels of activity are usually much greater than the support needs at lower levels of activity. For example, the advertising needs of a company striving to increase sales by 25 percent would probably be much greater than if no sales increase was planned. Thus, fixed costs often move upward in steps as the activity level increases. This concept is illustrated in Exhibit 5–6, which depicts fixed costs and the relevant range.

Although discretionary fixed costs are most susceptible to adjustment according to changing needs, the step pattern depicted in Exhibit 5–6 also has application to committed fixed costs. As a company expands its level of activity, it may outgrow its present plant, or the key management core may need to be expanded. The result, of course, will be increased committed fixed costs as a larger plant is built and as new key management positions are created.

One's first reaction to the step pattern depicted in Exhibit 5–6 is to say that discretionary and committed fixed costs are really just step-variable costs. To some extent this is true, since *all* costs vary in the long run. There are two major differences, however, between the step-variable costs depicted earlier in Exhibit 5–3 and the fixed costs depicted in Exhibit 5–6.

The first difference is that the step-variable costs can be adjusted very quickly as conditions change, whereas once fixed costs have been set, they often can't be changed easily, even if they are discretionary in nature. A step-variable cost such as maintenance labor, for example, can be adjusted upward or downward very quickly by the hiring and firing of maintenance workers. By contrast, once a company has committed itself to a particular program, it becomes locked into the attendant fixed costs, at least for the budget period under consideration. Once an advertising contract has been

EXHIBIT 5–6

Fixed costs and the relevant range

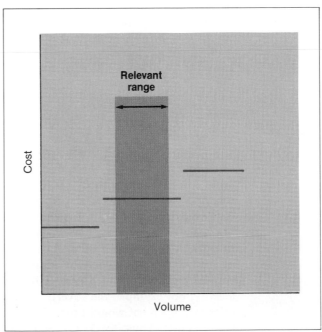

signed, for example, the company is locked into the attendant costs for the contract period.

The second difference is that the *width of the steps* depicted for step-variable costs is much narrower than the width of the steps depicted for the fixed costs in Exhibit 5–6. The width of the steps relates to volume or level of activity. For step-variable costs, the width of a step may be 40 hours of activity or less if one is dealing, for example, with maintenance labor cost. For fixed costs, however, the width of a step may be *thousands* or even *tens of thousands* of hours of activity. In essence, the width of the steps for step-variable costs is generally so narrow that these costs can be treated essentially as variable costs. The width of the steps for fixed costs, on the other hand, is so wide that these costs must generally be treated as being entirely fixed within the relevant range.

Mixed costs

A **mixed cost** is one that contains both variable and fixed cost elements. Mixed costs are also known as **semivariable costs.** At certain levels of activity, mixed costs may display essentially the same characteristics as a fixed cost; at other levels of activity, they may display essentially the same characteristics as a variable cost.

To continue the Premier Motor Company example, assume that the company leases a large part of the machinery used in its operations. The lease

EXHIBIT 5–7
Mixed cost behavior

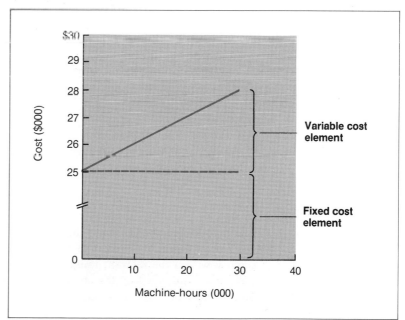

agreement calls for a flat annual lease payment of $25,000, plus 10 cents for each hour that the machines are operated during the year. If during a particular year the machines are operated a cumulative total of 30,000 hours, then the lease cost of the machines will be $28,000, made up of $25,000 in fixed cost plus $3,000 in variable cost. The concept of a mixed cost is shown graphically in Exhibit 5–7.

Even if the machines leased by the Premier Motor Company aren't used a single hour during the year, the company will still have to pay the minimum $25,000 charge. This is why the cost line in Exhibit 5–7 intersects the vertical cost axis at the $25,000 point. For each hour that the machines are used, the *total* cost of leasing will increase by 10 cents. Therefore, the total cost line slopes upward as the variable cost element is added onto the fixed cost element.

THE ANALYSIS OF MIXED COSTS

The concept of a mixed cost is important, since mixed costs are common to a wide range of firms. Examples of mixed costs include electricity, heat, repairs, telephone, and maintenance.

The fixed portion of a mixed cost represents the basic, minimum charge for just having a service *ready and available* for use. The variable portion represents the charge made for *actual consumption* of the service. As one would expect, the variable element varies in proportion to the amount of the service that is consumed.

For planning purposes, how does management handle mixed costs? The ideal approach would be to take each invoice as it comes in and break it down into its fixed and variable elements. As a practical matter, even if it were possible to make this type of minute breakdown, the cost of doing so would probably be prohibitive. Analysis of mixed costs is normally done on an aggregate basis, concentrating on the past behavior of a cost at various levels of activity. If this analysis is done carefully, good approximations of the fixed and variable elements of a cost can be obtained with a minimum of effort.

We will examine three methods of breaking mixed costs down into their fixed and variable elements—the *high-low method,* the *scattergraph method,* and the *least squares method.*

The high-low method

The **high-low method** of analyzing mixed costs requires that the cost involved (for example, maintenance) be observed at both high and low levels of activity within the relevant range. The difference in cost observed at the two extremes is divided by the change in activity in order to determine the amount of variable cost involved.

To illustrate, assume that maintenance costs for the Arco Company have been observed as follows within the relevant range of 5,000 to 8,000 direct labor-hours (DLH):

Month	Direct labor-hours	Maintenance cost incurred
January	5,500	$ 745
February	7,000	850
March	5,000	700
April	6,500	820
May	7,500	960
June	8,000	1,000
July	6,000	825

Since total maintenance cost increases as the activity level increases, it seems obvious that some variable cost element is present. To separate the variable cost element from the fixed cost element, we need to relate the change in direct labor-hours between the high and low points to the change that we observe in cost:

	Direct labor-hours	Maintenance cost incurred
High point observed	8,000	$1,000
Low point observed	5,000	700
Change observed	3,000	$ 300

$$\text{Variable rate} = \frac{\text{Change in cost}}{\text{Change in activity}} = \frac{\$300}{3,000} = \$0.10 \text{ per direct labor-hour}$$

Having determined that the variable rate is 10 cents per direct labor-hour, we can now determine the amount of fixed cost present. This is done by taking total cost at *either* the high or the low point and deducting the variable cost element. In the computation below, total cost at the high point of activity is used in computing the fixed cost element:

$$\text{Fixed cost element} = \text{Total cost} - \text{Variable cost element}$$
$$= \$1,000 - (\$0.10 \times 8,000 \text{ hours})$$
$$= \$200$$

Both the variable and fixed cost elements have now been isolated. The cost of maintenance within the relevant range analyzed can be expressed as being $200 plus 10 cents per direct labor-hour. This is sometimes referred to as a **cost formula.**

$$\left.\begin{array}{c}\text{Cost formula for maintenance, over}\\\text{the relevant range of 5,000 to}\\\text{8,000 direct labor-hours}\end{array}\right\} = \begin{array}{c}\text{\$200 fixed cost} + \text{\$0.10}\\\text{per direct labor-hour}\end{array}$$

The data used in this illustration are shown graphically in Exhibit 5–8. Three things should be noted in relation to this exhibit:

1. Notice that cost is always plotted on the vertical axis and that it is represented by the letter Y. Cost is known as the **dependent variable** since the amount of cost incurred during a period will be dependent on the level of activity for the period. (That is, as the level of activity increases, total cost will also increase.)

EXHIBIT 5–8
**High-low method of cost analysis
The Arco Company—maintenance cost**

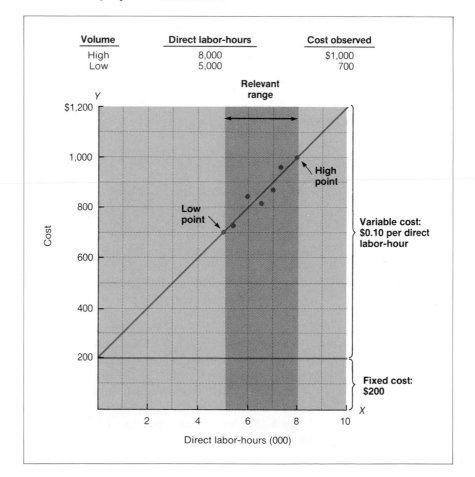

Volume	Direct labor-hours	Cost observed
High	8,000	$1,000
Low	5,000	700

2. Notice that activity (direct labor-hours in this case) is always plotted on the horizontal axis and that it is represented by the letter X. Activity is known as the **independent variable** since it controls the amount of cost that will be incurred during a period.

3. Notice that the relevant range is highlighted on the exhibit. In using a cost formula, the manager must remember that the formula will not be valid outside the relevant range from which the underlying data have been drawn.

The high-low method is very simple to apply, but it suffers from a major (and sometimes critical) defect in that it utilizes only two points in determining a cost formula. Generally, two points are not enough to produce accurate results in cost analysis work unless the points *happen* to fall in such a way as to represent a true average of all points of cost and activity. As one might suppose, only rarely will the two points in the high-low method happen to fall in just this way. For this reason, other methods of cost analysis that utilize a greater number of points will generally be more accurate than the high-low method in deriving a cost formula. If a manager chooses to use the high-low method, he or she should do so with a full awareness of the method's limitations.

The scattergraph method

In mixed cost analysis, the manager is trying to find the *average* rate of variability in a mixed cost. A more accurate way of doing this than the high-low method is to use the **scattergraph method,** which includes all points of observed cost data in the analysis through use of a graph. A graph much like the one that we used in Exhibit 5–8 is constructed, in which cost is shown on the vertical axis, and volume or rate of activity is shown on the horizontal axis. Costs observed at various levels of activity are then plotted on the graph, and a line is fitted to the plotted points. However, rather than just fitting the line to the high and low points, *all points* are considered in the placement of the line. This is done through simple visual inspection of the data, with the analyst taking care that the placement of the line is representative of all points, not just the high and low ones. Typically, the line is placed so that approximately equal numbers of points fall above and below it.

A graph of this type is known as a *scattergraph,* and the line fitted to the plotted points is known as a **regression line.** The regression line, in effect, is a line of averages, with the average variable cost per unit of activity represented by the slope of the line and the average fixed cost in total represented by the point where the regression line intersects the cost axis.

To illustrate how a scattergraph is prepared, assume that Western Company has recorded costs for water over the last eight months as follows:

Water consumed (000 gallons)	Total cost
12.	$260
15.	270
10.	230
9.	220
11.	250
13.	240
8.	220
14.	260

The observed costs for water at the various activity levels have been plotted on a graph in Exhibit 5–9, and a regression line has been fitted to the plotted data by visual inspection. Note that the regression line has been placed in such a way that approximately equal numbers of points fall above and below it.

Since the regression line strikes the cost axis at the $150 point, that amount

EXHIBIT 5–9
A completed scattergraph

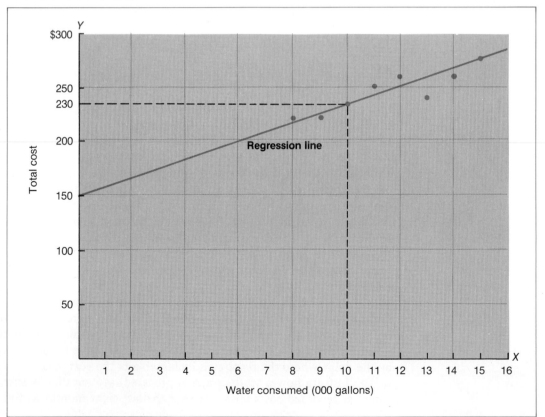

represents the fixed cost element. The variable cost element would be $8 per 1,000 gallons of water consumed, computed as follows:

Total cost observed for 10,000 gallons of water consumed
  (a point falling on the regression line in Exhibit 5–9). $230
Less fixed cost element   150
Variable cost element . . . . $ 80

    $80 ÷ 10,000 gallons = $0.008 per gallon, or $8 per thousand gallons.

Thus, the cost formula for water would be $150 per month plus $8 per thousand gallons of water consumed.

A scattergraph can be an extremely useful tool in the hands of an experienced analyst. Quirks in cost behavior due to strikes, bad weather, breakdowns, and so on, become immediately apparent to the trained observer, and he or she can make appropriate adjustment to the data in fitting the regression line. Many cost analysts would argue that a scattergraph should be the beginning point in all cost analyses, due to the benefits to be gained from having the data visually available in graph form.

The least squares method

The **least squares method** is a more sophisticated approach to the scatter-graph idea. Rather than fitting a regression line through the scattergraph data by simple visual inspection, the least squares method fits the line by statistical analysis.

The least squares method is based on computations that find their foundation in the equation for a straight line. A straight line can be expressed in equation form as:

$$Y = a + bX$$

with a as the fixed element and b as the degree of variability, or the slope of the line. From this basic equation, and given a set of observations, n, two simultaneous linear equations can be developed that will fit a regression line to a linear array of data. The equations are:[1]

$$\Sigma XY = a\Sigma X + b\Sigma X^2 \qquad\qquad (1)$$
$$\Sigma Y = na + b\Sigma X \qquad\qquad\qquad (2)$$

where

    a = fixed cost
    b = variable rate
    n = number of observations
    X = activity measure (hours, etc.)
    Y = total mixed cost observed

---

[1] The Appendix contains an alternative approach to the least squares method.

An example of least squares The application of the least squares method can best be seen through a detailed example. Let us assume that a company is anxious to break its power (electrical) costs down into basic variable and fixed cost elements. Over the past year, power costs *(Y)* have been observed as shown in the tabulation below. The number of hours of machine time logged *(X)* in incurring these costs is also shown in the tabulation.

Month	Machine-hours (000) (X)	Power costs (Y)	XY	X²
January	9	$ 3,000	$ 27,000	81
February	8	2,500	20,000	64
March	9	2,900	26,100	81
April	10	2,900	29,000	100
May	12	3,600	43,200	144
June	13	3,400	44,200	169
July.	11	3,200	35,200	121
August	11	3,300	36,300	121
September	10	3,000	30,000	100
October	8	2,600	20,800	64
November	7	2,300	16,100	49
December	8	2,600	20,800	64
	116	$35,300	$348,700	1,158

Substituting these amounts in the two linear equations given earlier, we have:

$$\Sigma XY = a\Sigma X + b\Sigma X^2 \qquad (1)$$
$$\Sigma Y = na + b\Sigma X \qquad (2)$$

$$\$348,700 = 116a + 1,158b \qquad (1)$$
$$\$\ 35,300 = 12a + 116b \qquad (2)$$

In order to solve the equations, it will be necessary to eliminate one of the terms. The *a* term can be eliminated by multiplying equation (1) by 12, by multiplying equation (2) by 116, and then by subtracting equation (2) from equation (1). These steps are shown below:

Multiply equation (1) by 12: $\$4,184,400 = 1,392a + 13,896b$
Multiply equation (2) by 116: $\$4,094,800 = 1,392a + 13,456b$
Subtract (2) from (1): $\$89,600 = \qquad\qquad 440b$
$\$203.64 = b$

Therefore, the variable rate for power cost is $203.64 for each thousand machine-hours of operating time (or $0.20364 per hour). The fixed cost of power can be obtained by substituting the value for term *b* in either equation (1) or equation (2). We will use equation (2) since the numbers are smaller and easier to deal with:

$$\$35,300 = 12a + 116b \qquad (2)$$
$$\$35,300 = 12a + 116(\$203.64)$$
$$\$35,300 = 12a + \$23,622.24$$
$$\$11,677.76 = 12a$$
$$\$973.15 = a$$

The fixed cost for power is $973.15 per month. The cost formula for the mixed cost is therefore $973.15 per month plus $203.64 per thousand machine-hours worked.

$$\left. \begin{array}{l} \text{Cost formula for power over} \\ \text{the relevant range of 7,000} \\ \text{to 13,000 machine-hours} \end{array} \right\} = \begin{array}{l} \$973.15 \text{ fixed cost} + \$203.64 \\ \text{per thousand machine-} \\ \text{hours } (\$0.20364 \text{ per hour}) \end{array}$$

In terms of the linear equation $Y = a + bX$, the cost formula can be expressed as:

$$Y = \$973.15 + \$203.64X$$

where activity (X) is expressed in thousands of machine-hours. To show how the cost formula is used for planning purposes, if it is expected that 10,500 machine-hours will be worked during the coming month, expected power costs will be:

Variable costs:
10.5 thousand machine-hours × $203.64 . .	$2,138.22
Fixed costs	973.15
Total expected power costs	$3,111.37

What does least squares mean? The term *least squares* means that the sum of the squares of the deviations from the plotted points to the regression line *is smaller* than would be obtained from any other line fitted to the data. This idea can be illustrated as shown in Exhibit 5–10.

Notice from the exhibit that the deviations from the plotted points to the regression line are measured vertically on the graph. They are not measured perpendicular to the regression line. Least squares will have been attained when $\Sigma(Y - Y_1)^2$ is at the lowest possible figure. At the point of least squares, the best possible fit of a regression line to the plotted points will have been achieved in terms of slope and placement of the line.

The use of judgment in cost analysis

Although a cost formula has the appearance of exactness, the user should recognize that the breakdown of any mixed cost by any of the three techniques that we have discussed involves a substantial amount of estimating. The breakdowns represent *good approximations* of the fixed and variable elements

EXHIBIT 5–10
The concept of least squares

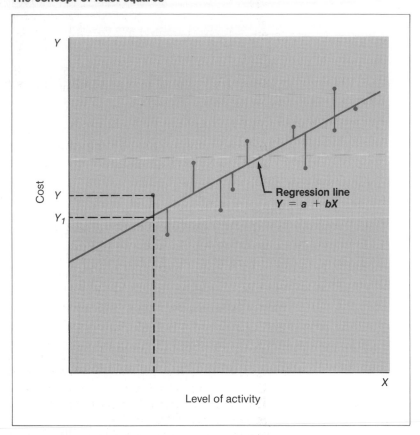

involved; they should not be construed as being precise analyses. Managers must be ready to step in at any point in their analysis of a cost and to adjust their computations for judgment factors that in their view are critical to a proper understanding of the mixed cost involved. However, the fact that computations are not exact, and involve estimates and judgment factors, does not prevent data from being useful and meaningful in decision making. The managers who wait to make a decision until they have perfect data available will rarely have an opportunity to demonstrate their decision-making ability.

Multiple regression analysis

In all of our computations involving mixed costs, we have assumed a single causative factor as the basis for the behavior of the variable element. That causative factor has been the volume or rate of some activity, such as direct labor-hours, machine-hours, production, or sales. This assumption is acceptable for many mixed costs, but in some situations there may be more than one causative factor involved in the behavior of the variable element. For example, in a shipping department the cost of freight-out might depend on both the number of units shipped and the weight of the units as dual causative factors. In a situation such as this, the equation for a simple regression would have to be expanded to include the additional variable:

$$Y = a + bX + cW$$

where W = the weight of a unit and c = the factor of variability. When dealing with an expanded equation such as this one, the simple regression analysis that we have been doing is no longer adequate. A **multiple regression analysis** is necessary. Although the added variable or variables will make the computations more complex, the principles involved are the same as in a simple regression such as we have been doing. Because of the complexity of the computations involved, multiple regression is generally done with the aid of a computer.

Engineering approach to cost study

Some firms use the engineering approach to the study of cost behavior. Essentially, this approach involves a quantitative analysis of what cost behavior should be, based on the industrial engineer's evaluation of the production methods to be used, the materials specifications, labor needs, equipment needs, efficiency of production, power consumption, and so on. The engineering approach must be used in those situations where no past experience is available on activity and costs. In addition, it is often used in tandem with the methods we have discussed above in order to sharpen the accuracy of cost analysis. An NAA (National Association of Accountants) research report of actual business practices describes the use of the engineering approach as follows:

> The industrial engineering approach to determination of how costs should vary with volume proceeds by systematic study of materials, labor, services, and facilities needed at varying volumes. The aim is to find the best way to obtain the desired production. These studies generally make use of past experience, but it is used as a guide or as a check upon the results obtained by direct study of the production methods and facilities. Where no past experience is available, as with a new product, plant, or method, this approach can be applied to estimate the changes in cost that will accompany changes in volume.[2]

THE CONTRIBUTION FORMAT

Once the manager has separated costs into fixed and variable elements, what does he or she do with the data? To answer this question will require

---

[2] National Association of Accountants, Research Report No. 16, "The Analysis of Cost-Volume-Profit Relationships" (New York, 1960), p. 17.

most of the remainder of this book, since virtually everything the manager does rests in some way on an understanding of cost behavior. One immediate and very significant application of the ideas we have developed, however, is found in a new format to the income statement known as the **contribution approach.** The unique thing about the contribution approach is that it provides the manager with an income statement geared directly to cost behavior.

Why a new income statement format?

The **traditional approach** to the income statement, such as illustrated in Chapter 2 and such as you studied in financial accounting, is not organized in terms of cost behavior. Rather, it is organized in a "functional" format—emphasizing the functions of production, administration, and sales in the classification and presentation of cost data. No attempt is made to distinguish between the behavior of costs included under each functional heading. Under the heading "Administrative expense," for example, one can expect to find both variable and fixed costs lumped together.

Although an income statement prepared in the functional format may be useful for external reporting purposes, it has serious limitations so far as usefulness internally to the manager is concerned. Internally, the manager needs cost data organized in a format that will facilitate the carrying out of major responsibilities of planning, control, and decision making. As we shall see in chapters ahead, these responsibilities are discharged most effectively when cost data are available in a fixed and variable format. The contribution approach to the income statement has been developed in response to this need.

The contribution approach

Exhibit 5–11 presents a model of the contribution approach to the income statement, along with the traditional approach with which you are already familiar.

Notice that the contribution approach separates costs into fixed and variable categories, first deducting variable expenses from sales to obtain what is known as the *contribution margin.* The term **contribution margin** means what remains from total sales revenues, after deducting variable expenses, that can be used *to contribute* toward the covering of fixed expenses and then toward profits for the period.

The contribution approach to the income statement is widely used as an internal planning and decision-making tool. Its emphasis on costs by behavior facilitates cost-volume-profit analysis, such as we shall be doing in the following chapter. The approach is also very useful in appraisal of management performance, in segmented reporting of profit data, in budgeting, and in organizing data pertinent to all kinds of special decisions, such as product line analysis, pricing, use of scarce resources, and make or buy analyses. All of these topics are covered in later chapters.

EXHIBIT 5–11
Comparison of the contribution income statement with the traditional income statement

Traditional approach (costs organized by function)			Contribution approach (costs organized by behavior)			
Sales		$12,000	Sales.			$12,000
Less cost of goods sold . .		6,000*	Less variable expenses:			
Gross margin.		6,000	Variable production . . .	$2,000		
Less operating expenses:			Variable selling	600		
Selling	$3,100*		Variable administrative . .	400	3,000	
Administrative	1,900*	5,000	Contribution margin			9,000
Net income		$ 1,000	Less fixed expenses:			
			Fixed production	4,000		
			Fixed selling	2,500		
			Fixed administrative . . .	1,500	8,000	
			Net income.			$ 1,000

* Contains both variable and fixed expenses. This is the income statement for a *manufacturing* firm; thus, when the income statement is placed in the contribution format, the ''cost of goods sold'' figure is divided between variable production costs and fixed production costs. If this were the income statement for a *merchandising* firm (which simply purchases completed goods from a supplier), then the ''cost of goods sold'' would *all* be variable.

SUMMARY

Managers analyze cost behavior in order to have a basis for predicting how costs will respond to changes in activity levels throughout the organization. We have looked at three types of cost behavior—variable, fixed, and mixed. In the case of mixed costs, we have studied three methods of breaking a mixed cost into its basic variable and fixed elements. The high-low method is the simplest of the three, having as its underlying assumption that the rate of variability is constant per unit of activity. When the rate of variability in a mixed cost is not constant, an average rate of variability must be computed. This can be done by either the scattergraph method or the least squares method. Both methods require the construction of a regression line, the slope of which represents the average rate of variability in the mixed cost being analyzed. The least squares method is the more accurate of the two in that it uses statistical analysis to fit a regression line to an array of data.

Managers use costs organized by behavior as a basis for many decisions. To facilitate this use, costs are often prepared in a contribution format. The unique thing about the contribution format is that it classifies costs on the income statement by cost behavior rather than by the functions of production, administration, and sales.

KEY TERMS FOR REVIEW

Activity base A measure of effort, such as production, sales, or miles driven by salespersons, that operates as a causal factor in the incurrence of variable costs.

178

Committed fixed costs Those fixed costs that relate to the investment in plant, equipment, and the basic organizational structure of a firm.

Contribution approach An income statement format that is geared to cost behavior in that costs are separated into variable and fixed categories rather than being separated according to the functions of production, sales, and administration.

Contribution margin The amount remaining from sales revenues after variable expenses have been deducted.

Cost formula A quantitative expression of the fixed and variable elements of a cost. This expression is generally in the form of the linear equation $Y = a + bX$.

Cost structure The relative proportion of fixed, variable, and mixed costs found within an organization.

Curvilinear costs The economist's expression of the relationship between cost and activity in an organization.

Dependent variable Total cost is the dependent variable as represented by the letter Y in the equation $Y = a + bX$.

Discretionary fixed costs Those fixed costs that arise from annual decisions by management to spend in certain fixed cost areas, such as advertising and research.

High-low method A method of breaking a mixed cost into its variable and fixed elements by fitting a regression line to the high and low points in a group of observed data.

Independent variable Activity is the independent variable as represented by the letter X in the equation $Y = a + bX$.

Least squares method A method of breaking a mixed cost into its variable and fixed elements by use of statistical analysis.

Mixed cost A cost that contains both variable and fixed cost elements. Also see *Semivariable cost.*

Multiple regression analysis An analytical method required in those situations where more than one causative factor is involved in the behavior of the variable element of a mixed cost.

Regression line A line fitted to a group of plotted points such that the slope of the line represents the average variable cost per unit of activity and the point where the line intersects the cost axis represents the average total fixed cost.

Relevant range That range of activity over which assumptions relative to variable and fixed cost behavior are valid.

Scattergraph method A method of breaking a mixed cost into its variable and fixed cost elements by fitting a regression line to a group of plotted points by visual inspection.

Semivariable cost A cost that contains both variable and fixed cost elements. Also see *Mixed cost.*

Step-variable cost A cost (such as the cost of a maintenance worker) that is obtainable only in large pieces and that increases and decreases only in response to fairly wide changes in the activity level.

Traditional approach An income statement format in which costs are organized and presented according to the functions of production, sales, and administration.

REVIEW PROBLEM ON COST BEHAVIOR

Consider the following costs of X Company over the relevant range of 5,000 to 20,000 units produced:

	Units produced			
	5,000	10,000	15,000	20,000
Variable costs	$ 20,000	$?	$?	$?
Fixed costs	180,000	?	?	?
Total costs	$200,000	$?	$?	$?
Cost per unit:				
Variable	$?	$?	$?	$?
Fixed	?	?	?	?
Total cost per unit	$?	$?	$?	$?

Required: Compute the missing amounts.

Solution: The variable cost per unit of product can be computed as:

$$\$20,000 \div 5,000 \text{ units} = \$4 \text{ per unit}$$

Therefore, in accordance with the behavior of variable and fixed costs, the missing amounts are:

	Units produced			
	5,000	10,000	15,000	20,000
Variable costs	$ 20,000	$ 40,000	$ 60,000	$ 80,000
Fixed costs	180,000	180,000	180,000	180,000
Total costs	$200,000	$220,000	$240,000	$260,000
Cost per unit:				
Variable	$ 4	$ 4	$ 4	$ 4
Fixed	36	18	12	9
Total cost per unit	$ 40	$ 22	$ 16	$ 13

Observe that the variable costs increase in total proportionately with increases in the number of units produced but remain constant at $4 on a per unit basis. On the other hand, the fixed costs by definition do not change in total with changes in the level of output. They remain constant at $180,000. With increases in production, however, they decrease on a per unit basis, dropping from $36 per unit when 5,000 units are produced to only $9 per unit when 20,000 units are produced. *Because of this troublesome aspect of fixed costs, they are most easily (and most safely) dealt with on a total basis, rather than on a unit basis, in cost analysis work.*

APPENDIX: ALTERNATIVE APPROACH TO LEAST SQUARES

Some managers prefer an alternative approach to the least squares method that does not require use of the equations given in the chapter. Assume that a firm wishes to develop a cost formula for its maintenance expense. The company has determined that the variable portion of maintenance is incurred as a function of the number of machine-hours worked. Data on machine-hours and attendant maintenance expense for the first six months of 19x1 are given in Exhibit 5–12. The exhibit also contains computations showing how a mixed cost can be broken down into its basic variable and fixed cost elements by the alternative approach.

As shown in the exhibit, the cost formula for maintenance expense is $100 fixed cost plus 20 cents per machine-hour. Or, it can be expressed in equation form as:

$$Y = \$100 + \$0.20X$$

There are six basic steps to computing a cost formula by this method. The reader should trace these six steps back through the computations in Exhibit 5–12.

Step 1: Determine the average level of activity $(\overline{X})$ and the average amount of cost $(\overline{Y})$ for the period of time being analyzed. In Exhibit 5–12, machine-hours average 500 hours per month (3,000 hours ÷ 6 months = 500 hours) and power costs average $200 per month ($1,200 ÷ 6 months = $200).

EXHIBIT 5–12

Alternative approach to least squares analysis

Month	Machine-hours (X)	Maintenance expense (Y)	Difference from average Machine-hours (X')	Difference from average Maintenance expense (Y')	X'Y'	X'²
January	400	$ 180	−100	−$20	+$ 2,000	10,000
February	575	215	+ 75	+ 15	+ 1,125	5,625
March	350	170	−150	− 30	+ 4,500	22,500
April	475	195	− 25	− 5	+ 125	625
May	550	210	+ 50	+ 10	+ 500	2,500
June	650	230	+150	+ 30	+ 4,500	22,500
Total	3,000	$1,200	−0−	−0−	$12,750	63,750
Average	500 (X̄)	$ 200 (Ȳ)				

Variable rate: $\dfrac{\Sigma X'Y'}{\Sigma X'^2} = \dfrac{\$12,750}{63,750} = \$0.20$ per machine-hour

Total fixed cost: $\overline{Y} = a + b\overline{X}$
$\$200 = a + \$0.20(500 \text{ hours})$
$a = \$200 - \$100$
$a = \$100$

Step 2: Compute the difference between the actual activity for each month and the average activity computed in step 1, and enter this difference in a column labeled X'. Then compute the difference between the actual cost for each month and the average cost, and enter this difference in a second column labeled Y'. Use plus (+) and minus (−) notations to signify whether monthly amounts are greater or less than the average.

Step 3: For each month, multiply the amount in the X' column times the amount in the Y' column and enter the result in a column labeled $X'Y'$. (In obtaining the data for the $X'Y'$ column, remember that algebraically a minus times a minus is a plus, but a minus times a plus is a minus.)

Step 4: Square the X' amount for each month, and enter the result in a new column labeled X'^2.

Step 5: Compute the variable rate by the formula:

$$\frac{\Sigma X'Y'}{\Sigma X'^2} = \text{Variable rate}$$

Step 6: Compute the total fixed cost by substituting in the equation:

$$\overline{Y} = a + b\overline{X}$$

where $\overline{Y}$ = the average cost observed, a = the total fixed cost that you are seeking, b = the variable rate computed in step 5, and $\overline{X}$ = the average activity level observed.

QUESTIONS

5–1. Distinguish between (a) a variable cost, (b) a fixed cost, and (c) a mixed cost.

5–2. What effect does an increase in volume have on—
   a. Unit fixed costs?
   b. Unit variable costs?
   c. Total fixed costs?
   d. Total variable costs?

5–3. Define the following terms: (a) cost behavior and (b) relevant range.

5–4. What is meant by an "activity base" when dealing with variable costs? Give several examples of activity bases.

5–5. Distinguish between (a) a variable cost, (b) a mixed cost, and (c) a step-variable cost. Chart the three costs on a graph, with activity plotted horizontally and cost plotted vertically.

5–6. The accountant often assumes a strictly linear relationship between cost and volume. How can this practice be defended in face of the fact that many variable costs are curvilinear in form?

5–7. Distinguish between discretionary fixed costs and committed fixed costs.

5–8. Classify the following fixed costs as normally being either committed (C) or discretionary (D):

a. Depreciation on buildings.
b. Advertising.
c. Research.
d. Insurance.
e. The president's salary.
f. Management development and training.

5–9. What factors are contributing to the trend toward increasing numbers of fixed costs, and why is this trend significant from a managerial accounting point of view?

5–10. Does the concept of the relevant range have application to fixed costs? Explain.

5–11. What is the major disadvantage of the high-low method? Under what conditions would this analytical method provide an accurate cost formula?

5–12. What methods are available for determining the average rate of variability in a mixed cost? Which method is most accurate? Why?

5–13. What is meant by a regression line? Give the general formula for a regression line. Which term represents the variable cost? The fixed cost?

5–14. Once a regression line has been drawn, how does one determine the fixed cost element? The variable cost element?

5–15. What is meant by the term *least squares?*

5–16. What is the difference between single regression analysis and multiple regression analysis?

5–17. What is the difference between the contribution approach to the income statement and the traditional approach to the income statement?

5–18. What is meant by contribution margin? How is it computed?

EXERCISES

E5–1. The number of X rays taken and X ray costs over the last nine months in Beverly Hospital are given below:

Month	X rays taken	X ray costs
January	6,250	$28,000
February	7,000	29,000
March	5,000	23,000
April	4,250	20,000
May	4,500	22,000
June	3,000	17,000
July	3,750	18,000
August	5,500	24,000
September	5,750	26,000

Required: 1. Using the high-low method, determine the formula for X ray costs.
2. What X ray costs would you expect to be incurred during a month in which 4,600 X rays are taken?

E5–2. Refer to the data in Exercise 5–1.

Required: 1. Prepare a scattergraph using the data from Exercise 5–1. Plot cost on the vertical axis and activity on the horizontal axis. Fit a regression line to your plotted points by visual inspection.

2. What is the approximate monthly fixed cost for X rays? The approximate variable cost per X ray taken?
3. Scrutinize the points on your graph, and explain why the high-low method would or would not yield an accurate cost formula in this situation.

E5–3. Speedy Parcel Service operates a fleet of delivery trucks in a large metropolitan area. A careful study by the company's cost analyst has determined that if a truck is driven 120,000 miles during a year, the operating cost is 11.6 cents per mile. If a truck is driven only 80,000 miles during a year, the operating cost increases to 13.6 cents per mile.

Required:
1. Using the high-low method, determine the variable and fixed cost elements of the annual cost of truck operation.
2. Express the variable and fixed costs in the form $Y = a + bX$.
3. If a truck were driven 100,000 miles during a year, what total cost would you expect to be incurred?

E5–4. Perkins Company experiences considerable fluctuation in its utilities costs from month to month according to the number of machine-hours worked in its factory. The company has plotted utilities cost at various levels of activity on a graph, and the plotted points indicate that total utilities cost is a mixed cost in the form $Y = a + bX$. Machine-hours of activity and total utilities cost over the last six months are given below:

Month	Machine-hours (000)	Total utilities cost
January	9	$14,000
February	12	17,000
March	16	20,000
April	21	23,000
May	18	21,000
June	14	19,000

Required: Using the least squares method, determine the cost formula for utilities cost. It is not necessary to prepare a graph. (The variable rate you compute will be the rate per thousand machine-hours of activity. It can be left in this form, or you can convert it to a per hour basis by dividing the variable rate you compute by 1,000.)

E5–5. Laxal Company manufactures and sells a single product. The company typically operates within a relevant range of 60,000 to 100,000 units produced and sold each year. A partially completed schedule of the company's total and per unit costs over this range is given below:

	Units produced and sold		
	60,000	80,000	100,000
Total variable costs	$150,000	?	?
Total fixed costs	360,000	?	?
Total costs	$510,000	?	?
Cost per unit:			
Variable cost	?	?	?
Fixed cost	?	?	?
Total cost per unit	?	?	?

Required:
1. Complete the schedule of the company's total and unit costs above.
2. Assume that the company produces and sells 90,000 units during a year. The selling price is $7.50 per unit. Prepare an income statement in the contribution format for the year.

E5–6. The data below have been taken from the cost records of the Atlanta Processing Company. The data relate to the cost of operating one of the company's processing facilities at various levels of activity:

Month	Units processed	Total cost
January	8,000	$14,000
February	4,500	10,000
March	7,000	12,500
April	9,000	15,500
May	3,750	10,000
June	6,000	12,500
July	3,000	8,500
August	5,000	11,500

Required:
1. Prepare a scattergraph by plotting the above data on a graph. Plot cost on the vertical axis and activity on the horizontal axis. Fit a regression line to your plotted points by visual inspection.
2. What is the approximate monthly fixed cost? The approximate variable cost per unit processed? Show computations.

E5–7. Resort Inns, Inc., has a total of 2,000 rooms in its nationwide chain of motels. On the average, 80 percent of the rooms are occupied each month. The company's operating costs are $7 per occupied room per day at this occupancy level, assuming a 30-day month. This $7 cost figure contains both variable and fixed cost elements. During October, the occupancy rate was only 65 percent. Some $318,000 in operating costs were incurred during the month.

Required:
1. Determine the variable cost per occupied room per day.
2. Determine the total fixed operating costs per month.
3. Assume an occupancy rate of 70 percent. What total operating costs would you expect the company to incur?

E5–8. The management of Micro Devices, Inc., has observed selling costs in the company to be as follows over the last nine months:

Month	Units sold (000)	Selling costs
January	8	$ 70,000
February	10	73,000
March	11	76,000
April	12	81,000
May	14	84,000
June	19	98,000
July	23	107,000
August	21	102,000
September	17	92,000

The Micro Devices management would like to know the amount of variable selling cost per unit and the total fixed selling cost per month.

Required:
1. Using the least squares method, compute the variable selling cost per unit sold and the total fixed cost per month. (Since the "Units sold" above are in thousands of units, the variable rate you compute will also be in thousands of units. To convert your answer to a variable rate per unit, divide it by 1,000.)
2. Express the cost data in (1) above in the form $Y = a + bX$.
3. If the company sells 18,000 units next month, what would be the expected total selling costs? Show computations.

E5-9.   The Alpine House, Inc., is a large retailer of winter sports equipment. An income statement for the company's Ski Department for the most recent quarter is presented below:

THE ALPINE HOUSE, INC.
Income Statement—Ski Department
For the Quarter Ended March 31, 19x5

Sales		$150,000
Less cost of goods sold		90,000
Gross margin		60,000
Less operating expenses:		
Selling expenses	$30,000	
Administrative expenses	10,000	40,000
Net income		$ 20,000

Skis sell, on the average, for $150 per pair. Variable selling expenses are $10 per pair of skis sold. The remaining selling expenses are fixed. The administrative expenses are 20 percent variable and 80 percent fixed. The company does not manufacture its own skis; it purchases them from a supplier for $90 per pair.

Required:
1. Prepare an income statement for the quarter, using the contribution approach.
2. For every pair of skis sold during the quarter, what was the contribution toward covering fixed expenses and toward earning profits?

PROBLEMS

P5-10.   **High-low method; contribution income statement.**   Over the years, Franklin Company, a merchandising firm, has kept track of revenues and expenses at various levels of monthly sales. Revenues and expenses for three recent months are given below:

FRANKLIN COMPANY
Income Statements at Various Levels of Sales

	April	May	June
Sales in units	2,000	2,500	3,000
Sales revenue	$200,000	$250,000	$300,000
Less cost of goods sold	80,000	100,000	120,000
Gross margin	120,000	150,000	180,000
Less operating expenses:			
Shipping expense	30,000	33,000	36,000
Advertising expense	25,000	25,000	25,000
Salaries and commissions	46,000	50,000	54,000
Depreciation expense	12,000	12,000	12,000
Total operating expenses	113,000	120,000	127,000
Net income before income taxes	$ 7,000	$ 30,000	$ 53,000

Required:
1. Identify each of the company's expenses (including cost of goods sold) as being either variable, fixed, or mixed.
2. By use of the high-low method, separate each mixed expense into variable and fixed elements. State the cost formula for each mixed expense.
3. Redo the Company's income statement at the 2,500-unit level of activity by placing the revenue and expense data in the contribution format.

P5–11. **High-low method of cost analysis.** Marsden Company's total factory overhead costs fluctuate considerably from year to year according to the number of direct labor-hours worked in its factory. These costs at high and at low levels of activity for recent years are given below:

	Level of activity	
	Low	**High**
Direct labor-hours.	60,000	80,000
Total factory overhead costs	$244,000	$282,000

The factory overhead costs above consist of indirect materials, rent, and maintenance. The company has analyzed these costs at the 60,000 direct labor-hours level of activity and has determined that at this activity level these costs exist in the following proportions:

Indirect materials (V)	$ 90,000 .625
Rent (F)	100,000
Maintenance (M)	54,000 .375
Total factory overhead costs	$244,000

V = variable; F = Fixed; M = mixed.

For planning purposes, the company wants to break down the maintenance cost into its variable and fixed cost elements.

Required:
1. Determine how much of the $282,000 factory overhead cost at the high level of activity above consists of maintenance cost. (Hint: To do this, it may be helpful to first determine how much of the $282,000 consists of indirect materials and rent. Think about the behavior of variable and fixed costs within the relevant range!)
2. By means of the high-low method of cost analysis, determine the cost formula for maintenance.
3. Express the company's maintenance costs in the linear equation form $Y = a + bX$.
4. What *total* overhead costs would you expect the company to incur at an operating level of 70,000 direct labor-hours?

P5–12. **Least squares method of cost analysis; graphing.** State University operates a large evening school program and requires its academic departments to report student credit hours and operating costs on a monthly basis. Data reported by the art department over the last five months follow:

Month	Student credit hours	Operating costs
September.	750	$13,500
October.	850	14,500
November	500	12,750
December	600	12,500
January	400	11,750
	3,100	$65,000

Required: 1. Compute the variable operating cost per student credit hour and the total fixed operating cost per month for the art department. Use the least squares method.
2. Express the cost data derived in (1) above in the linear equation form $Y = a + bX$. How much cost would you expect the art department to incur if 700 student credit hours were reported in a month? (Round to the nearest dollar.)
3. Prepare a scattergraph, and fit a regression line to the plotted points using the cost formula derived in (1) above.

P5–13.   Least squares analysis; contribution income statement.   "If we expect to stay competitive, we need better information for planning purposes and for control of our costs," said Mark Davis, president of Argyle Company. "The industry literature I've been reading lately says that the way to get better information is to use a contribution-type income statement that separates fixed and variable costs." Accordingly, Mr. Davis has directed the accounting department to prepare the following analysis:

Cost	Cost formula
Cost of goods sold	$28 per unit
Sales commissions . . .	12% of sales
Advertising expense.	$150,000 per month
Administrative salaries	$80,000 per month
Billing expense	?
Depreciation expense	$31,000 per month

The accounting department feels that billing expense is a mixed cost, containing both fixed and variable cost elements. A tabulation has been made of billing expense and sales over the last several months, as follows:

Month	Units sold (000)	Billing expense
January	8	$15,200
February	10	17,000
March	13	19,400
April	16	21,800
May	14	20,000
June	11	18,200

Mr. Davis would like a cost formula developed for billing expense so that a contribution-type income statement can be prepared for management's use.

Required: 1. Using the least squares method, derive a cost formula for billing expense. (Since the "Units sold" above are in thousands of units, the variable rate you compute will also be in thousands of units. It can be left in this form, or you can convert your variable rate to a per unit basis by dividing it by 1,000.)

2. Assume that the company plans to sell 15,000 units during July at a selling price of $60 per unit. Prepare a budgeted income statement for the month, using the contribution format.

P5–14. **High-low method of cost analysis.** Golden Company's total overhead costs at various levels of activity are presented below:

Month	Machine-hours	Total overhead costs
March	50,000	$174,000
April	40,000	150,200
May.	60,000	197,800
June	70,000	221,600

Assume that the overhead costs above consist of utilities, supervisory salaries, and maintenance. The proportion of these costs at the 40,000 machine-hour level of activity is:

Utilities (V)	$ 52,000
Supervisory salaries (F)	40,000
Maintenance (M)	58,200
Total overhead costs	$150,200

V = variable; F = fixed; M = mixed.

The company wants to break down the maintenance cost into its basic variable and fixed cost elements.

Required: 1. As shown above, overhead costs in June amounted to $221,600. Determine how much of this consisted of maintenance cost. (Hint: To do this, it may be helpful to first determine how much of the $221,600 consisted of utilities and supervisory salaries. Think about the behavior of variable and fixed costs within the relevant range!)
2. By means of the high-low method, determine the cost formula for maintenance.
3. Express the company's total overhead costs in the linear equation form $Y = a + bX$.
4. What total overhead costs would you expect to be incurred at an operating activity level of 45,000 machine-hours?

P5–15. **Identifying cost patterns.** Below are a number of cost behavior patterns that might be found in a company's cost structure. The vertical axis on each graph represents cost, and the horizontal axis on each graph represents level of activity (volume).

Required: 1. For each of the following situations, identify the graph that illustrates the cost pattern involved. Any graph may be used more than once.
   a. Cost of raw materials, where the cost decreases by 5 cents per unit for each of the first 100 units purchased, after which it remains constant at $2.50 per unit.
   b. Electricity bill—a flat fixed charge, plus a variable cost after a certain number of kilowatt-hours are used.
   c. City water bill, which is computed as follows:

First 1,000,000 gallons or less	$1,000 flat fee
Next 10,000 gallons.	0.003 per gallon used
Next 10,000 gallons.	0.006 per gallon used
Next 10,000 gallons.	0.009 per gallon used
Etc.	Etc.

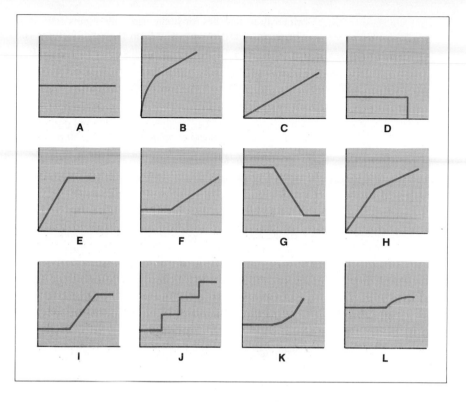

d. Depreciation of equipment, where the amount is computed by the straight-line method. When the depreciation rate was established, it was anticipated that the obsolescence factor would be greater than the wear and tear factor.

e. Rent on a factory building donated by the city, where the agreement calls for a fixed fee payment unless 200,000 labor hours are worked, in which case no rent need be paid.

f. Salaries of maintenance workers, where one maintenance worker is needed for every 1,000 hours of machine-hours or less (that is, 0 to 1,000 hours requires one maintenance worker, 1,001 to 2,000 hours requires two maintenance workers, etc.)

g. Cost of raw material used.

h. Rent on a factory building donated by the county, where the agreement calls for rent of $100,000 less $1 for each direct labor-hour worked in excess of 200,000 hours, but a minimum rental payment of $20,000 must be paid.

i. Use of a machine under a lease, where a minimum charge of $1,000 is paid for up to 400 hours of machine time. After 400 hours of machine time, an additional charge of $2 per hour is paid up to a maximum charge of $2,000 per period.

2. How would a knowledge of cost behavior patterns such as those above be of help to a manager in analyzing the cost structure of his firm?

(CPA, adapted)

P5–16. **Contribution versus traditional income statement.** The House of Organs, Inc., purchases organs from a well-known manufacturer and distributes them at a retail level, primarily to families for home use. The organs sell, on the average, for $3,500 each. The average cost of an organ from the manufacturer is $2,250.

The House of Organs, Inc., has always kept careful records of its costs. The costs that the company incurs in a typical month are presented below:

Costs	Cost formula
Selling:	
Advertising	$4,000 per month
Adjustment and tuning of delivered organs	$30 per organ sold
Freight on delivered organs.	$75 per organ sold
Insurance on delivered organs.	$90 per organ sold
Sales salaries	$2,000 per month, plus 4% of sales dollars
Depreciation.	$3,000 per month
Utilities.	$600 per month
Administrative:	
Salaries	$5,000 per month
Depreciation.	$900 per month
Clerical.	$800 per month, plus $15 per organ sold

During December 19x3, the company sold and delivered 40 organs.

Required:

1. Prepare an income statement for the month of December 19x3, using the traditional format, with costs organized by function.
2. Redo (1), this time using the contribution format, with costs organized by behavior. Show costs and revenues on both a total and a per unit basis down through contribution margin.
3. Refer to the income statement you prepared in (2). Why might it be misleading to show the fixed costs on a per unit basis?

P5–17. **Scattergraph and least squares.** In the past, the Big Piney Resort has had great difficulty in predicting its costs at various levels of activity through the year. The reason is that the company has never attempted to study its cost structure by analyzing cost behavior patterns. The president has now become convinced that such an analysis is necessary if the company is to maintain its profits and its competitive position. Accordingly, an analysis of cost behavior patterns has been undertaken.

The company has managed to identify variable and fixed costs in all areas of its operation except for food services. Costs in this area do not seem to exhibit either a strictly variable or a strictly fixed pattern. Food costs over the past several months, along with the number of meals served, are given below:

Month	Number of meals served (000)	Total food cost
January.	4	$18,000
February	5	21,000
March	6	23,700
April.	10	33,000
May.	12	35,000
June.	11	32,900
July.	9	30,000
August.	8	26,000
September	7	27,000

The president feels that the costs above must contain a mixture of variable and fixed cost elements. He has assigned you the responsibility of determining whether this is correct.

Required: 1.   Prepare a scattergraph using the data given above. Place cost on the vertical axis and activity (meals served) on the horizontal axis. Fit a regression line to the plotted points by simple visual inspection.
2.   Is the president correct in assuming that food costs contain both variable and fixed cost elements? If so, what is the approximate total fixed cost and the approximate variable cost per meal served?
3.   By use of the least squares method, determine the variable and fixed cost elements in total food cost. (Since "Number of meals served" is in thousands of meals, the variable rate you compute will also be in thousands of meals. It can be left in this form, or you can convert your variable rate to a per meal basis by dividing it by 1,000.)
4.   From the data determined in (3) above, express the cost formula for food in linear equation form.

P5–18.   **Least squares analysis; contribution income statement.**   The Alden Company has decided to use the contribution approach to the income statement internally for planning purposes. The company has analyzed its expenses and developed the following cost formulas:

Cost	Cost formula
Cost of goods sold	$20 per unit sold
Advertising expense.	$170,000 per quarter
Sales commissions	5% of sales
Administrative salaries	$80,000 per quarter
Shipping expense	?
Depreciation expense	$50,000 per quarter

Management has concluded that shipping expense is a mixed cost, containing both variable and fixed cost elements. Units sold and the related shipping expense over the last eight quarters are given below:

Quarter	Units sold (000)	Shipping expense
19x1:		
First	16	$160,000
Second	18	175,000
Third	23	210,000
Fourth	19	180,000
19x2:		
First	17	170,000
Second	20	190,000
Third	25	230,000
Fourth	22	205,000

Management would like a cost formula derived for shipping expense so that a budgeted income statement using the contribution approach can be prepared for the next quarter.

Required: 1.   Using the least squares method, derive a cost formula for shipping expense. (Since the "Units sold" above are in thousands of units, the variable rate you compute will also be in thousands of units. It can be left in this form, or you can convert your variable rate to a per unit basis by dividing it by 1,000.)

2. Assume that in the first quarter, 19x3, the company plans to sell 21,000 units at a selling price of $50 per unit. Prepare an income statement for the quarter, using the contribution format.

P5–19. **Mixed cost analysis by three methods.** Pleasant View Hospital has just hired a new chief administrator who is anxious to employ sound management and planning techniques in the business affairs of the hospital. Accordingly, she has directed her assistant to summarize the cost structure existing in the various departments so that data will be available for planning purposes.

The assistant is unsure how to classify the utilities costs in the radiology department since these costs do not exhibit either strictly variable or fixed cost behavior. Utilities costs are very high in this department due to a large CAT scanner that draws a large amount of power and is kept running at all times. The scanner can't be turned off due to the long warm-up period required for its use. When the scanner is used to scan a patient, it consumes an additional burst of power. The assistant has accumulated the following data on utilities costs and use of the scanner since the first of the year:

Month	Number of scans	Utilities cost
January	60	$2,200
February	70	2,600
March	90	2,900
April	120	3,300
May	100	3,000
June	130	3,600
July	150	4,000
August	140	3,600
September	110	3,100
October	80	2,500

The chief administrator has informed her assistant that the utilities cost is probably a mixed cost that will have to be broken down into its variable and fixed cost elements by use of a scattergraph. The assistant feels, however, that if an analysis of this type is necessary, then the high-low method should be used, since it is easier and quicker. The controller has suggested that statistical least squares is the best approach.

Required:
1. Using the high-low method, determine the cost formula for utilities. Express the formula in the form $Y = a + bX$. (The variable rate should be stated in terms of cost per scan.)
2. Prepare a scattergraph by plotting the above data on a graph. (The number of scans should be placed on the horizontal axis, and utilities cost should be placed on the vertical axis.) Fit a regression line to the plotted points by visual inspection, and determine the cost formula for utilities.
3. Using the least squares method, calculate the cost formula for utilities. Again express the formula in the form $Y = a + bX$. (Round the variable rate to two decimal places.)
4. Refer to the graph prepared in (2). Explain why in this case the high-low method would be the least accurate of the three methods in deriving a cost formula.

P5–20. **Manufacturing statements; high-low method of cost analysis.** NuWay, Inc., manufactures a single product. Selected cost data from the company's records for two recent years are given below:

	Level of activity	
	19x1—low	19x3—high
Equivalent number of units produced	40,000	70,000
Cost of goods manufactured	$1,372,000	$2,156,000
Work in process inventory, beginning	140,000	190,000
Work in process inventory, ending	160,000	170,000
Direct materials cost per unit	8	8
Direct labor cost per unit	12	12
Manufacturing overhead cost, total	?	?

The company's manufacturing overhead cost consists of both variable and fixed cost elements. In order to have data available for planning, management wants to determine how much of the overhead cost is variable with units produced and how much of it is fixed per year.

Required: 1. For both 19x1 and 19x3, determine the amount of manufacturing overhead cost added to production. The company had no under- or overapplied overhead in either year. (Hint: A useful way to proceed might be to construct a schedule of cost of goods manufactured.)

2. By means of the high-low method of cost analysis, determine the cost formula for manufacturing overhead. Express the variable portion of the cost formula in terms of a variable rate per unit of product.

3. If 60,000 units are produced during a period, what would be the cost of goods manufactured, assuming that work in process inventories remain unchanged?

P5–21. **Mixed cost analysis by three methods.** The Sebolt Wire Company heats copper ingots to very high temperatures by placing the ingots in a large heat coil. The heated ingots are then run through a shaping machine that shapes the soft ingot into wire. Due to the long heat-up time involved, the coil is never turned off. When an ingot is placed in the coil, the temperature is raised to an even higher level, and then the coil is allowed to drop to the "waiting" temperature between ingots. Management needs to know the variable cost of power involved in heating an ingot and to know the fixed cost of power during "waiting" periods. The following data on ingots processed and power costs are available:

Month	Ingots	Power cost
January	900	$4,000
February	650	3,300
March	500	2,500
April	800	3,500
May	1,000	4,500
June	1,200	4,600
July	750	3,600
August	600	3,000
September	850	3,750
October	700	3,250
November	950	4,000
December	1,300	5,000

Required:

1. Using the high-low method, calculate the cost formula for power cost. Express the formula in the form $Y = a + bX$. (Carry the variable rate to three decimal places.)
2. Prepare a scattergraph by plotting ingots processed and power cost on a graph. Fit a regression line to the plotted points by visual inspection, and determine the cost formula for power cost.
3. Using the least squares method, calculate the cost formula for power cost. Again express the formula in the form $Y = a + bX$. (Round the variable rate to two decimal places.)
4. Comment on the accuracy and usefulness of the data derived by each of the methods (1)–(3) above.

P5–22. **Regression analysis; graphing.** The Ramon Company manufactures a wide range of products at several plant locations. The Franklin plant, which manufactures electrical components, has been experiencing difficulties with fluctuating monthly overhead costs. The fluctuations have made it difficult to estimate the level of overhead that will be incurred for any one month.

Management wants to be able to estimate overhead costs accurately in order to better plan its operational and financial needs. A trade association publication to which Ramon Company subscribes indicates that for companies manufacturing electrical components, overhead tends to vary with direct labor-hours.

One member of the accounting staff has proposed that the cost behavior pattern of the overhead costs be determined. Then overhead costs could be predicted from the budgeted direct labor-hours.

Another member of the accounting staff has suggested that a good starting place for determining the cost behavior pattern of overhead costs would be an analysis of historical data. The historical cost behavior pattern would provide a basis for estimating future overhead costs. The methods that have been proposed for determining the cost behavior pattern include the high-low method, the scattergraph method, simple linear regression, multiple regression, and exponential smoothing. Of these methods, Ramon Company has decided to employ the high-low method, the scattergraph method, and simple linear regression. Data on direct labor-hours and the respective overhead costs incurred have been collected for the past two years. The raw data are as follows:

	19x1		19x2	
Month	**Direct labor-hours**	**Overhead costs**	**Direct labor-hours**	**Overhead costs**
January	20,000	$84,000	21,000	$86,000
February	25,000	99,000	24,000	93,000
March	22,000	89,500	23,000	93,000
April	23,000	90,000	22,000	87,000
May	20,000	81,500	20,000	80,000
June	19,000	75,500	18,000	76,500
July	14,000	70,500	12,000	67,500
August	10,000	64,500	13,000	71,000
September	12,000	69,000	15,000	73,500
October	17,000	75,000	17,000	72,500
November	16,000	71,500	15,000	71,000
December	19,000	78,000	18,000	75,000

All equipment in the Franklin plant is leased under an arrangement calling for a flat fee up to 19,500 direct labor-hours of activity in the plant, after which rental charges are assessed on an hourly basis. Rental expense is a major item of overhead cost.

Required:

1. Using the high-low method, determine the cost formula for overhead in the Franklin plant.
2. Repeat (1) above, this time using the least squares method. Your assistant has computed the following amounts, which may be helpful in your analysis:

Equation method:

$$\Sigma X = 435,000$$
$$\Sigma Y = \$1,894,000$$
$$\Sigma XY = \$35,170,500,000$$
$$\Sigma X^2 = 8,275,000,000$$

Alternative method:

Twenty-four month average:

$$X = 18,125$$
$$Y = \$78,917$$
$$\Sigma X'Y' = \$841,750,000$$
$$\Sigma X'^2 = 390,625,000$$

3. Prepare a scattergraph, including on it all data for the two-year period. Fit a regression line to the plotted points by visual inspection. (It is not necessary to compute variable and fixed cost elements from your regression line.)
4. Assume that the Franklin plant works 22,500 direct labor-hours during a month. Compute the expected overhead cost for the month, using the cost formulas developed above with:
   a. The high low method.
   b. The least squares method.
   c. The scattergraph method [read the expected costs directly off the graph prepared in (3) above].
5. Of the three proposed methods, which one should the Ramon Company use to estimate monthly overhead costs in the Franklin plant? Explain fully, indicating the reasons why the other methods are less desirable.
6. Would the relevant range concept probably be more or less important in the Franklin plant than in most companies? (CMA, adapted)

6 Cost-Volume-Profit Relationships

Learning objectives

After studying Chapter 6, you should be able to:

Explain how changes in activity affect contribution margin and net income.

Compute the contribution margin ratio (C/M ratio) and use it to compute changes in contribution margin and net income.

Explain and compute operating leverage.

Show the effects on contribution margin of changes in variable costs, fixed costs, selling price, and volume.

Compute the break-even point by both the equation method and the unit contribution method.

Prepare a cost-volume-profit (CVP) graph and explain the significance of each of its components.

Compute the margin of safety (M/S) and explain its significance.

Explain the effects of shifts in the sales mix on contribution margin and on the break-even point.

Define or explain the key terms listed at the end of the chapter.

Cost-volume-profit (CVP) analysis involves a study of the interrelationship between the following factors:

1. Prices of products.
2. Volume or level of activity.
3. Per unit variable costs.
4. Total fixed costs.
5. Mix of products sold.

CVP analysis is a key factor in many decisions, including choice of product lines, pricing of products, marketing strategy, and utilization of productive facilities. The concept is so pervasive in managerial accounting that it touches on virtually everything that a manager does. Because of its wide range of usefulness, CVP analysis is undoubtedly the best tool the manager has for discovering the untapped profit potential that may exist in an organization.

THE BASICS OF COST-VOLUME-PROFIT (CVP) ANALYSIS

Our study of CVP analysis begins where our study of cost behavior in the preceding chapter left off—with the contribution income statement. The contribution income statement has a number of interesting characteristics that can be helpful to the manager in trying to judge the impact on profits of changes in selling price, cost, or volume. To demonstrate these characteristics, we shall use the income statement of the Norton Company, a small manufacturer of microwave ovens:

NORTON COMPANY
Contribution Income Statement
For the Month of June 19xx

	Total	Per unit
Sales (400 ovens)	$100,000	$250
Less variable expenses	60,000	150
Contribution margin	40,000	$100
Less fixed expenses	35,000	
Net income	$ 5,000	

For purposes of discussion, we shall assume that the Norton Company produces only one model of oven.

Notice that the company expresses its sales, variable expenses, and contribution margin on a per unit basis as well as in total. This is commonly done on income statements prepared for management's internal use, since, as we shall see, it facilitates profitability analysis.

Contribution margin

As explained in Chapter 5, contribution margin means how much is left from sales revenue, after covering variable expenses, that is contributed toward the covering of fixed expenses and then toward profits for the period. Notice the sequence here—contribution margin is used first to cover the fixed expenses, and then whatever remains after the fixed expenses are covered goes toward profits. If the contribution margin is not sufficient to cover the fixed expenses, then a loss occurs for the period. To illustrate, assume that by the middle of a particular month the Norton Company has been able to sell only one oven. At that point, the company's income statement will appear as follows:

	Total	Per unit
Sales (1 oven)	$ 250	$250
Less variable expenses	150	150
Contribution margin	100	$100
Less fixed expenses	35,000	
Net loss	$(34,900)	

For each additional oven that the company is able to sell during the month, $100 more in contribution margin will become available to help cover the fixed expenses. If a second oven is sold, for example, then the total contribution margin will increase by $100 (to a total of $200) and the company's loss will decrease by $100, to $34,800:

	Total	Per unit
Sales (2 ovens)	$ 500	$250
Less variable expenses	300	150
Contribution margin	200	$100
Less fixed expenses	35,000	
Net loss	$(34,800)	

If enough ovens can be sold to generate $35,000 in contribution margin, then all of the fixed costs will be covered and the company will have managed to at least *break even* for the month—that is, to show neither profit nor loss but just cover all of its costs. To reach this **break-even point,** the company will have to sell 350 ovens in a month, since each oven sold yields $100 in contribution margin:

	Total	Per unit
Sales (350 ovens)	$87,500	$250
Less variable expenses	52,500	150
Contribution margin	35,000	$100
Less fixed expenses	35,000	
Net income	$ 0	

Computation of the break-even point is discussed in detail later in the chapter; for the moment, we can note that it can be defined either as the point where total sales revenue equals total expenses, variable and fixed, or as the point where total contribution margin equals total fixed expenses.

Once the break-even point has been reached, net income will increase by the contribution margin per unit for each additional unit sold. If 351 ovens are sold in a month, for example, then we can expect that the net income for the month will be $100, since the company will have sold 1 oven more than the number needed to break even:

	Total	Per unit
Sales (351 ovens)	$87,750	$250
Less variable expenses	52,650	150
Contribution margin	35,100	$100
Less fixed expenses	35,000	
Net income	$ 100	

If 352 ovens are sold (2 ovens above the break-even point), then we can expect that the net income for the month will be $200, and so forth. To know what the profits will be at various levels of activity, therefore, it is not necessary for a manager to prepare a whole series of income statements. The manager can simply take the number of units to be sold over the break-even point and multiply that number by the unit contribution margin. The result will represent the anticipated profits for the period. Or, if an increase in sales is planned and the manager wants to know what the impact of that increase will be on profits, he or she can simply multiply the increase in units sold by the unit contribution margin. The result will be the expected increase in profits. To illustrate, if the Norton Company is selling 400 ovens per month and plans to increase sales to 425 ovens per month, the impact on profits will be:

Increased number of ovens to be sold	25
Contribution margin per oven	× $100
Increase in net income	$2,500

As proof:

	Sales volume 400 ovens	425 ovens	Difference 25 ovens	Per unit
Sales	$100,000	$106,250	$6,250	$250
Less variable expenses	60,000	63,750	3,750	150
Contribution margin	40,000	42,500	2,500	$100
Less fixed expenses	35,000	35,000	–0–	
Net income	$ 5,000	$ 7,500	$2,500	

To summarize the series of examples in this section, we can say that the contribution margin first goes to cover an organization's fixed expenses, and that the potential loss represented by these fixed expenses is reduced successively by the unit contribution margin for each incremental unit sold up to the break-even point. Once the break-even point has been reached, then overall net income is increased by the unit contribution margin for each incremental unit sold from that point forward.

Contribution margin ratio (C/M ratio)

In addition to being expressed on a per unit basis, revenues, variable expenses, and contribution margin for the Norton Company can also be expressed on a percentage basis:

	Total	Per unit	Percent
Sales (400 ovens)	$100,000	$250	100
Less variable expenses	60,000	150	60
Contribution margin	40,000	$100	40
Less fixed expenses	35,000		
Net income	$ 5,000		

The percentage of contribution margin to total sales is referred to either as the **contribution margin ratio** (C/M ratio) or as the **profit-volume ratio** (P/V ratio). This ratio is extremely useful in that it shows how contribution margin will be affected by a given dollar change in total sales. To illustrate, notice that the Norton Company has a C/M ratio of 40 percent. This means that for each dollar increase in sales, total contribution margin will increase by 40 cents ($1 sales × C/M ratio of 40 percent). Net income will also increase by 40 cents, assuming that there are no changes in fixed costs.

As this illustration suggests, *the impact on net income of any given dollar change in total sales can be computed in seconds by simply applying the C/M ratio to the dollar change.* If the Norton Company plans a $30,000 increase in sales during the coming month, for example, management can expect contribution margin to increase by $12,000 ($30,000 increased sales × C/M ratio of 40 percent). As we noted above, net income will increase by a like amount if the fixed costs do not change. As proof:

	Sales volume			
	Present	Expected	Increase	Percent
Sales	$100,000	$130,000	$30,000	100
Less variable expenses	60,000	78,000*	18,000	60
Contribution margin	40,000	52,000	12,000	40
Less fixed expenses	35,000	35,000	–0–	
Net income	$ 5,000	$ 17,000	$12,000	

* $130,000 × 60% = $78,000.

Many managers find the C/M ratio easier to work with than the unit contribution margin figure, particularly where a company has multiple product lines. This is because an item in ratio form facilitates comparisons between products. Other things equal, the manager will search out those product lines that have the highest C/M ratios. The reason, of course, is that for a given dollar increase in sales these product lines will yield the greatest amount of contribution margin toward the covering of fixed costs and toward profits.

Cost structure

We stated in the preceding chapter that *cost structure* refers to the relative proportion of fixed and variable costs in an organization. We also stated that an organization often has some latitude in trading off between fixed and variable costs. Such a trade-off is possible, for example, by automating facilities rather than using direct labor workers.

Which cost structure is best—high variable costs and low fixed costs, or the opposite? No categorical answer to this question is possible; we can simply note that there may be advantages either way, depending on the specific circumstances involved. To illustrate, the income statements of two companies are given below. Notice that the two companies have opposite cost structures—Company X has high variable costs and low fixed costs, with the opposite true for Company Y.

	Company X		Company Y	
	Amount	Percent	Amount	Percent
Sales	$100,000	100	$100,000	100
Less variable expenses	60,000	60	30,000	30
Contribution margin	40,000	40	70,000	70
Less fixed expenses	30,000		60,000	
Net income	$ 10,000		$ 10,000	

The question as to which company has the best cost structure depends on many factors, including the long-run trend in sales, year-to-year fluctuations in the level of sales, and the attitude of the managers toward risk. If sales are expected to trend above $100,000 in the future, then Company Y probably has the best cost structure, since its C/M ratio is higher and its profits will therefore increase more rapidly as sales increase. For example, assume that each company experiences a 10 percent increase in sales. The new income statements will be:

	Company X		Company Y	
	Amount	Percent	Amount	Percent
Sales	$110,000	100	$110,000	100
Less variable expenses	66,000	60	33,000	30
Contribution margin	44,000	40	77,000	70
Less fixed expenses	30,000		60,000	
Net income	$ 14,000		$ 17,000	

As we would expect, for the same dollar increase in sales, Company Y has experienced a greater increase in net income, due to its higher C/M ratio.

On the other hand, if $100,000 represents maximum sales, and if sales can be expected to drop below $100,000 from time to time, then Company X probably has the best cost structure. Its fixed costs are lower, and it will not lose contribution margin as rapidly as sales fall off, due to its lower C/M ratio. If sales fluctuate above and below $100,000, it becomes more difficult to tell which company is in a better position.

In the matter of risk, Company Y with its high fixed costs will incur losses much more quickly than Company X if recessionary conditions strike the industry. By the same token, since Company Y has low variable costs, it will reap huge profits as compared to Company X in prosperous times or if unexpected demand stimulates sales in the industry.

In sum, Company Y will experience wider movements in net income as changes take place in sales, with greater profits in good years and greater losses in bad years. Company X will enjoy somewhat greater stability in net income, but it will do so at the risk of losing substantial profits if sales trend upward in the long run.

Operating leverage

To the scientist, leverage explains how one is able to move a large object with a small force. To the manager, leverage explains how one is able to achieve a large increase in profits (in percentage terms) with only a small increase in sales and/or assets. One type of leverage that the manager uses to do this is known as *operating leverage.*[1]

Operating leverage is a measure of the extent to which fixed costs are being used in an organization. It is greatest in companies that have high fixed costs and low per unit variable costs. Conversely, operating leverage is lowest in companies that have low fixed costs and high per unit variable costs. If a company has high operating leverage (that is, high fixed costs and low per unit variable costs), then profits will be very sensitive to changes in sales. Just a small percentage increase in sales can yield a large percentage increase in profits.

Operating leverage can be illustrated by returning to the data in the preceding section. Company Y has greater fixed costs and smaller per unit variable costs than does Company X, although *total* costs are the same in the two companies at a $100,000 sales level. Observe that with a 10 percent increase in sales (from $100,000 to $110,000 in each company), net income in Company Y increases by 70 percent (from $10,000 to $17,000), whereas net income in Company X increases by only 40 percent (from $10,000 to $14,000). Thus, for a 10 percent increase in sales, Company Y experiences a much greater percentage increase in profits than does Company X. The reason is that

---

[1] There are two types of leverage—operating and financial. Financial leverage is discussed in Chapter 17.

Company Y has greater operating leverage as a result of its greater amount of fixed costs.

The **degree of operating leverage** existing in a company at a given level of sales can be measured by the following formula:

$$\frac{\text{Contribution margin}}{\text{Net income}} = \text{Degree of operating leverage}$$

The degree of operating leverage is a measure, at a given level of sales, of how a percentage change in sales volume will affect profits. To illustrate, the degree of operating leverage existing in Companies X and Y at a $100,000 sales level would be:

$$\text{Company X:} \quad \frac{\$40,000}{\$10,000} = 4$$

$$\text{Company Y:} \quad \frac{\$70,000}{\$10,000} = 7$$

By interpretation, these figures tell us that *for a given percentage change in sales* we can expect a change four times as great in the net income of Company X and a change seven times as great in the net income of Company Y. Thus, if sales increase by 10 percent, then we can expect the net income in company X to increase by four times this amount, or by 40 percent, and the net income in Company Y to increase by seven times this amount, or by 70 percent.

	(1) Percent increase in sales	(2) Degree of operating leverage	(1) × (2) Percent Increase in net income
Company X	10	4	40
Company Y	10	7	70

These computations explain why the 10 percent increase in sales mentioned earlier caused the net income of Company X to increase from $10,000 to $14,000 (an increase of 40 percent), and the net income of Company Y to increase from $10,000 to $17,000 (an increase of 70 percent).

The degree of operating leverage in a company is greatest at sales levels near the break-even point and decreases as sales and profits rise. This can be seen from the tabulation below, which shows the degree of operating leverage in Company X at various sales levels.

Sales	$80,000	$100,000	$150,000	$200,000
Less variable expenses	48,000	60,000	90,000	120,000
Contribution margin (a)	32,000	40,000	60,000	80,000
Less fixed expenses	30,000	30,000	30,000	30,000
Net income (b)	$ 2,000	$ 10,000	$ 30,000	$ 50,000
Degree of operating leverage, (a) ÷ (b)	16	4	2	1.6

Thus, a 10 percent increase in sales would increase profits by only 16 percent (10% × 1.6) if the company were operating at a $200,000 sales level, as compared to the 40 percent increase we computed earlier at the $100,000 sales level. The degree of operating leverage will continue to decrease the farther the company moves from its break-even point. At the break-even point, the degree of operating leverage will be infinitely large.

The operating leverage concept provides the manager with a tool that can signify quickly what impact various percentage changes in sales will have on profits, without the necessity of preparing detailed income statements. As shown by our examples, the effects of operating leverage can be dramatic. If a company is fairly near its break-even point, then even small increases in sales can yield large increases in profits. *This explains why management will often work very hard for only a nominal increase in sales volume.* If the degree of operating leverage is 5, then a 6 percent increase in sales would translate into a 30 percent increase in profits.

Some applications of CVP concepts

The concepts that we have developed on the preceding pages have many applications in planning and decision making. We will return now to the example of the Norton Company (a manufacturer of microwave ovens) to illustrate some of these applications. The Norton Company's basic cost and revenue data are:

	Per unit	Percent
Sales price	$250	100
Less variable expenses	150	60
Contribution margin	$100	40

Recall that fixed expenses are $35,000 per month.

Change in fixed costs and sales volume Assume that the Norton Company is currently selling 400 ovens per month (monthly sales of $100,000). The sales manager feels that a $10,000 increase in the monthly advertising budget would increase monthly sales by $30,000. Should the advertising budget be increased?

Solution:

Expected total contribution margin:	
$130,000 × 40% C/M ratio	$52,000
Present total contribution margin:	
$100,000 × 40% C/M ratio	40,000
Incremental contribution margin	12,000
Change in fixed costs:	
Less incremental advertising expense	10,000
Increased net income	$ 2,000

Yes, the advertising budget should be increased.

Since in this case only the fixed costs and the sales volume are changing, the solution can be presented in even shorter format, as follows:

Alternative solution:

Incremental contribution margin:
$30,000 × 40% C/M ratio $12,000
Less incremental advertising expense 10,000
Increased net income. . . . . $ 2,000

Notice that this approach does not depend on a knowledge of what sales were previously and that it is unnecessary under either approach to prepare an income statement. Both of the solutions above involve **incremental analysis** in that they consider only those items of cost or revenue that will change if the new program is implemented. Although in each case a new income statement could have been prepared, most managers would prefer the incremental approach. The reason is that it is simpler and more direct, and it permits the decision maker to focus attention on the specific items involved in the decision.

Change in variable costs and sales volume Refer to the original data. Assume again that the Norton Company is currently selling 400 ovens per month. Management is contemplating the use of less costly components in the manufacture of the ovens, which would reduce variable costs by $25 per oven. However, the sales manager predicts that the lower overall quality would reduce sales to only 350 ovens per month. Should the change be made?

Solution:

The $25 decrease in variable costs will cause the contribution margin per unit to increase from $100 to $125.

Expected total contribution margin:
350 ovens × $125 . . . . $43,750
Present total contribution margin:
400 ovens × $100 40,000
Increase in total contribution margin . . . . . . $ 3,750

Yes, the less costly components should be used in the manufacture of the ovens. Since the fixed costs will not change, net income will increase by the $3,750 increase in contribution margin shown above.

Change in fixed cost, sales price, and sales volume Refer to the original data. Assume again that the Norton Company is currently selling 400 ovens per month. In order to increase sales, management would like to cut the selling price by $20 per oven and increase the advertising budget by $15,000 per month. Management feels that if these two steps are taken, unit sales will increase by 50 percent. Should the changes be made?

Solution:

A decrease of $20 per oven in the selling price will cause the unit contribution margin to decrease from $100 to $80.

Expected total contribution margin:
400 ovens × 150% × $80 . . . . $48,000
Present total contribution margin:
400 ovens × $100 40,000
Incremental contribution margin 8,000
Change in fixed costs:
Less incremental advertising expense 15,000
Reduction in net income . . . . $ (7,000)

No, the changes should not be made. The same solution can be obtained by preparing comparative income statements:

	Present 400 ovens per month		Expected 600 ovens per month		
	Total	Per unit	Total	Per unit	Difference
Sales	$100,000	$250	$138,000	$230	$38,000
Less variable expenses	60,000	150	90,000	150	30,000
Contribution margin	40,000	$100	48,000	$ 80	8,000
Less fixed expenses	35,000		50,000*		15,000
Net income (loss)	$ 5,000		$ (2,000)		$ (7,000)

* $35,000 + $15,000 = $50,000.

Notice that the answer is the same as that obtained by the incremental analysis above.

Change in variable cost, fixed cost, and sales volume Refer to the original data. Assume again that the Norton Company is currently selling 400 ovens per month. The sales manager would like to place the sales staff on a commission basis of $15 per oven sold, rather than on flat salaries that now total $6,000 per month. The sales manager is confident that the change will increase monthly sales by 15 percent. Should the change be made?

Solution: Changing the sales staff from a salaried basis to a commission basis will affect both fixed and variable costs. Fixed costs will decrease by $6,000, from $35,000 to $29,000. Variable costs will increase by $15, from $150 to $165, and the unit contribution margin will decrease from $100 to $85.

Expected total contribution margin:
400 ovens × 115% × $85 . . . . $39,100
Present total contribution margin:
400 ovens × $100 40,000
Decrease in total contribution margin. . . . . (900)
Change in fixed costs:
Add salaries avoided if a commission is paid 6,000
Increase in net income . . . . $ 5,100

Yes, the changes should be made. Again, the same answer can be obtained by preparing comparative income statements:

	Present 400 ovens per month		Expected 460 ovens per month		Difference: increase or (decrease) in net income
	Total	Per unit	Total	Per unit	
Sales	$100,000	$250	$115,000*	$250	$ 15,000
Less variable expenses	60,000	150	75,900	165	(15,900)
Contribution margin	40,000	$100	39,100	$ 85	(900)
Less fixed expenses	35,000		29,000		6,000
Net income	$ 5,000		$ 10,100		$ 5,100

* 400 ovens × 115% = 460 ovens.
  460 ovens × $250 = $115,000.

Change in regular sales price

Change in regular sales price   Refer to the original data. Assume again that the Norton Company is currently selling 400 ovens per month. The company has an opportunity to make a bulk sale of 150 ovens to a wholesaler if an acceptable price can be worked out. This sale would not disturb regular sales currently being made. What price per oven should be quoted to the wholesaler if the Norton Company wants to increase its monthly profits by $3,000?

Solution:

Variable cost per oven	$150
Desired profits per oven:	
$3,000 ÷ 150 ovens	20
Quoted price per oven	$170

Notice that no element of fixed cost is included in the computation. This is because the Norton Company's regular business puts it beyond the break-even point, and the fixed costs are therefore covered. Thus, the quoted price on the special order only needs to be large enough to cover the variable costs involved with the order and to provide the desired $3,000 contribution margin. As shown above, this is $170 per unit, consisting of $150 in variable costs and $20 per unit in contribution margin.

If the Norton Company had been operating at a loss rather than at a profit, then this would have meant that a portion of the fixed costs was not being covered by regular sales. In this case, it would have been necessary to quote a price on the 150 new units that was high enough to include these unrecovered fixed costs (as represented by the loss), in addition to the variable costs and the desired profit on the sale.

Importance of the contribution margin

As stated in the introduction to the chapter, CVP analysis seeks the most profitable combination of variable costs, fixed costs, selling price, and sales volume. The examples that we have just provided show that the effect on the contribution margin is a major consideration in deciding on the most profitable combination of these factors. We have seen that profits can sometimes be improved by reducing the contribution margin, if fixed costs can be reduced by a greater amount. More commonly, however, we have seen that the way to improve profits is to increase the total contribution margin figure. Sometimes this can be done by reducing the selling price and thereby increasing volume; sometimes it can be done by increasing fixed costs (such as advertising) and thereby increasing volume; and sometimes it can be done by trading off variable and fixed costs with appropriate changes in volume. Many other combinations of factors are possible.

The size of the unit contribution margin figure (and the size of the C/M ratio) will have a heavy influence on what steps a company is willing to take to improve profits. For example, the greater the unit contribution margin for a product, the greater is the amount that a company will be willing to spend in order to increase sales of the product by a given percentage. This explains in part why companies with high unit contribution margins (such as auto manufacturers) advertise so heavily, while companies with low unit contribution margins (such as dishware manufacturers) tend to spend much less for advertising.

In short, the effect on the contribution margin holds the key to most cost-revenue decisions in a company.

BREAK-EVEN ANALYSIS

CVP analysis is sometimes referred to simply as break-even analysis. This is unfortunate, because break-even analysis is just one part of the entire CVP concept. However, it is often a key part, and it can give the manager many insights into the data with which he or she is working.

As a basis for discussion, we will continue with the example of the Norton Company. Recall that the selling price is $250 per oven, the variable expenses are $150 per oven, and the fixed costs total $35,000 per month.

Break-even computations

Earlier in the chapter, we stated that the break-even point can be defined equally well as the point where total sales revenue equals total expenses, variable and fixed, or as the point where total contribution margin equals total fixed expenses. As suggested by these two definitions of the break-even point, break-even analysis can be approached in two ways—first, by what is called the *equation method;* and second, by what is called the *unit contribution method.*

The equation method   The **equation method** centers on the contribution approach to the income statement illustrated earlier in the chapter. The format of this statement can be expressed in equation form as:

$$\text{Sales} = \text{Variable expenses} + \text{Fixed expenses} + \text{Profits}$$

At the break-even point, profits will be zero. Therefore, the break-even point can be computed by finding that point where sales just equal the total of the variable expenses plus the fixed expenses. For the Norton Company, this would be:

$$\text{Sales} = \text{Variable expenses} + \text{Fixed expenses} + \text{Profits}$$

$$\$250X = \$150X + \$35,000 + 0$$
$$\$100X = \$35,000$$
$$X = 350 \text{ ovens}$$

where:

$X =$ break-even point in ovens
$\$250 =$ unit sales price
$\$150 =$ unit variable expenses
$\$35,000 =$ total fixed expenses

After the break-even point in units sold has been computed, the break-even point in sales dollars can be computed by multiplying the break-even level of units by the sales price per unit:

$$350 \text{ ovens} \times \$250 = \$87,500$$

At times, the *dollar* relationship between variable expenses and sales may not be known. In these cases, if one knows the *percentage* relationship between variable expenses and sales, then the break-even point can still be computed, as follows:

$$\text{Sales} - \text{Variable expenses} + \text{Fixed expenses} + \text{Profits}$$

$$X = 0.60X + \$35,000 + 0$$
$$0.40X = \$35,000$$
$$X = \$87,500$$

where:

$X =$ break-even point in sales dollars
$0.60 =$ variable expenses as a percentage of sales
$\$35,000 =$ total fixed expenses

Firms often have data available only in percentage form, and the approach we have just illustrated must then be used to find the break-even point. Notice that use of percentages in the equation yields a break-even point in sales dollars rather than in units sold. The break-even point in units sold would be:

$$\$87,500 \div \$250 = 350 \text{ ovens}$$

The unit contribution method The **unit contribution method** is actually just a variation of the equation method already described. The approach centers on the idea discussed earlier that each unit sold provides a certain amount of contribution margin that goes toward the covering of fixed costs. To find how many units must be sold to break even, one must divide the total fixed costs by the contribution margin being generated by each unit sold:

$$\frac{\text{Fixed expenses}}{\text{Unit contribution margin}} = \text{Break-even point}$$

Each oven that the Norton Company sells generates a contribution margin of $100 ($250 selling price, less $150 variable expenses). Since the total fixed expenses are $35,000, the break-even point is:

$$\frac{\text{Fixed expenses}}{\text{Unit contribution margin}} = \frac{\$35,000}{\$100} = 350 \text{ ovens}$$

If only the percentage relationship between variable expenses, contribution margin, and sales is known, the computation becomes:

$$\frac{\text{Fixed expenses}}{\text{C/M ratio}} = \frac{\$35,000}{40\%} = \$87,500$$

This approach to break-even analysis is particularly useful in those situations where a company has multiple product lines and wishes to compute a single break-even point for the company as a whole. More is said on this point in a later section titled "The concept of sales mix."

CVP relationships in graphical form

The cost data relating to the Norton Company's microwave ovens can be expressed in graphical form by preparing a **cost-volume-profit (CVP) graph.** A CVP graph can be very helpful in that it highlights CVP relationships over wide ranges of activity and gives managers a perspective that can be obtained in no other way. Such graphing is sometimes referred to as preparing a **break-even chart.** This is correct to the extent that the break-even point is clearly shown on the graph. The reader should be aware, however, that a graphing of CVP data highlights CVP relationships throughout the *entire* relevant range—not just at the break-even point.

Preparing the CVP graph Preparing a CVP graph (sometimes called a *break-even chart*) involves three steps. These steps are keyed to the graph in Exhibit 6–1.

1. Draw a line parallel to the volume axis, to represent total fixed expenses. For the Norton Company, total fixed expenses are $35,000.
2. Choose some volume of sales above zero, and plot the point representing total expenses (fixed and variable) at that activity level. In Exhibit 6–1, we have chosen a sales volume of 600 ovens. Total expenses at that activity level would be:

Fixed expenses	$ 35,000
Variable expenses (600 ovens × $150)	90,000
Total expenses	$125,000

EXHIBIT 6–1
Preparing the CVP graph

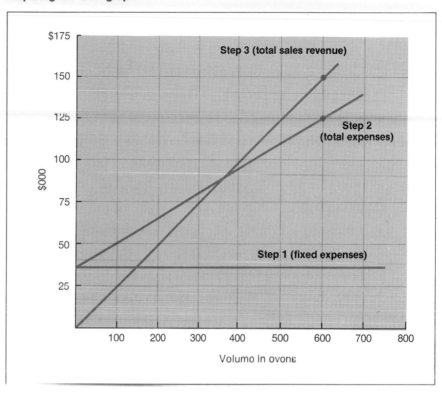

After the point has been plotted, draw a line through it back to the point where the fixed expenses line intersects the dollars axis.

3. Choose some volume of sales above zero and plot the point representing total sales dollars at that activity level. In Exhibit 6–1, we have again chosen a sales volume of 600 ovens. Sales at that activity level total $150,000 (600 ovens × $250). Draw a line through this point back to the origin.

The interpretation of the completed CVP graph is given in Exhibit 6–2. The anticipated profit or loss at any given level of sales is measured by the vertical distance between the total revenue line (sales) and the total expenses line (variable expenses plus fixed expenses).

The break-even point is where the total revenue and total expenses lines cross. The break-even point of 350 ovens in Exhibit 6–2 agrees with the break-even point obtained for the Norton Company in earlier computations.

An alternative format Some managers prefer an alternative format to the CVP graph, as illustrated in Exhibit 6–3.

Note that the total revenue and total expenses lines are the same as in Exhibit 6–2. However, the new format in Exhibit 6–3 places the fixed expenses above the variable expenses, thereby allowing the contribution margin to

EXHIBIT 6-2
The completed CVP graph

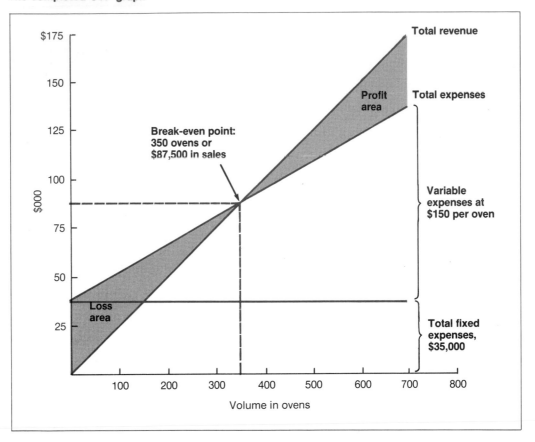

be depicted on the graph. Otherwise, the graphs in the two exhibits are the same.

The profitgraph Another approach to the CVP graph is presented in Exhibit 6–4. This approach, called a **profitgraph,** is preferred by some managers because it focuses more directly on how profits change with changes in volume. It has the added advantage of being easier to interpret than the more traditional approaches illustrated in Exhibits 6–2 and 6–3. It has the disadvantage, however, of not showing as clearly how costs are affected by changes in the level of sales.

The profitgraph is constructed in two steps. These steps are illustrated in Exhibit 6–4.

1. Locate total fixed expenses on the vertical axis, assuming zero level of activity. This point will be in the "loss area," equal to the total fixed expenses expected for the period.

EXHIBIT 6–3
Alternative format to the CVP graph

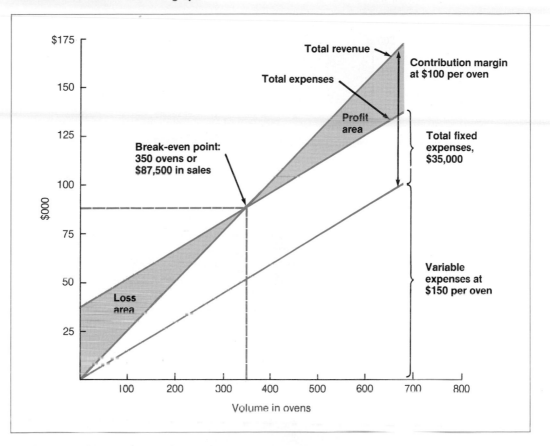

2. Plot a point representing expected profit or loss at any chosen level of sales. In Exhibit 6–4, we have chosen to plot the point representing expected profits at a sales volume of 600 ovens. At this activity level, expected profits are:

Sales (600 ovens × $250)	$150,000
Less variable expenses	
(600 ovens × $150)	90,000
Contribution margin	60,000
Less fixed expenses	35,000
Net income	$ 25,000

After this point is plotted, draw a line through it back to the point on the vertical axis representing total fixed expenses. The interpretation of the completed profitgraph is given in Exhibit 6–5. The break-even point is where the profit line crosses the break-even line.

EXHIBIT 6–4
Preparing the profitgraph

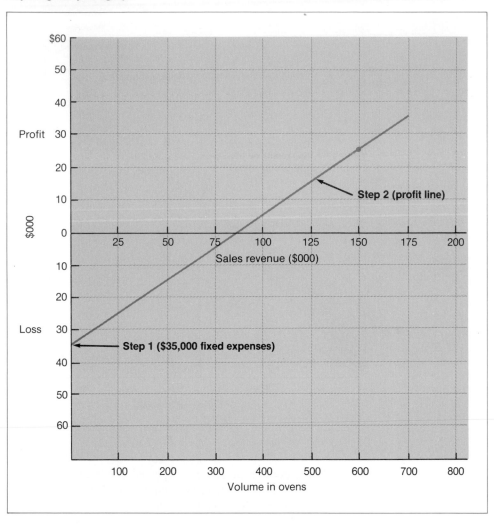

The vertical distance between the two lines represents the expected profit or loss at any given level of sales volume. This vertical distance can be translated directly into dollars by referring to the profit and loss figures on the vertical axis.

Target net profit analysis

CVP formulas can be used to determine the sales volume required to meet a target net profit figure. Suppose that the Norton Company would like to earn a target net profit of $40,000 per month. How many ovens would have to be sold?

EXHIBIT 6–5
The completed profitgraph

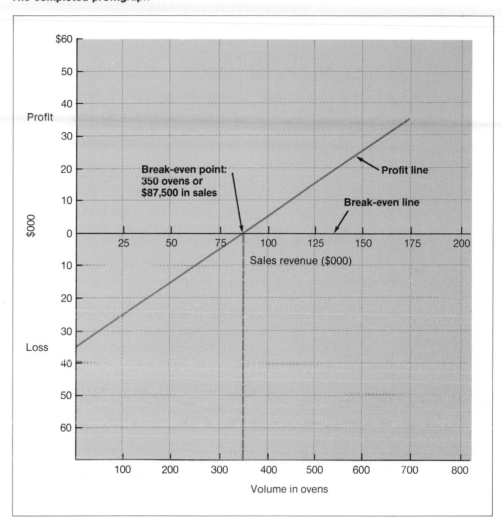

The CVP equation One approach to the solution would be to use the CVP equation. The target net profit requirement can be added into the basic equation data, and the solution will then show what level of sales is necessary to cover all expenses and yield the target net profit.

$$\text{Sales} = \text{Variable expenses} + \text{Fixed expenses} + \text{Profits}$$

$$\$250X = \$150X + \$35,000 + \$40,000$$
$$\$100X = \$75,000$$
$$X = 750 \text{ ovens}$$

where:

$$X = \text{number of ovens sold}$$
$$\$250 = \text{unit sales price}$$
$$\$150 = \text{unit variable expenses}$$
$$\$35,000 = \text{total fixed expenses}$$
$$\$40,000 = \text{target net profit}$$

Thus, the target net profit can be achieved by selling 750 ovens per month, which represents $187,500 in total sales ($250 × 750 ovens).

The unit contribution approach A second approach would be to expand the unit contribution formula to include the target net profit requirement:

$$\frac{\$35,000 \text{ fixed expenses} + \$40,000 \text{ target net profit}}{\$100 \text{ contribution margin per oven}} = 750 \text{ ovens}$$

This approach is simpler and more direct than using the CVP equation. In addition, it shows clearly that once the fixed costs are covered, the unit contribution margin is fully available for meeting profit requirements.

The margin of safety (M/S)

The **margin of safety (M/S)** can be defined as the excess of budgeted (or actual) sales over the break-even volume of sales. It states the amount by which sales can drop before losses begin to be incurred in an organization. The formula for its calculation is:

$$\text{Total sales} - \text{Break-even sales} = \text{Margin of safety (M/S)}$$

Computations involving the M/S are presented in Exhibit 6–6. Notice that the two companies in the exhibit have equal sales and net income figures but that Alpha Company has an M/S of $40,000, whereas Beta Company has an M/S of only $20,000. The difference in the M/S can be traced to the fact that the two companies have very different cost structures. Beta Company has higher fixed costs and thus will incur losses more quickly than Alpha Company if sales drop off. As indicated by the M/S, if sales drop by only $20,000, Beta Company will be at its break-even point, whereas sales can drop by $40,000 before Alpha Company will be at its break-even point.

The M/S can also be expressed in percentage form. This percentage is obtained by dividing the M/S in dollar terms by total sales:

$$\frac{\text{M/S in dollars}}{\text{Total sales}} = \text{M/S percentage}$$

Exhibit 6–6 contains the M/S expressed in percentage form for both Alpha Company and Beta Company. The M/S can also be expressed in terms of units of product (if a company is a single-product firm) by dividing the M/S in dollars by the unit selling price.

EXHIBIT 6–6
Margin of safety (M/S)

	Alpha Company		Beta Company	
	Amount	**Percent**	**Amount**	**Percent**
Sales	$200,000	100	$200,000	100
Less variable expenses	150,000	75	100,000	50
Contribution margin	50,000	25	100,000	50
Less fixed expenses	40,000		90,000	
Net income	$ 10,000		$ 10,000	
Break-even point:				
$40,000 ÷ 25%.	$160,000			
$90,000 ÷ 50%.			$180,000	
M/S in dollars (total sales less break-even sales):				
$200,000 − $160,000.	40,000			
$200,000 − $180,000.			20,000	
M/S in percentage form (M/S in dollars divided by total sales):				
$40,000 ÷ $200,000	20%			
$20,000 ÷ $200,000			10%	

If the M/S is low, as in Beta Company, what does management do to correct the problem? There is no universal answer to this question, other than to point out that management's efforts must be directed either toward reducing the break-even point or toward increasing the overall level of sales in the company. In short, the M/S is a tool designed to point out a problem (or the lack of one), the solution to which must be found by analyzing the company's cost structure and by applying the general CVP techniques that have been illustrated in this chapter.

STRUCTURING SALES COMMISSIONS

Some firms base salespersons' commissions on contribution margin generated rather than on sales generated. The reasoning goes like this: Since contribution margin represents the amount of sales revenue available to cover fixed expenses and profits, a firm's well-being will be maximized when contribution margin is maximized. By tying salespersons' commissions to contribution margin, the salespersons are automatically encouraged to concentrate on the element that is of most importance to the firm. There is no need to worry about what mix of products the salespersons sell, because they will *automatically* sell the mix of products that will maximize the base on which their commissions are to be paid. That is, if salespersons are aware that their commissions will depend on the amount of contribution margin that they are able to generate, then they will use all of the experience, skill, and expertise at their command to sell the mix of products that will maximize the contribution margin base. In effect, by maximizing their own well-being, they automatically maximize the well-being of the firm.

As a further step, some firms deduct from the total contribution margin generated by salespersons the amount of the traveling, entertainment, and other expenses that are incurred. This encourages the salespersons to be sensitive to their own costs in the process of making sales.

THE CONCEPT OF SALES MIX

The preceding sections have given us some insights into the principles involved in CVP analysis, as well as some selected examples of how these principles are used by the manager. Before concluding our discussion, it will be helpful to consider one additional application of the ideas that we have developed—the use of CVP concepts in analyzing sales mix.

The definition of sales mix

Sales mix can be defined as the relative combination of products represented in total sales. Managers try to achieve that combination, or mix, that will yield the greatest amount of profits. Most companies have several products, and these products are often not equally profitable. Where this is true, profits will depend to some extent on the sales mix that the company is able to achieve. Profits will be greater if high-margin items make up a relatively large proportion of total sales than if sales consist mostly of low-margin items.

Changes in the sales mix can cause interesting (and sometimes confusing) variations in a company's profits. A shift in the sales mix from high-margin items to low-margin items can cause total profits to decrease even though total sales increase. Conversely, a shift in the sales mix from low-margin items to high-margin items can cause the reverse effect—total profits may increase even though total sales decrease. Given the possibility of these types of variations in profits, one measure of the effectiveness of a company's sales force is the sales mix that it is able to generate. It is one thing to achieve a particular sales volume; it is quite a different thing to sell the most profitable mix of products.

Sales mix and break-even analysis

If a company is selling more than one product, break-even analysis is somewhat more complex than that discussed earlier in the chapter. The reason is that different products will have different selling prices, different costs, and different contribution margins. Consequently, the break-even point will depend on the mix in which the various products are sold. To illustrate, assume that a company has two product lines—line A and line B. For 19x1, the company's sales, costs, and break-even point were as shown in Exhibit 6–7.

EXHIBIT 6–7
Multiple-product break-even analysis

	Line A		Line B		Total	
	Amount	**Percent**	**Amount**	**Percent**	**Amount**	**Percent**
Sales	$20,000	100	$80,000	100	$100,000	100
Less variable expenses	15,000	75	40,000	50	55,000	55
Contribution margin	$ 5,000	25	$40,000	50	45,000	45
Less fixed expenses					27,000	
Net income					$ 18,000	

Computation of the break-even point:

$$\frac{\text{Fixed expenses, }\$27,000}{\text{Average C/M ratio, }45\%} = \$60,000$$

As shown in the exhibit, the break-even point is $60,000 in sales. This is computed by dividing the fixed costs by the company's *average* C/M ratio of 45 percent. But $60,000 in sales represents the break-even point for the company only so long as the sales mix does not change. *If the sales mix changes, then the break-even point will also change.* We can illustrate this by assuming that in 19x2, the following year, the sales mix shifts away from the more profitable line B (which has a 50 percent C/M ratio), toward the less profitable line A (which has only a 25 percent C/M ratio). Assume that sales in 19x2 are as shown in Exhibit 6–8.

Although sales have remained unchanged at $100,000, the sales mix is exactly the reverse of what it was in the prior exhibit, with the bulk of the sales now coming from line A rather than from line B. Notice that this shift in the sales mix has caused both the average C/M ratio and total profits to drop sharply from the prior year—the average C/M ratio has dropped from 45 percent in 19x1 to only 30 percent in 19x2, and net income has dropped from $18,000 to only $3,000. In addition, with the drop in the

EXHIBIT 6–8
Multiple-product break-even analysis: A shift in sales mix (see Exhibit 6–7)

	Line A		Line B		Total	
	Amount	**Percent**	**Amount**	**Percent**	**Amount**	**Percent**
Sales	$80,000	100	$20,000	100	$100,000	100
Less variable expenses	60,000	75	10,000	50	70,000	70
Contribution margin	$20,000	25	$10,000	50	30,000	30
Less fixed expenses					27,000	
Net income					$ 3,000	

Computation of the break-even point:

$$\frac{\text{Fixed expenses, }\$27,000}{\text{Average C/M ratio, }30\%} = \$90,000$$

average C/M ratio, the company's break-even point is no longer $60,000 in sales. Since the company is now realizing less average contribution margin per dollar of sales, it takes more sales to cover the same amount of fixed costs. Thus, the break-even point has increased from $60,000 to $90,000 in sales per year.

In preparing a break-even analysis, some assumption must be made concerning the sales mix. Usually the assumption is that it will not change. However, if the manager knows that shifts in various factors (consumer tastes, market share, and so forth) are causing shifts in the sales mix, then these factors must be explicitly considered in any CVP computations. Otherwise, the manager may be making decisions on the basis of outmoded or faulty data.

Sales mix and per unit contribution margin

Sometimes the sales mix is measured in terms of the average per unit contribution margin. To illustrate, assume that a company has two products— X and Y. During 19x1 and 19x2, sales of products X and Y were as shown in Exhibit 6–9.

Two things should be noted about the data in this exhibit. First, note that the sales mix in 19x1 was 1,000 units of product X and 3,000 units of product Y. This sales mix yielded $3.50 in average per unit contribution margin.

Second, note that the sales mix in 19x2 shifted to 2,000 units for both products, although *total* sales remained unchanged at 4,000 units. This sales mix yielded $4 in average per unit contribution margin, an increase of 50 cents per unit over the prior year.

What caused the increase in average per unit contribution margin between the two years? The answer is the shift in sales mix toward the more profitable product X. Although total volume (in units) did not change, total and per unit contribution margin changed simply because of the change in sales mix.

EXHIBIT 6–9

Sales mix and per unit contribution margin analysis

	Contribution margin per unit	Total units sold		Total contribution margin	
		19x1	19x2	19x1	19x2
Product X	$5	1,000	2,000	$ 5,000	$10,000
Product Y	3	3,000	2,000	9,000	6,000
		4,000	4,000	$14,000	$16,000
Average per unit contribution margin ($14,000 ÷ 4,000 units)				$3.50	
Average per unit contribution margin ($16,000 ÷ 4,000 units)					$4

LIMITING ASSUMPTIONS IN CVP ANALYSIS

Several limiting assumptions must be made when using data for CVP analysis. These assumptions are:

1. That the behavior of both revenues and costs is linear throughout the entire relevant range. The economists would differ from this view. They would say that changes in volume will trigger changes in both revenues and costs in such a way that relationships will not remain linear.
2. That costs can be accurately divided into variable and fixed elements.
3. That the sales mix is constant.
4. That inventories do not change in break-even computations (this assumption is considered further in Chapter 7).
5. That worker productivity and efficiency do not change throughout the relevant range.
6. That the value of a dollar received today is the same as the value of a dollar received in any future year (the time value of money is considered in Chapter 14).

SUMMARY

The analysis of CVP relationships is one of management's most significant responsibilities. Basically, it involves finding the most favorable combination of variable costs, fixed costs, selling price, sales volume, and mix of products sold. We have found that trade-offs are possible between types of costs, as well as between costs and selling price, and between selling price and sales volume. Sometimes these trade-offs are desirable, and sometimes they are not. CVP analysis provides the manager with a powerful tool for identifying those courses of action that will and will not improve profitability.

The concepts developed in this chapter represent a *way of thinking* rather than a mechanical set of procedures. That is, in order to put together the optimum combination of costs, selling price, and sales volume, the manager must train himself or herself to think in terms of the unit contribution margin, the break-even point, the C/M ratio, the sales mix, and the other concepts developed in this chapter. These concepts are dynamic in that a change in one will trigger changes in others—changes that may not be obvious on the surface. Only by learning to *think* in CVP terms can the manager move with assurance toward the firm's profit objectives.

KEY TERMS FOR REVIEW

Break-even chart The relationship between revenues, costs, and level of activity in an organization presented in graphical form. Also see *Cost-volume-profit (CVP) graph*.

Break-even point That level of activity at which an organization neither earns a profit nor incurs a loss.

Contribution margin ratio The contribution margin per unit expressed as a percentage of the selling price per unit.

Cost-volume-profit (CVP) graph The relationship between revenues, costs, and level of activity in an organization, presented in graphical form. Also see *Break-even chart*.

Degree of operating leverage A measure, at a given level of sales, of how a percentage change in sales volume will affect profits. The degree of operating leverage is computed by dividing contribution margin by net income.

Equation method A method of computing the break-even point that relies on the equation: Sales = Variable expenses + Fixed expenses + Profits.

Incremental analysis An analytical approach that focuses only on those items of revenue, cost, and volume that will change as a result of a decision in an organization.

Margin of safety (M/S) The excess of budgeted (or actual) sales over the break-even volume of sales.

Operating leverage A measure of the extent to which fixed costs are being used in an organization. The greater the fixed costs, the greater is the operating leverage available and the greater is the sensitivity of net income to changes in sales.

Profitgraph An alternative form of the cost-volume-profit graph that focuses more directly on how profits change with changes in volume.

Profit-volume ratio See *Contribution margin ratio*.

Sales mix The relative combination of products represented in total sales.

Unit contribution method A method of computing the break-even point in which the fixed costs are divided by the contribution margin per unit.

QUESTIONS

6-1. Cost-volume-profit (CVP) analysis is a study of the interaction of a number of factors. Name the factors involved.

6-2. What is meant by a product's contribution margin ratio (C/M ratio)? How is this ratio useful in the planning of business operations?

6-3. Able Company and Baker Company are competing firms. Each company sells a single product, widgets, in the same market at a price of $50 per widget. Variable costs are the same in each company—$35 per widget. Able Company has discovered a way to reduce its variable costs by $4 per unit and has decided to pass half of this cost savings on to its customers in the form of a lower price. Although Baker Company has not been able to reduce its variable costs, it must also lower its selling price in order to remain competitive with Able Company. If each company sells 10,000 units per year, what will be the effect of the changes on each company's profits?

6-4. Often the most direct route to a business decision is to make an incremental analysis based on the information available. What is meant by an "incremental analysis"?

6-5. Company A's cost structure includes costs that are mostly variable, whereas Company B's cost structure includes costs that are mostly fixed. In a time of increasing sales, which company will tend to realize the most rapid increase in profits? Explain.

6-6. What is meant by the term *operating leverage?*

6–7.   A 10 percent decrease in the selling price of a product will have the same impact on net income as a 10 percent increase in the variable expenses. Do you agree? Why or why not?

6–8.   "Changes in fixed costs are much more significant to a company than changes in variable costs." Do you agree? Explain.

6–9.   What is meant by the term *break-even point?*

6–10. Name three approaches to break-even analysis. Briefly explain how each approach works.

6–11. Why is the term *break-even chart* a misnomer?

6–12. In response to a request from your immediate supervisor, you have prepared a CVP graph portraying the cost and revenue characteristics of your company's product and operations. Explain how the lines on the graph would change if *(a)* the selling price per unit decreased, *(b)* fixed costs increased throughout the entire range of activity portrayed on the graph, and *(c)* variable costs per unit increased.

6–13. Using the following notations, write out the correct formula for computing the break-even level of sales in units: S = sales in units, SP = selling price per unit, FC = total fixed costs, and VC = variable cost per unit. Is the formula you have derived the formula for the equation method or the formula for the unit contribution method?

6–14. Al's Auto Wash charges $2 to wash a car. The variable costs of washing a car are 15 percent of sales. Fixed costs total $1,020 monthly. How many cars must be washed each month for Al to break even?

6–15. What is meant by the margin of safety (M/S)?

6–16. Companies X and Y are in the same industry. Company X is highly automated, whereas Company Y relies primarily on labor in the manufacture of its products. If sales in the two companies are about the same, which would you expect to have the lowest M/S? Why?

6–17. What is meant by the term *sales mix?* CVP analysis includes some inherent, simplifying assumptions. What assumption is usually made concerning sales mix?

6–18. Explain how a shift in the sales mix could result in both a higher break-even point and a lower net income.

EXERCISES

E6–1.   Pringle Company manufactures and sells a single product. The company's sales and expenses for a recent month follow:

	Total	Per unit
Sales	$600,000	$40
Less variable expenses	420,000	28
Contribution margin	180,000	$12
Less fixed expenses	150,000	
Net income	$ 30,000	

Required: 1.   What is the monthly break-even point in units sold and in sales dollars?

2.   Without resorting to computations, what is the total contribution margin at the break-even point?

3.   How many units would have to be sold each month to earn a minimum target net income of $18,000? Use the unit contribution method. Prove your answer by preparing a contribution income statement at the target level of sales.

4.   Refer to the original data. Compute the company's M/S in both dollar and percentage terms.

5.   What is the company's C/M ratio? If monthly sales increase by $80,000, by how much would you expect monthly net income to increase?

E6–2.   The Super Sales Company is the exclusive distributor for a new product. The product sells for $60 per unit and has a C/M ratio of 40 percent. The company's fixed expenses are $360,00 per year.

Required: 1.   What are the variable expenses per unit?

2.   Using the equation method:

   a.   What is the break-even point in units and in sales dollars?

   b.   What sales level in units and in sales dollars is required to earn an annual profit of $90,000?

   c.   Assume that through negotiation with the manufacturer the Super Sales Company is able to reduce its variable expenses by $3 per unit. What is the company's new break-even point in units and in sales dollars?

3.   Repeat (2) above, using the unit contribution method.

E6–3.   The Hartford Symphony Guild is planning its annual dinner-dance. The dinner-dance committee has assembled the following expected costs for the event:

Dinner (per person)	$ 18
Favors and program (per person) . . .	2
Orchestra	2,800
Rental of ballroom	900
Professional entertainment	
during intermission	1,000
Tickets and advertising	1,300

The committee members would like to charge $35 per person for the evening's activities.

Required: 1.   Compute the break-even point for the dinner-dance (in terms of the number of persons that must attend).

2.   Assume that last year only 300 persons attended the dinner-dance. If the same number attend this year, what price per ticket must be charged in order to break even?

3.   Refer to the original data ($35 ticket price per person). Prepare a cost-volume-profit graph for the dinner-dance. Number of persons should be placed on the horizontal *(X)* axis, and dollars should be placed on the vertical *(Y)* axis. (Note: Exercise 6–4 has further requirements for the data in this exercise.)

E6–4.   (This exercise is a continuation of Exercise 6–3.) Refer to the data in Exercise 6–3.

Required: 1.   Prepare a profitgraph for the dinner-dance.

2.   If the dinner-dance committee charges $40 per person rather than $35, will this cause the slope of the profit line to be steeper or flatter? Explain.

E6-5.   Dorsey Company is one of several producers of a part used in the small appliance industry. The company is currently producing and selling 120,000 parts a year. The selling price is $4 per part, variable expenses are $2.50 per part, and fixed expenses are $150,000 per year.

Required: 1.   Compute the break-even point in units and in sales dollars.
2.   After a study of the market, the president is convinced that a 5 percent reduction in the unit selling price will result in a 20 percent increase in the number of parts sold. Prepare two contribution income statements, one under present operating conditions and one as operations would appear after the proposed changes. Show two column headings on each statement, one for total and one for per unit data.
3.   Refer to the data in (2) above. Show the effect of the proposed changes on net income, using the incremental approach illustrated in the text.
4.   Refer to the data in (2) above. How many units would have to be sold at the new selling price to yield the net income currently being earned?

E6-6.   The Superior Door Company manufactures and sells prehung doors to home builders. The doors are sold for $30 each. Variable costs are $21 per door, and fixed costs total $60,000 per year. The company is currently selling 8,000 doors per year.

Required: 1.   Compute the degree of operating leverage at the present level of sales.
2.   Management is confident that the company can sell 10,000 doors next year (an increase of 2,000 doors, or 25 percent, over current sales). Compute:
a.   The expected percentage increase in net income for next year.
b.   The expected total dollar net income for next year.

E6-7.   Fill in the missing amounts in each of the eight case situations below. Each case is independent of the others. (Hint: One way to find the missing amounts would be to prepare a contribution income statement for each case, enter the known data, and then compute the missing items.)
a.   Assume that only one product is being sold in each of the four following case situations:

Case	Units sold	Sales	Variable expenses	Contribution margin per unit	Fixed expenses	Net income (loss)
1. . .	15,000	$180,000	$120,000	$?	$ 50,000	$?
2. . .	?	100,000	?	10	32,000	8,000
3. . .	10,000	?	70,000	13	?	12,000
4. . .	6,000	300,000	?	?	100,000	(10,000)

b.   Assume that more than one product is being sold in each of the four following case situations:

Case	Sales	Variable expenses	Average contribution margin (percent)	Fixed expenses	Net income (loss)
1 . . .	$500,000	$?	20	$?	$ 7,000
2 . . .	400,000	260,000	?	100,000	?
3 . . .	?	?	60	130,000	20,000
4 . . .	600,000	420,000	?	?	(5,000)

E6–8.   Porter Company's most recent income statement is shown below:

	Total	Per unit
Sales (30,000 units)	$150,000	$5
Less variable expenses . . .	90,000	3
Contribution margin	60,000	$2
Less fixed expenses	50,000	
Net income	$ 10,000	

Required: Prepare a new income statement under each of the following conditions (consider each case independently):
1. The sales volume increases by 15 percent.
2. The selling price decreases by 50 cents per unit, and the sales volume increases by 20 percent.
3. The selling price increases by 50 cents per unit, fixed expenses increase by $10,000, and the sales volume decreases by 5 percent.
4. Variable expenses increase by 20 cents per unit, the selling price increases by 12 percent, and the sales volume decreases by 10 percent.

E6–9.   Each of the following situations is independent.

1. Toomey Company's income statement for a recent year is given below:

Sales	$750,000	100%
Less variable expenses . . .	450,000	60
Contribution margin	300,000	40%
Less fixed expenses	200,000	
Net income	$100,000	

Compute the total variable expenses at the break-even point.
2. Wathen Company sold 25,000 units of product last year and realized a contribution margin of $3 on each unit sold. Fixed costs last year totaled $65,000. This year fixed costs are expected to total $80,000 due to increased advertising. If the contribution margin remains unchanged at $3 per unit, how many units will have to be sold this year to earn the same income before taxes as last year?
3. Zeppo, Inc., manufactures and sells a single product. The company is experiencing a slack in demand and suffered a loss in its most recent year, as shown below:

Sales (12,000 units)	$240,000
Less variable expenses . . .	150,000
Contribution margin	90,000
Less fixed expenses	100,000
Net loss	$ (10,000)

Regular sales in the coming year are expected to be about 12,000 units, the same as last year. A foreign distributor has offered to purchase an additional 4,000 units "if the price is right." What price should be quoted to the distributor if the company wants to make an overall profit of $5,000 in the coming year? (This sale would not disturb regular business.)

PROBLEMS

P6–10. **Basic CVP analysis, with graphing.** Shirts Unlimited operates a chain of shirt stores around the country. The stores carry many styles of shirts that are all sold at the same price. In order to encourage sales personnel to be aggressive in their sales efforts, the company pays a substantial sales commission on each shirt sold. Sales personnel also receive a small basic salary.

The following cost and revenue data relate to Store 36 and are typical of one of the company's many outlets:

	Per shirt
Sales price.	$ 20.00
Variable expenses:	
Invoice cost.	$ 9.50
Sales commission	2.50
Total variable expenses.	$ 12.00
Fixed expenses (per year):	
Rent	$ 30,000
Advertising	20,000
Salaries	50,000
Total fixed expenses.	$100,000

Shirts Unlimited is a fairly new organization. The company has asked you, as a member of its planning group, to assist in some basic analysis of its stores and company policies.

Required:
1. Calculate the annual break-even point in dollar sales and in unit sales for Store 36.
2. Prepare a CVP graph showing cost and revenue data for Store 36. Clearly indicate the break-even point on the graph.
3. If 12,000 shirts are sold in a year, what would be Store 36's net income or loss?
4. The company is considering paying the store manager of Store 36 an incentive commission of 50 cents per shirt (in addition to the salespersons' commissions). If this change is made, what will be the new break-even point in dollar sales and in unit sales?
5. Refer to the original data. As an alternative to (4) above, the company is considering paying the store manager 50 cents commission on each shirt sold in excess of the break-even point. If this change is made, what will be the store's net income or loss if 15,000 shirts are sold in a year?
6. Refer to the original data. The company is considering eliminating sales commissions entirely in its stores and increasing fixed salaries by $26,000 annually.
   a. If this change is made, what will be the new break-even point in dollar sales and in unit sales in Store 36?
   b. Would you recommend that the change be made? Explain.

P6–11. **Interpretive questions on the CVP graph.** A cost-volume-profit graph, as illustrated on the next page, is a useful technique for showing relationships between costs, volume, and profits in an organization.

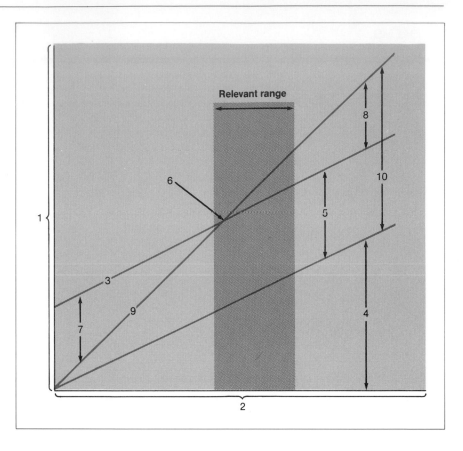

Required: 1. Identify the numbered components in the cost-volume-profit graph.
2. State the effect of each of the following actions on line 3, line 9, and the break-even point. For line 3 and line 9, state whether the action will cause the line to:

      Remain unchanged.
      Shift upward.
      Shift downward.
      Have a steeper slope (i.e., rotate upward).
      Have a flatter slope (i.e., rotate downward).
      Shift upward *and* have a steeper slope.
      Shift upward *and* have a flatter slope.
      Shift downward *and* have a steeper slope.
      Shift downward *and* have a flatter slope.

In the case of the break-even point, state whether the action will cause the break-even point to:

      Remain unchanged.
      Increase.
      Decrease.
      Probably change, but the direction is uncertain.

Treat each case independently.

x. *Example.* Fixed costs are reduced by $5,000 per period.

> *Answer* (see choices above): Line 3: Shift downward.
> Line 9: Remain unchanged.
> Break-even point: Decrease.

a. The unit selling price is increased from $18 to $20.
b. Unit variable costs are decreased from $12 to $10.
c. Fixed costs are increased by $3,000 per period.
d. Two thousand more units are sold during the period than were budgeted.
e. Due to paying salespersons a commission rather than a flat salary, fixed costs are reduced by $8,000 per period and unit variable costs are increased by $3.
f. Due to an increase in the cost of materials, both unit variable costs and the selling price are increased by $2.
g. Advertising costs are increased by $10,000 per period, resulting in a 10 percent increase in the number of units sold.
h. Due to automating an operation previously done by workers, fixed costs are increased by $12,000 per period and unit variable costs are reduced by $4.

P6–12.   **Sales mix assumptions; break-even analysis.**   Marlin Company has been operating for only a few months and is just starting a budgeting and planning program. The company sells three products—A, B, and C. Budgeted sales by product and in total for the coming month are shown below:

	Product								Total	
	A		**B**		**C**				**Total**	
Percentage of total sales .	48%		20%		32%				100%	
Sales.	$240,000	100%	$100,000	100%	$160,000	100%			$500,000	100%
Less variable expenses .	72,000	30	80,000	80	88,000	55			240,000	48
Contribution margin . . .	$168,000	70%	$ 20,000	20%	$ 72,000	45%			260,000	52%
Less fixed expenses . .									223,600	
Net income.									$ 36,400	

Break-even sales: $\dfrac{\text{Fixed expenses, \$223,600}}{\text{C/M ratio, 0.52}} = \$430,000$

As shown by these data, net income is budgeted at $36,400 for the month, and break-even sales at $430,000.

Assume that actual sales for the month total $500,000 as planned. Actual sales by product are: A, $160,000; B, $200,000; and C, $140,000.

Required: 1. Prepare a contribution income statement for the month based on actual sales data. Present the income statement in the format shown above.
2. Compute the break-even sales for the month, based on your actual data.
3. Considering the fact that the company met its $500,000 sales budget for the month, the president is shocked at the results shown on your income statement in (1). Prepare a brief memo for the president explaining why both the operating results and break-even sales are different from what was budgeted.

P6–13. **Graphing; incremental analysis; operating leverage.** Teri Hall has recently opened Sheer Elegance, Inc., a store specializing in fashionable stockings. Ms. Hall has just completed a course in managerial accounting at the state university, and she believes that she can apply certain aspects of the course to her business. She is particularly interested in adopting the cost-volume-profit approach to decision making. Thus, she has prepared the following analysis:

Sales price per pair of stockings.	$2.00
Variable expense per pair of stockings	0.80
Contribution margin per pair of stockings.	$1.20

Fixed expenses per year:	
Building rental	$12,000
Equipment depreciation	3,000
Selling	30,000
Administrative	15,000
Total fixed expenses	$60,000

Required:
1. How many pairs of stockings must be sold to break even? What does this represent in total dollar sales?
2. Prepare a CVP graph for the store. Indicate the break-even point on the graph.
3. How many pairs of stockings must be sold in order to earn a $9,000 target net income for the first year?
4. Ms. Hall now has one full-time and one part-time salesperson working in the store. It will cost her an additional $8,000 per year to convert the part-time position to a full-time position. Ms. Hall believes that the change would bring in an additional $20,000 in sales each year. Should she convert the position? Use the incremental approach (do not prepare an income statement).
5. Refer to the original data. Actual operating results for the first year are as follows:

Sales	$125,000
Less variable expenses	50,000
Contribution margin	75,000
Less fixed expenses	60,000
Net income	$ 15,000

    a. What is the store's operating leverage?
    b. Ms. Hall is confident that with some effort she can increase sales by 20 percent next year. What would be the expected percentage increase in net income? Use the operating leverage concept to compute your answer.

P6–14. **Basics of CVP analysis.** Stratford Company makes a product that sells for $15 per unit. Variable costs are $6 per unit, and fixed costs total $180,000 annually.

Required: Answer the following independent questions:
1. What is the product's C/M ratio?
2. Use the C/M ratio to determine the break-even point in sales dollars.
3. The company estimates that sales will increase by $45,000 during the coming year due to increased demand. By how much should net income increase?
4. Assume that the operating results for last year were:

Sales	$360,000
Less variable expenses	144,000
Contribution margin	216,000
Less fixed expenses	180,000
Net income	$ 36,000

    a. Compute the degree of operating leverage at the current level of sales.

    b. The president expects sales to increase by 15 percent next year. By how much should net income increase?

5. Refer to the original data. Assume that the company sold 28,000 units last year. The sales manager is convinced that a 10 percent reduction in the selling price, combined with a $70,000 increase in advertising expenditures, would cause annual sales in units to increase by 50 percent. Prepare two contribution income statements, one showing the results of last year's operations and one showing what the results of operations would be if these changes were made. Would you recommend that the company do as the sales manager suggests?

6. Refer to the original data. Assume again that the company sold 28,000 units last year. The president feels that it would be unwise to change the selling price. Instead, he wants to increase the sales commission by $1 per unit. He thinks that this move, combined with some increase in advertising, would increase annual sales by 25 percent. By how much could advertising be increased with profits remaining unchanged? Do not prepare an income statement; use the incremental analysis approach.

7. Refer to the original data. Assume that due to a slack in demand the company is selling only 23,000 units per year. An order has been received from a wholesale distributor who wants to purchase 4,000 units on a special price basis. What unit price would have to be quoted to the distributor if the company wants to double its current profits? (Present sales would not be disturbed by this special order.)

P6–15.   **Basics of CVP analysis.**   Memofax, Inc., produces a single product. Sales have been very erratic, with some months showing a profit and some months showing a loss. The company's income statement for the most recent month is given below:

Sales (14,000 units at $20) . . .	$280,000
Less variable expenses	196,000
Contribution margin	84,000
Less fixed expenses	90,000
Net loss	$ (6,000)

Required:

1. Compute the company's C/M ratio and its break-even point in both units and dollars.

2. The sales manager feels that a $10,000 increase in the monthly advertising budget, combined with an intensified effort by the sales staff, will result in a $60,000 increase in monthly sales. If the sales manager is right, what will be the effect on the company's monthly net income or loss? (Use the incremental approach in preparing your answer.)

3. The president is convinced that a 10 percent reduction in the selling price, combined with an increase of $30,000 in the monthly advertising budget, will cause unit sales to double. What will the new income statement look like if these changes are adopted?

4. Refer to the original data. The company's advertising agency thinks that a new package for the company's product would help sales. The new package being proposed would increase packaging costs by $0.60 per unit. Assuming no other changes in cost behavior, how many units would have to be sold each month to earn a profit of $4,500?

5. Refer to the original data. By automating certain operations, the company could reduce variable expenses by $2 per unit. However, fixed costs would increase by $38,000 per month.

    a. Compute the new C/M ratio and the new break-even point in both units and dollars.

    b. Assume that the company expects to sell 20,000 units next month. Prepare two income statements, one assuming that operations are not automated and one assuming that they are.

    c. Would you recommend that the company automate its operations? Explain.

6. Refer to the original data. A large distributor has offered to make a bulk purchase of 5,000 units each month on a special price basis. Variable selling expenses of $1.50 per unit could be avoided on this sale. What price per unit should Memofax, Inc., quote to this distributor if Memofax desires to make an overall net income of $10,000 each month for the company as a whole? (Present sales would not be disturbed by this order.)

P6–16. **The case of the suddenly appearing fixed costs.** The Marbury Stein Shop sells steins from all parts of the world. The owner of the shop, Mr. Marbury, is thinking of expanding his operations by hiring local college students, on a commission basis, to sell steins bearing the school emblem at the local college.

These steins must be ordered from the manufacturer three months in advance, and because of the unique emblem of each college, they cannot be returned. The steins would cost Mr. Marbury $3 each with a minimum order of 100 steins. Any additional steins would have to be ordered in increments of 25.

Since this expansion plan would not require additional facilities, Mr. Marbury's only costs for the project would be the costs of the steins and the costs of the sales commissions. The selling price of the steins would be $6.50. The sales commission would be $1.50 per stein.

Required: 1. In order to make the investment worthwhile, Mr. Marbury would require a $750 profit for the first six months of the venture. What level of sales in units and in dollars would be required to reach this target net income?

           2. Assuming that the venture is undertaken and that an order is placed, what would be the break-even point in units and in dollar sales? Explain the reasoning behind your answer. Assume an order of 100 steins.

P6–17. **Sensitivity analysis of net income; changes in volume.** Minden Company's marketing expert, Mr. Rand, believes that the firm can increase sales by 5,000 units for each $2 per unit reduction in selling price. The company's present selling price is $80 per unit, and variable expenses are $50 per unit. Fixed expenses are $600,000 per year. The present sales volume is 30,000 units.

Required: 1. *a.* What is the present yearly net income?

               b. What is the present break-even point in units and in dollar sales?

           2. *a.* Assuming that Mr. Rand is correct, what is the *maximum* profit that the firm could generate yearly? At how many units and at what selling price per unit would the firm generate this profit?

               b. What would be the break-even point in units and in dollar sales using the selling price you have determined above?

P6–18. **Changes in cost structure.** (This problem requires a maximum of thought and a minimum of pencil pushing.) The May 19x1 income statement for Frieden Company is given below:

Sales (10,000 units)	$100,000
Less variable expenses	70,000
Contribution margin	30,000
Less fixed expenses	24,000
Net income	$ 6,000

Frieden Company has ample unused capacity and is studying various ways of improving profits.

Required: Each of the situations below is independent of the others. Provide the information requested.

1. New equipment has come onto the market that would allow Frieden Company to automate a portion of its operations. Variable costs could be reduced by $3 per unit. However, fixed costs would increase by $30,000 each month.

   a. Prepare two contribution-type income statements, one showing present operations and one showing how operations would appear if the new equipment is purchased. On each statement show an amount column, a per unit column, and a percent column. Do not show percentages for the fixed costs.

   b. As a manager, what factor would be paramount in your mind in deciding whether to purchase the new equipment? (You may assume that plenty of funds are available to make the purchase.)

2. Refer to the original data. The company is thinking about changing its marketing method. Under the new method, sales would increase by 15 percent each month and net income would increase by one third. Fixed costs could be slashed to only $15,000 per month. Compute the break-even point for the company before and after the change in marketing method.

3. Refer to the original data. Due to a sudden and unprecedented surge in demand, the company's sales increased by 25 percent during June 19x1. During that month, net income increased by $3,000, or by 50 percent. By how much should net income have increased? Would you congratulate management for an outstanding performance, or would you chastise management for not doing its job well during the period? Explain.

P6–19.   **Sales mix; break-even analysis.** Topper Sports, Inc., produces high-quality sports equipment. The company's racket division manufactures three tennis rackets—the Standard, the Deluxe, and the Pro—that are widely used in amateur play. Selected information on the rackets is given below:

	Standard	Deluxe	Pro
Selling price per racket	$40.00	$60.00	$90.00
Variable expenses per racket:			
Production	22.00	27.00	31.50
Selling (5% of selling price)	2.00	3.00	4.50

All sales are made through the company's own retail outlets. The cost records show that the following fixed costs are assignable to the racket division:

	Per month
Fixed production costs	$120,000
Advertising expense	100,000
Administrative salaries	50,000
Total	$270,000

Sales, in units, over the past two months have been:

	Standard	Deluxe	Pro	Total
April	2,000	1,000	5,000	8,000
May.	8,000	1,000	3,000	12,000

Required:

1. Using the contribution approach, prepare an income statement for April and an income statement for May, with the following headings:

	Total		Standard		Deluxe		Pro	
	Amount	Percent	Amount	Percent	Amount	Percent	Amount	Percent
Sales . . .								
Etc. . . .								

Place the fixed expenses only in the total column. Do not show percentages for the fixed expenses.

2. Upon seeing the income statements in (1), the president stated, "I can't believe this! We sold 50 percent more rackets in May than in April, yet profits went down. It's obvious that costs are out of control in that division." What other explanation can you give for the drop in net income?

3. Compute the racket division's break-even point in dollars for the month of April.

4. Has May's break-even point in dollars gone up or down from April's break-even point? Explain without computing a break-even point for May.

5. Assume that sales of the Standard racket increase by $20,000. What would be the effect on net income? What would be the effect if Pro racket sales increased by $20,000? Do not prepare income statements; use the incremental analysis approach in determining your answer.

P6–20. **Sales mix; commission structure; break-even point.** Carbex, Inc., produces cutlery sets out of high-quality wood and steel. The company makes a standard cutlery set and a deluxe set and sells them to retail department stores throughout the country. The standard set sells for $60, and the deluxe set sells for $75. The variable expenses associated with each set are given below (in cost per set):

	Standard	Deluxe
Production expenses	$15.00	$30.00
Sales commissions (15% of sales price) . . .	9.00	11.25

The company's fixed expenses each month are:

Advertising	$90,000
Depreciation	35,000
Administrative	60,000

Salespersons are paid on a commission basis in order to encourage them to be aggressive in their sales efforts. Mary Parsons, the financial vice president, watches sales commissions carefully and has noted that they have risen steadily over the last year. For this reason, she was shocked to find that even though sales have increased, profits for the current month—May 19x2—are down substantially from May of the previous year. Sales, in sets, for May over the last two years are given below:

	Total	Standard	Deluxe
May 19x1. . .	6,000	4,000	2,000
May 19x2. . .	6,000	1,000	5,000

Required: 1. *a.* Prepare an income statement for May 19x1 and an income statement for May 19x2. Use the contribution format, with the following headings:

	Standard		Deluxe		Total	
	Amount	Percent	Amount	Percent	Amount	Percent
Sales. . .						
Etc. . . .						

Place the fixed expenses only in the total column. Do not show percentages for the fixed expenses.

b. Explain why there is a difference in net income between the two months, even though the same *total* number of sets was sold in each month.

2. What can be done to the sales commissions to optimize the sales mix?

3. *a.* Using May 19x1's figures, what was the break-even point for the month in sales dollars?

b. Has May 19x2's break-even point gone up or down from that of May 19x1? Explain your answer without calculating the break-even point for May 19x2.

P6–21. **Changing levels of fixed and variable costs.** Novelties, Inc., produces and sells highly faddish products directed toward the teenage market. A new product has come onto the market that the company is anxious to produce and sell. Enough capacity exists in the company's plant to produce 15,000 units each month. Variable costs to manufacture and sell one unit would be $1.60, and fixed costs would total $16,000 per month.

The marketing department predicts that demand for the product will exceed the 15,000 units that the company is able to produce. Additional production capacity can be rented from another company at a fixed cost of $3,500 per month. Variable costs in the rented facility would total $1.75 per unit, due to somewhat less efficient operations than in the main plant. The product will sell for $2.50 per unit.

Required: 1. What is the monthly break-even point in units and in dollar sales?

2. How many units must be sold in order to make a profit of $3,750 each month?

3. If the sales manager receives a bonus of 10 cents per unit sold in excess of the break-even point, how many units must be sold each month in order to earn a return of 10 percent on the monthly investment in fixed costs?

P6–22. **Detailed income statement; CVP sensitivity analysis.** The most recent income statement for Alpine, Inc., appears below:

ALPINE, INC.
Income Statement
For the Year Ended June 30, 19x1

Sales (35,000 units at $5)		$175,000
Less cost of goods sold:		
Direct materials.	$35,000	
Direct labor	26,250	
Factory overhead	53,100	114,350
Gross margin		60,650
Less operating expenses:		
Selling expense:		
Variable:		
Sales commissions $14,000		
Shipping 3,500	17,500	
Fixed (advertising, salaries). . .	30,000	
Administrative expense:		
Variable	1,750	
Fixed	18,000	67,250
Net loss		$ (6,600)

All variable expenses vary in terms of units sold, except for sales commissions, which are based on sales dollars. Variable factory overhead is 50 cents per unit. Alpine, Inc.'s plant has a capacity of 60,000 units.

Management is very disappointed with 19x1's operating results. Several possible courses of action are being studied to determine what should be done to make 19x2 profitable.

Required:

1. Redo Alpine, Inc.'s 19x1 income statement in the contribution format. Show a total and a per unit column. Allow enough space to enter the solution to (2) below.

2. *a.* For 19x2, the sales manager would like to reduce the unit selling price by 10 percent. He is certain that this would fill the plant to capacity.

   b. For 19x2, the executive vice president would like to increase the unit selling price by 10 percent, increase the sales commission to 12 percent of sales, and increase advertising by $25,000. She thinks that this would trigger a 60 percent increase in volume. Prepare two contribution income statements, one showing what profits would be under the sales manager's proposal and one showing what profits would be under the executive vice president's proposal. On each statement, include both total and per unit columns.

3. Refer to the original data. The president thinks it would be unwise to change the unit selling price. Instead, he wants to use less costly materials in manufacturing units of product, thereby reducing unit costs by 25 cents. How many units would have to be sold in 19x2 to earn a target profit of $12,000?

4. Refer to the original data. Alpine, Inc.'s advertising agency thinks that the problem lies in inadequate promotion. How much may advertising be increased and still allow the company to earn a target return of 5 percent on sales of 50,000 units?

5. Refer to the original data. The company has been approached by an overseas distributor who wants to purchase 15,000 units on a special price basis. There would be no sales commission on these units; however, shipping costs would be doubled. In addition, a foreign import duty of $4,500 would have to be paid by

Alpine, Inc., on behalf of the overseas distributor. What unit price would have to be quoted on the 15,000 units by Alpine, Inc., to allow the company to earn a profit of $10,500 on total operations? Regular business would not be disturbed by the special order.

P6–23. **Break-even analysis with step fixed costs.** Wymont Hospital operates a general hospital that rents space and beds to separate departments such as pediatrics, maternity, and surgery. Wymont Hospital charges each separate department for common services to its patients such as meals and laundry and for administrative services such as billing and collections. Space and bed rentals are fixed for the year.

For the year ended June 30, 19x7, the pediatrics department at Wymont Hospital charged its patients an average of $65 per day, had a capacity of 60 beds, operated 24 hours per day for 365 days, and had total revenue of $1,138,800.

Expenses charged by the hospital to the pediatrics department for the year were as follows:

	Basis for allocation	
	Patient days	**Bed capacity**
Dietary	$ 42,952	
Janitorial		$ 12,800
Laundry	28,000	
Laboratory	47,800	
Pharmacy	33,800	
Repairs and maintenance	5,200	7,140
General administrative services		131,760
Rent		275,320
Billings and collections	87,000	
Other	18,048	25,980
	$262,800	$453,000

The only personnel directly employed by the pediatrics department are supervising nurses, nurses, and aides. The hospital has minimum personnel requirements based on total annual patient days. Hospital requirements, beginning at the minimum expected level of operation, follow:

Annual patient days	Aides	Nurses	Supervising nurses
10,000–14,000	21	11	4
14,001–17,000	22	12	4
17,001–23,725	22	13	4
23,726–25,550	25	14	5
25,551–27,375	26	14	5
27,376–29,200	29	16	6

These staffing levels represent full-time equivalents, and it should be assumed that the pediatrics department always employs only the minimum number of required full-time equivalent personnel.

Annual salaries for each class of employee are: supervising nurses, $18,000; nurses, $13,000; and aides, $5,000. Salary expense for the year ended June 30, 19x7 was $72,000, $169,000, and $110,000 for supervising nurses, nurses, and aides, respectively.

Required:
1. Compute the following:
   a. The number of patient days in the pediatrics department for the year ended June 30, 19x7. (Each day a patient is in the hospital is known as a "patient day.")
   b. The variable cost per patient day for the year ended June 30, 19x7.
   c. The total fixed costs, including both allocated fixed costs and personnel costs, in the pediatrics department for each level of operation shown above (i.e., total fixed costs at the 10,000–14,000 patient-day level of operation, total fixed costs at the 14,001–17,000 patient-day level of operation, etc.).
2. Using the data computed in (1) and using any other data as needed, compute the *minimum* number of patients days required for the pediatrics department to break even. You may assume that variable and fixed cost behavior and that revenue per patient day will remain unchanged in the future.
3. Determine the minimum number of patient days required for the pediatrics department to earn an annual profit of $80,000. (CPA, heavily adapted)

P6–24. **Case on plant expansion; break-even analysis.** "In my opinion, it will be a mistake if that new plant is built," said Robert Simons, controller and financial vice president of Tanka Toys. "Why, if that plant was in existence right now, we would be reporting a loss of $37,800 for the year [1986] rather than a profit, and 1986 sales have been the best in the history of the company."

Mr. Simons was speaking of a new, highly automated production plant that Tanka Toys is considering building. The company was organized only eight years ago, but it has become one of the leaders in the industry due to innovative toys that it has designed and marketed. Annual sales since inception of the company, along with net income as a percentage of sales, are presented below:

1979	$ 699,000	6.9%
1980	857,000	6.7
1981	1,071,000	6.8
1982	1,360,000	5.5
1983	1,845,000	5.7
1984	1,476,000	1.7
1985	2,860,000	3.2
1986	3,800,000	3.4

Although the company has always been profitable, in recent years rising costs have cut into its profit margins. The main production plant was constructed in 1981, but growth has been greater than anyone anticipated, making it necessary to rent additional production and storage space in various locations around the country. This spreading out of production facilities has caused costs to rise, particularly since the company is somewhat limited in the amount of automated equipment that it can use and therefore must rely on training a large number of new workers each year during peak production seasons.

Tanka Toys produces about 75 percent of its toys between April and September and only about 25 percent during the remainder of the year. This seasonal production pattern is followed by many toy manufacturers, since it saves on storage costs and reduces the chances of toy obsolescence due to style changes. Other toy manufacturers produce evenly throughout the year, thereby maintaining a stable work force. Alice Clark, manufacturing vice president of Tanka Toys, is pushing the new plant very hard, since it would permit Tanka Toys to produce on a more even basis, as well as to automate many hand operations and thereby dramatically reduce variable costs.

Although total toy sales are quite stable, individual toy manufacturers can experience wide fluctuations from year to year according to how well their toys are received by the market. For example, Tanka Toys "missed the market" on one of its toy lines in 1984, causing a sharp drop in sales and profits, as shown above. Other manufacturers have experienced even sharper drops in sales, some on a prolonged basis, and Tanka Toys feels fortunate in the sales stability that it has enjoyed.

Mr. Simons points out that although variable costs will be reduced by the new plant, fixed costs will rise steeply, to $1,400,000 per year. On the other hand, fixed costs are now only $450,000 per year. Mr. Simons is confident (and Ms. Clark agrees) that with stringent cost control variable expenses can be held at 82 percent of sales if the company continues with its present production setup. Variable expenses will be 65 percent of sales if the new plant is built.

Ms. Clark points out that marketing projections predict only a 10 percent annual growth rate in sales if the company continues with its present production setup, whereas sales growth is expected to be as much as 15 percent annually if the new plant is built. The new plant would provide ample capacity to meet projected sales needs for many years into the future. Economies of expansion dictate, however, that any expansion undertaken be made in one step, since expansion by stages is too costly to be a feasible alternative.

Required: 1. Assuming that the company continues with its present production setup:
  a. Compute the break-even point in sales dollars.
  b. Prepare a contribution income statement for each of the years 1987–90, assuming that sales growth is 10 percent per year as expected (i.e., 1987 sales are 110 percent of 1986 sales, and so forth). Assume that cost behavior patterns remain stable over the four-year period.
  c. Refer to the computations in *(b)* above. Compute the operating leverage and the M/S for each year. (Express the M/S in percentage terms.)

2. Assuming that the company builds the new plant, redo the computations in (1) above. (Assume a growth rate of 15 percent per year.)

3. Prepare a CVP graph for Tanka Toys, showing on the graph the cost-revenue data for both the present plant and the proposed new plant.

4. Compute the level of sales at which profits would be equal with either the old or the new plant. Show this point on the graph that you prepared in (3) above.

5. Refer to the original data. Assume that Tanka Toys "misses the market" in 1987 and that sales fall by 20 percent (the same rate that sales fell in 1984). Compute the net profit or loss for 1987 with and without the new plant.

6. Refer to the original data. Suppose that the company is anxious to earn a profit of at least 7 percent of sales. At what sales level will this be achieved if the new plant is built?

7. Based on the data in (1)–(6) above, evaluate the risks and merits of building the new plant and recommend to management the course of action that you think should be taken. Be prepared to defend your recommendation in class.

P6–25. **Break-even and sales mix.** Wesco Electronics manufactures two products—tape recorders and electronic calculators—and sells them nationally to wholesalers and retailers. The Wesco management is very pleased with the company's performance for the current fiscal year. Projected sales through December 31, 19x7, indicate that 70,000 tape recorders and 140,000 electronic calculators will be sold this year. The projected earnings statement, which appears below, shows that Wesco will exceed its earnings goal of 9 percent on sales after taxes.

WESCO ELECTRONICS
Projected Earnings Statement
For the Year Ended December 31, 19x7

	Tape recorders		Electronic calculators		
	Total amount ($000)	Per unit	Total amount ($000)	Per unit	Total ($000)
Sales	$1,050	$15.00	$3,150	$22.50	$4,200.0
Production costs:					
Materials	280	4.00	630	4.50	910.0
Direct labor	140	2.00	420	3.00	560.0
Variable overhead	140	2.00	280	2.00	420.0
Fixed overhead	70	1.00	210	1.50	280.0
Total production costs	630	9.00	1,540	11.00	2,170.0
Gross margin	$ 420	$ 6.00	$1,610	$11.50	2,030.0
Fixed selling and administrative expenses					1,040.0
Net income before income taxes					990.0
Income taxes (55%)					544.5
Net income					$ 445.5

The tape recorder business has been fairly stable the last few years, and the company does not intend to change the tape recorder price. However, the competition among manufacturers of electronic calculators has been increasing. Wesco's calculators have been very popular with consumers. In order to sustain this interest in its calculators and to meet the price reductions expected from competitors, management has decided to reduce the wholesale price of its calculator from $22.50 to $20 per unit effective January 1, 19x8. At the same time, the company plans to spend an additional $57,000 on advertising during fiscal year 19x8. As a consequence of these actions, management estimates that 80 percent of its total revenue will be derived from calculator sales, as compared to 75 percent in 19x7. As in prior years, the sales mix is assumed to be the same at all volume levels.

The total fixed overhead costs will not change in 19x8, nor will the variable overhead cost rates (applied on a direct labor-hour base). However, the cost of materials and direct labor is expected to change. The cost of solid-state electronic components will be cheaper in 19x8. Wesco estimates that material costs will drop 10 percent for the tape recorders and 20 percent for the calculators in 19x8. However, direct labor costs for both products will increase 10 percent in the coming year.

Required:
1. How many tape recorder and electronic calculator units did Wesco Electronics have to sell in 19x7 to break even?
2. What volume of sales is required if Wesco Electronics is to earn a profit in 19x8 equal to 9 percent on sales after taxes?
3. How many tape recorder and electronic calculator units will Wesco have to sell in 19x8 to break even? (CMA, adapted)

PART 2

Uses of
Managerial
Accounting
Data

7 Segmented Reporting and the Contribution Approach to Costing

Learning objectives

After studying Chapter 7, you should be able to:

Explain how costs are allocated to segments of an organization when the contribution approach is used.

Differentiate between direct fixed costs and common fixed costs.

Compute the segment margin and explain how it differs from the contribution margin.

Prepare a segmented income statement using the contribution approach.

Explain how direct costing differs from absorption costing and compute the cost of a unit of product under each method.

Describe how fixed overhead costs are deferred in inventory and released from inventory under absorption costing.

Prepare income statements using both absorption costing and direct costing and reconcile the two net income figures.

Define or explain the key terms listed at the end of the chapter.

One aspect of the accountant's work centers on the problem of allocating costs to various parts of an organization. Cost allocation is necessary to provide useful and relevant data for three purposes:

1. For product costing and for pricing.
2. For appraisal of managerial performance.
3. For making special decisions.

In allocating costs, the accountant can use either of two approaches. One approach, known as absorption costing, was discussed at length in Chapter 3. The other, generally called the contribution approach to costing, was introduced in the preceding chapter in conjunction with our discussion of cost-volume-profit (CVP) analysis. The purpose of this chapter is to study the contribution approach in greater depth. We have already seen how it can be used in making a variety of special decisions. We shall now see how it can be used in preparing segmented statements for management's use, and how the cost of a unit of product or the cost of a service is computed under this costing method.

SEGMENTED REPORTING

To operate effectively, managers must have a great deal more information available to them than that provided by a single income statement. Some product lines may be profitable, and some may be unprofitable; some salespersons may be more effective than others; some sales territories may have a poor sales mix or may be overlooking sales opportunities; or some producing divisions may be ineffectively using their capacity and/or resources. To uncover problems such as these, the manager needs statements that focus on the *segments* of the company. The preparation of such statements is known as **segmented reporting.**

A **segment** can be defined as any part or activity of an organization about which a manager seeks cost data. Examples of segments would include sales territories, manufacturing divisions, producing departments and operations, and groups or lines of products. One of the most valuable uses of the contribution approach to costing is for preparation of segmented reports that can be used for profitability analysis of various segments of an organization.

Differing levels of segmented reports

Segmented reports can be prepared for activity at many different levels of an organization and in differing formats. Exhibit 7–1 illustrates three levels of segmented reports, presented in a format that is widely used. Observe from the exhibit that the total company is first segmented in terms of divisions. Then one of these divisions, Division 2, is further segmented in terms of the product lines sold within the division. In turn, one of these product lines, the regular model, is further segmented in terms of the territories in which it is sold.

EXHIBIT 7–1
Segmented income statements

Segments defined as divisions:

		Segments	
	Total company	**Division 1**	**Division 2**
Sales	$500,000	$300,000	$200,000
Less variable expenses:			
Variable cost of goods sold	180,000	120,000	60,000
Other variable expenses	50,000	30,000	20,000
Total variable expenses	230,000	150,000	80,000
Contribution margin	270,000	150,000	120,000
Less direct fixed expenses	170,000	90,000	80,000*
Divisional segment margin	100,000	$ 60,000	$ 40,000
Less common fixed expenses	25,000		
Net income	$ 75,000		

Segments defined as product lines of Division 2:

		Segments	
	Division 2	**Deluxe model**	**Regular model**
Sales	$200,000	$ 75,000	$125,000
Less variable expenses:			
Variable cost of goods sold	60,000	20,000	40,000
Other variable expenses	20,000	5,000	15,000
Total variable expenses	80,000	25,000	55,000
Contribution margin	120,000	50,000	70,000
Less direct fixed expenses	70,000	30,000	40,000
Product line segment margin	50,000	$ 20,000	$ 30,000
Less common fixed expenses	10,000		
Divisional segment margin	$ 40,000		

Segments defined as sales territories for one product line of Division 2:

		Segments	
	Regular model	**Home sales**	**Foreign sales**
Sales	$125,000	$100,000	$ 25,000
Less variable expenses:			
Variable cost of goods sold	40,000	32,000	8,000
Other variable expenses	15,000	5,000	10,000
Total variable expenses	55,000	37,000	18,000
Contribution margin	70,000	63,000	7,000
Less direct fixed expenses	25,000	15,000	10,000
Territorial segment margin	45,000	$ 48,000	$ (3,000)
Less common fixed expenses	15,000		
Product line segment margin	$ 30,000		

* Notice that this $80,000 in direct fixed expense is divided into two parts—$70,000 direct and $10,000 common—when Division 2 is broken down into product lines. The reasons for this are discussed in a later section, "Direct costs can become common."

Notice that as we go from one segmented report to another, we are looking at smaller and smaller pieces of the company. This is a widely used approach to segmented reporting. If management desired, Division 1 could also be segmented into smaller pieces in the same way as we have segmented Division 2, thereby providing a detailed look at all aspects and levels of the company's operations.

The benefits accruing to the manager from a series of reports such as those contained in Exhibit 7–1 are very great. By carefully examining trends and results in each segment, the manager will be able to gain considerable insight into the company as a whole, and perhaps will discover opportunities and courses of action that would otherwise have remained hidden from view.

Basic allocation concepts

Segmented reports for internal use are typically prepared in the contribution format, as shown in Exhibit 7–1. The same costing guidelines are used in preparing these statements as are used in preparing contribution-type statements generally, with one exception. This lies in the handling of the fixed costs. Notice from the exhibit that the fixed costs are divided into two parts on a segmented statement—one part labeled *direct* and the other part labeled *common*. Only those fixed costs labeled direct are charged to the various segments. If a fixed cost cannot be traced directly to some segment, then it is treated as a common cost and kept separate from the segments themselves. Thus, under the contribution approach, a cost is never arbitrarily assigned to a segment of an organization.

In sum, two guidelines are followed in assigning costs to the various segments of a company under the contribution approach:

1. First, according to cost behavior patterns (that is, variable and fixed).
2. Second, according to whether the costs are *directly traceable* to the segments involved.

We will now consider various parts of Exhibit 7–1 in greater depth.

Sales and contribution margin

In order to prepare segmented statements, it is necessary to keep records of sales and variable expenses by segment, as well as in total for the organization. With sales and variable expense information available, a contribution margin figure can be computed for each separate segment, as illustrated in Exhibit 7–1.

Recall from the prior chapter that the contribution margin is an extremely useful piece of data to the manager—particularly for determining the effect on net income of increases and decreases in sales volume. If sales volume goes up or down, the impact on net income can easily be computed by simply multiplying the unit contribution margin figure by the change in units sold or by multiplying the change in sales dollars by the C/M ratio. Segmented statements give the manager the ability to make such computations on a product-by-product, division-by-division, or territory-by-territory basis, thereby providing the information needed to shore up areas of weakness or to capitalize on areas of strength.

It is important to keep in mind that *the contribution margin is basically a short-run planning tool.* As such, it is especially valuable in decisions relating to temporary uses of capacity, to special orders, and to short-term product line promotion. Decisions relating to the short run usually involve only variable costs and revenues, which of course are the very elements involved in contribution margin. By carefully monitoring segment contribution margins and segment contribution margin ratios, the manager will be in a position to make those short-run decisions that will maximize the contribution of each segment to the overall profitability of the organization.

The importance of fixed costs

The emphasis that we place on the usefulness of the contribution margin should not be taken as a suggestion that fixed costs are not important. *Fixed costs are very important in any organization.* What the contribution approach does imply is that *different costs are needed for different purposes.* For one purpose, variable costs and revenues alone may be adequate for a manager's needs; for another purpose, his or her needs may encompass the fixed costs as well.

The breaking apart of fixed and variable costs also emphasizes to management that the costs are controlled differently and that these differences must be kept clearly in mind for both short-run and long-run planning. Moreover, the grouping of fixed costs under the contribution approach highlights the fact that net income emerges only after the fixed costs have been covered. It also highlights the fact that after the fixed costs have been covered, net income will increase to the extent of the contribution margin generated on each additional unit sold. All of these concepts are useful to the manager *internally* for planning purposes.

Direct and common fixed costs

Direct fixed costs can be defined as those fixed costs that can be identified with a particular segment and that arise because of the existence of the segment. **Common fixed costs** can be defined as those fixed costs that cannot be identified with any particular segment but rather arise because of overall operating activities. In order to be assigned to segments, a common fixed cost would have to be allocated on some highly arbitrary basis, such as sales dollars. Common costs are also known as *indirect costs.*

In Chapter 2, the following guidelines were given in distinguishing between direct and indirect (common) costs:

1. If a cost can be obviously and physically traced to a unit of product or some other organizational segment, then it is a direct cost with respect to that segment.

2. If a cost must be allocated in order to be assigned to a unit of product or some other organizational segment, then it is an indirect (common) cost with respect to that segment.

Examples of direct fixed costs would include advertising outlays made in behalf of a particular segment, the salary of a segment manager (such as a product line supervisor), and depreciation of buildings and equipment acquired for use in a particular segment. Examples of common fixed costs would include corporate image advertising (from which many segments may benefit), salaries of top administrative officers, and depreciation of facilities shared by more than one segment.

Identifying direct fixed costs

The distinction that we have drawn between direct and common fixed costs is crucial in segmented reporting, since direct fixed costs are charged to the segments, whereas common fixed costs are not, as mentioned earlier. As the reader may suppose, in an actual situation it is sometimes hard to determine whether a cost should be classified as direct or common. One widely used rule of thumb is to treat as direct costs *only those costs that would disappear if the segment itself disappeared.* For example, if Division 1 in Exhibit 7–1 were discontinued, then it is unlikely that the division manager would be retained. Since she would disappear with her division, then her salary should be classified as a direct fixed cost of the division. On the other hand, the president of the company undoubtedly would continue even if Division 1 were dropped. Therefore, his salary is common to both divisions. The same idea can be expressed in another way: *treat as direct costs only those costs that are added as a result of the creation of a segment.*

There will always be some costs that fall between the direct and common categories, and considerable care and good judgment will be required for their proper classification. The important point is to resist the temptation to allocate arbitrarily. From a managerial point of view, *any arbitrary allocation of common costs would simply destroy the value of the segment margin as a guide to long-run segment profitability.*

Direct costs can become common

Fixed costs that are direct on one segmented report may become common if the company is divided into smaller segments. This is because there are limits to how finely a cost may be separated without resorting to arbitrary allocation. The more finely segments are defined, the more costs there are that become common.

This concept can be seen in Exhibit 7–1. Notice from the exhibit that when segments are defined as divisions, Division 2 has $80,000 in direct fixed expenses. Only $70,000 of this amount remains direct, however, when we narrow our definition of a segment from divisions to that of the product lines within Division 2. Notice that the other $10,000 then becomes a common cost of these product lines.

		Segments	
	Total company	**Division 1**	**Division 2**
Contribution margin.	$270,000	$150,000	$120,000
Less direct fixed expenses	170,000	90,000	80,000

		Segments	
	Division 2	**Deluxe model**	**Regular model**
Contribution margin.	$120,000	$ 50,000	$ 70,000
Less direct fixed expenses	70,000	30,000	40,000
Product line segment margin . . .	50,000	$ 20,000	$ 30,000
Less common fixed expenses . . .	10,000		
Divisional segment margin	$ 40,000		

Why would $10,000 of direct fixed costs become common costs when the division is divided into product lines? The $10,000 could be depreciation on Division 2's plant building. This depreciation would be a *direct* cost when we are speaking of the division as a whole, but it would be *common* to the product lines produced within the building because both lines would share in the building's use. Any allocation of the depreciation between the two product lines would have to be on some arbitrary basis. To avoid this, we would treat the depreciation on the building as a common cost when Division 2 is segmented into product lines.

The $70,000 that remains a direct fixed cost even after the division is segmented into product lines would consist of amounts that can be identified directly with the product lines on a nonarbitrary basis. It might consist of advertising, for example, expended for product line promotion, of which $30,000 was expended for promotion of the deluxe model and $40,000 was expended for promotion of the regular model. Product line advertising would be a direct fixed cost of the division as a whole, and it would still be a direct cost when looking only at the product lines within the division, since it could be assigned to the lines without the necessity of making an arbitrary allocation.

Segment margin

Observe from Exhibit 7–1 that the **segment margin** is obtained by deducting the direct fixed costs of a segment from the segment's contribution margin. It represents the margin available after a segment has covered all of its own direct costs that can be applied toward the organization's common costs and then toward profits. *The segment margin is viewed as being the best gauge of the long-run profitability of a segment,* since only those costs directly traceable to the segment are used in its computation. If in the long run a segment can't cover its own direct expenses, then that segment probably should not be retained (unless it is essential to sales in other segments). Notice from Exhibit 7–1, for example, that one sales territory (foreign) has a negative segment margin. This means that the segment is not covering its own direct costs and thus is not contributing to the overall profits of the company. In fact, it is detracting from profits in that its loss must be covered by other segments.[1]

From a decision-making point of view, the segment margin is most useful in those decisions relating to long-run needs and performance, such as capacity changes, long-run pricing policy, and segment return on investment. By contrast, as we noted earlier, the contribution margin is most useful in decisions relating to the short run, such as pricing of special orders and utilization of existing capacity through short-term promotional campaigns.

To emphasize this point, refer to the data in Exhibit 7–2. Here we have an income statement segmented by product lines. Notice that all three product lines are covering their own direct costs and thus have positive segment margins.

EXHIBIT 7–2
Income statement segmented by product lines

	Total		Product A		Product B		Product C	
Sales.	$100,000	100%	$30,000	100%	$50,000	100%	$20,000	100%
Less variable expenses	46,000	46	9,000	30	25,000	50	12,000	60
Contribution margin .	54,000	54	21,000	70	25,000	50	8,000	40
Less direct fixed expenses	30,000	30	15,000	50	10,000	20	5,000	25
Product line segment margin.	24,000	24	$ 6,000	20%	$15,000	30%	$ 3,000	15%
Less common fixed expenses	15,000	15						
Net income.	$ 9,000	9%						

Which is the company's best product? The answer depends on your point of reference. In terms of *long-run performance,* product B is the company's best product. Note that it is generating a $15,000 segment margin each period, which by itself is adequate to cover all of the company's common fixed costs. Product B's segment margin ratio is also very high (30 percent), which indicates that its overall direct costs are low in relation to sales. Thus, as shown by its segment margin data, product B represents the company's best product in terms of long-run performance.

---

[1] Retention or elimination of product lines and other segments is covered in depth in Chapter 13.

In terms of *short-run* promotional campaigns or *short-run* capacity utilization, however, management might prefer product A over product B. The reason is that product A has a higher contribution margin ratio than product B. Note that product A's C/M ratio is 70 percent as compared to only 50 percent for product B. Thus, product A will generate a greater amount of contribution margin for a given increase in sales than will product B. As we learned in Chapter 6, the greater the amount of contribution margin that a company is able to generate, the more quickly it will cover its fixed costs or increase its profits.

Of course, in making short-run decisions of this type, management will need to consider other factors as well, such as available capacity, the degree of market saturation, and the amount of sales that can be generated per dollar of advertising. But other factors equal, in short-run promotional decisions or in capacity utilization decisions, management will focus on those products that will generate the greatest amount of contribution margin toward the covering of fixed costs.

To summarize, in evaluating the long-run performance of a segment, the manager will look at the segment margin and at the segment margin ratio. In short-run decision making, however (such as a two-week promotional campaign), the manager will look for the segments that will generate the greatest amount of contribution margin for the effort expended. Typically, this will be the segments that have the highest C/M ratios.

Common fixed costs

Notice both from Exhibit 7–1 and Exhibit 7–2 that no attempt has been made to allocate the common fixed costs to the various segments. Common fixed costs are not allocated to segments but simply deducted in total amount to arrive at the net income for the company as a whole.[2] The managerial accountant contends that nothing is added to the overall usefulness of a segmented statement by allocating the common costs among segments. Rather, the accountant would argue that such allocations tend to *reduce* the usefulness of segmented statements. The reason is that arbitrary allocations draw attention away from the costs that a segment manager has control over and that should form a basis for appraising his or her performance as a segment manager.

Moreover, it is argued that any attempt to allocate common fixed costs among segments may result in misleading data or may obscure important relationships between segment revenues and segment earnings. Backer and McFarland state the problem as follows:

---

[2] For external reporting purposes, the Financial Accounting Standards Board requires that all common costs be allocated among segments on a "reasonable" basis. FASB, *Statement of Financial Accounting Standards No. 14* "Financial Reporting for Segments of a Business Enterprise" (Stamford, Conn., 1976), par. 10(d).

A characteristic of all arbitrary allocations is that they lack universality. Sooner or later circumstances arise in which allocation procedures break down and yield misleading or even absurd results.[3]

Backer and McFarland point out that arbitrary allocations of common fixed costs often result in a segment *appearing* to be unprofitable, whereas it may be contributing substantially above its own direct costs toward the overall profitability of the firm. In such cases, the allocated costs may lead to the unwise elimination of a segment and to a *decrease* in total profits for the firm.

Varying breakdowns of total sales

In order to obtain more detailed information, a company may show total sales broken down into several different segment arrangements. For example, a company may show total sales segmented in three different ways: first, segmented according to divisions; second, segmented according to product lines, without regard to the divisions in which the products are sold; and third, segmented according to the sales territories in which the sales were made. In each case, the sum of the sales by segments would add up to total company sales; the variation in segment arrangements would simply give management the power to look at the total company from several different directions. This type of segmented reporting provides much the same perspective as looking at a beautiful landscape from several different views—from every view you see something you didn't see before.

After this type of segmentation of total sales has been made, many companies then go ahead and break each segment down more finely, such as we illustrated earlier in Exhibit 7–1 and such as is illustrated graphically in Exhibit 7–3. With the availability of the computer, the type of segmentation that we describe here is well within the reach of most companies today.

To illustrate how total sales can be divided into more than one segment arrangement, assume that the Fairfield Company sells two products, X and Y, in two sales territories, the East and the West. Cost and revenue data on the products and the sales territories follow:

1. Selling price, variable expenses, and contribution margin per unit:

	X	Y
Selling price per unit	$10	$6
Variable expense per unit	6	4
Contribution margin per unit . . .	$ 4	$2

---

[3] Morton Backer and Walter B. McFarland, *External Reporting for Segments of a Business* (New York: National Association of Accountants, 1968), p. 23.

EXHIBIT 7–3

Graphical presentation of segmented reporting—the Detroit Motor Company

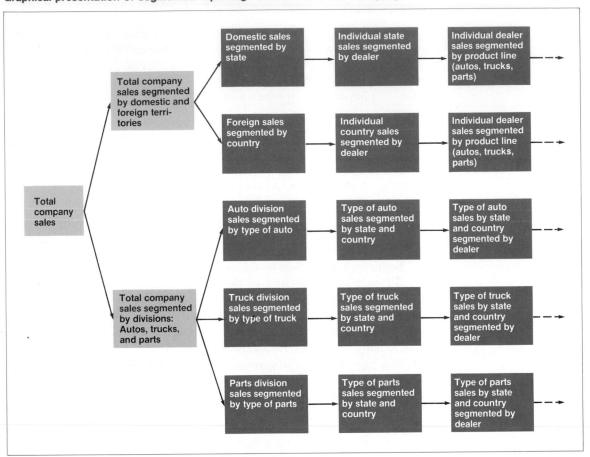

2. Sales in units during 19x1 were:

	Sales territory		Total sales
	East	**West**	
Product X sales	3,000	7,000	10,000
Product Y sales	6,000	9,000	15,000

3. Fixed costs incurred during 19x1 were:

	Product line		Sales territory	
	X	**Y**	**East**	**West**
Fixed production costs	$8,000	$6,000	—	—
Fixed selling costs	—	—	$12,000	$10,000
Fixed administrative costs	2,000	1,500	2,200	2,300

EXHIBIT 7–4

Total sales segmented by product lines and by sales territories

Total Sales Presented by Product Lines

	Total firm	Product X	Product Y
Sales	$190,000	$100,000	$90,000
Less variable expenses	120,000	60,000	60,000
Contribution margin.	70,000	40,000	30,000
Less direct fixed expenses:			
Production	14,000	8,000	6,000
Administration—product lines	3,500	2,000	1,500
Total direct fixed expenses	17,500	10,000	7,500
Product line segment margin	52,500	$ 30,000	$22,500
Less common fixed expenses:			
Selling—sales territories	22,000		
Administration—sales territories.	4,500		
General administration	9,000		
Total common fixed expenses	35,500		
Net income	$ 17,000		

Total Sales Presented by Sales Territories

		Sales territory	
	Total firm	East	West
Sales	$190,000	$66,000*	$124,000*
Less variable expenses	120,000	42,000†	78,000†
Contribution margin.	70,000	24,000	46,000
Less direct fixed expenses:			
Selling—sales territories	22,000	12,000	10,000
Administration—sales territories.	4,500	2,200	2,300
Total direct fixed expenses	26,500	14,200	12,300
Territorial segment margin	43,500	$ 9,800	$ 33,700
Less common fixed expenses:			
Production	14,000		
Administration—product lines	3,500		
General administration	9,000		
Total common fixed expenses	26,500		
Net income	$ 17,000		

	Total	East	West
* Sales by sales territory:			
Product X sales at $10 per unit	$100,000	$30,000	$ 70,000
Product Y sales at $6 per unit	90,000	36,000	54,000
Total sales, as above.	$190,000	$66,000	$124,000
† Variable expenses by sales territory:			
Product X variable expenses, at $6 per unit.	$ 60,000	$18,000	$ 42,000
Product Y variable expenses, at $4 per unit.	60,000	24,000	36,000
Total variable expenses, as above	$120,000	$42,000	$ 78,000

In addition, the company had $9,000 in fixed general administrative costs during 19x1 that cannot be charged directly to any segment.

Exhibit 7–4 presents total sales for the company for 19x1, broken down first between product lines and second between sales territories. Notice from the exhibit that although the product lines are about equally profitable, this equality does not carry over to the sales territories. The West is much more profitable than the East. Thus, the segmented statements point to management areas that may be in need of attention.

In summary, segmented reporting gives a company the ability to look at itself from many different directions. Some of the ways in which cost and profitability data can be generated include:

1. By division.
2. By product line.
3. By salesperson.
4. By sales territory.
5. By region of the country.
6. By domestic and foreign operations.

As we have noted, each of these segments can in turn be broken down into many parts. Indeed, the number of possible directions in which segments can be defined is limited only by one's imagination or by the needs of the firm.

INVENTORY VALUATION UNDER THE CONTRIBUTION APPROACH—DIRECT COSTING

As discussed in Chapter 3, absorption costing allocates a portion of fixed manufacturing overhead to each unit produced during a period, along with variable manufacturing costs. Since absorption costing mingles variable and fixed costs together, units of product costed by that method are not well suited for inclusion in a contribution-type income statement. This has led to an alternative costing method that focuses on cost behavior in computing unit costs. This alternative method is called *direct costing*. It harmonizes fully with the contribution approach and is widely used by manufacturing companies and other organizations in their preparation of contribution-type income statements.

Direct costing

Under **direct costing,** only those costs of production that vary directly with activity are treated as product costs. This would include direct materials, direct labor, and the variable portion of manufacturing overhead. Fixed manufacturing overhead is not treated as a product cost under this method; rather, it is treated as a period cost and, like selling and administrative expenses, is charged off in its entirety against revenue each period. Consequently, the inventory cost of a unit of product under the direct costing method contains no element of fixed overhead cost.

Although it is widely used, the term *direct costing* is really a misnomer. More accurate terms for this costing method would be **variable** or **marginal costing,** since it centers on the notion that only variable production costs should be added to the cost of goods produced. The term *direct costing* is so firmly embedded in the literature and in everyday usage, however, that it seems unlikely that any change in terminology will be made.

Absorption costing

As we learned in Chapter 3, **absorption costing** treats *all* costs of production as product costs, regardless of whether they are variable or fixed in nature. Thus, unlike direct costing, absorption costing allocates a portion of the fixed manufacturing overhead to each unit of product, along with the variable manufacturing costs. The cost of a unit of product under the absorption costing method therefore consists of direct materials, direct labor, and *both* variable and fixed overhead.

To complete this summary comparison of direct and absorption costing, we need to consider briefly the handling of selling and administrative expenses. These expenses are never treated as product costs, regardless of the costing method in use. Thus, under either direct or absorption costing, selling and administrative expenses are always treated as period costs and deducted from revenues as incurred.

Unit cost computations

To illustrate the computation of unit costs under both direct and absorption costing, assume the following data:

The Boley Company produces a single product. The cost characteristics of the product and of the manufacturing plant are given below:

Number of units produced each year	6,000
Variable costs per unit:	
Direct materials	$ 2
Direct labor	4
Variable manufacturing overhead	1
Variable selling and administrative expense	3
Fixed cost per year:	
Manufacturing overhead	30,000
Selling and administrative expense	10,000

Required:
1. Compute the cost of a unit of product under absorption costing.
2. Compute the cost of a unit of product under direct costing.

Solution:

Absorption Costing

Direct materials	$ 2
Direct labor	4
Variable overhead	1
Total variable production cost	7
Fixed overhead ($30,000 ÷ 6,000 units of product)	5
Total cost per unit	$12

Direct Costing

Direct materials	$ 2
Direct labor.	4
Variable overhead	1
Total cost per unit.	$ 7

(The $30,000 fixed overhead will be charged off in total against income as a period expense along with the fixed selling and administrative expense.)

Under the absorption costing method, notice that *all* production costs, variable and fixed, have been added to the cost of units produced during the period. Thus, if the company sells a unit of product and absorption costing is being used, then $12 (consisting of $7 variable cost and $5 fixed cost) will be deducted on the income statement as cost of goods sold. Similarly, any unsold units will be carried as inventory on the balance sheet at $12 each.

Under the direct costing method, notice that only the variable production costs have been added to the cost of units produced during the period. Thus, if the company sells a unit of product, only $7 will be deducted as cost of goods sold, and unsold units will be carried in the balance sheet inventory account at only $7 each.

The controversy over fixed overhead cost

Probably no subject in all of managerial accounting has created as much controversy among accountants as has direct costing. The controversy isn't over whether costs should be separated as between variable and fixed in matters relating to planning and control. Rather, the controversy is over the theoretical justification for excluding fixed overhead costs from the cost of units produced and therefore from inventory.

Advocates of direct costing argue that fixed overhead costs relate to the *capacity* to produce rather than to the actual production of units of product in a given year. That is, they argue that costs for facilities and equipment, insurance, supervisory salaries, and the like, represent costs of being *ready* to produce and therefore will be incurred regardless of whether any actual production takes place during the year. For this reason, advocates of direct costing feel that such costs should be charged against the period rather than against the product.

Advocates of absorption costing argue, on the other hand, that so far as product costing is concerned, it makes no difference whether a manufacturing cost is variable or fixed. They argue that fixed overhead costs such as depreciation and insurance are just as essential to the production process as are the variable costs, and therefore cannot be ignored in costing units of product. They argue that to be fully costed, each unit of product must bear an equitable portion of *all* manufacturing costs.

Although this difference in the handling of fixed overhead might seem slight, it can have a substantial impact on both the clarity and the usefulness of statement data, as we shall see in the following sections.

Comparison of absorption and direct costing

Income statements prepared under the absorption and direct costing approaches are shown in Exhibit 7–5. In preparing these statements, we use the data for the Boley Company presented earlier, along with other information about the company as given below:

Beginning inventory in units.	–0–
Units produced	6,000
Units sold	5,000
Ending inventory in units	1,000
Selling price per unit	$ 20
Selling and administrative expenses:	
Variable per unit	$ 3
Fixed per year	10,000

	Absorption costing	Direct costing
Cost of a unit of product:		
Direct materials	$ 2	$ 2
Direct labor	4	4
Variable overhead	1	1
Fixed overhead ($30,000 ÷ 6,000 units)	5	—
Total cost per unit	$12	$ 7

Several points should be noted from the statements in Exhibit 7–5:

1. Under the absorption costing method, it is possible to defer a portion of the fixed overhead costs of the current period to future periods through the inventory account (known as fixed overhead cost deferred in inventory). Notice that the company produced 6,000 units during the current period but sold only 5,000 units, thus leaving 1,000 units unsold at the end of the period. Recall that under the absorption costing method each unit produced during the period was assigned $5 in fixed overhead cost ($30,000 fixed overhead cost ÷ 6,000 units = $5). Therefore, each of the 1,000 units going into inventory at the end of the period has $5 in fixed overhead cost attached to it, or a total of $5,000 for the 1,000 units involved. This amount of fixed overhead cost of the current period is thereby deferred in inventory to the next period, when, hopefully, these units will be taken out of inventory and sold. The deferral of fixed overhead cost we are talking about can be seen clearly by analyzing the $12,000 ending inventory figure under the absorption costing method:

Variable manufacturing costs: 1,000 units × $7	$ 7,000
Fixed overhead costs: 1,000 units × $5.	5,000
Total inventory value	$12,000

In summary, of the $30,000 in fixed overhead cost incurred during the period, only $25,000 (5,000 units sold × $5) has been included in cost of goods sold. The remaining $5,000 (1,000 units *not* sold × $5) has been deferred in inventory to the next period.

2. Under the direct costing method, fixed overhead costs are not included as part of the cost of units produced but rather are expensed in total ($30,000)

260

EXHIBIT 7–5
Comparison of direct and absorption costing

Absorption Costing

Sales (5,000 units × $20)		$100,000
Cost of goods sold:		
Beginning inventory	$ –0–	
Cost of goods manufactured (6,000 units × $12)	72,000	
Goods available for sale	72,000	
Less ending inventory (1,000 units × $12)	12,000	60,000
Gross margin		40,000
Less selling and administrative expense ($15,000 total variable plus $10,000 fixed)		25,000
Net income		$ 15,000

> Note the difference in ending inventories. Fixed overhead cost at $5 per unit is included under the absorption approach. This explains the difference in ending inventory and in net income (1,000 units × $5 = $5,000).

Direct Costing

Sales (5,000 units × $20)		$100,000
Less variable expenses:		
Variable cost of goods sold:		
Beginning inventory	$ –0–	
Variable manufacturing costs (6,000 units × $7)	42,000	
Goods available for sale	42,000	
Less ending inventory (1,000 units × $7)	7,000	
Variable cost of goods sold	35,000	
Variable selling and administrative expense (5,000 units × $3)	15,000	50,000
Contribution margin		50,000
Less fixed costs:		
Fixed overhead costs	30,000	
Fixed selling and administrative expenses	10,000	40,000
Net income		$ 10,000

as a period cost, along with the selling and administrative expenses. This explains why the ending inventory value under direct costing is $5,000 lower than it is under absorption costing. Under the direct costing method, only the variable manufacturing costs have been added to the cost of units produced and therefore included in inventory:

Variable manufacturing costs: 1,000 units × $7 . . . . . . $7,000

This difference in ending inventories also explains the difference in net income reported under the two costing methods. Since part of the fixed overhead costs of the period have been deferred in inventory under the absorption costing method, net income is $5,000 *higher* under that method than it is under the direct costing method.

3. Notice that the absorption costing income statement makes no distinction between fixed and variable costs; therefore, it is not well suited for CVP computations, which we have emphasized as being important to good

planning and control. In order to generate data for CVP analysis, it would be necessary to spend considerable time reworking and reclassifying the absorption statement.

4. The direct costing approach to costing units of product blends very well with the contribution approach to the income statement, since both concepts are based on the idea of classifying costs by behavior. The direct costing data in Exhibit 7–5 could be used immediately in CVP computations.

The definition of an asset

Essentially, the difference between the absorption approach and the direct costing approach centers on the matter of timing. Direct costing advocates say that fixed manufacturing costs should be released against revenues immediately in total, whereas absorption costing advocates say that fixed manufacturing costs should be released against revenues bit by bit as units of product are sold. Any units of product not sold under absorption costing result in fixed costs being inventoried and carried forward *as assets* to the next period. The solution to the controversy as to which costing method is "right" should therefore rest in large part on whether fixed costs added to inventory fall within the definition of an asset as this concept is generally viewed in accounting theory.

What is an asset? A cost is normally viewed as being an asset if it can be shown that it has revenue-producing powers, or if it can be shown that it will be beneficial in some way to operations in future periods. In short, a cost is an asset if it can be shown that it has *future service potential* that can be identified. For example, insurance prepayments are viewed as being assets, since they have future service potential. The prepayments acquire protection that can be used in future periods to guard against losses that might otherwise hinder operations. If fixed production costs added to inventory under absorption costing are indeed properly called assets, then they too must meet this test of service potential.

The absorption costing view Advocates of absorption costing argue that fixed production costs added to inventory do, indeed, have future service potential. They take the position that if production exceeds sales, then a benefit to future periods is created in the form of an inventory that can be carried forward and sold, resulting in a future inflow of revenue. They argue that *all costs* involved in the creation of inventory should be carried forward as assets—not just the variable costs. The fixed costs of depreciation, taxes, insurance, supervisory salaries, and so on, are just as essential to the creation of units of product as are the variable costs. It would be just as impossible to create units of product in the absence of equipment as it would be to create them in the absence of raw materials or in the absence of workers to operate the machines. In sum, until the fixed production costs have been recognized and attached, units of product have not been fully costed. Both variable and fixed costs become inseparably attached as units are produced and *remain* inseparably attached regardless of whether the units are sold immediately or carried forward as inventory to generate revenue in future periods.

The direct costing view   Direct costing advocates argue that a cost has service potential and is therefore an asset *only if its incurrence now will make it unnecessary to incur the same cost again in the future.* Service potential is therefore said to hinge on the matter of *future cost avoidance.* If the incurrence of a cost now will have no effect on whether or not the same cost will be incurred again in the future, then that cost is viewed as having no relevance to future events. It is argued that such a cost can in no way represent a future benefit or service.

For example, the prepayment of insurance is viewed as being an asset because the cash outlays made when the insurance is acquired make it unnecessary to sustain the same outlays again in the future periods for which insurance protection has been purchased. In short, by making insurance payments now, a company *avoids* having to make payments in the future. Since prepayments of insurance result in *future cost avoidance,* the prepayments qualify as assets.

This type of cost avoidance does not exist in the case of fixed production costs. The incurrence of fixed production costs in one year in no way reduces the necessity to incur the same costs again in the following year. Since the incurrence of fixed production costs does not result in *future cost avoidance,* the costs of one year can have no relevance to future events and therefore cannot possibly represent a future benefit or service. Direct costing advocates argue, therefore, that no part of the fixed production costs of one year should ever be carried forward as an asset to the following year. Such costs do not result in future cost avoidance—the key test for any asset.[4]

Extended comparison of income data

Having gained some insights into the conceptual differences between absorption and direct costing, we are now prepared to take a more detailed look at the differences in the income data generated by these two approaches to cost allocation. Exhibit 7–6 presents data covering a span of three years. In the first year, production and sales are exactly equal. In the second year, production exceeds sales. In the third year, the tables are reversed, with sales exceeding production.

Certain generalizations can be drawn from the data in this exhibit:

1. When production and sales are equal, the same net income will be realized regardless of whether absorption or direct costing is being used (see year 1 in Exhibit 7–6). The reason is that when production and sales are equal, there is no chance for fixed overhead costs to be deferred in inventory or released from inventory under absorption costing.

[4] For further discussion, see David Green, Jr., "A Moral to the Direct Costing Controversy?" *Journal of Business* 33, no. 3 (July 1960), pp. 218–26; and Charles T. Horngren and George H. Sorter, "Direct Costing for External Reporting," *Accounting Review* 36, no. 1 (January 1961), pp. 88–93.

EXHIBIT 7-6
Absorption costing versus direct costing—extended income data

Basic Data

Sales price per unit	$ 12
Variable manufacturing costs per unit (direct materials, direct labor, and variable overhead).	5
Fixed manufacturing overhead costs (total)	24,000

Cost of producing one unit of product:

Under direct costing:	
Variable manufacturing costs.	$ 5

Under absorption costing:	
Variable manufacturing costs.	$ 5
Fixed overhead costs (based on a normal production volume of 8,000 units per year—$24,000 ÷ 8,000)	3
Total absorption costs	$ 8

Selling and administrative expenses are assumed, for simplicity, to be all fixed at $25,000 per year.

	Year 1	Year 2	Year 3	Three years together
Opening inventory in units	–0–	–0–	1,000	–0–
Units produced during the year	8,000	8,000	8,000	24,000
Units sold during the year	8,000	7,000	9,000	24,000
Ending inventory in units	–0–	1,000	–0–	–0–

Direct Costing

	Year 1	Year 2	Year 3	Three years together
Sales	$96,000	$84,000	$108,000	$288,000
Less variable expenses.	40,000*	35,000*	45,000*	120,000
Contribution margin	56,000	49,000	63,000	168,000
Less fixed expenses:				
Manufacturing overhead.	24,000	24,000	24,000	72,000
Selling and administrative expenses. . . .	25,000	25,000	25,000	75,000
Total fixed expenses	49,000	49,000	49,000	147,000
Net income	$ 7,000	$ –0–	$ 14,000	$ 21,000

Absorption Costing

	Year 1	Year 2	Year 3	Three years together
Sales	$96,000	$84,000	$108,000	$288,000
Opening inventory.	–0–	–0–	8,000	8,000
Cost of goods manufactured	64,000	64,000	64,000	192,000
Goods available for sale	64,000	64,000	72,000	200,000
Ending inventory	–0–	8,000	–0–	8,000
Cost of goods sold	64,000	56,000	72,000	192,000
Gross margin	32,000	28,000	36,000	96,000
Selling and administrative expenses	25,000	25,000	25,000	75,000
Net income	$ 7,000	$ 3,000	$ 11,000	$ 21,000

* Variable expenses:
   Year 1: 8,000 units sold × $5 = $40,000.
   Year 2: 7,000 units sold × $5 = $35,000.
   Year 3: 9,000 units sold × $5 = $45,000.

2. When production exceeds sales, the net income reported under absorption costing will generally be greater than the net income reported under direct costing (see year 2 in Exhibit 7–6). The reason is that when more is produced than is sold, part of the fixed overhead costs are deferred in inventory under absorption costing, as discussed earlier. In year 2, for example, $3,000 of fixed overhead cost (1,000 units × $3 per unit) has been deferred in inventory under the absorption approach. Only that portion of fixed overhead cost not deferred in inventory has been charged against income.

Under direct costing, however, all of the fixed overhead costs have been charged against income. The result is that net income is $3,000 lower under direct costing than it is under absorption costing. Exhibit 7–7 contains a reconciliation of the direct costing and absorption costing net income figures.

3. When sales exceed production, the net income reported under the absorption costing approach will generally be less than the net income reported under the direct costing approach (see year 3 in Exhibit 7–6). The reason is that when more is sold than is produced, inventories are drawn down and fixed overhead costs that were previously deferred in inventory under absorption costing are released and charged against income (known as **fixed overhead cost released from inventory**). In year 3, for example, the $3,000 in fixed overhead cost deferred in inventory under the absorption approach in the prior year is released from inventory through the sales process and charged against income. As a result, the cost of goods sold for year 3 contains not only all of the fixed overhead costs for year 3 (since all that was produced in year 3 was sold in year 3) but $3,000 of the fixed overhead costs of year 2 as well.

By contrast, under direct costing only the fixed overhead costs of year 3 have been charged against year 3. The result is that net income under direct costing is $3,000 higher than it is under absorption costing. Exhibit 7–7 contains a reconciliation of the direct costing and absorption costing net income figures.

4. Over an *extended* period of time, the net income figures reported under absorption costing and direct costing will tend to be the same. The reason is that over the long run sales can't exceed production, nor can production

EXHIBIT 7–7

Reconciliation of direct costing and absorption costing—net income data from Exhibit 7–6

	Year 1	Year 2	Year 3
Direct costing net income	$7,000	$ –0–	$14,000
Add: Fixed overhead costs deferred in inventory under absorption costing (1,000 units × $3 per unit).	—	3,000	—
Deduct: Fixed overhead costs released from inventory under absorption costing (1,000 units × $3 per unit)	—	—	(3,000)
Absorption costing net income.	$7,000	$3,000	$11,000

much exceed sales. The shorter the time period, the more the net income figures will tend to vary.

Sales constant, production fluctuates

Exhibit 7–8 presents a reverse situation from that depicted in Exhibit 7–6. In Exhibit 7–6, we made production constant and allowed sales to fluctuate from period to period. In Exhibit 7–8, sales are constant and production

EXHIBIT 7–8
Sensitivity to changes in production and sales

Basic Data

Sales price per unit	$ 10
Variable manufacturing costs per unit	4
Fixed manufacturing overhead costs (total)	24,000
Selling and administrative expenses (all assumed, for simplicity, to be fixed)	5,000

	Year 1	Year 2	Year 3
Number of units produced	6,000	8,000	4,000
Number of units sold	6,000	6,000	6,000
Cost of producing one unit:			
Under direct costing (variable manufacturing costs only)	$4	$4	$ 4
Under absorption costing:			
Variable manufacturing costs	$4	$4	$ 4
Fixed overhead costs ($24,000 total spread in each year over the number of units produced)	4	3	6
Total cost per unit	$8	$7	$10

Direct Costing

	Year 1	Year 2	Year 3
Sales (6,000 units)	$60,000	$60,000	$60,000
Less variable expenses (6,000 units)	24,000	24,000	24,000
Contribution margin	36,000	36,000	36,000
Less fixed expenses:			
Manufacturing overhead	24,000	24,000	24,000
Selling and administrative expenses	5,000	5,000	5,000
Total fixed expenses	29,000	29,000	29,000
Net income	$ 7,000	$ 7,000	$ 7,000

Absorption Costing

	Year 1	Year 2	Year 3
Sales (6,000 units)	$60,000	$60,000	$60,000
Opening inventory	–0–	–0–	14,000
Cost of goods manufactured	48,000	56,000	40,000
Goods available for sale	48,000	56,000	54,000
Ending inventory	–0–	14,000	–0–
Cost of goods sold (6,000 units)	48,000	42,000	54,000
Gross margin	12,000	18,000	6,000
Less selling and administrative expenses	5,000	5,000	5,000
Net income	$ 7,000	$13,000	$ 1,000

fluctuates. Our purpose in Exhibit 7–8 is to observe the effect of changes in production on net income under both absorption and direct costing.

Direct costing Net income is *not* affected by changes in production under direct costing. Notice from Exhibit 7–8 that net income is the same for all three years under the direct costing approach, although production exceeds sales in one year and is less than sales in another year. In short, the only thing that can affect net income under direct costing is a change in sales—a change in production has no impact when direct costing is in use.

Absorption costing Net income *is* affected by changes in production when absorption costing is in use. Notice from Exhibit 7–8 that net income goes up in year 2, in response to the increase in production for that year, and goes down in year 3, in response to the drop in production for that year. The reason for this effect can be traced to the shifting of fixed overhead cost between periods through the inventory account under absorption costing.

When production exceeds sales, units of product are carried forward as inventory to the next period. These units of product take a portion of the current period's fixed costs forward to the next period with them, thereby relieving the current period of costs and causing its income to rise in comparison with past periods. This effect can be observed in year 2 in Exhibit 7–8. Even though the same number of units was sold in year 2 as was sold in year 1, year 2's net income was substantially higher due to the shifting of part of its fixed costs into year 3.

The reverse effect occurs in year 3. Since sales exceed production in year 3, that year is forced to cover all of its own fixed overhead costs as well as the fixed overhead costs carried forward in inventory from year 2. The result is a substantial drop in net income during year 3, as shown in Exhibit 7–8.

Opponents of absorption costing argue that this shifting of fixed overhead cost between periods can be confusing to a manager and can cause him or her either to misinterpret data or to make faulty decisions. The reader may recall from Chapter 3 that one way to overcome problems of this type is to use *normalized* overhead rates. Even if normalized overhead rates are used, the same problems can arise if the under- or overapplied overhead resulting from production being out of balance with sales is taken to cost of goods sold. The only way to avoid the problems entirely is to use normalized overhead rates and to place any under- or overapplied overhead in a balance sheet clearing account of some type. However, this is rarely done in practice.

CVP analysis and absorption costing

Absorption costing is widely regarded as a product costing method. Many firms use the absorption approach exclusively because of its focus on "full" costing of units of product. If the approach has a weakness, it is to be found in its inability to dovetail well with CVP analysis under certain conditions.

To illustrate, refer again to Exhibit 7–6. Let us compute the break-even point for the firm represented by the data in this exhibit. To obtain the break-even point, we divide total fixed costs by the contribution margin per unit:

Sales price per unit	$12
Variable costs per unit	5
Contribution margin per unit	$ 7
Fixed overhead costs.	$24,000
Fixed selling and administrative costs	25,000
Total fixed costs	$49,000

$$\frac{\text{Total fixed costs}}{\text{Contribution margin per unit}} = \frac{\$49,000}{\$7} = 7,000 \text{ units}$$

We have computed the break-even point to be 7,000 units sold. Notice from Exhibit 7–6 that in year 2 the firm sold exactly 7,000 units, the break-even volume. Under the contribution approach, using direct costing, the firm does exactly break even in year 2, showing zero net income or loss. *Under absorption costing, however, the firm shows a positive net income of $3,000 for year 2.* How can this be so? How can absorption costing produce a positive net income when the firm sold exactly the break-even volume of units?

The answer lies in the fact that in year 2 under absorption costing, $3,000 in fixed overhead costs were deferred in inventory and did not appear as charges against income. By deferring these fixed overhead costs in inventory, the firm was able to show a profit even though it sold exactly the break-even volume of units. This leads us to a general observation about absorption costing. The only way that absorption costing data can be used in a break-even analysis is to assume that inventories will not change. Unfortunately, such an assumption often falls far short of reality.

Absorption costing runs into similar kinds of difficulty in other areas of CVP analysis and often requires considerable manipulation of data before figures are available that are usable for decision-making purposes.

External reporting and income taxes

For external reporting on financial statements, a company is required to cost units of product by the absorption costing method. In like manner, the absorption costing method must be used in preparing tax returns. In short, the contribution approach is limited to *internal* use by the managers of a company.

The majority of accountants would agree that absorption costing *should* be used in external reporting. That is, most accountants feel that for *external reporting* purposes, units of product *should* contain a portion of fixed manufacturing overhead, along with variable manufacturing costs. The absorption costing argument that a unit of product is not fully costed until it reflects a portion of the fixed costs of production is difficult to refute, particularly as it applies to the preparing of information to be reported to stockholders and others.

The contribution approach finds its greatest application internally as an assist to the manager in those situations where the absorption costing data are not well suited for CVP analysis or are not well suited for a segment-type analysis, such as was covered earlier in the chapter. No particular problems are created by using *both* costing methods—the contribution method internally and the absorption method externally. As we demonstrated earlier in Exhibit 7–7, the adjustment from direct costing net income to absorption costing net income is a simple one and can be made in a few hours' time at year-end in order to produce an absorption costing net income figure for use on financial statements.

ADVANTAGES OF THE CONTRIBUTION APPROACH

As stated in the preceding section, many accountants feel that under the appropriate circumstances there are certain advantages to be gained from using the contribution approach (with direct costing) internally, even if the absorption approach is used externally for reporting purposes. These advantages have been summarized by the National Association of Accountants as follows:[5]

1. CVP relationship data wanted for profit planning purposes are readily obtained from the regular accounting statements. Hence management does not have to work with two separate sets of data to relate one to the other.
2. The profit for a period is not affected by changes in absorption of fixed expenses resulting from building or reducing inventory. Other things remaining equal (for example, selling prices, costs, sales mix), profits move in the same direction as sales when direct costing is in use.
3. Manufacturing cost and income statements in the direct cost form follow management's thinking more closely than does the absorption cost form for these statements. For this reason, management finds it easier to understand and to use direct cost reports.
4. The impact of fixed costs on profits is emphasized because the total amount of such cost for the period appears in the income statement.
5. Marginal income figures facilitate relative appraisal of products, territories, classes of customers, and other segments of the business without having the results obscured by allocation of joint fixed costs.
6. Direct costing ties in with such effective plans for cost control as standard costs and flexible budgets.[6] In fact, the flexible budget is an aspect of direct costing, and many companies thus use direct costing methods for this purpose without recognizing them as such.
7. Direct cost constitutes a concept of inventory cost that corresponds closely

---

[5] National Association of Accountants, *Research Series No. 23,* "Direct Costing" (New York, 1953), p. 55.

[6] Standard costs and flexible budgets are covered in Chapters 9 and 10.

with the current out-of-pocket expenditure necessary to manufacture the goods.

SUMMARY

Cost allocation problems exist in every company. The contribution approach attempts to handle these problems by defining segments of an organization and by classifying costs as being either direct or common to the segments. Only those costs that are direct to the segments are allocated. Costs that are not direct to the segments are treated as common costs and are not allocated.

The contribution approach also classifies costs by behavior. For this reason, those costs traceable *directly* to a segment are classified as between variable and fixed. Deducting total variable costs from sales yields a contribution margin, which is highly useful in short-run planning and decision making. The direct fixed costs of a segment are then deducted from the contribution margin, yielding a segment margin. The segment margin is highly useful in long-run planning and decision making. Segments can be arranged in many ways—by sales territory, by division, by product line, by salesperson, and so on.

In costing units of product in a manufacturing firm, the contribution method with direct costing adds only the variable manufacturing costs to units of product. The fixed manufacturing costs are taken directly to the income statement as expenses of the period.

Although the contribution approach cannot be used externally either for financial reporting or for tax purposes, it is often used internally by management. Its popularity internally can be traced in large part to the fact that it dovetails well with CVP concepts that are often indispensable in profit planning and decision making.

REVIEW PROBLEM ON ABSORPTION AND DIRECT COSTING

Dexter Company produces and sells a single product. Selected cost and operating data relating to the product for a recent year are given below:

Opening inventory in units	–0–
Units produced during the year	10,000
Units sold during the year	8,000
Ending inventory in units	2,000
Selling price per unit.	$ 50
Selling and administrative costs:	
Variable per unit	5
Fixed per year	70,000
Manufacturing costs:	
Variable per unit:	
Direct materials	12
Direct labor	6
Variable overhead	2
Fixed per year	100,000

Required: 1. Assume that the company uses absorption costing.

    a. Compute the manufactured cost of one unit of product.

    b. Prepare an income statement for the year.

2. Assume that the company uses direct costing.

    a. Compute the manufactured cost of one unit of product.

    b. Prepare an income statement for the year.

3. Reconcile the direct costing and absorption costing net income figures.

Solution: 1. *a.* Under absorption costing, all manufacturing costs, variable and fixed, are added to the cost of a unit of product:

Direct materials	$12
Direct labor	6
Variable overhead	2
Fixed overhead ($100,000 ÷ 10,000 units)	10
Total cost per unit	$30

    b. The absorption costing income statement follows:

Sales (8,000 units × $50)		$400,000
Cost of goods sold:		
Opening inventory	$ –0–	
Add cost of goods manufactured		
(10,000 units × $30)	300,000	
Goods available for sale	300,000	
Less ending inventory (2,000 units × $30)	60,000	240,000
Gross margin		160,000
Less selling and administrative expense		110,000*
Net income		$ 50,000

* Variable (8,000 units × $5)	$ 40,000
Fixed per year	70,000
Total	$110,000

2. *a.* Under direct costing, only the variable manufacturing costs are added to the cost of a unit of product:

Direct materials	$12
Direct labor	6
Variable overhead	2
Total cost per unit	$20

    b. The direct costing income statement follows. Notice that the variable cost of goods sold is computed in a simpler, more direct manner than it was in the example provided earlier in Exhibit 7–5. On a direct costing income statement, either approach is acceptable.

Sales (8,000 units × $50)		$400,000
Less variable expenses:		
Variable cost of goods sold		
(8,000 units × $20)	$160,000	
Variable selling and administrative		
expense (8,000 units × $5)	40,000	200,000
Contribution margin.		200,000
Less fixed expense:		
Fixed overhead cost for the year	100,000	
Fixed selling and administrative expense	70,000	170,000
Net income		$ 30,000

3. The reconciliation of the direct and absorption costing net income figures follows:

Direct costing net income	$30,000
Add: Fixed overhead costs deferred in	
inventory under absorption costing	
(2,000 units × $10)	20,000
Absorption costing net income	$50,000

KEY TERMS FOR REVIEW

Absorption costing A costing method that includes a portion of fixed manufacturing overhead in the cost of a unit of product, along with direct materials, direct labor, and variable overhead.

Common fixed cost A cost that cannot be identified with any particular segment but rather which exists to serve the needs of several segments taken together.

Direct costing A costing method that includes only variable manufacturing costs—direct materials, direct labor, and variable overhead—in the cost of a unit of product. Also see *Marginal costing.*

Direct fixed cost A cost that can be identified with a particular segment and that arises because of the existence of that segment.

Fixed overhead cost deferred in inventory The portion of the fixed overhead cost of a period that goes into inventory under the absorption costing method as a result of production exceeding sales.

Fixed overhead cost released from inventory The portion of the fixed overhead cost of a *prior* period that becomes an expense of the current period under the absorption costing method as a result of sales exceeding production.

Marginal costing Another term for direct costing. See *Direct costing.*

Segment Any part or activity of an organization about which the manager seeks cost data.

Segment margin The amount remaining from the sales of a segment after the segment has covered all of its own direct costs, variable and fixed.

Segmented reporting An income statement or other report in an organization in which data are divided according to product lines, division, territories or similar organizational segments.

Variable costing Another term for direct costing. See *Direct costing.*

QUESTIONS

7–1. Define a segment of an organization. Give several examples of segments.

7–2. How does the contribution approach attempt to assign costs to segments of an organization?

7–3. Distinguish between a direct cost and a common cost. Give several examples of each.

7–4. How does the manager benefit from having the income statement in a segmented format?

7–5. Explain how the segment margin differs from the contribution margin. Which concept is most useful to the manager? Why?

7–6. Why aren't common costs allocated to segments under the contribution approach?

7–7. How is it possible for a cost that is direct under one segment arrangement to become a common cost under another segment arrangement?

7–8. What is the basic difference between absorption costing and direct costing?

7–9. Are selling and administrative expenses treated as product costs or as period costs under direct costing?

7–10. Explain how fixed overhead costs are shifted from one period to another under absorption costing.

7–11. What arguments can be advanced in favor of treating fixed overhead costs as product costs?

7–12. What arguments can be advanced in favor of treating fixed overhead costs as period costs?

7–13. If production and sales are equal, which method would you expect to show the highest net income, direct costing or absorption costing? Why?

7–14. If production exceeds sales, which method would you expect to show the highest net income, direct costing or absorption costing? Why?

7–15. If fixed overhead costs are released from inventory under absorption costing, what does this tell you about the level of production in relation to the level of sales?

7–16. What special assumption must be made in order to compute a break-even point under absorption costing?

7–17. Under absorption costing, how is it possible to increase net income without increasing sales?

7–18. What limitations are there to the use of direct costing?

EXERCISES

E7–1. Caltec, Inc., produces and sells two products. During 19x1, 10,000 units of product A and 12,000 units of product B were produced and sold. Revenue and cost information relating to the products follows:

	Product A	Product B
Selling price per unit	$ 8.00	$ 10.00
Variable expenses per unit	3.20	7.00
Direct fixed expenses (total)	40,000	12,000

Common fixed expenses in the company total $18,000 annually.

Required: Prepare an income statement segmented by product lines. Show both "Amount" and "Percent" columns for the company as a whole and for each of the product lines.

E7–2. Marple Company operates two divisions, X and Y. A segmented income statement for the company's most recent year is given below:

	Total company		Segments			
			Division A		Division B	
Sales	$500,000	100%	$200,000	100%	$300,000	100%
Less variable expenses	220,000	44	70,000	35	150,000	50
Contribution margin	280,000	56	130,000	65	150,000	50
Less direct fixed expenses	150,000	30	90,000	45	60,000	20
Divisional segment margin	130,000	26	$ 40,000	20%	$ 90,000	30%
Less common fixed expenses . . .	70,000	14				
Net income	$ 60,000	12%				

Required:
1. By how much would the company's net income increase if Division B increased its sales by $40,000 per year? Assume no change in cost behavior patterns in the company.
2. Refer to the original data. Assume that sales in Division A increase by $50,000 next year and that sales in Division B remain unchanged. Assume no change in fixed costs in the divisions or in the company.
   a. Prepare a new segmented income statement for the company, using the format above. Show both amounts and percentages.
   b. Notice from your income statement that the contribution margin ratio for Division A has remained unchanged at 65 percent (the same as in the data above) but that the segment margin ratio has changed. How do you explain the change in the segment margin ratio?

E7–3. Refer to the data in Exercise 7–2. Assume that Division B's sales by product line are:

	Division B		Segments			
			Product X		Product Y	
Sales	$300,000	100%	$100,000	100%	$200,000	100%
Less variable expenses	150,000	50	40,000	40	110,000	55
Contribution margin	150,000	50	60,000	60	90,000	45
Less direct fixed expenses . . .	48,000	16	28,000	28	20,000	10
Product line segment margin . . .	102,000	34	$ 32,000	32%	$ 70,000	35%
Less common fixed expenses . .	12,000	4				
Divisional segment margin. . . .	$ 90,000	30%				

The company would like to initiate an intensive promotional campaign on one of the two products during the next month. The campaign would cost $5,000. Marketing studies indicate that such a campaign would increase sales of product X by $25,000 or increase sales of product Y by $30,000.

Required: 1. On which of the products would you recommend that the company focus its promotional campaign? Show computations to support your answer.

2. In exercise 7–2, Division B shows $60,000 in direct fixed expenses. What happened to the $60,000 in this exercise?

E7–4. You have a client who operates a large retail self-service grocery store that has a full range of departments. The management has encountered difficulty in using accounting data as a basis for decisions as to possible changes in departments operated, products, marketing methods, and so forth. List several overhead costs, or costs not applicable to a particular department, and explain how the existence of such costs (sometimes called *common costs* or *joint costs*) complicates and limits the use of accounting data in making decisions in such a store.   (CPA adapted)

E7–5. Bovine Company experienced a loss for last month, as shown by the following income statement:

Sales	$500,000
Less variable expenses . . .	282,500
Contribution margin	217,500
Less fixed expenses	225,000
Net income (loss)	$ (7,500)

In order to pinpoint the problem, the president has asked for an income statement segmented by product line. Accordingly, the accounting department has developed the following cost and revenue data:

	Product A	Product B	Product C
Sales	$150,000	$100,000	$250,000
Contribution margin ratio . . .	30%	60%	45%
Direct fixed expenses	$ 60,000	$ 35,000	$ 90,000

Required: 1. Prepare an income statement segmented by products, as desired by the president.

2. The marketing department feels that sales of product B could be increased by 50 percent if advertising were increased by $10,000 monthly. Would you recommend the increased advertising? Show computations.

E7–6. Selected information on the operations of Diston Company for 19x8 is given below:

Opening inventory in units	–0–
Units produced during the year	25,000
Units sold during the year	20,000
Ending inventory in units	5,000
Variable costs per unit:	
Direct materials	$4
Direct labor	7
Variable overhead	1
Variable selling expenses	2
Fixed costs per year:	
Manufacturing overhead	$200,000
Selling and administrative expenses . .	90,000

The company produces and sells a single product. Work in process inventories are nominal and can be ignored.

Required: 1. Assume that the company uses absorption costing. Compute the cost of one unit of product.
2. Assume that the company uses direct costing. Compute the cost of one unit of product.

E7–7. Refer to the data in Exercise 7–6. An income statement prepared under the absorption costing method for 19x8 follows:

Sales (20,000 units × $30)		$600,000
Cost of goods sold:		
Opening inventory	$ –0–	
Cost of goods manufactured (25,000 units × $?) . . .	500,000	
Goods available for sale	500,000	
Less ending inventory (5,000 units × $?)	100,000	400,000
Gross margin		200,000
Less selling and administrative expenses:		
Variable selling	40,000	
Fixed selling and administrative	90,000	130,000
Net income		$ 70,000

Required: 1. Determine how much of the $100,000 ending inventory above consists of fixed overhead cost deferred in inventory to the next period.
2. Prepare an income statement for 19x8, using the direct costing method. (Note that the company's product sells for $30 per unit.) How do you explain the difference in net income between the two costing methods?

E7–8. Amcor, Inc., produces and sells a single product. The following costs relate to its production and sale:

Variable costs per unit:	
Direct materials	$10
Direct labor	5
Variable manufacturing overhead	2
Variable selling and administrative expenses . . .	4
Fixed costs per year:	
Manufacturing overhead	$ 90,000
Selling and administrative expenses	150,000

During the last year, 30,000 units were produced and 28,000 units were sold. The Finished Goods inventory account at the end of the year shows a balance of $34,000 for the 2,000 unsold units.

Required: 1. Is the company using absorption costing or direct costing to cost units in the Finished Goods inventory account? Show computations to support your answer.
2. Assume that the company wishes to prepare financial statements for the year to issue to its stockholders.
    a. Is the $34,000 figure for finished goods inventory the correct figure to use on these statements for external reporting purposes? Explain.
    b. At what dollar amount *should* the 2,000 units be carried in inventory for external reporting purposes?

E7–9. Morey Company was organized just one year ago. The results of the company's first year of operations are shown below (absorption costing basis):

MOREY COMPANY
Income Statement

Sales (6,000 units at $15)		$90,000
Less cost of goods sold:		
Opening inventory	$ –0–	
Cost of goods produced (8,000 units at $10)	80,000	
Goods available for sale	80,000	
Ending inventory (2,000 units at $10).	20,000	60,000
Gross margin.		30,000
Less selling and administrative expenses		23,000
Net income		$ 7,000

The selling and administrative expenses are all fixed. The company's $10 unit cost is computed as follows:

Direct materials	$ 3
Direct labor.	2
Variable factory overhead.	1
Fixed factory overhead ($32,000 ÷ 8,000)	4
Total unit cost	$10

Required: 1. Redo the company's income statement in the contribution format using direct costing.

2. Reconcile any difference between the net income shown on the direct costing income statement you have prepared and the net income shown on the absorption costing income statement above.

E7–10. Maxwell, Inc., manufactures and sells a single product. The following costs are available for 19x5, the company's first year of operation:

Variable costs per unit:	
Direct materials	$2
Direct labor.	7
Variable manufacturing overhead . . .	1
Variable selling and administrative . . .	3
Fixed costs (annual):	
Manufacturing overhead	$60,000
Selling and administrative.	40,000

During 19x5, the company produced 12,000 units and sold 10,000 units. The selling price is $25 per unit.

Required: 1. Assume that the company uses absorption costing.
   a. Compute the cost of one unit of product.
   b. Prepare an income statement for 19x5.

2. Assume that the company uses direct costing.
   a. Compute the cost of one unit of product.
   b. Prepare an income statement for 19x5.

PROBLEMS

Problems 7–11 through 7–19 deal primarily with segmented reporting issues; problems 7–20 through 7–28 deal primarily with absorption versus direct costing issues.

P7–11. **Basic segmented statement.** Diversified Products, Inc., has recently acquired a small publishing company that Diversified Products intends to operate as one of its subsidiaries. The newly acquired company has three books that it offers for sale—a cookbook, a travel guide, and a handy speller. Each book sells for $10. It costs $3 to print a cookbook, $4 to print a travel guide, and $2 to print a handy speller. Sales commissions are 10 percent of sales for any book.

The publishing company's income statement for the most recent month is given below:

	Total company		Cookbook	Travel Guide	Handy speller
Sales	$200,000	100.0%	$60,000	$100,000	$40,000
Less expenses:					
Printing costs	66,000	33.0	18,000	40,000	8,000
Sales commissions	20,000	10.0	6,000	10,000	4,000
Advertising	25,000	12.5	9,000	13,000	3,000
Salaries and wages	27,000	13.5	12,000	7,000	8,000
Equipment depreciation.	20,000	10.0	6,000	10,000	4,000
Warehouse rent	10,000	5.0	3,000	5,000	2,000
General administration	27,000	13.5	9,000	9,000	9,000
Total expenses.	195,000	97.5	63,000	94,000	38,000
Net income	$ 5,000	2.5%	$ (3,000)	$ 6,000	$ 2,000

The following additional information is available about the company:

a. The same equipment is used to print all three books, and the same warehouse is used to store the books awaiting sale. Therefore, these costs have been allocated to the product lines on a basis of sales dollars.

b. The general administration costs above relate to administration of the company as a whole; therefore, they have been allocated equally among the three product lines.

c. All other costs are direct to the product lines.

Diversified Products is anxious to improve on the company's 2.5 percent return on sales. Therefore, management has decided to eliminate the cookbook, since it is not returning a profit, and to focus all available resources on promoting the travel guide, since it is the most profitable line.

Required: 1. Prepare a new segmented income statement for the month, using the contribution approach. Show both an "Amount" column and a "Percent" column for the company as a whole and for each product line.

2. Do you agree with management's decision:
   a. To eliminate the cookbook line? Explain.
   b. To focus all available resources on promoting the travel guide? Explain. (You may assume that an ample market is available for all three products.)

3. What additional points would you bring to the attention of management that might help to improve sales or profits?

P7–12. **Segmented reporting** The most recent monthly income statement for Reston Company is given below:

RESTON COMPANY
Income Statement

Sales	$100,000
Less variable expenses	55,000
Contribution margin .	45,000
Less fixed expenses .	41,000
Net income	$ 4,000

Management is very disappointed with the company's performance and is wondering what can be done to improve overall profits. By examining sales and cost records, you have determined the following:

a. The company is divided into two sales territories—Central and Eastern. Sixty percent of monthly sales come from the Central territory, and $30,000 of the variable expenses are traceable to the Central territory. Fixed expenses of $14,000 and $12,000 are traceable to the Central and Eastern territories, respectively.

b. The company sells two products—Awls and Pows—in each sales territory. Sales of Awls and Pows totaled $10,000 and $30,000, respectively, in the Eastern territory last month. Variable expenses are 40 percent of the selling price for Awls and 70 percent for Pows. Cost records show that $4,000 of the Eastern territory's fixed expenses are assignable directly to Awls and $5,000 to Pows.

Required: 1. Prepare segmented income statements such as illustrated in Exhibit 7–1, first showing the total company broken down between sales territories, and then showing the Eastern territory broken down by product line. Show both "Amount" and "Percent" columns for the company in total and for the segments.

2. Looking at the data contained in the segmented statements, what seems to be a major problem in the Eastern territory?

P7–13. **Analyzing segmented statements.** Profits in Wiley Company have been poor for some time. In an effort to improve the company's operating performance, the executive committee has requested that the monthly income statement be segmented by sales territory. Accordingly, the company's accounting department has prepared the following statement for October 19x3, the most recent month of activity:

	Territory A	Territory B	Territory C
Sales	$250,000	$100,000	$150,000
Less territorial expenses:			
Cost of goods sold	75,200	30,000	43,600
Salaries and wages	30,000	14,000	39,250
Utilities.	12,500	11,500	12,000
Advertising	40,000	20,000	40,000
Freight-out	9,800	5,000	5,900
Depreciation of buildings and equipment	15,000	14,500	15,250
Total territorial expenses.	182,500	95,000	156,000
Territorial income (loss) before corporate expenses	67,500	5,000	(6,000)
Less corporate expenses:			
Advertising (general)	10,000	4,000	6,000
General and administrative expense	15,000	15,000	15,000
Total corporate expenses	25,000	19,000	21,000
Net income (loss).	$ 42,500	$ (14,000)	$ (27,000)

The company is a wholesale distributor of industrial tools. It purchases tools from the manufacturer and distributes them in the eastern part of the United States. The three territories are about the same size. Each territory has its own manager and sales staff.

Required: 1. What are the advantages of the statement format above from the point of view of *(a)* the territory managers and *(b)* the executive committee?

2. What are the disadvantages or weaknesses of the statement format illustrated above?

3. Explain how the corporate expenses have been allocated to the territories. Do you agree with these allocations? Explain.

4. Prepare a new segmented income statement for October 19x3, using the contribution approach. Show a "Total" column as well as data for each territory. Include percentages on your statement. You may assume that all expenses are fixed except cost of goods sold and freight-out.

5. Analyze the statement that you prepared in (4) above. What points that might help to improve the company's performance would you be particularly anxious to bring to the attention of the executive committee?

P7–14. **Multiple segmented income statements.** Heritage Company has started segmenting its income statements in order to provide more useful data for management. The company's income statement segmented by divisions for May 19x7 is given below:

	Total company	Office products division	Home products division
Sales	$1,000,000	$700,000	$300,000
Less variable expenses:			
Production.	290,000	140,000	150,000
Other	100,000	70,000	30,000
Total variable expenses . .	390,000	210,000	180,000
Contribution margin	610,000	490,000	120,000
Less direct fixed expenses. . .	350,000	250,000	100,000
Divisional segment margin . . .	260,000	$240,000	$ 20,000
Less common fixed expenses. .	170,000		
Net income	$ 90,000		

Management is very concerned with the poor performance of the home products division. To help pinpoint the problem, the president has asked for additional information on the division. The following data are available on the three products that the division manufactures and sells:

		Product line		
	Total	A	B	C
Sales.	$300,000	$150,000	$50,000	$100,000
Variable production costs as a percentage of sales	—	50%	38%	56%
Other variable expenses as a percentage of sales	—	10%	12%	9%
Direct fixed expenses	$ 90,000	$ 33,000	$17,000	$ 40,000

Required: 1. Prepare a segmented income statement for the home products division, with segments defined by products. Use the contribution approach and the format shown in Exhibit 7–1. Show both an "Amount" and a "Percent" column for the division in total and for each product line.

2. The president now wants more information about product line C. This product is sold in two sales markets—the East and the West. Sales and other data about the two markets follow:

	Total	Sales market	
		East	West
Sales.	$100,000	$75,000	$25,000
Variable production costs as a percentage of sales . . .	—	56%	56%
Other variable expenses as a percentage of sales	—	8%	12%
Direct fixed expenses	$ 26,000	$12,000	$14,000

Prepare a segmented income statement for product line C, with segments defined as markets. Again use the format in Exhibit 7–1 and show both "Amount" and "Percent" columns.

3. Scrutinize the statements you have prepared in (1) and (2). What points should be brought to the attention of management?

4. Assume that the president wants more information about the West sales market. Suggest ways in which this market might be further segmented.

P7–15. **Multiple segmented income statements.** Kelvin Products, Inc.'s income statement segmented by divisions for last year is given below:

	Total company	Divisions	
		Plastics	Glass
Sales	$1,500,000	$900,000	$600,000
Less variable expenses	700,000	400,000	300,000
Contribution margin	800,000	500,000	300,000
Less direct fixed expenses:			
Advertising.	300,000	180,000	120,000
Depreciation	140,000	92,000	48,000
Administration	220,000	118,000	102,000
Total	660,000	390,000	270,000
Divisional segment margin . . .	140,000	$110,000	$ 30,000
Less common fixed expenses . .	100,000		
Net income	$ 40,000		

Top management doesn't understand why the glass division has such a low segment margin when its sales are only one third less than sales in the plastics division. Accordingly, management has directed that the glass division be further segmented into product lines. The following information is available on the product lines in the glass division:

	Product line		
	X	Y	Z
Sales	$200,000	$300,000	$100,000
Direct fixed expenses:			
Advertising	30,000	42,000	48,000
Depreciation	10,000	24,000	14,000
Administration	14,000	21,000	7,000
Variable expenses as a			
percentage of sales . .	65%	40%	50%

Analysis shows that $60,000 of the glass division's administration expenses are common to the product lines.

Required: 1. Prepare a segmented income statement for the glass division, with segments defined as product lines. Use the contribution approach and the format shown in Exhibit 7–1. Show both an "Amount" and a "Percent" column for the division in total and for each product line.

2. Management is very surprised by product line Z's poor showing and would like to have the product line segmented by market. The following information is available about the two markets in which product line Z is sold:

	Markets	
	Domestic	Foreign
Sales	$60,000	$40,000
Direct fixed expenses:		
Advertising	18,000	30,000
Variable expenses as a		
percentage of sales . .	50%	50%

All of product line Z's depreciation and administration expenses are common to the markets in which the product is sold. Prepare a segmented income statement for product line Z, with segments defined as markets. Again use the format in Exhibit 7–1 and show both "Amount" and "Percent" columns.

3. Refer to the statement prepared in (1) above. The sales manager wants to run a special promotional campaign on one of the products over the next month. A market study indicates that such a campaign would increase sales of product line X by $40,000 or sales of product line Y by $30,000. The campaign would cost $8,000. Show computations to determine which product line should be chosen.

P7–16. **Total sales segmented by product line and by sales territory.** Selected information relating to the operations of Stratford Company for a recent month is given below:

| | Product line | | | |
	A	B	C	Total
Sales in units	10,000	20,000	11,000	41,000
Selling price per unit	$ 15	$ 12	$ 10	$ —
Variable cost per unit for production, administration, and sales.	6	9	8	—
Depreciation of production equipment. . .	6,000	8,000	4,000	18,000
Product line supervisor	3,000	4,000	2,000	9,000
General factory overhead—fixed	—	—	—	30,000
Selling expenses—fixed	—	—	—	60,000
Administrative expense—fixed	—	—	—	40,000

Depreciation and product line supervisor costs are direct to the product lines. Other fixed costs are common to the product lines.

Required:

1. Prepare a segmented income statement for the month, with the company segmented by product line. Show both "Amount" and "Percent" columns. (Round percentages to one decimal place.)

2. The company's products are sold throughout the United States in three sales territories—the East, the Midwest, and the West. The percentage of product line sales made in each of the three territories is given below, along with other data:

| | Sales territory | | | |
	East	Midwest	West	Total
Product line A.	40%	50%	10%	100%
Product line B.	40	40	20	100
Product line C.	20	20	60	100
Selling expenses—fixed	$14,000	$16,000	$30,000	$60,000
Administrative expenses—fixed. . .	7,000	8,000	10,000	25,000

Notice that all $60,000 of the company's fixed selling expenses are direct to the sales territories and that $25,000 of the company's $40,000 fixed administrative expenses are direct to the sales territories. The remaining $15,000 of the fixed administrative expenses relate to overall company administration and are therefore common to the sales territories. The fixed costs relating to factory overhead, depreciation of production equipment, and product line supervision are also common to the sales territories; do *not* allocate these fixed costs to the sales territories—treat them as common costs.

  a. Prepare another segmented income statement for the month, this time showing the total company segmented by sales territory. Again show both "Amount" and "Percent" columns on your statement. (Round percentages to one decimal place.)

  b. Comment on the profitability of the various sales territories. What factors would you be particularly anxious to bring to the attention of management?

P7–17. Segmented reporting; expansion analysis. Meredith Company produces and sells three products (A, B, and C), which are sold in a local market and a regional market. At the end of the first quarter of the current year, the following absorption basis income statement has been prepared:

MEREDITH COMPANY
Income Statement
For the First Quarter

	Total	Local	Regional
Sales	$1,300,000	$1,000,000	$300,000
Cost of goods sold	1,010,000	777,000	233,000
Gross margin	290,000	223,000	67,000
Selling expenses	105,000	60,000	45,000
Administrative expenses. . .	52,000	40,000	12,000
Total expenses	157,000	100,000	57,000
Net income	$ 133,000	$ 123,000	$ 10,000

Management has expressed special concern with the regional market because of the extremely poor return on sales. This market was entered a year ago because of excess capacity. It was originally believed that the return on sales would improve with time, but after a year no noticeable improvement can be seen from the results in the above quarterly statement.

In attempting to decide whether to eliminate the regional market, the following information has been gathered:

	Products		
	A	B	C
Sales	$500,000	$400,000	$400,000
Variable manufacturing expenses as a percentage of sales	40%	35%	30%
Variable selling expenses as a percentage of sales.	3	2	2
Fixed manufacturing expenses traceable directly to the product lines	$190,000	$150,000	$210,000

	Sales by markets	
Product	Local	Regional
A	$ 400,000	$100,000
B	300,000	100,000
C	300,000	100,000
Total sales . . .	$1,000,000	$300,000

The administrative expenses shown on the income statement above are common to both the markets and the product lines. They have been allocated to the markets above on a basis of sales dollars. The selling expenses shown on the income statement above are all direct to the markets, as shown. Inventory levels are nominal and can be ignored.

Required: 1. Prepare a segmented income statement for the quarter using the contribution approach, segmented into local and regional markets.
2. Assuming that there are no alternative uses for the company's present capacity, would you recommend dropping the regional market? Why or why not?
3. Prepare another segmented income statement for the quarter, again using the

contribution approach, but this time segmented by product line. (Do not allocate the fixed selling expenses to the product lines; treat these as common costs.)

4. Assume that product lines B and C are both at full capacity. The company would like to add sufficient additional capacity to double the output of one of these product lines. Overall cost relationships for the added capacity would follow the same cost behavior patterns as with present capacity for each product line. The company's executive committee has decided to double the capacity of product C because of its higher C/M ratio. Explain why you do or do not agree with this decision.   (CMA, adapted)

P7–18. **Analyzing segmental statements.** "Rats! We're still in the red," said Jana Andrews, executive vice president of the Ashland Company. "I know," said Steve Clark, the controller. "Just look at this income statement for March. At least placing it in a segmented format this month tells us where our problem is. We've got to forget about Districts A and B and zero in on District C." The statement to which Mr. Clark was referring is shown below:

	Total company	District A	District B	District C
Sales @ $20 per unit	$1,000,000	$300,000	$500,000	$200,000
Less cost of goods sold @ $9 per unit . . .	450,000	135,000	225,000	90,000
Gross margin	550,000	165,000	275,000	110,000
Less operating expenses:				
Marketing expenses:				
Freight-out.	51,250	11,250	25,000	15,000
Warehouse depreciation*.	80,000	24,000	40,000	16,000
Sales commissions	60,000	18,000	30,000	12,000
Sales salaries.	30,000	12,000	10,000	8,000
District advertising	75,000	20,000	25,000	30,000
National advertising*	115,000	34,500	57,500	23,000
Total marketing expenses	411,250	119,750	187,500	104,000
Administrative expenses:				
District management salaries	40,000	12,000	15,000	13,000
Central office administrative expenses* . .	100,000	30,000	50,000	20,000
Total administrative expenses	140,000	42,000	65,000	33,000
Total operating expenses	551,250	161,750	252,500	137,000
Net income (loss)	$ (1,250)	$ 3,250	$ 22,500	$ (27,000)

* Allocated on a basis of sales dollars.

The company is a retail organization that sells a single product. The product is sold in three districts, as shown above. Additional information on the company follows:

a. The sales and administrative offices are centrally located, being about the same distance from each district.

b. Each district specifies on the sales order what freight method is to be used (by truck, rail, or air). All goods are shipped from a central warehouse. Freight is a variable cost and it is direct to the districts; differences in amounts above are reflective of the different freight methods used.

c. All salespersons are paid a base salary of $500 per month, plus a commission of 6 percent of sales. There are 24 salespersons in District A, 20 in District B, and 16 in District C.

d. Each district manager must arrange his or her own district advertising program. The national advertising is provided by the central office.

e. It costs the central office $5 to process an order from any of the districts. During March, District A had 3,000 orders, District B had 1,500 orders, and District C had 500 orders. Although the $5 per order processing cost is variable and is traceable directly to the districts, this cost for March has been included in the "Central office administrative expenses" above. The remainder of the "Central office administrative expenses" are fixed and relate to general administrative assistance provided to all parts of the organization.

f. Inventories are negligible and can be ignored.

Required:

1. Garth Hansen, the president, has asked that the income statement be redone in the contribution format, which he heard about in a recent industry convention. Prepare the income statement as requested by Mr. Hansen.

2. Compute the contribution margin per order for each district. What problems does this computation suggest?

3. The manager of District B would like to spend an extra $25,000 next month in a special promotional campaign. If sales increase by $100,000 as a result, would the expenditure be justified?

4. Analyze the data in the statement you prepared in (1) above. What points should be brought to the attention of management?

P7–19. **Segmented statements; product line analysis.** "The situation is slowly turning around," declared Bill Aiken, president of Datex, Inc. "This $42,500 loss for June is our smallest yet. If we can just strengthen lines A and C somehow, we'll soon be making a profit." Mr. Aiken was referring to the company's latest monthly income statement, presented below (absorption costing basis):

DATEX, INC.
Income Statement

	Total	Line A	Line B	Line C
Sales	$1,000,000	$400,000	$250,000	$350,000
Cost of goods sold	742,500	300,000	180,000	262,500
Gross margin	257,500	100,000	70,000	87,500
Less operating expenses:				
Selling	150,000	60,000	22,500	67,500
Administrative	150,000	60,000	37,500	52,500
Total operating expenses	300,000	120,000	60,000	120,000
Net income (loss)	$ (42,500)	$ (20,000)	$ 10,000	$(32,500)

"How's that new business graduate doing that we just hired?" asked Mr. Aiken. "He's supposed to be well trained in internal reporting; can he help us pinpoint what's wrong with lines A and C?" "He claims it's partly the way we make up our segmented statements," declared Margie Nelson, the controller. "Here are a lot of data he's prepared on what he calls direct and common costs that he thinks we ought to be isolating in our reports." The data to which Ms. Nelson was referring are shown below:

	Line A	Line B	Line C
Variable costs:*			
Production (materials, labor, and variable overhead)	20%	30%	25%
Selling	5	5	5
Direct fixed costs:			
Production.	$100,000	$30,000	$70,000
Selling†.	40,000	10,000	50,000

* As a percentage of line sales.
† Salaries and advertising. Advertising contracts are signed annually.

a. Fixed production costs total $500,000 per month. Part of this amount is traceable directly to the product lines, as shown in the tabulation above. The remainder is common to the product lines.

b. All administrative costs are common to the three product lines.

c. Work in process and finished goods inventories are nominal and can be ignored.

d. Lines A and B each sell for $100 per unit, and line C sells for $80 per unit. Strong market demand exists for all three products.

"I don't get it," said Mr. Aiken. "Our CPAs assure us that we're following good absorption costing methods in our cost allocations, and we're segmenting our statements like they want us to do. So what could be wrong?"

At that moment, John Young, the production superintendent, came bursting into the room. "Word has just come that Fairchild Company, the supplier of our type B4 chips, has just gone out on strike. The trade says that they'll be out for at least a month, and our inventory of B4 chips is low. We'll have to cut back production of either line A or B, since that chip is used in both products." (A single B4 chip is used per unit of each product.) Mr. Aiken looked at the latest monthly statement and declared, "Thank goodness for these segmented statements. It's pretty obvious that we should cut back production of line A. Pass the word, and concentrate all of our B4 chip inventory on production of line B."

Required:

1. Prepare a new segmented income statement, segmented by product line, using the contribution approach. Show both "Amount" and "Percent" columns for each of the product lines.

2. Do you agree with Mr. Aiken's decision to cut back production of line A? Why or why not?

3. Assume that the company's executive committee is considering the elimination of line C, due to its poor showing. If you were serving on this committee, what points would you make for or against elimination of the line?

4. Line C is sold in both a home and a foreign market, with sales and cost data as follows:

	Home market	Foreign market
Sales	$300,000	$50,000
Direct fixed costs:		
Selling.	10,000	40,000

The fixed production costs of line C are considered to be common to the markets in which the product is sold. Variable expense relationships in the markets are the same as those shown in the main body of the problem for line C.

    a. Prepare a segmented income statement showing line C segmented by markets.

    b. What points revealed by this statement would you be particularly anxious to bring to the attention of management?

P7–20. **Straightforward direct costing statements.** Milex Company was organized on January 1, 19x8. During its first two years of operation, the company reported net income as follows (absorption costing basis):

	19x8	19x9
Sales (@ $25)	$400,000	$500,000
Less cost of goods sold:		
Opening inventory	–0–	32,000
Add cost of goods manufactured (@ $16) . . .	288,000	288,000
Goods available for sale	288,000	320,000
Less ending inventory (@ $16)	32,000	–0–
Cost of goods sold	256,000	320,000
Gross margin	144,000	180,000
Less selling and administrative expenses* . . .	118,000	130,000
Net income	$ 26,000	$ 50,000

    * $3 per unit variable; $70,000 fixed per year.

The company's $16 unit cost is computed as follows:

Direct materials	$ 6
Direct labor	3
Variable manufacturing overhead	2
Fixed manufacturing overhead ($90,000 ÷ 18,000 units) . .	5
Total cost per unit	$16

Production and cost data for the two years are:

	19x8	19x9
Units produced . . .	18,000	18,000
Units sold	16,000	20,000

Required: 1. Prepare an income statement for each year in the contribution format, using direct costing.

    2. Reconcile the absorption costing and the direct costing net income figures for each year.

P7–21. **Straightforward comparison of costing methods.** High Country, Inc., produces and sells many recreational products. The company has just opened a new plant to produce a folding camp cot that will be marketed throughout the United States. The following cost and revenue data relate to May 19x8, the first month of the plant's operation:

Opening inventory	–0–
Units produced	10,000
Units sold	8,000
Sales price per unit	$ 75
Selling and administrative expenses:	
Variable per unit	6
Fixed (total)	200,000

Manufacturing costs:
Direct materials cost per unit.   20
Direct labor cost per unit   8
Variable overhead cost per unit. . . .   2
Fixed overhead (total)   100,000

Management is anxious to see how profitable the new camp cot will be and has asked that an income statement be prepared for the month.

Required: 1.   Assume that the company uses absorption costing.
        a.   Determine the cost to produce one unit of product.
        b.   Prepare an income statement for the month.
    2.   Assume that the company uses the contribution approach with direct costing.
        a.   Determine the cost to produce one unit of product.
        b.   Prepare an income statement for the month.
    3.   Explain the reason for any difference in the ending inventory under the two costing methods and the impact of this difference on reported net income.

P7–22.   **A comparison of costing methods.**   Advance Products, Inc., has just organized a new division to manufacture and sell specially designed tables for mounting and using personal computers. The company's new plant is highly automated and thus requires high annual fixed costs, as shown in the schedule below:

Manufacturing costs:
Variable cost per unit:
   Direct materials . . . . $ 50
   Direct labor   36
   Variable overhead   4
Fixed overhead costs (total) . . .   240,000

Selling and administrative costs:
   Variable . . . .   15% of sales
   Fixed (total) $160,000

During 19x9, the first year of operations, the following activity was recorded:

Units produced.   4,000
Units sold   3,200
Selling price per unit. . . $250

Required: 1.   Compute the cost of a single unit of product under:
        a.   Absorption costing.
        b.   Direct costing.
    2.   Prepare an income statement for the year, using absorption costing.
    3.   Prepare an income statement for the year, using direct costing.
    4.   Assume that in order to continue operations into the second year, the company must obtain a loan from its bank. As a member of top management, which of the statements that you have prepared in (2) and (3) above would you prefer to take with you as you negotiate with the bank?
    5.   Reconcile the absorption costing and direct costing net income figures in (2) and (3) for the year.

P7–23.   **Preparation and reconciliation of direct costing statements.**   Linden Company was organized on May 1, 19x1. The company manufactures and sells a single product. Cost data for the product follow:

Variable cost per unit:

Direct materials	$ 6
Direct labor.	12
Variable factory overhead.	4
Variable selling and administrative . . .	3
Total variable cost per unit.	$25

Fixed cost per month:

Factory overhead	$240,000
Selling and administrative.	180,000
Total fixed cost per month	$420,000

The product sells for $40 per unit. Production and sales data for May and June are:

	Units produced	Units sold
May . . .	30,000	26,000
June . . .	30,000	34,000

Income statements prepared by the accounting department, using absorption costing, are presented below:

	May 19x1	June 19x1
Sales.	$1,040,000	$1,360,000
Less cost of goods sold:		
Opening inventory	–0–	120,000
Cost of goods manufactured	900,000	900,000
Goods available for sale	900,000	1,020,000
Less ending inventory	120,000	–0–
Cost of goods sold	780,000	1,020,000
Gross margin	260,000	340,000
Less selling and administrative expenses . .	258,000	282,000
Net income.	$ 2,000	$ 58,000

Required:

1. Determine the cost of a single unit of product under:
   a. Absorption costing.
   b. Direct costing.
2. Prepare income statements for May and June using the contribution approach, with direct costing.
3. Reconcile the direct costing and absorption costing net income figures.
4. The company's accounting department has determined the break-even point to be 28,000 units per month, computed as follows:

$$\frac{\text{Fixed cost per month}}{\text{Unit contribution margin}} = \frac{\$420,000}{\$15} = 28,000 \text{ units}$$

Upon receiving this figure, the president commented, "There's something peculiar here. The controller says that the break-even point is 28,000 units per month. Yet we sold only 26,000 units in May, and the income statement we received showed a $2,000 profit. Which figure do we believe?" Prepare a brief explanation of what happened on the May income statement.

P7–24. **Prepare and reconcile direct costing statements; sales constant, production varies.** "This makes no sense at all," said Bill Sharp, president of Essex Company. "We sold the same number of units this year as we did last year, yet our profits have more than doubled. Who made the goof—the computer or the people who operate it?" The statements to which Mr. Sharp was referring are shown below (absorption costing basis):

	19x1	19x2
Sales (20,000 units each year)	$700,000	$700,000
Less cost of goods sold.	460,000	400,000
Gross margin	240,000	300,000
Less selling and administrative expenses. . .	200,000	200,000
Net income	$ 40,000	$100,000

The company was organized on January 1, 19x1, so the statements above show the results of its first two years of operation. In the first year, the company produced and sold 20,000 units; in the second year, the company again sold 20,000 units, but it increased production in order to have a stock of units on hand, as shown below:

	19x1	19x2
Production in units.	20,000	25,000
Sales in units	20,000	20,000
Variable production cost per unit . . .	$ 8	$ 8
Fixed overhead costs (total)	300,000	300,000

Fixed overhead costs are applied to units of product *on a basis of each year's production.* (The company produces and sells a single product.) Variable selling and administrative expenses are $1 per unit sold.

Required:
1. Compute the cost of a single unit of product for each year under:
   a. Absorption costing.
   b. Direct costing.
2. Prepare an income statement for each year, using the contribution approach with direct costing.
3. Reconcile the direct costing and absorption costing net income figures for each year.
4. Explain to the president why, under absorption costing, the net income for 19x2 was higher than the net income for 19x1, although the same number of units was sold in each year.

P7–25. **Absorption and direct costing; production constant, sales fluctuate.** Sandi Scott obtained a patent on a small electronic device and organized Scott Products, Inc., in order to produce and sell the device. During the first month of operations, the device was very well received on the market, so Ms. Scott looked forward to a healthy profit from sales. For this reason, she was surprised to see a loss for the month on her income statement. This statement was prepared by her accounting service, which takes great pride in providing its clients with timely financial data. The statement follows:

SCOTT PRODUCTS, INC.
Income Statement

Sales (40,000 units)		$200,000
Less variable expenses:		
Variable cost of goods sold*	$80,000	
Selling and administrative expenses. . .	30,000	110,000
Contribution margin		90,000
Less fixed expenses:		
Fixed manufacturing overhead.	75,000	
Selling and administrative expenses. . .	20,000	95,000
Net loss		$ (5,000)

* Consists of direct materials, direct labor, and variable overhead.

Ms. Scott is very discouraged over the loss shown for the month, particularly since she had planned to use the statement to encourage investors to purchase stock in the new company. A friend, who is a CPA, insists that the company should be using absorption costing rather than direct costing. He argues that if absorption costing had been used, the company would probably have reported a nice profit for the month.

Selected cost data relating to the product and to the first month of operations follow:

Units produced	50,000
Units sold	40,000
Variable costs per unit:	
Direct materials	$1.00
Direct labor	0.80
Variable overhead	0.20
Variable selling and administrative expense . . .	0.75

Required: 1. Complete the following:

    a. Compute the cost of a unit of product under absorption costing.

    b. Redo the company's income statement for the month, using absorption costing.

    c. Reconcile the direct and absorption costing net income figures.

2. Was the CPA correct in suggesting that the company really earned a "profit" for the month? Explain.

3. During the second month of operations, the company again produced 50,000 units but sold 60,000 units. (Assume no change in total fixed costs.)

    a. Prepare an income statement for the month, using direct costing.

    b. Prepare an income statement for the month, using absorption costing.

    c. Reconcile the direct costing and absorption costing net income figures.

P7–26. **Absorption costing; direct costing; shifting of fixed overhead.** Memotec, Inc., was organized on January 2, 19x1, to manufacture and sell a unique electronic part. Operating results for the first three years of activity were as follows (absorption costing basis):

	19x1	19x2	19x3
Sales	$300,000	$240,000	$300,000
Cost of goods sold:			
Opening inventory	–0–	–0–	76,000
Cost of goods manufactured	220,000	228,000	212,000
Goods available for sale	220,000	228,000	288,000
Less ending inventory	–0–	76,000	53,000
Cost of goods sold	220,000	152,000	235,000
Gross margin	80,000	88,000	65,000
Selling and administrative expenses . . .	70,000	64,000	70,000
Net income	$ 10,000	$ 24,000	$ (5,000)

Sales dropped sharply in 19x2 due to heavy foreign competition. The company had not anticipated this competition, so production was up in 19x2, even though sales for the year were down. Production was decreased in 19x3 in order to work down inventories, as shown below:

	19x1	19x2	19x3
Production in units . . .	20,000	24,000	16,000
Sales in units	20,000	16,000	20,000

Additional information about the company follows:

a. Variable manufacturing costs were $2 per unit in each year. Fixed manufacturing costs totaled $180,000 per year.

b. Fixed manufacturing costs are applied to units of product on a basis of each year's production. (That is, a new fixed overhead rate is computed each year, as in Exhibit 7–8.)

c. Variable selling and administrative expenses were $1.50 per unit sold in each year. Fixed selling and administrative expenses totaled $40,000 each year.

d. Assume a FIFO inventory flow.

Required:
1. Prepare income statements for each year using the contribution approach, with direct costing.
2. Refer to the absorption costing income statements above.
   a. Compute the cost to produce one unit of product in each year under absorption costing. (Show how much of this cost is variable and how much is fixed.)
   b. Reconcile the direct costing and absorption costing net income figures for each year.
3. Refer again to the absorption costing income statements. Explain why net income was higher in 19x2 than it was in 19x1 under the absorption approach, in light of the fact that fewer units were sold in 19x2 than in 19x1.
4. Refer again to the absorption costing income statements. Explain why the company suffered a loss in 19x3 but reported a profit for 19x1, although the same number of units was sold in each year.

P7–27. The case of the perplexed president. Budgeted sales for Advance Products, Inc., for the four quarters of 19x3 are given below, along with actual sales for the first two quarters of the year:

	First	Second	Third	Fourth
Budgeted sales in units . . .	10,000	12,000	12,000	14,000
Actual sales in units	10,000	12,000	—	—

The income statements for the first two quarters are presented below:

ADVANCE PRODUCTS, INC.
Income Statement
For the First Two Quarters

	First quarter		Second quarter	
Sales		$200,000		$240,000
Cost of goods sold:				
Opening inventory	$ 40,000		$ 60,000	
Cost of goods produced	120,000		80,000	
Goods available for sale	160,000		140,000	
Less ending inventory	60,000		20,000	
Cost of goods sold	100,000		120,000	
Add underapplied overhead . . .	—	100,000	24,000	144,000
Gross margin		100,000		96,000
Less selling and administrative				
expenses		80,000		90,000
Net income		$ 20,000		$ 6,000

Mr. Walter Ovard, the president of Advance Products, Inc., was looking forward to receiving the second-quarter income statement. He knew that the sales budget of 12,000 units sold had been met during the second quarter and that this represented a substantial increase in sales over the first quarter. He was especially happy about the increase in sales, since Advance Products, Inc., was about to approach its bank for additional loan money for expansion purposes. He anticipated that the strong second-quarter showing would be a real plus in persuading the bank to extend the additional credit.

For this reason, Mr. Ovard was shocked when he received the second quarter income statement above, which showed a substantial drop in net income from the first quarter. He was sure that there had to be an error somewhere and immediately called the controller into his office to find the problem. The controller stated, "That net income figure is correct, Walt. I agree that sales went up during the quarter, but the problem is in production. You see, we budgeted to produce 12,000 units each quarter, but a strike in one of our supplier's plants forced us to cut production back to only 8,000 units in the second quarter. That's what caused the drop in net income."

Mr. Ovard was angered by the controller's explanation. "I call you in here to find out why income dropped when sales went up, and you talk about production! So what if production was off? What does that have to do with the sales we made? If sales go up, then income ought to go up. If your statements can't show a simple thing like that, then we're spending too much money in your area!"

Fixed manufacturing overhead amounts to $72,000 each quarter. Variable manufacturing costs are $4 per unit. The fixed overhead is applied to units of product at a rate of $6 per unit, based on budgeted production of 12,000 units each quarter. Any under- or overapplied overhead is taken to cost of goods sold. Variable selling and administrative expenses are $5 per unit sold. There were 4,000 units in inventory to start the first quarter. The company uses a FIFO cost flow.

Required: 1. How would you have explained the drop in net income to Mr. Ovard?
         2. Prepare income statements for each quarter using the contribution approach with direct costing.

3. Reconcile the absorption costing and direct costing net income figures for each quarter.

P7–28. **Absorption and direct costing; uneven production; break even.** As vice president of sales for Porter Company, Cindy Hales would like to be able to predict how profits will change with changes in sales volume. She is confused by the monthly income statements for the last quarter, which show decreasing profits even though sales increased from 50,000 units in April to 55,000 units in May and 60,000 units in June. Ms. Hales is particularly disturbed by the $45,000 loss shown for June. Monthly income statements for the quarter are shown below:

PORTER COMPANY
Monthly Income Statements

	April	May	June
Sales	$500,000	$550,000	$600,000
Less cost of goods sold:			
Opening inventory	25,000	100,000	125,000
Cost applied to production:			
Variable production cost	130,000	120,000	80,000
Fixed production cost	195,000	180,000	120,000
Goods available for sale	350,000	400,000	325,000
Less ending inventory	100,000	125,000	25,000
Cost of goods sold	250,000	275,000	300,000
Under- or (overapplied) fixed overhead cost	(15,000)	—	60,000
Cost of goods sold at actual	235,000	275,000	360,000
Gross margin	265,000	275,000	240,000
Less selling and administrative expenses*	245,000	265,000	285,000
Net income (loss)	$ 20,000	$ 10,000	$ (45,000)

* Contains both variable and fixed expenses. Use the high-low method to compute the variable and fixed elements.

Ms. Hales is convinced that there must be a better way to report profit data to management so that changes in profits are more closely correlated with changes in sales volume. Sales and production data for the quarter follow:

	April	May	June
Sales in units	50,000	55,000	60,000
Production in units	65,000	60,000	40,000

Five thousand units were in inventory at the beginning of April. Fixed overhead cost is applied to production based on a budgeted production volume of 60,000 units each month. Actual fixed production costs totaled $540,000 for the quarter and were incurred evenly throughout the quarter.

Required:
1. Prepare an income statement for each month, using direct costing.
2. Compute the break-even point under:
   a. Direct costing.
   b. Absorption costing.

3. Explain to Ms. Hales why profits have moved erratically over the three-month period and why they have not been more closely correlated with changes in sales volume.

4. Reconcile the direct costing and absorption costing net income figures for each month.

8 Profit Planning

Learning objectives

After studying Chapter 8, you should be able to:

Define budgeting and explain the difference between planning and control.

Enumerate the principal advantages of budgeting.

Diagram and explain the master budget interrelationships.

Prepare a sales budget, including a computation of expected cash receipts.

Prepare a production budget.

Prepare a direct materials purchases budget, including a computation of expected cash disbursements.

Prepare a manufacturing overhead budget and a selling and administrative expense budget.

Prepare a cash budget, along with a budgeted income statement and a budgeted balance sheet.

Compute the economic order quantity and the reorder point.

Define or explain the key terms listed at the end of the chapter.

In this chapter, we focus our attention on those steps taken by business organizations to achieve certain desired levels of profits—a process that is generally called *profit planning*. In our study, we shall see that profit planning is accomplished through the preparation of a number of budgets, which, when combined, form an integrated business plan known as the *master budget*. We shall find that the data going into the preparation of the master budget focus heavily on the future, rather than on the past.

THE BASIC FRAMEWORK OF BUDGETING

Definition of budgeting

A **budget** is a detailed plan outlining the acquisition and use of financial and other resources over some given time period. It represents a plan for the future expressed in formal quantitative terms. The act of preparing a budget is called *budgeting*. The use of budgets to control a firm's activities is known as *budgetary control*.

The **master budget** is a summary of all phases of a company's plans and goals for the future. It sets specific targets for sales, production, distribution, and financing activities, and it generally culminates in a projected statement of net income and a projected statement of cash position. In short, it represents a comprehensive expression of management's plans for the future and how these plans are to be accomplished.

Nearly everyone budgets

Nearly everyone prepares and uses budgets of some sort, even though many of the people who do so may not recognize what they are doing as budgeting. For example, most people make estimates of the income to be realized over some future time period and plan expenditures for food, clothing, housing, and so on, accordingly. As a result of this planning, spending will usually be restricted by limiting it to some predetermined, allowable amount. In this type of action, a budget is used as a control device. At other times, individuals use estimates of income and expenditures to predict what their financial condition will be at some specific future time. The budgets involved here may exist only in the mind of the individual, but they are budgets nonetheless in that they involve plans of how resources will be acquired and used over some specific time period.

The budgets of a business firm serve much the same functions as the budgets prepared informally by individuals. Business budgets tend to be more detailed and to involve more work in preparation (mostly because they are formal rather than informal), but they are similar to the budgets prepared by individuals in most other respects. Like personal budgets, they assist in planning and controlling expenditures; they also assist in predicting operating results and financial condition in future periods.

Difference between planning and control

The terms *planning* and *control* are often confused, and occasionally they are used in such a way as to suggest that they mean the same thing. Actually, they are two quite distinct concepts. **Planning** involves the development of future objectives and the preparation of various budgets to achieve these objectives. **Control** involves the steps taken by management to assure that the objectives set down at the planning stage are attained, and to assure that all parts of the organization function in a manner consistent with organizational policies. To be completely effective, a good budgeting system must provide for *both* planning and control. Good planning without effective control is time wasted. On the other hand, unless plans are laid down in advance, there are no objectives toward which control can be directed.

Advantages of budgeting

There is an old saying to the effect that "a man is usually down on what he isn't up on." Managers who have never tried budgeting or attempted to find out what benefits might be available through the budget process are usually quick to state that budgeting is a waste of time. These managers may argue that even though budgeting may work well in *some* situations, it would never work well in their companies because of the complexities and uncertainties involved. Yet these managers will be constantly planning (albeit on an informal basis). Most managers will have well-defined thoughts about what they want to accomplish and when they want it accomplished. The difficulty is that unless they have some way of communicating their thoughts and plans to others, the only way their companies will ever attain the desired objectives will be through accident. Even though such companies may attain a certain degree of success without budgets, they never attain the heights that could have been reached had the efforts of the entire organization been coordinated by means of a detailed system of budgets.

One of the great values of budgeting is that it requires managers to give planning top priority among their duties. Moreover, budgeting provides managers with a vehicle for communicating their plans in an orderly way throughout an entire organization. No one has any doubt about what the managers want to accomplish or how they want it done. Other benefits of budgeting are:

1. It provides managers with a way to *formalize* their planning efforts.
2. It provides definite goals and objectives that serve as *benchmarks* for evaluating subsequent performance.
3. It uncovers potential *bottlenecks* before they occur.
4. It *coordinates* the activities of the entire organization by *integrating* the plans and objectives of the various parts. By so doing, budgeting ensures that the plans and objectives of the parts are consistent with the broad goals of the entire organization.

Consider the following situation encountered by the author:

Company X is a mortgage banking firm. For years, the company operated with virtually no system of budgets whatever. Management contended that budgeting wasn't well suited to the firm's type of operation. Moreover, management pointed out that the firm was already profitable. Indeed, outwardly it gave every appearance of being a well-managed, smoothly operating organization. A careful look within, however, disclosed that day-to-day operations were far from smooth, and often approached chaos. The average day was nothing more than an exercise in putting out one brush fire after another. The Cash account was always at crisis levels. At the end of a day, no one ever knew whether enough cash would be available the next day to cover required loan closings. Departments were uncoordinated, and it was not uncommon to find that one department was pursuing a course that conflicted with the course pursued by another department. Employee morale was low, and turnover was high. Employees complained bitterly that when a job was well done, nobody ever knew about it.

Company X was bought out by a new group of stockholders who required that the company establish an integrated budgeting system to control operations. Within one year's time, significant changes were evident. Brush fires were rare. Careful planning virtually eliminated the problems that had been experienced with cash, and departmental efforts were coordinated and directed toward predetermined overall company goals. Although the employees were wary of the new budgeting program initially, they became "converted" when they saw the positive effects that it brought about. The more efficient operations caused profits to jump dramatically. Communication increased throughout the organization. When a job was well done, everybody knew about it. As one employee stated, "For the first time, we know what the company expects of us."

Responsibility accounting

Most of what we say in the remainder of this chapter and in Chapters 9, 10, and 11 following centers on the concept of *responsibility accounting*. The basic idea behind **responsibility accounting** is that each manager's performance should be judged by how well he or she manages those items directly under his or her control. To judge a manager's performance in this way, the costs (and revenues) of an organization must be carefully scrutinized and classified according to the various levels of management under whose control the costs rest. Each level of management is then charged with those costs under its care, and the managers at each level are held responsible for variations between budgeted goals and actual results. In effect, responsibility accounting *personalizes* the accounting system by looking at costs from a *personal control* standpoint, rather than from an *institutional* standpoint. This concept is central to any effective profit planning and control system.

We will look at responsibility accounting in more detail in Chapters 9,

10, and 11. For the moment, we can summarize the overall idea by noting that it rests on three basic premises. The first premise is that costs can be organized in terms of levels of management responsibility. The second premise is that the costs charged to a particular level are controllable at that level by its managers. And the third premise is that effective budget data can be generated as a basis for evaluating actual performance. This chapter on profit planning is concerned with the third of these premises, in that its purpose is to show the steps involved in budget preparation.

Choosing a budget period

Budgets covering acquisition of land, buildings, and other items of capital equipment (often called **capital budgets**) generally have quite long time horizons and may extend 30 years or more into the future. The later years covered by such budgets may be quite indefinite, but at least management is kept planning ahead sufficiently to ensure that funds will be available when purchases of equipment become necessary. As time passes, capital equipment plans that were once somewhat indefinite come more sharply into focus, and the capital budget is updated accordingly. Without such long-term planning, an organization can suddenly come to the realization that substantial purchases of capital equipment are needed, but find that no funds are available to make the purchases.

Operating budgets are ordinarily set to cover a one-year period. The one-year period should correspond to whatever fiscal year the company is following, so that the budget figures can be compared with the actual results. Many companies divide their budget year into four quarters. The first quarter is then subdivided into months, and monthly budget figures are established. These near-term figures can usually be established with considerable accuracy. The last three quarters are carried in the budget at quarterly totals only. As the year progresses, the figures for the second quarter are broken down into monthly amounts, then the third quarter figures are broken down, and so forth. This approach has the advantage of requiring a constant review and reappraisal of budget data.

Continuous or perpetual budgets are becoming very popular. A continuous or perpetual budget is one that covers a 12-month period but which is constantly adding a new month on the end as the current month is completed. Advocates of continuous budgets state that this approach to budgeting is superior to other approaches in that it keeps management thinking and planning a full 12 months ahead. Thus, it stabilizes the planning horizon. Under other budget approaches, the planning horizon becomes shorter as the year progresses.

The self-imposed budget

The success of any budget program will be determined in large part by the way in which the budget itself is developed. Generally, the most successful budget programs are those that permit managers with responsibility over cost control to prepare their own budget estimates, as illustrated in Exhibit 8–1. This approach to preparing budget data is particularly important if the budget is to be used in controlling a manager's activities after it has been developed. If a budget is forced on a manager from above, it will probably generate resentment and ill will rather than cooperation and increased productivity.

When managers prepare their own budget estimates, the budgets that they prepare become *self-imposed* in nature. Certain distinct advantages arise from the **self-imposed budget:**

1. Individuals at all levels of the organization are recognized as members of the team, whose views and judgments are valued by top management.
2. The person in direct contact with an activity is in the best position to make budget estimates. Therefore, budget estimates prepared by such persons tend to be more accurate and reliable.
3. A person is much more apt to work at fulfilling a budget that he has set himself than he is to work at fulfilling a budget imposed on him from above.
4. A sclf-imposed budget contains its own unique system of control in that if people are not able to meet budget specifications, they have only themselves to blame. On the other hand, if a budget is imposed on them from above, they can always say that the budget was unreasonable or unrealistic to start with, and therefore was impossible to meet.

EXHIBIT 8–1

The initial flow of budget data

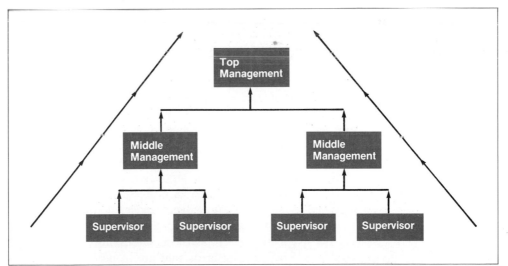

The initial flow of budget data is from lower levels of responsibility to higher levels of responsibility. Each person with responsibility for cost control will prepare his or her own budget estimates and submit them to the superior. These estimates are consolidated as they move upward in the organization.

Once self-imposed budgets are prepared, are they subject to any kind of review? The answer is yes. Even though individual preparation of budget estimates is critical to a successful budgeting program, such budget estimates cannot necessarily be accepted without question by higher levels of management. If no system of checks and balances is present, the danger exists that self-imposed budgets will be too loose and allow too much freedom in activities. The result will be inefficiency and waste. Therefore, before budgets are accepted, they must be carefully reviewed by immediate superiors. If changes from the original budget seem desirable, the items in question are discussed and compromises are reached that are acceptable to all concerned.

In essence, all levels of an organization work together to produce the budget. Since top management is generally unfamiliar with detailed, day-to-day cost matters, it will rely on subordinates to provide detailed budget information. On the other hand, top management has a perspective on the company as a whole that is vital in making broad policy decisions in budget preparation. Each level of responsibility in an organization contributes in the way that it best can in a *cooperative* effort to develop an integrated budget document.

The matter of human relations

Whether or not a budget program is accepted by lower management personnel will be reflective of (1) the degree to which top management accepts the budget program as a vital part of the company's activities, and (2) the way in which top management uses budgeted data.

If a budget program is to be successful, it must have the complete acceptance and support of the persons who occupy key management positions. If lower or middle management personnel sense that top management is lukewarm about budgeting, or if they sense that top management simply tolerates budgeting as a necessary evil, then their own attitudes will reflect a similar lack of enthusiasm. Budgeting is hard work, and if top management is not enthusiastic about and committed to the budget program, then it is unlikely that anyone else in the organization will be either.

In administering the budget program, it is particularly important that top management not use the budget as a "club" to pressure employees or as a way to find someone to "blame" for a particular problem. This type of negative emphasis will simply breed hostility, tension, and mistrust rather than greater cooperation and productivity. Unfortunately, research suggests that the budget is often used as a pressure device and that great emphasis is placed on "meeting the budget" under all circumstances.[1]

Rather than being used as a pressure device, the budget should be used as a positive instrument to assist in establishing goals, in measuring operating results, and in isolating areas that are in need of extra effort or attention.

---

[1] Paul J. Carruth, Thurrell O. McClendon, and Milton R. Ballard, "What Supervisors Don't Like about Budget Evaluations," *Management Accounting* 64, no. 8 (February 1983), p. 42.

Any misgivings that employees have about a budget program can be overcome by meaningful involvement at all levels and by proper use of the program over a period of time. Administration of a budget program requires a great deal of insight and sensitivity on the part of management. The ultimate objective must be to develop the realization that the budget is designed to be a positive aid in achieving both individual and company goals.

Management must keep clearly in mind that the human dimension in budgeting is of key importance. It is easy for the manager to become preoccupied with the technical aspects of the budget program to the exclusion of the human aspects. Accountants are particularly open to criticism in this regard. Indeed, the study cited earlier found that use of budget data in a rigid and inflexible manner was the greatest single complaint of persons whose performance was being evaluated through the budget process.[2] In light of these facts, management should remember that the purposes of the budget are to motivate employees and to coordinate efforts. Preoccupation with the dollars and cents in the budget, or being rigid and inflexible in budget administration, can only lead to frustration of these purposes.

The budget committee

A standing **budget committee** will usually be responsible for overall policy matters relating to the budget program and for coordination in the preparation of the budget itself. This committee generally consists of the president; vice presidents in charge of various functions such as sales, production, and purchasing; and the controller. Difficulties and disputes between segments of the organization in matters relating to the budget are resolved by the budget committee. In addition, the budget committee approves the final budget and receives periodic reports on the progress of the company in attaining budgeted goals.

The master budget—a network of interrelationships

The master budget is a network consisting of many separate budgets that are interdependent. This network is illustrated in Exhibit 8–2.

The sales budget   Nearly all other parts of the master budget are dependent in some way on the sales budget. A **sales budget** is a detailed schedule of expected sales for coming periods; it is usually expressed in both dollars and units. Once the sales budget has been set, a decision can be made on the level of production that will be needed to support sales, and the production budget can be set as well. The production budget then becomes a key factor in the determination of other budgets, including the direct materials budget, the direct labor budget, and the manufacturing overhead budget. These budgets, in turn, are needed to assist in formulating a cash budget for the budget

---

[2] Ibid.

EXHIBIT 8–2
The master budget interrelationships

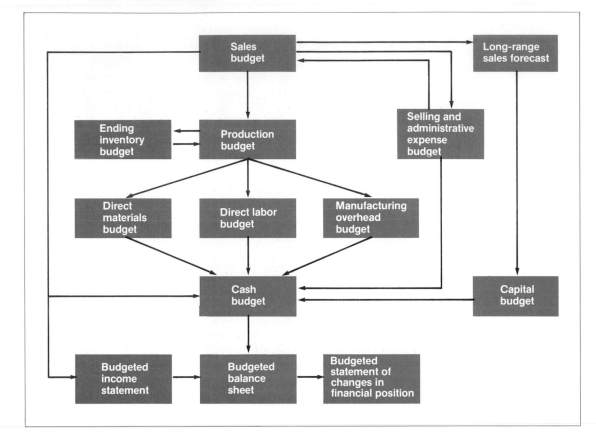

period. In essence, the sales budget triggers a chain reaction that leads to the development of many other budget figures in an organization.

As shown in the exhibit, the selling and administrative expense budget is both dependent on and a determinant of the sales budget. This reciprocal relationship arises from the fact that sales will in part be determined by the funds available for advertising and sales promotion.

The cash budget Once the operating budgets (sales, production, and so on) have been established, the cash budget and other financial budgets can be prepared. A **cash budget** is a detailed plan showing how cash resources will be acquired and used over some specified time period. Notice from Exhibit 8–2 that all of the operating budgets, including the sales budget, have an impact of some type on the cash budget. In the case of the sales budget, the impact comes from the planned cash receipts to be received on sales. In the case of the other budgets, the impact comes from the planned cash expenditures within the budgets themselves.

Sales forecasting—a critical step

Since nearly all budgets are derived from it in some way, the sales budget is the key to the entire budgeting process. If the sales budget is sloppily done, then the entire master budget will be worthless and a waste of time and effort.

The sales budget is prepared from the *sales forecast*. A **sales forecast** is broader than a sales budget, generally encompassing potential sales for the entire industry, as well as potential sales for the firm preparing the forecast. Factors that are considered in making a sales forecast include:

1. Past experience in terms of sales volume.
2. Prospective pricing policy.
3. Unfilled order backlogs.
4. Market research studies.
5. General economic conditions.
6. Industry economic conditions.
7. Movements of economic indicators such as gross national product, employment, prices, and personal income.
8. Advertising and product promotion.
9. Industry competition.
10. Market share.

Sales results from prior years are used as a starting point in preparing a sales forecast. Forecasters examine sales data in relation to various factors, including prices, competitive conditions, availability of supplies, and general economic conditions. Projections are then made into the future, based on those factors that the forecasters feel will be significant over the budget period. In-depth discussions generally characterize the gathering and interpretation of all data going into the sales forecast. These discussions, held at all levels of the organization, develop perspective and assist in assessing the significance and usefulness of data.

Statistical tools such as regression analysis, trend and cycle projection, and correlation analysis are widely used in sales forecasting. In addition, some firms have found it useful to build econometric models of their industry or of the nation to assist in forecasting problems. Such models hold great promise for improving the overall quality of budget data.

PREPARING THE MASTER BUDGET

To show how the separate budgets making up the master budget are developed and integrated, we focus now on Meredith Company. Meredith Company produces and sells a single product that we will call product A. Each year the company prepares the following budget documents:

1. A sales budget, including a computation of expected cash receipts.
2. A production budget.
3. A direct materials budget, including a computation of expected cash payments for raw materials.

4. A direct labor budget.
5. A manufacturing overhead budget.
6. An ending finished goods inventory budget.
7. A selling and administrative expense budget.
8. A cash budget.
9. A budgeted income statement.
10. A budgeted balance sheet.

These budgets for the year 19x1 are illustrated in Schedules 1 through 10 following.

The sales budget

The *sales budget* is the starting point in preparing the master budget. As shown earlier in Exhibit 8–2, nearly all other items in the master budget, including production, purchases, inventories, and expenses, depend on it in some way.

The sales budget is constructed by multiplying the expected sales in units by the sales price. Schedule 1 below contains the sales budget for Meredith Company for 19x1, by quarters. Notice from the schedule that the company plans to sell 6,000 units during the year, with sales peaking out in the third quarter.

Generally, the sales budget is accompanied by a computation of expected cash receipts for the forthcoming budget period. This computation is needed to assist in preparing the cash budget for the year. Expected cash receipts are composed of collections on sales made to customers in prior periods, plus collections on sales made in the current budget period. Schedule 1 below also contains a computation of expected cash collections for Meredith Company.

Schedule 1

MEREDITH COMPANY
Sales Budget
For the Year Ended December 31, 19x1

| | Quarter | | | | |
	1	2	3	4	Year
Expected sales in units	1,000	1,800	2,000	1,200	6,000
Selling price per unit	× $150	× $150	× $150	× $150	× $150
Total sales	$150,000	$270,000	$300,000	$180,000	$900,000

Schedule of Expected Cash Collections

	1	2	3	4	Year
Accounts receivable, 12/31/x0	$100,000				$100,000
First quarter sales ($150,000)	60,000	$ 90,000			150,000
Second quarter sales ($270,000)		108,000	$162,000		270,000
Third quarter sales ($300,000)			120,000	$180,000	300,000
Fourth quarter sales ($180,000)				72,000	72,000
Total cash collections	$160,000	$198,000	$282,000	$252,000	$892,000

Note: Forty percent of a quarter's sales is collected in the quarter of sale; the remaining 60 percent is collected in the quarter following.

The production budget

After the sales budget has been prepared, the production requirements for the forthcoming budget period can be determined and organized in the form of a **production budget.** Sufficient goods will have to be available to meet sales needs and provide for the desired ending inventory. A portion of these goods will already exist in the form of a beginning inventory. The remainder will have to be produced. Therefore, production needs can be determined by adding budgeted sales (in units or in dollars) to the desired ending inventory (in units or in dollars), and deducting the beginning inventory (in units or in dollars) from this total. Schedule 2 below contains a production budget for Meredith Company.

Schedule 2

MEREDITH COMPANY
Production Budget
For the Year Ended December 31, 19x1
(in units)

		Quarter			
	1	2	3	4	Year
Expected sales (Schedule 1)	1,000	1,800	2,000	1,200	6,000
Add: Desired ending inventory of finished goods*	180	200	120	300‡	300
Total needs	1,180	2,000	2,120	1,500	6,300
Less: Beginning Inventory of finished goods†	200	180	200	120	200
Units to be produced.	980	1,820	1,920	1,380	6,100

* Ten percent of the next quarter's sales.
† The same as the prior quarter's *ending* inventory.
‡ Estimated.

Students are often surprised to learn that firms budget the level of their ending inventories. Budgeting of inventories is a common practice, however. If inventories are not carefully planned, the levels remaining at the end of a period may be excessive, causing an unnecessary tie-up of funds and an unneeded expense of carrying the unwanted goods. On the other hand, without proper planning, inventory levels may be too small, thereby requiring crash production efforts in following periods, and perhaps loss of sales due to inability to meet shipping schedules.

Inventory purchases—merchandising firm

Meredith Company is a manufacturing firm, so it prepares a production budget, as shown in Schedule 2. If it were a *merchandising* firm, then instead of a production budget it would prepare a *merchandise purchases budget* showing the amount of goods to be purchased from its suppliers during the period. The merchandise purchases budget is in the same basic format as the production budget, except that it shows goods to be purchased rather than goods to be produced, as shown below:

```
Budgeted cost of goods sold (in units
     or in dollars).  .  .  .  .  .  .  .  .  .  .  .  .  .  .  .  .  .  .   XXXXX
Add: Desired ending merchandise inventory  .  .  .  .  .   XXXXX
     Total needs .  .  .  .  .  .  .  .  .  .  .  .  .  .  .  .  .  .  .  .   XXXXX
Less: Beginning merchandise inventory .  .  .  .  .  .  .   XXXXX
Required purchases (in units or in dollars)  .  .  .  .  .  .   XXXXX
```

The merchandising firm would prepare an inventory purchases budget such as this one for each item carried in stock. Some large retail organizations make such computations on a frequent basis (particularly at peak seasons) in order to ensure that adequate stocks are on hand to meet customer needs.

The direct materials budget

Returning to the Meredith Company example, after production needs have been computed, a **direct materials budget** should be prepared to show the materials that will be required in the production process. Sufficient raw materials will have to be available to meet production needs, and to provide for the desired ending raw materials inventory for the budget period. Part of this raw materials requirement will already exist in the form of a beginning raw materials inventory. The remainder will have to be purchased from suppliers. In sum, the format for computing raw materials needs is:

```
Raw materials needed to meet the production schedule .  .  .  .  .  .   XXXXX
Add desired ending inventory of raw materials .  .  .  .  .  .  .  .  .   XXXXX
     Total raw materials needs  .  .  .  .  .  .  .  .  .  .  .  .  .  .  .  .   XXXXX
Less beginning inventory of raw materials .  .  .  .  .  .  .  .  .  .  .   XXXXX
Raw materials to be purchased  .  .  .  .  .  .  .  .  .  .  .  .  .  .  .   XXXXX
```

Preparing a budget of this kind is one step in a company's overall **material requirements planning (MRP)**. MRP is an operations research tool that employs the computer to assist the manager in overall materials and inventory planning. The objective of MRP is to ensure that the right materials are on hand, in the right quantities, and at the right time to support the production process. The detailed operation of MRP is covered in most operations research textbooks; for this reason, it will not be considered further here, other than to point out that the concepts we are discussing are an important part of the overall MRP technique.

Schedule 3 contains a direct materials purchases budget for Meredith Company. Notice that materials requirements are first determined in units (pounds, gallons, and so on) and then translated into dollars by multiplying by the appropriate unit cost.

The direct materials budget is usually accompanied by a computation of expected cash disbursements for raw materials. This computation is needed

Schedule 3

MEREDITH COMPANY
Direct Materials Budget
For the Year Ended December 31, 19x1

	Quarter				
	1	2	3	4	Year
Units to be produced (Schedule 2)	980	1,820	1,920	1,380	6,100
Raw material needs per unit (pounds)	× 2	× 2	× 2	× 2	× 2
Production needs (pounds)	1,960	3,640	3,840	2,760	12,200
Add desired ending inventory of raw materials* (pounds).	910	960	690	520	520
Total needs (pounds)	2,870	4,600	4,530	3,280	12,720
Less beginning inventory of raw materials (pounds)	490	910	960	690	490
Raw materials to be purchased (pounds)	2,380	3,690	3,570	2,590	12,230
Raw materials cost per pound	× $5	× $5	× $5	× $5	× $5
Cost of raw materials to be purchased	$11,900	$18,450	$17,850	$12,950	$61,150

Schedule of Expected Cash Disbursements

Accounts payable, 12/31/x0	$ 6,275				$ 6,275
First-quarter purchases ($11,900).	5,950	$ 5,950			11,900
Second quarter purchases ($18,450).		9,225	$ 9,225		18,450
Third-quarter purchases ($17,850).			8,925	$ 8,925	17,850
Fourth-quarter purchases ($12,950)				6,475	6,475
Total cash disbursements	$12,225	$15,175	$18,150	$15,400	$60,950

Note: Fifty percent of a quarter's purchases are paid for in the quarter of purchase; the remaining 50 percent are paid for in the quarter following.

* Twenty-five percent of the next quarter's production needs. For example, the second-quarter production needs are 3,640 pounds. Therefore, the desired ending inventory for the first quarter would be 25 percent × 3,640 pounds = 910 pounds. The ending inventory of 520 pounds for the fourth quarter is estimated.

to assist in developing a cash budget. Disbursements for raw materials will consist of payments for prior periods, plus payments for purchases for the current budget period. Schedule 3 contains a computation of expected cash disbursements for Meredith Company.

The direct labor budget

The **direct labor budget** is also developed from the production budget. Direct labor requirements must be computed so that the company will know whether sufficient labor time is available to meet production needs. By knowing in advance just what will be needed in the way of labor time throughout the budget year, the company can develop plans to adjust the labor force as the situation may require. Firms that neglect to budget run the risk of facing labor shortages or having to hire and fire at awkward times. Erratic labor policies lead to insecurity and inefficiency on the part of employees.

To compute direct labor requirements, the number of units of finished product to be produced each period (month, quarter, and so on) is multiplied by the number of direct labor-hours required to produce a single unit. Many different types of labor may be involved. If so, then computations should be by type of labor needed. The hours of direct labor time resulting from these computations can then be multiplied by the direct labor cost per hour to obtain budgeted total direct labor costs. Schedule 4 following contains such computations for Meredith Company.

Schedule 4

MEREDITH COMPANY
Direct Labor Budget
For the Year Ended December 31, 19x1

	Quarter				
	1	2	3	4	Year
Units to be produced (Schedule 2)	980	1,820	1,920	1,380	6,100
Direct labor time per unit (hours)	× 5	× 5	× 5	× 5	× 5
Total hours of direct labor time needed	4,900	9,100	9,600	6,900	30,500
Direct labor cost per hour	× $10	× $10	× $10	× $10	× $10
Total direct labor cost	$49,000	$91,000	$96,000	$69,000	$305,000

The manufacturing overhead budget

The **manufacturing overhead budget** should provide a schedule of all costs of production other than direct materials and direct labor. These costs should be broken down by cost behavior for budgeting purposes, and a predetermined overhead rate developed. This rate will be used to apply manufacturing overhead to units of product throughout the budget period. In the case of Meredith Company, the contribution approach to costing is being used internally for planning purposes, so only variable overhead is included in the predetermined overhead rate.

A computation showing budgeted cash disbursements for manufacturing overhead should be made for use in developing the cash budget. The critical thing to remember in making this computation is that depreciation is a non-cash charge. Therefore, any depreciation charges included in manufacturing overhead must be deducted from the total in computing expected cash payments.

We will assume that the variable overhead rate is $2 per direct labor-hour, and that fixed overhead costs are budgeted at $18,300 per quarter, of which $4,000 represents depreciation. All overhead costs involving cash disbursements are paid for in the quarter incurred. The manufacturing overhead budget, by quarters, and the expected cash disbursements, by quarters, are both shown in Schedule 5.

Schedule 5

MEREDITH COMPANY
Manufacturing Overhead Budget
For the Year Ended December 31, 19x1

| | Quarter | | | | |
	1	2	3	4	Year
Budgeted direct labor-hours	4,900	9,100	9,600	6,900	30,500
Variable overhead rate	× $2	× $2	× $2	× $2	× $2
Budgeted variable overhead	$ 9,800	$18,200	$19,200	$13,800	$ 61,000
Budgeted fixed overhead	18,300	18,300	18,300	18,300	73,200
Total budgeted overhead	28,100	36,500	37,500	32,100	134,200
Less depreciation.	4,000	4,000	4,000	4,000	16,000
Cash disbursements for overhead	$24,100	$32,500	$33,500	$28,100	$118,200

Cost of a unit of product

After completing Schedules 1–5, sufficient data will have been generated to compute the cost of a unit of finished product. This computation is needed for two reasons: first, to know how much to charge as cost of goods sold on the budgeted income statement; and second, to know what value to place on the balance sheet for the ending finished goods inventory.

For Meredith Company, the cost of a unit of finished product is $82, consisting of $10 of direct materials, $50 of direct labor, and $22 of manufacturing overhead. The computations behind these figures are shown below in Schedule 6.

Schedule 6

MEREDITH COMPANY
Ending Finished Goods Inventory Budget
For the Year Ended December 31, 19x1

Item	Quantity	Cost	Total
Production cost per unit:			
Direct materials	2 pounds	$5.00 per pound	$10
Direct labor	5 hours	$10.00 per hour	50
Manufacturing overhead	5 hours	$4.40 per hour*	22
			$82
Budgeted finished goods inventory:			
Ending finished goods inventory in units (Schedule 2).			300
Total production cost per unit (see above).			× $82
Ending finished goods inventory in dollars.			$24,600

* $134,200 ÷ 30,500 hours = $4.40.

The selling and administrative expense budget

The **selling and administrative expense budget** contains a listing of anticipated expenses for the budget period that will be incurred in areas other than manufacturing. The budget will be made up of many smaller, individual budgets submitted by various persons having responsibility for cost control in selling and administrative matters. If the number of expense items is very large, separate budgets may be needed for the selling and administrative functions.

Schedule 7

MEREDITH COMPANY
Selling and Administrative Expense Budget
For the Year Ended December 31, 19x1

	Quarter				
	1	**2**	**3**	**4**	**Total**
Budgeted sales in units	1,000	1,800	2,000	1,200	6,000
Variable selling and administrative expense per unit*	× $3	× $3	× $3	× $3	× $3
Budgeted variable expense	$ 3,000	$ 5,400	$ 6,000	$ 3,600	$ 18,000
Fixed selling and administrative expense:					
Advertising	20,000	20,000	20,000	20,000	80,000
Executive salaries	40,000	40,000	40,000	40,000	160,000
Insurance	—	12,600	—	—	12,600
Property taxes	—	—	—	7,400	7,400
Total budgeted selling and administrative expenses	$63,000	$78,000	$66,000	$71,000	$278,000

* Commissions, clerical, and freight-out.

Schedule 7 contains the selling and administrative expense budget for Meredith Company for 19x1.

The cash budget

The cash budget pulls together much of the data developed in the preceding steps, as illustrated earlier in Exhibit 8–2. The reader should restudy this exhibit before reading on.

The cash budget is composed of four major sections:

1. The receipts section.
2. The disbursements section.
3. The cash excess or deficiency section.
4. The financing section.

The receipts section consists of the opening cash balance added to whatever is expected in the way of cash receipts during the budget period. Generally, the major source of receipts will be from sales, as discussed earlier.

The disbursements section consists of all cash payments that are planned for the budget period. These payments will include raw materials purchases, direct labor payments, manufacturing overhead costs, and so on, as contained in their respective budgets. In addition, other cash disbursements such as income taxes, capital equipment purchases, and dividend payments will also be included.

The cash excess or deficiency section consists of the difference between the cash receipts section totals and the cash disbursements section totals. If a deficiency exists, the company will need to arrange for borrowed funds from its bank. If an excess exists, funds borrowed in previous periods can be repaid or the idle funds can be placed in short-term investments.

The financing section provides a detailed account of the borrowings and repayments projected to take place during the budget period. It also includes a detail of interest payments that will be due on money borrowed. Banks are becoming increasingly insistent that firms in need of borrowed money give long advance notice of the amounts and times that funds will be needed. This permits the banks to plan and helps to assure that funds will be ready when needed. Moreover, careful planning of cash needs via the budgeting process avoids unpleasant surprises for companies as well. Few things are more disquieting to an organization than to run into unexpected difficulties in the Cash account. A well-coordinated budgeting program eliminates uncertainty as to what the cash situation will be two months, six months, or a year from now.

The cash budget should be broken down into time periods that are as short as feasible. Many firms budget cash on a weekly basis, and some larger firms go so far as to plan daily cash needs. The more common planning horizons are geared to monthly or quarterly figures. The cash budget for Meredith Company for 19x1 is shown on a quarterly basis in Schedule 8.[3]

The budgeted income statement

A budgeted income statement can be prepared from the data developed in Schedules 1–8. *The budgeted income statement is one of the key schedules in the budget process.* It is the document that tells how profitable operations are anticipated to be in the forthcoming period. After it has been developed, it stands as a benchmark against which subsequent company performance can be measured.

Schedule 9 below contains a budgeted income statement for Meredith Company for 19x1.

---

[3] Meredith Company has an open line of credit with its bank, which can be used as needed to bolster the cash position. Borrowings and repayments must be in round $1,000 amounts, and interest is 10 percent per annum. Interest is computed and paid on the principal as the principal is repaid. All borrowings take place at the beginning of a quarter, and all repayments are made at the end of a quarter.

Schedule 8

MEREDITH COMPANY
Cash Budget
For the Year Ended December 31, 19x1

	Schedule	Quarter 1	2	3	4	Total year
Cash balance, beginning		$ 19,000	$ 10,675	$ 10,000	$ 10,350	$ 19,000
Add receipts:						
Collections from customers	1	160,000	198,000	282,000	252,000	892,000
Total cash available before current financing		179,000	208,675	292,000	262,350	911,000
Less disbursements:						
Direct materials	3	12,225	15,175	18,150	15,400	60,950
Direct labor	4	49,000	91,000	96,000	69,000	305,000
Manufacturing overhead	5	24,100	32,500	33,500	28,100	118,200
Selling and administrative	7	63,000	78,000	66,000	71,000	278,000
Income taxes	9	15,000	15,000	15,000	15,000	60,000
Equipment purchases		30,000	12,000	—	—	42,000
Dividends		5,000	5,000	5,000	5,000	20,000
Total disbursements		198,325	248,675	233,650	203,500	884,150
Excess (deficiency) of cash available over disbursements		(19,325)	(40,000)	58,350	58,850	26,850
Financing:						
Borrowings (at beginning)		30,000*	50,000	—	—	80,000
Repayments (at ending)		—	—	(45,000)	(35,000)	(80,000)
Interest (at 10% per annum)		—	—	(3,000)†	(2,625)	(5,625)
Total financing		30,000	50,000	(48,000)	(37,625)	(5,625)
Cash balance, ending		$ 10,675	$ 10,000	$ 10,350	$ 21,225	$ 21,225

* The company requires a minimum cash balance of $10,000. Therefore, borrowing must be sufficient to cover the cash deficiency of $19,325 and to provide for the minimum cash balance of $10,000. All borrowings and all repayments of principal are in round $1,000 amounts.

† The interest payments relate only to the principal being repaid at the time it is repaid. For example, the interest in quarter 3 relates only to the interest due on the $30,000 principal being repaid from quarter 1 borrowing and on the $15,000 principal being repaid from quarter 2 borrowing, as follows:

$30,000 × 10% × 9 months	. . . . . .	$2,250
$15,000 × 10% × 6 months	. . . . . .	750
Total interest being paid.	. . . . . .	$3,000

Schedule 9

MEREDITH COMPANY
Budgeted Income Statement
For the Year Ended December 31, 19x1

	Schedule	
Sales (6,000 units at $150)	1	$900,000
Less cost of goods sold (6,000 units at $82)	6	492,000
Gross margin		408,000
Less selling and administrative expense	7	278,000
Net operating income		130,000
Less interest expense	8	5,625
Income before taxes		124,375
Less income taxes	*	60,000
Net income		$ 64,375

* Estimated.

The budgeted balance sheet

The budgeted balance sheet is developed by beginning with the current balance sheet and adjusting it for the data contained in the other budgets. A budgeted balance sheet for Meredith Company for 19x1 is presented in Schedule 10. The company's beginning-of-year balance sheet, from which the budgeted balance sheet in Schedule 10 has been derived in part, is presented below:

MEREDITH COMPANY
Balance Sheet
December 31, 19x0

Assets

Current assets:		
Cash	$ 19,000	
Accounts receivable	100,000	
Raw materials inventory (490 pounds)	2,450	
Finished goods inventory (200 units)	16,400	
Total current assets		$137,850
Plant and equipment:		
Land	30,000	
Buildings and equipment	250,000	
Accumulated depreciation	(74,000)	
Plant and equipment, net		206,000
Total assets		$343,850

Liabilities and Stockholders' Equity

Current liabilities:		
Accounts payable (raw materials)		$ 6,275
Stockholders' equity:		
Common stock, no par	$200,000	
Retained earnings	137,575	
Total stockholders' equity		337,575
Total liabilities and stockholders' equity		$343,850

Schedule 10

MEREDITH COMPANY
Budgeted Balance Sheet
December 31, 19x1

Assets

Current assets:

Cash.	$ 21,225	(a)
Accounts receivable	108,000	(b)
Raw materials inventory	2,600	(c)
Finished goods inventory.	24,600	(d)
Total current assets		$156,425

Plant and equipment:

Land.	30,000	(e)
Buildings and equipment	292,000	(f)
Accumulated depreciation	(90,000)	(g)
Plant and equipment, net		232,000
Total assets		$388,425

Liabilities and Stockholders' Equity

Current liabilities:

Accounts payable (raw materials) . . .	$ 6,475	(h)

Stockholders' equity:

Common stock, no par	$200,000	(i)
Retained earnings	181,950	(j)
Total stockholders' equity.		381,950
Total liabilities and stockholders' equity. .		$388,425

Explanation of December 31, 19x1, balance sheet figures:

a. The ending cash balance, as projected by the cash budget in Schedule 8.

b. Sixty percent of fourth-quarter sales, from Schedule 1 ($180,000 × 60% = $108,000).

c. From Schedule 3, the ending raw materials inventory will be 520 pounds. This material costs $5 per pound. Therefore, the ending inventory in dollars will be 520 pounds × $5 = $2,600.

d. From Schedule 6.

e. From the December 31, 19x0, balance sheet (no change).

f. The December 31, 19x0, balance sheet indicated a balance of $250,000. During 19x1, $42,000 additional equipment will be purchased (see Schedule 8), bringing the December 31, 19x1, balance to $292,000.

g. The December 31, 19x0, balance sheet indicated a balance of $74,000. During 19x1, $16,000 of depreciation will be taken (see Schedule 5), bringing the December 31, 19x1, balance to $90,000.

h. One half of the fourth-quarter raw materials purchases, from Schedule 3.

i. From the December 31, 19x0, balance sheet (no change).

j. December 31, 19x0, balance	$137,575
Add net income, from schedule 9 . . .	64,375
	201,950
Deduct dividends paid, from Schedule 8.	20,000
December 31, 19x1, balance.	$181,950

ZERO-BASE BUDGETING

Zero-base budgeting has received great attention recently as a new approach to the budgeting process. The **zero-base budget** gets its name from the fact that managers are required to start at zero budget levels every year and justify all costs as if the programs involved were being initiated for the first time. By this, we mean that no costs are viewed as being ongoing in nature; the manager must start at the ground level each year and present justification for all costs in the proposed budget, regardless of the type of cost involved. This is done in a series of "decision packages" in which the manager ranks all of the activities in the department according to relative importance, going from those that he or she considers essential to those that he or she considers of least importance. Presumably, this allows top management to evaluate each decision package independently and to pare back in those areas that appear less critical or that do not appear to be justified in terms of the cost involved.

This process differs from traditional budgeting, in which budgets are generally initiated on an incremental basis; that is, the manager starts with last year's budget and simply adds to it (or subtracts from it) according to anticipated needs. The manager doesn't have to start at the ground each year and justify ongoing costs (such as salaries) for existing programs.

In a broader sense, zero-base budgeting isn't really a new concept at all. Managers have always advocated in-depth reviews of departmental costs. The only difference is the frequency with which this review is carried out. Zero-base budgeting says that it should be done annually; critics of the zero-base idea say that this is too often and that such reviews should be made only every five years or so. These critics say that annual in-depth reviews are too time-consuming and too costly to be really feasible, and that in the long run such reviews probably cannot be justified in terms of the cost savings involved. In addition, it is argued that annual reviews soon become mechanical and that the whole purpose of the zero-base idea is then lost.

The question of frequency of zero-base reviews must be left to the judgment of the individual manager. In some situations, annual zero-base reviews may be justified; in other situations, they may not because of the time and cost involved. Whatever the time period chosen, however, most managers would agree that zero-base reviews can be helpful and should be an integral part of the overall budgeting process.

THE NEED FOR FURTHER BUDGETING MATERIAL

The material covered in this chapter represents no more than an introduction into the vast area of budgeting and profit planning. Our purpose has been to present an overview of the budgeting process and to show how the various operating budgets build on each other in guiding a firm toward its profit objectives. However, the matter of budgeting and profit planning is so critical to the intelligent management of a firm in today's business environment that we can't stop with simply an overview of the budgeting process. We need to look more closely at budgeting to see how it helps managers in the day-to-day conduct of business affairs. We will do this by studying standard costs and flexible budgets in the following two chapters and by introducing the concept of performance reporting. In Chapter 11, we will expand on these ideas by looking at budgeting and profit planning as tools for control of decentralized operations and as facilitating factors in judging managerial performance.

In sum, the materials in the following two chapters build on the budgeting and profit planning foundation that has been laid in this chapter by expanding on certain concepts that have been introduced and by refining others. The essential thing to keep in mind at this point is that the material covered in this chapter does not conclude our study of budgeting and profit planning, but rather just introduces the ideas.

KEY TERMS FOR REVIEW

Budget A detailed plan outlining the acquisition and use of financial and other resources over some given time period.

Budget committee A group of key management persons who are responsible for overall policy matters relating to the budget program and for coordinating the preparation of the budget itself.

Capital budget A budget covering the acquisition of land, buildings, and items of equipment; such a budget may have a time horizon extending 30 years or more into the future.

Cash budget A detailed plan showing how cash resources will be acquired and used over some specific time period.

Continuous or perpetual budget A budget that covers a 12-month period but is constantly adding a new month on the end as the current month is completed.

Control Those steps taken by management to ensure that the objectives set down at the budget planning stage are attained and to ensure that all parts of the organization function in a manner consistent with organizational policies.

Direct labor budget A detailed plan showing labor requirements over some specific time period.

Direct materials budget A detailed plan showing the amount of raw material that must be purchased during a period to meet both production and inventory needs.

Manufacturing overhead budget A detailed plan showing all the costs of production, other than direct materials and direct labor, from which the company's predetermined overhead rate is developed.

Master budget An interdependent network consisting of the various budgets in an organization.

Material requirements planning (MRP) An operations research tool that employs the computer to assist the manager in overall materials and inventory planning.

Planning The development of objectives in an organization and the preparation of various budgets to achieve these objectives.

Production budget A detailed plan showing the number of units that must be produced during a period in order to meet both sales and inventory needs.

Responsibility accounting A system of accounting in which costs are assigned to various managerial levels according to where control of the costs is deemed to rest, with the managers then held responsible for differences between budgeted and actual results.

Sales budget A detailed schedule of expected sales in both units and dollars over some specified time period.

Sales forecast A schedule of expected sales for an entire industry or for a model line of a particular product.

Self-imposed budget A method of budget preparation in which managers with responsibility over cost control prepare their own budget figures; these budget figures are reviewed by the managers' supervisors, and any questions are then resolved in face-to-face meetings.

Selling and administrative expense budget A detailed schedule of planned expenses that will be incurred in areas other than manufacturing during a budget period.

Zero-base budget A method of budgeting in which managers are required to start at zero budget levels every year and to justify all costs as if the programs involved were being initiated for the first time.

APPENDIX: ECONOMIC ORDER QUANTITY AND THE REORDER POINT

As stated in the main body of the chapter, inventory planning and control are an essential part of a budgeting system. We have seen that inventory levels are not left to chance but rather are carefully planned for, in terms of both opening and closing balances. Major questions that we have left unanswered are, "How does the manager know what inventory level is 'right' for the firm?" and "Won't the level that is 'right' vary from organization to organization?" The purpose of this section is to examine the inventory control methods available to the manager for answering these questions.

Costs associated with inventory

Three groups of costs are associated with inventory. The first group represents the **costs of ordering inventory.** The second group represents the **costs of carrying inventory.** The third group represents the costs of not carrying *sufficient* inventory. Examples of costs associated with each group are given below:

Costs of ordering inventory:
1. Clerical costs.
2. Transportation costs.

Costs of carrying inventory:
1. Storage space costs.
2. Handling costs.
3. Property taxes.
4. Insurance.
5. Obsolescence losses.
6. Interest on capital invested in inventory.

Costs of not carrying sufficient inventory:

1. Customer ill will.
2. Quantity discounts foregone.
3. Erratic production (expediting of goods, extra setup, etc.).
4. Inefficiency of production runs.
5. Added transportation charges.
6. Lost sales.

In a broad conceptual sense, the "right" level of inventory to carry is that which will minimize the total of these three classes of costs. This is not easily done, however, since certain of these costs are in direct conflict with one another. Notice, for example, that as inventory levels increase, the costs of carrying inventory will also increase, but the costs of not carrying sufficient inventory will decrease. In working toward total cost minimization, therefore, the manager must balance off the three groups of costs against one another. The problem really has two dimensions—how much to order (or how much to produce in a production run) and how often to do it.

Computing the economic order quantity

The "how much to order" is commonly referred to as the **economic order quantity.** It is the order size that will result in a minimization of the first two classes of costs above. We will consider two approaches to computing the economic order quantity—the tabular approach and the formula approach.

The tabular approach

Given a certain annual consumption of an item, a firm might place a few orders each year of a large quantity each, or it might place many orders of a small quantity each. Placing only a few orders would result in low ordering costs but in high inventory carrying costs, since the average inventory level would be very large. On the other hand, placing many orders would result in high ordering costs but in low inventory carrying costs, since in this case the average inventory level would be quite small. As stated above, the economic order quantity seeks the order size that will balance off these two classes of costs. To show how it is computed, assume that a manufacturer uses 3,000 subassemblies in the manufacturing process each year. The subassemblies are purchased from a supplier at a cost of $20 each. Other cost data are given below:

Inventory carrying costs, per unit, per year. . . . . . $ 0.80
Cost of placing a purchase order 10.00

Exhibit 8–3 contains a tabulation of the total costs associated with various order sizes for the subassemblies. Notice that total annual cost is lowest (and is equal) at the 250- and 300-unit order sizes. The economic order quantity will lie somewhere between these two points. We could locate it

EXHIBIT 8–3
Tabulation of costs associated with various order sizes

Symbol*		Order size in units								
		25	50	100	200	250	300	400	1,000	3,000
O/2	Average inventory in units	12.5	25	50	100	125	150	200	500	1,500
Q/O	Number of purchase orders	120	60	30	15	12	10	7.5	3	1
C(O/2)	Annual carrying cost at $0.80 per unit . .	$ 10	$ 20	$ 40	$ 80	$100	$120	$160	$400	$1,200
P(Q/O)	Annual purchase order cost at $10 per order .	1,200	600	300	150	120	100	75	30	10
T	Total annual cost	$1,210	$620	$340	$230	$220	$220	$235	$430	$1,210

* Symbols:
O = Order size in units (see headings above).
Q = Annual quantity used, in units (3,000 in this example).
C = Annual cost of carrying one unit in stock.
P = Cost of placing one order.
T = Total annual cost.

EXHIBIT 8–4

Graphical solution to economic order size

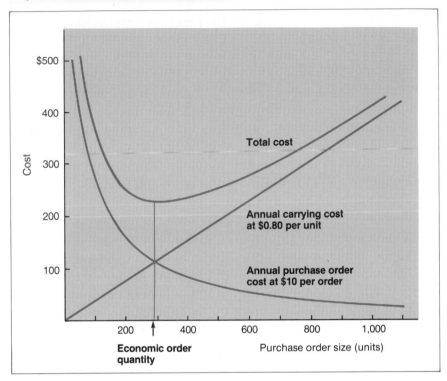

precisely by adding more columns to the tabulation, and we would in time zero in on 274 units as being the exact economic order quantity.

The cost relationships from this tabulation are shown graphically in Exhibit 8–4. Notice from the graph that total annual cost is minimized at that point where annual carrying costs and annual purchase order costs are equal. The same point identifies the economic order quantity, since the purpose of the computation is to find the point of exact trade-off between these two classes of costs.

Observe from the graph that total cost shows a tendency to flatten out between 200 and 400 units. Most firms look for this minimum cost range and choose an order size that falls within it, rather than choosing the exact economic order quantity. The primary reason is that suppliers will often ship goods only in round-lot sizes.

The formula approach

The economic order quantity can also be found by means of a formula. The formula is (derived by calculus):

$$0 = \sqrt{\frac{2\ QP}{C}}$$

where:

> 0 = the order size in units
> Q = the annual quantity used in units
> P = the cost of placing one order
> C = the annual cost of carrying one unit in stock

Substituting with the data used in our preceding example, we have:

> Q = 3,000 subassemblies used per year
> P = $10 cost to place one order
> C = $0.80 cost to carry one subassembly in stock for one year

$$0 = \sqrt{\frac{2(3,000)(\$10)}{\$0.80}} = \sqrt{\frac{\$60,000}{\$0.80}} = \sqrt{75,000}$$

$$0 = 274 \text{ (the economic order quantity)}$$

Although data can be obtained very quickly using the formula approach, it has the drawback of not providing as great a range of information as the methods discussed above.

Production runs

The economic order quantity concept can also be applied to the problem of determining the economic **production run size.** Deciding when to start and when to stop production runs is a problem that has plagued manufacturers for years. The problem can be solved quite easily by inserting the **setup cost** for a new production run into the economic order quantity formula in place of the purchase order cost. The setup cost includes the labor and other costs involved in getting facilities ready for a run of a different production item.

To illustrate, assume that the Chittenden Company has determined that the following costs are associated with one of its product lines:

> Q = 15,000 units produced each year
> P = $150 setup costs to change a production run
> C = $2 to carry one unit in stock for one year

What is the optimal production-run size for this product line? It can be determined by using the same formula as is used to compute the economic order quantity:

$$0 = \sqrt{\frac{2(15,000)(\$150)}{\$2}} = \sqrt{\frac{\$4,500,000}{\$2}} = \sqrt{2,250,000}$$

$$0 = 1,500 \text{ (economic production-run size in units)}$$

The Chittenden Company will minimize its overall costs by producing in runs of 1,500 units each.

Reorder point and safety stock

We stated earlier that the inventory problem has two dimensions—how much to order and how often to do it. The "how often to do it" involves what are commonly termed the *reorder point* and the *safety stock,* and seeks to find the optimal trade-off between the second two classes of inventory costs outlined earlier (the costs of carrying inventory and the costs of not carrying sufficient inventory).

The **reorder point** tells the manager when to place an order or when to initiate production to replenish depleted stocks. It is dependent on three factors—the economic order quantity (or economic production-run size), the *lead time,* and the rate of usage during the lead time. The **lead time** can be defined as the interval between the time that an order is placed and the time that the order is finally received from the supplier or from the production line.

Constant usage during the lead time

If the rate of usage during the lead time is known with certainty, the reorder point can be determined by the following formula:

Reorder point = Lead time × Average daily or weekly usage

To illustrate the formula's use, assume that a company's economic order quantity is 500 units, that the lead time is 3 weeks, and that the average weekly usage is 50 units.

Reorder point = 3 weeks × 50 units per week = 150 units

The reorder point would be 150 units. That is, the company will automatically place a new order for 500 units when inventory stocks drop to a level of 150 units, or three weeks' supply, left on hand.

Variable usage during the lead time

The previous example assumed that the 50 units per week usage rate was constant and was known with certainty. Although some firms enjoy the luxury of certainty, the more common situation is to find considerable variation in the rate of usage of inventory items from period to period. If usage varies from period to period, the firm that reorders in the way computed above may soon find itself out of stock. A sudden spurt in demand, a delay in delivery, or a snag in processing an order may cause inventory levels to be depleted before a new shipment arrives.

Companies that experience problems in demand, delivery, or processing of orders have found that they need some type of buffer to guard against stockouts. Such buffers are usually called *safety stocks.* **Safety stocks** serve as a kind of insurance against greater than usual demand and against problems in the ordering and delivery of goods. Their size is determined by deducting *average usage* from the *maximum usage* that can reasonably be expected during a period. For example, if the firm in the preceding example was faced with a situation of variable demand for its product, it would compute a safety stock as follows:

Maximum expected usage per week	65 units
Average usage per week	50
Excess	15 units
Lead time	× 3 weeks
Safety stock	45 units

The reorder point is then determined by *adding the safety stock to the average usage during the lead time.* In formula form, the reorder point would be:

Reorder point

$$= (\text{Lead time} \times \text{Average daily or weekly usage}) + \text{Safety stock}$$

Computation of the reorder point by this approach is shown both numerically and graphically in Exhibit 8–5.

EXHIBIT 8–5
Determining the reorder point—variable usage

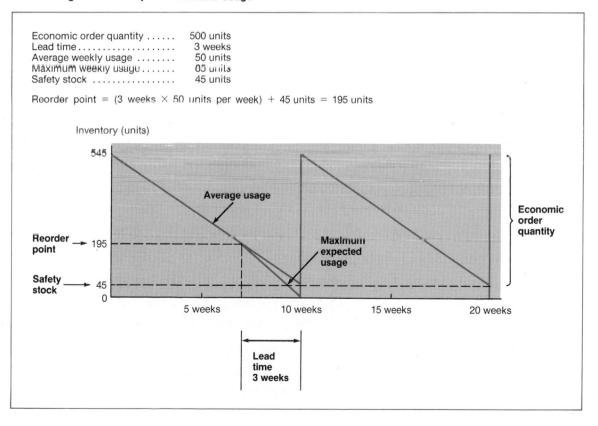

Economic order quantity	500 units
Lead time	3 weeks
Average weekly usage	50 units
Maximum weekly usage	65 units
Safety stock	45 units

Reorder point = (3 weeks × 50 units per week) + 45 units = 195 units

Thus, the company will place a new order for 500 units when inventory stocks drop to a level of 195 units left on hand.

KEY TERMS FOR REVIEW (APPENDIX)

Economic order quantity The order size for materials that will result in a minimization of the costs of ordering inventory and carrying inventory.

Economic production-run size The number of units produced in a production run that will result in a minimization of setup costs and the costs of carrying inventory.

Inventory carrying costs Those costs that result from having inventory in stock, such as rental of storage space, handling costs, property taxes, insurance, and interest on funds.

Inventory ordering costs Those costs associated with the acquisition of inventory, such as clerical costs and transportation costs.

Lead time The interval between the time that an order is placed and the time that the order is finally received from the supplier.

Reorder point The point in time when an order must be placed to replenish depleted stocks; it is determined by multiplying the lead time by the average daily or weekly usage.

Safety stock The difference between average usage of materials and maximum usage of materials that can reasonably be expected during the lead time.

Setup costs Labor and other costs involved in getting facilities ready for a run of a different production item.

QUESTIONS

8–1. What is a budget? What is budgetary control?

8–2. Discuss some of the major benefits to be gained from budgeting.

8–3. What is meant by the term *responsibility accounting?*

8–4. "Budgeting is designed primarily for organizations that have few complexities and uncertainties in their day-to-day operations." Do you agree? Why or why not?

8–5. What is a master budget? Briefly describe its contents.

8–6. Which is a better basis for judging actual results, budgeted performance or past performance? Why?

8–7. Why is the sales forecast always the starting point in budgeting?

8–8. Is there any difference between a sales forecast and a sales budget? Explain.

8–9. "As a practical matter, planning and control mean exactly the same thing." Do you agree? Explain.

8–10. Describe the flow of budget data in an organization. Who are the participants in the budgeting process, and how do they participate?

8–11. "To a large extent, the success of a budget program hinges on education and good salesmanship." Do you agree? Explain.

8–12. What is a self-imposed budget? What are the major advantages of self-imposed budgets? What caution must be exercised in their use?

8–13. In structuring a cash budget, what important factors must be considered in planning cash collections from sales? In planning cash disbursements to suppliers?

8–14. How can budgeting assist a firm in its employment policies?

8–15. "The principal purpose of the cash budget is to see how much cash the company will have in the bank at the end of the year." Do you agree? Explain.

8–16. How does zero-base budgeting differ from traditional budgeting?

8–17. List at least three costs associated with a company's inventory policy that do not appear as an expense on the income statement.

8–18. What three classes of costs are associated with a company's inventory policy? Which of these classes of costs is the most difficult to quantify?

8–19. What trade-offs in costs are involved in computing the economic order quantity?

8–20. "Managers are more interested in a minimum cost *range* than they are in a minimum cost point." Explain.

8–21. Define *lead time* and *safety stock*.

EXERCISES

E8–1. Warner Company has budgeted the sales of its product over the next four months as follows:

	Sales in units
July	30,000
August	45,000
September	60,000
October	50,000

The company is now in the process of preparing a production budget for the third quarter. Past experience has shown that end-of-month inventories of finished goods must equal 10 percent of the next month's sales. The inventory at the end of June was 3,000 units.

Required: Prepare a production budget for the third quarter showing the number of units to be produced each month and for the quarter in total.

E8–2. Micro Products, Inc., has developed a very powerful electronic calculator. Each calculator requires three small "chips" in its manufacture. The chips cost $8 each and are purchased from an overseas supplier. Micro Products has prepared a production budget for the calculator by quarters for 19x5 and for the first quarter of 19x6, as shown below:

	19x5				19x6
	First	**Second**	**Third**	**Fourth**	**First**
Budgeted production, in number of calculators	6,000	9,000	15,000	10,000	7,000

The chip used in production of the calculator is often hard to get, so it is necessary for the company to carry large inventories as a precaution against stockouts. For this reason, the inventory of chips at the end of a quarter must be equal to 25 percent of the following quarter's production needs. Some 4,500 chips will be on hand to start the first quarter of 19x5.

Required: Prepare a materials purchases budget for chips by quarter and in total for 19x5. Show your budget both in number of chips and in dollars.

E8–3. Peak sales for Midwest Products, Inc., occur in August. The company's sales budget for the third quarter of 19x8, showing these peak sales, is given below:

	July	August	September	Total
Budgeted sales	$80,000	$100,000	$70,000	$250,000

From past experience, the company has learned that 30 percent of a month's sales are collected in the month of sale, that another 60 percent is collected in the month following sale, and that the remaining 10 percent is collected in the second month following sale. Bad debts are negligible and can be ignored. May sales totaled $60,000, and June sales totaled $65,000 .

Required:
1. Prepare a schedule of budgeted cash collections from sales, by month and in total, for the third quarter.
2. Assume that the company will prepare a budgeted balance sheet as of September 30. Compute the accounts receivable as of that date.

E8–4. A cash budget, by quarters, is given below. Fill in the missing amounts (000 omitted). The company requires a minimum cash balance of at least $5,000 to start each quarter.

	1	2	3	4	Year
Cash balance, beginning	$ 6	$?	$?	$?	$?
Add collections from customers	?	?	96	?	323
Total cash available.	71	?	?	?	?
Less disbursements:					
Purchase of inventory	35	45	?	35	?
Operating expenses	?	30	30	?	113
Equipment purchases	8	8	10	?	36
Dividends	2	2	2	2	?
Total disbursements.	?	85	?	?	?
Excess (deficiency) of cash available over disbursements	(2)	?	11	?	?
Financing:					
Borrowings	?	15	—	—	?
Repayments (including interest)*	—	—	(?)	(17)	(?)
Total financing	?	?	?	?	?
Cash balance, ending	$?	$?	$?	$?	$?

* Interest will total $1,000 for the year.

E8–5. Greatday, Inc., makes a product that has peak sales in June of each year. The company has prepared a sales budget for the second quarter of 19x5, as shown below:

	April	May	June	Total
Budgeted sales	$600,000	$750,000	$900,000	$2,250,000

The company is in the process of preparing a cash budget for the second quarter and must determine the expected cash collections by month. To this end, the following information has been assembled:

Collections on sales:
70% in month of sale
20% in month following sale
8% in second month following sale
2% uncollectible

The company gives a 2 percent cash discount for payments made by customers during the month of sale. The accounts receivable balance to start the quarter is $195,000, of which $45,000 represents uncollected February sales and $150,000 represents uncollected March sales.

Required:

1. What were the total sales for February? For March?
2. Prepare a schedule showing the budgeted cash collections from sales, by month and in total, for the second quarter.

E8–6. Calgon Products needs a cash budget for the month of September 19x4. The following information is available:

a. The cash balance on September 1 is $9,000.
b. Actual sales for July and August and expected sales for September are:

	July	August	September
Cash sales.	$ 5,000	$ 5,250	$ 6,500
Credit sales	25,000	30,000	40,000
Total sales	$30,000	$35,250	$46,500

Credit sales are collected over a three-month period in the ratio 10 percent in the month of sale, 70 percent in the month following sale, and 18 percent in the second month following sale, with 2 percent uncollectible.

c. Purchases of inventory will total $25,000 for September. Twenty percent of a month's purchases are paid during the month of purchase. Accounts payable for August purchases total $16,000, which will be paid in September.
d. Selling and administrative expenses are budgeted at $14,000 for September. Of this amount, $5,000 is for depreciation.
e. Dividends of $6,000 will be paid during September, and equipment costing $12,000 will be purchased.
f. The company must maintain a minimum cash balance of $5,000. An open line of credit is available from the company's bank to bolster the cash position as needed.

Required:

1. Prepare a schedule of expected cash collections for the month of September.
2. Prepare a schedule of expected cash payments to suppliers during September for inventory purchases.
3. Prepare a cash budget for the month of September. Indicate in the financing section any borrowing that will be necessary during the month.

E8–7. (Appendix) Classify the following as either (a) costs of carrying inventory or (b) costs of not carrying sufficient inventory:

1. Airfreight on a rush order of a critical part needed in production.
2. Interest paid on investment funds.
3. State and local taxes on personal property.

4. Spoilage of perishable goods.
5. Excessive setup costs.
6. Customers lost through inability of the company to make prompt delivery.
7. Quantity discounts lost as a result of purchasing in small lots.
8. Fire insurance on inventory.
9. Loss sustained when a competitor comes out with a less expensive, more efficient product.
10. A general feeling of ill will among customers, due to broken delivery promises.

E8–8. (Appendix) Castleberry Manufacturing Company uses 5,400 units of part MV–4 each year. The cost of placing one order for part MV–4 is $10. Other costs associated with part MV–4 are:

	Annual cost per part
Insurance.	$0.12
Property taxes	0.05
Interest on funds invested	0.10
Other	0.03
Total cost.	$0.30

Required: Compute the economic order quantity for part MV–4.

E8–9. (Appendix) Selected information relating to an inventory item carried by the Santos Company is given below:

Economic order quantity	700 units
Maximum weekly usage	60 units
Lead time	4 weeks
Average weekly usage.	50 units

Santos Company is trying to determine the proper safety stock to carry on this inventory item, and the proper reorder point.

Required:
1. Assume that no safety stock is to be carried. What is the reorder point?
2. Assume that a full safety stock is to be carried.
   a. What would be the size of the safety stock in units?
   b. What would be the reorder point?

E8–10. (Appendix) The Baldwin Company uses 8,000 units of a certain part each year.

Required:
1. The company has determined that it costs $40 to place an order for the part from the supplier and $4 to carry one part in inventory each year. Compute the economic order quantity for the part.
2. Assume that the Baldwin Company's ordering costs increase to $50 per order. What will be the effect on the economic order quantity? Show computations.
3. Assume that the Baldwin Company's carrying costs increase to $5 per part. (Ordering costs remain unchanged at $40.) What will be the effect on the economic order quantity? Show computations.
4. In (2) and (3) above, why does an increase in cost cause the economic order quantity to go up in one case and to go down in the other?

PROBLEMS

P8–11. **Production and purchases budgets.** Tonga Toys manufactures and distributes a number of products to retailers. One of these products, Playclay, requires three pounds of material A in the manufacture of each unit. The company is now planning raw materials needs for the third quarter of 19x7. Peak sales of Playclay occur in the third quarter of each year. In order to keep production and shipments moving smoothly, the company has the following inventory requirements:

a. The finished goods inventory on hand at the end of each month must be equal to 5,000 units plus 30 percent of the next month's sales. The finished goods inventory on June 30 is budgeted to be 17,000 units.

b. The raw materials inventory on hand at the end of each month must be equal to one half of the following month's production needs for raw materials. The raw materials inventory on June 30 for material A is budgeted to be 64,500 pounds.

c. The company maintains no work in process inventories.

A sales budget for Playclay for the last six months of 19x7 is given below:

	Budgeted sales in units
July	40,000
August	50,000
September	70,000
October	35,000
November	20,000
December	10,000

Required: 1. Prepare a production budget for Playclay for the months July–October.
2. Examine the production budget that you have prepared. Why will the company produce more units than it sells in July and August and less units than it sells in September and October?
3. Prepare a budget showing the quantity of material A to be purchased for July, August, and September 19x7 and for the quarter in total.

P8–12. **Cash budget.** Mary Roberts, president of Crestline Products, has just approached the company's bank with a request for a $30,000, 90-day loan. The purpose of the loan is to assist the company in building inventories in support of peak April sales. Since the company has had some difficulty in paying off its loans in the past, the loan officer has asked for a cash budget to help determine whether the loan should be made. The following data are available for the months April–June, during which the loan will be used:

a. On April 1, the start of the loan period, the cash balance will be $26,000. Accounts receivable on April 1 will total $151,500, of which $141,000 will be collected during April and $7,200 will be collected during May. The remainder will be uncollectible.

b. Past experience shows that 20 percent of a month's sales are collected in the month of sale, 75 percent in the month following sale, and 4 percent in the second month following sale. Budgeted sales and expenses for the period follow:

	April	May	June
Sales	$200,000	$300,000	$250,000
Merchandise purchases	120,000	180,000	150,000
Payroll	9,000	9,000	8,000
Lease payments.	15,000	15,000	15,000
Advertising	70,000	80,000	60,000
Equipment purchases	8,000	—	—
Depreciation	10,000	10,000	10,000

c. Merchandise purchases are paid in full during the month following purchase. Accounts payable for merchandise purchases on March 31, which will be paid during April, total $108,000.

d. In preparing the cash budget, assume that the loan will be made in April and repaid in June. Interest on the loan will total $2,250.

Required: 1. Prepare a schedule of budgeted cash collections for April, May, and June and for the three months in total.

2. Prepare a cash budget, by month and in total, for the three-month period.

3. If the company needs a minimum cash balance of $20,000 to start each month, can the loan be repaid as planned? Explain.

P8–13. **Production and direct materials budgets.** A sales budget is given below for one of the products manufactured by Vincent, Ltd.:

Month	Sales budget in units
July	18,000
August	20,000
September	24,000
October	26,000
November	19,000
December	16,000

The inventory of finished goods at the end of each month must be equal to 5,000 units plus 10 percent of the next month's sales. On June 30, the finished goods inventory totaled 6,800 units.

Each unit of product requires three ounces of a special liquid extract known as SV–6. Sometimes the extract is in short supply; for this reason, the company has a policy of maintaining an inventory at the end of each month equal to one half of the next month's production needs. This requirement was met on July 1 of the current year.

Required: Prepare a budget showing the quantity of SV–6 to be purchased each month from July–September and for the three-month period in total. (Hint: Remember that a production budget must be prepared before a materials purchases budget can be prepared.)

P8–14. **Master budget.** The balance sheet of Phototec, Inc., as of May 31, 19x4, is given below:

PHOTOTEC, INC.
Balance Sheet
May 31, 19x4
Assets

Cash	$ 8,000
Accounts receivable, customers	27,000
Inventory	46,000
Plant and equipment, net of depreciation	200,000
Total assets	$281,000

Liabilities and Equity

Accounts payable, suppliers	$ 40,000
Note payable	8,000
Capital stock, no par	150,000
Retained earnings	83,000
Total liabilities and equity	$281,000

Phototec, Inc., has never budgeted before, and for this reason it is limiting its master budget planning horizon to just one month—June 19x4. The company has assembled the following budgeted information relating to the month of June:

a. Sales are budgeted at $150,000. Of these sales, $60,000 will be for cash; the remainder will be credit sales. Fifty percent of credit sales are collected in the month the sales are made, and the remainder is collected in the following month. All of the May 31 accounts receivable will be collected during June.

b. Purchases of inventory are expected to total $80,000 during the month, all on account. Forty percent of all purchases are paid for in the month of purchase; the remainder is paid in the following month. All of the May 31 accounts payable to suppliers will be paid during June.

c. The June 30 inventory balance is budgeted at $36,000.

d. Operating expenses for June are budgeted at $50,000, exclusive of depreciation. These expenses will all be paid in cash. Depreciation is budgeted at $2,500 for the month.

e. Equipment costing $15,000 will be acquired on June 30. The company will give a note payable to its bank in order to obtain funds to cover the equipment cost. The note will be due in one year.

f. The note payable at May 31 will be paid in June, with $250 interest. (All of the interest relates to the month of June.)

Required: 1. Prepare a cash budget for June 19x4. Support your budget with schedules showing budgeted cash receipts and budgeted cash payments for inventory purchases.

2. Prepare a budgeted income statement for June 19x4. Use the traditional income statement format. Ignore income taxes.

3. Prepare a budgeted balance sheet as of June 30, 19x4.

P8–15. **Planning bank financing by means of a cash budget.** The president of Univax, Inc., has just approached the company's bank seeking short-term financing for the coming year, 19x2. The bank has stated that the loan request must be accompanied by a detailed cash budget that shows the quarters in which financing will be needed, as well as the amounts that will be needed, and the quarters in which repayments can be made.

In order to provide this information for the bank, the president has directed that the following data be gathered from which a cash budget can be prepared:

a. Budgeted sales and merchandise purchases for 19x2, as well as actual sales and purchases for the last quarter of 19x1, are:

	Sales	Merchandise purchases
19x1:		
Fourth quarter actual.	$300,000	$180,000
19x2:		
First quarter budgeted	400,000	260,000
Second quarter budgeted	500,000	310,000
Third quarter budgeted	600,000	370,000
Fourth quarter budgeted	480,000	240,000

b. The company typically collects 33 percent of a quarter's sales before the quarter ends and another 65 percent in the following quarter. The remainder is uncollectible. This pattern of collections is now being experienced in the actual data for the 19x1 fourth quarter.

c. Some 20 percent of a quarter's merchandise purchases are paid for within the quarter. The remainder is paid in the quarter following.

d. Operating expenses for 19x2 are budgeted quarterly at $90,000 plus 12 percent of sales. Of the fixed amount, $20,000 each quarter is depreciation.

e. The company will pay $10,000 in cash dividends each quarter.

f. Equipment purchases will be made as follows during the year: $80,000 in the second quarter and $48,500 in the third quarter.

g. The Cash account contained $20,000 at the end of 19x1. The company must maintain a minimum cash balance of at least $18,000.

h. Any borrowing will take place at the beginning of a quarter, and any repayments will be made at the end of a quarter at an annual interest rate of 10 percent. Interest is paid only when principal is repaid. All borrowings and all repayments of principal must be in round $1,000 amounts. Interest payments can be in any amount.

i. At present, the company has no loans outstanding.

Required:
1. Prepare the following, by quarter and in total, for the year 19x2:
   a. A schedule of budgeted cash collections on sales.
   b. A schedule of budgeted cash payments for merchandise purchases.
2. Compute the expected cash payments for operating expenses, by quarter and in total, for the year 19x2.
3. Using the data from parts (1) and (2) and other data as needed, prepare a cash budget for 19x2, by quarter and in total for the year. Show clearly on your budget the quarter(s) in which borrowing will be needed and the quarter(s) in which repayments can be made, as requested by the company's bank.

P8–16. Master budget preparation. Nordic Company prepares its master budget on a quarterly basis. The following data have been assembled to assist in preparation of the master budget for the second quarter of 19x6:

a. As of March 31, 19x6 (the end of the prior quarter), the company's balance sheet showed the following account balances:

Cash	$ 9,000	
Accounts receivable	48,000	
Inventory	12,600	
Plant and equipment	200,000	
Accounts payable		$ 18,300
Capital stock		180,000
Retained earnings		71,300
	$269,600	$269,600

b. Actual sales for March and budgeted sales for April–July are as follows:

March (actual)	$60,000
April	70,000
May.	85,000
June	90,000
July.	50,000

c. Sales are 20 percent for cash and 80 percent on credit. All credit sale terms are n/30; therefore, accounts are collected in the month following sale. The accounts receivable at March 31 are a result of March credit sales.

d. The company's gross profit rate is 40 percent of sales.

e. Monthly expenses are budgeted as follows: salaries and wages, $7,500 per month; freight-out, 6 percent of sales; advertising, $6,000 per month; depreciation, $2,000 per month; other expense, 4 percent of sales.

f. At the end of each month, inventory is to be on hand equal to 30 percent of the following month's sales needs, stated at cost.

g. Half of a month's inventory purchases are paid for in the month of purchase and half in the following month.

h. Equipment purchases during the quarter will be as follows: April, $11,500; and May, $8,250.

i. Dividends totaling $4,000 will be declared and paid in June.

j. The company must maintain a minimum cash balance of $8,000. An open line of credit is available at a local bank. All borrowing is done at the beginning of a month, and all repayments are made at the end of a month. Borrowings and repayments of principal must be in multiples of $1,000. Loan repayments are on a FIFO basis. Interest is paid only at the time of repayment of principal; however, *any interest on unpaid loans should be properly accrued when statements are prepared.* The interest rate is 12 percent per annum. (Figure interest on whole months, e.g., $\frac{1}{12}$, $\frac{2}{12}$.)

Required: Using the data above, complete the following statements and schedules for the second quarter:

1. Schedule of expected cash collections:

	April	May	June	Total
Cash sales	$14,000			
Credit sales	48,000			
Total collections	$62,000			

2. *a.* Inventory purchases budget:

	April	May	June	Total
Budgeted cost of goods sold	$42,000*	$51,000		
Add: Desired ending inventory	15,300†			
Total needs	57,300			
Deduct: Opening inventory	12,600			
Required purchases	$44,700			

* For April sales: $70,000 sales × 60% cost ratio = $42,000.
† $51,000 × 30% = $15,300.

b. Schedule of cash disbursements for purchases:

	April	May	June	Total
For March purchases	$18,300			$18,300
For April purchases	22,350	$22,350		44,700
For May purchases				
For June purchases				
Total cash disbursements	$40,650			

3. Schedule of cash disbursements for expenses:

	April	May	June	Total
Salaries and wages	$ 7,500			
Freight-out	4,200			
Advertising	6,000			
Other expenses	2,800			
Total cash disbursements	$20,500			

4. Cash budget:

	April	May	June	Total
Cash balance, beginning	$ 9,000			
Add cash collections	62,000			
Total cash available	71,000			
Less disbursements:				
For inventory purchases	40,650			
For operating expenses	20,500			
For equipment purchases	11,500			
For dividends	—			
Total disbursements	72,650			
Excess (deficiency) of cash	(1,650)			
Financing:				
Etc.				

5. Prepare an income statement for the quarter ending June 30. (Use the functional format in preparing your income statement.)

6. Prepare a balance sheet as of June 30.

P8–17. **Evaluating a company's budget procedures.** Rouge Corporation is a medium-sized company in the steel fabrication industry with six divisions located in different geographic sectors of the United States. Considerable autonomy in operational management is permitted in the divisions, due in part to the distance between corporate headquarters in St. Louis and five of the six divisions. Corporate management establishes divisional budgets using data for the prior year adjusted for industry and economic changes expected for the coming year. Budgets are prepared by year and by quarter, with top management attempting to recognize problems unique to each division in the divisional budget-setting process. Once the year's divisional budgets have been set by corporate management, they cannot be modified by division management.

The budget for calendar year 1986 projects total corporate net income before taxes of $3,750,000 for the year, including $937,500 for the first quarter. Results of first-quarter operations presented to corporate management in early April showed corporate net income of $865,000, which was $72,500 below the projected net income for the quarter. The St. Louis division operated at 4.5 percent above its projected divisional net income, while the other five divisions showed net incomes with variances ranging from 1.5 to 22 percent below budgeted net income.

Corporate management is concerned with the first-quarter results because it believes strongly that differences between divisions had been recognized. An entire day in late November of last year had been spent presenting and explaining the corporate and divisional budgets to the division managers and their division controllers. A mid-April meeting of corporate and division management generated unusual candor. All five out-of-state division managers cited reasons why the first-quarter results in their respective divisions represented effective management and was the best that could be expected. Corporate management has remained unconvinced and informs division managers that "results will be brought into line with the budget by the end of the second quarter."

Required:
1. Identify the major defects in the procedures employed by Rouge Corporation's corporate management in preparing and implementing the divisional budgets.
2. Discuss the behavioral problems that may arise by requiring Rouge Corporation's division managers to meet the quarterly budgeted net income figures as well as the annual budgeted net income. (CMA, adapted)

P8–18. Cash budget. Janus Products, Inc., is a merchandising firm that sells binders, paper, and other school supplies. The company is planning its cash needs for the third quarter of 19x6. In the past, Janus Products has had to borrow money during the third quarter in order to support peak sales of back-to-school materials, which occur during August. The following information has been assembled to assist in preparing a cash budget for the quarter:

a. Budgeted monthly income statements for July–October 19x6 are:

	July	August	September	October
Sales	$40,000	$70,000	$50,000	$45,000
Cost of goods sold	24,000	42,000	30,000	27,000
Gross margin	16,000	28,000	20,000	18,000
Less operating expenses:				
Selling expense	7,200	11,700	8,500	7,300
Administrative expense*	5,600	7,200	6,100	5,900
Total operating expenses	12,800	18,900	14,600	13,200
Net income	$ 3,200	$ 9,100	$ 5,400	$ 4,800

* Includes $2,000 depreciation each month.

b. Sales are 20 percent for cash and 80 percent on credit.

c. Credit sales are collected over a three-month period in the ratio of 10 percent in the month of sale, 70 percent in the month following sale, and 20 percent in the second month following sale. May sales totaled $30,000, and June sales totaled $36,000.

d. Inventory purchases are paid for within 15 days. Therefore, 50 percent of a month's inventory purchases are paid for in the month of purchase. The remaining 50 percent is paid in the following month. Accounts payable for inventory purchases at June 30 total $11,700.

e. The company maintains its ending inventory levels at 75 percent of the cost of the merchandise to be sold in the following month. The merchandise inventory at June 30 is $18,000.

f. Equipment costing $4,500 will be purchased in July.

g. Dividends of $1,000 will be declared and paid in September.

h. The cash balance on June 30 is $8,000; the company must maintain a cash balance of at least this amount at all times.

i. The company can borrow from its bank as needed to bolster the cash account. Borrowings must be in multiples of $1,000. All borrowings take place at the beginning of a month, and all repayments are made at the end of a month. The interest rate is 12 percent per annum. Compute interest on whole months ($\frac{1}{12}$, $\frac{2}{12}$, and so on).

Required:
1. Prepare a schedule of budgeted cash collections from sales for each of the months July, August, and September and for the quarter in total.
2. Prepare the following for merchandise inventory:
   a. An inventory purchases budget for each of the months July, August, and September.
   b. A schedule of expected cash disbursements for inventory for each of the months July, August, and September and for the quarter in total.
3. Prepare a cash budget for the third quarter of 19x6. Show figures by month as well as for the quarter in total. Show borrowings from the company's bank and repayments to the bank as needed to maintain the minimum cash balance.

P8–19. Master budget preparation. Actual sales for June and budgeted sales for July–October 19x2 are presented below for the Newark Company:

June (actual)	$40,000
July	50,000
August . . . . . . \	64,000
September.	80,000
October.	36,000

The company is preparing its master budget for the third quarter. The following information is available:

a. Sales are 40 percent for cash and 60 percent on credit. All credit sale terms are n/30; therefore, accounts are collected in the month following sale. The accounts receivable at June 30 are a result of June credit sales.

b. The gross profit rate is 30 percent of sales.

c. Monthly expenses are as follows: salaries and wages, 15 percent of sales; rent, $2,200 per month; and other expenses (excluding depreciation), 5 percent of sales. Depreciation is $1,000 per month.

d. At the end of each month, inventory is to be on hand equal to 75 percent of the following month's sales needs, stated at cost.

e. All inventory purchases are on terms of 2/15, n/30; therefore, half of a month's purchases are paid for in the month of purchase and half in the following month. All purchase discounts are taken and treated as "Other income" on the income statement. (Purchase discounts are not recorded until payment is made.) The accounts payable at June 30 are a result of June purchases of inventory.

f. Equipment costing $2,500 will be purchased in August.

g. The company must maintain a minimum cash balance of $5,000. An open line of credit is available at a local bank. All borrowing is done at the beginning of a month, and all repayments are made at the end of a month. Borrowings and repayments of principal must be in multiples of $1,000. Loan repayments are on a FIFO basis. Interest is paid only at the time of repayment of principal; however, any interest on unpaid loans should be properly accrued when statements are prepared. The interest rate is 12 percent per annum. (Figure interest on whole months—$\frac{1}{12}$, $\frac{2}{12}$, and so forth.)

h. Dividends of $1,500 will be declared and paid in September.

i. Balances in various balance sheet accounts at June 30 follow:

Cash	$ 6,000
Accounts receivable	24,000
Inventory	26,250
Plant and equipment, net	150,000
Accounts payable	16,625
Capital stock	175,000
Retained earnings	14,625

Required: Using the data above, complete the following statements and schedules:

1. Schedule of expected cash collections:

	July	August	September	Total
Cash sales	$20,000			
Credit sales	24,000			
Total collections	$44,000			

2. a. Purchases budget:

	July	August	September	Total
Budgeted cost of goods sold	$35,000*	$44,800		
Add: Desired ending inventory	33,600†			
Total needs	68,600			
Deduct: Opening inventory	26,250			
Required purchases	$42,350			

* For July sales: $50,000 sales × 70% cost ratio = $35,000.
† $44,800 × 75% = $33,600.

b. Schedule of cash disbursements for purchases:

	July	August	September	Total
For June purchases	$16,625			$16,625
For July purchases	21,175	$21,175		42,350
For August purchases				
For September purchases				
Total	37,800			
Less 2% discount	756			
Net cash disbursements	$37,044			

3. Schedule of cash disbursements for expenses:

	July	August	September	Total
Salaries and wages	$ 7,500			
Rent	2,200			
Other expenses	2,500			
Total cash disbursements	$12,200			

4. Cash budget:

	July	August	September	Total
Cash balance, beginning	$ 6,000			
Add cash collections	44,000			
Total cash available	50,000			
Less disbursements:				
For inventory purchases	37,044			
For expenses	12,200			
For equipment purchases	—			
For dividends	—			
Total disbursements	49,244			
Excess (deficiency) of cash	756			
Financing:				
Etc.				

5. Prepare an income statement for the quarter ending September 30. (Use the functional format in preparing your income statement.)
6. Prepare a balance sheet as of September 30.

P8–20. **Production budget; purchases budget; income statement.** Amcor Products, Inc., produces and sells a very popular fertilizer called Greenex. The company is in the process of preparing budgeted data on Greenex for the second quarter of 19x4. The following data are available:

a. The company expects to sell 45,000 bags of Greenex during the second quarter of 19x4. The selling price is $10 per bag.
b. Each bag of Greenex requires 5 pounds of a material called Nitro and 15 pounds of a material called Mixo.
c. Inventory levels are planned as follows:

	Beginning of quarter	End of quarter
Finished bags of Greenex.	12,000	9,000
Material Nitro—pounds.	65,000	52,500
Material Mixo—pounds.	115,000	95,000
Empty bags.	30,000	20,000

d. Nitro costs 60 cents per pound; Mixo costs 10 cents per pound; and empty bags cost 80 cents each.

e. It requires six minutes of direct labor time to process and fill one bag of Greenex. Labor cost is $7.50 per hour.

f. Variable manufacturing overhead costs are 45 cents per bag. Fixed manufacturing overhead costs total $60,000 per quarter.

g. Variable selling and administrative expenses are 5 percent of sales. Fixed selling and administrative expenses total $35,000 per quarter.

Required:

1. Prepare a production budget for Greenex for the second quarter.

2. Prepare a raw materials purchases budget for Nitro, Mixo, and empty bags for the second quarter. Show the budgeted purchases in dollars as well as in pounds or bags.

3. Compute the budgeted cost to manufacture one bag of finished Greenex. (Include only variable manufacturing costs, as illustrated in the chapter.)

4. Prepare a budgeted income statement for Greenex for the second quarter. Use the contribution approach and show both per unit and total cost data.

P8–21. **Quarterly cash budget.** As part of the company's overall planning program, the controller of the Lambert Company, Ltd., prepares a cash budget by quarters each year.

The company's operations consist solely of processing and canning the yearly crop of peaches. As this is a seasonal commodity, all manufacturing operations take place in the quarter of October through December. Sales are made throughout the year, and the company's fiscal year ends on June 30.

The sales forecast for the coming year is as follows:

First quarter (July–September 19x1)	$ 780,000
Second quarter (October–December 19x1)	1,500,000
Third quarter (January–March 19x2)	780,000
Fourth quarter (April–June 19x2).	780,000

All sales are on account. The beginning balance of receivables is expected to be collected during the first quarter. It is anticipated that subsequent collections will follow the pattern of two thirds collected in the quarter of sales, the remaining one third in the quarter following.

Purchases of peaches are scheduled as follows: $240,000 in the first quarter and $720,000 in the second quarter. Payment is made in the quarter of purchase.

Direct labor of $700,000 is incurred and paid in the second quarter.

Factory overhead cost (paid in cash during quarter it is incurred) is $860,000 in the second quarter. The standby (fixed) amount in each of the other three quarters is $200,000.

Selling and administrative expenses, incurred and paid, amount to $100,000 per quarter during the year.

To finance its seasonal working capital needs, the company has obtained a line of short-term credit with the Royal Toronto Bank. The company maintains a minimum cash balance of $8,000 and borrows and repays only in multiples of $5,000. It repays as soon as it is able to do so without impairing the minimum cash balance. Interest is at 8 percent and is paid at the time of loan repayment. It is assumed that all borrowing is done at the beginning of a quarter, and the repayments are made at the end of a quarter. (Round interest calculations to nearest $1,000.)

The company plans to spend the following amounts on equipment:

Third quarter	$150,000
Fourth quarter	50,000

Account balances as of July 1, 19x1, were:

Cash	$ 8,000
Accounts receivable	25,000

Required:
1. Prepare a schedule of budgeted cash collections on sales.
2. Prepare a cash budget by quarter and for the year in total ending June 30, 19x2.
3. Comment briefly on the nature and purpose of cash budgets for management.

(SMA, adapted)

P8–22. Evaluating a company's budget procedures. Springfield Corporation operates on a calendar-year basis. It begins the annual budgeting process in late August, when the president establishes targets for the total dollar sales and net income before taxes for the next year.

The sales target is given to the marketing department, where the marketing manager formulates a sales budget by product line in both units and dollars. From this budget, sales quotas by product line in units and dollars are established for each of the corporation's sales districts.

The marketing manager also estimates the cost of the marketing activities required to support the target sales volume and prepares a tentative marketing expense budget.

The executive vice president uses the sales and profit targets, the sales budget by product line, and the tentative marketing expense budget to determine the dollar amounts that can be devoted to manufacturing and corporate office expense. The executive vice president prepares the budget for corporate expenses, and then forwards to the production department the product-line sales budget in units and the total dollar amount that can be devoted to manufacturing.

The production manager meets with the factory managers to develop a manufacturing plan that will produce the required units when needed within the cost constraints set by the executive vice president. The budgeting process usually comes to a halt at this point because the production department does not consider the financial resources allocated to be adequate.

When this standstill occurs, the vice president of finance, the executive vice president, the marketing manager, and the production manager meet to determine the final budgets for each of the areas. This normally results in a modest increase in the total amount available for manufacturing costs, while the marketing expense and corporate office expense budgets are cut. The total sales and net income figures proposed by the president are seldom changed. Although the participants are seldom pleased with the compromise, these budgets are final. Each executive then develops a new detailed budget for the operations in his or her area.

None of the areas has achieved its budget in recent years. Sales often run below the target. When budgeted sales are not achieved, each area is expected to cut costs so that the president's profit target can still be met. However, the profit target is seldom met because costs are not cut enough. In fact, costs often run above the original budget in all functional areas. The president is disturbed that Springfield has not been able to meet the sales and profit targets. He hired a consultant with considerable experience with companies in Springfield's industry. The consultant reviewed the budgets for the past four years. He concluded that the product-line sales budgets were reasonable and that the cost and expense budgets were adequate for the budgeted sales and production levels.

Required:
1. Discuss how the budgeting process as employed by Springfield Corporation contributes to the failure to achieve the president's sales and profit targets.
2. Suggest how Springfield Corporation's budgeting process could be revised to correct the problems.
3. Should the functional areas be expected to cut their costs when sales volume falls below budget? Explain your answer. (CMA, adapted)

P8-23. Cash budget for month. The treasurer of Househall Company, Ltd., states, "Our monthly financial budget shows me our cash surplus or deficiency and assures me that an unexpected cash shortage will not occur."

A cash budget is now being prepared for the month of May 19x5. The following information has been gathered to assist in preparing the budget:

a. Budgeted sales and production requirements are:

Budgeted sales	$650,000
Production requirements:	
Raw materials to be used	301,000
Direct labor cost	85,000

The raw materials inventory is budgeted to increase by $6,000 during the month; other inventories will not change.

b. Customers are allowed a 2 percent cash discount on accounts paid within 10 days after the end of the month of sale. Only about 50 percent of the payments made in the month following sale fall within the discount period.

c. Accounts receivable outstanding at April 30 were:

Month	Sales	Accounts receivable at April 30	Percentage of sales uncollected at April 30	Percentage to be collected in May
January	$340,000	$ 8,500	2½%	?
February	530,000	31,800	6%	?
March	470,000	47,000	10%	?
April	550,000	550,000	100%	?

Bad debts are negligible. All January receivables outstanding will have been collected by the end of May, and the collection pattern since the time of sale will be the same in May as in previous months.

d. Raw materials purchases are paid in the month following purchase, and $320,000 in accounts payable for purchases was outstanding at the end of April.

e. Accrued wages on April 30, 19x5, were $11,000. All May payroll amounts will be paid within the month of May.

f. Budgeted operating expenses and overhead costs for May are:

Overhead and other charges:

Indirect labor	$34,000	
Real estate taxes.	1,500	
Depreciation	25,000	
Utilities	1,500	
Wage benefits.	9,000	
Fire insurance.	1,500	
Amortization of patents.	5,000	
Spoilage of materials in the warehouse	1,500	$79,000
Sales salaries		45,000
Administrative salaries.		15,000

g. Real estate taxes are paid in August each year.
h. Utilities are billed and paid within the month.
i. The $9,000 monthly charge above for "Wage benefits" includes:

Unemployment insurance (payable monthly)	$1,350
Canada pension plan (payable monthly)	820
Holiday pay, which represents $\frac{1}{12}$ of the annual cost (May holidays will require $2,040)	1,100
Company pension fund, including $\frac{1}{12}$ of a $10,800 adjustment paid in January 19x5	5,000
Group insurance (payable quarterly, with the last payment having been made in February)	730

j. Fire insurance premiums are payable in January, in advance.
k. Freight-out costs for May will be $1,000, all payable during the month.
l. The cash balance on April 30, 19x5, was $5,750.

Required:
1. Prepare a schedule showing expected cash collections for May 19x5.
2. Prepare a cash budget for May 19x5 in good form. Ignore income taxes.
3. Comment briefly on the treasurer's statement quoted at the beginning of the problem. (SMA, adapted)

P8–24. **Integrated operating budgets.** The West division of Vader Corporation produces an intricate component part used in Vader's major product line. The division manager has recently been concerned about a lack of coordination between purchasing and production personnel and believes that a monthly budgeting system would be better than the present system.

West's division manager has decided to develop budget information for the third quarter of the current year as a trial before the budget system is implemented for an entire fiscal year. In response to the division manager's request for data that could be used to develop budget information, the division controller accumulated the following data.

Sales

Sales through June 30, 19x7, the first six months of the current year, are 24,000 units. Actual sales in units for May and June and estimated unit sales for the next five months are detailed as follows:

May (actual)	4,000
June (actual)	4,000
July (estimated)	5,000
August (estimated)	6,000
September (estimated).	7,000
October (estimated)	7,500
November (estimated)	8,000

West division expects to sell 65,000 units during the year ending December 31, 19x7.

Direct material

Data regarding the materials used in the component are shown in the following schedule. The desired monthly ending inventory for all direct materials is to have sufficient materials on hand to provide for 50 percent of the next month's production needs.

Direct material	Units of direct materials per finished component	Cost per unit	Inventory level 6/30/x7
No. 101.	6 ounces	$2.40	35,000 ounces
No. 211.	4 pounds	5.00	30,000 pounds

Direct labor

Each component must pass through three processes to be completed. Data regarding the direct labor are as follows:

Process	Direct labor-hours per finished component	Cost per direct labor-hour
Forming . . . . :	0.80	$8.00
Assembly . . . . . . , . . .	2.00	5.50
Finishing.	0.25	6.00

Factory overhead

The division produced 27,000 components during the six-month period through June 30, 19x7. The actual variable overhead costs incurred during this six-month period are shown below. The division controller believes that the variable overhead costs will be incurred at the same rate during the last six months of 19x7.

Supplies	$ 59,400
Electricity.	27,000
Indirect labor	54,000
Other	8,100
Total variable overhead	$148,500

The fixed-overhead costs incurred during the first six months of 19x7 amounted to $93,500. Fixed-overhead costs are budgeted for the full year as follows:

Supervision	$ 60,000
Taxes	7,200
Depreciation	86,400
Other	32,400
Total fixed overhead	$186,000

Finished goods inventory

The desired monthly ending inventory in units of completed components is 80 percent of the next month's estimated sales. There are 4,000 finished units in inventory on June 30, 19x7.

Required:
1. Prepare a production budget for the West division for the third quarter ending September 30, 19x7. Show computations by month and in total for the quarter.
2. Prepare a direct materials purchases budget in units and in dollars for each type of material for the third quarter ending September 30, 19x7. Again show computations by month and in total for the quarter.
3. Prepare a direct labor budget in hours and in dollars for the third quarter ending September 30, 19x7. This time it is *not* necessary to show monthly figures; show quarterly totals only.
4. Assume that the company plans to produce a total of 65,000 units for the year. Prepare a factory overhead budget for the six-month period ending December 31, 19x7. Again, it is *not* necessary to show monthly figures. (CMA, adapted)

P8–25. **Master budget with supporting budgets.** You have just been hired as a new management trainee by Quik-Flik Sales Company, a nationwide distributor of a revolutionary new cigarette lighter. The company has an exclusive franchise on distribution of the lighter, and sales have grown so rapidly over the last few years that it has become necessary to add new members to the management team. You have been given direct responsibility for all planning and budgeting. Your first assignment is to prepare a master budget for the next three months, starting April 1. You are anxious to make a favorable impression on the president and have assembled the information below.

The company desires a minimum ending cash balance each month of $10,000. The lighters are forecast to sell for $8 each. Recent and forecast sales in units are:

January (actual).	20,000	June	60,000
February (actual)	24,000	July.	40,000
March (actual)	28,000	August.	36,000
April	35,000	September	32,000
May.	45,000		

The large buildup in sales before and during the month of June is due to Father's Day. Ending inventories are supposed to equal 90 percent of the next month's sales in units. The lighters cost the company $5 each.

Purchases are paid for as follows: 50 percent in the month of purchase and the remaining 50 percent in the following month. All sales are on credit, with no discount, and payable within 15 days. The company has found, however, that only 25 percent of a month's sales are collected by month-end. An additional 50 percent is collected in the month following, and the remaining 25 percent is collected in the second month following. Bad debts have been negligible.

The company's monthly operating expenses are given below:

Variable:	
Sales commissions	$1 per lighter
Fixed:	
Wages and salaries	$36,000
Utilities	1,000
Insurance expired.	1,200
Depreciation	1,500
Miscellaneous	2,000

All operating expenses are paid during the month, in cash, with the exception of depreciation and insurance expired. New fixed assets will be purchased during May for $25,000 cash. The company declares dividends of $12,000 each quarter, payable in the first month of the following quarter. The company's balance sheet at March 31 is given below:

Assets

Cash	$ 14,000
Accounts receivable ($48,000 February sales;	
$168,000 March sales)	216,000
Inventory (31,500 units)	157,500
Unexpired insurance	14,400
Fixed assets, net of depreciation	172,700
Total assets	$574,600

Liabilities and Stockholders' Equity

Accounts payable, purchases	$ 85,750
Dividends payable	12,000
Capital stock, no par	300,000
Retained earnings	176,850
Total liabilities and stockholders' equity	$574,600

The company can borrow money from its bank at 12 percent annual interest. All borrowing must be done at the beginning of a month, and repayments must be made at the end of a month. Repayments of principal must be in round $1,000 amounts. Borrowing (and payments of interest) can be in any amount.

Interest is computed and paid at the end of each quarter on all loans outstanding during the quarter. Round all interest payments to the nearest whole dollar. Compute interest on whole months ($\frac{1}{12}$, $\frac{2}{12}$, and so forth). The company wishes to use any excess cash to pay loans off as rapidly as possible.

Required:

Prepare a master budget for the three-month period ending June 30. Include the following detailed budgets:

1. *a.* A sales budget by month and in total.
    b. A schedule of budgeted cash collections from sales and accounts receivable, by month and in total.
    c. A purchases budget in units and in dollars. Show the budget by month and in total.
    d. A schedule of budgeted cash payments for purchases, by month and in total.
2. A cash budget. Show the budget by month and in total.
3. A budgeted income statement for the three-month period ending June 30. Use the contribution approach.
4. A budgeted balance sheet as of June 30.

P8–26. **Tabulation approach to EOQ.** (Appendix) Yales Jewelers, Inc., purchases 30,000 one-quarter-carat diamonds each year for various mountings. Pertinent information relating to the diamonds is given below:

Purchase cost per diamond	$200
Cost to carry one diamond in inventory for one year	5
Cost of placing one order to the company's supplier	40

The maximum order that the insurance company will permit is 1,500 diamonds. The minimum order that the supplier will permit is 300 diamonds, with all orders required to be in multiples of 300 diamonds. The company has been purchasing in the maximum allowable volume of 1,500 diamonds per order.

Required:
1. By use of the tabulation approach to EOQ, determine the volume in which the company should be placing its diamond orders.
2. Compute the annual cost savings that will be realized if the company purchases in the volume you have determined in (1) above, as compared to its present purchase policy.

P8–27. **Economic order quantity and safety stock.** (Appendix). Myron Metal Works, Inc., uses a small casting in one of its finished products. The castings are purchased from a foundry located in another state. In total, Myron Metal Works, Inc., purchases 24,000 castings per year at a cost of $8 per casting.

The castings are used evenly throughout the year in the production process on a 360-day-per-year basis. The company estimates that it costs $60 to place a single purchase order and about $2 to carry one casting in inventory for a year. The high carrying costs result from the need to keep the castings in carefully controlled temperature and humidity conditions, and from the high cost of insurance.

Delivery from the foundry generally takes 6 days, but it can take as much as 10 days. The days of delivery time and the percentage of their occurrence are shown in the following tabulation:

Delivery time (days)	Percentage of occurrence
6.	75
7.	10
8.	5
9.	5
10.	5
	100

Required:
1. Compute the economic order quantity.
2. Assume that the company is willing to assume the risk of being out of stock 15 percent of the time. What would be the safety stock? The reorder point?
3. Assume that the company is willing to assume the risk of being out of stock only 5 percent of the time. What would be the safety stock? The reorder point?
4. Assume a 5 percent stockout risk as stated in (3) above. What would be the total cost of ordering and carrying inventory for one year?

P8–28. **Economic order quantity and safety stock.** (Appendix) Pearl Manufacturing Company uses 100,000 units of material A each year. The material is used evenly throughout the year in the company's production process. A recent cost study indicates that it costs 60 cents to carry one unit of material A in stock for a year. The company estimates that the cost of placing an order for material A is $75.

On the average, it takes six days to receive an order from the supplier. Sometimes, orders do not arrive for 9 days, and at rare intervals (about 1 percent of the time) they do not arrive for 11 days. Each unit of material A costs the Pearl Manufacturing Company $4. The company works an average of 360 days per year. Round all figures to the nearest whole unit.

Required:
1. Compute the economic order quantity.
2. What size safety stock would you recommend for material A? Why?

    3. What is the reorder point for material A in units?

    4. Compute the *total cost* associated with ordering and carrying material A for a year.

P8–29. **EOQ computations.** (Appendix) SaPane Company is a regional distributor of automobile window glass. With the introduction of the new subcompact car models and the expected high level of consumer demand, management recognizes a need to determine the total inventory cost associated with maintaining an optimal supply of replacement windshields for the new subcompact cars introduced by each of the three major manufacturers. SaPane is expecting a daily demand for 36 windshields. The purchase price of each windshield is $50.

    Other costs associated with ordering and maintaining an inventory of these windshields are as follows:

a. The historical ordering costs incurred in the purchase order department for placing and processing orders are shown below:

Year	Orders placed and processed	Total ordering costs
1982.	20	$12,300
1983.	55	12,475
1984.	100	12,700

    Management expects the ordering costs to increase 16 percent over the amounts and rates experienced during the last three years.

b. The windshield manufacturer charges SaPane a $75 shipping fee per order.

c. A clerk in the receiving department receives, inspects, and secures the windshields as they arrive from the manufacturer. This activity requires eight hours per order received. This clerk has no other responsibilities and is paid at the rate of $9 per hour. Related variable overhead costs in this department are applied at the rate of $2.50 per hour.

d. Additional warehouse space will have to be rented to store the new windshields. Space can be rented as needed in a public warehouse at an estimated cost of $2,500 per year plus $5.35 per windshield.

e. Breakage cost is estimated to be 6 percent of the cost per windshield.

f. Taxes and fire insurance on the inventory are $1.15 per windshield.

g. The desired rate of return on the investment in inventory is 21 percent of the purchase price.

    Six working days are required from the time an order is placed with the manufacturer until it is received. SaPane uses a 300-day workyear when making economic order quantity computations.

Required: Calculate the following values for SaPane Company.

    1. The value for ordering cost that should be used in the EOQ formula.

    2. The value for storage cost that should be used in the EOQ formula.

    3. The economic order quantity.

    4. The minimum annual cost at the economic order quantity point.

    5. The reorder point in units.   (CMA, adapted)

P8–30. **Inventory control systems.** (Appendix) You have been engaged to install an accounting system for the Dexter Corporation. Among the inventory control features that Dexter desires in the system are indicators of "how much" to order "when." The following information is furnished for one item, called a duosonic, that is carried in inventory:

a. Duosonics are sold by the gross (12 dozen) at a list price of $800 per gross, FOB shipper. Dexter receives a 40 percent trade discount off list price on purchases in gross lots.

b. Freight cost is $20 per gross from the shipping point to Dexter's plant.

c. Dexter uses about 5,000 duosonics during a 259-day production year but must purchase a total of 36 gross per year to allow for normal breakage. Minimum and maximum usages are 12 and 28 duosonics per day, respectively.

d. Normal delivery time to receive an order is 20 working days from the date that a purchase request is initiated. A stockout (complete exhaustion of the inventory) of duosonics would stop production, and Dexter would purchase duosonics locally at list price rather than shut down.

e. The cost of placing an order is $30.

f. Space storage cost is $24 per year per average gross in storage.

g. Insurance and taxes are approximately 12 percent of the net delivered cost of average inventory, and Dexter expects a return of at least 8 percent on its average investment. (Ignore ordering costs and carrying costs in making these computations.)

Required:

1. Prepare a schedule computing the total annual cost of duosonics based on uniform order lot sizes of one, two, three, four, five, and six gross of duosonics. (The schedule should show the total annual cost according to each lot size.) Indicate the economic order quantity.

2. Prepare a schedule computing the minimum stock reorder point for duosonics. This is the point below which reordering is necessary to guard against a stockout. Factors to be considered include average lead period usage and safety stock requirements. (CPA, adapted)

9 Control through Standard Costs

Learning objectives

After studying Chapter 9, you should be able to:

Distinguish between ideal standards and practical standards.

Explain how direct materials standards and direct labor standards are set.

Enumerate the advantages and disadvantages of using standard costs.

Compute the direct materials price and quantity variances and explain their significance.

Compute the direct labor rate and efficiency variances and explain their significance.

Compute the variable overhead spending and efficiency variances.

Explain how the manager would determine whether a variance constituted an "exception" that would require his or her attention.

Prepare journal entries to record standard costs and variances.

Define or explain the key terms listed at the end of the chapter.

In attempting to control costs, managers have two types of decisions to make—decisions relating to prices paid and decisions relating to quantities used. Managers are expected to pay the lowest possible prices, consistent with the quality of output desired, in attaining the objectives of their firms. In attaining these objectives, managers are also expected to consume the minimum quantity of whatever resources they have at their command, again consistent with the quality of output desired. Breakdowns in control over either price or quantity will lead to excessive costs and to deteriorating profit margins.

How do managers attempt to control price paid and quantity used? Managers could personally examine every transaction that takes place, but this obviously would be an inefficient use of management time. The answer to the control problem lies in *standard costs*.

STANDARD COSTS—MANAGEMENT BY EXCEPTION

A *standard* can be defined as a benchmark or "norm" for measuring performance. Standards are found in many facets of day-to-day life. Students who wish to enter a college or university are often required to perform at a certain level on a standard achievement exam as a condition for admittance; the autos we drive are built under exacting engineering standards; and the food we eat is prepared under standards of both cleanliness and nutritional content. Standards are also widely used in managerial accounting. Here the standards relate to the *cost* and *quantity* of inputs used in manufacturing goods or in providing services.

Cost and quantity standards are set by managers for the three elements of cost input—materials, labor, and overhead—that we have discussed in preceding chapters. *Quantity standards* say how much of a cost element, such as labor time or raw materials, should be used in producing a single unit of product or in providing a unit of service. *Cost standards* say what the cost of this amount of time or these materials should be. Actual quantities and actual costs of inputs are measured against these standards to see whether operations are proceeding within the limits that management has set. If either the quantity or the cost of inputs exceeds the bounds that management has set, attention is directed to the difference, thereby permitting the manager to focus his or her efforts where they will do the most good. This process is called **management by exception.**

Who uses standard costs?

Manufacturing, service, food, and not-for-profit organizations all make use of standards (in terms of either costs or quantities) to some extent. Auto service centers, for example, often set specific labor time standards for the completion of certain work tasks, such as installing a carburetor or doing a valve job, and then measure actual performance against these standards. Fast-food outlets such as McDonald's have exacting standards as to the quantity of meat going into a sandwich, as well as standards for the cost of the meat. Hospitals have standard costs (for food, laundry, and other items) for each occupied bed per day, as well as standard time allowances for the performing of certain routine activities, such as laboratory tests. In short, the business student is likely to run into standard cost concepts in virtually any line of business that she or he may enter.

The broadest application of the standard cost idea is probably found in manufacturing firms, where standards relating to materials, labor, and overhead are developed in detail for each separate product line. These standards are then organized into a **standard cost card** that tells the manager what the final, manufactured cost should be for a single unit of product. In the following section, we provide a detailed example of the setting of standard costs and the preparation of a standard cost card.

SETTING STANDARD COSTS

The setting of standard costs is more an art than a science. It requires the combined thinking and expertise of all persons who have responsibility over prices and quantities of inputs. In a manufacturing setting, this would include the managerial accountant, the purchasing agent, the industrial engineer, production supervisors, and line managers.

The beginning point in setting standard costs is a rigorous look at past experience. The managerial accountant can be of great help in this task by preparing data on the cost characteristics of prior years' activities at various levels of operations. A standard for the future must be more than simply a projection of the past, however. Data must be adjusted and modified in terms of changing economic patterns, changing demand and supply characteristics, and changing technology. Past experience in certain costs may be distorted due to inefficiencies. To the extent that such inefficiencies can be identified, the data must be appropriately adjusted. The manager must realize that the past is of value only insofar as it helps to predict the future. In short, standards must be reflective of efficient *future* operations, not inefficient *past* operations.

Ideal versus practical standards

Should standards be attainable all of the time, only part of the time, or should they be so tight that they become, in effect, "the impossible dream"? Opinions among managers vary, but standards tend to fall into one of two categories—either ideal or practical.

Ideal standards are those that can be attained only under the best circumstances. They allow for no machine breakdowns or work interruptions, and call for a level of effort that can be attained only by the most skilled and efficient employee working at peak effort 100 percent of the time. Some managers feel that such standards have a motivational value. These managers argue that even though an employee knows he will never stay within the standard set, it is a constant reminder to him of the need for ever-increasing efficiency and effort. Few fims use ideal standards. Most managers are of the opinion that ideal standards tend to discourage even the most diligent workers. Moreover, when ideal standards are used, variances from standards have little meaning. The reason is that the variances contain elements of "normal" inefficiencies, not just the abnormal inefficiencies that managers would like to have isolated and brought to their attention.

Practical standards can be defined as standards that are "tight but attainable." They allow for normal machine breakdown time and employee rest periods, and are such that they can be attained through reasonable, though highly efficient, efforts by the average worker at a task. Variances from such a standard are very useful to management in that they represent deviations that fall outside of normal, recurring inefficiencies, and signal a need for management attention. Furthermore, practical standards can serve multiple purposes. In addition to signaling abnormal deviations in costs, they can also be used in forecasting cash flows and in planning inventory. By contrast, ideal standards cannot be used in forecasting and planning; they do not allow for normal inefficiencies, and therefore result in unrealistic planning and forecasting figures.

Throughout the remainder of this chapter, we will assume the use of practical rather than ideal standards.

Setting direct materials standards

As stated earlier, managers prepare separate standards for the price and quantity of inputs. The **standard price per unit** for direct materials should reflect the final, delivered cost of the materials, net of any discounts taken. For example, the standard price of a pound of material A might be determined as follows:

Purchase price, top grade, in 500-pound quantities	$3.80
Freight, by truck, from the supplier's plant	0.28
Receiving and handling	0.05
Less purchase discount	(0.13)
Standard price per pound	$4.00

Notice that the standard price reflects a particular grade of material (top grade), purchased in particular lot sizes (500 pounds), and delivered by a particular type of carrier (truck). Allowances have also been made for handling and discounts. If all proceeds according to plans, the net standard price of a pound of material A should therefore be $4.

The **standard quantity per unit** for direct materials should reflect the amount of material going into each unit of finished product, as well as an allowance for unavoidable waste, spoilage, and other normal inefficiencies. To illustrate, the standard quantity of material A going into a unit of product might be determined as follows:

Per bill of materials, in pounds	2.7
Allowance for waste and spoilage, in pounds	0.2
Allowance for rejects, in pounds	0.1
Standard quantity per unit of product, in pounds	3.0

A **bill of materials** is simply a list that shows the quantity of each item of material going into a unit of finished product. It is a handy source for determining the basic material input per unit, but it must be adjusted for waste and other factors, as shown above, in determining the full standard quantity per unit of product. "Rejects" represents the direct material contained in units of product that are rejected at final inspection. The cost of this material must be added back to good units.

Once the price and quantity standards have been set, the standard cost of material A per unit of finished product can be computed as follows:

$$3.0 \text{ pounds} \times \$4 = \$12 \text{ per unit}$$

This $12 cost figure will appear as one item on the standard cost card of the product under consideration.

Setting direct labor standards

Direct labor price and quantity standards are usually expressed in terms of labor rate and labor-hours. The **standard rate per hour** for direct labor would include not only wages earned but also an allowance for fringe benefits and other labor-related costs. The computation might be as follows:

Basic wage rate per hour	$10
Employment taxes at 10% of the basic rate	1
Fringe benefits at 30% of the basic rate	3
Standard rate per direct labor-hour	$14

Many companies prepare a single standard rate for all employees in a department, even though the actual wage rates may vary somewhat between employees due to seniority or other reasons. This simplifies the use of standard costs and also permits the manager to monitor the use of employees within departments. More is said on this point a little later. If all proceeds according to plans, the direct labor rate for our mythical company should average $14 per hour.

The standard direct labor time required to complete a unit of product (generally called the **standard hours per unit**) is perhaps the single most difficult standard to determine. One approach is to divide each operation performed on the product into elemental body movements (such as reaching, pushing, and turning over). Published tables of standard times for such movements are available. These times can be applied to the movements and then added together to determine the total standard time allowed per operation. Another approach is for an industrial engineer to do a time and motion study, actually clocking the time required for certain tasks. As stated earlier, the standard time developed must include allowances for coffee breaks, personal needs of employees, cleanup, and machine downtime. The resulting standard time might appear as follows:

Basic labor time per unit, in hours	1.9
Allowance for breaks and personal needs	0.1
Allowance for cleanup and machine downtime	0.3
Allowance for rejects	0.2
Standard hours per unit of product	2.5

Once the rate and time standards have been set, the standard labor cost per unit of product can be computed as follows:

$$2.5 \text{ hours} \times \$14 = \$35 \text{ per unit}$$

This $35 cost figure will appear along with direct materials as one item on the standard cost card of the product under consideration.

Setting variable overhead standards

As with direct labor, the price and quantity standards for variable overhead are generally expressed in terms of rate and hours. The rate represents *the variable portion of the predetermined overhead rate* discussed in Chapter 3; the hours represent whatever hours base is used to apply overhead to units of product (often direct labor-hours, as we learned in Chapter 3). To illustrate, if the variable portion of the predetermined overhead rate was $3, and if overhead was applied to units of product on a basis of direct labor-hours, the standard variable overhead cost per unit of product in our example would be:

$$2.5 \text{ hours} \times \$3.00 = \$7.50 \text{ per unit}$$

A more detailed look at the setting of overhead standards is reserved until Chapter 10.

To summarize our example on the setting of standard costs, the completed standard cost card for one unit of product in our mythical company is presented in Exhibit 9–1. Observe that the **standard cost per unit** is computed by multiplying the standard quantity or hours by the standard price or rate.

EXHIBIT 9–1
Standard cost card—variable production cost

Inputs	(1) Standard quantity or hours	(2) Standard price or rate	Standard cost (1) × (2)
Direct materials	3.0 pounds	$ 4.00	$12.00
Direct labor	2.5 hours	14.00	35.00
Variable overhead	2.5 hours	3.00	7.50
Total standard cost per unit			$54.50

Are standards the same as budgets?

Essentially, standards and budgets are the same thing. The only distinction between the two terms is that a standard is a *unit* amount, whereas a budget is a *total* amount. That is, the standard cost for materials in a unit of product may be $5. If 1,000 units of the product are to be produced during a period, then the budgeted cost of materials is $5,000. In effect, a standard may be viewed as being the *budgeted cost for one unit of product.*

Advantages of standard costs

A number of distinct advantages can be cited in favor of using standard costs in an organization.

1. As stated earlier, the use of standard costs makes possible the concept of management by exception. So long as costs remain within the standards set, no attention by management is needed. When costs fall outside the standards set, then the matter is brought to the attention of management at once as an "exception." Management by exception makes possible more productive use of management time.

2. Standard costs facilitate cash planning and inventory planning.

3. So long as standards are set on a "practical" basis, they promote economy and efficiency in that employees normally become very cost and time conscious. In addition, wage incentive systems can be tied to a system of standard costs once the standards have been set.

4. In income determination, a system of standard costs may be more economical and simpler to operate than a historical cost system. Standard cost cards can be kept for each product or operation, and costs for material, labor, and manufacturing overhead charged out according to the standards set. This greatly simplifies the bookkeeping process.

5. Standard costs can assist in the implementation of "responsibility accounting," in which responsibility over cost control is assigned, and the extent to which that responsibility has been discharged can be evaluated through performance reports.

Disadvantages of standard costs

Although the advantages of using standard costs are significant, we must recognize that certain difficulties can be encountered by the manager in applying the standard cost idea. Moreover, improper use of standard costs and the management by exception principle can lead to adverse behavioral problems in an organization. Managers cite the following as being either problems or potential problems in using standard costs:

1. Difficulty may be experienced in determining which variances are "material" or significant in amount. (Ways to overcome this problem are discussed later in the chapter.)

2.   By focusing only on variances above a certain level (that is, on variances that are considered to be material in amount), other useful information, such as trends, may not be noticed at an early stage.

3.   If management performance evaluation is tied to the exception principle, subordinates may be tempted to cover up negative exceptions or not report them at all. In addition, subordinates may not receive reinforcement for the positive things they do, such as controlling or reducing costs charged to their area of responsibility, but may only receive reprimands for those items that exceed the acceptable cost standards. Thus, subordinate morale may suffer because of the lack of positive reinforcement for work well done.

4.   The management by exception technique may also affect supervisory employees in an unsatisfactory manner. Supervisors may feel that they are not getting a complete review of operations because they are always just keying in on problems. In addition, supervisors may feel that they are constantly being critical of their subordinates, that is, always "running them down." This may have a negative impact on supervisory morale.[1]

These potential problems suggest that considerable care must be exercised by the manager in organizing and administering a standard cost system. It is particularly important that the manager focus on the positive, rather than on the negative, and that work that is well done be appropriately recognized.

A GENERAL MODEL FOR VARIANCE ANALYSIS

One reason for separating standards into two categories—price and quantity—is that control decisions relating to price paid and quantity used will generally fall at different points in time. In the case of raw materials, for example, control over price paid comes at the time of purchase. By contrast, control over quantity used does not come until the raw materials are used in production, which may be many weeks or months after the purchase date. In addition, control over price paid and quantity used will generally be the responsibility of two different managers and will therefore need to be assessed independently. As we have stressed earlier, no manager should be held responsible for a cost over which he or she has no control. It is important, therefore, that we separate price considerations from quantity considerations in our approach to the control of costs.

The general model

A general model exists that is very useful in variance analysis. A **variance** is the difference between *standard* prices and quantities and *actual* prices and quantities. This model, which deals with variable costs, helps to distinguish between *price variances* and *quantity variances,* as well as showing

---

[1] Institute of Management Accounting, *Certificate in Management Accounting Examination* (New York: National Association of Accountants, June 1979), p. 26.

EXHIBIT 9–2
A general model for variance analysis—variable production costs

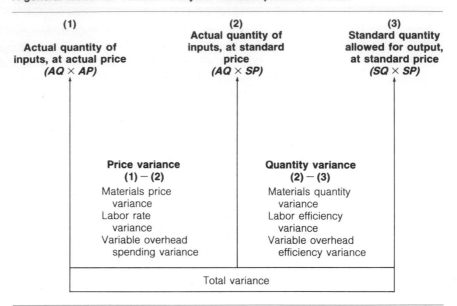

(1) **Actual quantity of inputs, at actual price** **(AQ × AP)**	(2) **Actual quantity of inputs, at standard price** **(AQ × SP)**	(3) **Standard quantity allowed for output, at standard price** **(SQ × SP)**

**Price variance
(1) − (2)**
Materials price
  variance
Labor rate
  variance
Variable overhead
  spending variance
	**Quantity variance
	(2) − (3)**
	Materials quantity
	  variance
	Labor efficiency
	  variance
	Variable overhead
	  efficiency variance	

Total variance		

how each of these variances is computed.[2] The model is presented in Exhibit 9–2.

Three things should be noted from the exhibit. First, note that a price variance and a quantity variance can be computed for all three variable cost elements—direct materials, direct labor, and variable manufacturing overhead—even though the variance is not called by the same name in all cases. For example, a price variance is called a *materials price variance* in the case of direct materials but a *labor rate variance* in the case of direct labor and an *overhead spending variance* in the case of variable manufacturing overhead.

Second, note that even though a price variance may be called by different names, it is computed in exactly the same way regardless of whether one is dealing with direct materials, direct labor, or variable manufacturing overhead. The same is true with the quantity variance.

And third, note that variance analysis is actually a matter of input-output analysis. The inputs represent the actual quantity of direct materials, direct labor, and variable manufacturing overhead used; the output represents the good production of the period, expressed in terms of the *standard quantity or hours of input allowed* in its manufacture (see column 3 in Exhibit 9–2). By **standard quantity allowed** or **standard hours allowed,** we mean the amount of direct materials, direct labor, or variable manufacturing overhead *that*

---

[2] Variance analysis of fixed costs is reserved until Chapter 10.

should *have been used* to produce what was produced during the period. This might be more or less than what was *actually* used, depending on the efficiency or inefficiency of operations.

With this general model as a foundation, we will now examine the price and quantity variances in more detail.

USING STANDARD COSTS—DIRECT MATERIAL VARIANCES

To illustrate the computation and use of direct material variances, we will return to the standard cost data for direct materials contained in Exhibit 9–1. This exhibit shows the standard cost of direct materials per unit of product in our mythical company to be:

$$3.0 \text{ pounds} \times \$4 = \$12$$

We will assume that during June the company purchased 6,500 pounds of material at a cost of \$3.80 per pound, including freight and handling costs, and net of the quantity discount. All of the material was used in the manufacture of 2,000 units of product. The computation of the price and quantity variances for the month is shown in Exhibit 9–3.[3]

A variance is unfavorable if the actual price or quantity exceeds the standard price or quantity; a variance is favorable if the actual price or quantity is less than the standard.

EXHIBIT 9–3

Variance analysis—direct materials

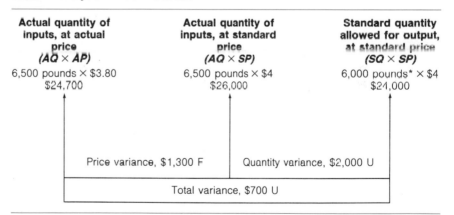

Actual quantity of inputs, at actual price (AQ × AP)	Actual quantity of inputs, at standard price (AQ × SP)	Standard quantity allowed for output, at standard price (SQ × SP)
6,500 pounds × \$3.80 \$24,700	6,500 pounds × \$4 \$26,000	6,000 pounds* × \$4 \$24,000

Price variance, \$1,300 F	Quantity variance, \$2,000 U
Total variance, \$700 U	

* 2,000 units × 3.0 pounds per unit = 6,000 pounds.
F = Favorable.
U = Unfavorable.

---

[3] This exhibit shows the computation of the price and quantity variances when all materials purchased during a period are used in production and none remain in inventory at period-end. See the review problem at the end of the chapter for a computation of the price and quantity variances when only part of the materials purchased during a period is used in production during that period.

Materials price variance—a closer look

A **materials price variance** measures the difference between what is paid for a given quantity of materials and what should have been paid according to the standard that has been set. From Exhibit 9–3, this difference can be expressed by the following formula:

$$(AQ \times AP) - (AQ \times SP) = \text{Materials price variance}$$

The formula can be factored into simpler form as:

$$AQ(AP - SP) = \text{Materials price variance}$$

Some managers prefer this simpler formula, since it permits variance computations to be made very quickly. Using the data from Exhibit 9–3 in this formula, we have:

$$6{,}500 \text{ pounds } (\$3.80 - \$4.00) = \$1{,}300$$

Notice that the answer is the same as that yielded in the exhibit. If the company wanted to put these data into a performance report, they would appear as follows:

MYTHICAL COMPANY
Performance Report—Purchasing Department

Item purchased	(1) Quantity purchased	(2) Actual price	(3) Standard price	(4) Difference in price (2) − (3)	Total price variance (1) × (4)	Explanation
Material A	6,500 pounds	$3.80	$4.00	$0.20	$1,300 F	Second-grade materials purchased, rather than top grade

F = Favorable.
U = Unfavorable.

Isolation of variances　At what point should variances be isolated and brought to the attention of management? The answer is, the earlier the better. One of the basic reasons for utilizing standard costs is to facilitate cost control. Therefore, the sooner deviations from standard are brought to the attention of management, the sooner problems can be evaluated and corrected. If long periods are allowed to elapse before variances are computed, costs that could otherwise have been controlled may accumulate to the point of doing significant damage to profits. Most firms compute the materials price variance, for example, when materials are purchased rather than when the materials are placed into production. This permits earlier isolation of the variance, since materials may lay in the warehouse for many months before being used in production. Isolating the price variance when materials are purchased also permits the company to carry its raw materials in the inventory accounts at standard cost. This greatly simplifies the process of costing materials as they are later placed into production.[4]

Once a performance report has been prepared, what does management do with the price variance data? The variances should be viewed as "red flags," calling attention to the fact that an exception has occurred that will require some follow-up effort. Normally, the performance report itself will contain some explanation of the reason for the variance, as shown above.

Responsibility for the variance Who is responsible for the materials price variance? Generally speaking, the purchasing agent has control over the price to be paid for goods and is therefore responsible for any price variances. Many factors control the price paid for goods, including size of lots purchased, delivery method used, quantity discounts available, rush orders, and the quality of materials purchased. To the extent that the purchasing agent can control these factors, he or she is responsible for seeing that they are kept in agreement with the factors anticipated when the standard costs were initially set. A deviation in any factor from what was intended in the initial setting of a standard cost can result in a price variance. For example, purchase of second-grade materials rather than top-grade materials would result in a favorable price variance, since the lower-grade materials would generally be less costly (but perhaps less suitable for production).

There may be times, however, when someone other than the purchasing agent is responsible for a materials price variance. Production may be scheduled in such a way, for example, that the purchasing agent is required to obtain delivery by airfreight, rather than by truck, or he or she may be forced to buy in uneconomical quantities. In these cases, the production manager would bear responsibility for the variances that develop.

A word of caution is in order. Variance analysis should not be used as an excuse to conduct witch hunts or as a means of beating line managers over the head. The emphasis must be on the control function in the sense of *supporting* the line managers and *assisting* them in meeting the goals that they have participated in setting for the company. In short, the emphasis must be positive rather than negative. Excessive dwelling on what has already happened, particularly in terms of trying to find someone to "blame," can often be destructive to the goals of an organization.

Materials quantity variance—a closer look

The **materials quantity variance** measures the difference between the quantity of materials used in production and the quantity that should have been used according to the standard that has been set. Although the variance is concerned with the physical usage of materials, it is generally stated in dollar

---

[4] See the Appendix for an illustration of journal entries in a standard cost system.

terms, as shown in Exhibit 9–3. The formula for the materials quantity variance is:

$$(AQ \times SP) - (SQ \times SP) = \text{Materials quantity variance}$$

Again, the formula can be factored into simpler terms:

$$SP(AQ - SQ) = \text{Materials quantity variance}$$

Using the data from Exhibit 9–3 in the formula, we have:

$$\$4(6{,}500 \text{ pounds} - 6{,}000 \text{ pounds*}) = \$2{,}000 \text{ U}$$

* 2,000 units × 3.0 pounds per unit = 6,000 pounds.

The answer, of course, is the same as that yielded in Exhibit 9–3. The data would appear as follows if a formal performance report were prepared:

MYTHICAL COMPANY
Performance Report—Production Department

Type of materials	(1) Standard price	(2) Actual quantity	(3) Standard quantity allowed	(4) Difference in quantity (2) − (3)	Total quantity variance (1) × (4)	Explanation
Material A	$4	6,500 pounds	6,000 pounds	500 pounds	$2,000 U	Second-grade materials, unsuitable for production

U = Unfavorable.
F = Favorable.

The materials quantity variance is best isolated at the time that materials are placed into production.[5] Materials are drawn for the number of units to be produced, according to the standard bill of materials for each unit. Any additional materials are usually drawn on an excess materials requisition slip, which is different in color from the normal requisition slips. This procedure calls attention to the excessive usage of materials *while production is still in process* and permits opportunity for early control of any developing problem.

Excessive usage of materials can result from many factors, including faulty machines, inferior quality of materials, untrained workers, and poor supervision. Generally speaking, it is the responsibility of the production department to see that material usage is kept in line with standards. There may be times, however, when the *purchasing* department may be responsible for an unfavorable material quantity variance. If the purchasing department obtains materials of inferior quality in an effort to economize on price, the materials may

[5] If a company uses process costing, then it may be necessary in some situations to compute the materials quantity variance on a periodic basis as production is *completed*. This is because under process costing it is sometimes difficult to know in advance what the output will be for a period. We assume the use of a job-order costing system throughout this chapter (including all assignment materials).

prove to be unsuitable for use on the production line and may result in excessive waste. Thus, purchasing rather than production would be responsible for the quantity variance.

USING STANDARD COSTS—DIRECT LABOR VARIANCES

To illustrate the computation and use of direct labor variances, we will use the standard cost data for direct labor contained in Exhibit 9–1. This exhibit shows the standard cost of direct labor per unit of product in our mythical company to be:

$$2.5 \text{ hours} \times \$14 = \$35$$

We will assume that during June the company recorded 4,500 hours of direct labor time. The actual cost of this labor time was $64,350 (including employment taxes and fringe benefits), or an average of $14.30 per hour. Recall that the company produced 2,000 units of product during June. The computation of the labor rate and efficiency variances for the month is shown in Exhibit 9–4.

EXHIBIT 9–4
Variance analysis—direct labor

Actual hours of input, at the actual rate (AH × AR)	Actual hours of input, at the standard rate (AH × SR)	Standard hours allowed for output, at the standard rate (SH × SR)
4,500 hours × $14.30 $64,350	4,500 hours × $14 $63,000	5,000 hours* × $14 $70,000
	Rate variance, $1,350 U	Efficiency variance, $7,000 F
	Total variance, $5,650 F	

* 2,000 units × 2.5 hours per unit = 5,000 hours.
F = Favorable.
U = Unfavorable.

Notice that the column headings in Exhibit 9–4 are the same as those used in the prior two exhibits, except that in Exhibit 9–4 the terms *hours* and *rate* are used in place of the terms *quantity* and *price*.

Labor rate variance—a closer look

As explained earlier, the price variance for direct labor is commonly termed a **labor rate variance.** This variance measures any deviation from standard in the average hourly rate paid to direct labor workers. From Exhibit 9–4, the formula for the labor rate variance is:

$$(AH \times AR) - (AH \times SR) = \text{Labor rate variance}$$

The formula can be factored into simpler form as:

$$AH(AR - SR) = \text{Labor rate variance}$$

Using the data from Exhibit 9–4 in the formula, we have:

$$4,500 \text{ hours } (\$14.30 - \$14.00) = \$1,350 \text{ U}$$

In many firms, the rates paid workers are set by union contract; therefore, rate variances, in terms of amounts paid to workers, tend to be almost nonexistent. Rate variances can arise, though, through the way labor is used. Skilled workers with high hourly rates of pay can be given duties that require little skill and call for low hourly rates of pay. This type of misallocation of the work force will result in unfavorable labor rate variances, since the actual hourly rate of pay will exceed the standard rate authorized for the particular task being performed. A reverse situation exists when unskilled or untrained workers are assigned to jobs. The lower pay scale for these workers will result in favorable rate variances, although the workers may be highly inefficient in terms of output. Finally, unfavorable rate variances can arise from overtime work at premium rates if any portion of the overtime premium is added to the direct labor account.

Who is responsible for controlling the labor rate variance? Since rate variances generally arise as a result of how labor is used, those supervisors in charge of effective utilization of labor time bear responsibility for seeing that labor rate variances are kept under control.

Labor efficiency variance—a closer look

The quantity variance for direct labor, more commonly called the **labor efficiency variance,** measures the productivity of labor time. No variance is more closely watched by management, since increasing productivity of labor time is a vital key to reducing unit costs of production. From Exhibit 9–4, the formula for the labor efficiency variance is:

$$(AH \times SR) - (SH \times SR) = \text{Labor efficiency variance}$$

Factored into simpler terms, the formula is:

$$SR(AH - SH) = \text{Labor efficiency variance}$$

Using the data from Exhibit 9–4 in the formula, we have:

$$\$14(4,500 \text{ hours} - 5,000 \text{ hours*}) = \$7,000 \text{ F}$$

* 2,000 units × 2.5 hours per unit = 5,000 hours.

Causes of the labor efficiency variance include poorly trained workers; poor quality materials, requiring more labor time in processing; faulty equipment, causing breakdowns and work interruptions; and poor supervision of workers. The managers in charge of production would generally be responsible for control of the labor efficiency variance. However, the variance might be chargeable to purchasing if the acquisition of poor materials resulted in excessive labor processing time.

USING STANDARD COSTS—VARIABLE OVERHEAD VARIANCES

The variable portion of manufacturing overhead can be analyzed and controlled using the same basic variance formulas that are used in analyzing direct materials and direct labor. In order to lay a foundation for the following chapter, where we discuss overhead control at length, it will be helpful at this time to illustrate the analysis of variable overhead using these basic formulas. As a basis for discussion, we will again use the cost data found in Exhibit 9–1. The exhibit shows the standard variable overhead cost per unit of product in our mythical company to be:

$$2.5 \text{ hours} \times \$3.00 = \$7.50$$

We will assume that the total actual variable overhead cost for the month of June was $13,950. Recall from our earlier discussion that 4,500 hours of direct labor time were recorded during the month and that the company produced 2,000 units of product. Exhibit 9–5 contains an analysis of the variable overhead variances.

Notice the similarities between Exhibits 9–4 and 9–5. These similarities arise from the fact that direct labor-hours are being used as a base for allocating overhead to units of product; thus, the same hours figures appear in Exhibit 9–5 for variable overhead as in Exhibit 9–4 for direct labor. The main difference between the two exhibits is in the standard hourly rate being used, which is much lower for variable overhead.

EXHIBIT 9–5
Variance analysis—variable overhead

Actual hours of input, at the actual rate (AH × AR)	Actual hours of input, at the standard rate (AH × SR)	Standard hours allowed for output, at the standard rate (SH × SR)
$13,950	4,500 hours × $3 $13,500	5,000 hours* × $3 $15,000

Spending variance, $450 U	Efficiency variance, $1,500 F

Total variance, $1,050 F

* 2,000 units × 2.5 hours per unit = 5,000 hours.
F = Favorable.
U = Unfavorable.

Overhead variances—a closer look

The variable overhead spending and efficiency variances, like the direct materials and direct labor variances, can be expressed in formula format. For the **spending variance,** the formula is:

$$(AH \times AR) - (AH \times SR) = \text{Variable overhead spending variance}$$

Or, factored into simpler terms:

$$AH(AR - SR) = \text{Variable overhead spending variance}$$

For the **efficiency variance,** the formula is:

$$(AH \times SR) - (SH \times SR) = \text{Variable overhead efficiency variance}$$

Or, factored into simpler terms:

$$SR(AH - SH) = \text{Variable overhead efficiency variance}$$

Using the data from Exhibit 9–5, we see that the computation of the variances using these formulas would be:

Spending variance: 4,500 hours ($3.10* − $3.00) = $450 U
Efficiency variance: $3.00 (4,500 hours − 5,000 hours†) = $1,500 F

* $13,950 ÷ 4,500 hours = $3.10.
† 2,000 units × 2.5 hours per unit = 5,000 hours.

We will reserve further discussion of the variable overhead spending and efficiency variances until Chapter 10, where overhead analysis is discussed in depth.

Before proceeding further, it will be helpful for the reader to pause at this point and go back and review the data contained in Exhibits 9–1 through 9–5. These exhibits and the accompanying text discussion represent a comprehensive, integrated illustration of standard setting and variance analysis.

GRAPHICAL ANALYSIS OF THE PRICE AND QUANTITY VARIANCES

The way in which the price and quantity variances are computed can lead to a problem between the purchasing and production departments. The problem can best be seen by presenting these two variances in graphical form. To do this, we will assume that a company uses 4 pounds of material X in the manufacture of a unit of product. During a recent period, the company produced 450 units, using 2,000 pounds of material X in the process. Variances for the period are summarized below and then presented in graphical form in Exhibit 9–6.

Summary of data—material X

Standard price per pound	$2.00
Actual price per pound	$2.15
Standard quantity for production of 450 units of product (4 pounds per unit × 450 units)	1,800 pounds
Actual quantity used in production of 450 units of product	2,000 pounds

Summary of variances—material X

$$AQ(AP - SP) = \text{Materials price variance}$$
$$2{,}000 \text{ pounds } (\$2.15 - \$2.00) = \$300 \text{ U}$$

$$SP(AQ - SQ) = \text{Materials quantity variance}$$
$$\$2(2{,}000 \text{ pounds} - 1{,}800 \text{ pounds}) = \$400 \text{ U}$$

EXHIBIT 9–6
Graphical analysis of price and quantity variances

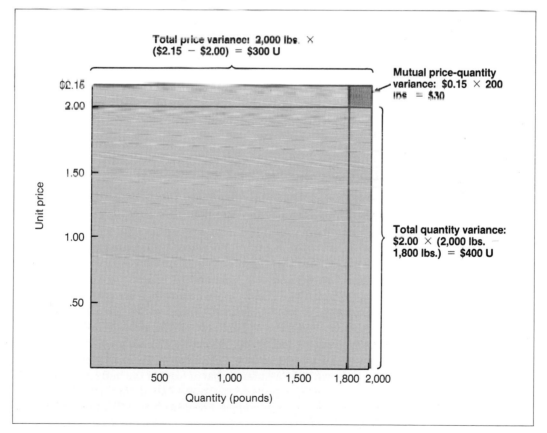

The problem referred to can arise from the upper right corner of the graph in Exhibit 9–6. This corner represents a **mutual price-quantity variance,** although we have shown it to be part of the price variance in our computations above. The purchasing agent may contend that it is unfair to charge her for the $30 mutual price-quantity variance represented in this corner, since it has arisen only because of the inefficient use of materials by the production department. If the production department had produced at standard and used only the 1,800 pounds of materials called for, then the extra 200 pounds of materials wouldn't have been purchased in the first place and the extra $30 of variance would not have arisen. The purchasing agent may argue, therefore, that the $30 mutual price-quantity variance should be charged to production, not to purchasing.

We should note that a dispute of this type is likely to arise only if the price and quantity variances are computed at the same time. The more typical situation is for the price variance to be computed at the time materials are purchased and for the quantity variance to be computed somewhat later, when the materials are used. Thus, when the two variances are computed at different times, it is unlikely that purchasing will ever raise any questions as to how efficiently the materials have been used.

It can be argued that even if the two variances are computed at the same time, the mutual price-quantity variance should still be included as part of the price variance. The reason is that purchasing is responsible for the acquisition of *any* materials needed in production and should ensure that the materials are purchased according to the standard prices that have been set. As we noted earlier, a price variance should be charged to production only if the variance arises from rush orders or similar problems caused by poor scheduling of production activities.

VARIANCE ANALYSIS AND MANAGEMENT BY EXCEPTION

Variance analysis and performance reports provide a vehicle for implementation of the concept of *management by exception.* Simply put, management by exception means that the manager's attention must be directed toward those parts of the organization where things are not proceeding according to plans. Since a manager's time is limited, every hour must be used as effectively as possible and time and effort must not be wasted looking after those parts of the organization where things are going smoothly.

The budgets and standards discussed in this chapter and in the preceding chapter represent the "plans" of management. If all goes smoothly, then costs would be expected to fall within the budgets and standards that have been set. To the extent that this happens, the manager is free to spend time elsewhere, with the assurance that at least in the budgeted areas all is proceeding according to expectations. To the extent that actual costs and revenues do not conform to the budget, however, a signal comes to the manager that an "exception" has occurred. This exception comes in the form of a variance from the budget or standard that was originally set.

The major question at this point is, "Are *all* variances to be considered exceptions that will require the attention of management?" The answer is no. If every variance were considered an exception, then management would get little else done other than chasing down nickel-and-dime differences. Obviously, some criteria are needed to determine when a variance has occurred that can properly be called an exception. We consider some of these criteria below.

Criteria for determining "exceptions"

It is probably safe to say that only by the rarest of coincidences will actual costs and revenues ever conform exactly to the budgeted pattern. The reason is that even though budgets may be prepared with the greatest of care, it will never be possible to develop budgeted data that contain the precise allowances necessary for each of the multitude of variables that can affect actual costs and revenues. For this reason, one can expect that in every period virtually every budgeted figure will produce a variance of some type when compared to actual cost data. How do managers decide which of these variances are worthy of their attention? We can identify at least four criteria that are used in actual practice: materiality, consistency of occurrence, ability to control, and nature of the item.

Materiality   Ordinarily, management will be interested only in those variances that are material in amount. To separate the material variances from the immaterial variances, firms often set guidelines, such as stating that any variance that differs from the budget by 5 percent or more will be considered a material variance. Notice that we say "differs" from the budget, not "exceeds" the budget. We say "differs" because management will be just as interested in those variances that are *under* the budget as it is in those that exceed it. The reason is that a level of spending that is under the budget can be just as critical to profitability as a level of spending that exceeds the budget. For example, if advertising is budgeted to be $100,000 during a period and only $80,000 is spent, this favorable spending variance could be damaging to profits because of insufficient promotion of the firm's products.

Generally, a guideline such as a 5 percent deviation from budget will not be sufficient to judge whether a variance is material. The reason is that a 2 percent variance in some costs could be far more critical to profits than a 10 percent variance in other costs. For this reason, a firm will often supplement the percentage guideline with some minimum absolute dollar figure, stating that even if a variance doesn't exceed the percentage guideline, it will still be considered material if it exceeds the minimum dollar figure. To illustrate, a firm might state that any variance will be considered material if it differs from the budget by 5 percent or more, or by $1,000.

Consistency of occurrence   Even if a variance never exceeds the minimum stated percentage or the minimum dollar amount, many firms want it brought to the attention of management if it comes *close* to these limits period after period. The thinking here is that the budget or standard may be out of date, and that adjustment to more current levels might improve overall profit planning. Or, some laxness in cost control may be present, warranting an occasional check by the relevant supervisor.

Ability to control   Some costs are largely out of the control of management, and in such cases even though variances may occur that are material in amount, no follow-up action on management's part is necessary. For example, utility rates and local tax rates are generally not controllable internally, and large variances resulting from rate increases will require little or no follow-up effort, even though these variances may be presented on the variance report for information purposes.

Nature of the item   By their very nature, some costs are much more critical to long-run profitability than others. One such cost is advertising. As mentioned above, underutilization of the advertising budget can have a severe adverse impact on sales, with a resulting loss of revenue that greatly outweighs any saving in advertising dollars. Another such cost is maintenance. Although inadequate maintenance may produce short-run savings in costs, these savings will probably be more than offset by future breakdowns, repairs, and loss of revenue from reduced productivity and efficiency.

Because of the critical nature of such costs as advertising and maintenance, the guidelines for determining whether a variance is material are usually much more stringent for these costs than for other costs. That is, variances in these areas are generally watched more closely by management than variances in other, less critical, areas. It may be that management will want to see *any* variance in certain key areas such as advertising and promotion. In addition, the normal guidelines may be reduced by half in other key areas such as maintenance and certain critical component parts.

Statistical analysis of random variances

The purpose of establishing criteria for separating material from immaterial variances is to isolate those variances that are *not* due to random causes, and that can and should be controlled by the company. The "5 percent of budget, or $1,000" approach described in the preceding section is a somewhat crude way of accomplishing this objective, although it is widely used. The approach is crude because it is based on rough guessing and on rules of thumb rather than on precise analysis.

A much more dependable way of separating random variances from variances that are controllable can be found in statistical analysis. This approach to segregating random variances has its basis in the idea that a budget or standard represents a *range* of acceptability, rather than a single point. Any variance falling within this range is considered to be due solely to random causes that either are not within the ability of management to control or that would be impractical to control. One author puts the idea this way:

Measured quality of manufactured product is always subject to a certain amount of variation as a result of chance. Some stable "system of chance causes" is inherent in any particular scheme of production and inspection. Variation within this stable pattern is inevitable. The reasons for variation outside this stable pattern [should] be discovered and corrected.[6]

How does a firm isolate the range within which variances from budget will be due to chance or random causes? This is done by means of statistical sampling of the population represented by the budgeted data. Random samples of the population are drawn, and the variances found in these samples are plotted on a *control chart* such as that illustrated in Exhibit 9–7. In effect, the upper and lower limits on the chart represent the normal distribution (bell-shaped curve), with the upper and lower limits generally being at least one standard deviation from the grand mean. Any variances falling within the upper and lower control limits will be due simply to chance occurrences and, therefore, either will not be within the ability of management to control or will not be large enough to warrant management time. Any variances falling outside these limits will not be due to random or chance causes and will be considered "exceptions" toward which management attention will need to be directed.

EXHIBIT 9–7
A statistical control chart

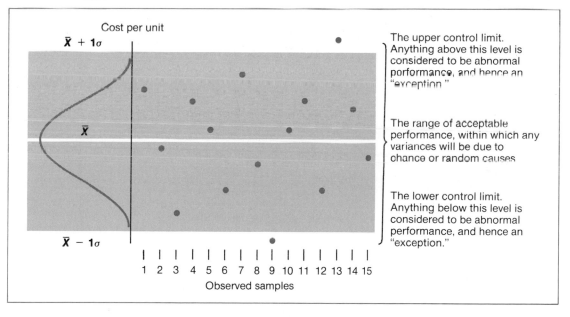

The value of a budgeting system is greatly increased if variances are analyzed by a statistical approach such as that described above, rather than by

---

[6] Eugene L. Grant and Richard L. Leavenworth, *Statistical Quality Control,* 4th ed. (New York: McGraw-Hill, 1972), p. 3. Used with permission of McGraw-Hill Book Company.

the "5 percent, or $1,000" approach described earlier. The reason, of course, is that the statistical approach eliminates guesswork and zeroes management in on those cost variations that are indeed within its ability to control.[7]

SUMMARY

Cost control centers in two areas—price paid and quantity used. The best way to effect control in these two areas is through use of standard costs. A standard can be viewed as being the budget for a single unit of product expressed in terms of either price or quantity.

Generally, standards are set by the cooperative effort of many people in an organization, including the accountant, the industrial engineer, and various levels of management. Standards are normally "practical" in nature, meaning that they can be attained by reasonable, though highly efficient, efforts. Such standards are generally felt to have a favorable motivational impact on employees.

Comparing standards against actual performance results in variances. If a variance falls outside the limits set by management, it is considered to be an exception toward which management time and attention must be directed. Ordinarily, the accounting system will be organized in such a way as to bring exceptions to the attention of management as early in time as possible in order that control may be maintained and corrections made before significant damage is done to profits.

REVIEW PROBLEM ON STANDARD COSTS

Xavier Company produces a single product. The standard costs for one unit of product are:

Direct material: 6 ounces at $0.50 per ounce	$ 3
Direct labor: 1.8 hours at $10 per hour	18
Variable overhead: 1.8 hours at $5 per hour	9
Total standard variable cost per unit	$30

During June, 2,000 units were produced. The costs associated with the month were:

Material purchased: 18,000 ounces at $0.60.	$10,800
Material used in production: 14,000 ounces	—
Direct labor: 4,000 hours at $9.75	39,000
Variable overhead costs incurred	20,800

[7] For further discussion of this and other statistical uses in cost analysis, see Joel S. Demski, *Information Analysis,* 2d. ed. (Reading, Mass: Addison-Wesley Publishing, 1980), chap. 6.

Materials variances

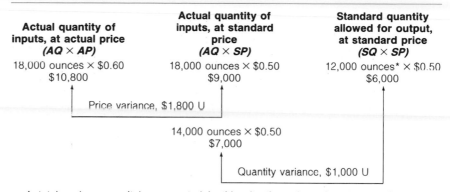

Actual quantity of inputs, at actual price (AQ × AP)	Actual quantity of inputs, at standard price (AQ × SP)	Standard quantity allowed for output, at standard price (SQ × SP)
18,000 ounces × $0.60 $10,800	18,000 ounces × $0.50 $9,000	12,000 ounces* × $0.50 $6,000

Price variance, $1,800 U

14,000 ounces × $0.50
$7,000

Quantity variance, $1,000 U

A total variance can't be computed in this situation, since the amount of materials purchased (18,000 ounces) differs from the amount of materials used in production (14,000 ounces).

* 2,000 units × 6 ounces = 12,000 ounces.

The same variances in shortcut format would be:

$$AQ(AP - SP) = \text{Materials price variance}$$
$$18,000 \text{ ounces } (\$0.60 - \$0.50) = \$1,800 \text{ U}$$

$$SP(AQ - SQ) = \text{Materials quantity variance}$$
$$\$0.50(14,000 \text{ ounces} - 12,000 \text{ ounces}) = \$1,000 \text{ U}$$

Notice that the price variance is computed on the entire amount of material purchased (18,000 ounces), whereas the quantity variance is computed only on the portion of this material used in production during the period (14,000 ounces). This is a common situation. The price variance is usually computed on whatever materials have been purchased. The quantity variance, however, can be computed only on that portion of the purchased materials *actually used* during the period. A quantity variance on the 4,000 ounces of materials above that were purchased during the period but *not* used in production (18,000 ounces purchased − 14,000 ounces used = 4,000 ounces unused) will be computed in a future period when these materials are drawn out of inventory and used in the production process.

Labor variances

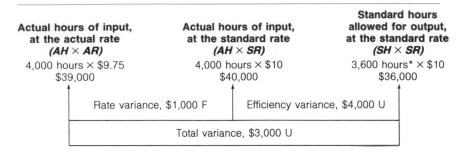

Actual hours of input, at the actual rate (AH × AR)	Actual hours of input, at the standard rate (AH × SR)	Standard hours allowed for output, at the standard rate (SH × SR)
4,000 hours × $9.75 $39,000	4,000 hours × $10 $40,000	3,600 hours* × $10 $36,000

Rate variance, $1,000 F   Efficiency variance, $4,000 U

Total variance, $3,000 U

* 2,000 units × 1.8 hours = 3,600 hours.

The same variances in shortcut format would be:

$$AH(AR - SR) = \text{Labor rate variance}$$
$$4,000 \text{ hours} \times (\$9.75 - \$10) = \$1,000 \text{ F}$$

$$SR(AH - SH) = \text{Labor efficiency variance}$$
$$\$10(4,000 \text{ hours} - 3,600 \text{ hours}) = \$4,000 \text{ U}$$

Variable overhead variances

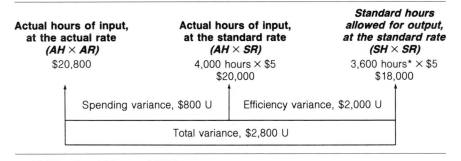

Actual hours of input, at the actual rate (AH × AR)	Actual hours of input, at the standard rate (AH × SR)	Standard hours allowed for output, at the standard rate (SH × SR)
$20,800	4,000 hours × $5 $20,000	3,600 hours* × $5 $18,000

Spending variance, $800 U   Efficiency variance, $2,000 U

Total variance, $2,800 U

* 2,000 units × 1.8 hours = 3,600 hours.

The same variances in shortcut format would be:

$$AH(AR - SR) = \text{Variable overhead spending variance}$$
$$4,000 \text{ hours} \times (\$5.20* - \$5.00) = \$800 \text{ U}$$

$$SR(AH - SH) = \text{Variable overhead efficiency variance}$$
$$\$5(4,000 \text{ hours} - 3,600 \text{ hours}) = \$2,000 \text{ U}$$

* $20,800 ÷ 4,000 hours = $5.20.

KEY TERMS FOR REVIEW

Bill of materials A listing of the type and quantity of each item of material required in the manufacture of a unit of product.

Ideal standards Standards that allow for no machine breakdowns or other work interruptions and that require peak efficiency at all times.

Labor efficiency variance A measure of the difference between the actual hours required to complete a task and the standard hours allowed, multiplied by the standard hourly rate.

Labor rate variance A measure of the difference between the actual hourly labor rate and the standard rate allowed, multiplied by the number of hours worked during the period.

Management by exception A system of management in which standards are set for various operating activities, with actual results then compared against these standards and any differences that are deemed significant brought to the attention of management as "exceptions."

Materials price variance A measure of the difference between the actual unit price paid for an item and the standard price that should have been paid, multiplied by the quantity purchased.

Materials quantity variance A measure of the difference between the actual quantity of materials used in production and the standard quantity allowed, multiplied by the standard price per unit of materials.

Mutual price-quantity variance An overlapping of the price and quantity variances caused by deviations in both price and quantity from the standards that have been set.

Practical standards Standards that allow for normal machine downtime and other work interruptions and that can be attained through reasonable, though highly efficient, efforts by the average worker at a task.

Standard cost card A detailed listing of the standard amounts of materials, labor, and overhead that should go into a unit of product, multiplied by the standard price or rate that has been set.

Standard cost per unit The expected cost of a unit of product as shown on the standard cost card.

Standard hours allowed The time that should have been taken to complete the period's output as computed by multiplying the number of units produced by the standard hours per unit.

Standard hours per unit The amount of labor time that should be required to complete a single unit of product, including allowances for breaks, machine downtime, cleanup, rejects, and other normal inefficiencies.

Standard price per unit The price that should be paid for a single unit of materials, including allowances for quality, quantity purchased, freight-in, receiving, and other such costs, net of any discounts allowed.

Standard quantity allowed The amount of materials that should have been used to complete the period's output as computed by multiplying the number of units produced by the standard quantity per unit.

Standard quantity per unit The amount of materials that should be required to complete a single unit of product, including allowances for normal waste, spoilage, rejects, and similar inefficiencies.

Standard rate per hour The labor rate that should be incurred per hour of labor time, including allowances for employment taxes, fringe benefits, and other such labor costs.

Variable overhead efficiency variance A measure of the difference between the actual activity (direct labor-hours, machine-hours, or some other base) of a period and the standard activity allowed, multiplied by the variable part of the predetermined overhead rate.

Variable overhead spending variance A measure of the difference between the actual variable overhead cost incurred during a period and the standard cost that should have been incurred, based on the actual activity of the period.

Variance The difference between standard prices and quantities and actual prices and quantities.

APPENDIX: GENERAL LEDGER ENTRIES TO RECORD VARIANCES

Although standard costs and variances can be computed and used by management without being formally entered into the accounting records, most organizations prefer to make formal entries, for three reasons. First, entry into the accounting records encourages early recognition of variances. As mentioned in the main body of the chapter, the earlier that variances can be recognized, the greater is their value to management in the control of costs. Second, formal entry tends to give variances a greater emphasis than is generally possible through informal, out-of-record computations. This emphasis gives a clear signal of management's desire to keep costs within the limits that have been set. And third, formal use of standard costs simplifies the bookkeeping process. By using standard costs within the accounting system itself, management eliminates the need to keep track of troublesome variations in actual costs and quantities, thereby providing for a flow of costs that is smoother, simpler, and more easily accounted for.

Direct materials variances

To illustrate the general ledger entries needed to record standard cost variances, we will return to the data contained in the review problem at the end of the chapter. The entry to record the purchase of direct materials would be:

```
Raw Materials (18,000 ounces at $0.50)  . . . . . . . . . .  9,000
Materials Price Variance (18,000 ounces at $0.10 U) . . . . .  1,800
    Accounts Payable (18,000 ounces at $0.60)  . . . . . .        10,800
```

Notice that the price variance is recognized when purchases are made, rather than when materials are actually used in production. This permits the price variance to be isolated early, and it also permits the materials to be carried in the inventory account at standard cost. As direct materials are later drawn from inventory and used in production, the quantity variance is isolated as follows:

Work in Process (12,000 ounces at $0.50)	6,000	
Materials Quantity Variance (2,000 ounces U at $0.50)	1,000	
Raw Materials (14,000 ounces at $0.50)		7,000

Thus, direct materials enter into the Work in Process account at standard cost, in terms of both price and quantity.

Notice that both the price variance and the quantity variance above are unfavorable, thereby showing up as debit (or additional cost) balances. If these variances had been favorable, they would have appeared as credit (or reduction in cost) balances, as in the case of the direct labor rate variance below.

Direct labor variances

Referring again to the cost data in the review problem at the end of the chapter, the general ledger entry to record the incurrence of direct labor cost would be:

Work in Process (3,600 hours at $10)	36,000	
Labor Efficiency Variance (400 hours U at $10)	4,000	
Labor Rate Variance (4,000 hours at $0.25 F)		1,000
Wages Payable (4,000 hours at $9.75)		39,000

Thus, as with direct materials, direct labor costs enter into the Work in Process account at standard, both in terms of the rate and in terms of the hours allowed for the production of the period.

Variable overhead variances

Variable overhead variances generally aren't recorded in the accounts separately, but rather are determined as part of the general analysis of overhead, which is discussed in Chapter 10.

QUESTIONS

9–1. What types of organizations make use of standard costs?

9–2. What is a quantity standard? What is a price standard?

9–3. What is the beginning point in setting a standard? Where should final responsibility for standard setting fall?

9–4. Why must a standard for the future be more than simply a projection of the past?

9–5. Distinguish between ideal and practical standards.

9–6. If employees are unable to meet a standard, what effect would you expect this to have on their productivity?

9–7. What is the difference between a standard and a budget?

9–8. What is meant by the term *variance?*

9–9. What is meant by the term *management by exception?*

9–10. Why are variances generally segregated in terms of a price variance and a quantity variance?

9–11. Who is generally responsible for the materials price variance? The materials quantity variance? The labor efficiency variance?

9–12. An examination of the cost records of the Chittenden Furniture Company indicates that the materials price variance is favorable but that the materials quantity variance is unfavorable by a substantial amount. What might this indicate?

9–13. What dangers lie in using standards as punitive tools?

9–14. "Our workers are all under labor contracts; therefore, our labor rate variance is bound to be zero." Discuss.

9–15. What effect, if any, would you expect poor quality materials to have on direct labor variances?

9–16. If variable manufacturing overhead is applied to production on a basis of direct labor-hours and the direct labor efficiency variance is unfavorable, will the variable overhead efficiency variance be favorable or unfavorable, or could it be either? Explain.

9–17. What factors are considered by management in determining whether a variance is properly called an exception?

9–18. What is a statistical control chart, and how is it used?

EXERCISES

E9–1. Sonne Company produces a perfume called Whim. The direct materials and direct labor standards for one bottle of Whim are given below:

	Standard quantity or hours	Standard price or rate	Standard cost
Direct materials	7.2 ounces	$2.50 per ounce	$18
Direct labor	0.4 hours	$10 per hour	4

During the most recent month, the following activity was recorded:

a. Twenty thousand ounces of material were purchased at a cost of $2.40 per ounce.
b. All of the material was used to produce 2,500 bottles of Whim.
c. Nine hundred hours of direct labor time were recorded at a total labor cost of $10,800.

Required: 1. Compute the direct materials price and quantity variances for the month.
2. Compute the direct labor rate and efficiency variances for the month.

E9–2. Refer to the data in Exercise 9–1. Assume that instead of producing 2,500 bottles of Whim during the month, the company produced only 2,000 bottles, using 16,000 ounces of material in the production process. (The rest of the material purchased remained in inventory.)

Required: Compute the direct materials price and quantity variances for the month.

E9–3.   Harmon Household Products, Inc., manufactures a number of consumer items for general household use. One of these products, a chopping board, requires an expensive hardwood in its manufacture. During a recent month, the company manufactured 4,000 chopping boards, using 11,000 board feet of hardwood in the process. The hardwood cost the company $18,700.

        The company's standards for one chopping board are 2.5 board feet of hardwood, at a cost of $1.80 per board foot.

Required: 1. What cost should have been incurred in the manufacture of the 4,000 chopping blocks? How much greater or less is this than the cost that was incurred?

          2. Break down the difference computed in (1) in terms of a materials price variance and a materials quantity variance.

E9–4.   Clark Equipment, Inc., produces machine tools for industry. The company uses standards to control its costs. The labor standards that have been set for one very popular machine tool are:

> Direct labor time per tool . . . . . . 15 minutes
> Direct labor rate per hour $5.20

During 19x5, the company worked 7,750 hours in order to produce 30,000 of these tools. The direct labor cost amounted to $39,525.

Required: 1. What direct labor cost should have been incurred in the manufacture of the 30,000 machine tools? By how much does this cost differ from the cost that was incurred?

          2. Break down the difference in cost from (1) above in terms of a labor rate variance and a labor efficiency variance.

          3. For each direct labor-hour worked, the company expects to incur $5 in variable overhead cost. This rate was experienced in 19x5. What effect did the efficiency (or inefficiency) of labor have on variable overhead cost in 19x5?

E9–5.   As business organizations grow in size and complexity, cost control becomes more difficult. A system to provide information and assist in cost control is imperative for effective management. Management by exception is one technique that is often used to foster cost control.

Required: 1. Describe how a standard cost system helps to make management by exception possible.

          2. Discuss the potential benefits of management by exception to an organization.

          3. Identify and discuss the behavioral problems that might occur in an organization using standard costs and management by exception.   (CMA, adapted)

E9–6.   Dawson Toys, Ltd., produces a toy called the Maze. The company has recently established a standard cost system to help control costs and has established the following standards for the Maze toy:

> Direct materials: 6 pieces per toy at $0.50 per piece.
> Direct labor: 1.3 hours per toy at $8 per hour.

During the month of July 19x6, the company produced 3,000 Maze toys. Production data for the month on the toy follow:

Direct materials: 25,000 pieces were purchased for use in production at a cost of $0.48 per piece. Some 5,000 of these pieces were still in inventory at the end of the month. Direct labor: 4,000 direct labor-hours were worked at a cost of $36,000.

Required:
1. Compute the following variances for the month:
   a. Direct materials price and quantity variances.
   b. Direct labor rate and efficiency variances.
2. Prepare a brief explanation of the significance and possible cause of each variance.

E9–7. Kelson Products manufactures a gasoline additive. Each bottle of additive requires two items of material, Benol and Protex, as described below:

a. Benol is purchased in 10-gallon containers at a cost of $60 per container. Freight is paid by the supplier. Discount terms of 2/10, n/30 are offered by the supplier, and Kelson Products takes all discounts.

b. Protex is purchased in 80-pound boxes at a cost of $30 per box. Kelson Products must pay all freight charges, which amount to $420 for an average shipment of 100 boxes. About 5 percent of the Protex is wasted in the production process.

Required:
1. Compute the following:
   a. The standard price of a quart of Benol.
   b. The standard price of a pound of Protex.
2. Assume that each bottle of additive requires 1.2 quarts of Benol and 0.6 pounds of Protex. Prepare a standard cost card showing the standard cost of material in a bottle of additive. (Carry computations to three decimal places.)

E9–8. The auto repair shop of Quality Motor Company uses standards to control labor time and labor cost in the shop. The standard labor cost for a motor tune-up is given below:

Job	Standard hours	Standard rate	Standard cost
Motor tune-up.	2.5	$9	$22.50

The record showing the time spent in the shop last week on motor tune-ups has been misplaced. However, the shop supervisor recalls that 50 tune-ups were completed during the week, and the controller recalls the following variance data relating to tune-ups:

Labor rate variance . . . . . . $87 F
Total labor variance . . . . . . 93 U

Required:
1. Determine the number of actual labor-hours spent on tune-ups last week.
2. Determine the actual hourly rate of pay for tune-ups last week.

(Hint: A useful way to proceed would be to work from known to unknown data either by using the variance formulas or by using the columnar format shown in Exhibit 9–4.)

E9–9. (Appendix) Aspen Products, Inc., began production of product A on April 1, 19x8. The company uses a standard cost system and has established the following standards for one unit of product A:

	Standard quantity	Standard price or rate	Standard cost
Direct materials	3.5 feet	$6 per foot	$21
Direct labor	0.4 hours	$10 per hour	4

During the month of April, the following activity was recorded relative to product A:

a. Purchased 7,000 feet of material at a cost of $5.75 per foot.
b. Used 6,000 feet of material to produce 1,500 units of product A.
c. Worked 725 direct labor-hours on product A at a cost of $8,120.

Required:

1. Compute the direct materials price and quantity variances for the month.
2. Compute the direct labor rate and efficiency variances for the month.
3. Prepare journal entries to record all activity relating to materials and labor for the month, and then post the entries to the T-accounts below:

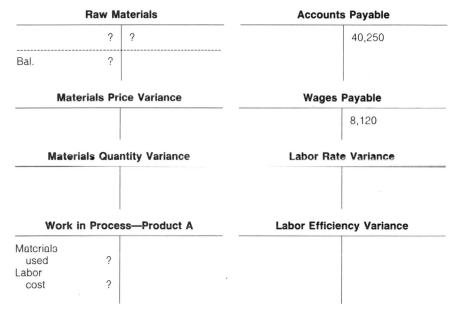

Raw Materials				Accounts Payable	
	?	?			40,250
Bal.	?				

Materials Price Variance		Wages Payable	
			8,120

Materials Quantity Variance		Labor Rate Variance	

Work in Process—Product A		Labor Efficiency Variance	
Materials used	?		
Labor cost	?		

PROBLEMS

P9–10. Straightforward variance analysis. Barberry, Inc., manufactures a product called Fruta. The company uses a standard cost system and has established the following standards for one unit of Fruta:

	Standard quantity	Standard price or rate	Standard cost
Direct materials	1.5 pounds	$6 per pound	$ 9.00
Direct labor	0.6 hours	$12 per hour	7.20
Variable overhead	0.6 hours	$2.50 per hour	1.50
			$17.70

During June 19x8, the following activity was recorded by the company relative to production of Fruta:

a. The company produced 3,000 units during the month.

b. A total of 8,000 pounds of material were purchased at a cost of $46,000.

c. There was no beginning inventory of materials on hand to start the month; at the end of the month, 3,000 pounds of material remained in the warehouse unused.

d. The company employs 10 persons to work on the production of Fruta. During June, each worked an average of 160 hours at an average rate of $12.50 per hour.

e. Variable overhead is assigned to Fruta on a basis of direct labor-hours. Variable overhead costs during June totaled $3,600.

The company's management is anxious to determine the efficiency of the activities surrounding the production of Fruta.

Required:

1. For materials used in the production of Fruta:
   a. Compute the price and quantity variances.
   b. The materials were purchased from a new supplier who is anxious to enter into a long-term purchase contract. Would you recommend that the company sign the contract? Explain.

2. For labor employed in the production of Fruta:
   a. Compute the rate and efficiency variances.
   b. In the past, the 10 persons employed in the production of Fruta consisted of four senior workers and six assistants. During June, the company experimented with five senior workers and five assistants. Would you recommend that the new labor mix be continued? Explain.

3. Compute the variable overhead spending and efficiency variances. What relationship can you see between this efficiency variance and the labor efficiency variance?

P9–11. Setting labor standards. The Mason Company is going to expand its punch press department. The company is about to purchase several new punch presses from Equipment Manufacturers, Inc. Equipment Manufacturers' engineers report that their mechanical studies indicate that for Mason's intended use, the output rate for one press should be 1,000 pieces per hour. The Mason Company has similar presses now in operation. At present, production from these presses averages 600 pieces per hour.

A detailed study of the Mason Company's experience shows that the average is derived from the following individual outputs:

Worker	Output per hour (pieces)
J. Smith	750
H. Brown	750
R. Jones	600
J. Hardy	550
P. Clark	500
B. Randall	450
Total	3,600
Average	600

Mason's management also plans to institute a standard cost accounting system in the near future. The company's engineers are supporting a standard based on 1,000 pieces per hour; the accounting department is arguing for a standard of 750 pieces per hour; and the department supervisor is arguing for a standard of 600 pieces per hour.

Required: 1. What arguments would each proponent be likely to use to support his or her case?
             2. Which alternative best reconciles the needs of cost control and motivation for improved performance? Explain the reasons for your choice.   (CMA, adapted)

P9–12.   **Computations from incomplete data.** Topaz Company produces a single product. The company has set standards as follows for materials and labor:

	Direct materials	Direct labor
Standard quantity or hours per unit	? pounds	2.5 hours
Standard price or rate	? per pound	$9 per hour
Standard cost per unit	?	$22.50

During the past month, the company purchased 6,000 pounds of direct materials at a cost of $16,500. All of this material was used in the production of 1,400 units of product. Direct labor cost totaled $28,500 for the month. The following variances have been computed:

Materials quantity variance . . . . $1,200 U
Total materials variance . . . .   300 F
Labor efficiency variance. . . . .   4,500 F

Required: 1. For direct materials:
             a. Compute the standard price per pound for materials.
             b. Compute the standard quantity allowed for materials for the month's production.
             c. Compute the standard quantity of materials allowed per unit of product.
             2. For direct labor:
             a. Compute the actual direct labor cost per hour for the month.
             b. Compute the labor rate variance.

(Hint: In completing the problem, it may be helpful to move from known to unknown data either by using the variance formulas or by using the columnar format shown in Exhibits 9–3 and 9–4.)

P9–13.   **The impact of variances on unit costs; basic variance analysis.** Sparks Company produces a number of products. The standards relating to one of these products are shown below, along with actual cost data for July 19x8 (per unit):

	Standard cost	Actual cost
Direct materials:		
Standard: 2.8 yards at $3.50 per yard	$ 9.80	
Actual: 2.75 yards at $3.60 per yard		$ 9.90
Direct labor:		
Standard: 0.8 hours at $9 per hour	7.20	
Actual: 0.9 hours at $8.50 per hour		7.65
Variable overhead:		
Budget: 0.8 hours at $2.50 per hour	2.00	
Actual: 0.9 hours at $2.40 per hour		2.16
Total cost per unit	$19.00	$19.71
Excess of actual unit cost over standard		$0.71

The production superintendent was disturbed when he saw these cost figures. He explained to one of his assistants, "This 71-cent variance doesn't look like much when you're talking about only one unit of product, but when you consider that we produce 50,000 of these a year, it can really add up fast. We need to isolate and correct the cost problem before any real damage is done to profits."

Actual production for the month was 4,000 units.

Required: 1. Compute the following variances for the month of July:
    a. Materials price and quantity.
    b. Labor rate and efficiency.
    c. Overhead spending and efficiency.
2. Show how much of the 71 cents excessive unit cost is traceable to each of the variances computed in (1) above.
3. Show how much of the 71 cents excessive unit cost is traceable to the inefficient use of labor time.

P9–14.   **Basic variance analysis.**   The Portland Company's Ironton Plant produces precast ingots for industrial use. Carlos Santiago, who was recently appointed general manager of the Ironton Plant, has just been handed the plant's income statement for October 19x4. The statement is shown below:

	Budgeted	Actual
Sales (5,000 ingots)	$250,000	$250,000
Less variable expenses:		
Variable cost of goods sold*	80,000	96,390
Variable selling expenses	20,000	20,000
Total variable expenses	100,000	116,390
Contribution margin	150,000	133,610
Less fixed expenses:		
Manufacturing overhead.	60,000	60,000
Selling and administrative expenses.	75,000	75,000
Total fixed expenses	135,000	135,000
Net income (loss)	$ 15,000	$ (1,390)

* Contains direct materials, direct labor, and variable overhead.

Mr. Santiago was shocked to see the loss for the month, particularly since sales were exactly as budgeted. He stated, "I sure hope the plant has a standard cost system in operation. If it doesn't, I won't have the slightest idea of where to start looking for the problem."

The plant does use a standard cost system, with the following standard variable cost per ingot:

	Standard quantity	Standard price or rate	Standard cost
Direct materials	4.0 pounds	$2.50 per pound	$10.00
Direct labor	0.6 hours	$9.00 per hour	5.40
Variable overhead . . . , ...	0.6 hours	$1.00 per hour	0.60
Total standard variable cost			$16.00

Mr. Santiago has determined that during the month of October the plant produced 5,000 units and incurred the following costs:

a. Purchased 25,000 pounds of materials at a cost of $2.95 per pound.

b. Used 19,800 pounds of materials in production. (Finished goods and work in process inventories are nominal and can be ignored.)

c. Worked 3,600 direct labor-hours at a cost of $8.70 per hour.

d. Incurred a variable overhead cost of $1.20 per hour, or a total cost of $4,320 for the month.

It is the company's policy to close all variances to cost of goods sold on a monthly basis.

Required:
1. Compute the following variances for the month:
   a. Direct materials price and quantity variances.
   b. Direct labor rate and efficiency variances.
   c. Variable overhead spending and efficiency variances.
2. Summarize the variances that you computed in (1) above, by showing the net overall favorable or unfavorable variance for the month. What impact did this figure have on the company's income statement?
3. Pick out the two most significant variances that you computed in (1) above. Explain to Mr. Santiago the possible causes of these variances, so that he will know where to concentrate his and his subordinates' time.

P9–15. **Multiple products; standard cost card; variance analysis.** Princeton Company produces two products, Lags and Zets, which pass through two operations. The company uses a standard cost system, with standard usage of materials and labor as follows for each product (on a per unit basis):

	Raw material		Standard labor time (hours)	
Product	X	Y	Operation 1	Operation 2
Lags	1.8 pounds	2.0 gallons	0.4 hours	1.6 hours
Zets.	3.0 pounds	4.5 gallons	0.7 hours	1.8 hours

Information relating to materials purchased and materials used in production during May 19x5 follows:

Material	Purchases	Purchase cost	Standard price	Used in production*
X.	14,000 pounds	$51,800	$3.50 per pound	8,500 pounds
Y.	15,000 gallons	19,500	1.40 per gallon	13,000 gallons

* Materials purchased but not used in production remain in inventory and will be used in production in a following period.

The following additional information is available:

a. The company recognizes price variances at the time of purchase of material.

b. The standard labor rate is $10 per hour in operation 1 and $9.50 per hour in operation 2.

c. During May 19x5, 2,400 direct labor-hours were worked in operation 1 at a total labor cost of $27,000, and 5,700 direct labor-hours were worked in operation 2 at a total labor cost of $59,850.

d. Production during May 19x5 was: 1,500 Lags and 2,000 Zets.

Required:

1. Prepare a standard cost card for each product showing the standard cost of direct materials and direct labor.

2. For materials, compute the following variances for May 19x5:
   a. The price variance for each type of material.
   b. The quantity variance for each type of material. Express the variance both in units (pounds or gallons) and in dollars.

3. For labor, compute the following variances for May 19x5:
   a. The labor rate variance for each operation.
   b. The labor efficiency variance for each operation. Express the variance both in hours and in dollars.

4. When might it be better to express variances in units (pounds, gallons, hours) rather than in dollars? In dollars rather than in units?

P9–16. **Preparation of a variance report.** Dolby, Inc., produces and sells high-quality cabinets for stereo speakers. The company's most recent income statement is given below:

DOLBY, INC.
Income Statement
For the Month Ended July 31, 19x7

	Budget	Actual	Variance
Sales (2,500 units)	$200,000	$200,000	—
Less variable expenses:			
Variable production costs	90,000	96,000	$6,000 U
Other variable expenses.	30,000	30,000	—
Total variable expenses	120,000	126,000	
Contribution margin	80,000	74,000	
Less fixed expenses:			
Production	28,000	28,000	—
Selling and administrative	32,000	32,000	—
Total fixed expenses	60,000	60,000	
Net income	$ 20,000	$ 14,000	$6,000 U

The company uses a standard cost system for planning and control purposes. The standard cost for one unit of product is given below:

Wood: 3.2 feet at $6 per foot	$19.20
Direct labor: 1.4 hours at $10 per hour	14.00
Variable overhead: 1.4 hours at $2 per hour	2.80
Total standard variable cost	$36.00

Management is somewhat unhappy with the standard cost system because difficulty is being experienced in interpreting the cost variance reports coming from accounting. A typical cost variance report is given below. The report relates to the $6,000 variance above for July:

DOLBY, INC.
Cost Variance Report—Variable Production Costs
For the Month of July 19x7

	Total	Per unit
Excess wood used in production	$1,400	$0.56
Excess direct labor cost incurred	4,400	1.76
Excess variable overhead cost incurred	200	0.08
Total excess cost incurred	$6,000	$2.40

The company has hired you, as an expert in cost analysis, to help management clarify the reports coming from accounting. You have found that 2,500 units of product were produced and sold during the month and that the following actual unit costs were incurred:

Wood: 3.04 feet at $6.50 per foot.
Direct labor: 1.6 hours at $9.85 per hour.
Variable overhead: 1.6 hours at $1.80 per hour.

Required:
1. What criticisms can be made of the cost variance reports currently being prepared by accounting?
2. Compute the following variances for July 19x7:
   a. Materials price and quantity.
   b. Labor rate and efficiency.
   c. Variable overhead spending and efficiency.
3. Prepare a new cost variance report for management; show your variances on both a total and a per unit basis.

P9–17. **Standards and variances from incomplete data.** Vitalite, Inc., produces a number of products, including a body-wrap kit. Standard variable costs relating to a single kit are given below:

	Standard quantity or hours	Standard price or rate	Standard cost
Direct materials.	?	$6 per yard	$?
Direct labor	?	?	?
Variable overhead.	?	$2 per hour	?
Total standard cost per kit			$42

During August 19x9, 500 kits were manufactured and sold. Selected information relating to the month's production is given below:

	Materials used	Direct labor	Variable overhead
Total standard cost*	$?	$8,000	$1,600
Actual costs incurred	10,000	?	1,620
Materials price variance	?		
Materials quantity variance	600 U		
Labor rate variance		?	
Labor efficiency variance		?	
Overhead spending variance			?
Overhead efficiency variance			?

* For the month's production.

The following additional information is available for March production of kits:

Actual direct labor-hours 900
Overhead is based on . . . . Direct labor-hours
Difference between standard and
actual cost per kit produced
during August . . . . $0.14 U

Required:
1. What was the total standard cost of the materials used during August?
2. How many yards of material are required at standard per kit?
3. What was the materials price variance for August?
4. What is the standard direct labor rate per hour?
5. What was the labor rate variance for the month? The labor efficiency variance?
6. What was the overhead spending variance for the month? The overhead efficiency variance?
7. Complete the standard cost card for one kit shown at the beginning of the problem.

P9–18. **Variance analysis; multiple lots.** Ricardo Shirts, Inc., manufactures short- and long-sleeved men's shirts for large stores. Ricardo produces a single-quality shirt in lots to each customer's order and attaches the store's label to each shirt. The standard direct costs for a dozen long-sleeved shirts include:

Direct materials: 24 yards at $0.65 . . . . . . $15.60
Direct labor: 3 hours at $7.25 . . . . . . 21.75

During April, Ricardo worked on three orders for long-sleeved shirts. Job cost records for the month disclose the following:

Lot	Units in lot (dozens)	Materials used (yards)	Hours worked
30.	1,000	24,100	2,980
31.	1,700	40,440	5,130
32.	1,200	28,825	2,890

The following additional information is available:

a. Ricardo purchased 95,000 yards of material during the month at a cost of $66,500.
b. Direct labor cost incurred amounted to $80,740 during April.

c. There was no work in process at April 1. During April, lots 30 and 31 were completed and all material was issued to lot 32, which was 80 percent completed as to labor.

Required: 1. Compute the materials price variance for April, and show whether the variance was favorable or unfavorable.
2. Determine the materials quantity variance for the month in both yards and dollars:
   a. For the company in total.
   b. For each lot worked on during the month.
3. Compute the labor rate variance for April, and show whether the variance was favorable or unfavorable.
4. Determine the labor efficiency variance for the month in both hours and dollars:
   a. For the company in total.
   b. For each lot worked on during the month.
5. In what situations might it be better to express variances in units (hours, yards, and so on) rather than in dollars? In dollars rather than in units?

(CPA, adapted)

P9–19.   **Setting materials and labor standards.**   The Scera Company manufactures trivets. The company is just starting to use standard costs. From accounting records, industrial engineering studies, and other sources, the following information has been developed:

a. The clocked labor time to produce one trivet (good or defective) is 1.5 hours.
b. Ten percent of all completed trivets are scrapped as defective. The scrapped trivets have no monetary value.
c. The materials required in the production of one trivet (good or defective) are:

Material	Quantity required per trivet	Invoice cost	Freight
H–4	3.6 qts *	$3 per qt.	$0.10 per qt.
H–11	2.7 lbs.	4 per lb.	0.20 per lb.

* After spillage or evaporation loss.

d. All materials are purchased subject to a 2 percent cash discount if paid within 10 days. All discounts are taken.
e. Only 80 percent of material H–4 finds its way into a trivet. The remainder is lost through spillage or evaporation.
f. The labor rate is $6 per hour.
g. Coffee breaks, cleanup, and so on, consume about 0.8 hours of labor time each eight-hour day. The company works a 40-hour week.

Required: 1. Compute the following for material:
   a. The standard quantity of material H–4 and the standard quantity of material H–11 for each acceptable trivet, allowing for the normal loss factors mentioned above.
   b. The standard cost per quart or pound for each type of material.
   c. Using the data from (a) and (b) above, compute the standard cost of each type of material per acceptable trivet.

2. Compute the following for labor:
   a. The standard labor time per acceptable trivet, again allowing for normal loss factors.
   b. The standard labor cost per acceptable trivet.

P9–20. **Determining standard costs; variance analysis.** Helix Company produces several products in its factory, including a karate robe. The company uses a standard cost system to assist in the control of costs. According to the standards that have been set for the robes, the factory should work 780 direct labor-hours each month and produce 1,950 robes. The standard costs associated with this level of production activity are:

	Total	Per unit of product
Direct materials.	$35,490	$18.20
Direct labor	7,020	3.60
Variable overhead (based on direct labor-hours)	2,340	1.20
		$23.00

During April 19x8, the factory worked only 760 direct labor-hours and produced 2,000 robes. The following actual costs were recorded during the month:

	Total	Per unit of product
Direct materials (6,000 yards)	$36,000	$18.00
Direct labor	7,600	3.80
Variable overhead	3,800	1.90
		$23.70

At standard, each robe should require 2.8 yards of material.

Required: Compute the following variances for April 19x8:
1. The materials price and quantity variances.
2. The labor rate and efficiency variances.
3. The variable overhead spending and efficiency variances.

P9–21. **Variances; unit costs; journal entries.** (Appendix) Vermont Mills, Inc., is a large producer of men's and women's clothing. The company uses standard costs for all of its products. The standard costs and actual costs for a recent period are given below for one of the company's product lines (per unit of product):

	Standard cost	Actual cost
Direct materials:		
Standard: 4.0 yards at $3.60 per yard	$14.40	
Actual: 4.4 yards at $3.35 per yard		$14.74
Direct labor:		
Standard: 1.6 hours at $4.50 per hour	7.20	
Actual: 1.4 hours at $4.85 per hour		6.79
Variable overhead:		
Standard: 1.6 hours at $1.80 per hour	2.88	
Actual: 1.4 hours at $2.15 per hour		3.01
Total cost per unit	$24.48	$24.54

During this period, the company produced 4,800 units of product. A comparison of standard and actual costs for the period on a total cost basis is given below:

Actual costs: 4,800 units at $24.54 . . . . $117,792
Standard costs: 4,800 units at $24.48 117,504
Difference in cost—unfavorable . . . . $ 288

There was no inventory of materials on hand to start the period. During the period, 21,120 yards of materials were purchased, all of which were used in production.

Required: 1. For direct materials:
  a. Compute the price and quantity variances for the period.
  b. Prepare journal entries to record all activity relating to direct materials for the period.
2. For direct labor:
  a. Compute the rate and efficiency variances.
  b. Prepare a journal entry to record the incurrence of direct labor cost for the period.
3. Compute the variable overhead spending and efficiency variances.
4. On seeing the $288 total cost variance, the company's president stated, "This variance of $288 is only 0.2 percent of the $117,504 standard cost for the period. It's obvious that our costs are well under control." Do you agree? Explain.
5. State the possible causes of each variance that you have computed.

P9–22. **Variance analysis; incomplete data; journal entries.** (Appendix) Topline Surf Boards manufactures a single product. The standard cost of one unit of this product is:

Direct materials: 6 feet at $1 . . . . $ 6.00
Direct labor: 1 hour at $4.50 . . . .   4.50
Variable overhead: 1 hour at $3 . . . .   3.00
Total standard variable cost per unit $13.50

During the month of October, 6,000 units were produced. Selected cost data relating to the month's production follow:

Material purchased: 60,000 feet at $0.95 . . . . $57,000
Material used in production: 38,000 feet . . . .   —
Direct labor: ?   hours at $?   per hour   27,950
Variable overhead cost incurred   20,475
Variable overhead efficiency variance . . . .   1,500 U

There was no beginning inventory of raw materials. The variable overhead rate is based on direct labor-hours.

Required:
1. For direct materials:
    a. Compute the price and quantity variances for the month.
    b. Prepare journal entries to record activity for the month.
2. For direct labor:
    a. Compute the rate and efficiency variances for the month.
    b. Prepare a journal entry to record labor activity for the month.
3. For variable overhead:
    a. Compute the spending variance for the month, and prove the efficiency variance given above.
    b. If overhead is applied to production on a basis of direct labor-hours, is it possible to have a favorable direct labor efficiency variance and an unfavorable overhead efficiency variance? Explain.
4. State the possible causes of each variance that you have computed.

P9–23. **Multiple products; journal entries.** (Appendix) Bestway Pharmaceutical Company produces two products, Milex and Silex, in Department 4. Materials and other inputs into each product are shown below:

	Per batch		Standard price or rate
	Milex	**Silex**	
Direct materials:			
Material A	2 pounds	1 pound	$4 per pound
Material B	—	3 pounds	3 per pound
Material C	1 gallon	1 gallon	5 per gallon
Direct labor	0.8 hours	1.5 hours	8 per hour
Variable overhead	0.8 hours	1.5 hours	3 per hour

During the month of March, the company produced 900 batches of Milex and 1,200 batches of Silex. The following additional information is available:

a. Materials purchased during the month:

	Amount (pounds)	Purchase cost
Material A	3,600	$14,940
Material B	3,800	10,830
Material C	—	—

b. Inventories on hand at the start of the month:

	Amount	Inventory cost
Material A	500 pounds	$ 2,000
Material B	400 pounds	1,200
Material C	2,500 gallons	12,500

c. Materials issued into production during the month:

	Amount	Cost
Material A	3,450 pounds	?
Material B	3,500 pounds	?
Material C	2,400 gallons	?

d. A total of 2,700 hours of direct labor time were recorded for the month; direct labor cost for the month was $20,250.

e. Variable overhead cost is allocated to production on a basis of direct labor-hours.

f. There was no work in process at the beginning or end of the month.

Required: 1. Determine the standard variable cost of one batch of each product.
2. For direct materials:
    a. Compute the price variance for each material purchased. Prepare a journal entry to record each purchase.
    b. Compute the quantity variance for the month for each material. Prepare journal entries to record the placing of materials into production.
3. For direct labor:
    a. Compute the rate and efficiency variances for the month.
    b. Prepare a journal entry to record the incurrence of direct labor cost for the month.
4. State the possible causes of each variance that you have computed.

P9–24. **Fragmentary data; journal entries; unit costs.** (Appendix)   You have just been hired by Barfex Company, which manufactures cough syrup. The syrup requires two materials, A and B, in its manufacture, and it is produced in batches. The company uses a standard cost system, with the controller preparing variances on a weekly basis. These variances are discussed at a meeting attended by all relevant managers. The meeting to discuss last week's variances is tomorrow; and since you will be working initially in the planning and control area, the president thinks that this would be a good chance for you to get acquainted with the company's control system and has asked that you attend and be prepared to participate fully in the discussion. Accordingly, you have taken home the controller's figure sheet containing last week's variances, as well as the ledger pages from which these variances were derived. You are sure that with a little study you will be able to make a sterling impression and be launched into a bright and successful career.

After completing your study that night, the weather being warm and humid, you leave your windows open upon retiring, only to arise the next morning horrified to discover that a sudden shower has obliterated most of the controller's figures (left lying on a table by an open window). Only the following fragments are readable:

	Raw Materials—A	
Bal. 6/1	600	
Bal. 6/7	1,380	

	Wages Payable	
		1,725

	Raw Materials—B	
Bal. 6/1	0	600
Bal. 6/7	200	

	Material A—Price Variance	
	220	

	Work in Process	
Bal. 6/1	0	
Material A	2,400	
Bal. 6/7	0	

	Material B—Quantity Variance	
		40

	Accounts Payable	
		4,240

	Labor Efficiency Variance	
	240	

Not wanting to admit your carelessness to either the president or the controller, you have decided that your only alternative is to reproduce the obliterated data. From your study last night, you recall the following:

a. The wages payable are only for direct labor.
b. The accounts payable are for purchases of both material A and material B.
c. The standard cost of material A is $6 per gallon, and the standard quantity is 5 gallons per batch of syrup.
d. Purchases last week were: material A, 550 gallons; and material B, 200 pounds.
e. The standard rate for direct labor is $8 per hour; a total of 230 actual hours were worked last week.

Required:
1. How many batches of syrup were produced last week? (Double-check this figure before going on!)
2. For material A:
   a. How many gallons were used in production last week?
   b. What was the quantity variance?
   c. What was the cost of material A purchased during the week?
   d. Prepare journal entries to record all activity relating to material A during the week.
3. For material B:
   a. What is the standard cost per pound of material B?
   b. How many pounds of material B were used in production last week? How many pounds should have been used at standard?
   c. What is the standard quantity of material B per batch?
   d. What was the price variance for material B?

   e. Prepare journal entries to record all activity relating to material B during the week.

 4. For direct labor:

   a. What were the standard hours allowed for last week's production?

   b. What are the standard hours per batch?

   c. What was the direct labor rate variance?

   d. Prepare a journal entry to record all activity relating to direct labor during the week.

 5. In terms of materials and labor, compute the standard cost of one batch of syrup.

10 Flexible Budgets and Overhead Analysis

Learning objectives

After studying Chapter 10, you should be able to:

Prepare a flexible budget and explain its advantages over the static budget approach.

Use flexible budget data to prepare a performance report containing (1) only a spending variance for overhead and (2) both a spending and an efficiency variance for overhead.

Explain the nature of the spending and efficiency variances for overhead and explain how they are controlled.

Properly apply overhead cost to units of product in a standard cost system.

Explain the significance of the denominator activity figure in determining the standard cost of a unit of product.

Compute and properly interpret the fixed overhead budget and volume variances.

Present variances on the income statement in the proper format.

Define or explain the key terms listed at the end of the chapter.

There are four problems involved in overhead cost control. First, manufacturing overhead is usually made up of many separate costs. Second, these separate costs are often very small in dollar amount, making it highly impractical to control them in the same way that direct materials and direct labor costs are controlled. Third, these small, separate costs are often the responsibility of different managers. And fourth, manufacturing overhead costs vary in behavior, some being variable, some fixed, and some mixed in nature.

Most of these problems can be overcome by use of a *flexible budget*. In this chapter, we study flexible budgets and their use in overhead cost control. We also expand the study of overhead variances that we started in Chapter 9.

FLEXIBLE BUDGETS

Characteristics of a flexible budget

The budgets that we studied in Chapter 8 were essentially static budgets in nature. A **static budget** has two characteristics:

1. It is geared toward only one level of activity.
2. Actual results are always compared against budgeted costs at the *original* budget activity level.

A **flexible budget** differs from a static budget on both of these points. First, it does not confine itself to only one level of activity, but rather is geared toward a *range* of activity. Second, actual results do not have to be compared against budgeted costs at the original budget activity level. Since the flexible budget covers a *range* of activity, if actual costs are incurred at a different activity level from what was originally planned, then the manager is able to construct a new budget, as needed, to compare against actual results. Hence, the term *flexible budget*. In sum, the characteristics of a flexible budget are:

1. It is geared toward *all* levels of activity within the relevant range, rather than toward only one level of activity.
2. It is *dynamic* in nature rather than static. A budget can be tailored for any level of activity within the relevant range, even after the period is over. That is, a manager can look at what activity level *was attained* during a period and then turn to the flexible budget to determine what costs *should have been* at that activity level.

Deficiencies of the static budget

To illustrate the difference between a static budget and a flexible budget, let us assume that the assembly operation of Rocco Company has budgeted to produce 10,000 units during March. The variable overhead budget that has been set is shown in Exhibit 10–1.

Let us assume that the production goal of 10,000 units is not met. The

EXHIBIT 10–1

ROCCO COMPANY
Static Budget
Assembly Operation
For the Month Ended March 31, 19x1

Budgeted production in units	10,000
Budgeted variable overhead costs:	
Indirect materials	$4,000
Lubricants.	1,000
Power	3,000
Total.	$8,000

company is able to produce only 9,000 units during the month. *If a static budget approach is used,* the performance report for the month will appear as shown in Exhibit 10–2.

What's wrong with this report? The deficiencies of the static budget can be explained as follows. A production manager has two prime responsibilities to discharge in the performance of his or her duties—*production control* and *cost control.* Production control is involved with seeing that production goals in terms of output are met. Cost control is involved with seeing that output is produced at the least possible cost, consistent with quality standards. These are different responsibilities, and they must be kept separate in attempting to assess how well the production manager is doing his or her job. The main difficulty with the static budget is that it fails completely to distinguish between the production control and the cost control dimensions of a manager's performance.

Of the two, the static budget does a good job of measuring only whether production control is being maintained. Look again at the data in Exhibit 10–2. The data on the top line relate to the production superintendent's

EXHIBIT 10–2

ROCCO COMPANY
Static Budget Performance Report
Assembly Operation
For the Month Ended March 31, 19x1

	Actual	Budget	Variance
Production in units	9,400	10,000	600 U
Variable overhead costs:			
Indirect materials.	$3,800	$4,000	$200 F*
Lubricants	950	1,000	50 F*
Power	2,900	3,000	100 F*
Total	$7,650	$8,000	$350 F*

* These cost variances are useless, since they have been derived by comparing actual costs at one level of activity against budgeted costs at a *different* level of activity.

responsibility for production control. These data for Rocco Company properly reflect the fact that production control was not maintained during the month. The company failed to meet its production goal by 600 units.

The remainder of the data in the report deal with cost control. These data are useless in that they are comparing apples with oranges. Although the production manager may be very proud of the favorable cost variances, they tell nothing about how well costs were controlled during the month. The problem is that the budget costs are based on an activity level of 10,000 units, whereas the actual costs were incurred at an activity level substantially below this (only 9,400 units). From a cost control point of view, it is total nonsense to try to compare costs at one activity level with costs at a different activity level. Such comparisons will always make a production manager look good so long as the actual production is less than the budgeted production.

How the flexible budget works

The basic idea of the flexible budget approach is that through a study of cost behavior patterns, a budget can be prepared that is geared to a *range* of activity, rather than to a single level. The basic steps in preparing a flexible budget are:

1. Determine the relevant range over which activity is expected to fluctuate during the coming period.
2. Analyze costs that will be incurred over the relevant range in terms of determining cost behavior patterns (variable, fixed, mixed).
3. Separate costs by behavior, determining the formula for variable and mixed costs, as discussed in Chapter 5.
4. Using the formula for the variable portion of the costs, prepare a budget showing what costs will be incurred at various points throughout the relevant range.

To illustrate, let us assume that Rocco Company's production normally fluctuates between 8,000 and 11,000 units each month. A study of cost behavior patterns over this relevant range has revealed the following formulas for the variable portion of overhead:

Cost	Variable cost formula (per unit)
Indirect materials	$0.40
Lubricants.	0.10
Power	0.30

Based on these cost formulas, a flexible budget for Rocco Company would appear as shown in Exhibit 10–3.

EXHIBIT 10-3

ROCCO COMPANY
Flexible Budget
Assembly Operation
For the Month Ended March 31, 19x1

Budgeted production in units. 10,000

Overhead costs	Cost formula (per unit)	Range of production in units			
		8,000	9,000	10,000	11,000
Variable costs:					
Indirect materials	$0.40	$3,200	$3,600	$4,000	$4,400
Lubricants	0.10	800	900	1,000	1,100
Power	0.30	2,400	2,700	3,000	3,300
Total variable costs. . . .	$0.80	$6,400	$7,200	$8,000	$8,800

Using the flexible budget   Once the flexible budget has been prepared, the manager is ready to compare actual results for a period against the comparable budget level anywhere within the relevant range. The manager isn't limited to a single budget level as with the static budget. To illustrate, let us again assume that Rocco company is unable to meet its production goal of 10,000 units during the month of March. As before, we will assume that only 9,400 units are produced. Under the flexible budget approach, the performance report would appear as shown in Exhibit 10-4.

In contrast to the performace report prepared earlier under the static budget approach (Exhibit 10-2), this performance report distinguishes clearly between production control and cost control. The production data at the top of the report indicate whether the production goal was met. The cost

Exhibit 10-4

ROCCO COMPANY
Performance Report
Assembly Operation
For the Month Ended March 31, 19x1

Budgeted production in units 10,000
Actual production in units 9,400

Overhead costs	Cost formula	Actual costs incurred 9,400 units	Budget based on 9,400 units	Variance
Variable costs:				
Indirect materials.	$0.40	$3,800	$3,760*	$ 40 U†
Lubricants	0.10	950	940	10 U†
Power	0.30	2,900	2,820	80 U†
Total variable costs	$0.80	$7,650	$7,520	$130 U†

* 9,400 units × $0.40 = $3,760. Other budget allowances are computed in the same way.
† These cost variances are usable in evaluating cost control, since they have been derived by comparing actual costs and budgeted costs at the *same* level of activity.

data at the bottom of the report tell how well costs were controlled for the 9,400 units that were actually produced.

Notice that all cost variances are *unfavorable,* as contrasted to the *favorable* cost variances on the performance report prepared earlier under the static budget approach. The reason for the change in variances is that by means of the flexible budget approach we are able to compare budgeted and actual costs at *the same activity level* (9,400 units produced), rather than being forced to compare budgeted costs at one activity level against actual costs at a different activity level. Herein lies the strength and dynamic nature of the flexible budget approach. By simply applying the cost formulas, it is possible to develop a budget *at any time* for *any* activity level within the relevant range. Thus, even if actual activity results in some odd figure that does not appear in the flexible budget, such as the 9,400 units above, budgeted costs can still be prepared to compare against actual costs. One simply develops a budget at the 9,400-unit level, as we have done, by using the cost formulas contained in the flexible budget. The result shows up in more usable variances.

The measure of activity—a critical choice

In the Rocco Company example, we chose to use units of production as the activity base for developing a flexible budget. Rather than units of production, we could have used some other base such as direct labor-hours or machine-hours. What is "best" in terms of an activity base will vary from firm to firm. At least three factors should be considered in the activity base decision:

1. The existence of a causal relationship between the activity base and overhead costs.
2. The avoidance of dollars in the activity base itself.
3. The selection of an activity base that is simple and easily understood.

Causal relationship There should be a direct causal relationship between the activity base and a company's variable overhead costs. That is, the variable overhead costs should vary as a result of changes in the activity base. In a machine shop, for example, one would expect power usage and other variable overhead costs to vary in relationship to the number of machine-hours worked. Machine-hours would therefore be the proper base to use in the flexible budget.

Other common activity bases include direct labor-hours, miles driven by salespersons, contacts made by salespersons, number of invoices processed, number of occupied beds in a hospital, and number of X rays given. Any one of these could be used as the base for preparing a flexible budget in the proper situation.

Do not use dollars Whenever possible, the activity base should be expressed in units rather than in dollars. If dollars are used, they should be standard dollars rather than actual dollars.

The problem with dollars is that they are subject to price-level changes, which can cause a distortion in the activity base if it is expressed in dollar terms. A similar problem arises when wage-rate changes take place if direct labor cost is being used as the activity base in a flexible budget. The change in wage rates will cause the activity base to change, even though a proportionate change may not take place in the overhead costs themselves. These types of fluctuations generally make dollars difficult to work with, and argue strongly for units rather than dollars in the activity base. The use of *standard* dollar costs rather than *actual* dollar costs overcomes the problem to some degree, but standard costs still have to be adjusted from time to time as changes in actual costs take place. On the other hand, *units* as a measure of activity (beds, hours, miles, and so on) are subject to few distorting influences and are less likely to cause problems in preparing and using a flexible budget.

Keep the base simple   The activity base should be simple and easily understood. A base that is not easily understood by the manager who works with it day by day will probably result in confusion and misunderstanding rather than serve as a positive means of cost control.

THE OVERHEAD PERFORMANCE REPORT—A CLOSER LOOK

A special problem arises in preparing overhead performance reports when the flexible budget is based on *hours* of activity (such as direct labor-hours) rather than on units of product. The problem relates to what hour base to use in constructing budget allowances on the performance report.

The problem of budget allowances

The nature of the problem can best be seen through a specific example. Assume that Donner Company is budgeting its activities for the month of June. The flexible budget that has been prepared is shown in Exhibit 10–5.

As shown in Exhibit 10–5, the company uses machine-hours as an activity base in its flexible budget and has budgeted to operate at an activity level

EXHIBIT 10–5

DONNER COMPANY
Flexible Budget

Budgeted machine-hours.   5,000

Overhead costs	Cost formula (per hour)	Machine-hours			
		3,000	4,000	5,000	6,000
Variable costs:					
Indirect labor	$0.80	$2,400	$3,200	$4,000	$4,800
Lubricants	0.30	900	1,200	1,500	1,800
Power	0.40	1,200	1,600	2,000	2,400
Total variable costs	$1.50	$4,500	$6,000	$7,500	$9,000

of 5,000 machine-hours during the month. Let us assume that two machine-hours are required to produce one unit of output. Under this assumption, budgeted production for the month is 2,500 units (5,000 budgeted machine-hours ÷ 2 hours per unit = 2,500 units). After the month is over, suppose the company finds that actual production for the month was 2,000 units and that it required 4,200 hours of machine time to produce these units. A summary of actual activity and costs for the month follows:

Number of machine-hours worked   4,200
Number of units produced   2,000

	Actual costs incurred
Indirect labor	$3,600
Lubricants	1,100
Power	2,300
Total actual costs	$7,000

In preparing a performance report for the month, what hour base should Donner Company use in computing budget allowances to compare against actual results? There are two possibilities. The company could use:

1. The 4,200 hours *actually worked* during the month.
2. The 4,000 hours that *should have been worked* during the month to produce 2,000 units of output (since it should take two hours to produce one unit).

Which base the company chooses will depend on how much detailed variance information it wants. As we learned in the preceding chapter, variable overhead can be analyzed in terms of a *spending* variance and an *efficiency* variance. The two bases provide different variance output.

Spending variance alone

If Donner Company chooses alternative 1 and bases its performance report on the 4,200 hours actually worked during the period, then the performance report will show only a spending variance for overhead. A performance report prepared in this way is shown in Exhibit 10–6.

The formula behind the spending variance was introduced in the preceding chapter. For review, that formula is:

$$(AH \times AR) - (AH \times SR) = \text{Variable overhead spending variance}$$

Or, in factored form:

$$AH(AR - SR) = \text{Variable overhead spending variance}$$

The report in Exhibit 10–6 is prepared around the first, or unfactored, format.

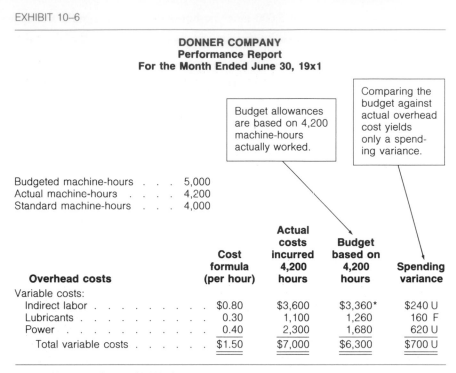

DONNER COMPANY
Performance Report
For the Month Ended June 30, 19x1

Budget allowances are based on 4,200 machine-hours actually worked.

Comparing the budget against actual overhead cost yields only a spending variance.

Budgeted machine-hours . . . 5,000
Actual machine-hours 4,200
Standard machine-hours . . . 4,000

Overhead costs	Cost formula (per hour)	Actual costs incurred 4,200 hours	Budget based on 4,200 hours	Spending variance
Variable costs:				
Indirect labor	$0.80	$3,600	$3,360*	$240 U
Lubricants	0.30	1,100	1,260	160 F
Power	0.40	2,300	1,680	620 U
Total variable costs	$1.50	$7,000	$6,300	$700 U

* 4,200 hours × $0.80 = $3,360. Other budget allowances are computed in the same way.

Interpreting the spending variance The overhead spending variance is affected by two things. First, a spending variance may occur simply because of price increases over what is shown in the flexible budget. For Donner Company, this means that prices paid for overhead items may have gone up during the month, resulting in unfavorable spending variances. This portion of the overhead spending variance is just like the price variance for raw materials.

Second, the overhead spending variance is affected by waste or excessive usage of overhead materials. A first reaction is to say that waste or excessive usage of materials ought to show up as part of the efficiency variance. But this isn't true so far as overhead is concerned. Waste or excessive usage will show up as part of the spending variance. The reason is that the Manufacturing Overhead account is charged with *all* overhead costs incurred during a period, including those costs that arise as a result of waste. Since the spending variance represents any difference between the standard rate per hour and the actual costs incurred, waste will automatically show up as part of this variance, along with any excessive prices paid for variable overhead items.

In sum, the overhead spending variance contains both price and quantity (waste) elements. These two elements could be broken out and shown separately on the performance report, but this is rarely done in actual practice.

Usefulness of the spending variance   Most firms consider the overhead spending variance to be highly useful. Generally, the price element in this variance will be small, so the variance permits a focusing of attention on that thing over which the supervisor probably has the greatest control—usage of overhead in production. In many cases, firms will limit their overhead analysis to the spending variance alone, feeling that the information it yields is sufficient for overhead cost control.

Both spending and efficiency variances

If Donner Company wants both a spending and an efficiency variance for overhead, then it should compute budget allowances for *both* 4,000 machine-hour and 4,200 machine-hour levels of activity. The 4,000 machine-hours would be the *standard hours allowed* for the month's production. As defined in the preceding chapter, standard hours represent the time that should have been taken to complete the period's output:

2,000 units × 2 standard hours per unit = 4,000 standard hours

A performance report prepared in this way is shown in Exhibit 10–7.

EXHIBIT 10–7

DONNER COMPANY
Performance Report
For the Month Ended June 30, 19x1

Budget allowances are based on 4,000 machine-hours—the time it *should have taken* to produce 2,000 units of output—as well as on the 4,200 *actual* machine-hours worked.

This approach yields both a spending and an efficiency variance.

Budgeted machine-hours   5,000
Actual machine-hours   4,200
Standard machine-hours   4,000

Overhead costs	Cost formula (per hour)	(1) Actual costs incurred 4,200 hours	(2) Budget based on 4,200 hours	(3) Budget based on 4,000 hours	Total variance (1) − (3)	Breakdown of the total variance — Spending variance (1) − (2)	Breakdown of the total variance — Efficiency variance (2) − (3)
Variable costs:							
Indirect labor	$0.80	$3,600	$3,360*	$3,200	$ 400 U	$240 U	$160 U
Lubricants	0.30	1,100	1,260	1,200	100 F	160 F	60 U
Power	0.40	2,300	1,680	1,600	700 U	620 U	80 U
Total variable costs	$1.50	$7,000	$6,300	$6,000	$1,000 U	$700 U	$300 U

* 4,200 hours × $0.80 = $3,360. Other budget allowances are computed in the same way.

Notice from the exhibit that the spending variance is the same as the spending variance shown in Exhibit 10–6. The performance report in Exhibit 10–7 has simply been expanded to include an efficiency variance as well. Together, the spending and efficiency variances make up the total variance, as explained in the preceding chapter.

Interpreting the efficiency variance The term *overhead efficiency variance* is a misnomer, since this variance has nothing to do with efficiency in the use of overhead. What the variance really measures is how efficiently the *base* underlying the flexible budget is being utilized in production. Recall from the preceding chapter that the variable overhead efficiency variance is a function of the difference between the actual hours utilized in production and the hours that should have been taken to produce the period's output:

$$(AH \times SR) - (SH \times SR) = \text{Variable overhead efficiency variance}$$

Or, in factored form:

$$SR(AH - SH) = \text{Variable overhead efficiency variance}$$

If more hours are worked than are allowed at standard, then the overhead efficiency variance will be unfavorable to reflect this inefficiency. As a practical matter, however, the inefficiency is not in the use of overhead *but rather in the use of the base itself.*

This point can be illustrated by looking again at Exhibit 10–7. Two hundred more machine-hours were used during the period than should have been used to produce the period's output. Each of these hours required the incurrence of $1.50 of variable overhead cost, resulting in an unfavorable variance of $300 (200 hours $\times$ $1.50 = $300). Although this $300 variance is called an overhead efficiency variance, it could better be called a machine-hours efficiency variance, since it measures the efficiency of utilization of machine time. However, the term *overhead efficiency variance* is so firmly ingrained in day-to-day use that a change is unlikely. Even so, the user must be careful to interpret the variance with a clear understanding of what it really measures.

Control of the efficiency variance Who is responsible for control of the overhead efficiency variance? Since the variance really measures efficiency in the utilization of the base underlying the flexible budget, whoever is responsible for control of this base is responsible for control of the variance. If the base is direct labor-hours, then the supervisor responsible for the use of labor time will be chargeable for any overhead efficiency variance.

FIXED COSTS AND THE FLEXIBLE BUDGET

Should the flexible budget contain fixed costs as well as variable costs? The term *flexible budget* implies variable costs only. As a practical matter, however, most firms include fixed overhead costs in the budget as well.

Exhibit 10–8 illustrates the flexible budget of Donner Company, which has been expanded to include the company's fixed overhead costs as well

EXHIBIT 10–8

DONNER COMPANY
Flexible Budget

Budgeted machine-hours 5,000

Overhead costs	Cost formula (per hour)	Machine-hours			
		3,000	4,000	5,000	6,000
Variable costs:					
Indirect labor.	$0.80	$ 2,400	$ 3,200	$ 4,000	$ 4,800
Lubricants.	0.30	900	1,200	1,500	1,800
Power .	0.40	1,200	1,600	2,000	2,400
Total variable costs.	$1.50	4,500	6,000	7,500	9,000
Fixed costs:					
Depreciation .		10,000	10,000	10,000	10,000
Supervisory salaries		16,000	16,000	16,000	16,000
Insurance .		4,000	4,000	4,000	4,000
Total fixed costs.		30,000	30,000	30,000	30,000
Total overhead costs.		$34,500	$36,000	$37,500	$39,000

as its variable overhead costs. Actually, the fixed portion of the budget is a *static budget* in that the amounts remain unchanged throughout the relevant range.

Fixed costs are often included in the flexible budget for at least two reasons. First, to the extent that a fixed cost is controllable by a manager, it should be included in the evaluation of his or her performance. Such costs should be placed on the manager's performance report, along with the variable costs for which he or she is responsible. And second, fixed costs are needed in the flexible budget for product costing purposes. Recall from Chapter 3 that overhead costs are added to units of product by means of the predetermined overhead rate. *The flexible budget provides the manager with the information needed to compute this rate.* In the remainder of this chapter, we discuss the use of the flexible budget for this purpose; in the process, we also demonstrate the preparation and use of fixed overhead variances.

FIXED OVERHEAD ANALYSIS

The analysis of fixed overhead differs considerably from the analysis of variable overhead, simply because of the difference in the nature of the costs involved. To provide a background for our discussion, we will first review briefly the need for, and computation of, predetermined overhead rates. This review will be helpful since the predetermined overhead rate plays a role in fixed overhead analysis. We will then show how fixed overhead variances are computed and make certain observations as to their usefulness to the manager.

Flexible budgets and overhead rates

Fixed costs come in large indivisible pieces that by definition do not change with changes in the level of activity. As we learned in Chapter 3, this creates a problem in product costing, since a given level of fixed overhead cost spread over a small number of units will result in a higher cost per unit than if the same amount of cost is spread over a large number of units. Consider the data in the table below:

Month	(1) Fixed overhead cost	(2) Number of units produced	Unit cost (1) ÷ (2)
January	$6,000	1,000	$6.00
February	6,000	1,500	4.00
March	6,000	800	7.50

Notice that the large number of units produced in February results in a low unit cost ($4), whereas the small number of units produced in March results in a high unit cost ($7.50). This problem arises only in connection with the fixed portion of overhead, since by definition the variable portion of overhead remains constant on a per unit basis, rising and falling in total proportionately with changes in the activity level. For product costing purposes, managers need to stabilize the fixed portion of unit cost so that a single unit cost figure can be used throughout the year without regard to month-by-month changes in activity levels. As we learned in Chapter 3, this stability can be accomplished through use of the predetermined overhead rate.

Denominator activity   The formula that we used in Chapter 3 to compute the predetermined overhead rate is given below, with one added feature. We have titled the estimated activity portion of the formula as being the **denominator activity**:

$$\frac{\text{Estimated total manufacturing overhead costs}}{\substack{\text{Estimated direct labor-hours or machine-hours} \\ \text{(denominator activity)}}} = \substack{\text{Predetermined} \\ \text{overhead rate}}$$

Recall from our discussion in Chapter 3 that once an estimated activity level (denominator activity) has been chosen, it remains unchanged throughout the year, even if actual activity later proves the estimate (denominator) to be somewhat in error. The reason for not changing the denominator, of course, is to maintain stability in the amount of overhead applied to each unit of product regardless of when it is produced during the year.

Computing the overhead rate   When we discussed predetermined overhead rates in Chapter 3, we did so without elaboration as to the source of the estimated data going into the formula. These data are normally derived from the flexible budget, with the denominator activity being the budgeted activity level for the forthcoming period, as shown in the budget. To illustrate, turn back to the flexible budget for Donner Company contained in Exhibit 10–8. Notice that the budgeted activity level for the forthcoming period is 5,000 machine-hours. As explained, *this becomes the denominator activity in the formula,* with the overhead cost (variable and fixed) at this activity level becoming the estimated overhead cost in the formula ($37,500 from Exhibit 10–8). In sum, the predetermined overhead rate for Donner Company will be:

$$\frac{\$37,500}{5,000 \text{ MH}} = \$7.50 \text{ per machine-hour}$$

Or, the company can break its predetermined overhead rate down into variable and fixed elements rather than using a single combined figure:

$$\text{Variable element } \frac{\$7,500}{5,000 \text{ MH}} = \$1.50 \text{ per machine-hour}$$

$$\text{Fixed element } \frac{\$30,000}{5,000 \text{ MH}} = \$6 \text{ per machine-hour}$$

For every standard machine-hour of operation, work in process will be charged with $7.50 of overhead, of which $1.50 will be variable overhead and $6 will be fixed overhead. If a unit of product takes two machine-hours to complete, then its cost will include $3 variable overhead and $12 fixed overhead, as shown on the standard cost card below:

Standard Cost Card—per Unit	
Direct materials (assumed)	$ 9.40
Direct labor (assumed)	10.60
Variable overhead (2 hours at $1.50)	3.00
Fixed overhead (2 hours at $6)	12.00
Total standard cost per unit	$35.00

In sum, the flexible budget provides the manager with both the overhead cost figure and the denominator activity figure needed in computing the predetermined overhead rate; thus, the flexible budget plays a key role in determining the amount of fixed and variable overhead cost that will be charged to units of product.

Overhead application in a standard cost system

To understand the fixed overhead variances, it is necessary first to understand how overhead is applied to work in process in a standard cost system. In Chapter 3, recall that we applied overhead to work in process on a basis of actual hours of activity (multiplied by the predetermined overhead rate). This procedure was correct, since at the time we were dealing with an actual

EXHIBIT 10–9

Applied overhead costs: Actual cost system versus standard cost system

Actual cost system		Standard cost system	
Manufacturing Overhead		**Manufacturing Overhead**	
Actual overhead costs incurred.	Applied overhead costs: Actual hours × Predetermined overhead rate.	Actual overhead costs incurred.	Applied overhead costs: Standard hours allowed for output × Predetermined overhead rate.
Under- or overapplied overhead		Under- or overapplied overhead	

cost system. However, we are now dealing with a standard cost system; and when standards are in operation, overhead is applied to work in process on a basis of the *standard hours allowed for the output of the period* rather than on a basis of the actual number of hours worked. This point is illustrated in Exhibit 10–9.

The reason for using standard hours to apply overhead to production in a standard cost system is to assure that every unit of product moving along the production line bears the same amount of overhead cost, regardless of any time variations that may be involved in its manufacture.

The fixed overhead variances

To illustrate the computation of fixed overhead variances, we will refer again to the flexible budget data for Donner Company contained in Exhibit 10–8.

Denominator activity in machine-hours	5,000
Budgeted fixed overhead costs	$30,000
Fixed portion of the predetermined overhead rate (computed earlier)	$6

Let us assume that the following actual operating results were recorded for the period:

Actual machine-hours	4,200
Standard machine-hours allowed*	4,000
Actual fixed overhead costs:	
Depreciation	$10,000
Supervisory salaries	17,200
Insurance	3,800
Total actual costs	$31,000

* For the actual production of the period.

From these data, two variances can be computed for fixed overhead—a *budget variance* and a *volume variance*. The variances are shown in Exhibit 10–10.

Notice from the exhibit that overhead has been applied to work in process on a basis of 4,000 standard hours allowed for the output of the period rather than on a basis of 4,200 actual hours worked. As stated earlier, this keeps unit costs from being affected by any efficiency variations.

EXHIBIT 10–10
Computation of the fixed overhead variances

Actual fixed overhead cost	Flexible budget fixed overhead cost	Fixed overhead cost applied to work in process
$31,000	$30,000*	4,000 standard hours × $6 = $24,000

Budget variance, $1,000 U	Volume variance, $6,000 U

Total variance, $7,000 U

* As originally budgeted (see Exhibit 10–8). This figure can also be expressed as: 5,000 denominator hours × $6 = $30,000.

The budget variance—a closer look

As illustrated in Exhibit 10–10, the **budget variance** represents the difference between actual fixed overhead costs incurred during the period and budgeted fixed overhead costs as contained in the flexible budget. The variance can also be presented in the following format:

Actual fixed overhead costs	$31,000
Budgeted fixed overhead costs (from the flexible budget in Exhibit 10–8)	30,000
Budget variance	$ 1,000 U

Although the budget variance is somewhat similar to the variable overhead spending variance, care must be exercised in how it is used. One must keep in mind that fixed costs are often beyond immediate managerial control. Therefore, rather than serving as a measure of managerial performance, in many cases the budget variance will be computed simply for information purposes in order to call management's attention to changes in price factors.

Fixed overhead costs and variances are often presented on the performance report, along with the variable overhead costs. To show how this is done, a performance report for Donner Company containing the fixed overhead

EXHIBIT 10–11
Fixed overhead costs on the performance report

DONNER COMPANY
Performance Report
For the Month Ended June 30, 19x1

Budgeted machine-hours 5,000
Actual machine-hours 4,200
Standard machine-hours allowed 4,000

Overhead costs	Cost formula	Actual costs 4,200 hours	Budget based on 4,200 hours	Spending or budget variance
Variable costs:				
Indirect labor	$0.80	$ 3,600	$ 3,360	$ 240 U
Lubricants	0.30	1,100	1,260	160 F
Power	0.40	2,300	1,680	620 U
Total variable costs	$1.50	7,000	6,300	700 U
Fixed costs:				
Depreciation		10,000	10,000	—
Supervisory salaries . . .		17,200	16,000	1,200 U
Insurance		3,800	4,000	200 F
Total fixed costs . . .		31,000	30,000	1,000 U
Total overhead costs . . .		$38,000	$36,300	$1,700 U

budget variance is found in Exhibit 10–11. (The variable overhead cost data in the exhibit are taken from Exhibit 10–6.)

The volume variance—a closer look

The **volume variance** is a measure of utilization of plant facilities. It is computed by comparing the denominator activity figure with the standard hours allowed for the output of the period and multiplying any difference by the fixed portion of the predetermined overhead rate:

$$\begin{array}{l}\text{Fixed portion of} \\ \quad\text{the predetermined} \\ \quad\text{overhead rate}\end{array} \times \left(\begin{array}{c}\text{Denominator} \\ \text{hours}\end{array} - \begin{array}{c}\text{Standard hours} \\ \text{allowed}\end{array}\right) = \begin{array}{c}\text{Volume} \\ \text{variance}\end{array}$$

Applying this formula to Donner Company, the volume variance would be:

$$\$6\ (5{,}000\ \text{MH} - 4{,}000\ \text{MH}) = \$6{,}000\ \text{unfavorable}$$

Note that this computation agrees with the volume variance as shown in Exhibit 10–10. At this point we should ask, "What caused a volume variance to arise in Donner Company, and what does the variance mean?" The cause of the variance can be explained as follows: If the company's activity level for the period had been 5,000 hours as planned, then work in process would have been charged with the full $30,000 in fixed costs contained in the flexible budget:

$$5,000 \text{ machine-hours} \times \$6 = \$30,000$$

But the activity level for the period (at standard) was only 4,000 hours, *so even though the full $30,000 in fixed costs would have been incurred, less than this amount would have been charged to work in process:*

$$4,000 \text{ machine-hours} \times \$6 = \$24,000$$

The difference between these two figures is the volume variance:

$$\$30,000 - \$24,000 = \$6,000$$

As stated earlier, the volume variance is a measure of utilization of available plant facilities. An unfavorable variance, as above, means that the company operated at an activity level *below* that planned for the period; a favorable variance would mean that the company operated at an activity level *greater* than that planned for the period. It is important to note that the volume variance does not measure over- or underspending. A company normally would incur the same dollar amount of fixed overhead cost regardless of whether the period's activity was above or below the planned (denominator) level. In short, the volume variance is an activity-related variance in that it is explainable only by activity and is controllable only through activity.

To summarize:

1. If the denominator activity and the standard hours allowed for the output of the period are the same, then there is no volume variance.
2. If the denominator activity is greater than the standard hours allowed for the output of the period, then the volume variance is unfavorable, signifying an underutilization of available facilities.
3. If the denominator activity is less than the standard hours allowed for the output of the period, then the volume variance is favorable, signifying an overutilization of available facilities.

Graphical analysis of fixed overhead variances

Some insights into the budget and volume variances can be gained through graphical analysis. The needed graph is presented in Exhibit 10–12.

As shown in the graph, fixed overhead cost is applied to work in process at the predetermined rate of $6 for each standard hour of activity. (The applied-cost line is the upward-sloping line on the graph.) Since a denominator level of 5,000 machine-hours was used in computing the $6 rate, the applied-cost line crosses the budgeted-cost line at exactly the 5,000 machine-hour point. Thus, if the denominator hours and the standard hours allowed for output are the same, there can be no volume variance, since the applied-cost line and the budgeted-cost line will exactly meet on the graph. It is only when the standard hours differ from the denominator hours that a volume variance can arise.

In the case at hand, the standard hours allowed for output (4,000 hours) are less than the denominator hours (5,000 hours); the result is an unfavorable

EXHIBIT 10–12

Graphical analysis of fixed overhead variances

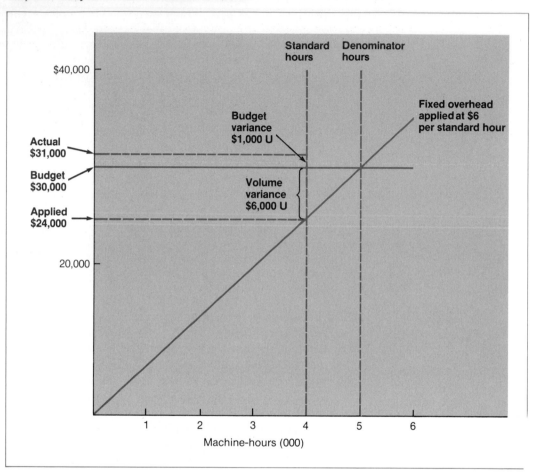

volume variance, since less cost was applied to production than was originally budgeted. If the tables had been reversed and the standard hours allowed for output had exceeded the denominator hours, then the volume variance on the graph would have been favorable.

Cautions in fixed overhead analysis

There can be no volume variance for variable overhead, since applied costs and budgeted costs are both dependent on activity and thus will always be moving together. The reason we get a volume variance for fixed overhead is that the incurrence of the fixed costs does not depend on activity; yet when applying the costs to work in process, we do so *as if* the costs were variable and depended on activity. This point can be seen from the graph in Exhibit 10–12. Notice from the graph that the fixed overhead costs are applied to work in process at a rate of $6 per hour *as if* they were indeed variable. Treating these costs as if they were variable is necessary for product costing purposes, but there are some real dangers here. The manager can easily become misled and start thinking of the fixed costs as if they were *in fact* variable.

The manager must keep clearly in mind that fixed overhead costs come in large, indivisible pieces. Any breakdown of such costs, though necessary for product costing purposes, is artificial in nature and has no significance in matters relating either to actual cost behavior or to cost control. This is why the volume variance, which arises as a result of treating fixed costs as if they were variable, is not a controllable variance from a spending point of view. The fixed overhead rate used to compute the variance is simply a derived figure needed for product costing purposes, but it has no significance in terms of cost control.

Because of these factors, some companies present the volume variance in physical units (hours) rather than in dollars. These companies feel that stating the variance in physical units gives management a clearer signal as to the cause of the variance and how it can be controlled.

PRESENTATION OF VARIANCES ON THE INCOME STATEMENT

To complete our discussion of standard costs and variance analysis, we will show how variances can be presented on the income statement. Even though the variances may have already been presented on individual managers' performance reports and fully analyzed as to causes, many companies find it helpful to present them on the income statement as well, so that top management can see the cumulative effect on profits.

To illustrate, assume that Donner Company had the following variances for the most recent month. (The variances for materials and labor are assumed; the variances for variable and fixed overhead are the ones computed for Donner Company earlier in the chapter.)

Direct materials price variance	$1,100 F
Direct materials quantity variance	400 U
Direct labor rate variance	1,200 U
Direct labor efficiency variance	500 F
Variable overhead spending variance (p. 408)	700 U
Variable overhead efficiency variance (p. 408)	300 U
Fixed overhead budget variance (p. 413)	1,000 U
Fixed overhead volume variance (p. 413)	6,000 U
Total variances	$8,000 U

An income statement for Donner Company containing the total of these variances is shown in Exhibit 10–13. Notice that the actual cost of goods sold on the statement exceeds the budgeted amount by $8,000, which agrees with the total of the variances summarized above. This type of presentation provides management with a clear picture of the impact of the variances

EXHIBIT 10–13
Variances on the income statement

DONNER COMPANY
Income Statement
For the Month Ended June 30, 19x1

2,000 units

	Budgeted	Actual	Variance
Sales ($50 per unit)	$100,000	$100,000	—
Less cost of goods sold (standard cost, $35 per unit*)	70,000	78,000	$ 8,000
Gross margin	30,000	22,000	(8,000)
Less operating expenses:			
Selling expense.	14,000	14,000	—
Administrative expense	6,000	6,000	—
Total operating expenses.	20,000	20,000	—
Net income	$ 10,000	$ 2,000	$(8,000)

* Taken from Donner Company's standard cost card found on page 411.

on profits—a picture that could not be obtained by looking at performance reports alone. In the case at hand, Donner Company's profits have been dramatically reduced by the variances that developed during the period.

We should note that separate presentation of variances on the income statement is generally done only on those income statements that are prepared for management's own internal use. Income statements prepared for external use (for stockholders and others) typically show only actual cost figures.

SUMMARY PROBLEM ON OVERHEAD ANALYSIS

(This problem provides a comprehensive review of all parts of Chapter 10, including the computation of under- or overapplied overhead and its breakdown into the various overhead variances.) A flexible budget for Aspen Company is given below:

Overhead costs	Cost formula (per DLH)	Direct labor-hours		
		4,000	6,000	8,000
Variable costs:				
Supplies	$0.20	$ 800	$ 1,200	$ 1,600
Indirect labor	0.30	1,200	1,800	2,400
Total variable costs	$0.50	2,000	3,000	4,000
Fixed costs:				
Depreciation.		4,000	4,000	4,000
Supervision		5,000	5,000	5,000
Total fixed costs		9,000	9,000	9,000
Total overhead costs		$11,000	$12,000	$13,000

Five hours of labor time are required per unit of product. The company has set denominator activity for the coming period at 6,000 hours (or 1,200 units). The computation of the predetermined overhead rate would be:

$$\text{Total } \frac{\$12,000}{6,000 \text{ DLH}} = \$2 \text{ per DLH}$$

$$\text{Variable element } \frac{\$3,000}{6,000 \text{ DLH}} = \$0.50 \text{ per DLH}$$

$$\text{Fixed element } \frac{\$9,000}{6,000 \text{ DLH}} = \$1.50 \text{ per DLH}$$

Assume the following actual results for the period:

Number of units produced	1,300
Actual direct labor-hours	6,800
Standard direct labor-hours allowed*	6,500
Actual variable overhead cost	$ 4,200
Actual fixed overhead cost.	9,400
Overhead cost applied to production	
(6,500 standard hours × $2)	13,000

* For 1,300 units of product.

Therefore, the company's manufacturing overhead account would appear as follows at the end of the period:

Manufacturing Overhead

Actual overhead costs	13,600*	13,000	Overhead costs applied
Underapplied overhead		600	

* $4,200 variable + $9,400 fixed = $13,600.

Required: Analyze the $600 underapplied overhead in terms of:

1. A variable overhead spending variance.
2. A variable overhead efficiency variance.
3. A fixed overhead budget variance.
4. A fixed overhead volume variance.

Variable overhead variances

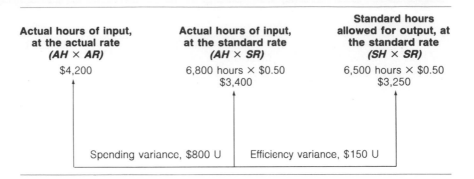

These same variances in the alternative format would be:

Variable overhead spending variance:

Actual variable overhead cost	$4,200
Actual inputs at the standard rate:	
6,800 hours × $0.50	3,400
Spending variance	$ 800 U

Variable overhead efficiency variance:

$$SR(AH - SH) = \text{Efficiency variance}$$

$$\$0.50(6{,}800 \text{ hours} - 6{,}500 \text{ hours}) = \$150 \text{ U}$$

Fixed overhead variances

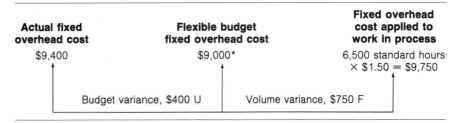

* Can be expressed as: 6,000 denominator hours × $1.50 = $9,000.

These same variances in the alternative format would be:

Fixed overhead budget variance:

$$\begin{array}{lr}
\text{Actual fixed overhead} & \$9,400 \\
\text{Budgeted fixed overhead} & 9,000 \\
\text{Budget variance} & \$\ \ 400\ U
\end{array}$$

Fixed overhead volume variance:

$$\begin{array}{c}
\text{Fixed portion of} \\
\text{the predetermined} \\
\text{overhead rate}
\end{array} \times \left(\begin{array}{c} \text{Denominator} \\ \text{hours} \end{array} - \begin{array}{c} \text{Standard} \\ \text{hours} \end{array} \right) = \begin{array}{c} \text{Volume} \\ \text{variance} \end{array}$$

$$\$1.50\ (6,000 \text{ hours} - 6,500 \text{ hours}) = \$750\ F$$

Summary of variances

A summary of the four overhead variances is given below:

$$\begin{array}{lr}
\text{Variable overhead:} & \\
\quad \text{Spending variance} & \$800\ U \\
\quad \text{Efficiency variance} & 150\ U \\
\text{Fixed overhead:} & \\
\quad \text{Budget variance} & 400\ U \\
\quad \text{Volume variance} & 750\ F \\
\text{Underapplied overhead} & \$600
\end{array}$$

Notice that the $600 summary variance figure agrees with the underapplied balance in the company's Manufacturing Overhead account. This agreement stands as proof of the accuracy of our variance analysis. *Each period* the under- or overapplied overhead balance should be analyzed as we have done above. These variances will help the manager to see where his or her time and the time of the subordinates should be directed for better control of costs and operations.

KEY TERMS FOR REVIEW

Budget variance A measure of the difference between budgeted fixed overhead costs (as contained in the flexible budget) and the actual fixed overhead costs incurred during a period.

Denominator activity The estimated activity figure used to compute the predetermined overhead rate.

Flexible budget A budget that is designed to cover a range of activity and that can be used to develop budgeted costs at any point within that range to compare against actual costs incurred.

Static budget A budget designed to cover only one level of activity and in which actual costs are always compared against budgeted costs at this one activity level.

Volume variance A measure of the difference between the amount of fixed overhead cost contained in the flexible budget and the amount of fixed overhead cost applied to work in process during a period.

QUESTIONS

10–1. What is a static budget?

10–2. What is a flexible budget, and how does it differ from a static budget? What is the main deficiency of the static budget?

10–3. What are the two prime responsibilities of the production manager? How do these two responsibilities differ?

10–4. Name three criteria that should be considered in choosing an activity base on which to construct a flexible budget.

10–5. In comparing budgeted data with actual data in a performance report for variable manufacturing overhead, what variance(s) will be produced if the budgeted data are based on actual hours worked? On both actual hours worked and standard hours allowed?

10–6. What is meant by the term *standard hours allowed?*

10–7. How does the variable manufacturing overhead spending variance differ from the materials price variance?

10–8. Why is the term *overhead efficiency variance* a misnomer?

10–9. "Fixed costs have no place in a flexible budget." Discuss.

10–10. In what way is the flexible budget involved in product costing?

10–11. What costing problem is created by the fact that fixed overhead costs come in large, indivisible chunks?

10–12. What is meant by the term *denominator level of activity?*

10–13. Why do we apply overhead to work in process on a basis of standard hours allowed in Chapter 10, when we applied it on a basis of actual hours in Chapter 3? What is the difference in costing systems between the two chapters?

10–14. In a standard cost system, what two variances can be computed for fixed overhead?

10–15. What does the fixed overhead budget variance measure? Is the variance controllable by management? Explain.

10–16. Under what circumstances would you expect the volume variance to be favorable? Unfavorable? Does the variance measure deviations in spending for fixed overhead items? Explain.

10–17. How might the volume variance be measured, other than in dollars?

10–18. What dangers are there in expressing fixed costs on a per unit basis?

10–19. In Chapter 3, you became acquainted with the concept of under- or overapplied overhead. What four variances can be computed from the under- or overapplied overhead total?

10–20. If factory overhead is overapplied for the month of August, would you expect the total of the overhead variances to be favorable or unfavorable? Why?

EXERCISES

E10–1. An incomplete flexible budget is given below:

Overhead costs	Cost formula	Direct labor-hours			
		6,000	8,000	10,000	12,000
Variable costs:					
Indirect materials.			$ 6,000		
Maintenance			4,800		
Utilities			1,200		
Total variable costs					
Fixed costs:					
Rent			10,000		
Supervisory salaries			20,000		
Insurance			8,000		
Total fixed costs					
Total overhead costs					

Required: Provide the missing information in the budget.

E10–2. The cost formulas for Swan Company's overhead costs are given below. The costs cover a range of 8,000 to 10,000 direct labor-hours.

Cost	Cost formula
Supplies.	$0.20 per direct labor-hour
Indirect labor	10,000 plus $0.25 per direct labor-hour
Utilities	0.15 per direct labor-hour
Maintenance	7,000 plus $0.10 per direct labor-hour
Depreciation	8,000

Required: Prepare a flexible budget in increments of 1,000 direct labor-hours. Include the fixed costs in your flexible budget.

E10–3. Murray Company's flexible budget is given below:

Overhead costs	Cost formula (per unit)	Number of units		
		10,000	12,000	14,000
Supplies	$0.20	$ 2,000	$ 2,400	$ 2,800
Maintenance.	0.80	8,000	9,600	11,200
Utilities.	0.10	1,000	1,200	1,400
Rework time.	0.40	4,000	4,800	5,600
Total overhead costs . .	$1.50	$15,000	$18,000	$21,000

During a recent period, the company produced 11,500 units. The variable overhead costs incurred were:

Supplies	$2,400
Maintenance.	8,000
Utilities.	1,100
Rework time.	5,300

The production budgeted for the period had been 12,000 units.

Required: 1. Prepare a performance report for the period. Indicate whether variances are favorable (F) or unfavorable (U).

2. Discuss the significance of the variances. Might some variances be the result of others? Explain.

E10–4. Operating at a normal level of 24,000 direct labor-hours, Trone Company produces 8,000 units of product. The direct labor wage rate is $6.30 per hour. Two pounds of raw materials go into each unit of product at a cost of $4.20 per pound. A flexible budget is used to plan and control overhead costs:

Flexible Budget Data

Overhead costs	Cost formula	Direct labor-hours 20,000	22,000	24,000
Variable costs.	$1.60	$ 32,000	$ 35,200	$ 38,400
Fixed costs		84,000	84,000	84,000
Total overhead costs		$116,000	$119,200	$122,400

Required: 1. Using 24,000 direct labor-hours as the denominator activity, compute the predetermined overhead rate and break it down into fixed and variable elements.

2. Complete the standard cost card below for one unit of product:

Direct materials, 2 pounds at $4.20 . . . . $8.40
Direct labor,   ? . . . . ?
Variable overhead, ? . . . . ?
Fixed overhead,   ? . . . . ?
    Total standard cost per unit . . . . $?

E10–5. Kohler Company's flexible budget (in condensed form) is given below:

Overhead costs	Cost formula (per direct labor-hour)	Direct labor-hours 12,000	15,000	18,000
Variable costs.	$1.80	$21,600	$27,000	$32,400
Fixed costs		60,000	60,000	60,000
Total overhead costs		$81,600	$87,000	$92,400

The following information is available for 19x8:

a. For 19x8, the company chose 15,000 direct labor-hours as the denominator level of activity for computing the predetermined overhead rate.
b. During 19x8, the company produced 9,500 units of product and worked 14,000 actual hours. The standard direct labor time per unit is 1.5 hours.
c. Actual overhead costs incurred during 19x8 were: variable overhead, $26,000; and fixed overhead, $60,450.

Required: 1. Compute the predetermined overhead rate used during 19x8. Divide it into fixed and variable elements.
2. Compute the standard hours allowed for the output of 19x8.
3. Compute the fixed overhead budget and volume variances for 19x8.

E10–6. Selected operating information on four different companies for the year 19x6 is given below:

	A	B	C	D
Full capacity direct labor-hours.	10,000	18,000	20,000	15,000
Budgeted direct labor-hours*	9,000	17,000	20,000	14,000
Actual direct labor-hours worked	9,000	17,800	19,000	14,500
Standard direct labor-hours allowed for actual production	9,500	16,000	20,000	13,000

* Denominator activity.

Required: In each case, state whether the company would have:
1. No volume variance.
2. A favorable volume variance.
3. An unfavorable volume variance.

Also state in each case why you chose (1), (2), or (3).

E10–7. Selected information relating to the fixed overhead costs of Westwood Company for 19x7 is given below:

Activity:
Number of units produced 9,500
Standard hours allowed per unit 2
Denominator activity (direct labor-hours) 20,000

Costs:
Actual fixed overhead costs incurred $79,000
Budget variance . . . . 1,000 F

Overhead cost is applied to products on a basis of direct labor-hours.

Required: 1. What was the fixed portion of the predetermined overhead rate for 19x7?
2. What were the standard hours allowed for 19x7 production?
3. What was the volume variance for 19x7?

E10–8. Weller Company's flexible budget (in condensed form) is given below:

	Cost formula (per DLH)	Direct labor-hours		
Overhead costs		8,000	9,000	10,000
Variable costs.	$1.05	$ 8,400	$ 9,450	$10,500
Fixed costs		24,800	24,800	24,800
Total overhead costs		$33,200	$34,250	$35,300

The following information is available:

a. For 19x1, a denominator activity of 8,000 direct labor-hours was chosen to compute the predetermined overhead rate.
b. At the 8,000 standard direct labor-hours level of activity, the company should produce 3,200 units of product.
c. During 19x1, the company's actual operating results were:

Number of units produced. 3,500
Actual direct labor-hours 8,500
Actual variable overhead costs . . . . $ 9,860
Actual fixed overhead costs $25,100

Required: 1. Compute the predetermined overhead rate for 19x1, and break it down into variable and fixed cost elements.
  2. What were the standard hours allowed for the output of 19x1?
  3. Compute the variable overhead spending and efficiency variances and the fixed overhead budget and volume variances for 19x1.

E10–9.   The standard cost card for the single product manufactured by Prince Company is given below:

Standard Cost Card—per Unit	
Direct materials, 3.5 feet at $4	$14.00
Direct labor, 0.8 hours at $9	7.20
Variable overhead, 0.8 hours at $2.50	2.00
Fixed overhead, 0.8 hours at $6	4.80
Total standard cost per unit	$28.00

During 19x8, the company produced 10,000 units of product and worked 8,200 actual direct labor-hours. Overhead cost is applied to production on a basis of direct labor-hours. Selected data relating to the company's operations for the year are shown below:

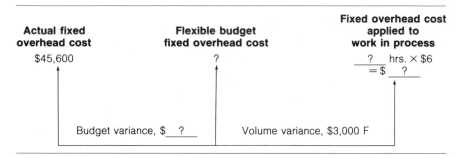

Required: 1. What were the standard hours allowed for 19x8 production?
  2. What was the amount of fixed overhead cost contained in the flexible budget for the year?
  3. What was the budget variance for the year?
  4. What denominator activity level did the company use in setting the predetermined overhead rate for the year?

PROBLEMS

P10–10.   **Materials, labor, and overhead variances.**   Dresser Company uses a standard cost system and sets predetermined overhead rates on a basis of direct labor-hours. The following data are taken from the company's flexible budget for 19x5:

Denominator activity (direct labor-hours)	9,000
Variable overhead cost	$34,200
Fixed overhead cost	63,000

A standard cost card showing the standard cost to produce one unit of the company's product is given below:

Direct materials, 4 pounds at $2.60	$10.40
Direct labor, 2 hours at $9.	18.00
Overhead, 120% of direct labor cost	21.60
Standard cost per unit	$50.00

During 19x5, the company produced 4,800 units of product and incurred the following costs:

Materials purchased, 30,000 pounds at $2.50	$75,000
Materials used in production (in pounds)	20,000
Direct labor cost incurred, 10,000 hours at $8.60	000,000
Variable overhead cost incurred	35,900
Fixed overhead cost incurred	64,800

Required:

1. Redo the standard cost card in a clearer, more usable format by detailing the variable and fixed overhead cost elements.
2. Prepare an analysis of the variances for materials and labor for the year.
3. Prepare an analysis of the variances for variable and fixed overhead for the year.
4. What effect, if any, does the choice of a denominator activity level have on unit costs? Is the volume variance a controllable variance from a spending point of view? Explain.

P10–11. **Overhead analysis.** High-Tech, Inc., produces a single product and uses a standard cost system to help in the control of costs. Overhead is applied to production on a basis of direct labor-hours. According to the company's flexible budget, the following overhead costs should be incurred at an activity level of 18,000 direct labor-hours (the denominator activity level chosen for 19x8):

Budgeted variable overhead costs	$ 31,500
Budgeted fixed overhead costs	72,000
Total overhead costs	$103,500

During 19x8, the following operating results were recorded:

Actual direct labor-hours worked	15,000
Standard direct labor-hours allowed	16,000
Actual variable overhead cost incurred	$26,500
Actual fixed overhead cost incurred	70,000

At the end of the year, the company's Manufacturing Overhead account contained the following data:

Manufacturing Overhead

Actual	96,500	92,000	Applied
	4,500		

Management would like to determine the cause of the $4,500 underapplied overhead before closing the amount to cost of goods sold.

Required:

1. Compute the predetermined overhead rate that would have been used during 19x8. Break it down into variable and fixed cost elements.

2. Show how the $92,000 "applied" figure in the Manufacturing Overhead account was computed.
3. Analyze the $4,500 underapplied overhead figure in terms of the variable overhead spending and efficiency variances and the fixed overhead budget and volume variances.
4. Explain the meaning of each variance that you computed in (3) above, and indicate how each variance is controlled.

P10–12. **Integration of materials, labor, and overhead variances.** "It certainly is nice to see that small variance on the income statement after all the trouble we've had lately in controlling manufacturing costs," said Linda White, vice president of Molina Company. "We need to congratulate everybody on a job well done." The income statement to which Ms. White was referring is shown below:

	20,000 Units		
	Budgeted	**Actual**	**Variance**
Sales	$1,200,000	$1,200,000	$ —
Less cost of goods sold (standard cost, $38 per unit)	760,000	762,250	2,250
Gross margin	440,000	437,750	(2,250)
Less operating expenses:			
Selling expenses	200,000	200,000	—
Administrative expenses	150,000	150,000	—
Total operating expenses	350,000	350,000	—
Net income	$ 90,000	$ 87,750	$(2,250)

The company produces and sells a single product. A standard cost card for the product follows:

Standard Cost Card—per Unit of Product

Direct materials, 4 yards at $3.50	$14
Direct labor, 1.5 hours at $8	12
Variable overhead, 1.5 hours at $2	3
Fixed overhead, 1.5 hours at $6	9
Standard cost per unit	$38

The following additional information is available for the year just completed:
a. The company manufactured and sold 20,000 units of product during the year.
b. A total of 78,000 yards of material were purchased during the year at a cost of $3.75 per yard. All of this material was used to manufacture the 20,000 units. There were no beginning or ending inventories for the year.
c. The company worked 32,500 direct labor-hours during the year at a cost of $7.80 per hour.
d. Overhead cost is applied to products on a basis of direct labor-hours. Data relating to overhead costs follow:

Denominator activity level (direct labor-hours)	25,000
Budgeted fixed overhead costs (from the flexible budget)	$150,000
Actual fixed overhead costs	148,000
Actual variable overhead costs	68,250

e. All variances are closed to cost of goods sold at the end of each year.

Required: 1. Compute the direct materials price and quantity variances for the year.
2. Compute the direct labor rate and efficiency variances for the year.
3. For overhead compute:
   a. The variable overhead spending and efficiency variances for the year.
   b. The fixed overhead budget and volume variances for the year.
4. Total the variances you have computed, and compare the net amount with the $2,250 variance on the income statement. Do you agree that everyone should be congratulated for a job well done? Explain.

P10–13. **Flexible budgets and overhead analysis.** The Rowe Company manufactures a variety of products in several departments. Budgeted costs for the company's finishing department have been set as follows for 19x2:

Variable costs:	
Direct materials	$ 600,000
Direct labor	450,000
Indirect labor	30,000
Utilities	50,000
Maintenance	20,000
Total variable costs	1,150,000
Fixed costs:	
Supervisory salaries	60,000
Insurance	5,000
Depreciation	190,000
Equipment rental	45,000
Total fixed costs	300,000
Total budgeted costs	$1,450,000
Budgeted direct labor-hours	?

After careful study, the company has determined that operating activity in the finishing department is best measured in direct labor hours. Direct labor cost is budgeted at $9 per hour. The cost formulas used to develop the budgeted costs above are valid over a relevant range of 40,000 to 60,000 direct labor-hours per year.

Required: 1. Prepare a flexible overhead budget in good form for the finishing department. Make your budget in increments of 10,000 hours. (The company does not include direct materials and direct labor costs in the flexible budget.)
2. Assume that the company computes predetermined overhead rates by department. Compute the rates, variable and fixed, that will be used by the finishing department during 19x2 to apply overhead costs to production.
3. Suppose that during 19x2 the following actual activity and costs are recorded in the finishing department:

Actual direct labor-hours worked	46,000
Standard direct labor-hours allowed	
for the output of the year	45,000
Actual variable overhead cost incurred	$ 89,700
Actual fixed overhead cost incurred	296,000

   a. A T-account for manufacturing overhead costs for 19x2 in the finishing department is given below. Determine the amount of applied overhead cost for the year, and compute the under- or overapplied overhead.

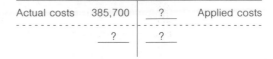

Manufacturing Overhead

Actual costs	385,700	?	Applied costs
		?	?

    b. Analyze the under- or overapplied overhead figure in terms of the variable overhead spending and efficiency variances and the fixed overhead budget and volume variances.

P10–14.   **Standard cost card and overhead analysis.** Wymont Company produces a single product and applies overhead to products on a basis of direct labor-hours. The company's condensed flexible budget is given below:

Overhead costs	Cost formula (per DLH)	Direct labor-hours 24,000	30,000	36,000
Variable costs	$2	$ 48,000	$ 60,000	$ 72,000
Fixed costs.		180,000	180,000	180,000
Total overhead costs.		$228,000	$240,000	$252,000

    The company's product requires 4 feet of direct material that has a standard cost of $3 per foot. The product requires 1.5 hours of direct labor time. The standard labor rate is $7 per hour.

    During 19x7, the company had planned to operate at a denominator activity level of 30,000 direct labor-hours and to produce 20,000 units of product. Actual activity and costs for the year were as follows:

Number of units produced	22,000
Actual direct labor-hours worked	35,000
Actual variable overhead cost incurred	$ 63,000
Actual fixed overhead cost incurred	181,000

Required: 1.   Compute the predetermined overhead rate that would have been used during 19x7. Break the rate down into variable and fixed elements.
    2.   Prepare a standard cost card for the company's product; show the details for all manufacturing costs on your standard cost card.
    3.   *a.*   Compute the standard hours allowed for 19x7 production.
          b.   Complete the following Manufacturing Overhead T-account for the year:

Manufacturing Overhead

?	?
?	?

    4.   Determine the reason for the under- or overapplied overhead from (3) above by computing the variable overhead spending and efficiency variances and the fixed overhead budget and volume variances.
    5.   Suppose the company had chosen 36,000 direct labor-hours as the denominator activity rather than 30,000 hours. State which, if any, of the variances computed in (4) would have changed, and explain how the variance(s) would have changed. No computations are necessary.

P10–15.   **Integration of materials, labor, and overhead variances.**   "Wow! Just look at the size of that variance," said John Baker, president of Marvel, Inc. "We've got to do something to get costs back under control." The variance to which Mr. Baker was referring is shown in the company's most recent income statement below:

	12,500 units		
	Budgeted	**Actual**	**Variance**
Sales	$1,000,000	$1,000,000	$ —
Less cost of goods sold (standard cost, $60 per unit)	750,000	795,000	45,000*
Gross margin.	250,000	205,000	(45,000)
Less operating expenses:			
Selling expenses.	120,000	120,000	—
Administrative expenses	70,000	70,000	—
Total operating expenses	190,000	190,000	—
Net income . . . :	$ 60,000	$ 15,000	$(45,000)

* Consists of the following variances:

Direct materials	$ 4,000 U
Direct labor	5,000 F
Manufacturing overhead	46,000 U
Total variance	$45,000 U

The company produces and sells a single product. A standard cost card for the product follows:

Standard Cost Card—per Unit of Product

Direct materials: 3 pounds at $4 per pound	$12
Direct labor: 2.5 hours at $10 per hour	25
Variable manufacturing overhead: 2.5 hours at $2 per hour	5
Fixed manufacturing overhead: 2.5 hours at $7.20 per hour*	18
Total standard cost per unit	$60

* Based on a denominator activity of 37,500 hours.

The following additional information is available for the period:

a.   The company purchased 40,000 pounds of materials during the period, at a cost of $3.85 per pound. All of the material was used to produce 12,500 units. There were no beginning or ending inventories.

b.   The company worked 30,000 actual direct labor-hours during the period, at an average cost of $10.25 per hour.

c.   The company incurred $62,000 in variable overhead cost during the period. Overhead is applied to products on a basis of direct labor-hours.

d.   The company incurred $271,500 in fixed overhead costs during the period; budgeted fixed overhead costs were $270,000. A denominator activity of 37,500 hours is used to set overhead rates.

e.   The company closes all variances to cost of goods sold each period, as shown in the income statement above.

Required: 1.   Compute the direct materials price and quantity variances for the period.
2.   Compute the direct labor rate and efficiency variances for the period.

3. Compute the variable overhead spending and efficiency variances and the fixed overhead budget and volume variances for the period.

4. Is the company's problem primarily one of poor control over costs? Explain.

P10-16. **Overhead analysis, with graphing.** For 19x5, the Eastwood Company has planned a denominator activity level of 15,000 direct labor-hours. At this level of activity, the following overhead costs are budgeted:

Variable costs	$18,000
Fixed costs	60,000

The company produces a single product that requires 2.5 hours to complete. The direct labor rate is $7 per hour. The product requires four pounds of raw materials, at $3.20 per pound. Overhead is applied to production on a basis of direct labor-hours.

Required:

1. Compute the predetermined overhead rate that the company will use during 19x5. Break the rate down into fixed and variable cost elements.

2. Prepare a standard cost card for one unit of product, using the following format:

Direct materials, 4 pounds at $3.20	$12.80
Direct labor, ?.	?
Variable costs,?.	?
Fixed costs, ?.	?
Total standard cost per unit	$?

3. Graph the following costs from an activity level of zero to 20,000 direct labor-hours:
   a. Budgeted fixed overhead (in total).
   b. Applied fixed overhead [applied at the hourly rate computed in (1) above].

4. Assume that during 19x5 the company works 14,500 actual direct labor-hours and produces 5,600 units of product. Actual fixed overhead costs are $61,500.
   a. Compute the fixed overhead budget and volume variances.
   b. Show the volume variance on the graph that you prepared in (3) above.

5. Assume that during 19x5 the company works 15,800 actual direct labor-hours and produces 6,200 units of product. Actual fixed overhead costs are again $61,500.
   a. Compute the fixed overhead budget and volume variances.
   b. Show the volume variance on the chart that you prepared in (3) above.

P10-17. **Selection of a denominator; overhead analysis.** The condensed flexible budget of the Scott Company for 19x2 is given below:

Overhead costs	Cost formula (per DLH)	Direct labor-hours		
		30,000	40,000	50,000
Variable costs	$2.50	$ 75,000	$100,000	$125,000
Fixed costs		320,000	320,000	320,000
Total overhead costs		$395,000	$420,000	$445,000

The company produces a single product that requires 2.5 direct labor-hours to complete. The direct labor wage rate is $7.50 per hour. Three yards of raw material are required for each unit of product, at a cost of $5 per yard.

Demand for the company's product differs widely from year to year. Expected actual activity for 19x2 is 50,000 direct labor-hours; long-run normal activity is 40,000 direct labor-hours per year.

Required: 1. Assume that the company chooses 40,000 direct labor-hours as the denominator level of activity. Compute the predetermined overhead rate, breaking it down into fixed and variable cost elements.

2. Assume that the company chooses 50,000 direct labor-hours as the denominator level of activity. Repeat the computations in (1) above.

3. Complete two standard cost cards as outlined below. Each card should relate to a single unit of product.

Denominator Activity: 40,000 DLH

Direct materials, 3 yards at $5	$15.00
Direct labor, ?	?
Variable overhead, ?	?
Fixed overhead, ?	?
Total standard cost per unit	$?

Denominator Activity: 50,000 DLH

Direct materials, 3 yards at $5	$15.00
Direct labor, ?	?
Variable overhead, ?	?
Fixed overhead, ?	?
Total standard cost per unit	$?

---

4. Assume that 48,000 actual hours are worked during 19x2, and that 18,500 units are produced. Actual overhead costs for the year are:

Variable costs	$124,800
Fixed costs	321,700
Total overhead costs	$446,500

  a. Compute the standard hours allowed for 19x2 production.

  b. Compute the missing items from the manufacturing overhead account below. Assume that the company uses 40,000 direct labor-hours (long-run normal activity) as the denominator activity figure in computing overhead rates, as you have used in (1) above.

Manufacturing Overhead

Actual costs	446,500	?	Applied costs
Underapplied overhead	?	?	Overapplied overhead

  c. Analyze your under- or overapplied overhead balance in terms of variable overhead spending and efficiency variances and fixed overhead budget and volume variances.

5. Looking at the variances that you have computed, what appears to be the major disadvantage of using long-run normal activity rather than expected actual activity as a denominator in computing the predetermined overhead rate? What advantages can you see to offset this disadvantage?

P10-18. Overhead analysis, with graphing.   A condensed flexible budget for the Eaton Company is given below:

Overhead costs	Cost formula (per DLH)	Direct labor-hours		
		8,000	10,000	12,000
Variable costs	$1.50	$ 12,000	$ 15,000	$ 18,000
Fixed costs		90,000	90,000	90,000
Total overhead costs		$102,000	$105,000	$108,000

The company produces a single product, which requires 2 hours of direct labor time to complete, at a rate of $5 per hour. Each unit of product requires 3 yards of material at $5.60 per yard. Overhead is applied to units of product on a basis of direct labor-hours. During the most recent period, the following actual costs and output were recorded:

Number of units produced	4,250
Actual direct labor-hours.	9,000
Actual fixed overhead cost	$88,500

Required: 1. Assume that the company computes predetermined overhead rates by using a denominator activity of 8,000 direct labor-hours.
   a. Compute the predetermined overhead rate, and break it down into variable and fixed cost elements.
   b. Prepare a standard cost card, showing the cost to produce one unit of product.
2. Refer to the original data. Assume that the company computes predetermined overhead rates by using a denominator activity of 12,000 direct labor-hours.
   a. Compute the predetermined overhead rate under this assumption, and break it down into variable and fixed cost elements.
   b. Prepare a standard cost card, showing the cost to produce one unit of product.
3. Refer to your computations in (1).
   a. Using these data, compute the budget and volume variances for the most recent period.
   b. Prepare a graph showing budgeted fixed costs throughout the relevant range and showing an applied overhead line for fixed costs from a zero level of activity through the denominator level of activity. Indicate on your graph the volume variance that you have just computed. In your own words, explain why a volume variance arises.
4. Refer to your computations in (2).
   a. Using these data, compute the budget and volume variances for the most recent period.
   b. Prepare another graph showing budgeted fixed overhead and applied fixed overhead, as well as the volume variance that you have just computed.
5. What are the implications of this problem regarding the setting of fixed overhead rates for product costing purposes? Are such rates useful control tools? Explain.

P10–19. **Comprehensive overhead analysis.** Carbo-Weld, Inc., produces a single product that requires two pounds of raw materials at a cost of $1.85 per pound and three hours of direct labor time at a rate of $5 per hour. Overhead costs are planned and controlled through a flexible budget, which is shown in condensed form below:

Overhead costs	Cost formula (per DLH)	Direct labor-hours		
		5,000	10,000	15,000
Variable costs.	$1.60	$ 8,000	$16,000	$24,000
Fixed costs		30,000	30,000	30,000
Total overhead costs		$38,000	$46,000	$54,000

Actual operating results for the most recent period are shown below:

Number of units produced	2,000
Actual direct labor-hours worked	5,600
Standard hours allowed for the output of the period.	?
Actual variable overhead cost	$10,080
Actual fixed overhead cost	$31,500

Required:

1. Assume that the company normally operates at an activity level of 10,000 standard direct labor-hours each period and that this figure is used as the denominator activity in computing predetermined overhead rates.
   a. Compute the predetermined overhead rate, and break it down into fixed and variable cost elements.
   b. Prepare a standard cost card, showing the standard cost to produce one unit of product.

2. Refer to the original data. Assume that the company decides to use 5,000 standard direct labor-hours as the denominator activity in computing predetermined overhead rates.
   a. Under this assumption, compute the predetermined overhead rate and break it down into fixed and variable cost elements.
   b. Prepare another standard cost card, showing the standard cost to produce one unit of product.

3. Refer to the computations you made in (1) above.
   a. Prepare a T-account for manufacturing overhead, and enter the actual overhead costs for the most recent period as shown in the original data to the problem. Determine the amount of overhead that would have been applied to production during the period, and enter this amount into the T-account.
   b. Compute the amount of under- or overapplied overhead for the period, and then analyze it in terms of the variable overhead spending and efficiency variances and the fixed overhead budget and volume variances.

4. Refer to the computations you made in (2) above.
   a. Prepare another T-account for manufacturing overhead, and again enter the actual overhead costs for the most recent period. Determine the amount of overhead that would have been applied to production during the period, and enter this amount into the T-account.
   b. Compute the amount of under- or overapplied overhead for the period, and then analyze it in terms of the variable overhead spending and efficiency variances and the fixed overhead budget and volume variances.

5. Firms are sometimes accused by competitors and others of selling products "below cost." What implications does this problem have for the "cost" of a unit of product so far as the setting of fixed overhead rates is concerned?

P10–20. **Incomplete data.** Each of the cases below is independent. You may assume that each company uses a standard cost system and that each company's flexible budget is based on standard direct labor-hours.

Item	Company X	Company Y
1. Denominator activity in hours	18,000	?
2. Standard hours allowed for units produced	?	28,000
3. Actual hours worked	?	27,500
4. Flexible budget variable overhead per direct labor-hour	$ 1.60	$?
5. Flexible budget fixed overhead (total)	?	?
6. Actual variable overhead cost	30,000	55,275
7. Actual fixed overhead cost	72,500	134,600
8. Variable overhead cost applied to production*	31,200	?
9. Fixed overhead cost applied to production*	?	126,000
10. Variable overhead spending variance	?	?
11. Variable overhead efficiency variance	800 U	1,000 F
12. Fixed overhead budget variance	500 U	?
13. Fixed overhead volume variance	?	9,000 U
14. Variable portion of the predetermined overhead rate	?	?
15. Fixed portion of the predetermined overhead rate	?	?
16. Underapplied or (overapplied) overhead	?	?

* Based on standard hours allowed for units produced.

Required: Compute the unknown amounts. (Hint: One way to proceed would be to use the columnar format for variance analysis found in Exhibit 9–5 for variable overhead and in Exhibit 10–10 for fixed overhead, fill in the known amounts above, and then compute the missing amounts by logic and analysis.)

P10–21. **Preparing a revised performance report.** Shipley Company has had a comprehensive budgeting system in operation for several years. Feelings vary among the managers as to the value and benefit of the system. The line supervisors are very happy with the reports being prepared on their performance, but upper management often expresses dissatisfaction over the reports being prepared on various phases of the company's operations. A typical performance report for a recent period is shown below:

SHIPLEY COMPANY
Performance Report—Milling Department
For the Quarter Ended June 30, 19x6

	Actual	Budget	Variance
Units produced	25,000	30,000	
Variable overhead:			
Indirect labor	$ 20,000	$ 22,500	$2,500 F
Supplies	5,400	6,000	600 F
Utilities	27,000	30,000	3,000 F
Rework time	14,000	15,000	1,000 F
Total variable costs	66,400	73,500	7,100 F
Fixed overhead:			
Maintenance	61,000	60,000	1,000 U
Inspection	90,000	90,000	—
Total fixed costs	151,000	150,000	1,000 U
Total overhead costs	$217,400	$223,500	$6,100 F

After receiving a copy of this performance report, the supervisor of the milling department stated, "No one can complain about my department; our variances have been favorable for over a year now. We've saved the company thousands of dollars by our excellent cost control."

The "budget" data above are taken from the department's flexible budget and represent the original planned level of activity for the quarter.

Required:
1. The production superintendent is uneasy about the performance reports being prepared and would like you to evaluate their usefulness to the company.
2. What changes, if any, would you recommend be made in the performance report above in order to give the production superintendent better insight into how well the supervisor is doing his job?
3. Prepare a new performance report for the quarter, incorporating any changes you suggested in (2).

P10–22. **Flexible budget and performance report.** The Durrant Company has had great difficulty in controlling overhead costs. At a recent convention, the president heard about a control device for overhead costs known as a flexible budget, and he has hired you to implement this budgeting program in the Durrant Company. After some effort, you develop the following cost formulas for the company's machining department. These costs are based on a normal operating range of 10,000 to 20,000 machine-hours per month:

Cost	Cost formula
Machine setup	$0.20 per machine-hour
Lubricants	1.00 per machine-hour plus $8,000 per month
Utilities	0.70 per machine-hour
Indirect labor	0.60 per machine-hour plus $20,000 per month
Depreciation	32,000 per month

During March 19x3, the first month after your preparation of the above data, the machining department worked 18,000 machine-hours and produced 9,000 units of product. The actual costs of this production were:

Machine setup	$ 4,800
Lubricants	24,500
Utilities	12,000
Indirect labor	32,500
Depreciation	32,000
Total costs	$105,800

There were no variances in the fixed costs. The department had originally been budgeted to work 20,000 machine-hours during March 19x3.

Required:
1. Prepare a flexible budget for the machining department in increments of 5,000 hours. Make the flexible budget inclusive enough to be used for both control and product costing purposes.
2. Prepare a performance report for the machining department for the month of March. Include both fixed and variable costs in the report (in separate sections). Show only a spending variance on the report.
3. What additional information would you need to have in order to compute an overhead efficiency variance for the department?
4. Explain to the president how the flexible budget might be used for product costing purposes as well as for cost control purposes.

P10–23. **Spending and efficiency variances; evaluating a performance report.** Ronald Davis, superintendent of the milling department of Mason Company, is very happy with his performance report for the past month. The report is shown below:

MASON COMPANY
Performance Report—Milling Department

	Budget	Actual	Variance
Direct labor-hours	12,000	10,000	
Variable overhead:			
Indirect materials	$13,200	$12,500	$ 700 F
Utilities	1,800	1,200	600 F
Machine setup	3,000	2,900	100 F
Maintenance	4,800	4,700	100 F
Total variable costs	22,800	21,300	1,500 F
Fixed overhead:			
Supervision	9,000	9,000	—
Maintenance	6,500	6,800	300 U
Depreciation	12,000	12,000	—
Total fixed costs	27,500	27,800	300 U
Total overhead costs	$50,300	$49,100	$1,200 F

Upon receiving a copy of this report, John Arnold, the production manager, commented, "I've been getting these reports for months now, and I still can't see how they help me assess efficiency and cost control in that department. I agree that the budget for the month was 12,000 direct labor-hours, but that represents 6,000 units of product (since it should take two hours to produce one unit). The department produced only 4,600 units during the month, and took 10,000 hours of direct labor time to do it. Why do most of the variances turn up favorable?"

Required:
1. In answer to Mr. Arnold's question, why do most of the variances turn up favorable? Evaluate the performance report.

2. Prepare a new performance report that will help Mr. Arnold assess efficiency and cost control in the milling department. (Hint: Exhibit 10–7 may be helpful in structuring your report; include both variable and fixed costs in the report.)

P10–24. Detailed performance report. The cost formulas for variable overhead costs in a machining operation are given below:

Variable overhead cost	Cost formula (per machine-hour)
Power	$0.30
Setup time	0.20
Polishing wheels	0.16
Maintenance.	0.18
Total	$0.84

During the month of August, the machining operation was scheduled to work 11,250 machine-hours and to produce 4,500 units of product. The standard machine time per unit of product is 2.5 hours. A strike near the end of the month forced a curtailment of production. Actual results for the month were:

Actual machine-hours worked 9,250
Actual number of units produced 3,600

Actual costs for the month were:

	Total actual costs	Per machine-hour
Power.	$2,405	$0.26
Setup time	2,035	0.22
Polishing wheels	1,110	0.12
Maintenance	925	0.10
Total cost.	$6,475	$0.70

Required: Prepare a performance report for the machining operation for the month of August. Use column headings in your report as shown below:

Overhead item	Cost formula	Actual costs incurred 9,250 hours	Budget based on ? hours	Budget based on ? hours	Total variance	Breakdown of the total variance	
						Spending variance	Efficiency variance

P10–25. Preparing and analyzing a detailed performance report. Weil Products, Inc., operates a number of production plants throughout the country. The company's Lindon Plant has been in operation for 15 months. Performance in the plant during the first six months was affected by the usual problems associated with a new operation. Although operations are now running smoothly, the Lindon Plant has not been able to produce profits on a consistent basis. As the production requirements to meet sales demand have increased, the profit performance has deteriorated.

At a staff meeting attended by the plant general manager, the corporate controller, and the corporate budget director, the plant production manager commented that production in the plant changes somewhat from month to month according to sales demand. He noted that this makes it more difficult to control manufacturing expenses. He further noted that the overhead budget for the plant, included in the company's annual profit plan, was static in nature and thus was not useful for judging the plant's performance because of the month-to-month changes in operating levels. The meeting resulted in a decision to redo the budget on a flexible basis and to prepare a report each month that would compare actual manufacturing expenses with budgeted expenses based on actual direct labor-hours in the plant.

The plant production manager and the plant accountant studied the cost patterns for recent months, as well as volume and cost data from other Weil plants. Then they prepared the following flexible budget schedule:

Overhead costs	Per direct labor-hour	Direct labor-hours		
		150,000	200,000	250,000
Variable costs:				
Indirect labor	$0.80	$120,000	$160,000	$200,000
Supplies.	0.13	19,500	26,000	32,500
Power	0.07	10,500	14,000	17,500
Total variable costs	$1.00	150,000	200,000	250,000
Fixed costs:				
Supervisory labor		64,000	64,000	64,000
Heat and light.		15,000	15,000	15,000
Property taxes.		5,000	5,000	5,000
Total fixed costs		84,000	84,000	84,000
Total overhead costs		$234,000	$284,000	$334,000

The plant expected to work 200,000 planned production hours in a typical month, which at standard would result in 50,000 units of output.

The manufacturing expense reports prepared for the first three months after the flexible budget program was approved were pleasing to the plant production manager. They showed that except for small variations, the manufacturing expenses were in line with the flexible budget allowances. This is also reflected in the report prepared for November, which is presented below, when 50,500 units were manufactured. However, the plant is still not producing an adequate profit (due in part to excessive overhead costs), and management is beginning to wonder whether the flexible budget was a good idea after all.

LINDON PLANT
Manufacturing Expense Report
November 19x5

220,000 actual direct labor production hours

Overhead costs	Actual costs	Budgeted costs	(Over) under budget
Variable costs:			
Indirect labor	$177,000	$176,000	$(1,000)
Supplies	27,400	28,600	1,200
Power	16,000	15,400	(600)
Total variable costs	220,400	220,000	(400)
Fixed costs:			
Supervisory labor	65,000	64,000	(1,000)
Heat and light.	15,500	15,000	(500)
Property taxes	5,000	5,000	—
Total fixed costs	85,500	84,000	(1,500)
Total overhead costs	$305,900	$304,000	$(1,900)

Required:
1. From the standpoint of cost control, explain the advantages of the flexible budget approach over the static budget approach.
2. Criticize the overhead expense report above. How could the report be improved to provide management with more information about overhead costs?
3. Prepare a new overhead expense report for November. On your report, show the total excess over standard incurred for manufacturing expense items during the month. Analyze this total excess amount into those variances due to:
   a. Spending (or budget).
   b. Efficiency.
4. Explain what the management of the Lindon Plant should do to reduce:
   a. The spending (or budget) variance.
   b. The efficiency variance.   (CMA, adapted)

P10–26. **Comprehensive problem: flexible budget; performance report.** Elgin Company has recently introduced budgeting as an integral part of its corporate planning process. An inexperienced member of the accounting staff was given the assignment of constructing a flexible budget for overhead costs and prepared it in the format shown below:

Percentage of capacity	80%	100%
Machine-hours	40,000	50,000
Utilities.	$ 41,000	$ 49,000
Supplies	4,000	5,000
Indirect labor	8,000	10,000
Maintenance.	37,000	41,000
Supervision	10,000	10,000
Total overhead costs	$100,000	$115,000

The company assigns overhead costs to production on a basis of machine-hours. The cost formulas used to prepare the budgeted figures above are relevant over a range of 80 to 100 percent of capacity and relate to monthly usage of overhead cost items. The managers who will be working under these budgets have control over both fixed and variable overhead costs.

Required:

1. Redo the company's flexible budget, presenting it in better format as illustrated in Exhibit 10–8. Show the budgeted costs at 80, 90, and 100 percent levels of capacity. (Use the high-low method to separate fixed and variable costs.)

2. Express the flexible budget prepared in (1) above in cost formula form, using a single cost formula to express all overhead costs.

3. During May 19x7, the company operated at 86 percent of capacity in terms of actual machine-hours recorded in the factory. Actual overhead costs incurred during the month were:

Utilities	$ 42,540
Supplies	6,450
Indirect labor	9,890
Maintenance	35,190
Supervision	10,000
Total actual costs	$104,070

There were no variances in the fixed costs. Prepare a performance report for May 19x7. Include both fixed and variable costs in your report (in separate sections). Structure your report so that it shows only a spending variance for overhead. The company originally budgeted to work 40,000 machine-hours during the month; standard hours allowed for the month's production totaled 41,000 machine-hours.

4. Explain the possible causes of the spending variance for supplies.

5. Compute an efficiency variance for *total* variable overhead cost, and explain the nature of the variance.

11 Control of Decentralized Operations

Learning objectives

After studying Chapter 11, you should be able to:

Explain how a pyramiding system of reports is used to communicate information between various levels of responsibility in an organization.

Enumerate the benefits to be gained by decentralization in an organization.

Differentiate between cost centers, profit centers, and investment centers and explain how performance is measured in each.

Compute return on investment (ROI) by means of the ROI formula and show how changes in sales, expenses, and assets affect an organization's ROI.

Compute the residual income and enumerate the strengths and weaknesses of this method of measuring managerial performance.

Use the transfer pricing formula to compute an appropriate transfer price between segments of an organization under conditions of (1) full capacity and (2) idle capacity.

Define or explain the key terms listed at the end of the chapter.

In this chapter, we expand our knowledge of performance reports by looking more closely at responsibility accounting. This concept was first introduced in Chapter 8 and has been the "why" behind most of our work with budgets and performance reports in preceding chapters. We shall now use the responsibility accounting concept to show how the reports developed in these chapters fit together into an integrated reporting system. In the process, we will extend the technique of performance reporting to the company as a whole and demonstrate methods of evaluating the performance of top management.

RESPONSIBILITY ACCOUNTING

Responsibility accounting centers on the idea that an organization is simply a group of individuals working toward common goals. The more each individual can be assisted in the performance of his or her tasks, the better chance the organization has of reaching the goals it has set. As we have seen in preceding chapters, responsibility accounting recognizes each person in an organization who has any control over cost or revenue to be a *separate responsibility center* whose stewardship must be defined, measured, and reported upward in the organization. One author expresses the idea this way:

In effect, the system personalizes the accounting statements by saying, "Joe, this is what you originally budgeted and this is how you performed for the period with actual operations as compared against your budget." By definition it [responsibility accounting] is a system of accounting which is tailored to an organization so that costs are accumulated and reported by levels of responsibility within the organization. Each supervisory area in the organization is charged *only* with the cost for which it is responsible and over which it has control.[1]

Although the idea behind responsibility accounting is not new, the implementation of the idea on a widespread basis is quite recent and has come about in response to the manager's need for better and more efficient ways to control operations.

The functioning of the system

In order to broaden our perspective of how a responsibility accounting system functions, we will consider selected data relating to Potter Company. Potter Company is part of the Western Division of General Products, Inc., a broadly diversified firm with interests in many product areas. A partial organization chart for Potter Company is shown in Exhibit 11–1. The data on this chart form the basis for exhibits found on the following pages.

Although the concepts underlying responsibility accounting apply equally well to all parts of an organization, we will concentrate our discussion on the shaded area of Potter Company's organization chart. It depicts the line

---

[1] John A. Higgins, "Responsibility Accounting," *Arthur Andersen Chronicle*, April 1952, p. 94.

EXHIBIT 11–1

Organization chart—Potter Company

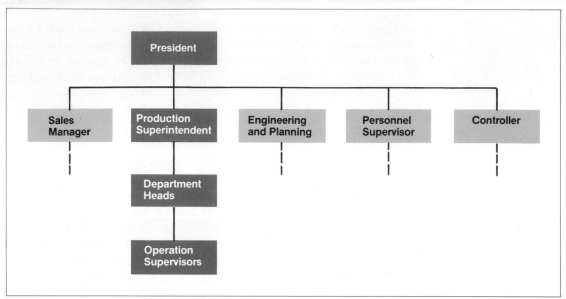

of responsibility for the production activities of the firm. This line of responsibility begins with the operation supervisors and moves upward in the organization, with each successive level having greater overall responsibility than the level that preceded it. To see how this concept of an upward-flowing, broadening line of responsibility can be integrated into the accounting statements, refer to Exhibit 11–2.

Exhibit 11–2 provides us with a bird's-eye view of the structuring of reports in a responsibility accounting system. Notice that the performance reports *start at the bottom and build upward,* with each manager receiving information on his own performance as well as on the performance of each manager under him in the chain of responsibility. We will now start at the bottom of this chain and follow it upward to show how the reports are used by the various levels of management.

The flow of information

The responsibility accounting system depicted in Exhibit 11–2 is structured around four levels of responsibility. The number of levels of responsibility will vary from company to company, according to organizational structure and needs.

Fourth level of responsibility The fourth, or lowest, level of responsibility is that of the wiring operation supervisor. The performance report prepared for the supervisor will be similar to the performance reports discussed

EXHIBIT 11–2

POTTER COMPANY
An Overview of Responsibility Accounting

President's report:

The president's performance report summarizes all company data. Since variances are given, the president can trace the variances downward through the company as needed to determine where his and his subordinates' time can best be spent.

Responsibility center:	Budget	Actual	Variance
Sales manager	X	X	X
Production superintendent	$26,000	$29,000	$3,000 U
Engineering and planning	X	X	X
Personnel supervisor	X	X	X
Controller	X	X	X
	$54,000	$61,000	$7,000 U

Production superintendent:

The performance of each department head is summarized for the production superintendent. The totals on the superintendent's performance report are then passed upward to the next level of responsibility.

Responsibility center:	Budget	Actual	Variance
Cutting department	X	X	X
Machining department	X	X	X
Finishing department	$11,000	$12,500	$1,500 U
Packaging department	X	X	X
	$26,000	$29,000	$3,000 U

Finishing department head:

The performance report of each supervisor is summarized on the performance report of the department head. The department totals are then summarized upward to the production superintendent.

Responsibility center:	Budget	Actual	Variance
Sanding operation	X	X	X
Wiring operation	$ 5,000	$ 5,800	$ 800 U
Assembly operation	X	X	X
	$11,000	$12,500	$1,500 U

Wiring operation supervisor:

The supervisor of each operation receives a performance report on his or her center of responsibility. The totals on these reports are then communicated upward to the next higher level of responsibility.

Variable costs:	Budget	Actual	Variance
Direct materials	X	X	X
Direct labor	X	X	X
Manufacturing overhead	X	X	X
	$ 5,000	$ 5,800	$ 800 U

in the two preceding chapters. This report will show budgeted data, actual data, and variances in terms of materials, labor, and overhead. This information will be communicated upward to the department head, along with detailed variance analyses.

Third level of responsibility The third level of responsibility is that of the finishing department head who oversees the work of the wiring operation supervisor as well as the work of the other supervisors in this department. Notice from Exhibit 11–2 that the department head will receive summarized data from each of the operations within the department. If the department head desires to know the reasons behind the variances reported in these summaries (such as the $800 variance in the wiring operation), he or she can look at the detailed, individual performance reports prepared on the separate operations.

Second level of responsibility The second level of responsibility is that of the production superintendent who has responsibility for all producing department activities. Notice from Exhibit 11–2 that the summarized totals from the performance report of the finishing department head are reported upward to the production superintendent, along with summarized totals from the performance reports of other departments. In addition to the summarized totals, the production superintendent will undoubtedly also require that detailed copies of the performance reports themselves be furnished to him, as well as detailed copies of the performance reports from all separate operations within the departments. The availability of these reports will permit the production superintendent to go right to the heart of any problem in cost control. This, of course, is the implementation of the management by exception principle discussed in earlier chapters. By having variances from budget highlighted on each performance report, the production superintendent is able to see where his or her time and the time of the department heads and supervisors can best be spent.

First level of responsibility The president of a company has ultimate responsibility for all costs and revenues. On his or her performance report, therefore, the activities of all phases of the business must be summarized for review.

The president may require that copies of the detailed performance reports from *all* levels of responsibility be supplied to him. On the other hand, he may concern himself only with broad results, leaving the more detailed data for the scrutiny of the managers of the lower responsibility centers, such as the production superintendent. Thus, the system provides a great deal of flexibility and can be expanded or contracted in terms of data provided to suit the needs and interests of the particular manager involved.

In the absence of a responsibility accounting system, managers are left with little more than a "seat-of-the-pants" feel for what is going on in their own areas of responsibility, as well as those of their subordinates. In today's highly competitive business environment, a seat-of-the-pants feel for how well costs are being controlled is rarely sufficient to sustain profitable operations.

EXHIBIT 11–3

General Products, Inc., organization—an expansion of the responsibility accounting concept

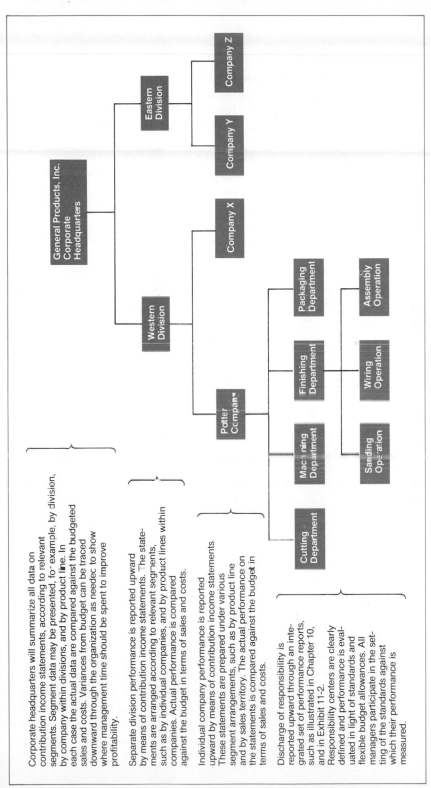

Corporate headquarters will summarize all data on contribution income statements, according to relevant segments. Segment data may be presented, for example, by division, by company within divisions, and by product line. In each case the actual data are compared against the budgeted sales and costs. Variances from budget can be traced downward through the organization as needed to show where management time should be spent to improve profitability.

Separate division performance is reported upward by means of contribution income statements. The statements are arranged according to relevant segments, such as by individual companies, and by product lines within companies. Actual performance is compared against the budget in terms of sales and costs.

Individual company performance is reported upward by means of contribution income statements. These statements are prepared under various segment arrangements, such as by product line and by sales territory. The actual performance on the statements is compared against the budget in terms of sales and costs.

Discharge of responsibility is reported upward through an integrated set of performance reports, such as illustrated in Chapter 10, and in Exhibit 11–2. Responsibility centers are clearly defined and performance is evaluated in light of standards and flexible budget allowances. All managers participate in the setting of the standards against which their performance is measured.

Expanding the responsibility accounting idea

We have indicated earlier that Potter Company is a part of the Western Division of General Products, Inc. Exhibit 11–3 on the preceding page shows more clearly just how Potter Company fits into the structure of the General Products, Inc., organization.

This exhibit illustrates a further expansion of the responsibility accounting idea. Notice from the exhibit that contribution income statements are used to report company-level performance to the divisional manager and to report divisional performance to corporate headquarters.

On a corporate headquarters level, all data are summarized into various segment arrangements for an overall performance evaluation of the entire corporate structure (see Exhibit 11–3). Since variances from budgeted sales and costs are shown on the contribution income statements, managers at the various levels of responsibility can see clearly where profit objectives are not being met. An illustration of a contribution income statement with variances is presented in Exhibit 11–4. Income statements of this type are prepared at both the company and division levels and then consolidated on a corporate level.

EXHIBIT 11–4

GENERAL PRODUCTS, INC.
Contribution Income Statement Comparing
Budgeted Data with Actual Data
(in thousands)

	Budget	Actual	Variance
Sales	$100,000	$97,000	$3,000 U
Variable expenses:			
Variable cost of sales	45,000	46,000	1,000 U
Other variable expenses	15,000	14,500	500 F
Total variable expenses	60,000	60,500	500 U
Contribution margin	40,000	36,500	3,500 U
Less fixed expenses:			
Selling	13,000	13,000	—
Administrative	4,000	4,300	300 U
Manufacturing	13,000	13,700	700 U
Total fixed expenses	30,000	31,000	1,000 U
Net income	$ 10,000	$ 5,500	$4,500 U

The benefits of decentralization

Managers have found that a responsibility accounting system functions most effectively in an organization that is *decentralized*. **A decentralized organization** is one in which decision making is not confined to a few top executives but rather is spread throughout the organization, with managers at various levels making key operating decisions relating to their sphere of responsibility. Decentralization must be viewed in terms of degree, since all organizations are decentralized to some extent out of economic necessity. At one extreme, a strongly decentralized organization is one in which there are few, if any, constraints on the freedom of a manager to make a decision, even at the lowest levels. At the other extreme, a strongly centralized organization is one in which little freedom exists to make a decision other than at top levels of management. Although most firms today fall somewhere between these two extremes, there is a pronounced tendency toward the decentralized end of the spectrum.

Many benefits are felt to accrue from decentralization. These benefits include the following:

1. By spreading the burden of decision making among many levels of management, top management is relieved of much day-to-day problem solving and is left free to concentrate on long-range planning and on coordination of efforts.
2. Allowing managers greater decision-making control over their segments provides excellent training as these managers rise in the organization. In the absence of such training, managers may be ill-prepared to function in a decision-making capacity as they are given greater responsibility.
3. Added responsibility and decision-making authority often result in increased job satisfaction and provide greater incentive for the manager to put forth his or her best efforts.
4. Decisions are best made at that level in an organization where a problem arises. Members of top management are often in a poor position to make decisions in matters relating to the everyday operation of a given segment, since they are not intimately acquainted with the problems or local conditions that may exist.
5. Decentralization provides a more effective basis for measuring a manager's performance, since it typically leads to the creation of profit and investment centers. Profit and investment centers and the measurement of management performance are discussed in the following section.

Investment, profit, and cost centers

In a decentralized organization, the responsibility accounting system is structured around a number of centers, such as are depicted in Exhibit 11–5 for General Products, Inc. These consist of investment centers, profit centers, and cost centers, each of which defines a particular area of responsibility in an organization.[2]

---

[2] Some organizations also identify "revenue centers," which are responsible for sales activities only (products are shipped directly from the plant or from a warehouse as orders are submitted). An example of such a revenue center would be a Sears catalog outlet. Other companies would consider this to be just another type of profit center, since costs of some kind (salaries, rent, utilities) are usually present.

EXHIBIT 11–5
Investment, profit, and cost centers—General Products, Inc.

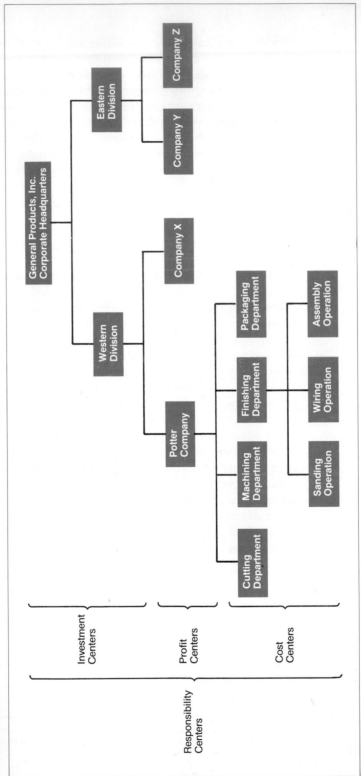

Responsibility center A **responsibility center** is any point within an organization where control over the incurrence of cost or the generating of revenue is found. Such a point could be an individual, an operation, a department, a company, a division, or the entire organization itself.

Cost center A **cost center** is any responsibility center that has control over the incurrence of cost. A cost center has no control over sales or over the generating of revenue.

Profit center By contrast to a cost center, a **profit center** has control over both cost and revenue. Potter Company, for example, would be a profit center in the General Products, Inc., organization, since it would be concerned with marketing its goods as well as producing them.

Investment center An **investment center** is any responsibility center within an organization that has control over cost and revenue and also over investment funds. The corporate headquarters of General Products, Inc., would clearly be an example of an investment center. Corporate officers have ultimate responsibility for seeing that production and marketing goals are met. In addition, they have responsibility for seeing that adequate facilities are available to carry out the production and marketing functions, and for seeing that adequate working capital is available for operating needs. Whenever a segment of an organization has control over investment in such areas as physical plant and equipment, receivables, inventory, and entry into new markets, then it is termed an *investment center*. Potter Company itself could be an investment center if it were given control over investment funds for some of these purposes. In the more usual situation, however, Potter Company would be a profit center within the larger organization, with most (or all) investment decisions being made at the divisional or central headquarters levels.

The reader should be cautioned that in everyday business practice the distinction between a profit center and an investment center is sometimes blurred, and the term *profit center* is often used to refer to either one. Thus, a company may refer to one of its segments as being a profit center when in fact the manager has full control over investment decisions in the segment. For purposes of our discussion, we will continue to maintain a distinction between the two, as made above.

Measuring management performance

These concepts of responsibility accounting are very important, since they assist in defining a manager's sphere of responsibility and also in determining how performance will be evaluated.

Cost centers are evaluated by means of performance reports, in terms of meeting cost standards that have been set. Profit centers are evaluated by means of contribution income statements, in terms of meeting sales and cost objectives. Investment centers are also evaluated by means of contribution income statements, but normally in terms of the *rate of return* that they are able to generate on *invested funds*. In the following section, we discuss rate of return as a tool for measuring managerial performance in an investment center.

RATE OF RETURN FOR MEASURING MANAGERIAL PERFORMANCE

The development of concepts such as investment centers, profit centers, and cost centers is largely a result of the rapid growth of decentralization in corporate structures. As mentioned earlier, in a decentralized organization managers are given a great deal of autonomy in directing the affairs in their particular areas of responsibility. So great is this autonomy that the various profit and investment centers are often viewed as being virtually independent businesses, with their managers having about the same control over decisions as if they were in fact running their own independent firms. With this autonomy, fierce competition often develops among managers, with each striving to make his or her operation the "best" in the company.

Competition is particularly keen when it comes to passing out funds for expansion of product lines, or for introduction of new product lines. How do top managers in corporate headquarters go about deciding who gets new investment funds as they become available, and how do these managers decide which investment centers are most profitably using the funds that have already been entrusted to their care? One of the most popular ways of making these judgments is to measure the rate of return that investment center managers are able to generate on their assets. This can be done through the **return on investment (ROI)** formula.

The ROI formula

To understand the concepts behind the ROI formula, refer to the funds flow model illustrated in Exhibit 11–6.

As shown in the exhibit, as a dollar leaves the central pool of cash, it is invested in inventory. The inventory is then sold, and an account receivable is created, which is subsequently collected from the customer. Upon collection from the customer, the dollar that was started through the system is returned to the central pool of cash from which it began its journey. This dollar will bring back with it whatever additional pennies the customer has been willing to pay above the cost of the goods that he or she purchased. Thus, the seller's profitability will at least in part be measured by the number of these additional pennies, which we will call the **margin** earned.

But a moment's reflection will indicate that a firm's profitability is also dependent on another factor. Realizing that a dollar going through the system will bring back a certain number of additional pennies with it, we will be anxious to send that dollar through the system as many times during the period as we possibly can. The number of trips a dollar makes through the system during a period is known as the **turnover.** Thus, we can see that a firm's profitability will be a product of the margin (number of pennies brought back by a dollar in one trip through the system) multiplied by the turnover

EXHIBIT 11–6
The funds flow model

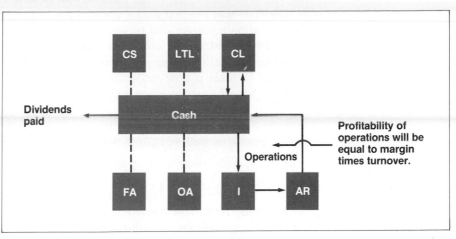

CS = capital stock; LTL = long-term liabilities; CL = current liabilities; FA = fixed assets; OA = other assets; I = inventory; and AR = accounts receivable.

(number of times a dollar makes the trip through the system during the period). This line of reasoning gives rise to the ROI formula:

$$\text{Margin} \times \text{Turnover} = \text{Profitability, or ROI}$$

Factors underlying rate of return

Armed with a conceptual perspective of the ROI formula, we can now examine the detailed factors making up the margin and turnover elements:

$$\text{Margin} \times \text{Turnover} = \text{ROI}$$

$$\text{Margin} = \frac{\text{Net operating income}}{\text{Sales}} \qquad \text{Turnover} = \frac{\text{Sales}}{\text{Average operating assets}}$$

Therefore,

$$\frac{\text{Net operating income}}{\text{Sales}} \times \frac{\text{Sales}}{\text{Average operating assets}} = \text{ROI}$$

In the past, managers have tended to focus only on the margin earned and have ignored the turnover of assets. To some degree at least, the margin earned can be a valuable measure of a manager's performance. Standing alone, however, it overlooks one very crucial area of a manager's responsibility—the control of investment in operating assets. Excessive funds tied up in operating assets can be just as much of a drag on profitability as excessive operating expenses. One of the real advantages of the ROI formula is that it forces the manager to control his or her investment in operating assets as well as to control expenses, the gross profit rate, and sales volume.

Du Pont was the first major corporation to recognize the importance of looking at both margin *and* turnover in assessing the performance of a manager. To it must go the credit for pioneering the ROI concept. Monsanto Company and other major corporations have followed Du Pont's lead, and the ROI formula is now recognized as one of the best single measures of a manager's performance when that manager has control of an investment center. It blends together many aspects of the manager's responsibilities into a single figure that can be compared against the return of competing investment centers, as well as against that of other firms in the industry.

Net operating income and operating assets defined

The reader may have noticed in the ROI formula above that in computing the margin percentage, *net operating income* was used rather than simply net income. **Net operating income** is income before interest and taxes. In business jargon, it is sometimes referred to as *EBIT* (earnings before interest and taxes). The reader should become familiar with these terms. The reason for using net operating income in the formula is that the income figure used should be consistent with the base to which it is applied. Notice that the base in the turnover part of the formula consists of *operating assets*. Thus, to be consistent we use net operating income in computing the margin figure.

Operating assets would include cash, accounts receivable, inventory, fixed assets, and all other assets held for productive use in the organization. Examples of assets that would not be included in the operating assets category (that is, examples of *non*operating assets) would include land being held for future use, or a factory building being rented to someone else. The operating assets base used in the formula is typically computed as the average between the beginning and the end of the year.

CONTROLLING THE RATE OF RETURN

When being measured by the ROI formula, a manager can improve profitability in three ways:

1. By increasing sales.
2. By reducing expenses.
3. By reducing assets.

To illustrate how the rate of return can be controlled by each of these three actions, let us assume the following data for an investment center:

Net operating income	$ 10,000
Sales	100,000
Average operating assets	50,000

The rate of return generated by the investment center would be:

$$\frac{\text{Net operating income}}{\text{Sales}} \times \frac{\text{Sales}}{\text{Average operating assets}} = \text{ROI}$$

$$\frac{\$10,000}{\$100,000} \times \frac{\$100,000}{\$50,000} = \text{ROI}$$

$$10\% \times 2 = 20\%$$

As we stated earlier, in order to improve the ROI figure the manager must (1) increase sales, (2) reduce expenses, or (3) reduce the operating assets.

Approach 1: Increase sales Assume that the manager in our example is able to increase sales from $100,000 to $110,000. Assume further that either because of good cost control or because most costs in the company are fixed, the net operating income increases even more rapidly, going from $10,000 to $12,000 per period. The operating assets remain constant.

$$\frac{\$12,000}{\$110,000} \times \frac{\$110,000}{\$50,000} = \text{ROI}$$

$$10.91\% \times 2.2 = 24\% \text{ (as compared to 20\% above)}$$

Approach 2: Reduce expenses Assume that the manager is able to reduce expenses by $1,000, so that net operating income increases from $10,000 to $11,000. Both sales and operating assets remain constant.

$$\frac{\$11,000}{\$100,000} \times \frac{\$100,000}{\$50,000} = \text{ROI}$$

$$11\% \times 2 = 22\% \text{ (as compared to 20\% above)}$$

Approach 3: Reduce assets Assume that the manager is able to reduce operating assets from $50,000 to $40,000. Sales and net operating income remain unchanged.

$$\frac{\$10,000}{\$100,000} \times \frac{\$100,000}{\$40,000} = \text{ROI}$$

$$10\% \times 2.5 = 25\% \text{ (as compared to 20\% above)}$$

A clear understanding of these three approaches to improving the ROI figure is critical to the effective management of an investment center. We will now look at each approach in more detail.

Increase sales

In first looking at the ROI formula, one is inclined to think that the sales figure is neutral, since it appears as the denominator in the margin computation and as the numerator in the turnover computation. We *could* cancel out the sales figure, but we don't do so for two reasons. First, this would tend to draw attention away from the fact that the rate of return is a function of *two* variables, margin and turnover. And second, it would tend to conceal the fact that a change in sales can affect *either* the margin or the turnover in an organization. To explain, a change in sales can affect the *margin* if expenses increase or decrease at a different rate than sales. For example, a company may be able to keep a tight control on its costs as its sales go up, thereby allowing the net operating income to increase more rapidly than sales and thus allowing the margin percentage to rise. Or, a company may have many fixed expenses that will remain constant as sales go up, thereby again allowing a rapid increase in the net operating income and causing the margin percentage to rise. Either (or both) of these factors could have been responsible for the increase in the margin percentage from 10 percent to 10.91 percent illustrated in approach 1 above.

Further, a change in sales can affect the *turnover* if sales either increase or decrease without a proportionate increase or decrease in the operating assets. In approach 1 above, for example, sales increased from $100,000 to $110,000, but the operating assets remained unchanged. As a result, the turnover increased from 2 to 2.2 for the period.

In sum, because a change in sales can affect either the margin or the turnover in a company, such changes are particularly significant to the manager in his or her attempts to control the ROI figure.

Reduce expenses

Often the easiest route to increased profitability and to a stronger ROI figure is to simply cut the "fat" out of an organization through a concerted effort to control expenses. When profit margins begin to be squeezed, this is generally the first line of attack by a manager. The discretionary fixed costs usually come under scrutiny first, and various programs are either curtailed or eliminated in an effort to cut costs. Firms under extreme pressures to reduce expenses have gone so far as to eliminate coffee breaks, under the reasoning that nothing could more emphatically impress the staff with the need to be cost conscious.

One of the most common ways to reduce variable expenses is to use less costly inputs of materials. Another way is to automate processes as much as possible, particularly where large volumes of units are involved.

Reduce operating assets

Managers have always been sensitive to the need to control sales, operating expenses, and operating margins. They have not always been equally sensitive, however, to the need to control investment in operating assets. Firms that have adopted the ROI approach to measuring managerial performance report that one of the first reactions on the part of investment center managers is to trim down their investment in operating assets. The reason, of course, is that these managers soon realize that an excessive investment in operating assets will reduce the asset turnover and hurt the rate of return. As these managers pare down their investment in operating assets, funds are released that can be used elsewhere in the organization. Consider the following actual situation:

X Company, a firm located in a western state, is a manufacturer of high-quality cast-iron pipe. A few years ago a large conglomerate acquired a controlling interest in the stock of X Company, and X Company became an investment center of the larger organization. The parent company measured the performance of the investment center managers by the ROI formula. X Company managers quickly found that their performance was below that of other investment centers within the organization. Because of their mediocre performance, X Company managers realized that they were in a poor position to compete for new investment funds. As one step in an effort to improve the rate of return, the company took a hard look at its investment in operating assets. As a result, it was able to reduce inventory alone by nearly 40 percent. This resulted in several million dollars becoming available for productive use elsewhere in the company. Within two years' time, the rate of return being generated by X Company improved dramatically. The controller of X Company, speaking at a management development conference, stated that the company had always been profitable in terms of net income to sales, so there really had been no incentive to watch the investment in operating assets prior to being put under the ROI microscope.

What approaches are open to an investment center manager in attempts to control the investment in operating assets? One approach is to pare out obsolete and redundant inventory. The computer has been extremely helpful in this regard, making perpetual inventory methods more feasible as well as facilitating the use of statistical methods of inventory control, such as those discussed in Chapter 8. Another approach is to devise various methods of speeding up the collection of receivables. For example, many firms now employ the lockbox technique by which customers in distant states remit directly to local post office boxes. The funds are received and deposited by a local banking institution in behalf of the payee firm. This can greatly speed up the collection process, thereby reducing the total investment required to carry accounts receivable. (The released funds are typically used to pay amounts due to short-term creditors.) As the level of investment in receivables is reduced, the asset turnover is increased.

The problem of allocated expenses and assets

In decentralized organizations such as General Products, Inc., it is common practice to allocate to the separate divisions the expenses incurred in operating corporate headquarters. When such allocations are made, a very thorny question arises as to whether these allocated expenses should be considered in the divisions' rate of return computations.

It can be argued on the one hand that allocated expenses should be included in rate of return computations, since they represent the value of services rendered to the divisions by central headquarters. On the other hand, it can be argued that they should not be included, since the divisional managers have no control over the incurrence of the expenses and since the "services" involved are often of questionable value, or are hard to pin down.

At the very least, *arbitrary* allocations should be avoided in rate of return computations. If arbitrary allocations are made, great danger exists of creating a bias for or against a particular division. Expense allocations should be limited to the cost of those *actual* services provided by central headquarters that the divisions would *otherwise* have had to provide for themselves. The amount of expense allocated to a division should not exceed the cost that the division would have incurred if it had provided the service for itself.

These same guidelines apply to asset allocations from central corporate headquarters to the separate·divisions. Assets relating to overall corporate operations should not be included as part of the divisional operating assets in divisional ROI computations, unless there are clear and traceable benefits to the divisions from the assets involved. As before, any type of arbitrary allocations (such as allocations on the basis of sales dollars) should be avoided.

THE CONCEPT OF RESIDUAL INCOME

In our discussion, we have assumed that the purpose of an investment center should be to maximize the rate of return that it is able to generate on operating assets. There is another approach to measuring performance in an investment center, which focuses on a concept known as **residual income.** Residual income is the net operating income that an investment center is able to earn *above* some minimum rate of return on operating assets. When residual income is used to measure performance, the purpose is to maximize the total amount of residual income, *not* to maximize the overall ROI figure.

Consider the following data for two comparable divisions:

	Performance measured by—	
	Rate of return (Division A)	Residual income (Division B)
Average operating assets	$100,000 *(a)*	$100,000
Net operating income	$ 20,000 *(b)*	$ 20,000
ROI, *(b)* ÷ *(a)*.	20%	
Minimum required rate of return is assumed to be 15% (15% × $100,000)		15,000
Residual income		$ 5,000

Notice that Division B has a positive residual income of $5,000. The performance of the manager of Division B is assessed according to how large or how small this residual income figure is from year to year. The larger the residual income figure, the better is the performance rating received by the division's manager.

Motivation and residual income

Many companies view residual income as being a better measure of performance than rate of return. They argue that the residual income approach encourages managers to make profitable investments that would be rejected by managers being measured by the ROI formula. To illustrate, assume that each of the divisions above is presented with an opportunity to make an investment of $25,000 in a new project that would generate a return of 18 percent on invested assets. The manager of Division A would probably reject this opportunity. Note from the tabulation above that his division is already earning a return of 20 percent on its assets. If he takes on a new project that provides a return of only 18 percent, then his overall ROI will be reduced, as shown below:

	Present	New project	Overall
Average operating assets *(a)*	$100,000	$25,000	$125,000
Net operating income *(b)*	$ 20,000	$ 4,500*	$ 24,500
ROI, *(b)* ÷ *(a)*	20%	18%	19.6%

* $25,000 × 18% = $4,500.

Since the performance of the manager of this division is being measured according to the *maximum* rate of return that he is able to generate on invested assets, he will be unenthused about any investment opportunity that reduces his current ROI figure. He will tend to think and act along these lines, even though the opportunity he rejects might have benefited the company *as a whole.*

On the other hand, the manager of Division B will be very anxious to accept the new investment opportunity. The reason is that she isn't concerned about maximizing her rate of return. She is concerned about maximizing her residual income. Any project that provides a return greater than the minimum required 15 percent will be attractive, since it will add to the *total amount* of the residual income figure. Under these circumstances, the new investment opportunity with its 18 percent return will clearly be attractive, as shown below:

	Present	New project	Overall
Average operating assets	$100,000	$25,000	$125,000
Net operating income	$ 20,000	$ 4,500*	$ 24,500
Minimum required rate of return is again assumed to be 15%	15,000	3,750†	18,750
Residual income	$ 5,000	$ 750	$ 5,750

* $25,000 × 18% = $4,500.
† $25,000 × 15% = $3,750.

Thus, by accepting the new investment project, the manager of Division B will increase her division's overall residual income figure and thereby show an improved performance as a manager. The fact that her division's overall ROI might be lower as a result of accepting the project is immaterial, since performance is being evaluated by residual income, not ROI. The well-being of both the manager and the company as a whole will be maximized by accepting all investment opportunities down to the 15 percent cutoff rate.

Divisional comparison and residual income

The residual income approach has one major disadvantage. It can't be used to compare the performance of divisions of different sizes, since by its very nature it creates a bias in favor of larger divisions. That is, one would expect larger divisions to have more residual income than smaller divisions, not necessarily because they are better managed, but simply because of the bigger numbers involved.

As an example, consider the residual income computations for Small Division and Large Division below. Observe that Large Division has slightly more residual income than Small Division, but that it has $1,000,000 in operating assets to work with as compared to only $250,000 in operating assets for Small Division. Thus, Large Division's greater residual income probably is more a result of its size than a result of the quality of its management. In fact, it appears that Small Division is better managed, since it has been able to generate nearly as much residual income with only one-fourth as much in operating assets available for use.

	Small Division	Large Division
Average operating assets *(a)*	$250,000	$1,000,000
Net operating income	$ 40,000	$ 120,000
Minimum required return: 10% × *(a)*	25,000	100,000
Residual income	$ 15,000	$ 20,000

TRANSFER PRICING

Special problems arise in applying the rate of return or residual income approaches to performance evaluation whenever segments of a company do business with each other. The problems revolve around the question of what **transfer price** to charge between the segments. A transfer price can be defined as the price charged when one segment of a company provides goods or services to another segment of the company.

The need for transfer prices

Assume that a vertically integrated firm has three divisions. The three divisions are:

Mining Division.
Processing Division.
Manufacturing Division.

The Mining Division mines raw materials that are transferred to the Processing Division. After processing, the Processing Division transfers the processed materials to the Manufacturing Division. The Manufacturing Division then includes the processed materials as part of its finished product.

In this example, we have two transfers of goods between divisions within the same company. What price should control these transfers? Should the price be set so as to include some "profit" element to the transferring division? Should it be set so as to include only the accumulated costs to that point? Or should it be set at yet another figure? The choice of a transfer price can be complicated by the fact that each division may be supplying portions of its output to outside customers, as well as to sister divisions. Another complication is that the price charged by one division becomes a cost to the other division, and the higher this cost, the lower will be the purchasing division's rate of return. Thus, the purchasing division would like the transfer price to be low, whereas the selling division would like it to be high, perhaps even charging the same "market" price internally as it charges to outside customers.

As the reader may guess, the problem of what transfer price to set between segments of a company has no easy solution and often leads to protracted and heated disputes between investment center managers. Yet some transfer price *must* be set if data are to be available for performance evaluation of the various parts or divisions of a company. In practice, three general approaches are used in setting transfer prices:

1. Set transfer prices at cost using:
   a. Variable cost.
   b. Full (absorption) cost.
2. Set transfer prices at the market price.
3. Set transfer prices at a negotiated market price.

In the following sections, we consider each of these approaches to the transfer pricing problem.

Transfer prices at cost

Many firms make transfers between divisions on a basis of the accumulated cost of the goods being transferred, thus ignoring any profit element to the selling division. A transfer price computed in this way might be based only on the variable costs involved, or fixed costs might also be considered and the transfer price thus based on full (absorption) costs accumulated to the point of transfer. Although the cost approach to setting transfer prices is relatively simple to apply, it has some major defects. These can be brought out by the following illustration:

Assume that a multidivisional company has a Relay Division that manufactures an electrical relay widely used as a component part by various governmental contractors. The relay requires $12 in variable costs to manufacture and sells for $20. Each relay requires one direct labor-hour to complete, and the division has a capacity of 50,000 relays per year.

The company also has a Motor Division. This division has developed a new motor requiring an electrical relay, but this relay is different from the one presently being manufactured by the Relay Division. In order to acquire the needed relay, the Motor Division has two alternatives:

1. The new relay can be purchased from an outside supplier at a price of $15 per relay, based on an order of 50,000 relays per year.
2. The new relay can be manufactured by the company's Relay Division. This would require that the Relay Division give up its present business, since manufacture of the new relay would require all of its capacity. One direct labor-hour would be required to produce each relay (the same time as that required by the old relay). Variable manufacturing costs would total $10 per relay.

In addition to the relay, each motor would require $25 in other variable cost inputs. The motors would sell for $60 each.

Should the Relay Division give up its present relay business and start producing the new relays for the Motor Division, or should it continue its present business and let the Motor Division purchase the new relays from the outside supplier? Let us assume first that the Motor Division decides to purchase the new relays from the outside supplier at $15 each, thereby permitting the Relay Division to continue to produce and sell the old relay. Partial income statements are given at the top of Exhibit 11–7 to show the effects of this decision on each division and on the company as a whole. Notice from the exhibit (alternative 1) that each division will have a positive contribution margin, and that the company as a whole will have a contribution margin of $1,400,000 for the year if this alternative is accepted.

Let us assume second that the Motor Division purchases the new relays internally from the Relay Division at a transfer price of $10 per relay (the Relay Division's variable costs per unit). This would require that the Relay Division give up its present outside business. On the surface this would seem to be a good decision, since the variable costs to the Relay Division would be only $10 for the new relay as compared to $12 for the old relay, and since the Motor Division would otherwise have to purchase the new relays from the outside supplier at $15 each. But this illusion quickly vanishes when we look at the data at the bottom of Exhibit 11–7 (alternative 2). Notice that this alternative would reduce the contribution margin for the company as a whole by $150,000 per year.

Herein lies one of the defects of the cost approach to setting transfer prices: Cost-based transfer prices can lead to dysfunctional decisions in a company because this approach has no built-in mechanism for telling the manager when transfers should or should not be made between divisions. In the case at hand, transfers should *not* be made; the Relay Division should go on selling the old relay to the governmental contractors, and the Motor

EXHIBIT 11–7

Effects of pricing transfers between divisions at cost

Alternative 1: The Motor Division purchases the new relays from the outside supplier at $15 each; the Relay Division continues to produce and sell the old relays.

	50,000 units per year		
	Relay Division	**Motor Division**	**Total company**
Sales (at $20 per old relay and $60 per motor, respectively)	$1,000,000	$3,000,000	$4,000,000
Less variable expenses (at $12 per old relay and $40* per motor, respectively)	600,000	2,000,000	2,600,000
Contribution margin	$ 400,000	$1,000,000	$1,400,000

Alternative 2: The Motor Division purchases the new relays from the Relay Division at an internal transfer price of $10 per relay (the Relay Division's variable cost of producing the new relay). This requires that the Relay Division give up its present outside business.

	Relay Division	Motor Division	Total company
Sales (at $10 per new relay and $60 per motor, respectively)	$ 500,000	$3,000,000	$3,000,000‡
Less variable expenses (at $10 per new relay and $35† per motor, respectively)	500,000	1,750,000	1,750,000‡
Contribution margin	–0–	$1,250,000	$1,250,000
Decrease in contribution margin for the company as a whole if alternative 2 is accepted			$ 150,000

* $15 outside supplier's cost per new relay + Other variable costs of $25 per motor = $40 per motor.
† $10 internal transfer price per new relay + Other variable costs of $25 per motor = $35 per motor.
‡ The $500,000 in intracompany sales has been eliminated.

Division should buy the new relay from the outside supplier. Although this is obvious after seeing the income statement data in Exhibit 11–7, such matters can be obscured when dealing with multiproduct divisions. Thus, as a result of using cost as a transfer price, profits for the company as a whole may be adversely affected and the manager may never know about it.

Exhibit 11–7 also illustrates another defect associated with cost-based transfer prices: The only division that will show any profits is the one that makes the final sale to an outside party. Other divisions, such as the Relay Division in the bottom portion of Exhibit 11–7, will show no profits for their efforts; thus, evaluation by the ROI formula or by the residual income approach will not be possible.

Another serious criticism of cost-based transfer prices lies in their general inability to provide incentive for control of costs. If the costs of one division are simply passed on to the next, then there is little incentive for anyone to control costs. The final selling division is simply burdened with the accumulated waste and inefficiency of intermediate processors and will be penalized with a rate of return that is deficient in comparison to that of competitors. Experience has shown that unless costs are subject to some type of competitive pressures at transfer points, waste and inefficiency almost invariably develop.

Despite these shortcomings, cost-based transfer prices are in fairly common use. Advocates argue that they are easily understood and highly convenient to use. If transfer prices are to be based on cost, then the costs should be standard costs rather than actual costs. This will at least avoid the passing on of inefficiency from one division to another.

A general formula for computing transfer prices

A general formula exists that can be used by the manager as a starting point in computing the appropriate transfer price between divisions or segments in a multidivisional company.[3] The formula is that *the transfer price should be equal to the unit variable costs of the good being transferred, plus the contribution margin per unit that is lost to the selling division as a result of giving up outside sales.* The formula can be expressed as:

Transfer price = Variable costs per unit + Lost contribution margin per unit on outside sales

Applying this formula to the data in the preceding section, the proper transfer price for the Relay Division to charge for the new relay would be:

Transfer price = $10 (the variable costs of the new relay) + $8 (the contribution margin per unit lost to the Relay Division as a result of giving up outside relay sales: $20 selling price − $12 variable costs = $8 lost contribution margin on the old relays)

Transfer price = $18 per unit

Upon seeing this transfer price, it becomes immediately obvious to management that no transfers should be made between the two divisions, since the Motor Division can buy its relays from an outside supplier at only $15 each. Thus, the transfer price enables management to reach the correct decision and to avoid any adverse effect on profits.

A transfer price computed by the above formula is one based on competitive market conditions. The remainder of our discussion will be directed toward the setting of market-based transfer prices.

Transfers at market price: General considerations

Some form of competitive **market price** is generally regarded as the best approach to the transfer pricing problem. One reason is that this approach dovetails very well with the profit center concept and makes profit-based performance evaluation feasible at many levels of an organization. By using

---

[3] For background discussion, see Ralph L. Benke, Jr., and James Don Edwards, "Transfer Pricing: Techniques and Uses," *Management Accounting* 61, no. 12 (June 1980), pp. 44–46.

market prices to control transfers, *all* divisions or segments are able to show profits for their efforts—not just the final division in the chain of transfers. The market price approach also helps the manager to decide when transfers should be made, as we saw earlier, and tends to lead to the best decisions involving transfer questions that may arise on a day-to-day basis.

The market price approach is designed for use in highly decentralized organizations. By this we mean that it is used in those organizations where divisional managers have enough autonomy in decision making so that the various divisions can be viewed as being virtually independent businesses with independent profit responsibility. The idea in using market prices to control transfers is to create the competitive market conditions that would exist if the various divisions were *indeed* separate firms and engaged in arm's-length, open-market bargaining. To the extent that the resulting transfer prices reflect actual market conditions, divisional operating results provide an excellent basis for evaluating managerial performance.

The National Association of Accountants describes other advantages and the overall operation of the market price approach as follows:

> Internal procurement is expected where the company's products and services are superior or equal in design, quality, performance, and price, and when acceptable delivery schedules can be met. So long as these conditions are met, the receiving unit suffers no loss and the supplier unit's profit accrues to the company. Often the receiving division gains advantages such as better control over quality, assurance of continued supply, and prompt delivery.[4]

In addition to the formula given earlier, there are certain guidelines that should be followed when using market prices to control transfers between divisions. These guidelines are:

1. The buying division must purchase internally so long as the selling division meets all bona fide outside prices and wants to sell internally.
2. If the selling division does not meet all bona fide outside prices, then the buying division is free to purchase outside.
3. The selling division must be free to reject internal business if it prefers to sell outside.[5]
4. An impartial board must be established to help settle disagreements between divisions over transfer prices.

Transfers at market price: Well-defined intermediate market

Not all companies or divisions face the same market conditions. Sometimes the only customer a division has for its output is a sister division. In other situations, an **intermediate market** may exist for part or all of a division's output. By intermediate market, we mean that a market exists in which an

---

[4] National Association of Accountants, *Research Series No. 30,* "Accounting for Intra-Company Transfers" (New York, Association of Accountants, June 1956), pp. 13–14.

[5] Ibid., p. 14. Outside products may provide the selling division with a greater return (as in the case of the Relay Division in our earlier example).

item can be sold *immediately* and *in its present form* to outside customers, if desired, rather than being transferred to another division for use in its manufacturing process. Thus, if an intermediate market exists, a division will have a choice between selling its products to outside customers on the intermediate market or selling them to other divisions within the company. In this section, we consider transfer pricing in those situations where intermediate markets are strong and well defined.

Let us assume that Division A of International Company has a product that can be sold either to Division B or to outside customers in an intermediate market. The cost and revenue structures of the two divisions are given below:

Division A		Division B	
Intermediate selling price		Final market price outside	$100
if sold outside.	$25	Transfer price from Division A	
Variable costs	15	(or outside purchase price).	25
		Variable costs added in Division B	40

What transfer price should control transfers between the two divisions? In this case, the answer is easy; the transfer price should be $25—the price that Division A can get by selling on the intermediate market and the price that Division B would otherwise have to pay to purchase the desired goods from an outside supplier in the intermediate market. This price can also be obtained by applying the formula developed earlier:

Transfer price = Variable costs per unit + Lost contribution margin per unit on outside sales

Transfer price = $15 + ($25 − $15 = $10)
Transfer price = $25

The choices facing the two divisions are shown graphically in Exhibit 11–8. (Start at the bottom of the exhibit and follow the arrows upward.)

So long as Division A receives a transfer price of $25 per unit from Division B, it will be willing to sell all of its output internally. In selling to Division B, Division A will be just as well off as if it had sold its product outside at the $25 price. In like manner, so long as the price charged by outside suppliers is not less than $25 per unit, Division B will be willing to pay that price to Division A. The $25 per unit intermediate market price, therefore, serves as an acceptable transfer price between the two divisions. The results of transfers at this price can be summarized as follows:

	Division A	Division B	Entire company
Sales price per unit	$25	$100	$100
Variable costs added per unit	15	40	55
Transfer cost per unit	—	25	—
Contribution margin per unit	$10	$ 35	$ 45

EXHIBIT 11–8
Transfers at market price: Well-defined intermediate market

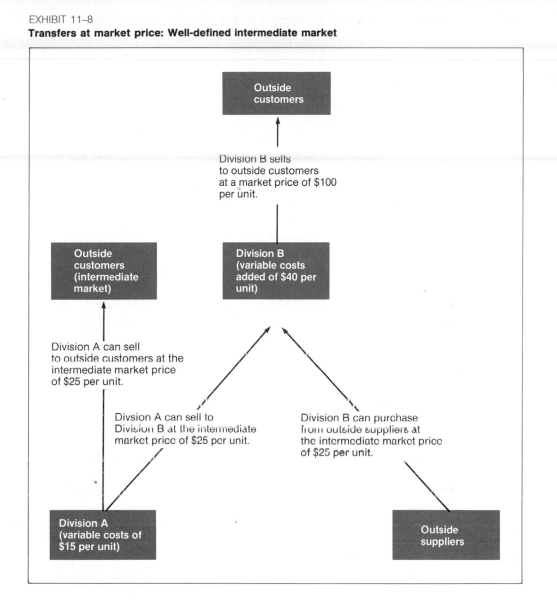

The contribution margin realized for the entire company is $45 per unit. By using the $25 intermediate market price to control intracompany transfers, the firm is able to show that a portion of this margin accrues from the efforts of Division A and that a portion accrues from the efforts of Division B. These data will then serve as an excellent basis for evaluating managerial performance in the divisions, using the rate of return or residual income approaches.

Transfers at market price: Price changes in the intermediate market

In the preceding section, we assumed that there was complete price agreement in the intermediate market, and therefore that Division B could purchase the needed goods from an outside supplier at the same $25 price as being charged by Division A. In reality, complete price agreement often doesn't exist, or it may be upset by some suppliers deciding to cut their prices for various reasons. Returning to the example in the preceding section, let us assume that an outside supplier has offered to supply the goods to Division B for only $20 per unit, rather than at the normal $25 intermediate market price being charged by Division A. Should Division B accept this offer, or should Division A cut its price to $20 to keep Division B's business? The answer will depend on whether Division A (the selling division) is operating at full or at partial capacity.

Selling division at full capacity One reason for using market price in transfer pricing is to guard against setting transfer prices below the selling division's opportunity costs. (Recall from Chapter 2 that opportunity cost can be defined as the potential benefit that is lost or sacrificed when the choice of one course of action requires the giving up of an alternative course of action.) If the selling division is already selling all that it can produce to outside customers, then the division's opportunity cost is the purchase price that these customers are willing to pay. The reason is that in accepting inside business, the selling division would have to give up outside business and sacrifice the revenues that could have been received on the outside sales. *Thus, when the selling division is at full capacity, the transfer price should never be less than this opportunity cost, or the selling division will suffer, and the company as a whole may suffer as well.*

This means that if Division A in our example is able to sell externally all that it can produce at the $25 intermediate market price, then this is its opportunity cost, and it should not sell to Division B for less. We can prove the accuracy of this statement by applying the formula used earlier:

Transfer price = Variable costs per unit + Lost contribution margin per unit on outside sales

Transfer price = $15 + ($25 outside selling price − $15 variable costs = $10 lost contribution margin per unit)

Transfer price = $25

In sum, Division A should continue to sell on the intermediate market at $25 per unit and Division B should accept the outside supplier's offer of $20 per unit, assuming that the outside supplier can meet required quality standards and delivery schedules.

Selling division with idle capacity If the selling division has substantial idle capacity, then a different situation exists. Under these conditions, the opportunity cost *may* be zero (depending on what alternative uses the selling division has for its idle capacity). Even if the opportunity cost is zero, many managers would argue that the transfer price should still be based on prevailing market prices, to the extent that these prices can be determined accurately and fairly. Other managers would argue that idle capacity combined with an opportunity cost of zero, or near zero, calls for a negotiation of the transfer price downward from prevailing market rates, so that both the buyer and the seller can profit from the intracompany business.

Under idle capacity conditions, so long as the selling division can receive a price greater than its variable costs (at least in the short run), all parties will benefit by keeping business inside the company rather than having the buying division go outside. The accuracy of this statement can be shown by returning to the example in the preceding section. Assume again that an outside supplier offers to sell the needed goods to Division B at $20 per unit. In this case, however, we will assume that Division A has enough idle capacity to supply all of Division B's needs, with no prospects for additional outside sales at the current $25 intermediate market price. Using our formula, the transfer price between Divisions A and B should be:

Transfer price = Variable costs per unit + Lost contribution margin per
unit on outside sales

Transfer price = $15 + –0–
Transfer price = $15

The $15 variable cost figure above actually represents a *lower limit* for a transfer price, and as a practical matter the transfer price between the two divisions would probably be the $20 price being quoted to Division B from the outside. But would Division A be *required* to meet the $20 price? The answer is no. The guidelines given earlier indicate that the selling division is not required to sell internally. Rather than accept a $20 price for its goods, Division A may prefer to let its capacity remain idle and search for other, more profitable products.

If Division A decides not to reduce its price to $20 to meet outside competition, should Division B be forced to continue to pay $25 and to buy internally? The answer again is no. The guidelines given earlier state that if the selling division is not willing to meet all bona fide outside prices, then the buying division is free to go outside to get the best price it can. However, if the selling division has idle capacity and the buying division purchases from an outside supplier, then **suboptimization**[6] will result for the selling division, possibly for the buying division, and certainly for the company as a whole. In our example, if Division A refuses to meet the $20 price, then *both it and the company as a whole will lose $5 per unit in potential contribution margin ($20 − $15 = $5).* In short, where idle capacity exists, every effort should be made to negotiate a price acceptable to both the buyer and the seller that will keep business within the company as a whole.

---

[6] By *suboptimization,* we mean that overall profitability will be less than it could have been.

Transfers at negotiated market price

Where an intermediate market price exists, it represents an *upper limit* on the charge that can be made on transfers between divisions. In many situations, a lesser price can be justified. For example, selling and administrative expenses may be less when intracompany sales are involved, or the volume of units may be large enough to justify quantity discounts. In addition, we have already seen that a price below the prevailing market price may be justified when the selling division has idle capacity.

Situations such as those just described can probably be served best by some type of **negotiated market price.** A negotiated market price is one agreed upon between the selling and buying divisions that reflects unusual or mitigating circumstances. Possibly the widest use of negotiated market prices is in those situations where no intermediate market prices are available. For example, one division may require an item that is not available from any outside source and therefore must be produced internally. Under these circumstances, the buying division must negotiate with another division in the company and agree to a transfer price that is attractive enough to the other division to cause it to take on the new business.

To summarize, a negotiated market price is appropriate when:

1. Costs such as selling or administrative expenses can be avoided on internal sales.
2. The volume of units to be transferred is large enough to justify quantity discounts.
3. The selling division has idle capacity.
4. The item needed by the buying division is not available from any outside source and therefore must be produced internally by another division.

As stated earlier, negotiated market prices are used most widely in those situations relating to (4) above where no intermediate market exists for an item. To provide an example of how a transfer price would be set in such a situation, consider the following data:

Division X has developed a new product that requires a custom-made fitting. Another division in the company, Division Y, has both the experience and the equipment necessary to produce the fitting. Division X has approached Division Y for a quoted unit price based on the production of 5,000 fittings per year.

Division Y has determined that the fitting would require variable costs of $8 per unit. However, in order to have time to produce the fitting, Division Y would have to reduce production of product A by 3,500 units per year. Product A sells for $45 per unit and has variable costs of $25 per unit. What transfer price should Division Y quote to Division X for the new fittings? Employing our formula, we get:

$$\text{Transfer price} = \text{Variable costs per unit} + \text{Lost contribution margin per unit on outside sales}$$

The lost contribution margin per unit would be:

Selling price of product A	$	45
Variable costs of product A		25
Contribution margin of product A		20
Unit sales of product A given up	×	3,500
Total contribution margin lost	$	70,000

$$\frac{\$70{,}000 \text{ contribution margin lost on product A}}{5{,}000 \text{ fittings to be manufactured for Division X}} = \frac{\$14 \text{ lost contribution}}{\text{margin per fitting}}$$

Transfer price = $8 variable costs + $14 lost contribution margin
Transfer price = $22 per fitting

Thus, the transfer price quoted by Division Y should not be less than $22 per fitting. Division Y might quote a higher price if it wants to increase its overall profits (at the expense of Division X), but it should not quote less than $22, or the profits of the company as a whole will suffer. If Division X is not happy with the $22 price, it can get a quote from an outside manufacturer for the fitting.

If Division Y in our example has idle capacity, then the appropriate transfer price is less clear. The lower limit for a transfer price would be the $8 variable costs, as discussed earlier. However, no division wants to simply recover its costs, so the actual transfer price would undoubtedly be greater than $8, according to what could be negotiated between the two divisional managers. In situations such as this, the selling division will often add some "target" markup figure to its costs in quoting a transfer price to the buying division.

Divisional autonomy and suboptimization

A question often arises as to how much autonomy should be granted to divisions in setting their own transfer prices and in making decisions concerning whether to sell internally or to sell outside. Should the divisional heads have complete authority to make these decisions, or should top corporate management step in if it appears that a decision is about to be made that would result in suboptimization? For example, if idle capacity exists in the selling division and divisional managers are unable to agree on a transfer price, should top corporate management step in and *force* settlement of the dispute?

Efforts should always be made, of course, to bring disputing managers together. But the almost unanimous feeling among top corporate executives is that divisional heads should not be forced into an agreement over a transfer price. That is, if a particular divisional head flatly refuses to change his or her position in a dispute, *then this decision should be respected* even if it results in suboptimization. This is simply the price that is paid for the concept of divisional autonomy. If top corporate management steps in and forces the decisions in difficult situations, then the concepts that we have been developing in this chapter largely evaporate and the company simply becomes a centralized operation with decentralization of only minor decisions and responsibilities. In short, if a division is to be viewed as an autonomous unit with independent profit responsibility, then it must have control over its own destiny—even to the extent of having the right to make bad decisions.

We should note, however, that if a division consistently makes bad decisions, the results will soon have an impact on its rate of return and the divisional manager may find himself having to defend the division's performance. Even so, his right to get himself into an embarrassing situation must be respected if the divisional concept is to operate successfully. The overwhelming experience of multidivisional companies is that divisional autonomy and independent profit responsibility lead to much greater success and profitability than do closely controlled, centrally administered operations. Part of the price of this success and profitability is an occasional situation of suboptimization due to pettiness, bickering, or just plain managerial stubbornness.

SUMMARY

Responsibility accounting centers on the notion that any point within an organization having control over cost or revenue is a responsibility center. The way in which the various responsibility centers discharge their control over cost or revenue is communicated upward in an organization, from lower levels of responsibility to higher levels of responsibility, through a system of integrated performance reports.

Those responsibility centers having control over cost are known as cost centers; those having control over both cost and revenue are known as profit centers; and those having control over cost, revenue, and investment funds are known as investment centers. The ROI formula is widely regarded as a method of evaluating performance in an investment center because it summarizes into one figure many aspects of an investment center manager's responsibilities. As an alternative to the ROI formula, some companies use residual income as a measure of investment center performance. These companies argue that the residual income approach encourages profitable investment in many situations where the ROI approach might discourage investment.

Transfer pricing relates to the price to be charged in a transfer of goods or an exchange of services between two units (such as divisions) within an organization. A transfer price can be based on the cost of the goods being transferred, on the intermediate market price of the goods being transferred, or on a price negotiated between the buying and selling divisions. The predominant feeling is that the best transfer price is some version of market price—either intermediate or negotiated—to the extent that such a price exists or can be determined for the good or service involved. The use of market price or negotiated market price in transfers between units facilitates performance evaluation by permitting both the buyer and the seller to be treated as independent, autonomous units.

REVIEW PROBLEM ON TRANSFER PRICING

Case A

Collyer products, Inc., has a Valve Division that manufactures and sells a standard valve as follows:

Capacity in units	100,000
Selling price to outside cutomers	
on the intermediate market	$30
Variable costs per unit	16
Fixed costs per unit (based on capacity)	9

The company has a Pump Division that could use this valve in the manufacture of one of its pumps. The Pump Division is currently purchasing 10,000 valves per year from an overseas supplier at a cost of $29 per valve.

Required:

1. Assume that the Valve Division has ample idle capacity to handle all of the Pump Division's needs. What should be the transfer price between the two divisions?
2. Assume that the Valve Division is selling all that it can produce to outside customers on the intermediate market. What should be the transfer price between the two divisions? At this price, will any transfers be made?
3. Assume again that the Valve Division is selling all that it can produce to outside customers on the intermediate market. Also assume that $3 in variable expenses can be avoided on intracompany sales, due to reduced selling costs. What should be the transfer price between the two divisions?

Solution—Case A:

1. Since the Valve Division has idle capacity, it is not necessary to give up any outside sales in order to take on the Pump Division's business. Therefore, applying the transfer pricing formula, we get:

Transfer price = Variable costs per unit + Lost contribution margin per unit on outside sales

Transfer price = $16 + $ –0–
Transfer price = $16

However, a transfer price of $16 represents a minimum price to cover the Valve Division's variable costs. The actual transfer price would undoubtedly fall somewhere between this amount and the $29 that the Pump Division is currently paying for its valves. Thus, we have a transfer price *range* in this case of from $16 to $29 per unit, depending on negotiations between the two divisions.

2. Since the Valve Division is selling all that it can produce on the intermediate market, it would have to give up some of these outside sales in order to take on the Pump Division's business. Applying the transfer pricing formula, we get:

$$\text{Transfer price} = \text{Variable costs per unit} + \text{Lost contribution margin per unit on outside sales}$$

Transfer price $= \$16 + \$14*$
Transfer price $= \$30$

* \$30 selling price $-$ \$16 variable costs $=$ \$14 contribution margin per unit.

Since the Pump Division can purchase valves from an outside supplier at only \$29 per unit, no transfers will be made between the two divisions.

3. Applying the transfer pricing formula, we get:

$$\text{Transfer price} = \text{Variable costs per unit} + \text{Lost contribution margin per unit on outside sales}$$

Transfer price $= \$13* + \$14$
Transfer price $= \$27$

* \$16 variable expenses $-$ \$3 variable expenses avoided $=$ \$13.

Case B

Refer to the original data in case A above. Assume that the Pump Division needs 20,000 special valves per year that are to be supplied by the Valve Division. The Valve Division's variable costs to manufacture and ship the special valve would be \$20 per unit. In order to produce these special valves, the Valve Division would have to give up one half of its production of the regular valves (that is, cut its production of the regular valves from 100,000 units per year to 50,000 units per year). You can assume that the Valve Division is selling all of the regular valves that it can produce to outside customers on the intermediate market.

Required: If the Valve Division decides to produce the special valves for the Pump Division, what transfer price should it charge per valve?

Solution—Case B: In order to produce the 20,000 special valves, the Valve Division will have to give up sales of 50,000 regular valves to outside customers. The lost contribution margin on the 50,000 regular valves will be:

$$50,000 \text{ valves} \times \$14 \text{ per unit} = \$700,000$$

Spreading this lost contribution margin over the 20,000 special valves, we get:

$$\frac{\$700,000 \text{ lost contribution margin}}{20,000 \text{ special valves}} = \$35 \text{ per unit}$$

Using this amount in the transfer pricing formula, we get the following transfer price per unit on the special valves:

$$\text{Transfer price} = \text{Variable costs per unit} + \text{Lost contribution margin per unit on outside sales}$$

Transfer price $= \$20 + \$35$
Transfer price $= \$55$

Thus, the Valve Division must charge a transfer price of $55 per unit on the special valves in order to be as well off as if it just continued to manufacture and sell the regular valves on the intermediate market. If the Valve Division wishes to increase its profits, it could charge more than $55 per valve, but it must charge at least $55 in order to maintain its present level of profits.

KEY TERMS FOR REVIEW

Cost center A responsibility center that has control over the incurrence of cost but has no control over the generation of revenue or the use of investment funds.

Decentralization The delegation of decision-making authority throughout an organization by allowing managers at various operating levels to make key decisions relating to their areas of responsibility.

Intermediate market A market in which an item can be sold immediately and in its present form to outside customers rather than just being transferred to another division for use in its manufacturing process.

Investment center A responsibility center which has control over the incurrence of cost and over the generating of revenue and that also has control over the use of investment funds.

Margin A percentage figure computed by dividing net operating income by sales.

Market price The price being charged for an item on the open (intermediate) market.

Negotiated market price A transfer price agreed upon between buying and selling divisions that reflects unusual or mitigating circumstances.

Net operating income The income of an organization before interest and income taxes have been deducted.

Operating assets Cash, accounts receivable, inventory, fixed assets, and all other assets held for productive use in an organization.

Profit center A responsibility center that has control over the incurrence of cost and the generating of revenue but has no control over the use of investment funds.

Residual income The net operating income that an investment center is able to earn above some minimum rate of return on its operating assets.

Responsibility center Any point in an organization that has control over the incurrence of cost, the generating of revenue, or the use of investment funds.

Return on investment (ROI) A measure of profitability in an organization that is computed by multiplying the margin by the turnover.

Suboptimization An overall level of profitability that is less than an organization is capable of earning.

Transfer price The price charged when one division provides goods or services to another division of an organization.

Turnover An operating ratio computed by dividing sales by the average operating assets.

478

QUESTIONS

11–1. Describe the general flow of information in a responsibility accounting system.

11–2. What is meant by the term *responsibility center?* Could a responsibility center be a person as well as a department, and so on? Does the concept of a responsibility center apply to nonmanufacturing as well as to manufacturing activities?

11–3. What is meant by the term *decentralization?*

14–4. What benefits are felt to result from decentralization in an organization?

11–5. Distinguish between a cost center, a profit center, and an investment center.

11–6. How is performance in a cost center generally measured? Performance in a profit center? Performance in an investment center?

11–7. What is meant by the terms *margin* and *turnover?*

11–8. In what way is the ROI formula a more exacting measure of performance than the ratio of net income to sales?

11–9. When the ROI formula is being used to measure performance, what three approaches to improving the overall profitability are open to the manager?

11–10. The sales figure could be canceled out in the ROI formula, leaving simply net operating income over operating assets. Since this abbreviated formula would yield the same ROI figure, why leave sales in?

11–11. A student once commented to the author, "It simply is not possible for a decrease in operating assets to result in an increase in profitability. The way to increase profits is to *increase* the operating assets." Discuss.

11–12. X Company has high fixed expenses and is currently operating somewhat above the break-even point. From this point on, will percentage increases in net income tend to be greater than, about equal to, or less than percentage increases in total sales? Why? (Ignore income taxes.)

11–13. What is meant by residual income?

11–14. In what way can ROI lead to dysfunctional decisions on the part of the investment center manager? How does the residual income approach overcome this problem?

11–15. Division A has operating assets of $100,000, and Division B has operating assets of $1,000,000. Can residual income be used to compare performance in the two divisions? Explain.

11–16. What is meant by the term *transfer price,* and why are transfer pricing systems needed?

11–17. Why are cost-based transfer prices in widespread use? What are the disadvantages of cost-based transfer prices?

11–18. If a market price for a product can be determined, why is it generally considered to be the best transfer price?

11–19. Under what circumstances might a negotiated market price be a better approach to pricing transfers between divisions than the actual market price?

11–20. In what ways can suboptimization result if divisional managers are given full autonomy in setting, accepting, and rejecting transfer prices?

EXERCISES

E11–1. Selected operating data for two divisions of York Company are given below:

	Eastern Division	Western Division
Sales	$1,000,000	$1,750,000
Average operating assets	500,000	500,000
Net operating income	90,000	105,000
Property, plant, and equipment	250,000	200,000

Required:
1. Compute the rate of return for each division, using the ROI formula.
2. So far as you can tell from the data available, which divisional manager seems to be doing the better job? Why?

E11–2. Melbourne Products, Inc., has two divisions, A and B. Selected data on the two divisions follow:

	Division A	Division B
Sales	$2,000,000	$4,000,000
Net operating income	150,000	350,000
Average operating assets	1,000,000	2,500,000

Required:
1. Compute the return on investment (ROI) for each division. (Carry computations to two decimal places.)
2. Assume that the company evaluates performance by use of residual income and that the minimum required return for any division is 12 percent. Compute the residual income for each division.
3. Is Division B's greater amount of residual income an indication that it is better managed? Explain.

E11–3. Nelcro Company's Electrical Division produces a high-quality transformer. Sales and cost data on the transformer follow:

Selling price per unit on the intermediate market	$40
Variable costs per unit	21
Fixed costs per unit (based on capacity)	9
Capacity in units	50,000

Nelcro Company has an Audio Division that would like to begin purchasing this transformer from the Electrical Division. The Audio Division is currently purchasing 10,000 transformers each year from another manufacturer at a cost of $40 per transformer, less a 5 percent quantity discount.

Required:
1. Assume that the Electrical Division is now selling only 40,000 transformers each year to outside customers on the intermediate market. If it begins to sell to the Audio Division, and if each division is to be treated as an independent investment center, what transfer price would you recommend? Why?
2. Assume that the Electrical Division is selling all of the transformers it can produce to outside customers on the intermediate market. Would this change your recommended transfer price? Explain.

E11–4. Listed below are three charges found on the monthly report of a division that manufactures and sells products primarily to outside customers. Divisional performance is evaluated by the use of ROI. You are to state which, if any, of the following charges are consistent with the responsibility accounting concept. Support each answer with a brief explanation.

1. A charge (at 10 percent of division sales) for the cost of operating general corporate headquarters.
2. A charge for goods purchased from another division. The charge is based on the competitive market price for the goods.
3. A charge for the use of the corporate computer facility. The charge is determined by taking actual annual computer department costs and allocating an amount to each division based on the ratio of its use to total corporate use.

(CMA, adapted)

E11–5. Provide the missing data in the following tabulation:

| | Division | | |
	A	B	C
Sales	$800,000	$?	$?
Net operating income	56,000	?	40,000
Average operating assets	?	125,000	?
Margin	?	4%	8%
Turnover	?	6	?
ROI	14%	?	20%

E11–6. Division A manufactures a product that can be sold either to Division B or to outside customers. During 19x8, the following activity occurred in Division A:

Number of units:
Produced during the year 5,000
Sold to outside customers 4,000
Sold to Division B 1,000
Selling price per unit $100
Cost of production per unit 80

Sales to Division B were at the same price as sales to outside customers. The units purchased by Division B were processed further at a cost of $120 per unit and then sold to outside customers for $250 each.

Required: 1. Prepare income statements for 19x8 for Division A, Division B, and the company as a whole.
2. Assume that Division A's manufacturing capacity is 5,000 units. In 19x9, Division B wants to purchase 2,000 units from Division A, rather than only 1,000 units as in 19x8. (Units are not available from outside sources.) Should Division A sell the 1,000 additional units to Division B or continue to sell them to outside customers? Explain why this would or would not make any difference from the point of view of the company as a whole.

E11–7. Supply the missing data in the tabulation below:

	Division		
	A	B	C
Sales	$400,000	$750,000	$600,000
Net operating income	?	45,000	?
Average operating assets	160,000	?	150,000
ROI.	20%	18%	?
Minimum required rate of return:			
Percentage	15%	?	12%
Dollar amount	$?	$ 50,000	$?
Residual income	?	?	6,000

E11–8. In each of the cases below, assume that Division X has a product that can be sold either to outside customers on an intermediate market or to Division Y for use in its production process.

	Case	
	A	B
Division X:		
Capacity in units	100,000	100,000
Number of units being sold on the		
intermediate market	100,000	80,000
Selling price per unit on the		
intermediate market	$50	$35
Variable costs per unit	30	20
Fixed costs per unit (based on capacity)	8	6
Division Y:		
Number of units needed for production	20,000	20,000
Purchase price per unit now being paid		
to an outside supplier	$47	$34

Required: 1. Refer to the data in case A above. Assume that $2 per unit in variable selling costs can be avoided on intracompany sales.

   a. Using the transfer pricing formula, determine the transfer price that Division X should charge on any sales to Division Y.

   b. Will any transfers be made between the two divisions? Explain.

2. Refer to the data in case B above. Within what range should the transfer price be set for any sales between the two divisions? (Use the transfer pricing formula as needed.)

E11–9. Selected sales and operating data for three companies are given below:

	Company		
	A	B	C
Sales	$6,000,000	$10,000,000	$8,000,000
Average operating assets	1,500,000	5,000,000	2,000,000
Net operating income.	300,000	900,000	180,000
Stockholders' equity	1,000,000	3,500,000	1,500,000
Minimum required rate of return	15%	18%	12%

Required: 1. Compute the ROI for each company.
2. Compute the residual income for each company.
3. Assume that each company is presented with an investment opportunity that would yield a rate of return of 17 percent.
   a. If performance is being measured by ROI, which company or companies will probably accept the opportunity? Reject? Why?
   b. If performance is being measured by residual income, which company or companies will probably accept the opportunity? Reject? Why?

PROBLEMS

P11–10.   **ROI; comparison of company performance.**   Comparative data on three companies in the same industry are given below:

	Company		
	A	**B**	**C**
Sales	$900,000	$200,000	$?
Net operating income	90,000	20,000	?
Average operating assets	450,000	?	2,000,000
Margin	?	?	0.5%
Turnover	?	?	2
ROI.	?	1%	?

Required: 1. What advantages can you see in breaking down the ROI computation into two separate elements, margin and turnover?
2. Fill in the missing information above, and comment on the relative performance of the three companies in as much detail as the data permit. Make *specific recommendations* on steps to be taken to improve the return on investment, where needed.

(Adapted from National Association of Accountants,
Research Report No. 35, p. 34)

P11–11.   **The appropriate transfer price; well-defined intermediate market.**   Electronic Products, Inc., has just purchased a small company that specializes in the manufacture of electronic tuners that are used as a component part in TV sets. Electronic Products, Inc., is a decentralized company and will treat the newly acquired company as an autonomous division with full profit responsibility. The new Tuner Division has the following cost per tuner:

Variable expenses	$11
Fixed overhead (based on a capacity of 10,000 tuners per month)	6
Total cost per tuner	$17

The division's selling price is $20 per tuner.

Electronic Products, Inc., also has an Assembly Division that assembles TV sets. The division is currently purchasing 3,000 tuners from an overseas supplier at a cost of $20 per tuner, less a 10 percent quantity discount. The president of Electronic Products, Inc., is anxious to have the Assembly Division begin purchasing its tuners from the newly acquired Tuner Division in order to "keep the profits within the corporate family."

Required: For (1)–(3) below, assume that the Tuner Division can sell all of its output to outside TV manufacturers at its quoted prices. *Each question is independent.*

1. If the Assembly Division purchases 3,000 tuners per month from the Tuner Division, what price should control the transfers? Why?
2. If the Tuner Division meets the price of the overseas supplier and sells 3,000 turners to the Assembly Division each month, what will be the effect on the profits of the company as a whole?
3. If the intermediate market price for tuners is $20, is there any reason why the Tuner Division should sell to the Assembly Division for less than $20? Explain.

For (4)–(7) below, assume that the Tuner Division is currently selling only 6,000 turners each month to outside TV manufacturers at the stated $20 price.

4. If the Assembly Division purchases 3,000 tuners per month from the Tuner Division, what price should control the transfers? Why?
5. Suppose that the overseas supplier drops its price (net of the quantity discount) to only $16 per tuner. Should the Tuner Division meet this price? Explain. If the Tuner Division does not meet the $16 price, what will be the effect on the profits of the company as a whole?
6. Refer to (5) above. If the Tuner Division refuses to meet the $16 price, should the Assembly Division be required to purchase from the Tuner Division at a higher price, for the good of the company as a whole? Explain.
7. What is the lowest price that the Tuner Division could accept from the Assembly Division and still be better off profitwise?

P11–12.   **Basic transfer pricing computations.**   In cases 1–3 below, assume that Division A has a product that can be sold either to Division B or to outside customers on an intermediate market. (Further information on case 4 is given in the "required" material.) Treat each case independently.

	Case			
	1	2	3	4
Division A:				
Capacity in units	50,000	300,000	100,000	200,000
Number of units now being sold to outside customers on the intermediate market	50,000	300,000	70,000	200,000
Selling price per unit on the intermediate market	$100	$40	$60	$45
Variable costs per unit	60	20	35	30
Fixed costs per unit (based on capacity)	25	8	15	6
Division B:				
Number of units needed annually	10,000	25,000	20,000	60,000
Purchase price now being paid to an outside supplier	—	$39	$60*	—

* Before any quantity discount.

Required: 1.   Refer to case 1 above. A study has indicated that Division A can avoid $5 per unit in variable costs on any sales to Division B. Use the transfer pricing formula to determine what transfer price should be charged on any sales between the two divisions.

2. Refer to case 2 above. Assume that Division A can avoid $4 per unit in variable costs on any sales to Division B.

   a. Again use the transfer pricing formula to compute an appropriate transfer price.

   b. Would you expect any disagreement between the two divisional managers over what the transfer price should be? Explain.

3. Refer to case 3 above. Assume that Division B is now receiving a 5 percent quantity discount from the outside supplier.

   a. Within what range should the transfer price be set for any sales between the two divisions?

   b. Assume that Division A offers to sell 20,000 units to Division B for $52 per unit and that Division B refuses the price. What will be the loss in potential profits to Division A? Division B? The company as a whole?

4. Refer to case 4 above. Assume that Division B wants Division A to provide it with 60,000 units of a *different* product from the one that Division A is now producing. The new product would require $25 per unit in variable costs and would require that Division A cut back production of its present product by 30,000 units annually. Use the transfer pricing formula to determine what transfer price per unit Division A should charge Division B for the new product.

P11–13. **ROI and residual income.** Billings Products, Inc., is a decentralized organization with five autonomous divisions. The divisions are evaluated on the basis of the return that they are able to generate on invested assets, with year-end bonuses given to the divisional managers who have the highest ROI figures. Operating results for the company's Office Products Division for the most recent year are given below:

Sales	$10,000,000
Less variable expenses	6,000,000
Contribution margin	4,000,000
Less fixed expenses	3,200,000
Net operating income	$ 800,000
Divisional operating assets	$ 4,000,000

The company had an overall ROI of 15 percent last year (considering all divisions). The Office Products Division has an opportunity to add a new product line that would require an additional investment in operating assets of $1,000,000. The cost and revenue characteristics of the new product line per year would be:

Sales	$2,000,000
Variable expenses	60% of sales
Fixed expenses	$640,000

16%
ROI

Required:

1. a. Compute the Office Products Division's ROI for the most recent year; also compute the ROI as it will appear if the new product line is added.

   b. As manager of the Office Products Division, would you accept or reject the new product line? Explain.

2. As the president of Billings Products, Inc., would you want the Office Products Division to accept or reject the new product line? Explain.

3. Suppose that the company views a return of 12 percent on invested assets as being the minimum that any division should earn, and that performance is evaluated by the residual income approach.

   a. Compute the Office Products Division's residual income for the most recent year; also compute the residual income as it will appear if the new product line is added.

b. Under these circumstances, as manager of the Office Products Division, would you accept or reject the new product line? Explain.

P11–14. **Basic transfer pricing computations.** Unless indicated otherwise, assume that each of the following situations is independent:

1. Given the following data for a product manufactured by Division A:

Selling price on the intermediate market	$40
Variable costs per unit	25
Fixed costs per unit (based on capacity)	10
Capacity in units	50,000

Assume that Division A is selling all it can produce to outside customers on the intermediate market. If it sells to Division B, $2 in variable costs per unit can be avoided. Division B is currently purchasing the units from an outside supplier at $37 per unit. From the point of view of the company as a whole, any sales made by Division A to Division B should be priced at what amount per unit?

2. Refer to the data in (1) above. Would you expect any transfers to take place between the two divisions? Explain.

3. Given the following data for product A, which is produced and sold by Division X:

Selling price on the intermediate market	$75
Variable costs per unit of product A	50
Fixed costs per unit (based on capacity)	16
Capacity in units of product A	25,000

Division X is currently operating at full capacity, producing 25,000 units of product A each period and selling them to outside customers. Division Y would like Division X to start producing 5,000 units of a new product—product B—for it each period. This would require that Division X cut back production of product A by 40 percent, to only 15,000 units each period. Division X has estimated the following cost per unit for the new product B:

Selling price to Division Y	$?
Variable costs per unit of product B	80
Fixed costs per unit	32

Division X would use existing personnel and equipment to produce product B. What transfer price should Division X charge Division Y for each unit of product B?

P11–15. **ROI analysis.** The income statement for Westex, Inc., for its most recent period is given below:

	Total	Unit
Sales	$1,000,000	$50.00
Less variable expenses	600,000	30.00
Contribution margin	400,000	20.00
Less fixed expenses	320,000	16.00
Net operating income	80,000	4.00
Less income taxes (40%)	32,000	1.60
Net income	$ 48,000	$ 2.40

The company had average operating assets of $500,000 during the period.

Required: 1. Compute the company's return on investment for the period, using the ROI formula.

For each of the following questions, indicate whether the margin and turnover will increase, decrease, or remain unchanged as a result of the events described, and then compute the new ROI figure. Consider each question separately, starting in each case from the original ROI computed in (1) above.

2. The company is able to achieve a cost savings of $10,000 per period by using less costly raw material inputs.
3. By using the computer to control inventory purchases, the company is able to reduce the average level of inventory by $100,000. (The released funds are used to pay off bank loans.)
4. Sales are increased by $100,000; operating assets remain unchanged.
5. The company issues bonds and uses the proceeds to purchase $125,000 in machinery and equipment. Interest on the bonds is $15,000 per period. Sales remain unchanged. The new, more efficient equipment reduces production costs by $5,000 per period.
6. The company invests $180,000 of cash (received on accounts receivable) in a plot of land that is to be held for possible future use as a plant site.
7. Obsolete items of inventory carried on the records at a cost of $20,000 are scrapped and written off as a loss, since they are unsalable.

P11–16. **Choosing an appropriate transfer price.** Top-Value Products, Inc., has just acquired a small company that manufactures electrical pumps. The company will operate as a division of Top-Value Products, Inc., under the name of the Pump Division. The pumps that are manufactured by the Pump Division are used primarily in dishwashers and are sold to various dishwasher manufacturers across the nation. The pumps sell for $60 each. Top-Value Products, Inc., has an Appliances Division that manufactures dishwashers, and the president of Top-Value products, Inc., feels that the Appliances Division should begin to purchase its pumps from the newly acquired Pump Division.

The Appliances Division is currently purchasing 30,000 pumps each year from an outside supplier. The price is $57 per pump, which represents the normal $60 price less a 5 percent quantity discount.

The Pump Division's cost per pump is given below:

Direct materials	$20
Direct labor	14
Variable overhead	6
Fixed overhead	5*
Total cost per pump	$45

* Based on 100,000 units capacity.

The president of Top-Value Products, Inc., is unsure what transfer price should control sales between the two divisions.

Required: 1. Assume that the Pump Division has sufficient idle capacity to supply 30,000 pumps each year to the Appliances Division. Explain why each of the following transfer prices would or would not be an appropriate price to charge the Appliances Division on the intracompany sales:

           a. $60.00.
           b. $57.00.
           c. $48.50.
           d. $45.00.
           e. $40.00.

2. Assume that the Pump Division is currently selling all the pumps it can produce to outside customers. Under these circumstances, explain why each of the transfer prices given in (1a) through (1e) above would or would not be an appropriate price to charge the Appliances Division on the intracompany sales.

P11–17.   **Transfer pricing; well-defined intermediate market; ROI.**   The Baka Motor Works has just acquired a new Battery Division. The Battery Division produces a standard 12-volt battery that it sells to retail outlets at a competitive price of $15. The retail outlets purchase about 1,200,000 batteries a year. Since the Battery Division has a capacity of 2,000,000 batteries a year, top management is thinking that it might be wise for the company's Automotive Division to start purchasing batteries from the newly acquired Battery Division.

The Automotive Division now purchases 600,000 batteries a year from an outside supplier, at a price of $14 per battery. The discount from the competitive $15 price is a result of the large quantity purchased.

The Battery Division's cost per battery is shown below:

Direct materials	$ 6
Direct labor	2
Variable overhead	1
Fixed overhead	2*
Total cost	$11

* Based on 1,200,000 batteries.

Both divisions are to be treated as investment centers, and their performance is to be evaluated by the ROI formula.

Required: 1. *a.* What transfer price would you recommend? Why?
      b. If the transfer price you recommend is accepted, what will be the effect on the profits of the company as a whole? Show computations.
      c. If the transfer price you recommend is accepted, would you expect the ROI in the Battery Division to increase, decrease, or remain unchanged? Why? (No computations are necessary.) What would be the effect on the ROI of the Automotive Division? Explain.

   2. Assume that the Battery Division is now selling 2,000,000 batteries a year to retail outlets.
      a. What transfer price would you recommend? Why? Will any transfers take place between the two divisions?
      b. If the Battery Division decides to sell to the Automotive Division for $14 per battery, what will be the effect on the profits of the company as a whole? Show computations.

P11–18.   **Negotiated transfer price.**   Pella Company has several independent divisions. The company's Compressor Division produces a high-quality compressor that is sold to various users. The division's income statement for the most recent month, in which 500 compressors were sold, is given below:

	Total	Unit
Sales	$125,000	$250
Less cost of goods sold	75,000	150
Gross margin	50,000	100
Less selling and administrative expenses	30,000	60
Divisional net income	$ 20,000	$ 40

As shown above, it costs the division $150 to produce a compressor. This figure consists of the following costs:

Direct materials	$ 50
Direct labor	60
Overhead (50% fixed)	40
Total cost	$150

The division has fixed selling and administrative expenses of $25,000 per month and variable selling and administrative expenses of $10 per compressor.

Another division of Pella Company, the Home Products Division, uses compressors as a component part of air-conditioning systems that it installs. The Home Products Division has asked the Compressor Division to sell it 40 compressors each month of a somewhat different design. The Compressor Division has estimated the following cost for each of the new compressors:

Direct materials	$ 60
Direct labor	90
Overhead (two thirds fixed)	75
Total cost	$225

In order to produce the new compressors, the Compressor Division would have to reduce production of its present compressors by 100 units per month. However, all variable selling and administrative expenses could be avoided on the intracompany business. Fixed overhead costs would not change.

Required:

1. What price should be charged by the Compressor Division for the new compressor? Show all computations.
2. Suppose the Home Products Division has found a supplier that will provide the new compressors for only $350 each. If the Compressor Division meets this price, what will be the effect on the profits of the company as a whole?

P11–19. **Cost-volume-profit analysis; ROI; transfer pricing.** The Bearing Division of Timkin Company produces a small bearing that is used by a number of companies as a component part in the manufacture of their products. The Timkin Company operates its divisions as autonomous units, giving its divisional managers great discretion in pricing and other decisions. Each division is expected to generate a return on its assets of at least 12 percent. The Bearing Division has operating assets as follows:

Cash	$ 10,000
Accounts receivable	60,000
Inventories	105,000
Plant and equipment (net)	125,000
Total assets	$300,000

The bearings are sold for $4 each. Variable costs are $2.50 per bearing, and fixed costs total $234,000 each period. The division's capacity is 200,000 bearings each period.

Required:
1. How many bearings must be sold each period for the division to obtain the desired rate of return on its assets?
   a. What is the margin earned at this sales level?
   b. What is the turnover of assets at this sales level?
2. The divisional manager is considering two ways of increasing the ROI figure:
   a. Market studies suggest that an increase in price to $4.25 per bearing would result in sales of 160,000 units each period. The decrease in units sold would allow the division to reduce its investment in assets by $10,000, due to the lower level of inventories and receivables that would be needed to support sales. Compute the margin, turnover, and ROI if these changes are made.
   b. Other market studies suggest that a reduction in price to $3.75 per bearing would result in sales of 200,000 units each period. However, this would require an increase in total assets of $10,000, due to the somewhat larger inventories and receivables that would be carried. Compute the margin, turnover, and ROI if these changes are made.
3. Refer to the original data. Assume that the normal volume of sales is 180,000 bearings each period at a price of $4 per bearing. Another division of the Timkin Company is currently purchasing 20,000 bearings each period from an overseas supplier at $3.25 per bearing. The manager of the Bearing Division says that this price is "ridiculous" and refuses to meet it, since doing so would result in a loss of $0.42 per bearing for her division:

Selling price		$3.25
Cost per bearing:		
Variable cost	$2.50	
Fixed cost ($234,000 ÷ 200,000 bearings)	1 17	3 67
Loss per bearing		($ .42)

You may assume that sales to the other division would require an increase of $25,000 in the total assets carried by the Bearing Division. Would you recommend that the Bearing Division meet the $3.25 price and start selling 20,000 bearings per period to the other division? Support your answer with ROI computations.

P11–20. **Negotiated transfer price.** Zobel Machine Products, Inc., has a Castings Division, which does casting work of various types. The company also has a Machine Tool Division, which has asked the Castings Division to provide it with 20,000 special castings each year on a continuing basis. The special casting would require $12 per unit in variable production costs.

In order to have time and space to produce the new casting, the Castings Division would have to cut back production of another casting—the HS7—that it is currently producing. The company now produces and sells 100,000 units of the HS7 each year. Production and sales of this casting would drop by 25 percent if the new casting were produced.

The HS7 sells for $40 per unit and requires $18 per unit in variable production costs. Boxing and shipping costs of the HS7 are $6 per unit. Boxing and shipping costs for the new special casting would be only $1 per unit, thereby saving the company $5 per unit in cost. Some $240,000 in fixed production costs in the Castings Division are now being covered by the HS7 casting; 25 percent of these costs would have to be covered by the new casting if it were produced and sold to the Machine Tool Division. However, total fixed costs in the Castings Division would not change.

Required: What transfer price per casting should the Castings Division charge the Machine Tool Division for the special casting? Show all computations in good form.

P11–21.   **Negotiated transfer price.**   National Industries is a diversified corporation with separate and distinct operating divisions. Each division's performance is evaluated on the basis of total dollar profits and return on division investment.

The WindAir Division manufactures and sells air conditioner units. The coming year's budgeted income statement, based on a sales volume of 15,000 units, appears below.

WINDAIR DIVISION
Budgeted Income Statement
For the 1985–1986 Fiscal Year

	Per unit	Total ($000)
Sales revenue	$400	$6,000
Manufacturing costs:		
Compressor	70	1,050
Other raw materials	37	555
Direct labor	30	450
Variable overhead	45	675
Fixed overhead	32	480
Total manufacturing costs	214	3,210
Gross margin	186	2,790
Operating expenses:		
Variable selling	18	270
Fixed selling	19	285
Fixed administrative	38	570
Total operating expenses	75	1,125
Net income before taxes	$111	$1,665

WindAir Division's manager believes that sales can be increased if the unit selling price of the air conditioners is reduced. A market research study conducted by an independent firm at the request of the manager indicates that a 5 percent reduction in the selling price ($20) would increase sales volume 16 percent, or 2,400 units. WindAir has sufficient production capacity to manage this increased volume with no increase in fixed costs.

At present, WindAir uses a compressor in its units that it purchases from an outside supplier at a cost of $70 per compressor. The division manager of WindAir has approached the manager of the Compressor Division regarding the sale of a compressor unit to WindAir. The Compressor Division currently manufactures and sells a unit exclusively to outside firms that is similar to the unit used by WindAir. The specifications of the WindAir compressor are slightly different, which would reduce the Compressor Division's raw material cost by $1.50 per unit. In addition, the Compressor Division would not incur any variable selling costs in the units sold to WindAir. The manager of WindAir wants all of the compressors it uses to come from one supplier and has offered to pay $50 for each compressor unit.

The Compressor Division has the capacity to produce 75,000 units. The coming year's budgeted income statement for the Compressor Division, shown below, is based on a sales volume of 64,000 units without considering WindAir's proposal.

COMPRESSOR DIVISION
Budgeted Income Statement
For the 1985–1986 Fiscal Year

	Per unit	Total ($000)
Sales revenue	$100	$6,400
Manufacturing costs:		
Raw materials	12	768
Direct labor	8	512
Variable overhead	10	640
Fixed overhead	11	704
Total manufacturing costs	41	2,624
Gross margin	59	3,776
Operating expenses:		
Variable selling	6	384
Fixed selling	4	256
Fixed administrative	7	448
Total operating expenses	17	1,088
Net income before taxes	$ 42	$2,688

Required:
1. Should WindAir Division institute the 5 percent price reduction on its air conditioner units even if it cannot acquire the compressors internally for $50 each? Support your conclusion with appropriate calculations.
2. Without prejudice to your answer to (1) above, assume that WindAir needs 17,400 units. Should the Compressor Division be willing to supply the compressor units for $50 each? Support your conclusions with appropriate calculations.
3. As the manager of the Compressor Division, what is the minimum transfer price that you could charge for the new compressor? Show computations.
4. Without prejudice to your answer to (1) above, assume that WindAir needs 17,400 units. Would it be in the best interest of National Industries for the Compressor Division to supply the compressor units at $50 each to the WindAir Division? Support your conclusions with appropriate calculations.

(CMA, adapted)

P11–22. Critique of a performance evaluation program. The ATCO Company purchased the Dexter Company three years ago. Prior to the acquisition, Dexter manufactured and sold plastic products to a wide variety of customers. Dexter has since become a division of ATCO, and now it manufactures plastic components only for products made by ATCO's Macon Division. Macon sells its products to hardware wholesalers.

ATCO's corporate management gives the Dexter Division management a considerable amount of authority in running the division's operations. However, corporate management retains authority for decisions regarding capital investments, price setting of all products, and the quantity of each product to be produced by the Dexter Division.

ATCO has a formal performance evaluation program for the management of all its divisions. The performance evaluation program relies heavily on each division's return on investment. The income statement of Dexter Division presented below provides the basis for the evaluation of Dexter's divisional management.

DEXTER DIVISION OF ATCO COMPANY
Income Statement
For the Year Ended October 31, 19x5
(in thousands)

Sales			$4,000
Costs and expenses:			
Product costs:			
Direct materials		$ 500	
Direct labor		1,100	
Factory overhead		1,300	
Total product costs		2,900	
Less increase in inventory		350	2,550
Engineering and research			120
Shipping and receiving			240
Division administration:			
Manager's office		210	
Cost accounting		40	
Personnel		82	332
Corporate costs:			
Computer		48	
General services		230	278
Total costs and expenses			3,520
Divisional operating income			$ 480
Net plant investment			$4,000
Return on investment			12%

The financial statements for the divisions are prepared by the corporate accounting staff. The corporate general services costs are allocated on the basis of sales dollars, and the computer department's actual costs are apportioned among the divisions on the basis of use. The net division investment includes division fixed assets at net book value (cost less depreciation), division inventory, and corporate working capital apportioned to the divisions on the basis of sales dollars.

Required:
1. Discuss fully whether the financial reporting and performance evaluation program discussed above is an appropriate basis for measuring performance in the Dexter Division.
2. Based on your response to (1) above, recommend appropriate revisions of the financial information and reports used to evaluate the performance of Dexter's divisional management. If revisions are not necessary, explain why this is so.

(CMA, adapted)

P11–23. **Transfer pricing; divisional performance; behavioral problems.** Stanco, Inc., is a decentralized organization containing five divisions. The company's Electronics Division produces a variety of electronics items, including an XL5 circuit board. The division (which is operating at capacity) sells the XL5 circuit board to regular customers for $12.50 each. The circuit boards have a variable production cost of $8.25 each.

The company's Clock Division has asked the Electronics Division to supply it with a large quantity of XL5 circuit boards for only $9 each. The Clock Division, which is operating at only 60 percent of capacity, will put the circuit boards into a timing device that it will produce and sell to a large oven manufacturer. The cost of the timing device being manufactured by the Clock Division follows:

XL5 circuit board (desired cost)	$ 9.00
Other purchased parts (from outside vendors)	30.00
Direct labor	16.50
Variable overhead.	4.25
Fixed overhead and administrative costs	10.00
Total cost per timing device	$69.75

The manager of the Clock Division feels that she can't quote a price greater than $70 per timing device to the oven manufacturer if her division is to get the job. As shown above, in order to keep the price at $70 or less, she can't pay more than $9 per unit to the Electronics Division for the XL-5 circuit boards. Although the $9 price for the XL-5 circuit boards represents a substantial discount from the normal $12.50 price, she feels that the price concession is necessary in order for her division to get the oven manufacturer contract and thereby keep its core of highly trained people.

The company uses ROI and dollar profits in measuring divisional performance.

Required: 1. Assume that you are the manager of the Electronics Division. Would you recommend that your division supply the XL5 circuit boards to the Clock Division for $9 each as requested? Why or why not? Show all computations. (Ignore income taxes.)

2. Would it be to the short-run economic advantage of the company as a whole for the Electronics Division to supply the Clock Division with the circuit boards for $9 each? Explain your answer. (Ignore income taxes.)

3. Discuss the organizational and manager behavior problems, if any, inherent in this situation. As the Stanco, Inc., company controller, what would you advise the company's president to do in this situation?

(Written by the author, based on a problem appearing on the CMA examination)

P11–24. Negotiated transfer price. PortCo Products is a divisionalized furniture manufacturer. The divisions are autonomous segments, with each division being responsible for its own sales, costs of operations, working capital management, and equipment acquisition. Each division serves a different market in the furniture industry. Because the markets and products of the divisions are so different, there have never been any transfers between divisions.

The Commercial Division manufactures equipment and furniture that is purchased by the restaurant industry. The division plans to introduce a new line of counter and chair units that feature a cushioned seat for the counter chairs. John Kline, the division manager, has discussed the manufacture of the cushioned seat with Russ Fiegel of the Office Division. They both believe that a cushioned seat currently made by the Office Division for use on its deluxe office stool could be modified for use on the new counter chair. Consequently, Kline has asked Fiegel for a price for 100-unit lots of the cushioned seat. The following conversation took place about the price to be charged for the cushioned seats.

Fiegel: John, we can make the necessary modifications to the cushioned seat easily. The raw materials used in your seat are slightly different and should cost about

10 percent more than those used in our deluxe office stool. However, the labor time should be the same because the seat fabrication operation is basically the same. I would price the seat at our regular rate—full cost plus 30 percent markup.

Kline: That's higher than I expected, Russ. I was thinking that a good price would be your variable manufacturing costs. After all, your capacity costs will be incurred regardless of this job.

Fiegel: John, I'm at capacity. By making the cushion seats for you, I'll have to cut my production of deluxe office stools. Of course, I can increase my production of economy office stools. The labor time freed by not having to fabricate the frame or assemble the deluxe stool can be shifted to the frame fabrication and assembly of the economy office stool. Fortunately, I can switch my labor force between these two models of stools without any loss of efficiency. As you know, overtime is not a feasible alternative in our community. I'd like to sell it to you at variable cost, but I have excess demand for both products. I don't mind changing my product mix to the economy model if I get a good return on the seats I make for you. Here are my standard costs for the two stools and a schedule of my manufacturing overhead. [See below.]

Kline: I guess I see your point, Russ, but I don't want to price myself out of the market. Maybe we should talk to corporate to see if they can give us any guidance.

OFFICE DIVISION
Standard Costs and Prices

	Deluxe office stool		Economy office stool
Raw materials:			
Framing	$ 8.15		$ 9.76
Cushioned seat:			
Padding	2.40		—
Vinyl	4.00		—
Molded seat (purchased)	—		6.00
Direct labor:			
Frame fabrication (0.5 × $7.50/DLH)	3.75	(0.5 × $7.50/DLH)	3.75
Cushion fabrication (0.5 × $7.50/DLH)	3.75		—
Assembly* (0.5 × $7.50/DLH)	3.75	(0.3 × $7.50/DLH)	2.25
Manufacturing:			
Overhead (1.5 DLH × $12.80/DLH)	19.20	(0.8 DLH × $12.80/DLH)	10.24
Total standard cost	$45.00		$32.00
Selling price (30% markup)	$58.50		$41.60

* Attaching seats to frames and attaching rubber feet.

OFFICE DIVISION
Manufacturing Overhead Budget

Overhead item	Nature	Amount
Supplies	Variable—at current market prices	$ 420,000
Indirect labor	Variable	375,000
Supervision	Nonvariable	250,000
Power.	Use varies with activity; rates are fixed	180,000
Heat and light	Nonvariable—same regardless of production.	140,000
Property taxes and	Nonvariable—any change in amounts or rates	
insurance.	is independent of production	200,000
Depreciation	Fixed dollar total	1,700,000
Employee benefits . . .	20% of supervision, direct and indirect labor	575,000
Total overhead		$3,840,000
Capacity in DLH		300,000
Overhead rate/DLH . . .		$12.80

Required: 1. Assume that you are the corporate controller. What transfer price would you recommend for a 100-unit lot of seats? Show all computations.

2. Which alternative transfer pricing system—full cost, variable manufacturing cost, or variable cost plus lost contribution margin—would be best as the underlying concept for an intracompany transfer pricing policy? Explain your answer.

(CMA, adapted)

P11–25. **Transfer pricing with and without idle capacity.** Division X manufactures an electronic relay device that can be sold either to outside customers or to Division Y. Selected operating data on the two divisions are given below:

```
Division X:
    Unit selling price to outside customers  . . . . . .  $    30
    Variable production cost per unit  . . . . . . . .          16
    Variable selling and administrative
        expense per unit . . . . . . . . . . . . .              4
    Fixed production cost in total. . . . . . . . . .      500,000*
Division Y:
    Outside purchase price per unit (before
        any quantity discount)  . . . . . . . . . . .          30
```

* Capacity 100,000 units per year.

Division Y now purchases the relay from an outside supplier at the regular $30 intermediate price less a 10 percent quantity discount. Since the relay manufactured by Division X is of the same quality and type used by Division Y, consideration is being given to buying internally rather than from the outside supplier.

The controller of Division X has determined that $2 in variable selling and administrative costs can be avoided on any intracompany sales. Top management wants to treat each division as an autonomous unit with independent profit responsibility.

Required: 1. Assume that Division X is currently selling only 60,000 units per year to outside customers and that Division Y needs 40,000 units per year.

a. What is the highest transfer price that can be justified between the two divisions? Explain.

b. What is the lowest transfer price that can be justified between the two divisions? Explain.

  c. Assume that Division Y finds an outside supplier that will sell the needed relays for only $25 per unit. Should Division Y be required to meet this price? Explain.

  d. Refer to the original data. Assume that Division X decides to raise its price to $35 per unit. If Division Y is forced to pay this price and to start purchasing from Division X, will this result in greater or less total corporate profits? How much per unit?

  e. Under the circumstances posed in *(d)* above, should Division Y be forced to purchase from Division X? Explain.

2. Assume that Division X can sell all that it produces to outside customers. Repeat *(a)* through *(e)* above.

12

Pricing of Products and Services

Learning objectives

After studying Chapter 12, you should be able to:

Explain how the price of a product or service is obtained by using the economist's total revenue and total cost concepts and marginal revenue and marginal cost concepts.

Define price elasticity and explain how it impacts on the pricing decision.

Compute the target selling price for a product by use of cost-plus pricing under either the absorption or the contribution approach.

Derive the markup percentage needed to achieve a target ROI for a product.

Compute the target selling price for a service by use of time and material pricing.

Make special pricing decisions under the contribution approach, using the range of flexibility concept.

Define or explain the key terms listed at the end of the chapter.

Many firms have no pricing problems at all. They make a product that is in competition with other, similar products for which a market price already exists. Customers will not pay more than this price, and there is no reason for any firm to charge less. Under these circumstances, no price calculations are necessary. Any firm entering the market simply charges the price that the market directs it to accept. To a large extent, farm products follow this type of pattern. In these situations, the question isn't what price to charge; the question is simply how much to produce.

In this chapter, we are concerned with the more common situation in which a firm is faced with the problem of setting its own prices, as well as deciding how much to produce. The pricing decision is considered by many to be the single most important decision that a manager has to make. The reason is that the pricing of products isn't just a marketing decision or a financial decision; rather, it is a decision touching on *all* aspects of a firm's activities, and as such it affects the entire enterprise. Since the prices charged for a firm's products largely determine the quantities customers are willing to purchase, the setting of prices dictates the inflows of revenues into a firm. If these revenues consistently fail to cover all the costs of the firm, then in the long run the firm cannot survive. This is true regardless of how carefully costs may be controlled or how innovative the managers of the firm may be in the discharge of their other responsibilities.

Cost is a key factor in the pricing decision. As we have already seen, however, *cost* is a somewhat fluid concept that is sometimes hard to pin down. Our purpose in this chapter is to look at some of the cost concepts developed in earlier chapters and to see how these concepts can be applied in the pricing decision. This chapter is not intended to be a comprehensive guide to pricing; rather, its purpose is to integrate those cost concepts with which we are already familiar into a general pricing framework.

THE ECONOMIC FRAMEWORK FOR PRICING

A large part of microeconomic theory (theory of the firm) is devoted to the matter of pricing. In order to establish a framework for the pricing decision, it will be helpful to review certain concepts of microeconomic theory. This review will also assist us in showing the relationship between the models involved in microeconomic theory and the concept of incremental analysis discussed in preceding chapters.

Total revenue and total cost curves

Microeconomic theory states that the best price for a product is the price that maximizes the difference between total revenue and total costs. The economist illustrates this concept by constructing a model such as that shown in Exhibit 12–1.

This model is based on a number of assumptions. The economist assumes,

EXHIBIT 12–1

Total revenue and total cost curves

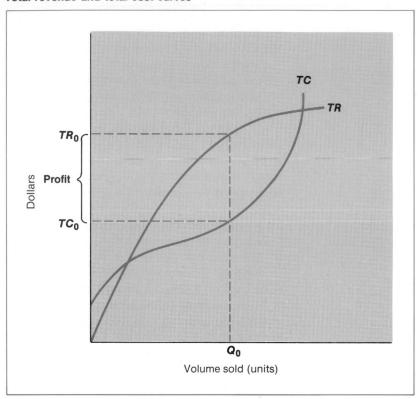

Volume sold (units)

first, that it is not possible to sell an unlimited number of units at the same price. If an unlimited number of units could be sold at the same price, then the total revenue *(TR)* curve would appear as a straight line, beginning at the origin of the graph. Since the economist assumes that at some point price reductions will be necessary to sell more units, the *TR* curve is shown increasing at a decreasing rate as quantity sold increases. That is, as price is reduced to stimulate more sales, total revenue will continue to increase for each unit sold, but the *rate* of this increase will begin to decline. As price is reduced more and more, the increase in total revenue will continue to decline, as depicted by the flattening tendency in the *TR* curve in the exhibit.

The total cost *(TC)* curve in Exhibit 12–1 assumes that the cost of producing additional units of product is not constant, but rather increases as attempts are made to squeeze more and more production out of a given set of productive facilities. So long as the rate of this increase is less than the rate of increase in total revenue, the company can profit by producing and selling more units of product. At some point, however, the rate of increase in total cost will become equal to the rate of increase in total revenue—that is, at some point the two lines will become parallel to each other. At this point, the increase to total cost from producing and selling one more unit of product is exactly equal to the increase to total revenue from that unit of product, and its production and sale yield zero increase in total profits in the firm. This point is shown in the graph in Exhibit 12–1 as quantity Q_0, representing the optimum volume of production and sales for the firm.

At Q_0 volume of units, the difference between total revenue and total cost is maximized. If we move to the right of Q_0 volume, then total cost is increasing more rapidly than total revenue, and therefore total profits would be decreased. If we move to the left of Q_0 volume, then total revenue is increasing more rapidly than total cost, and the company can profit by further expanding output up to Q_0 level of activity. In sum, Q_0 represents the optimum volume of sales for the firm, and the correct price to charge is the price that will allow the firm to sell this volume of units.

Marginal revenue and marginal cost curves

These same concepts can be shown in terms of marginal revenue and marginal cost. **Marginal revenue** can be defined as the addition to total revenue resulting from the sale of one additional unit of product. **Marginal cost** can be defined as the addition to total cost resulting from the production and sale of one additional unit of product. The economist expresses these concepts in model form as shown in Exhibit 12–2.

The marginal revenue (MR) and marginal cost (MC) curves in Exhibit 12–2 have their basis in the economist's assumption that the total revenue and total cost curves behave in the way depicted earlier in Exhibit 12–1. That is, the marginal revenue and marginal cost curves are derived by measuring the rate of *change* in total revenue and total cost at various levels of activity, and by plotting this change in graph form. Since the total revenue curve in Exhibit 12–1 depicts a declining rate of increase in total revenue, the marginal revenue curve in Exhibit 12–2 slopes downward to the right. And since the total cost curve in Exhibit 12–1 depicts total cost as first increasing at a decreasing rate, then flattening out somewhat, and then increasing at an increasing rate, the marginal cost curve in Exhibit 12–2 slopes downward initially, bottoms out, and then slopes upward to the right. As discussed in Chapter 2, the economist's marginal concept is basically the same as the accountant's incremental concept.

The optimum price to charge is determined by the intersection of the marginal revenue and the marginal cost curves. The intersection of these two curves occurs at volume Q_0. This is the same volume as shown earlier in Exhibit 12–1, depicting the point of maximum difference between total revenues and total costs. At volume Q_0, price P_0 should be charged for each unit sold.

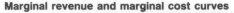

EXHIBIT 12–2
Marginal revenue and marginal cost curves

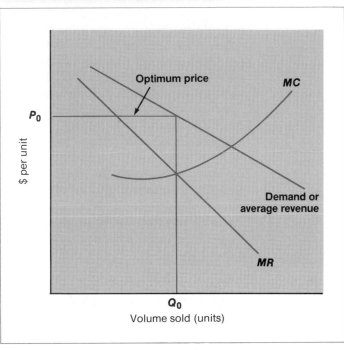

Elasticity of demand

A product's price elasticity is a key concept in any pricing decision. **Price elasticity** measures the degree to which volume of sales is affected by a change in price per unit. Demand for a product is price inelastic if a change in price has little or no effect on the volume of units sold. Demand is price elastic if a change in price has a substantial effect on the volume of units sold. Salt is a good example of a product that tends to be price inelastic. Raising or lowering the price of salt would probably have little or no effect on the amount of salt sold in a given year.

Whether demand for a product tends to be price elastic or price inelastic can be a crucial factor in a decision relating to a change in price. The problem is that measuring the degree of price elasticity is an extremely difficult thing to do. It's one thing to observe generally that a given product tends to be price elastic, and it's another thing to determine the exact *degree* of that elasticity—that is, to determine what change in volume of sales will take place as a result of specific changes in price. Yet this is exactly the kind of information that managers need in their pricing decisions, and the kind of information that they attempt to obtain by carefully planned marketing research programs.

Pricing decisions are further complicated by the fact that cross-elasticity often exists in the demand for certain products. *Cross-elasticity* measures the degree to which demand for one product is affected by a change in the price of a substitute product. For example, as the price of galvanized pipe goes up, consumers may switch to plastic pipe. One of the problems in measuring cross-elasticity is trying to identify the substitutes for a particular product, and the willingness of consumers to accept those substitutes in place of the product itself. Although problems of this type are often difficult to quantify, the concept of cross-elasticity of demand is an important concept and cannot be disregarded in the pricing decision.

Limitations of the general models

Although the models in Exhibits 12–1 and 12–2 do a good job of showing the general outlines of the incremental profit approach to pricing, they must be viewed as being only broad, conceptual guides in pricing decisions. There are several reasons why. First, the cost and revenue data available to managers are generally sufficient to provide only rough approximations of the shape of the various cost and revenue curves depicted in the models. As our methods of measurement are improved and refined in years to come, this situation may change, but at present managers usually have only a general idea of the shape of the demand curve that they are facing.

Second, the models are directly applicable only in conditions of **monopoly** (no directly competing product in the market) and **monopolistic competition** (many sellers of similar products, with no one seller having a large enough share of the market for other sellers to be able to discern the effect of its pricing decision on their sales). The models are not applicable between these two extremes, where the market is characterized by situations of **oligopoly** (a few large sellers competing directly with one another). The reason is that the models make no allowance for retaliatory pricing decisions by competing firms, and retaliatory pricing is a prime characteristic of oligopolistic industries.

A third limitation of the general models arises from the fact that price is just one element in the marketing of a product. Many other factors must also be considered that can have a significant impact on the number of units of a product that can be sold at a given price. Among these factors are promotional strategy, product design, intensity of selling effort, and the selection of distribution channels.

A final limitation of the general models is that even if business firms had a precise knowledge of the shape of their demand curves, we cannot automatically assume that they would price in such a way as to maximize profits. The reason is that this might bring accusations from the public of "profiteering" and "charging all that the traffic will bear." Rather than attempting to maximize profits, many firms seek only to earn a "satisfactory" profit for the company. They think in terms of a reasonable return on the investment that has been made in the company, and they strive to set prices in such a way as to earn that return. The concept of a satisfactory profit underlies the actions of a great many business firms today.

Although the limitations discussed above preclude the *direct* use of the economic pricing models in pricing decisions, these models are nonetheless highly useful in providing the general framework within which the price setter must work. They state the pricing problem in *conceptual* terms, and as such they constitute the starting point in any pricing decision.

PRICING STANDARD PRODUCTS

Not all pricing decisions are approached in the same way. Some pricing decisions relate to the pricing of standard products that are sold to customers in the routine day-to-day conduct of business activities. Other pricing decisions relate to special orders of standard or near-standard products, and still others relate to the pricing of special products that have been taken on in an effort to fill out unused productive capacity. In this section, we consider the pricing of standard products. The pricing of special orders of various types is reserved to a later section.

Cost-plus pricing formulas

In pricing standard products, the key concept is to recognize that selling prices must be sufficient in the long run to cover *all* costs of production, administration, and sales, both fixed and variable, as well as to provide for a reasonable return on the stockholders' investment, if a firm is to survive and grow. This point is often missed by some pricing enthusiasts who seem to imply in their writings that any price above variable or incremental costs is an acceptable price for any product under any circumstances.[1]

In setting normal long-run prices on standard products, *all costs* are relevant to the pricing decision and must be explicitly considered by the price setter if long-run profit goals are to be met. This means that a portion of the fixed costs (even if the fixed costs are sunk) must be considered along with the variable costs, and that the costs of administration and sales must be weighted in along with the costs of production as prices are set.

The most common approach to the pricing of standard products is to employ some type of **cost-plus pricing** formula.[2] The approach is to compute a "cost" base and then to add to this base some predetermined **markup** to arrive at a target selling price. The "cost" in cost-plus pricing is defined according to the method being used to cost units of product. In Chapters 3 and 7, we found that units of product can be costed in two different ways— by the absorption approach or by the contribution approach (with direct costing). We consider both costing methods below, and the approach that each takes to cost-plus pricing of standard products.

---

[1] For a discussion of the circumstances under which variable or incremental costs are useful as a pricing guide, see the section "Special pricing decisions."

[2] For a study documenting the use of cost-plus pricing, see Lawrence A. Gordon, Robert Cooper, Haim Falk, and Danny Miller, *The Pricing Decision* (New York: National Association of Accountants, 1981), p. 23.

The absorption approach

Under the absorption approach to cost-plus pricing, the cost base is defined as the cost to produce one unit of product. Selling and administrative costs are not included in this cost base, but rather are provided for through the markup that is added on to arrive at the target selling price. Thus, the markup must be high enough to cover these costs as well as to provide the company with a "satisfactory" profit margin.

To illustrate, let us assume that the Ritter Company is in the process of setting a selling price on one of its standard products, which has just undergone some slight modifications in design. The accounting department has accumulated the following cost data on the redesigned product:

	Per unit	Total
Direct materials	$6	
Direct labor	4	
Variable overhead	3	
Fixed overhead (based on 10,000 units)	7	$70,000
Variable selling and administrative expenses	2	
Fixed selling and administrative expenses		
(based on 10,000 units)	1	10,000

The first step is to compute the full cost to produce one unit of product. Once this cost has been determined, it becomes the base in the cost-plus pricing formula to which the desired markup can be added. For the Ritter Company, the cost to produce one unit of product is $20, computed as follows:

Direct materials	$ 6
Direct labor	4
Overhead ($3 variable plus $7 fixed, or 250%	
of direct labor cost)	10
Total absorption cost to manufacture one unit	$20

Let us assume that in order to obtain its target selling price, the Ritter Company has a general policy of adding a markup equal to 50 percent of the cost to manufacture. A price quotation sheet for the company prepared under this assumption is presented in Exhibit 12–3.

EXHIBIT 12–3
Price quotation sheet—absorption basis

Direct materials	$ 6
Direct labor	4
Overhead at 250% of direct labor cost	10
Total cost to manufacture	20
Markup to cover selling and administrative	
expenses and desired profit—50% of cost	
to manufacture	10
Target selling price	$30

As shown in Exhibit 12–3, even though this pricing approach is termed cost-plus, part of the costs involved are buried in the *plus,* or markup, part of the formula. The buried costs are those associated with the selling and administrative activities. These costs could be broken out separately and added to the cost base along with the cost to manufacture, but this is rarely done in actual practice. The reason centers on the difficulty that would be involved in making the necessary allocations among the various products of the firm. For example, the salary of the company president would be a common cost among all products. It would be a difficult task to try to allocate the president's salary in any meaningful way to these products. The great majority of firms feel that selling and administrative costs can be provided for adequately in final, target selling prices by simply expanding the markup over cost to manufacture to include them as well as the desired profit. This means, of course, that the markup must be structured with great care in order to ensure that it is sufficient to cover all that it is supposed to cover. More will be said on this point a little later.

If the Ritter Company produces and sells 10,000 units of its product at a selling price of $30 per unit, the income statement will appear as shown in Exhibit 12–4.

EXHIBIT 12–4

RITTER COMPANY
Income Statement
Absorption Basis

Sales (10,000 units at $30)	$300,000
Cost of goods sold (10,000 units at $20)	200,000
Gross margin.	100,000
Selling and administrative expenses (10,000 units at $2 variable and $1 fixed)	30,000
Net income	$ 70,000

The contribution approach

The contribution approach to cost-plus pricing differs from the absorption approach in that it emphasizes costs by behavior rather than by function. Thus, under the contribution approach the cost base consists of the variable expenses associated with a product, rather than the product's cost to manufacture. Included in this cost base are the variable selling and administrative expenses, as well as the variable manufacturing expenses. Since no element of fixed cost is included in the cost base, the markup that is added must be adequate to cover the fixed costs, as well as to provide the desired profit per unit.

To illustrate, refer again to the cost data for the Ritter Company. The base to use in cost-plus pricing under the contribution approach would be $15, computed as follows:

Direct materials	$ 6
Direct labor	4
Variable overhead	3
Variable selling and administrative expenses	2
Total variable expenses	$15

Let us assume that the Ritter Company has found that a markup of 100 percent of variable expenses is adequate to cover allocable fixed expenses and to provide the desired profit per unit. A price quotation sheet prepared under this assumption is shown in Exhibit 12–5.

EXHIBIT 12–5
Price quotation sheet—contribution basis

Direct materials	$ 6
Direct labor	4
Variable overhead	3
Variable selling and administrative expenses	2
Total variable expenses	15
Markup to cover fixed expenses and desired profit— 100% of variable expenses	15
Target selling price	$30

Notice again that even though this pricing method is termed *cost*-plus pricing, a portion of the costs are buried in the *plus,* or markup, part of the formula. In this case, however, the buried costs are the fixed costs rather than the selling and administrative costs. Again, the reason for not including the fixed costs in the cost base can be traced to the time and difficulty that would be involved in any attempt to allocate. As a practical matter, there is no way to equitably allocate many common fixed costs, as discussed in Chapter 7. Any attempt to do so may result in less usable cost data for pricing, rather than more usable data. In addition, many users of the contribution approach to pricing argue that keeping the cost base free of any element of fixed costs facilitates pricing in special and unusual situations. This point is discussed further in a following section dealing with special pricing problems.

Compare the contribution approach to cost-plus pricing in Exhibit 12–5 with the absorption approach in Exhibit 12–3. Although both approaches are employing the cost-plus concept, notice the difference in the way in which they handle the cost data and structure the price quotation sheet. Also notice that the Ritter Company can attain the *same* $30 target selling price by using either costing method.

In order to conclude the Ritter Company example, let us again assume that the company produces and sells 10,000 units of product at a selling price of $30 per unit. The company's income statement as it would appear under the contribution approach is shown in Exhibit 12–6.

EXHIBIT 12–6

RITTER COMPANY
Income Statement
Contribution Basis

Sales (10,000 units at $30)		$300,000
Less variable expenses (10,000 units at $15)		150,000
Contribution margin		150,000
Less fixed expenses:		
Production	$70,000	
Selling and administrative	10,000	80,000
Net income		$ 70,000

Determining the markup percentage

By far the most crucial element in the cost-plus pricing formulas is the percentage markup added to the cost base. We have found that under both the absorption and the contribution approaches some elements of cost are buried in the markup figure. This means that the markup must be sufficient to cover these buried costs, as well as to provide a satisfactory return on assets employed, if long-run profit goals are to be met. How does the manager determine the "right" markup percentage to use in setting target selling prices? The markup chosen is a function of a number of variables, one of which is the company's desired return on investment (ROI).

Markup formulas   ROI is widely used by firms as a basis for determining the appropriate markup to add to products. The approach is to set a target ROI figure and then to structure the markup so that this target figure is achieved. A formula exists that can be used to determine the appropriate markup percentage, given the ROI figure that management wishes to obtain for the organization. Assuming use of the absorption approach to costing, the formula is:

$$\text{Markup percentage} = \frac{\genfrac{}{}{0pt}{}{\text{Desired return on}}{\text{assets employed} } + \genfrac{}{}{0pt}{}{\text{Selling and adminis-}}{\text{istrative expenses}}}{\text{Volume in units } \times \text{Unit cost to manufacture}} \quad (1)$$

If the contribution approach to costing is used, the formula becomes:

$$\text{Markup percentage} = \frac{\genfrac{}{}{0pt}{}{\text{Desired return on}}{\text{assets employed}} + \text{Fixed costs}}{\text{Volume in units } \times \text{Unit variable expenses}} \quad (2)$$

Using the formulas   To show how the basic formula in (1) above is applied, assume that Hart Company has determined that an investment of $2,000,000 is necessary to produce and market 50,000 units of product X each year. The $2,000,000 investment would cover purchase of equipment and provide funds needed to carry inventories and accounts receivable. In all, the company's accounting department estimates that the following costs and activity will be associated with the manufacture and sale of product X:

Number of units sold annually	50,000
Required investment in assets	$2,000,000
Cost to manufacture one unit	30
Selling and administrative expenses	700,000

If Hart Company desires a 25 percent ROI, then the required markup for the product will be [using formula (1) above]:

$$\text{Markup percentage} = \frac{\text{Desired return on assets employed} + \text{Selling and administrative expenses}}{\text{Volume in units} \times \text{Unit cost to manufacture}}$$

$$\text{Markup percentage} = \frac{(25\% \times \$2,000,000) + \$700,000}{50,000 \text{ units} \times \$30}$$

$$= \frac{\$1,200,000}{\$1,500,000}$$

$$= 80\%$$

Using this markup percentage, the selling price of a unit of product X would be set at $54:

Cost to manufacture	$30
Add markup—80% × $30	24
Target selling price	$54

As proof that the $54 selling price for product X will permit Hart Company to achieve a 25 percent ROI, the company's income statement and a computation of its projected ROI are presented in Exhibit 12–7.

EXHIBIT 12–7
Income statement and ROI analysis—Hart Company

HART COMPANY
Budgeted Income Statement

Sales (50,000 units × $54)	$2,700,000
Less cost of goods sold (50,000 units × $30)	1,500,000
Gross margin	1,200,000
Less selling and administrative expenses	700,000
Net operating income	$ 500,000

Projected ROI (based on $2,000,000 in assets employed):

$$\frac{\text{Net operating income}}{\text{Sales}} \times \frac{\text{Sales}}{\text{Average operating assets}} = \text{ROI}$$

$$\frac{\$500,000}{\$2,700,000} \times \frac{\$2,700,000}{\$2,000,000} = \text{ROI}$$

$$18.52\%^* \times 1.35 = 25\%$$

* Rounded.

As a concluding note, in our example we have focused on formula (1) given earlier. Formula (2) is applied in the same way, except that it is used when the manager prefers to base markups on variable costs and to use the contribution approach in preparing statements.

Adjusting prices to market conditions

Although the cost-plus approach that we have been discussing can be of great assistance to the manager in determining target selling prices, care must be taken not to apply the cost-plus formulas too rigidly. The reason is that they tend to ignore the relationship between price and volume, and if applied too rigidly might result in less profits, rather than more profits, for the firm. For example, in the preceding illustration the competitive situation might be such for product X that a selling price of $54 would result in far less than 50,000 units being sold each year. On the other hand, at a $54 selling price, demand might be so great that the company would be swamped with orders.

In order to make cost-plus pricing formulas workable, companies usually do three things. First, they rarely price a product exactly at the target price suggested by the cost-plus formula. The costs used in the formula serve as a basis for establishing prices at their *lower limit*—the actual final selling price may be much higher than this minimum target figure. Many people have the mistaken notion that price is purely a function of cost, when in reality cost serves in large part simply to define the lower limit that can be set. Noncost factors, such as competitive position, promotional strategy, packaging, and ability to achieve long-term product differentiation, may permit a manager to set a price significantly higher than the minimum target figure provided by use of the cost formulas. The mark of real executives in pricing can be found in their ability to sense the market situation and to know when price adjustments can and should be made. If such executives sense that their competitive position is strong, they will adjust the prices upward; if they sense a strengthening of opposing competitive forces, then they will either shade the prices downward or attempt to further differentiate the product.

Second, the price setter must recognize that even if a particular margin has been obtainable for the last 20 or 30 years, this is no assurance that it will continue to be obtainable. For example, the neighborhood grocery stores suddenly discovered in the 1940s that the margins they had been obtaining for many decades were no longer obtainable because of the development of large chain supermarkets. In turn, the chain supermarkets discovered in the 1970s that the margins they had enjoyed for nearly three decades were being undercut by the self-service discount food outlets. In order to achieve target ROI figures, managers are often required to trade off some margin in order to achieve a higher turnover of assets, as we pointed out in our ROI discussion in Chapter 11. This means that markups must sometimes be reduced in the hope of stimulating the overall volume of sales.

Third, companies will not use the same markup for all product lines, but rather will vary the markup according to custom, need, or general industry practice. For example, one product line may carry a markup of 20 percent, whereas another may carry a markup of 60 percent. This is typical of clothing and department stores, where the percentage markup varies by department and occasionally even by item. Jewelry generally has a high markup, whereas stockings carry a relatively low markup.

Why use cost data in pricing?

If pricing executives end up setting prices according to how they sense the market, then an obvious question at this point is, "Why bother using cost data in the pricing decision?" Several reasons can be advanced in favor of computing target selling prices by means of the cost-plus formulas even if the resulting prices are later modified. First, in making pricing decisions, the manager is faced with a myriad of uncertainties. Cost-plus target prices represent a *starting point,* a way of perhaps removing some of the uncertainties and shedding some light on others. By this means, the manager may be able to feel his or her way more easily through the thicket and come up with a price that will be acceptable given the constraints at hand.

Second, cost might be viewed as a floor of protection, guarding the price setter from pricing too low and incurring losses. Although this line of reasoning is appealing and reassuring, the protection offered by the cost floor is more illusory than real. For one thing, we have already noted that neither the absorption approach nor the contribution approach includes all costs in the cost base. For another thing, unit cost depends on volume. This is because many costs are fixed, and unit cost will therefore depend on the number of units produced and sold. Even though selling prices may be set above total costs, losses may still be incurred if the volume of sales is less than estimated, thereby forcing per unit costs upward to the point that they exceed the selling price.

Third, formula-based target selling prices may give the price setter some insights into competitors' costs, or help him to predict what a competitive price will be. For example, if a company is operating in an industry where 30 percent markups over cost to manufacture are common, then the company may be able to assume that this same pattern will hold for new products, and thereby either predict competitors' prices or price in such a way as to gain quick acceptance of a new product line. On the other hand, by following standard markups over cost, a company may be able to largely *neutralize* the pricing issue and concentrate on competing in other ways, such as in delivery or in credit terms.

Finally, many firms have such a wide range of products that they simply don't have the time to do a detailed cost-volume-profit analysis on every item in every product line. Cost-plus pricing formulas provide a quick and direct way to reach at least a tentative price that can be further refined as time and circumstances permit.

TIME AND MATERIAL PRICING

Instead of computing prices by means of a cost-plus formula, some companies use an alternative approach called **time and material pricing.** Under this method, two pricing rates are established—one based on direct labor time and the other based on direct material used. In each case, the rate is constructed so that it includes an allowance for selling and administrative expenses, for other indirect costs, and for a desired profit. This pricing method is widely used in television and appliance repair shops, in automobile repair shops, in printing shops, and in similar types of service organizations. In addition, it is used by various kinds of professionals, including accountants, attorneys, physicians, and consultants.

Time component

The time component is typically expressed as a rate per direct labor-hour. The rate is computed by adding together three elements: (1) the direct costs of the employee, including salary and fringe benefits; (2) a pro rata allowance for selling and administrative expenses of the organization; and (3) an allowance for a desired profit per hour of employee time. In some organizations (such as a repair shop), the same hourly rate will be charged regardless of which employee is assigned to complete a job; in other organizations, the rate may vary by employee. For example, in an accounting firm, the rate charged for a new assistant accountant's time will generally be less than the rate charged for an experienced senior accountant or for a partner.

Material component

The material component is determined by adding a *material loading charge* to the invoice price of any materials used on the job. The **material loading charge** is designed to cover the costs of ordering, handling, and carrying materials in stock, plus a profit margin on the materials themselves. Typically, a material loading charge will fall somewhere between 30 percent and 50 percent of the invoice cost of the materials.

An example of time and material pricing

To provide a numerical example of time and material pricing, assume the following data:

The Quality Auto Shop uses time and material pricing for all of its repair work. The shop's time and material rates have been computed as follows:

Computing the time rate

The shop pays its mechanics an average of $8 per hour and incurs another $3 per hour for fringe benefits. The shop manager estimates that the following additional shop costs and selling and administrative expenses are incurred each year:

Shop supervision (including costs of supervisory fringe benefits).	$ 40,000
Supplies . .	16,000
Depreciation.	70,000
Miscellaneous selling and administrative expenses	90,000
Total	$216,000

The mechanics employed by the shop work a total of 24,000 hours per year. The manager feels that a reasonable profit for the shop can be computed on a basis of $5 per hour of mechanic's time. Using these data, the charge to customers for each hour of service time on a repair job would be:

Mechanics' pay per hour, including fringes ($8 + $3)	$11
Pro rata share of shop and other costs	9*
Desired profit per hour of mechanic time	5
Total charging rate per hour for service	$25

* $216,000 ÷ 24,000 hours = $9 per hour.

Computing the material loading charge

For materials, the shop incurs the following costs each year in ordering, handling, and storing parts:

Parts employees—wages and fringe benefits	$30,000
Utilities	16,000
Property taxes	4,800
Insurance	1,200
Rent	8,000
Total	$60,000

The invoice cost of parts used in the shop totals $240,000 per year. If the company desires a profit margin equal to 15 percent of the invoice cost of parts used, then the material loading charge would be computed as follows:

Charge for ordering, handling, and storing parts ($60,000 ÷ $240,000)	25% of invoice cost
Desired profit margin on parts	15% of invoice cost
Material loading charge	40% of invoice cost

Thus, the amount charged for parts on a job will consist of the invoice cost of the parts plus a material loading charge equal to 40 percent of this cost.

Billing a job

To complete our example, a repair job in the shop that required 2½ hours of labor time and $60 in parts would be priced as follows:

Labor time: 2½ hours × $25		$ 62.50
Materials used:		
Invoice cost	$60.00	
Material loading charge (40% × $60)	24.00	84.00
Total price of the job.		$146.50

Rather than using labor-hours as a basis for computing a time rate, a machine shop, a printing shop, or a similar organization might use machine-hours. Some organizations might charge a different rate per machine-hour, depending on the type of machine used.

PRICING NEW PRODUCTS

New products easily present the most challenging pricing problems, for the reason that the uncertainties involved are so great. If a new product is unlike anything currently on the market, then demand will be uncertain. If the new product is similar to products already being sold, then uncertainty will exist as to the degree of substitution that will develop between the new product and the already available products. Uncertainty will also exist over ultimate marketing costs, and so forth. In order to reduce the level of these uncertainties, a firm will often resort to some type of experimental or test marketing.

Test marketing of products

Many firms have used **test marketing** with great success in order to gain data relative to the pricing decision. The approach is to introduce the new product in selected areas only, generally at different prices in different areas. By this means, a company can gather data on the competition that the product will encounter, on the relationship between volume and price, and on the contribution to profits that can be expected at various selling prices and volumes of sales. A price can then be selected that will result in the greatest overall contribution to profits, or that seems best in relation to the company's long-run objectives.

Of course, test marketing is not the same thing as the full-scale production and marketing of a product, but it can provide highly useful information that can help to ensure that the full-scale effort will be successful. An added benefit can be found in the fact that through test marketing it may be possible to keep any errors in pricing on a small scale, rather than nationwide.

Pricing strategies

Two basic pricing strategies are available to the price setter in pricing new products. These pricing strategies are known as **skimming pricing** and **penetration pricing.**

Skimming pricing involves setting a high initial price for a new product, with a progressive lowering of the price as time passes and as the market broadens and matures. The purpose of skimming pricing is to maximize short-run profits. In effect, it represents a direct application of the economist's pricing models discussed earlier in the chapter.

Penetration pricing involves setting low initial prices in order to gain quick acceptance in a broad portion of the market. It calls for the sacrifice of some short-run profits in order to achieve a better long-run market position. Whether a firm adopts the skimming strategy or the penetration strategy will depend on what it is trying to accomplish and on which approach appears to offer the greatest chance for success.

For example, many new products have a certain novelty appeal that causes demand to be quite price inelastic. In these cases, high initial prices are often set and maintained until competitors develop competing products and begin price cutting. As sales volume becomes more sensitive to sales price, prices are slowly reduced until the point is reached where a penetration price is possible that permits access to a mass market. A good example of this type of skimming strategy can be found in the marketing of electronic calculators. Prices of hand-sized calculators started at about $300 in the early 1970s and dropped to less than $25 in about three years' time, finally permitting access to a market so wide that it included the purchasing of calculators for use in weekly grocery shopping. Television sets, stereo sets, automobiles, electronic ovens, and some drug products all went through a similar skimming pricing period before prices were eventually lowered to a mass market penetration level.

One strong argument in favor of skimming pricing is that it offers some protection against unexpected costs in the production and marketing of a product. If a new product is priced on a penetration basis and costs are unexpectedly high, then the company may be forced to raise prices later—not an easy thing to do when you are trying to gain wide market acceptance of a new product. On the other hand, if a new product is priced initially on a skimming level, the company has a layer of protection that can be used to absorb any unexpected costs or cost increases. Even if this later causes price reductions to be less than expected, the company will still be in the more favorable position of reducing prices rather than raising them.

Skimming pricing is most effective in those markets where entry is relatively difficult because of the technology or investment required. The easier that market entry becomes, the smaller is the likelihood that skimming can be carried off very effectively, or at least for a very long period of time. For example, skimming pricing was possible for many years in the computer industry because of technological barriers to entry. By contrast, it is doubtful whether skimming pricing was ever much of a factor in the marketing of household cleaning products.

Target costs and product pricing

Our discussion thus far has presumed that a product has already been developed, has been costed, and that it is ready to be marketed as soon as a price is set. In many cases, the sequence of events is just the reverse. That is, the company will already *know* what price should be charged, and the problem will be to *develop* a product that can be marketed profitably at the desired price. Even in this situation, where the normal sequence of events is reversed, cost is still a crucial factor. The company's approach will be to set **target costs** that can be used as guides in developing a product that can be sold within the desired price range.

This approach is used widely in the household appliance industry, where a company will determine in advance the price range in which it wants a particular product model to sell and then will set about to develop the model.

Component parts will be designed and then costed item by item to see whether the total cost is compatible with the target cost already set. If not, the parts will be redesigned and recosted, and features will be changed or eliminated until the expected costs fall within the desired targets. Prototypes will then be developed, and again costs will be carefully analyzed to be sure that the desired targets are being met. In these types of situations, the accountant can be of great help to management by continually pointing out the relationships between cost and volume, by segregating relevant costs where needed, and by assisting in the organization and interpretation of cost data.

To provide a numerical example of how to compute a target cost figure, assume the following situation:

Handy Appliance Company wants to produce a hand mixer that will sell for $29. In order to produce 25,000 mixers a year, an investment of $625,000 would be required. The company desires a 15 percent ROI. Selling and administrative costs associated with the mixer would total $200,000 per year. Given these data, the target cost to manufacture one mixer would be:

Projected sales (25,000 mixers × $29)		$725,000
Less required markup:		
Selling and administrative expenses	$200,000	
Desired ROI (15% × $625,000)	93,750	
Total markup.		293,750
Target cost to manufacture 25,000 mixers		$431,250

Target cost to manufacture one mixer: $431,250 ÷ 25,000 = $17.25

Thus, the company should produce the new mixer only if it can be manufactured at a target cost of $17.25 or less per unit.

SPECIAL PRICING DECISIONS

When faced with a pricing decision, which pricing method should the manager use—the absorption approach illustrated in Exhibit 12–3 or the contribution approach illustrated in Exhibit 12–5? If all pricing decisions were related to the pricing of *standard* products, the answer would be that it really wouldn't matter which method was used. We have already seen that the same target selling price for a standard product can be obtained using either method. The choice would probably depend on which method was otherwise being used to cost units of product. If the absorption method was otherwise in use, then it would be simpler to go ahead and use it as a basis for pricing decisions as well; the opposite would be the case if contribution costing was otherwise in use.

But all pricing decisions don't relate to standard products, or even to new standard products which fall into the same general category. Many pricing decisions relate to special or unusual situations. For example, a company may get a large order for a standard product but be asked to quote a special, one-time-only price. Or a special order may come in from a foreign customer who wants a special price on a standard item on a continuing basis because his or her order represents business that the company otherwise wouldn't have. A company may have substantial idle capacity and be faced with the problem of pricing special products that are not a part of the regular line and that are being produced on a limited basis. Finally, a company may be in a competitive bidding situation and forced to bid on many unlike jobs, some of which will be on a more or less continuing basis and others will be one-time-only affairs.

All of these situations present *special* pricing problems of one kind or another. Many managers feel that special pricing problems such as those above can be much more easily handled by the contribution approach to pricing than by the absorption approach. The reasons are twofold. First, advocates of the contribution approach argue that it provides the price setter with much more detailed information than does the absorption approach, and that the information it provides is structured in a way that parallels the way in which the price setter is used to thinking—in terms of cost-volume-profit relationships. And second, it is argued that the contribution approach provides the price setter with a flexible framework that is immediately adaptable to *any* pricing problem, without the necessity of doing a lot of supplementary analytical work.

Pricing a special order

In order to illustrate the adaptability of the contribution approach to special pricing situations, and to show how the data it presents guides the price setter in decisions, let us assume the following price quotation sheets for the Helms Company:

Absorption method		Contribution method	
Direct materials.	$ 6	Direct materials.	$ 6
Direct labor .	7	Direct labor .	7
Overhead at 100% of direct labor .	7	Variable overhead.	2
Total cost to manufacture	20	Variable selling and administrative .	1
Markup—20% .	4	Total variable expenses	16
Target selling price	$24	Markup—50% .	8
		Target selling price	$24

These price quotation sheets relate to a vacuum pump that the Helms Company manufactures and markets through jobbers. The company has never been able to sell all of the pumps that it can produce, and for this reason it is constantly on the lookout for new business. Let us assume that the Helms Company has just been approached by a foreign distributor who wants to purchase 10,000 pumps at a price of $19 per pump. Should the company accept the offer?

The absorption method The price quotation sheet prepared above by the absorption method is of little help in making the decision. If the Helms Company tries to relate the $20 "cost of manufacture" to the proposed $19 price, then the offer is clearly not attractive:

Sales (10,000 units at $19)	$190,000
Less absorption cost to manufacture (10,000 units at $20)	200,000
Net loss from the order	$ (10,000)

On the other hand, since there is idle capacity in the plant, management may be tempted to accept the offer. The dilemma is that no one really *knows* from looking at the price quotation sheet which course of action is best. The pricing system doesn't provide the essential keys that are needed to move in an intelligent way. As a result, whatever decision is made will be made either on a "seat of the pants" basis or only after much effort has been expended in trying to dig into the cost records for additional information.

The contribution method   By contrast, the price quotation sheet prepared by the contribution method provides the company with exactly the framework that it needs in making the decision. Since this price quotation sheet is organized by cost behavior, it dovetails precisely with cost-volume-profit concepts, and it enables the decision maker to reach his or her decisions without having to do all kinds of added digging and analytical work in the cost records.

Consider the Helms Company data. Since the company has idle capacity (for which there is apparently no other use), fixed overhead costs are irrelevant to the decision over whether to accept the foreign distributor's offer. Any amount received over unit variable costs (and any *incremental* fixed costs[3]) will increase overall profitability; therefore, rather than relating the proposed purchase price to the $20 "cost to manufacture," the company should relate it to the unit variable costs involved. This is easy to do if the regular price quotation sheet on a product is organized by cost behavior, such as shown above under the contribution method. In the case of the Helms Company, the unit variable costs are $16. Assuming that the unit variable costs associated with the special order will be the same as those associated with regular business, the analysis would be:

Sales (10,000 units at $19)	$190,000
Less variable expenses (10,000 units at $16)	160,000
Contribution margin promised by the order (and also increased net income, if the fixed costs don't change)	$ 30,000

In sum, by using the price quotation sheet prepared by the contribution method, the Helms Company will be able to see a clear-cut, short-run advantage to accepting the foreign distributor's offer. Before any final decision can be made, however, the Helms Company will have to weigh long-run considerations very carefully, particularly the impact that accepting this offer might have on future efforts to secure a position in foreign markets. Accepting the $19 price might seriously undermine future negotiations with foreign dealers and cause disruptions in the long-run profitability of the firm. The Helms Company may feel that it would be better to forego the short-run

---

[3] That is, any added fixed costs that are incurred solely as a result of the added sales.

$30,000 increase in contribution margin in order to protect its future long-run market position.

The essential point of our discussion is that the contribution approach to pricing contains a ready-made framework within which the price setter can operate in special pricing situations. By organizing costs in a way that is compatible with cost-volume-profit concepts, this approach to structuring price quotation sheets assists the manager in isolating those costs that are relevant in special pricing decisions and guides the manager in those decisions from a cost point of view.

The variable pricing model

The contribution approach to pricing can be presented in general model form, as shown in Exhibit 12–8.

EXHIBIT 12–8
The contribution approach to pricing: A general model

Variable costs (detailed)	. . . . . .	XXX	(Floor)	Range of flexibility
Fixed costs	. . . .	XXX		
Desired profit	. . . .	XXX		
Target selling price	. . . .	XXX	(Ceiling)	

The contribution approach provides a **ceiling** and a **floor** between which the price setter operates. The ceiling represents the price that the manager would *like* to obtain, and indeed *must* obtain on the bulk of the sales over the long run. But under certain conditions, the model shows that the manager can move within the **range of flexibility** as far down as the floor of variable costs in quoting a price to a prospective customer. What are the conditions under which a price based on variable costs alone might be appropriate? We can note three:

1. When idle capacity exists, as in the case of the Helms Company.
2. When operating under distress conditions.
3. When faced with sharp competition on particular orders under a competitive bidding situation.

When any of these conditions exist, it may be possible to increase overall profitability by pricing *some* jobs, products, or orders at *any amount* above variable costs, even if this amount is substantially less than the normal markup.

We will now examine each of the three special conditions listed above more closely to see how each relates to the range of flexibility depicted in Exhibit 12–8.

Idle capacity There is no need to be concerned about the range of flexibility depicted in Exhibit 12–8 so long as a company can sell all that it can produce at regular prices. That is, no company is going to sell at less than regular prices if regular prices are obtainable.

However, a different situation exists if a company has idle capacity that can't be used to expand regular sales at regular prices. Under these conditions, any use to which the idle capacity can be put that increases revenues more than variable costs (and any *incremental* fixed costs) will increase overall net income.

The use might come in the form of a special order for a regular product from a customer that the company does not usually supply (such as a foreign market). Or the use might come in the form of a slight modification of a regular product to be sold under a new customer's own brand name. Alternatively, the use might come in the form of a special order for a product that the company does not usually produce. In any of these situations, so long as the price received on the extra business exceeds the variable costs (and any *incremental* fixed costs) involved, overall net income will be increased by utilizing the idle capacity.

The Helms Company is a good example of the sort of situation we are talking about. The company has idle capacity, and there is no prospect of using the idle capacity for regular business. Under these conditions, nothing will be lost by quoting a price to the foreign distributor that is below full cost, or even relaxing the price down very close to the floor of variable costs, if necessary.

Distress conditions   Occasionally a company is forced to operate under distress conditions when the market for its product has been adversely affected in some way. For example, demand may virtually dry up overnight, forcing the company to drop its prices sharply downward. Under these conditions, any contribution that can be obtained to help cover fixed costs may be preferable to ceasing operations altogether. If operations cease, then *no* contribution will be available to apply toward fixed costs.

Competitive bidding   The pricing model illustrated in Exhibit 12–8 is particularly useful in competitive bidding situations. Competition is often hot and fierce in situations where bidding is involved, so companies can't afford to be inflexible in their pricing. Unfortunately, many companies refuse to cut prices in the face of stiff competition, adamantly stating that they price only on a "full cost" basis and don't want the business unless they can get a "decent price" for the work. There are several problems associated with taking this kind of position on pricing. First, it involves faulty logic. The so-called decent price is obtained by adding some markup onto "full cost." But cost is dependent on *volume* of sales, which in turn is dependent on selling price.

Second, as discussed in Chapter 11, there are *two* determinants of profitability—margin and turnover. The "decent price" attitude ignores the turnover factor and focuses entirely on the margin factor. Yet many companies have demonstrated that a more modest margin combined with a faster turnover of assets can be highly effective from a profitability point of view. One way to increase turnover, of course, is to be flexible in bidding by shading prices in situations where competition is keen.

Finally, in situations where fixed costs are high, a company can't *afford* to be inflexible in its pricing policies. Once an investment in plant and other fixed productive facilities has been made, a company's strategy must be to generate every dollar of contribution that it can to assist in the covering of these costs. Even if a company is forced to operate at an accounting loss, this might be preferable to having no contribution at all toward recovery of investment.

CRITICISMS OF THE CONTRIBUTION APPROACH TO PRICING

Not all managers are enthusiastic about the contribution approach to pricing. Some argue that the contribution approach, with its reliance on variable costs, can lead to setting prices too low and to eventual bankruptcy. These managers argue that the absorption approach to pricing is superior to the contribution approach since it includes an element of fixed overhead cost in the pricing base, whereas the contribution approach includes only the variable costs. Including an element of fixed overhead cost in the pricing base is said to make the absorption approach safer in terms of long-run pricing. Managers who argue in this way feel that if variable costs alone are used in pricing, the price setter may be misled into accepting *any* price over variable costs on a long-run basis for any product.

This argument can be criticized on several points. We should note first that the absorption approach to pricing excludes as many costs from the pricing base as does the contribution approach. It just excludes *different* costs. For example, the absorption approach doesn't consider selling and administrative costs at all in its base, since the base typically is made up entirely of "costs to manufacture." By contrast, the contribution approach does include variable selling and administrative expenses along with variable production expenses in developing a base for pricing.

Whether or not *any* pricing mechanism results in intelligent pricing decisions will depend in large part on the ability of the price setter to use the available data. As a practical matter, this means that pricing decisions must be restricted to managers who are qualified to make them. This point has been made very well in an NAA study of actual pricing practices:

> No instance of unprofitable pricing attributable to direct costing was reported, but on the contrary, opinion was frequently expressed to the effect that direct costing had contributed to better pricing decisions. However, companies restrict product cost and margin data to individuals qualified to interpret such data and responsible for pricing policy decisions.[4]

On the other hand, no matter how expert a decision maker may be, the decisions will be faulty if the cost information with which he or she is working is irrelevant, unclear, or inadequate. Firms that have adopted the contribution approach to pricing have found that the old pricing system often led to incorrect pricing decisions because of faulty data:

---

[4] National Association of Accountants, *Research Report No. 37,* "Current Applications of Direct Costing" (New York, January 1961), p. 55.

Instances were cited in which management had unknowingly continued selling products below out-of-pocket cost or had decided to withdraw from the market when a substantial portion of the period costs could have been recovered. . . .

In one interview . . . when direct costing was introduced, analysis demonstrated that contracts which would have contributed to period costs had often been refused at times when the company had a large amount of idle capacity.[5]

PRICE DISCRIMINATION

In structuring a pricing policy, firms must take care to keep their actions within the requirements of the various laws that deal with price setting and with price discrimination. The most widely known of these is the **Robinson-Patman Act** of 1936. The act forbids quoting different prices to competing customers unless the difference in price can be traced directly to "differences in the cost of manufacture, sale, or delivery resulting from the differing methods or quantities in which commodities are to such purchasers sold or delivered." Both the Federal Trade Commission and the courts have consistently held that "cost" is to be interpreted as full cost and not just incremental or variable costs. This means that in the case of *competing* customers for the *same* goods, price differences cannot be defended on the basis of covering incremental costs alone. Note, though, that we are talking about *competing* customers for the *same* goods. We are not talking about a competitive bidding situation, nor are we talking about a situation in which idle capacity might be used to produce for a noncompeting market or for some purpose other than production of regular products.

In addition to the Robinson-Patman Act, all states have laws prohibiting the sale of goods or services below "cost." Cost is normally either specified as full cost or is so interpreted by the regulating agencies. Although these state laws might appear to greatly restrict the flexibility of management in pricing decisions, they are often interpreted to apply to a company's products *as a whole,* rather than to individual products. For example, a store may be able to sell bread below cost (often called a "loss leader") so long as it sells its products *as a whole* over cost. These laws do suggest, however, that firms should keep careful records of their costs and of the way their prices are structured in order to be able to answer questions of regulatory bodies.

An international law relating to pricing exists in the form of the Anti-Dumping Law of 1932. This law prohibits the sale of products below cost in international markets. Again, "cost" is interpreted as full cost, including fully allocated fixed costs. The law is designed to protect a domestic manufacturer in its home market in those instances where it is in direct competition with a foreign supplier.

---

[5] Ibid.

SUMMARY

The general pricing models of the economist contain the basic framework for pricing decisions. Since these models are conceptual in nature, and since the specific information required for their direct application is rarely available, firms normally rely on pricing formulas to implement the ideas that the models contain. Pricing decisions can be divided into three broad groups:

1. Pricing standard products.
2. Pricing new products.
3. Pricing special orders.

The pricing of standard and new products is generally carried out through cost-plus pricing formulas. Such formulas require a cost base, to which a markup is added to derive a target selling price. Cost-plus pricing can be carried out equally well using either the absorption approach or the contribution approach.

Service-type organizations, such as repair shops and professional firms, use a pricing method known as time and material pricing. Under this approach, two pricing rates are established—one rate for time spent on a job, such as labor time or machine time, and another rate for materials used. In each case, the rate is structured so as to include a profit element as well as the direct costs of the time and material involved.

The pricing of special orders is somewhat different from the pricing of regular products or services in that in some situations full costs may not be applicable in setting prices. Circumstances may exist in which the price setter may be justified in pricing simply on a basis of variable or incremental costs. In these special pricing situations, price setters often find the contribution approach, with its emphasis on cost behavior, more useful than the absorption approach, which may require considerable reworking of data in order to generate the information needed for a pricing decision.

KEY TERMS FOR REVIEW

Ceiling A term used in relation to the range of flexibility that denotes the price that is obtained by adding a normal markup to the cost base in cost-plus pricing.

Cost-plus pricing A pricing method in which some predetermined markup is added to a cost base in determining a target selling price.

Floor A term used in relation to the range of flexibility that denotes the variable costs associated with a product.

Marginal cost A term used in economics that means the addition to total cost resulting from the production and sale of one additional unit of product.

Marginal revenue A term used in economics that means the addition to total revenue resulting from the sale of one additional unit of product.

Markup The amount added to a cost base in determining the target selling price in cost-plus pricing.

Material loading charge An amount added to the invoice cost of materials that is designed to cover (1) the costs of ordering, handling, and carrying the materials in stock and (2) a profit margin on the materials themselves.

Monopolistic competition A term used in economics that denotes a situation in which there are many sellers of similar products, with no one seller having a large enough share of the market for other sellers to be able to discern the effect of its pricing decisions on their sales.

Monopoly A term used in economics that denotes the absence of a directly competing product in the market.

Oligopoly A term used in economics that denotes a situation in which a few large sellers of a product are competing directly with one another.

Penetration pricing The setting of a low initial price for a product in order to gain quick acceptance in a broad portion of the market.

Price elasticity A term used in economics that means the degree to which volume of sales is affected by a change in price per unit.

Range of flexibility The range between the "floor" of variable costs and the "ceiling" of a normal target selling price in which a manager has to operate in special pricing decisions.

Robinson-Patman Act A federal law that prohibits discrimination in pricing between competing customers for a good or service.

Skimming pricing The setting of a high initial price for a product, with a progressive lowering of the price as time passes and as the market broadens and matures.

Target cost A maximum amount of production cost, which is used as a guide in developing a product that can be sold within a desired price range.

Test marketing The introduction of a product in selected areas in order to gain data on customer acceptance, volume of activity at various prices, and so forth.

Time and material pricing A pricing method, often used in service-type organizations, in which two pricing rates are established—one based on labor time and the other based on materials used.

QUESTIONS

12–1. Why does the economist depict a slowing down of the rate of increase in total revenue as more and more units are sold?

12–2. As depicted by the total revenue and total cost curves, what is the optimum point of production and what is the optimum price to be charged for a product?

12–3. According to the marginal revenue and marginal cost curves, what is the optimum point of production and what is the optimum price to charge for a product?

12–4. What is meant by price elasticity? Contrast a product that is price inelastic with a product that is price elastic.

12–5. Identify four limitations of the economic pricing models.

12–6. What costs are relevant in long-run pricing decisions?

12–7. What is meant by the term *cost-plus pricing?* Distinguish between the absorption and contribution approaches to cost-plus pricing.

12–8. In what sense is the term *cost-plus pricing* a misnomer?

12–9. "Full cost can be viewed as a floor of protection. If a firm always sets its prices above full cost, it will never have to worry about operating at a loss." Discuss.

12–10. In cost-plus pricing, what elements must be covered by the "markup" when the cost base consists of the cost to manufacture a product? What elements must be covered when the cost base consists of a product's variable expenses?

12–11. What is time and material pricing? What type of organization would use time and material pricing?

12–12. What is a material loading charge?

12–13. Distinguish between skimming pricing and penetration pricing. Which strategy would you probably use if you were introducing a new product that was highly price inelastic? Why?

12–14. What are *target costs,* and how do they enter into the pricing decision?

12–15. What problem is sometimes encountered in trying to price special orders under absorption costing?

12–16. Identify those circumstances under which the manager might be justified in pricing at any amount above variable costs.

12–17. In what ways does the Robinson-Patman Act influence pricing decisions?

EXERCISES

E12–1. Meridian Company must determine a target selling price for one of its products. Cost data relating to the product are given below:

	Per unit	Total
Direct materials	$ 6	
Direct labor	10	
Variable overhead	3	
Fixed overhead	5	$450,000
Variable selling and administrative expenses	1	
Fixed selling and administrative expenses	4	360,000

The costs above are based on an anticipated volume of 90,000 units produced and sold each period. The company uses cost-plus pricing, and it has a policy of obtaining target selling prices by adding a markup of 50 percent of cost to manufacture or by adding a markup of 80 percent of variable costs.

Required: 1. Assuming that the company uses absorption costing, compute the target selling price for one unit of product.

2. Assuming that the company uses the contribution approach to costing, compute the target selling price for one unit of product.

E12–2. Naylor Company is considering the introduction of a new product. As one step in its study of the new product, the company has gathered the following information:

526

| | 12,500 |
Number of units to be produced and sold each year 12,500
Cost to manufacture one unit of product . . . . $ 30
Projected annual selling and administrative
  expenses 60,000
Estimated investment required by the company 500,000
Desired ROI 18%

The company uses cost-plus pricing and the absorption costing method.

Required: 1. Compute the required markup in percentage terms.
2. Compute the target selling price per unit.

E12–3. Rolex, Inc., is anxious to introduce a new product on the market and is trying to determine what price to charge. The new product has required a $500,000 investment in equipment and working capital. The company wants a 10 percent ROI on all products. The following costs are traceable to the new product:

	Per unit	Annual total
Variable production costs (direct materials, direct labor, and variable overhead)	$19	—
Fixed overhead costs	—	$250,000
Variable selling and administrative expenses	1	—
Fixed selling and administrative expenses	—	150,000

The company uses cost-plus pricing and the contribution approach to costing.

Required: 1. Assume that the company expects to sell 50,000 units each year. What percentage markup would be required to achieve the target ROI? Using this markup, what would be the selling price per unit?
2. Repeat the computations in (1) above, assuming that the company expects to sell 30,000 units each year.

E12–4. The Riteway Plumbing Company does extensive plumbing repair work. The company incurs the following costs in its repair operations:

Plumbers:
  Wage rate per hour . . . . $ 15
  Fringe benefits per hour 3
  Desired profit per hour
    of plumber time. 4
Selling, administrative, and other
  costs of the repairs operation
  per year 160,000
Materials:
  Costs of ordering, handling,
    and storing parts . . . . 15% of invoice cost
  Desired profit on parts . . . . 30% of invoice cost

In total, the company logs 20,000 hours of repair time each year.

Required: 1. Assume that the company uses time and material pricing. Compute the time rate and the material loading charge that should be used to bill jobs.
2. One of the company's plumbers has just completed a repair job that required three hours of time and $40 in parts (invoice cost). Compute the amount that should be billed for the job.

E12–5.   Mead Company has always used the absorption approach for product costing and for pricing. The company's price quote sheet on its microwave oven is given below (per oven):

Direct materials	$ 75
Direct labor	60
Overhead ($5 variable + $40 fixed)	45
Total cost to manufacture.	$180
Markup: 33⅓%	60
Target selling price.	$240

The company incurs $10 in variable selling costs per unit and $150,000 annually in fixed selling and administrative costs. It produces and sells 5,000 ovens each year. The sales manager is curious as to what the price quote sheet would look like if the company used the contribution approach to pricing instead of the absorption approach.

Required: 1.   The accounting department has determined that the company would have to use a markup of 60 percent if the contribution approach were used in determining target selling prices. Prepare a price quote sheet for a microwave oven using the contribution approach.
2.   Identify the ceiling and the floor on the price quote sheet that you have prepared and explain their significance to the manager.
3.   Assume that the company has idle capacity and would like to run a special on microwave ovens for $179 each. Does it appear that this price would add to the company's overall profits? Explain.

E12–6.   To a large extent, the selling price that must be obtained on a product will be dependent on the number of units that can be sold. Consider the following data on a new product:

Variable production cost per unit	$	12
Variable selling and administrative expenses		
per unit		3
Fixed production cost (total)		480,000
Fixed selling and administrative expenses (total)		500,000
Desired markup		75%

The company uses the absorption method for product costing and for pricing.

Required: 1.   What would be the target selling price per unit if the company can produce and sell *(a)* 30,000 units each period, *(b)* 60,000 units each period?
2.   If the company charges the prices that you computed in (1) above, will it be assured that no losses will be sustained? Explain.

E12–7.   Reeder Company is contemplating entry into a new market. Costs and other information associated with the new product are given below:

Projected annual sales in units		30,000
Projected variable costs per unit:		
Production	$	12
Selling and administrative		3
Projected fixed costs in total:		
Production		175,000
Selling and administrative		85,000

As a first approximation to a selling price, the company normally uses a markup of 60 percent on variable costs, which represents the markup typically used in the industry.

Required:
1. Compute the target selling price for the new product, using the contribution approach.
2. Assume that the company will not add a new product line unless it promises a return on investment of at least 20 percent. The new product would require an investment in equipment and other assets totaling $500,000. What markup percentage would be required on the new product to provide the desired ROI? (Assume that the company uses the contribution approach to pricing.)

PROBLEMS

P12–8. **Percentage markups and price quotation sheets.** Aspen Company produces and markets a number of consumer products, including a toaster. Cost and revenue data on the toaster for 19x5, the most recent year, are given below:

	10,000 units sold	
	Total	Per unit
Sales	$300,000	$30
Cost of goods sold	180,000	18*
Gross margin	120,000	12
Selling and administrative expenses	70,000	7
Net income	$ 50,000	$ 5

* Contains $3 per unit in direct materials and $4 per unit in direct labor.

Fixed costs comprise $100,000 of cost of goods sold, and $50,000 of the selling and administrative expenses are fixed.

Required:
1. Using the data from the income statement above, do the following:
   a. Compute the percentage markup on cost being used by the company (that is, the gross margin as a percentage of cost of goods sold).
   b. Prepare a model price quotation sheet for a single unit of product using the absorption approach.
2. Recast the income statement for 19x5 in the contribution format, and then do the following:
   a. Compute the percentage markup based on variable cost (that is, the contribution margin as a percentage of variable costs).
   b. Prepare a model price quotation sheet for a single unit of product using the contribution approach.
3. Assume that the company has sufficient capacity to produce 12,500 toasters each year. J-Mart, a regional discount chain located in the East, is willing to make a bulk purchase of 2,500 toasters at a price of $15 per toaster, if the toasters are imprinted with the J-Mart name. The sale of these toasters would not disturb regular sales.
   a. Using the model price quotation sheet prepared in (1) above, should the offer be accepted? Explain.
   b. Explain how the model price quotation sheet prepared in (2) above can be helpful to the manager in making special pricing decisions. Using this sheet as a guide, should the offer be accepted? Show computations.

P12–9. **Computation of markup percentages.** Arborland Vineyards is in the process of developing a new wine. After considerable study, the following target costs have been set for a case of the new wine (based on 20,000 cases):

	Target costs per case	Target annual costs
Direct materials	$18.00	
Direct labor	3.60	
Variable overhead	2.40	
Fixed overhead—direct	6.00	$120,000
Variable selling	1.00	
Fixed selling and administrative	7.25	145,000

The company estimates that adding the new wine will require the following permanent investment of funds:

For working capital	$250,000
For equipment.	150,000
Total investment	$400,000

The company has a 15 percent target return on funds invested in a product. Cost-plus pricing is in use.

Required:
1. Assuming that the company uses absorption costing:
   a. Compute the markup percentage needed for the company to achieve its target ROI of 15 percent on funds invested in the new product.
   b. Using the markup percentage computed in (1a) above, compute the target selling price for a case of the new wine.
2. Assuming that the company uses the contribution approach:
   a. Compute the markup percentage needed for the company to achieve its target ROI of 15 percent on funds invested in the new product.
   b. Using the markup percentage computed in (2a) above, compute the target selling price for a case of the new wine.

P12–10. **Time and material pricing.** Superior TV Repair, Inc., employs five repair technicians who work a 40-hour week, 50 weeks per year. The company uses time and material pricing, and each year it reviews its rates in light of the actual costs incurred in the prior year. Actual costs incurred last year in connection with repair work and in connection with the company's parts inventory are given below:

	Repairs	Parts
Repair technicians—wages	$120,000	$ —
Repair service manager—salary	30,000	—
Parts manager—salary	—	26,000
Repairs and parts assistant—salary	8,000	4,000
Retirement benefits (20% of salaries and wages).	31,600	6,000
Health insurance (5% of salaries and wages).	7,900	1,500
Utilities	5,400	10,700
Truck operating costs.	27,000	—
Property taxes	950	3,200
Liability and fire insurance	400	1,800
Supplies	750	300
Rent—building	5,000	16,500
Depreciation—trucks and equipment.	18,000	—
Invoice cost of parts used	—	280,000
Total costs for the year	$255,000	$350,000

The company has a target profit of $4.50 per hour of repair service time and a target profit of 15 percent of the invoice cost of parts used. During the past year, the company billed repair service time at $27.50 per hour and added a material loading charge of 35 percent to parts. There is some feeling in the company that these rates may now be inadequate since costs have risen somewhat over the last year.

Required:
1. Using the data above, compute the following:
    a. The rate that should be charged per hour of repair service time. Your rate should contain three cost elements, as discussed in the body of the chapter.
    b. The material loading charge that should be used in billing jobs. The material loading charge should be expressed as a percentage of the invoice cost of parts and should contain two elements, as discussed in the body of the chapter.
2. Are the time and material rates that the company has been using adequate to cover its costs and yield the desired profit margins? Explain. (No computations are necessary.)
3. Assume that the company adopts the rates that you have computed in (1) above. What should be the total price charged on a repair job that requires 1½ hours of service time and $69.50 in parts?

P12–11. Computation of markup percentage; sensitivity analysis. Eureka Products, Inc., is in a highly competitive industry in which markups are about 45 percent of cost to manufacture. The company is anxious to introduce a new product line (now being sold by several competitors) that would require a $1,500,000 investment for the acquisition of needed equipment and for working capital purposes. The following estimated costs have been developed for the new product:

	Per unit	Total
Direct materials	$12	
Direct labor	20	
Variable overhead	3	
Fixed overhead	10	$300,000
Variable selling and administrative expense	5	
Fixed selling and administrative expense	14	420,000

These costs are based on the production and sale of 30,000 units per year. The company will not introduce a new product unless it is able to provide at least a 16 percent ROI.

Required:
1. Assume that the company uses absorption costing for product costing and for pricing. Determine the markup necessary to achieve the company's target ROI.
2. Would you recommend that the company take on the new product line? Explain.
3. Look at the formula used to compute the markup percentage in (1) above. If management wants to reduce the markup percentage in order to be more competitive and yet earn a 16 percent ROI, what lines of attack does the formula suggest that management can follow?

P12–12. Integrated problem: Markup percentages; price quote sheets; special order. Lemhi Products, Inc., manufactures a variety of electrical products. The company wants to introduce a new electric motor that would have the following cost characteristics (based on an activity level of 50,000 motors produced and sold each year):

	Per motor	Total
Direct materials	$18	
Direct labor	40	
Variable overhead	7	
Fixed overhead	20	$1,000,000
Variable selling expense.	5	
Fixed selling expense.	16	800,000

After careful study, the company has determined that production of the new motor would require an investment of $3,250,000 in order to purchase equipment, carry inventories, and provide for other working capital needs. The company desires a 20 percent return on investment for all new products.

Required: 1. Assume that the company uses the absorption costing method.
   a. Compute the markup percentage needed to achieve the company's desired 20 percent ROI.
   b. Using the markup percentage you have computed, prepare a price quote sheet for a single motor.
   2. Assume that the company uses the contribution approach to costing.
   a. Compute the markup percentage needed to achieve the company's desired 20 percent ROI.
   b. Using the markup percentage you have computed, prepare a price quote sheet for a single motor.
   3. Assume that production and sales drop off to only 45,000 motors per year due to a severe economic recession. A government contractor has offered to make a bulk purchase of 5,000 motors at a price of $82 per motor.
   a. Using the model price quote sheet prepared in (1b) above, should the offer be accepted? Explain.
   b. Explain how the model price quote sheet prepared in (2b) above can be helpful to the manager in making special pricing decisions. Using this sheet as a guide, should the offer be accepted? Explain.

P12–13.   Time and material pricing.   Midland Motors, Inc., is an automobile dealership that provides a service department for its customers. As part of this service department, the company maintains a large parts inventory in order to have parts on hand when needed for repair work. Although the service department always operates at capacity, it has never been very profitable, and management is concerned that the pricing rates in use may be too low ($25 per hour for mechanics' labor, plus a 35 percent material loading charge on parts).

An analysis of the costs incurred by the service department over the past year has revealed the following:

   a. The department employs one service manager over repair work who is paid $24,000 per year and one parts manager who is paid $21,000 per year. In addition, an office assistant is employed who is paid $10,000 per year. The assistant's time is divided 60 percent to repair work and 40 percent to parts work.
   b. Five mechanics are employed for repair work who work 40 hours per week, 50 weeks per year. Their combined wages totaled $90,000 for the past year.
   c. Retirement and vacation benefits equal 12 percent of salaries and wages; health insurance costs equal 5 percent of salaries and wages; and employment taxes

equal 10 percent of salaries and wages. (The company treats all of these items as employee fringe benefits.)

d. Insurance costs allocable to repair work totaled $8,900 for the past year, and insurance costs allocable to parts totaled $4,750.

e. Property taxes for the year on building, equipment, and inventories were allocable between repairs and parts as follows: repairs, $2,500; and parts, $3,000.

f. Costs for utilities incurred during the past year: repairs, $10,000; and parts, $2,500.

g. The repairs area incurred costs for cleaning supplies totaling $1,200 for the year.

h. Depreciation on building and equipment for the year totaled $68,000, of which $50,000 was allocable to repair work and $18,000 was allocable to parts.

i. The company has a target profit of $5 per hour of mechanics' work in the repair area and 15 percent of the invoice cost of parts in the parts area. Parts costing $200,000 were used in repair work during the year.

Required:

1. Compute the rate that should be charged per hour of mechanics' time, and the material loading charge that should be used (as a percentage of the invoice cost of parts). Your time rate should contain three cost elements, as discussed in the body of the chapter. Your material loading charge should contain two cost elements.

2. What should be the total price charged on a job that requires 3½ hours of mechanics' time and $60 in parts?

P12–14. Distress pricing. Advance Toys, Inc., manufactures a broad line of toys, games, and puzzles. In 19x1, the company obtained the manufacturing and distribution rights to a new puzzle called a Hubic Cube. New equipment costing $800,000 was purchased to produce the cubes. The equipment was estimated to be capable of producing 1,000,000 cubes before it would have to be replaced in 19x5. The company felt that the market for the Hubic Cube would be stable for several years and that there would be little competition, due to the complex nature of the production process. The cubes were priced as follows (per unit):

Direct materials	$0.80
Direct labor.	0.50
Overhead (⅙ variable)	1.20
Total cost to manufacture	2.50
Markup—60%	1.50
Target selling price	$4.00

Selling and administrative expenses relating to the cubes were:

Advertising and other fixed costs (per year)	$25,000
Commissions and shipping costs (per cube)	$0.10

In 19x1 and 19x2, the company produced and sold 300,000 Hubic Cubes each year. Early in 19x3, the market suddenly became flooded with similar cubes from several overseas sources, and the selling price quickly dropped to only $2.25 per cube.

The marketing vice president has recommended that the company stop producing the cubes and scrap the special equipment. "It would be insane to continue producing," she reasoned. "At a selling price of only $2.25 per cube, we would be losing $0.25 on every cube that comes off the production line, and that doesn't even consider our selling costs."

Required: 1. Redo the price quote sheet above by placing it in the contribution format. (The appropriate markup would be 150 percent.)

2. Assume that due to increased competition the company can expect to sell only 100,000 units per year even at the lower price. Do you agree with the vice president's recommendation to stop production and scrap the special equipment? Explain.

P12–15. **Pricing a bid.** Martin Instruments produces thermostats for industrial use. The company prices its thermostats by adding a markup of 75 percent to variable costs (so that the selling price is equal to 175 percent of variable costs). This pricing policy has worked very well over the years.

Martin Instruments has received an invitation to bid on a government order for 1,000 specially designed thermostats. The company has made the following cost estimates:

Direct materials	$ 70,000
Direct labor	50,000
Variable overhead	10,000
Allocated fixed overhead	20,000
Tools, dies, and other special production costs	30,000
Shipping costs	5,000
Special administrative costs	5,000
Total costs	$190,000
Cost per thermostat ($190,000 ÷ 1,000)	$190

Martin Instruments is now operating at capacity. If the company takes on the government order, it will have to forego regular sales of $210,000.

Required: 1. In terms of contribution margin sacrificed, what is the opportunity cost of accepting the government order?

2. What is the lowest price that Martin Instruments can bid on the government order without sacrificing current profits?

P12–16. **Distress pricing.** The Wasatch Mining Company purchased a mine for $1,000,000 in 19x1. The company then expended another $500,000 installing railroad tracks into the mine, setting up supporting beams, and purchasing equipment to process the ore coming out of the mine. The tracks, beams, and equipment were given a 10-year life. It was estimated that the mine contained 1,000,000 tons of ore. Active mining was started in 19x2 and continued through 19x5, with the following average yearly results:

Number of tons of ore mined per year	100,000
Mining costs per ton (exclusive of depletion and depreciation)	$4
Selling price per ton	7

In early 19x6, a competing company discovered massive deposits of the ore just a few miles from the Wasatch Mining Company's mine. As a result, the market was flooded with ore and the selling price dropped to $5 per ton. The president of the Wasatch Mining Company made a few quick computations and declared, "We'll have to close the mine. If we keep it open, we'll lose 50 cents a ton for every ton of ore we mine and sell. At a $5 selling price, it will be less costly to just close the doors and walk away from the place."

Required: 1. How did the president compute the 50 cents per ton loss?
2. Do you agree with the president's decision? Explain.

P12–17. **High-low analysis; special order.** Integrated Circuits, Inc. (ICI), is currently operating at 50 percent of capacity, producing 50,000 units annually of a patented electronic component. ICI has received an offer from a company in Yokohama, Japan, to purchase 30,000 components at $7 per unit, FOB ICI's plant. ICI has not previously sold components in Japan. Budgeted production costs for 50,000 and 80,000 units of output follow:

Units	50,000	80,000
Costs:		
Direct materials.	$ 75,000	$120,000
Direct labor	200,000	320,000
Factory overhead	125,000	140,000
Total costs	$400,000	$580,000
Cost per unit	$8.00	$7.25

The sales manager thinks that the order should be accepted, even if this results in a loss of $1 per unit, because the sale may build up future markets. The production manager does not wish to have the order accepted, primarily because the order would show a loss of 25 cents per unit when computed on the new average unit cost.

Required: 1. In terms of direct materials, direct labor, variable overhead, and fixed overhead, show the breakdown of the unit costs at the 50,000 and 80,000 unit levels of activity.
2. Assume that the normal target selling price is $10 per unit. Using the contribution approach, prepare a price quotation sheet for one unit of product. (The appropriate markup would be 66⅔ percent.) Indicate the ceiling, the floor, and the range of flexibility on your sheet.
3. On the basis of the information given in the problem and the information that you have computed above, should the order be accepted or rejected? Show computations to support your answer.
4. In addition to revenue and costs, what additional factors should be considered before making a final decision? (CPA, adapted)

P12–18. **Integrative problem: Standard costs; markup computations; pricing decisions.** Euclid Fashions, Inc., has designed a sports jacket that is about to be introduced on the market. A standard cost card has been prepared for the new jacket, as shown below:

	Standard quantity or hours	Standard price or rate	Standard cost
Direct materials.	2.0 yards	$ 4.60 per yard	$ 9.20
Direct labor	1.4 hours	10.00 per hour	14.00
Overhead (⅙ variable)	1.4 hours	12.00 per hour	16.80
Total standard cost per jacket			$40.00

The following additional information relating to the new jacket is available:
a. The only variable selling or administrative costs on the jackets will be $4 per jacket for shipping. Fixed selling and administrative costs will be (per year):

Salaries.	$ 90,000
Advertising and other	384,000
Total	$474,000

b. Since the company manufactures many products, it is felt that no more than 21,000 hours of labor time per year can be devoted to production of the new jackets.

c. An investment of $900,000 will be necessary to carry inventories and accounts receivable and to purchase some new equipment. The company desires a 24 percent return on investment in new product lines.

d. Overhead costs are allocated to products on a basis of direct labor-hours.

Required: 1. Assume that the company uses absorption costing.
    a. Compute the markup that the company needs on the jackets in order to achieve a 24 percent ROI.
    b. Using the markup you have computed, prepare a price quote sheet for a single jacket.
    c. Assume that the company is able to sell all of the jackets that it can produce. Prepare an income statement for the first year of activity, and compute the company's ROI for the year on the jackets, using the ROI formula from Chapter 11.

    2. Assume that the company uses the contribution approach.
    a. Compute the markup that the company needs on the jackets in order to achieve a 24 percent ROI.
    b. Using the markup you have computed, prepare a price quote sheet for a single jacket.
    c. Prepare an income statement for the first year of activity.

    3. After marketing the jackets for several years, the company is experiencing a falloff in demand due to an economic recession. A large retail outlet will make a bulk purchase of jackets if its label is sewn in and if an acceptable price can be worked out. Identify the range within which this price should fall.

P12–19. **Contribution approach to pricing.** E. Berg & Sons builds custom-made pleasure boats that range in price from $10,000 to $250,000. For the past 30 years, Mr. Berg, Sr., has determined the selling price of each boat by estimating the costs of materials, labor, and a prorated portion of the overhead, then adding 20 percent to these estimated costs.

For example, a recent price quotation was determined as follows:

Direct materials	$ 5,000
Direct labor	8,000
Overhead	2,000
	15,000
Plus 20%	3,000
Selling price	$18,000

The overhead figure was determined by estimating total overhead costs for the year and allocating them at 25 percent of direct labor.

If a customer rejected the price and business was slack, Mr. Berg, Sr., would often be willing to reduce his markup to as little as 5 percent over estimated costs. Thus, average markup for the year is estimated at 15 percent.

Mr. Ed Berg, Jr., has just completed a course on pricing and believes that the firm could use some of the techniques discussed in the course. The course emphasized the contribution approach to pricing, and Mr. Berg, Jr., feels that this approach would be helpful in determining the selling prices of the firm's custom-made pleasure boats.

Total overhead, which includes selling and administrative expenses for the year, has been estimated at $150,000, of which $90,000 is fixed and the remainder is variable in direct proportion to direct labor.

Required:

1. Assume that during a slack period the customer in the example rejected the $18,000 quotation and also rejected a $15,750 quotation (5 percent markup). The customer countered with a $15,000 offer.
   a. What is the difference in net income for the year between accepting and rejecting the customer's offer?
   b. What is the minimum selling price that Mr. Berg, Jr., could have quoted without reducing or increasing company net income?
2. What advantages does the contribution approach to pricing have over the approach used by Mr. Berg, Sr.?
3. What possible dangers are there, if any, to the contribution approach to pricing?
(CMA, adapted)

P12–20. Competitive bidding. The Tolby Machine Company designs and produces machine tools to customer specifications. The bulk of the company's business is obtained by competitive bidding. In the latter part of 19x5, the company was invited (along with several other companies) to bid on an order of 50 specially designed jigs needed by a manufacturing firm.

The Tolby Machine Company was very happy to receive the invitation to bid, since business had been very slow for over a year, with no prospects for improvement. The company estimated the following costs relating to the 50 jigs:

	Total	Per jig
Direct material	$ 50,000	$1,000
Direct labor	40,000	800
Variable overhead	10,000	200
Fixed overhead*	50,000	1,000
Design and cost study	5,000	100
Shipping	7,500	150
Total cost	$162,500	$3,250

* Allocated on a basis of machine-hours.

Based on these data, the company submitted a bid of $3,900 per jig. The price quotation sheet used to compute the bid is shown below:

Direct materials	$1,000
Direct labor	800
Manufacturing overhead	1,200
Total cost to manufacture	3,000
Markup desired—30%	900
Bid price per jig	$3,900

The manufacturer receiving the bid replied that the bid was too high and that no bid over $3,300 per jig would be considered. Upon hearing this, the president of the Tolby Machine Company stated, "That lets us out. Our cost is $3,250 per jig. At a bid price of $3,300, the profit we'd make wouldn't be worth the effort."

Required: What would you advise the Tolby Machine Company to do? Show computations in good form.

P12–21.   Special order; capacity utilization.   Tiffany Company manufactures several different styles of jewelry cases. Management estimates that during the third quarter of 19x6 the company will be operating at 80 percent of normal capacity. Because the company desires a higher utilization of plant capacity, it will consider a special order.

Tiffany has received special-order inquiries from two companies. The first inquiry is from JCP, Inc., which would like to market a jewelry case similar to one of Tiffany's cases. The JCP jewelry case would be marketed under JCP's own label. JCP, Inc., has offered Tiffany $5.75 per jewelry case for 20,000 cases to be shipped by October 1, 19x6. Cost data are given below for the Tiffany jewelry case that is similar to the jewelry case desired by JCP:

Regular selling price per unit.	$9.00
Costs per unit:	
Raw materials	$2.50
Direct labor, 0.5 hours at $6	3.00
Overhead, 0.25 machine-hours at $4	1.00
Total costs per unit	$6.50

According to the specifications provided by JCP, Inc., the special order case requires less expensive raw materials. Consequently, the raw materials will only cost $2.25 per case. Management has estimated that the remaining costs, labor time, and machine time will be the same as those for the Tiffany jewelry case.

The second special order, submitted by the Krage Company, was for 7,500 jewelry cases at $7.50 per case. These jewelry cases would be marketed under the Krage label and would have to be shipped by October 1, 19x6. The Krage jewelry case is different from any jewelry case in the Tiffany line. The estimated costs per unit of this case are as follows:

Raw materials	$3.25
Direct labor, 0.5 hours at $6	3.00
Overhead, 0.5 machine-hours at $4	2.00
Total costs per unit	$8.25

In addition, Tiffany will incur $1,500 in additional setup costs and will have to purchase a $2,500 special device to manufacture these cases. The device will be discarded once the special order has been completed.

The Tiffany manufacturing capabilities are limited to the total machine-hours available. The plant capacity under normal operations is 90,000 machine-hours per year, or 7,500 machine-hours per month. The budgeted fixed overhead for 19x6 amounts to $216,000. All manufacturing overhead costs (fixed and variable) are applied to production on the basis of machine-hours, at $4 per hour.

During the third quarter, Tiffany will be able to use all of its excess capacity to work on special orders. Management does not expect any repeat sales to be generated from either special order. Company practice precludes Tiffany from subcontracting any portion of an order when special orders are not expected to generate repeat sales.

Required: Should Tiffany Company accept either special order? Justify your answer, and show your calculations. (Hint: It may be helpful to distinguish between fixed and variable overhead.)   (CMA, adapted)

13 Relevant Costs for Decision Making

Learning objectives

After studying Chapter 13, you should be able to:

State a general rule for distinguishing between relevant and irrelevant costs in an organization.

Identify sunk costs and explain why they are not relevant in decision making.

Prepare an analysis showing whether a product line or other organizational segment should be dropped or retained.

Explain what is meant by a "make or buy" decision and prepare a well-organized make or buy analysis.

Make appropriate computations to determine the most profitable utilization of scarce resources in an organization.

Prepare an analysis showing whether joint products should be sold at the split-off point or processed further.

Construct a graph that shows the optimal solution to a linear programming problem.

Define or explain the key terms listed at the end of the chapter.

The making of decisions is one of the basic functions of a manager. The manager is constantly faced with problems of deciding what products to sell, what production methods to use, whether to make or buy component parts, what prices to charge, what channels of distribution to use, whether to accept special orders at special prices, and so forth. At best, decision making is a difficult and complex task. The difficulty of this task is usually increased by the existence of not just one or two but numerous courses of action that might be taken in any given situation facing a firm.

In decision making, *cost* is always a key factor. The costs of one alternative must be compared against the costs of other alternatives as one step in the decision-making process. The problem is that some costs associated with an alternative may not be *relevant* to the decision to be made. A **relevant cost** can be defined as a cost that is *applicable to a particular decision* in the sense that it will have a bearing on which alternative the manager selects.

To be successful in decision making, managers must have tools at their disposal to assist them in distinguishing between relevant and irrelevant costs so that the latter can be eliminated from the decision framework. The purpose of this chapter is to acquire these tools and to show their application in a wide range of decision-making situations.

COST CONCEPTS FOR DECISION MAKING

Three cost terms discussed in Chapter 2 are particularly applicable to this chapter. These terms are differential costs, opportunity costs, and sunk costs. The reader may find it helpful to turn back to Chapter 2 and refresh his or her memory of these terms before reading on.

Identifying relevant costs

What costs are relevant in decision making? The answer is easy. Any cost that is *avoidable* is relevant for decision purposes. An **avoidable cost** can be defined as a cost that can be eliminated as a result of choosing one alternative over another in a decision-making situation. *All* costs are considered to be avoidable, *Except:*

1. Sunk costs.
2. Future costs that *do not differ* between the alternatives at hand.

As we learned in Chapter 2, a **sunk cost** is a cost that has already been incurred and that cannot be avoided regardless of which course of action a manager may decide to take. As such, sunk costs have no relevance to future events and must be ignored in decision making. Similarly, if a cost will be incurred regardless of which course of action a manager may take, then the cost cannot possibly be of any help in deciding which course of action is best. Such a cost is not avoidable, and hence it is not relevant to the manager's decision.

Stated another way, *the relevant costs in a decision are those costs (and revenues) that are differential as between the alternatives being considered.* To identify those costs that are differential and therefore relevant, the manager's approach to cost analysis should include the following steps:

1. Assemble *all* of the costs associated with *each* alternative being considered.
2. Eliminate those costs that are sunk.
3. Eliminate those costs that do not differ between alternatives.
4. Make a decision based on the remaining costs. These costs will be the **differential** or **avoidable costs,** and hence the costs relevant to the decision to be made.

Different costs for different purposes

We need to recognize from the outset of our discussion that costs which are relevant in one decision situation are not necessarily relevant in another. Simply put, this means (as we've stated before) that *the manager needs different costs for different purposes.* For one purpose, a particular group of costs may be relevant; for another purpose, an entirely different group of costs may be relevant. Thus, in *each* decision situation the manager must examine the data at hand and then take the steps necessary to isolate the relevant costs. Otherwise, he or she runs the risk of being misled by irrelevant data.

The concept of "different costs for different purposes" is basic to managerial accounting; we shall see its application frequently in the pages that follow.

SUNK COSTS ARE NOT RELEVANT COSTS

One of the most difficult conceptual lessons that managers have to learn is that sunk costs are never relevant in decisions. The tendency to want to include sunk costs within the decision framework is especially strong in the case of book value of old equipment. We focus on book value of old equipment below, and then we consider other kinds of sunk costs in other parts of the chapter. We shall see that regardless of the kind of sunk cost involved, the conclusion is always the same—sunk costs are not avoidable, and therefore they must be eliminated from the manager's decision framework.

Book value of old equipment

Assume the following data:

Old machine		Proposed new machine	
Original cost	$10,000	List price new	$12,000
Remaining book value	8,000	Expected life	4 years
Remaining life	4 years	Disposal value in four years	–0–
Disposal value now	$ 3,000	Annual variable expenses	
Disposal value in four years	–0–	to operate	$15,500
Annual variable expenses		Annual revenue from sales	50,000
to operate	20,000		
Annual revenue from sales	50,000		

Should the old machine be disposed of and the new machine purchased? Some managers would say no, since disposal of the old machine would result in a "loss" of $5,000:

Old machine	
Remaining book value.	$8,000
Disposal value now.	3,000
Loss if disposed of now	$5,000

Given this potential loss if the old machine is sold, there is a general inclination for the manager to reason, "We've already made an investment in the old machine, so now we have no choice but to use it until our investment has been fully recovered." The manager will tend to think this way even though the new machine is clearly more efficient than the old machine. Although it may be appealing to think that an error of the past can be corrected by simply *using* the item involved, this, unfortunately, is not correct. The investment that has been made in the old machine is a sunk cost. The portion of this investment that remains on the company's books (the book value of $8,000) should not be considered in a decision about whether to buy the new machine. We can prove this assertion by the following analysis:

	Total costs and revenues— four years		
	Keep old machine	Differential costs	Purchase new machine
Sales	$200,000	–0–	$200,000
Variable expenses	(80,000)	$ 18,000	(62,000)
Cost (depreciation) of the new machine	–0–	(12,000)	(12,000)
Depreciation of the old machine, or book value write-off	(8,000)	–0–	(8,000)*
Disposal value of the old machine.	–0–	3,000	3,000*
Total net income over the four years	$112,000	$ 9,000	$121,000

* For external reporting purposes, the $8,000 remaining book value of the old machine and the $3,000 disposal value would be netted together and deducted as a single $5,000 "loss" figure.

Looking at all four years together, notice that the firm will be $9,000 better off by purchasing the new machine. Also notice that the $8,000 book value of the old machine had *no effect* on the outcome of the analysis. Since this book value is a sunk cost, it must be absorbed by the firm regardless of whether the old machine is kept and used or whether it is sold. If the old machine is kept and used, then the $8,000 book value is deducted in the form of depreciation. If the old machine is sold, then the $8,000 book value is deducted in the form of a lump-sum write-off. Either way, the company bears the same $8,000 deduction.

Focusing on relevant costs What costs in the example above are relevant in the decision concerning the new machine? Following the steps outlined earlier, we should eliminate (1) the sunk costs and (2) the future costs that do not differ between the alternatives at hand.

1. The sunk costs:
   a. The remaining book value of the old machine ($8,000).
2. The future costs that do not differ:
   a. The annual sales revenue ($50,000).
   b. The annual variable expenses (to the extent of $15,500).

The costs that remain will form the basis for a decision. The analysis is:

	Differential costs— four years
Reduction in variable expense promised by the new machine ($4,500* per year × 4 years)	$ 18,000
Cost of the new machine.	(12,000)
Disposal value of the old machine	3,000
Net advantage of the new machine	$ 9,000

* $20,000 − $15,500 = $4,500.

Note that the items above are the same as those in the middle column of the earlier analysis and represent those costs and revenues that are differential as between the two alternatives.

Depreciation and relevant costs   Since the book value of old equipment is not a relevant cost, there is a tendency to assume that depreciation of *any* kind is irrelevant in the decision-making process. This is not a correct assumption. Depreciation is irrelevant in decisions only if it relates to a sunk cost. Notice from the comparative income statements in the preceding section that the $12,000 depreciation on the new machine appears in the middle column as a relevant item in trying to assess the desirability of the new machine's purchase. By contrast, depreciation on the old machine does not appear as a relevant cost. The difference is that the investment in the new machine has *not yet been made,* and therefore it does not represent depreciation of a sunk cost.

FUTURE COSTS THAT DO NOT DIFFER ARE NOT RELEVANT COSTS

Any future cost that does not differ between the alternatives in a decision situation is not a relevant cost so far as that decision is concerned. As stated earlier, if a company is going to sustain the same cost regardless of what decision it makes, then that cost can in no way tell the company which decision is best. The only way a future cost can help in the decision-making process is by being different as between the alternatives under consideration.

An example of irrelevant future costs

To illustrate the irrelevance of future costs that do not differ, let us assume that a firm is contemplating the purchase of a new laborsaving machine.

The machine will cost $10,000 and have a 10-year useful life. The company's sales and cost structure on an annual basis with and without the new machine are shown below:

	Present costs	Expected costs with the new machine
Units produced and sold.	5,000	5,000
Sales price per unit	$ 10	$ 10
Direct materials cost per unit	4	4
Direct labor cost per unit.	3	2
Variable overhead cost per unit	1	1
Fixed costs, other	4,000	4,000
Fixed costs, new machine	–0–	1,000

The new machine promises a saving of $1 per unit in direct labor costs but will increase fixed costs by $1,000 per period. All other costs, as well as the total number of units produced and sold, will remain the same. Following the steps outlined earlier, the analysis is:

1. Eliminate the sunk costs. (No sunk costs are identified in this example.)
2. Eliminate the future costs (and revenues) that do not differ:
   a. The sales price per unit does not differ.
   b. The direct materials cost per unit does not differ.
   c. The variable overhead cost per unit does not differ.
   d. The total "fixed costs, other" do not differ.

This leaves just the per unit labor costs and the fixed costs associated with the new machine as being differential costs:

Savings in direct labor costs (5,000 units at a cost saving of $1 per unit)	$5,000
Less increase in fixed costs	1,000
Net annual cost savings promised by the new machine	$4,000

The accuracy of this solution can be proved by looking at *all* items of cost data (both those that are relevant and those that are not) under the two alternatives for a period and then comparing the net income results. This is done in Exhibit 13–1. Notice from the exhibit that we obtain the same $4,000 net advantage in favor of buying the new machine as we obtained earlier when we focused only on relevant costs. Thus, we can see that future costs that do not differ between alternatives are indeed irrelevant in the decision-making process and can be safely eliminated from the manager's decision framework.

Why isolate relevant costs?

In the preceding example, we used two different approaches to show that the purchase of the new machine was desirable. First, we considered only the relevant costs; and second, we considered all costs, both those that were

EXHIBIT 13–1
Differential cost analysis

	Present method	Differential costs	New machine
	\$50,000		\$50,000

(5,000 units produced and sold)

	Present method	Differential costs	New machine
Sales	\$50,000	–0–	\$50,000
Variable expenses:			
Direct materials	20,000	–0–	20,000
Direct labor	15,000	\$5,000	10,000
Variable overhead	5,000	–0–	5,000
Total variable expenses	40,000		35,000
Contribution margin	10,000		15,000
Less fixed expenses:			
Other	4,000	–0–	4,000
New machine	–0–	(1,000)	1,000
Total fixed expenses	4,000		5,000
Net income	\$ 6,000	\$4,000	\$10,000

relevant and those that were not. We obtained the same answer under both approaches. When students see that the same answer can be obtained under either approach, they often ask, "Why bother to isolate relevant costs when total costs will do the job just as well?" The isolation of relevant costs is desirable for at least two reasons.

First, only rarely will enough information be available to prepare a detailed income statement such as we have done in the preceding examples. Since normally only limited data are available, the decision maker *must* know how to recognize which costs are relevant and which are not. Assume, for example, that you are called upon to make a decision relating to a matter in a *single operation* of a multidepartmental, multiproduct firm. Under these circumstances, it would be virtually impossible to prepare an income statement of any type. You would have to rely on your ability to recognize which costs were relevant and which were not in order to assemble the data necessary to make a decision.

Second, the use of irrelevant costs mingled with relevant costs may confuse the picture and draw the decision maker's attention away from the matters that are really critical to the problem at hand. Furthermore, the danger always exists that an irrelevant piece of data may be used improperly, resulting in an incorrect decision. The best approach is to isolate the relevant items and to focus all attention directly on them and on their impact on the decison to be made.

Relevant cost analysis, combined with the contribution approach to the income statement, provides a powerful tool for making decisions in special, nonroutine situations. We will investigate various uses of this tool in the remaining sections of this chapter.

ADDING AND DROPPING PRODUCT LINES

The decisions relating to when to drop old product lines and when to add new product lines are among the stickiest that a manager has to make. In such decisions, many factors must be considered that are both qualitative and quantitative in nature. Ultimately, however, any final decision to drop an old product line or to add a new product line is going to hinge primarily on the impact the decision will have on net income. In order to assess this impact, it is necessary to make a careful analysis of the costs involved.

An illustration of cost analysis

As a basis for discussion, let us consider the product lines of the Discount Drug Company. The company has three major product lines—drugs, cosmetics, and housewares. Sales and cost information for the preceding month for each separate product line and for the store in total is given in Exhibit 13–2.

What can be done to improve the company's overall performance? One product line—housewares—shows a net loss for the month. Perhaps dropping this line would cause profits in the company as a whole to improve. In deciding whether the line should be dropped, management will need to reason as follows:

If the housewares line is dropped, then the company will lose $20,000 per month in contribution margin that is now available to help cover the fixed costs. By dropping the line, however, it may be possible to avoid certain of these fixed costs. It may be possible, for example, to discharge certain employees, or it may be possible to reduce advertising costs. If by dropping the housewares line the company is able to avoid more in fixed costs than it loses in contribution margin, then it will be better off if the line is eliminated, since overall net income should improve. On the other hand, if the company is not able to avoid as much in fixed costs as it loses in contribution margin,

EXHIBIT 13–2
Discount Drug Company product lines

	Total	Drugs	Cosmetics	Housewares
Sales	$250,000	$125,000	$75,000	$50,000
Less variable expenses. . . .	105,000	50,000	25,000	30,000
Contribution margin	145,000	75,000	50,000	20,000
Less fixed expenses:				
Salaries	50,000	29,500	12,500	8,000
Advertising	15,000	1,000	7,500	6,500
Utilities	2,000	500	500	1,000
Depreciation—fixtures . . .	5,000	1,000	2,000	2,000
Rent	20,000	10,000	6,000	4,000
Insurance.	3,000	2,000	500	500
General administrative . . .	30,000	15,000	9,000	6,000
Total fixed expenses . . .	125,000	59,000	38,000	28,000
Net income (loss).	$ 20,000	$ 16,000	$12,000	$ (8,000)

then the housewares line should be retained. In short, in order to identify the differential costs in decisions of this type, the manager must ask, "What costs can I avoid to offset my loss of revenue (or loss of contribution margin) if I drop this product line?"

As we have seen from our earlier discussion, not all costs are avoidable. Some of the costs associated with a product line may be sunk costs, for example; other costs may be allocated common costs that will not differ in total regardless of whether the product line is dropped or retained. To show how the manager should proceed in a product-line analysis, suppose that the management of the Discount Drug Company has analyzed the costs being charged to the three product lines and has determined the following:

1. The salaries represent salaries paid to employees working directly in each product-line area. All of the employees working in housewares can be discharged if the line is dropped.
2. The advertising represents direct advertising of each product line and is avoidable if the line is dropped.
3. The utilities represent utilities costs for the entire company. The amount charged to each product line represents an allocation based on space occupied.
4. The depreciation represents depreciation on fixtures used for display of the various product lines. Although the fixtures are nearly new, they are custom-built and will have little resale value if the housewares line is dropped.
5. The rent represents rent on the entire building housing the company; it is allocated to the product lines on a basis of sales dollars. The monthly rent of $20,000 is fixed under a long-term lease agreement.
6. The insurance represents insurance carried on inventories maintained within each of the three product-line areas.
7. The general administrative expense represents the costs of accounting, purchasing, and general management, which are allocated to the product lines on a basis of sales dollars. Total administrative costs will not change if the housewares line is dropped.

With this information, management can identify those costs that are avoidable and those costs that are not avoidable if the product line is dropped:

	Total cost	Not avoidable*	Avoidable
Salaries	$ 8,000		$ 8,000
Advertising	6,500		6,500
Utilities	1,000	$ 1,000	
Depreciation—fixtures	2,000	2,000	
Rent	4,000	4,000	
Insurance	500		500
General administrative	6,000	6,000	
Total fixed expenses	$28,000	$13,000	$15,000

* These costs represent either (1) sunk costs or (2) costs that will not change regardless of whether the housewares line is retained or discontinued.

To determine how dropping the line will affect the overall profits of the company, we can compare the contribution margin that will be lost against the costs that can be avoided if the line is dropped.

Contribution margin lost if the housewares
line is discontinued (see Exhibit 13–2) . . . . $(20,000)
Less fixed costs that can be avoided if the
housewares line is discontinued (see above) 15,000
Decrease in overall company net income . . . . $ (5,000)

In this case, the fixed costs that can be avoided by dropping the product line are less than the contribution margin that will be lost. Therefore, the housewares line should not be discontinued unless a more profitable use can be found for the floor and counter space that it is occupying.

A comparative format

Some managers prefer to approach decisions of this type by preparing comparative income statements showing the effects on the company as a whole of either keeping or dropping the product line in question. A comparative analysis of this type for the Discount Drug Company is shown in Exhibit 13–3.

As shown by column 3 in the exhibit, overall company net income will decrease by $5,000 each period if the housewares line is dropped. This is the same answer, of course, as we obtained in our earlier analysis.

EXHIBIT 13–3
A comparative format for product-line analysis

	Keep housewares	Drop housewares	Difference: Net income increase or (decrease)
Sales.	$50,000	–0–	$(50,000)
Less variable expenses	30,000	–0–	30,000
Contribution margin.	20,000	–0–	(20,000)
Less fixed expenses:			
Salaries	8,000	–0–	8,000
Advertising	6,500	–0–	6,500
Utilities	1,000	$ 1,000	–0–
Depreciation—fixtures	2,000	2,000	–0–
Rent	4,000	4,000	–0–
Insurance	500	–0–	500
General administrative	6,000	6,000	–0–
Total fixed expenses	28,000	13,000	15,000
Net income (loss)	$ (8,000)	$(13,000)	$ (5,000)

Beware of allocated fixed costs

Our conclusion that the housewares line should not be dropped seems to conflict with the data shown in Exhibit 13–2. Recall from the exhibit that the housewares line is showing a loss rather than a profit. Why keep a line that is showing a loss? The explanation for this apparent inconsistency lies at least in part with the common fixed costs that are being allocated to the product lines. As we observed in Chapter 7, one of the great dangers in allocating common fixed costs is that such allocations can make a product line (or other segment of a business) *look* less profitable than it really is. Consider the following example:

A bakery distributed its products through route salesmen, each of whom loaded a truck with an assortment of products in the morning and spent the day calling on customers in an assigned territory. Believing that some items were more profitable than others, management asked for an analysis of product costs and sales. The accountants to whom the task was assigned allocated all manufacturing and marketing costs to products to obtain a net profit for each product. The resulting figures indicated that some of the products were being sold at a loss, and management discontinued these products. However, when this change was put into effect, the company's overall profit declined. It was then seen that, by dropping some products, sales revenues had been reduced without commensurate reduction in costs because the joint manufacturing costs and route sales costs had to be continued in order to make and sell remaining products.[1]

The same thing has happened in the Discount Drug Company as happened in the bakery company. That is, by allocating the common fixed costs among all product lines, the Discount Drug Company has made the housewares line *look* as if it were unprofitable, whereas, in fact, dropping the line would result in a decrease in overall company net income. This point can be seen clearly if we recast the data in Exhibit 13–2 and eliminate the allocation of the common fixed costs. This recasting of data is shown in Exhibit 13–4.

Exhibit 13–4 gives us a much different perspective of the housewares line than does Exhibit 13–2. As shown in Exhibit 13–4, the housewares line is covering all of its own direct fixed costs and is generating a $3,000 segment margin toward covering the common fixed costs of the company. Unless another product line can be found that will generate a greater segment margin than this, then, as we have noted, the company will be better off to keep the housewares line. By keeping the line, the company will get at least some contribution toward the common fixed costs of the organization from the space it is occupying.

Finally, we should note that even in those situations where the contribution of a particular product line is small in comparison with other products, managers will often retain the line instead of replacing it, if the line is necessary to the sale of other products or if it serves as a "magnet" to attract customers. Bread, for example, is not an especially profitable line in food stores, but customers expect it to be available and many would undoubtedly shift their buying elsewhere if a particular store decided to stop carrying it.

---

[1] Walter B. McFarland, *Concepts for Management Accounting* (New York: National Association of Accountants, 1966), p. 46.

EXHIBIT 13–4

Discount Drug Company product lines—recast in contribution format (from Exhibit 13–2)

	Total	Drugs	Cosmetics	Housewares
Sales	$250,000	$125,000	$75,000	$50,000
Less variable expenses . . .	105,000	50,000	25,000	30,000
Contribution margin	145,000	75,000	50,000	20,000
Less direct fixed expenses:				
Salaries	50,000	29,500	12,500	8,000
Advertising	15,000	1,000	7,500	6,500
Depreciation—fixtures . . .	5,000	1,000	2,000	2,000
Insurance	3,000	2,000	500	500
Total	73,000	33,500	22,500	17,000
Product line segment margin . .	72,000	$ 41,500	$27,500	$ 3,000*
Less common fixed expenses:				
Utilities	2,000			
Rent	20,000			
General administrative . . .	30,000			
Total	52,000			
Net income	$ 20,000			

* If the housewares line is dropped, this $3,000 in segment margin will be lost to the company. In addition, we have seen that the $2,000 depreciation on the fixtures is a sunk cost that cannot be avoided. The sum of these two figures ($3,000 + $2,000 − $5,000) represents another way of obtaining the $5,000 figure that we found earlier would be the decrease in the company's overall profits if the housewares line were discontinued.

THE MAKE OR BUY DECISION

Many steps are involved in getting a finished product into the hands of a consumer. First, raw materials must be obtained through mining, drilling, growing crops, raising animals, and so forth. Second, these raw materials must be processed to remove impurities or to extract the desirable and usable materials from the bulk of materials available. Third, the usable materials must be fabricated into desired form to serve as basic inputs for manufactured products. Fourth, the actual manufacturing of the finished product must take place, with several products perhaps coming from the same basic raw material input (as, for example, several different items of clothing coming from the same basic cloth input). And finally, the finished product must be distributed to the ultimate consumer.

When a company is involved in more than one of these steps, it is said to be **vertically integrated.** Vertical integration is very common. Some firms go so far as to control *all* of the activities relating to their products, from the mining of raw materials or the raising of crops right up to the final distribution of finished goods. Other firms are content to integrate on a less grand scale, and perhaps they will produce only certain fabricated parts that go into their finished products.

A decision to produce a fabricated part internally, rather than to buy the part externally from a supplier, is often called a **make or buy decision.** Actually, any decision relating to vertical integration is a make or buy decision, since the company is deciding whether to meet its own needs internally rather than to buy externally.

The advantages of integration

Certain advantages arise from integration. The integrated firm is less dependent on its suppliers and may be able to ensure a smoother flow of parts and materials for production than the nonintegrated firm. For example, a strike against a major parts supplier might cause the operations of a nonintegrated firm to be interrupted for many months, whereas the integrated firm that is producing its own parts might be able to continue operations. Also, many firms feel that they can control quality better by producing their own parts and materials, rather than by relying on the quality control standards of outside suppliers. In addition, the integrated firm realizes profits from the parts and materials that it is "making" rather than "buying," as well as profits from its regular operations.

The advantages of integration are counterbalanced by a number of hazards. A firm that produces all of its own parts runs the risk of destroying long-run relationships with suppliers, which may prove harmful and disruptive to the firm. Once relationships with suppliers have been severed, they are often difficult to reestablish. If product demand becomes heavy, a firm may not have sufficient capacity to continue producing all of its own parts internally, but then it may experience great difficulty in its efforts to secure assistance from a severed supplier. In addition, changing technology often makes continued production of one's own parts more costly than purchasing them from the outside, but this change in cost may not be obvious to the firm. In sum, these factors suggest that although certain advantages may accrue to the integrated firm, the make or buy decision should be weighed very carefully before any move is undertaken that may prove to be costly in the long run.

An example of make or buy

How does a firm approach the make or buy decision? Basically, the matters that must be considered fall into two broad categories—qualitative and quantitative. Qualitative matters deal with issues such as those raised in the preceding section. Quantitative matters deal with cost—what is the cost of producing as compared to the cost of buying? Several kinds of costs may be involved here, including opportunity costs.

To provide an illustration, assume that Bonner Company is now producing a small subassembly that is used in the production of one of the company's main product lines. Bonner Company's accounting department reports the following "costs" of producing the subassembly internally:

	Per unit	8,000 units
Direct materials	$ 3	$ 24,000
Direct labor	4	32,000
Variable overhead	1	8,000
Supervisor's salary	3	24,000
Depreciation of special equipment	2	16,000
Allocated general overhead	5	40,000
Total cost	$18	$144,000

Bonner Company has just received an offer from an outside supplier who will provide 8,000 subassemblies a year at a firm price of $15 each. Should Bonner Company stop producing the subassemblies internally and start purchasing them from the outside supplier? To make this decision, the manager must again focus on the differential costs. As we have seen, the differential costs can be obtained by eliminating from the cost data those costs that are not avoidable; that is, by eliminating (1) the sunk costs and (2) the future costs that will continue regardless of whether the subassemblies are produced internally or purchased outside. The costs that remain after making these eliminations will be the costs that are avoidable to the company by purchasing outside. If these costs are less than the outside purchase price, then the company should continue to manufacture its own subassemblies and reject the outside supplier's offer. That is, the company should purchase outside only if the outside purchase price is less than the costs that can be avoided internally as a result of stopping production of the subassemblies.

Looking at the data above, notice first that depreciation of special equipment is one of the "costs" of producing the subassemblies internally. Since this equipment has already been purchased, this represents a sunk cost. Also notice that the company is allocating a portion of its general overhead costs to the subassemblies. Since these costs are common to all items produced in the factory, they will continue unchanged even if the subassemblies are purchased from the outside. These allocated costs, therefore, are not differential costs (since they will not differ between the make or buy alternatives), and they must be eliminated from the manager's decision framework along with the sunk costs.

The variable costs of producing the subassemblies (materials, labor, and variable overhead) are differential costs, since they can be avoided by buying the subassemblies from the outside supplier. If the supervisor can be discharged and his or her salary avoided by buying the subassemblies, then it too will be a differential cost and relevant to the decision. Assuming that both the variable costs and the supervisor's salary can be avoided by buying from the outside supplier, then the analysis takes the form shown in Exhibit 13–5.

EXHIBIT 13–5
Make or buy analysis

	Production "cost" per unit	Per unit differential costs		Total differential costs—8,000 units	
		Make	Buy	Make	Buy
Direct materials	$ 3	$ 3		$24,000	
Direct labor.	4	4		32,000	
Variable overhead	1	1		8,000	
Supervisor's salary	3	3		24,000	
Depreciation of special equipment.	2	—		—	
Allocation of general overhead	5	—		—	
Outside purchase price. . . .			$15		$120,000
Total cost.	$18	$11	$15	$88,000	$120,000
Difference in favor of continuing to make. . . .		$4		$32,000	

Since it costs $4 less per unit to continue to make the subassemblies, Bonner Company should reject the outside supplier's offer. There is one additional factor that the company may wish to consider before coming to a final decision, however. This factor is the opportunity cost of the space now being used to produce the subassemblies.

The matter of opportunity cost

If the space now being used to produce the subassemblies *would otherwise be idle,* then Bonner Company should continue to produce its own subassemblies and the supplier's offer should be rejected, as we stated above. Idle space that has no alternative use has an opportunity cost of zero.

But what if the space now being used to produce subassemblies would not sit idle, but rather could be used for some other purpose? In this case, the space would have an opportunity cost that would have to be considered in assessing the desirability of the supplier's offer. What would this opportunity cost be? It would be the segment margin that could be derived from the best alternative use of the space.

To illustrate, assume that the space now being used to produce subassemblies could be used to produce a new product line that would generate a segment margin of $50,000 per year. Under these conditions, Bonner Company would be better off to accept the supplier's offer and to use the available space to produce the new product line:

	Make	Buy
Differential cost per unit (see prior example)	$ 11	$ 15
Number of units needed annually	× 8,000	× 8,000
Total annual cost	88,000	120,000
Opportunity cost—segment margin foregone on a potential new product line	50,000	
Total cost	$138,000	$120,000
Difference in favor of purchasing from the outside supplier	$18,000	

Perhaps we should again emphasize that opportunity costs are not recorded in the accounts of an organization. They do not represent actual dollar outlays. Rather, they represent those economic benefits that are *forgone* as a result of pursuing some course of action. The opportunity costs of Bonner Company are sufficiently large in this case to make continued production of the subassemblies very costly from an economic point of view.

UTILIZATION OF SCARCE RESOURCES

Firms are often faced with the problem of deciding how scarce resources are going to be utilized. A department store, for example, has a limited amount of floor space and therefore cannot stock every product line that may be available. A manufacturing firm has a limited number of machine-hours and a limited number of direct labor-hours at its disposal. When capacity becomes pressed, the firm must decide which orders it will accept and which orders it will reject. In making these decisions, the contribution approach is necessary, since the firm will want to select the course of action that will maximize its *total* contribution margin.

Contribution in relation to scarce resources

To maximize total contribution margin, a firm may not necessarily want to promote those products that have the highest *individual* contribution margins. Rather, total contribution margin will be maximized by promoting those products or accepting those orders that promise the highest contribution margin *in relation to the scarce resources of the firm*. This concept can be demonstrated by assuming that a firm has two product lines, A and B. Cost and revenue characteristics of the two product lines are given below:

	A	B
Sales price per unit	$10	$12
Variable cost per unit	5	8
Contribution margin per unit	$ 5	$ 4
C/M ratio	50%	33%

Product line A appears to be much more profitable than product line B. It has a $5 per unit contribution margin as compared to only $4 per unit for product line B, and it has a 50 percent C/M ratio as compared to only 33 percent for product line B.

But now let us add one more piece of information—it takes two machine-hours to produce one unit of A and only one machine-hour to produce one unit of B. The firm has only 2,000 machine-hours of capacity available in the plant per period. If demand becomes strong, which orders should the firm accept, those for product line A or those for product line B? The firm should accept orders for product line B. Even though product line A has the highest *per unit* contribution margin, product line B provides the highest contribution margin in relation to the scarce resource of the firm, which in this case is machine-hours available.

	A	B
Contribution margin per unit (above) *(a)*	$5.00	$4
Machine-hours required to produce one unit *(b)*	2	1
Contribution margin per machine-hour, *(a) ÷ (b)*	$2.50	$4
Total contribution margin promised:		
Total machine-hours available	2,000	2,000
Contribution margin per machine-hour	× $2.50	× $4
Total contribution margin	$5,000	$8,000

This example shows clearly that looking at unit contribution margins alone is not enough; the contribution margin promised by a product line must be viewed in relation to whatever resource constraints a firm may be working under.

One of the most common resource constraints is advertising dollars available. Firms typically concentrate their efforts on those product lines that promise the greatest contribution margin per dollar of advertising expended. Another common resource constraint is floor space. Various discount retail outlets and discount food chains have utilized the concept of maximum contribution margin per square foot by concentrating on those product lines that have a rapid turnover, thereby generating large amounts of contribution in small amounts of space available.

The problem of multiple constraints

What does a firm do if it is operating under *several* scarce resource constraints? For example, a firm may have limited raw materials available, limited direct labor-hours available, limited floor space, and limited advertising dollars to spend on product promotion. How would it proceed to find the right combination of products to produce under such a variety of constraints? The proper combination or "mix" of products can be found by use of a quantitative method known as *linear programming*. Linear programming, a very powerful analytical tool, is illustrated in the Appendix to this chapter.

JOINT PRODUCT COSTS AND THE CONTRIBUTION APPROACH

The manufacturing processes of some firms are such that several end products are produced from a single raw material input. The meat-packing industry, for example, inputs a pig into the manufacturing process and comes out with a great variety of end products—bacon, ham, spare ribs, pork roasts, and so on. Firms that produce several end products from a common input (e.g., a pig) are faced with the problem of deciding how the cost of that input is going to be divided among the end products (bacon, ham, pork roasts, and so on) that result. Before we address ourselves to this problem, it will be helpful to define three terms—joint products, joint product costs, and split-off point.

Two or more products that are produced from a common input are known as **joint products.** The term **joint product costs** is used to describe those manufacturing costs that are incurred in producing joint products up to the split-off point. The **split-off point** is that point in the manufacturing process at which the joint products (bacon, ham, spare ribs, and so on) can be recognized as individual units of output. At that point, some of the joint products will be in final form, ready to be marketed to the consumer. Others will still need further processing on their own before they are in marketable form. These concepts are presented graphically in Exhibit 13–6.

EXHIBIT 13–6
Joint products

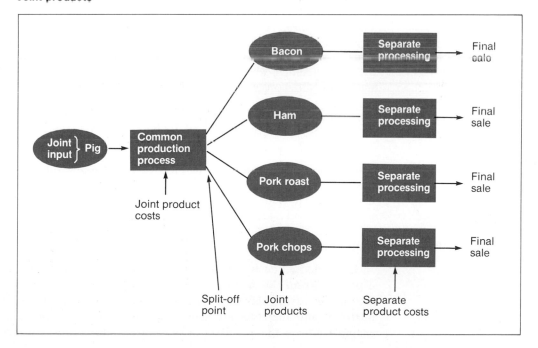

The pitfalls of allocation

Joint product costs are really common costs incurred to simultaneously produce a variety of end products. Traditional cost accounting books contain various approaches to allocating these common costs among the different products at the split-off point. The most usual approach is to allocate the joint product costs according to the relative sales value of the end products.

Although allocation of joint product costs is needed for some purposes, such as balance sheet inventory valuation, allocations of this kind should be used with great caution *internally* in the decision-making process. Unless a manager proceeds with care, he or she may be led into incorrect decisions as a result of relying on allocated common costs. Consider the following situation, which occurred in a firm several years ago:

A company located on the Gulf of Mexico is a producer of soap products. Its six main soap product lines are produced from common inputs. Joint product costs up to the split-off point constitute the bulk of the production costs for all six product lines. These joint product costs are allocated to the six product lines on the basis of the relative market value of each line at the split-off point.

The company has a waste product that results from the production of the six main product lines. Until a few years ago, the company loaded the waste onto barges and dumped it into the Gulf of Mexico, since the waste was thought to have no commercial value. The dumping was stopped, however, when the company's research division discovered that with some further processing the waste could be made commercially salable as a fertilizer ingredient. The further processing was initiated at a cost of $175,000 per year. The waste was then sold to fertilizer manufacturers at a total price of $300,000 per year.

The accountants responsible for allocating manufacturing costs included the sales value of the waste product along with the sales value of the six main product lines in their allocation of the joint product costs at the split-off point. This allocation resulted in the waste product being allocated $150,000 in joint product cost. This $150,000 allocation, when added to the further processing costs of $175,000 for the waste, caused the waste product to show a net loss:

Sales value of the waste product after further processing	$300,000
Less costs assignable to the waste product	325,000
Net loss	$ (25,000)

When presented with this analysis, the company's management decided that further processing of the waste was not desirable after all. The company went back to dumping the waste in the Gulf.

Sell or process further decisions

Joint product costs are irrelevant in decisions regarding what to do with a product from the split-off point forward. The reason is that by the time one arrives at the split-off point, the joint product costs have already been incurred, and therefore are sunk costs. In the case of the soap company example above, the $150,000 in allocated joint product costs should not have been permitted to influence what was done with the waste product from the split-off point forward. The analysis should have been:

	Dump in Gulf	Process further
Sales value	–0–	$300,000
Additional processing costs.	–0–	175,000
Contribution margin	–0–	$125,000
Advantage of processing further		$125,000

Decisions of this type are known as **sell or process further decisions.** As a general guide, it will always be profitable to continue processing a joint product after the split-off point *so long as the incremental revenue from such processing exceeds the incremental processing costs.* Joint product costs that have already been incurred up to the split-off point are sunk costs, and are always irrelevant in decisions concerning what to do from the split-off point forward.

To provide a detailed example of a sell or process further decision, assume that three products are derived from a single raw material input. Cost and revenue data relating to the products are presented in Exhibit 13–7, along with an analysis of which products should be sold at the split-off point and which should be processed further. As shown in the exhibit, products B and C should both be processed further; product A should be sold at the split-off point.

EXHIBIT 13–7
Sell or process further decision

	Product A	Product B	Product C
Sales value at the split-off point	$120,000	$150,000	$60,000
Sales value after further processing	160,000	240,000	90,000
Allocated joint product costs	80,000	100,000	40,000
Cost of further processing	50,000	60,000	10,000
Analysis of sell or process further:			
Sales value after further processing	$160,000	$240,000	$90,000
Sales value at the split-off point	120,000	150,000	60,000
Incremental revenue from further processing .	40,000	90,000	30,000
Cost of further processing	50,000	60,000	10,000
Profit (loss) from further processing	$ (10,000)	$ 30,000	$20,000

SUMMARY

The accountant is responsible for seeing that relevant, timely data are available to guide management in its decisions, particularly those decisions relating to special, nonroutine situations. Reliance by management on irrelevant data can lead to incorrect decisions, reduced profitability, and inability to meet stated objectives. *All* costs are relevant in decision making, *except:*

1. Sunk costs.
2. Future costs that will not differ between the alternatives under consideration.

The concept of cost relevance has wide application. In this chapter, we have observed its use in equipment replacement decisions, in make or buy decisions, in discontinuance of product line decisions, in joint product decisions, and in decisions relating to the effective use of scarce resources. This list does not include all of the possible applications of the relevant cost concept. Indeed, *any* decision involving costs hinges on the proper identification and use of those costs that are relevant, if the decision is to be made properly. For this reason, we shall continue to focus on the concept of cost relevance in the following two chapters, where we consider long-run investment decisions.

KEY TERMS FOR REVIEW

Avoidable cost Any cost that can be eliminated (in whole or in part) as a result of choosing one alternative over another in a decision-making situation. This term is synonymous with *relevant cost* and *differential cost.*

Differential cost Any cost that is present under one alternative in a decision-making situation but is absent in whole or in part under another alternative. This term is synonymous with *avoidable cost* and *relevant cost.*

Joint product costs Those manufacturing costs that are incurred up to the split-off point in producing joint products.

Joint products Two or more items that are produced from a common input.

Make or buy decision A decision as to whether an item should be produced internally or purchased from an outside supplier.

Relevant cost A cost that is applicable to a particular decision in the sense that it will have a bearing on which alternative the manager selects. This term is synonymous with *avoidable cost* and *differential cost.*

Sell or process further decision A decision as to whether a joint product should be sold at the split-off point or processed further and sold at a later time in a different form.

Split-off point That point in the manufacturing process where some or all of the joint products can be recognized as individual units of output.

Sunk cost Any cost that has already been incurred and that can't be changed by any decision made now or in the future.

Vertical integration The involvement by a company in more than one of the steps from extracting or otherwise securing basic raw materials to the manufacture and distribution of a finished product.

APPENDIX: LINEAR PROGRAMMING

Linear programming is a mathematical tool designed to assist management in making decisions in situations where constraining or limiting factors are present. The limiting factors might include, for example, a scarcity of raw materials needed in the production of a firm's products, or a plant with inadequate machine time to produce all of the products being demanded by a firm's customers. Linear programming is designed to assist the manager in putting together the "right mix" of products in situations such as these, so that the scarce resources of the firm (e.g., raw materials, machine time) can be utilized in a way that will maximize profits.

A graphical approach to linear programming

To demonstrate a linear programming analysis, let us assume the following data:

A firm produces two products, X and Y. The contribution margin per unit of X is $8, and the contribution margin per unit of Y is $10. The firm has 36 hours of production time available each period. It takes six hours of production time to produce one unit of X and nine hours of production time to produce one unit of Y.

The firm has only 24 pounds of raw material available for use in production each period. It takes six pounds of raw material to produce one unit of X and three pounds to produce one unit of Y.

Management estimates that no more than three units of Y can be sold each period. The firm is interested in maximizing contribution margin. What combination of X and Y should be produced and sold?

There are four basic steps in a linear programming analysis:

1. Determine the *objective function,* and express it in algebraic terms.
2. Determine the *constraints* under which the firm must operate, and express each constraint in algebraic terms (called a **constraint equation**).
3. Determine the *feasible production area* on a graph. This area will be bounded by the constraint equations derived in (2) above, after the constraint equations have been expressed on the graph in linear form.
4. Determine from the feasible production area that *product mix* which will maximize (or minimize) the objective function.

We shall now examine each of these steps in order by relating them to the data in the example above.

1. Determine the objective function, and express it in algebraic terms.

The objective function simply represents the goal that is to be achieved, expressed in terms of the variables involved. The goal might be to maximize total contribution margin, as in our example; alternatively, it might be to minimize total cost.

Looking at the data in our example, for each unit of X that is sold, $8 in contribution margin will be realized. For each unit of Y that is sold, $10 in contribution margin will be realized. Therefore, the total contribution margin for the firm can be expressed by the following **objective function equation:**

$$Z = \$8X + \$10Y \tag{1}$$

where Z = the total contribution margin that will be realized with an optimal mix of X and Y, X = the number of units of product X that should be produced and sold to yield the optimal mix, and Y = the number of units of product Y that should be produced and sold to yield the optimal mix.

2. Determine the constraints under which the firm must operate, and express each constraint in algebraic terms.

From the data in our example, we can identify three constraints. First, only 36 hours of production time are available. Since it requires six hours to produce one unit of X and nine hours to produce one unit of Y, this constraint can be expressed in the following form:

$$6X + 9Y \leq 36 \tag{2}$$

Notice the inequality sign ($\leq$) in the equation. This signifies that the total production of both X and Y taken together cannot *exceed* the 36 hours available, but that this production *could* require *less* than the 36 hours available.

The second constraint deals with raw material usage. Only 24 pounds are available each period. It takes six pounds of raw material to produce one unit of X and three pounds to produce one unit of Y. This constraint can be expressed in the following algebraic terms:

$$6X + 3Y \leq 24 \tag{3}$$

The third constraint deals with market acceptance of product Y. The market can absorb only three units of Y each period. This constraint can be expressed as follows:

$$Y \leq 3 \tag{4}$$

3. Determine the feasible production area on a graph.

A graph containing the constraint equations [equations (2)–(4) above] is presented in Exhibit 13–8. In placing these three equations on the graph, we have asked the questions "How much product X could be produced if all resources were allocated to it and none were allocated to product Y?" and "How much product Y could be produced if all resources were allocated to it and none were allocated to product X?" For example, consider equation (2), dealing with production capacity. A total of 36 hours of production time is available. If all 36 hours are allocated to product X, six units can be produced each period (since it takes 6 hours to produce one unit of X, and 36 hours are available). On the other hand, if all 36 hours are allocated

EXHIBIT 13–8

A linear programming graphical solution

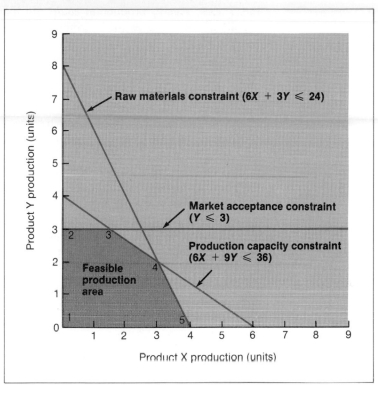

to product Y, then four units of Y can be produced each period (since it takes 9 hours to produce one unit of Y, and 36 hours are available).

If all production capacity is allocated to product X	If all production capacity is allocated to product Y
$6X + 0 \leq 36$	$0 + 9Y \leq 36$
$X = 6$	$Y = 4$

Therefore, the line on the graph in Exhibit 13–8 expressing the production constraint equation [equation (2)] extends from the six-unit point on the *X* axis to the four-unit point on the *Y* axis. Of course, production *could fall anywhere* on this constraint line; the points on the axes (6,4) simply represent the *extremes* that would be possible.

The equation associated with the raw materials constraint [equation (3)] has been placed on the graph through a similar line of reasoning. Since 24 pounds of raw material are available, the firm could produce either four units of X or eight units of Y if all of the raw material was allocated to one or the other (since it takes 6 pounds to produce a unit of X and 3 pounds to produce a unit of Y). Therefore, the line expressing the equation extends from the four-unit point on the X axis to the eight-unit point on the Y axis. Again, production *could fall anywhere* on this constraint line; the points on the axes (4, 8) simply represent the *extremes* that would be possible.

Since the third constraint equation [equation (4)] concerns only product Y, the line expressing the equation on the graph does not touch the X axis at all. It extends from the three-unit point on the Y axis and runs horizontal to the X axis, thereby signifying that regardless of the number of units of X that are produced, there can never be more than three units of Y produced.

Having now plotted on the graph the lines representing the three constraint equations, we have isolated the **feasible production area.** This area has been shaded on the graph. Notice that the feasible production area is formed by the lines of the constraint equations. Each line has served to limit the size of the area to some extent. The reason, of course, is that these lines represent *constraints* under which the firm must operate, and thereby serve to *limit* the range of choices available. The firm could operate *anywhere* within the feasible production area. One point within this area, however, represents an optimal mix of products X and Y that will result in a maximization of the objective function (contribution margin). Our task now is to find precisely where that point lies.

4. Determine from the feasible production area that product mix which will maximize the objective function.

The **optimal product mix** will always fall on a *corner* of the feasible production area. If we scan the graph in Exhibit 13–8, we can see that the feasible production area has five corners. The five corners will yield the following product mixes between X and Y (starting at the origin and going clockwise around the feasible production area):

	Units produced	
Corner	X	Y
1	0	0
2	0	3
3	1½	3
4	3	2
5	4	0

Which production mix is optimal? To answer this question, we will need to calculate the total contribution margin promised at each corner. We can do this by referring to the unit contribution margin data given in the objective function equation:

$$Z = \$8X + \$10Y \qquad (1)$$

This equation tells us that each unit of X promises $8 of contribution margin and that each unit of Y promises $10 of contribution margin. Relating these figures to the production mixes at the five corners, we find that the following total contribution margins are possible:

	X		Y		Total contribution margin
	$8(0)	+	$10(0)	=	$ 0
	8(0)	+	10(3)	=	30
	8(1½)	+	10(3)	=	42
	8(3)	+	10(2)	=	44
	8(4)	+	10(0)	=	32

The firm should produce three units of X and two units of Y. This production mix will yield a maximum contribution margin of $44. Given the constraints under which the firm must operate, it is not possible to obtain a greater total contribution margin than this amount. Any production mix different from three units of X and two units of Y will result in *less* total contribution margin.

Why always on a corner?

It was stated earlier that we will always find the optimal product mix on a *corner* of the feasible production area. Why does the optimal mix always fall on a corner? Look again at the objective function equation [equation (1)]. This equation expresses a straight line with a $-\frac{4}{5}$ slope. Place a ruler on the graph in Exhibit 13–8 extending from the 8 point on the Y axis to the 10 point on the X axis (a $-\frac{4}{5}$ slope). Now bring your ruler down toward the origin of the graph, taking care to keep it parallel to the line from which you started. Note that the first point which your ruler touches is the corner of the feasible production area showing a production mix of three units of X and two units of Y. Your ruler touches this point first because it is the farthest point from the origin in relation to the objective function line. Therefore, that point must yield the greatest total contribution margin for the firm. Any point closer to the origin would result in less total contribution margin.[2]

Direction of the constraint

Exhibit 13–8 shows the direction of all the constraints to be *inward* toward the origin of the graph. The direction of the constraint will always be inward,

---

[2] The objective function line could coincide with one of the lines bounding the feasible production area. In this case, a number of different product combinations would be possible, each resulting in the same total contribution margin. However, our statement that the solution will always be found on a corner is still true even under these conditions, since the product mix at the corners of the line would yield the same total contribution margin as any point on the line.

so long as the constraint equation is stated in terms of less than or equal to (≤).

The direction of the constraint will be *outward,* away from the origin of the graph, whenever the constraint equation is stated in terms of greater than or equal to (≥). To illustrate, assume the following constraint:

X weighs 4 ounces, and Y weighs 9 ounces. X and Y must be mixed in such a way that their total weight is at least 72 ounces

Constraint equation: $4X + 9Y \geq 72$ ounces

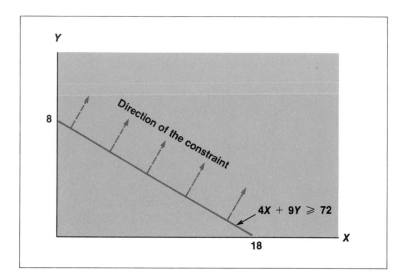

Since the direction of this constraint line is upward rather than downward, the feasible production area will be found *above* it rather than below it. Constraints expressed in terms of *greater than or equal to,* as illustrated above, can be found in any linear programming problem but are most common in *minimization* problems.

The simplex method

In our examples, we have dealt with only two products, X and Y. When more than two products are involved in a linear programming problem, the graphical method is no longer adequate to provide a solution. In these cases, a more powerful version of linear programming is needed. This more powerful version is commonly called the **simplex method.**

The simplex method is much more complex in its operation than is the graphical method; however, the principles underlying the two methods are the same. Generally, linear programming simplex solutions are carried out on the digital computer. The mechanics of the simplex method are covered in most advanced managerial accounting texts.

Applications of linear programming

Linear programming has been applied to an extremely wide range of problems in many different fields. Decision makers have found that it is by far the best tool available for combining labor, materials, and equipment to the best advantage of a firm. Although the use of linear programming has been most extensive in the industrial, agricultural, and military sectors, it has also been applied to problems in economics, engineering, and the sciences. Problems to which linear programming has been successfully applied include gasoline blending, production scheduling to optimize the use of total facilities, livestock feed blending to obtain a desired nutritional mix at the least cost, the routing of boxcars to desired points at the least cost, the selection of sites for electrical transformers, forestry maintenance, and the choice of flight paths for space satellites.

KEY TERMS FOR REVIEW (APPENDIX)

Constraint equation An equation expressing a limitation under which a firm must operate, such as limited materials available and limited machine time available.

Feasible production area The area on a linear programming graph, bounded by the constraint equations, within which production can take place.

Linear programming A mathematical tool designed to assist the manager in making decisions in situation where constraining or limiting factors are present.

Objective function equation An equation that expresses the goal that management is trying to achieve in a linear programming analysis; the goal might be, for example, to maximize the total contribution margin.

Optimal product mix That product mix which allows the firm to achieve the objective expressed in the objective function equation.

Simplex method A linear programming method that is designed to handle three or more variables in the objective function equation (for example, the optimal production mix of three or more products).

QUESTIONS

13–1. What is a "relevant cost"?

13–2. Define the following terms: incremental cost, opportunity cost, and sunk cost.

13–3. Are variable costs always relevant costs? Explain.

13–4. The book value of a machine (as shown on the balance sheet) is an asset to a company, but this same book value is irrelevant in decison making. Explain why this is so.

13–5. "Sunk costs are easy to spot—they're simply the fixed costs associated with a decision." Do you agree? Explain.

13–6. "Sometimes depreciation on equipment is a relevant cost in a decision, and sometimes it isn't." Do you agree? Explain.

13–7. "My neighbor offered me $25 for the use of my boat over the weekend, but I decided that renting it out is just too risky." What cost term would you use to describe the $25? Explain.

13–8. "Variable costs and differential costs mean the same thing." Do you agree? Explain.

13–9. "All future costs are relevant." Do you agree? Why?

13–10. Prentice Company is considering dropping one of its product lines. What costs of the product line would be relevant to this decision? Irrelevant?

13–11. Why is the term *avoidable cost* used in connection with product-line and make or buy decisions?

13–12. "If a product line is generating a loss, then that's pretty good evidence that the product line should be discontinued." Do you agree? Explain.

13–13. What is the danger in allocating common fixed costs among product lines or other segments of an organization?

13–14. What is meant by the term *make or buy?*

13–15. How does opportunity cost enter into the make or buy decision?

13–16. Give four examples of limiting or scarce factors that might be present in an organization.

13–17. How will the relating of product-line contribution margins to scarce resources help a company ensure that profits will be maximized?

13–18. Define the following terms: joint products, joint product costs, and split-off point.

13–19. What pitfalls are there in allocating common costs among joint products, from a decision-making point of view?

13–20. What guideline can be used in determining whether a joint product should be sold at the split-off point or processed further?

13–21. Airlines often offer reduced rates during certain times of the week to members of a businessperson's family if they accompany him or her on trips. How does the concept of relevant costs enter into the decision to offer reduced rates of this type?

13–22. Schloss Company has decided to use linear programming as a planning tool. The company can't decide whether to use marginal contribution per unit or gross profit per unit in its linear programming computations. Which would you suggest? Why?

13–23. Define *objective function* and *constraint* as these concepts relate to linear programming.

13–24. Sever Company produces two products. Product A has a contribution margin per unit of $10. Product B has a contribution margin per unit of $8. Explain why a linear programming analysis might suggest that the company produce more of product B than product A. (Ample market exists for either product.)

13–25. What is meant by the term *feasible production area?*

EXERCISES

E13–1. The costs associated with the acquisition and annual operation of a truck are given below:

Insurance.	$1,600
Licenses	250
Taxes (vehicle)	150
Garage rent for parking (per truck).	1,200
Depreciation ($9,000 ÷ 5 years)	1,800*
Gasoline, oil, tires, and repairs	0.07 per mile

* Based on obsolescence rather than on wear and tear.

Required: 1. Assume that Hollings Company has purchased one truck, and that the truck has been driven 50,000 miles during the first year. Compute the average cost per mile of owning and operating the truck.

2. At the beginning of the second year, Hollings Company is unsure whether to use the truck or leave it parked in the garage and have all hauling done commercially. (The state requires the payment of vehicle taxes even if the vehicle isn't used.) What costs above are relevant to this decision?

3. Assume that the company decides to use the truck during the second year. Near year-end an order is received from a customer over 1,000 miles away. What costs above are relevant in a decision between using the truck to make the delivery and having the delivery done commercially?

4. Occasionally the company could use two trucks at the same time. For this reason, some thought is being given to purchasing a second truck. The total miles driven would be the same as if only one truck were owned. What costs above are relevant to a decision over whether to purchase the second truck?

E13–2.   Listed below are a number of "costs" for the Swanson Company:

1. Direct labor.
2. Direct materials.
3. Variable production overhead.
4. Fixed production overhead (general).
5. Variable selling and administrative expense.
6. Fixed selling and administrative expense.
7. Book value of machine A.
8. Market value of machine A (current resale).
9. Market value of machine B (cost).
10. Rate of return available from outside investments.

Using the above list, indicate which "costs" are relevant for the following independent cases:

a. The Swanson Company wants to purchase machine B to replace machine A (machine A will be sold). Both machines have the same capacity and a remaining life of five years. Machine B will reduce direct materials costs by 15 percent, due to less waste. Other production costs will not change.

b. The Swanson Company wants to purchase machine B to increase production and sales. Machine A will continue to be used.

E13–3.   Dexter Products, Inc., manufactures and sells a number of items, including an overnight case. The company has been experiencing losses on the overnight case for some time, as shown on the income statement below:

DEXTER PRODUCTS, INC.
Income Statement—Overnight Cases
For the Month of April 19x5

Sales		$150,000
Less variable expenses:		
Variable manufacturing expenses	$46,000	
Sales commissions	9,000	
Freight-out	5,000	
Total variable expenses		60,000
Contribution margin		90,000
Less fixed expenses, direct and allocated:		
Salary of line manager	2,000	
General factory overhead	15,000*	
Depreciation of equipment (no resale value)	8,000	
Advertising—direct	48,000	
Purchasing department expenses	20,000†	
General office expenses	9,000†	
Total fixed expenses		102,000
Net loss		$ (12,000)

* Allocated on a basis of direct labor-hours.
† Allocated on a basis of sales dollars.

The discontinuance of the overnight cases would not affect sales of other product lines.

Required: Would you recommend that the company discontinue the manufacture and sale of overnight cases? Support your answer with appropriate computations.

E13–4. Markham Company is considering the purchase of a high-speed lathe to replace a standard lathe that is now in use. Selected information on the two machines is given below:

	Standard lathe	High-speed lathe
Original cost new	$40,000	$60,000
Accumulated depreciation to date	10,000	—
Current salvage value	8,000	—
Estimated cost savings each year over the standard lathe	—	15,000
Remaining years of useful life	5 years	5 years

Required: Prepare a computation covering the five-year period that will show the net advantage or disadvantage of purchasing the high-speed lathe. Ignore income taxes, and use only relevant costs in your analysis.

E13–5. Climate-Control, Inc., manufactures a variety of heating and air-conditioning units. The company is currently manufacturing all of its own component parts. An outside supplier has offered to produce and sell one component part to the company at a cost of $20 per part. In order to evaluate this offer, Climate-Control, Inc., has gathered the following information relating to its own "cost" of producing the part internally:

	Per part	15,000 parts per year
Direct materials	$ 6	$ 90,000
Direct labor	8	120,000
Variable manufacturing overhead	1	15,000
Fixed manufacturing overhead, direct	5*	75,000
Fixed manufacturing overhead, common,		
but allocated	10	150,000
Total cost	$30	$450,000

* 40 percent supervisory salaries; 60 percent depreciation of special equipment (no resale value).

Required: 1.   Assuming that the company has no alternative use for the facilities now being used to produce the part, should the outside supplier's offer be accepted? Show all computations.

2.   Assuming that a new product that will generate a segment margin of $65,000 per year could be produced if the part were purchased, should the offer be accepted? Show computations.

E13–6.   Banner Company produces three products, A, B, and C. The selling price, variable costs, and contribution margin for one unit of each product follow:

	A	B	C
Selling price	$60	$90	$80
Less variable expenses:			
Direct materials	27	14	40
Direct labor	12	32	16
Variable overhead	3	8	4
Total	42	54	60
Contribution margin	$18	$36	$20
Contribution margin ratio	30%	40%	25%

Due to a strike in the plant of one of its competitors, demand for the company's products far exceeds its capacity to produce. Management is trying to determine which product(s) to concentrate on next week in filling its backlog of orders. The direct labor rate is $8 per hour, and only 3,000 hours of labor time are available each week.

Required: 1.   Compute the amount of contribution margin that will be obtained per hour of labor time spent on each product.

2.   Which orders would you recommend that the company work on next week— the orders for product A, product B, or product C? Show computations.

E13–7.   Rolex Company manufactures three products from a common input in a joint processing operation. Joint processing costs up to the split-off point total $100,000 per year. The company allocates these costs to the joint products on the basis of their total sales value at the split-off point. These sales values are: proudct X, $50,000; product Y, $90,000; and product Z, $60,000.

Each product may be sold at the split-off point or processed further. Additional processing requires no special facilities. The additional processing costs and the sales value after further processing for each product (on an annual basis) are:

Product	Additional processing costs	Sales value
X	$35,000	$ 80,000
Y	40,000	150,000
Z	12,000	75,000

Required:　1.　Which product or products should be sold at the split-off point, and which product or products should be processed further? Show computations.

2.　What general statement can be made with respect to joint costs and the decision to process further?

E13–8.　Bill has just returned from a duck hunting trip. He has brought home eight ducks. Bill's wife detests cleaning ducks, and to discourage him from further duck hunting, she has presented him with the following cost estimate per duck:

Camper and equipment:	
Cost, $12,000. Usable for eight seasons, 10 hunting trips per season	$150
Travel expense (pickup truck):	
100 miles at $0.12 per mile (gas, oil, and tires—$0.07 per mile; depreciation and insurance—$0.05 per mile).	12
Shotgun shells (two boxes)	20
Boat:	
Cost $320. Usable for eight seasons, 10 hunting trips per season	4
Fine paid for speeding on the way to the river	25
Hunting license:	
Cost, $30 for the season, 10 hunting trips per season	3
Money lost playing poker:	
Loss, $18. (Bill plays poker every weekend.)	18
A fifth of Old Grandad:	
Cost, $8. (Used to ward off the cold.).	8
Total cost.	$240
Cost per duck ($240 ÷ 8 ducks)	$ 30

Required:　1.　Assuming that the duck hunting trip Bill has just completed is typical, what costs are relevant to a decision as to whether Bill should go duck hunting again this season?

2.　Discuss the wife's computation of the cost per duck.

13–9.　Royal Company manufactures 10,000 units of part R–3 each year for use on its production line. the cost per unit for part R–3 is:

Direct materials	$ 4.80
Direct labor	7.00
Variable overhead	3.20
Fixed overhead	10.00
Total cost	$25.00

An outside supplier has offered to sell 10,000 units of part R–3 each year to Royal Company for $23.50 per part. If Royal Company accepts this offer, the facilities now being used to manufacture part R–3 could be rented to another company at an annual rental of $40,000. In addition, $6 per unit of the fixed overhead being applied to part R–3 would be completely eliminated.

Required: Prepare computations to show the net dollar advantage or disadvantage of accepting the outside supplier's offer. (Written by the author, based on a question appearing on the CMA examination)

E13–10. The Regal Cycle Company manufactures three types of bicycles—a dirt bike, a 10-speed bike, and a touring bike. Data on sales and expenses for the past six months follow:

	Total	Dirt bikes	10-speed bikes	Touring bikes
Sales	$300,000	$90,000	$150,000	$60,000
Less variable manufacturing and selling expenses.	120,000	27,000	60,000	33,000
Contribution margin.	180,000	63,000	90,000	27,000
Less fixed expenses:				
Advertising, direct	33,000	10,000	14,000	6,000
Depreciation of special equipment	19,000	6,000	9,000	8,000
Salary of line supervisor	36,000	12,000	13,000	10,000
Common, but allocated*	60,000	18,000	30,000	12,000
Total fixed expenses.	148,000	46,000	66,000	36,000
Net income (loss)	$ 32,000	$17,000	$ 24,000	$ (9,000)

* Allocated on a basis of sales dollars.

Management is concerned about the continued losses shown by the touring bikes and wants a recommendation as to whether or not the line should be discontinued. The special equipment used to produce touring bikes has no resale value.

Required:
1. Should production and sale of the touring bikes be discontinued? Show computations to support your answer.
2. Recast the above data in a format that would be more usable to management in assessing the long-run profitability of the various product lines.

13–11. (Appendix) The Sweetwater Company manufactures two soft drinks, Zip and Pep. Each soft drink is manufactured in batches. The material requirements for a batch of each drink are as follows:

	Material A (gallons)	Material B (pounds)	Material C (ounces)
Zip usage per batch	10	24	40
Pep usage per batch	20	16	—
Total raw material available each week	8,000	9,600	12,000

Each batch of Zip yields a total contribution margin of $75; each batch of Pep yields a total contribution margin of $90. The company wants to maximize contribution margin.

Required:
1. Prepare equations to express the objective function and the constraints under which the company must operate.
2. Determine how many batches of Zip and how many batches of Pep should be produced each week. Use the linear programming graphical method, with Zip on the horizontal *(X)* axis and Pep on the vertical *(Y)* axis.

PROBLEMS

P13–12. **Dropping a tour; analysis of operating policy.** Blueline Tours, Inc., operates a large number of tours throughout the United States. A careful study has indicated that some of the tours are not profitable, and consideration is being given to dropping these tours in order to improve the company's overall operating performance.

One such tour is a two-day Historic Mansions bus tour conducted in the southern states. An income statement from a typical Historic Mansions tour is given below:

Ticket revenue (100 seats × 40% occupancy × $75 ticket price)	$3,000	100%
Less variable expenses ($22.50 per person)	900	30
Contribution margin	2,100	70%
Less tour expenses:		
Tour promotion	600	
Salary of bus driver	350	
Fee, tour guide	800	
Fuel for bus	125	
Depreciation of bus	450*	
Liability insurance, bus	200	
Overnight parking fee, bus	50	
Room and meals, bus driver and tour guide	75	
Bus maintenance and preparation	300	
Total tour expenses	2,950	
Net loss	$ (850)	

* Based on obsolescence.

The following additional information is available about the tour:

a. Bus drivers are paid fixed annual salaries; tour guides are paid for each tour conducted.

b. The "bus maintenance and preparation" cost above is an allocation of the salaries of mechanics and other service personnel who are responsible for keeping the company's fleet of buses in good operating condition.

Required: 1. Prepare an analysis showing what the impact will be on the company's profits if this tour is discontinued.

2. The company's tour director has been criticized because only about 50 percent of the seats on Blueline's tours are being filled as compared to an average of 60 percent for the industry. The tour director has explained that Blueline's average seat occupancy could be improved considerably by eliminating about 10 percent of the tours, but that doing so would reduce profits. Explain how this could happen.

P13–13. **Sell or process further decision.** (Prepared from a situation suggested by Professor John W. Hardy.) Lone Star Meat Packers is a major processor of beef and other meat products. The company has a large amount of T-bone steak on hand, and it is trying to decide whether to sell the T-bone steaks as they are initially cut or to process them further into filet mignon and the New York cut.

If the T-bone steaks are sold as initially cut, the company figures that a one-pound T-bone steak would yield the following profit:

Selling price ($2.25 per pound)	$2.25
Less joint product cost	1.80
Profit per pound	$0.45

Instead of being sold as initially cut, the T-bone steaks could be further processed into filet mignon and New York cut steaks. Cutting one side of a T-bone steak provides the filet mignon, and cutting the other side provides the New York cut. One 16-ounce T-bone steak thus cut will yield one 6-ounce filet mignon and one 8-ounce New York cut; the remaining ounces are waste. The cost of processing the T-bone steaks into these cuts is $0.25 per pound. The filet mignon can be sold for $4 per pound, and the New York cut can be sold for $2.80 per pound.

Required:
1. Determine the profit per pound from further processing the T-bone steaks.
2. Would you recommend that the T-bone steaks be sold as initially cut or processed further? Why?

P13–14. **Relevant cost analysis; book value.** The Matz Machine Shop purchased a new machine one year ago at a cost of $45,000. The machine has been very satisfactory, but the shop manager has just received information on a computer-controlled machine that is vastly superior to the machine that has been purchased. Comparative data on the two machines follow:

	Present machine	Proposed new machine
Purchase cost new	$45,000	$80,000
Estimated useful life new.	9 years	8 years
Annual straight-line depreciation	$ 5,000	$10,000
Remaining book value	40,000	
Salvage value now	10,000	
Annual costs to operate.	22,500	7,500

The shop manager would like to purchase the new machine, but his enthusiasm has been dampened considerably by the following computation:

Remaining book value of the old machine	$40,000
Less salvage value of the old machine	10,000
Net loss from disposal	$30,000

After considering the matter, the shop manager has commented to his assistant, "There's no way we can buy that new machine. If the boss found out that we took a loss on the old machine, somebody's head would roll."

Sales from the shop are expected to remain unchanged at $81,250 per year. Selling and administrative expenses will be $37,500 per year.

Required:
1. Prepare a summary income statement covering the next eight years, assuming:
    a. That the new machine is not purchased.
    b. That the new machine is purchased.
2. Determine the desirability of purchasing the new machine, using only relevant costs in your analysis.

P13–15. **Make or buy analysis.** "That old equipment for producing subassemblies is worn out," said Paul Taylor, president of Timkin Company. "We need to make a decision quickly." The company is trying to decide whether it should purchase new equipment and continue to make its subassemblies internally or whether it should discontinue production of its subassemblies and purchase them from an outside supplier. The alternatives are:

> Alternative 1: New equipment for producing the subassemblies can be purchased at a cost of $350,000. The equipment would have a five-year useful life (the company uses straight-line depreciation) and a $50,000 salvage value.
>
> Alternative 2: The subassemblies can be purchased from an outside supplier who has offered to provide them for $8 each under a five-year contract.

Timkin Company's present costs per unit of producing the subassemblies internally (with the old equipment) are given below. These costs are based on a current activity level of 40,000 subassemblies per year:

Direct materials	$ 2.75
Direct labor	4.00
Variable overhead	0.60
Fixed overhead ($0.75 supervision, $0.90 depreciation,	
and $2 general company overhead)	3.65
Total cost per unit	$11.00

The new equipment would be more efficient and, according to the manufacturer, would reduce direct labor costs and variable overhead costs by 25 percent. Supervision cost ($30,000 per year) and direct materials cost per unit would not be affected by the new equipment. The new equipment's capacity would be 60,000 subassemblies per year. The company has no other use for the space now being used to produce subassemblies.

Required: 1. The president is unsure what the company should do and would like an analysis showing what unit costs and what total costs would be under each of the two alternatives given above. Assume that 40,000 subassemblies are needed each year. Which course of action would you recommend to the president?

2. Would your recommendation in (1) above be the same if the company's needs were: *(a)* 50,000 subassemblies per year, or *(b)* 60,000 subassemblies per year? Show computations in good form.

3. What other factors would you recommend that the company consider before making a decision?

P13–16. **Relevant cost potpourri.** Unless otherwise indicated, each of the following parts is independent. In all cases, show computations to support your answer.

1. Morrell Company produces several products from the processing of krypton, a rare mineral. Material and processing costs total $30,000 per ton, one third of which is allocable to product A. The amount of product A received from a ton of krypton can either be sold at the split-off point or processed further at a cost of $15,000 and then sold for $60,000. The sales value of product A at the split-off point is $40,000. Should product A be processed further or sold at the split-off point?

2. Shelby Company produces three products, X, Y, and Z. Cost and revenue characteristics of the three products follow (per unit):

	X	Y	Z
Selling price	$40	$20	$36
Less variable expenses:			
Direct materials	15	5	10
Labor and overhead.	7	3	17
Total variable expenses.	22	8	27
Contribution margin.	$18	$12	$ 9
Contribution margin ratio	45%	30%	25%

Demand for the company's products is very strong, with far more orders on hand each month than the company has raw materials available to produce. The same material is used in each product. The material costs $2.50 per pound, with a maximum of 5,000 pounds available each month. Which orders would you advise the company to accept first, those for X, for Y, or for Z? Which orders second? Third?

3. For many years, Diehl Company has produced a small electrical part that it uses in the production of its standard line of diesel tractors. The company's cost of producing one part, based on a production level of 10,000 parts per year, is:

	Per part	Total
Direct materials.	$ 4.00	
Direct labor	2.75	
Variable overhead.	0.50	
Fixed overhead, direct	3.00	$30,000
Fixed overhead, common (allocated on a basis of labor-hours)	2.25	22,500
Total cost per part	$12.50	

An outside supplier has offered to supply the electrical parts to the Diehl Company for only $10 per part. The company has determined that one third of the direct fixed costs represent supervisory salaries and other costs that can be eliminated if the parts are purchased. The other two thirds of the direct fixed costs represent depreciation of special equipment that has no resale value. The decision would have no effect on the common fixed costs of the company, and the space being used to produce the parts would otherwise be idle. Show the dollar advantage or disadvantage of accepting the supplier's offer.

4. Glade Company produces a single product. The cost of producing and selling a single unit of this product at the company's normal activity level of 8,000 units per month is:

Direct materials	$2.50
Direct labor	3.00
Variable overhead	0.50
Fixed overhead	4.25
Variable selling and administrative expense	1.50
Fixed selling and administrative expense.	2.00

The normal selling price is $15 per unit. The company's capacity is 10,000 units per month. An order has been received from an overseas source for 2,000 units at a price of $12 per unit. This order would not disturb regular sales. If the order is accepted, by how much will monthly profits be increased or decreased? (The order would not change the company's total fixed costs.)

5. Refer to the data in (4). Assume that the company has 500 units of this product left over from last year, which are inferior to the current model. The units must be sold through regular channels at reduced prices. What unit cost figure is relevant for establishing a minimum selling price for these units? Explain.

P13–17. **Discontinuance of a department.** "We're got to eliminate Department A," said Rob Hunter, vice president of Pringle's Department Store. "It's a drag on the entire organization. If anyone needs proof, just look at last quarter's income statement." The statement to which Mr. Hunter was referring is shown below:

PRINGLE'S DEPARTMENT STORE
Income Statement
For the Quarter Ending March 31, 19x5

	Total	Department A	Department B	Department C
Sales	$1,500,000	$280,000	$700,000	$520,000
Less variable expenses	903,600	156,000	435,600	312,000
Contribution margin	596,400	124,000	264,400	208,000
Less fixed expenses:				
Direct advertising	97,500	26,000	40,000	31,500
General advertising*	30,000	5,600	14,000	10,400
Salaries	136,000	36,000	58,000	42,000
Rent on building†	76,500	19,000	31,500	26,000
Utilities	30,900	8,000	13,600	9,300
Employment taxes‡	20,400	5,400	8,700	6,300
Depreciation of fixtures	40,000	10,800	16,300	12,900
Insurance on inventory and fixtures	3,700	1,200	1,400	1,100
General office expenses	60,000	20,000	20,000	20,000
Service department expenses	45,000	15,000	15,000	15,000
Total fixed expenses	540,000	147,000	218,500	174,500
Net income (loss)	$ 56,400	$ (23,000)	$ 45,900	$ 33,500

* Allocated on a basis of sales dollars.
† Allocated on a basis of space occupied.
‡ Based on salaries paid directly in each department.

You have been assigned the task of making a recommendation to the president as to whether or not Department A should be eliminated. You have gathered the following information:

a. All departments are housed in the same building. The store leases the entire building at a fixed annual rental rate.

b. One of the employees in Department A is Mary Collins, who has been with the company for many years. If Department A is eliminated, Ms. Collins will be transferred to another department. Her salary is $4,000 per quarter.

c. If Department A is eliminated, the fixtures in the department will be transferred to the other departments.

d. If Department A is eliminated, the utilities bill will be reduced by about $7,000 per quarter.

e. One fourth of the insurance in Department A relates to the fixtures in the department; the remainder relates to the department's merchandise inventory.

f. The company has two service departments—purchasing and warehouse. If Department A is eliminated, the company can discharge one full-time and one part-time person from these departments. The combined salaries and other employment costs of these employees is $5,300 per quarter. General office expenses will not change.

Required: 1. Assume that the company has no alternative use for the space now being occupied by Department A. Prepare computations to show whether or not the department should be eliminated. (You may assume that eliminating Department A would have no effect on the sales of the other departments.)

2. Assume that the space being occupied by Department A is quite valuable and could be subleased at a rental rate of $60,000 per quarter. Would you advise the company to eliminate Department A and sublease the space? Show computations.

P13-18. **Utilization of scarce resources; product mix.**   Winkle Creations, Inc., manufactures a line of stuffed animals and a stuffed animal do-it-yourself kit. Sales are increasing, and management is concerned that the company may not have sufficient capacity to meet the expected demand for the coming year. The following sales and production data are available for planning purposes:

		Per unit		
Product	**Estimated demand next year (units)**	**Selling price**	**Direct materials**	**Direct labor**
Monkey	80,000	$20.00	$6.91	$5.60
Teddy bear	105,000	12.50	4.30	3.20
Panda	60,000	9.00	3.90	2.40
Beagle	48,000	14.75	6.50	4.00
Do-it-yourself kit	200,000	8.50	4.70	1.00

The following additional information is available:

a. Because of strong competition, the company feels that it can't increase its selling prices above those indicated.

b. The direct labor rate is $8 per hour; this rate is expected to remain unchanged during the coming year.

c. Fixed overhead costs total $640,000 per year. Variable overhead costs are equal to 25 percent of direct labor costs.

d. The company's plant has a capacity of 160,000 direct labor-hours per year on a single-shift basis. The company's present employees and equipment can produce all five products.

e. The company's present inventory of finished products is nominal and can be ignored.

f. All of the company's nonmanufacturing costs are fixed.

Required: 1. Determine the contribution margin for a unit of each product.

2. Determine the contribution margin that will be realized per direct labor-hour expended on each product.

3. Prepare a schedule showing the total direct labor-hours that will be required to produce the units estimated to be sold during the coming year.

4. Examine the data that you have computed in (1)–(3). Indicate the product and the number of units to be increased or decreased so that total production time is equal to the 160,000 production hours available.

5. Assume that the company does not want to reduce sales of any product. Identify ways in which the company could obtain the additional output and any problems that might be encountered.

P13–19. Discontinuance of a store. Thrifty Markets, Inc., operates three stores in a large metropolitan area. The company's segmented income statement for the last quarter is given below:

THRIFTY MARKETS, INC.
Income Statement
For the Quarter Ended March 31, 19x6

	Total	Uptown store	Downtown store	Westpark store
Sales	$2,500,000	$900,000	$600,000	$1,000,000
Cost of goods sold	1,450,000	513,000	372,000	565,000
Gross margin	1,050,000	387,000	228,000	435,000
Operating expenses:				
Selling expenses:				
Direct advertising	118,500	40,000	36,000	42,500
General advertising*	20,000	7,200	4,800	8,000
Sales salaries	157,000	52,000	45,000	60,000
Delivery salaries	30,000	10,000	10,000	10,000
Store rent	215,000	70,000	65,000	80,000
Depreciation of store fixtures	46,950	18,300	8,800	19,850
Depreciation of delivery equipment	27,000	9,000	9,000	9,000
Total selling expenses	614,450	206,500	178,600	229,350
Administrative expenses:				
Store management salaries	63,000	20,000	18,000	25,000
General office salaries*	50,000	18,000	12,000	20,000
Utilities	89,800	31,000	27,200	31,600
Insurance on fixtures and inventory	25,500	8,000	9,000	8,500
Employment taxes	36,000	12,000	10,200	13,800
General office—other*	25,000	9,000	6,000	10,000
Total administrative expenses	289,300	98,000	82,400	108,900
Total operating expenses	903,750	304,500	261,000	338,250
Net income (loss)	$ 146,250	$ 82,500	$ (33,000)	$ 96,750

* Allocated on a basis of sales dollars.

Management is very concerned about the Downtown Store's inability to show a profit, and consideration is being given to closing the store. The company has asked you to make a recommendation as to what course of action should be taken. The following additional information is available on the store:

a. The manager of the store has been with the company for many years; he would be retained and transferred to another position in the company if the store were closed. His salary is $6,000 per quarter.

b. The lease on the building housing the Downtown Store can be broken with no penalty.

c. The fixtures being used in the Downtown Store would be transferred to the other two stores if the Downtown Store were closed.

d. The company's employment taxes are 12 percent of salaries.

e. A single delivery crew serves all three stores. One delivery person could be discharged if the Downtown Store were closed; this person's salary is $3,000 per quarter.

f. One third of the Downtown Store's insurance relates to its fixtures.

g. The general office salaries and other expenses relate to the general management of Thrifty Markets, Inc. The employee in the general office who is responsible for the Downtown Store's accounting records would be discharged if the store were closed. This employee's salary is $5,000 per quarter.

Required:

1. Prepare a schedule showing the change in revenues and expenses and the impact on overall company net income that would result if the Downtown Store were closed.

2. Based on your computations in (1), what recommendation would you make to the management of Thrifty Markets, Inc.?

3. Assume that if the Downtown Store were closed, sales in the Uptown Store would increase by $200,000 per quarter due to loyal customers shifting their buying to the Uptown Store. The Uptown Store has ample capacity to handle the increased sales, and its gross profit rate is 43 percent. What effect would these factors have on your recommendation concerning the Downtown Store? Show computations.

P13–20. **Sell or process further decision.** Midwest Mills has a plant that can either mill wheat into a cracked wheat cereal or further mill the cracked wheat into flour. The company can sell all the cracked wheat cereal that it can produce at a selling price of $240 per ton. In the past, the company has sold only part of its cracked wheat as cereal and has retained the rest for further milling into the flour product. The flour has been selling for $295 per ton, but recently the price has become unstable and has dropped to $265 per ton.

Because of this price drop, the sales manager feels that the company should discontinue the milling of flour and concentrate its entire milling capacity on the milling of cracked wheat to sell as cereal. (The same milling equipment is used for both products.) Her feeling is based on the following analysis:

	Cracked wheat cost per ton		Flour cost per ton
Raw materials	$200	Cost of cracked wheat used in milling of flour	$230
Direct labor	12	Added milling costs:	
Overhead	18	Added materials	10
Total cost per ton	$230	Added labor	12
		Overhead	18
		Total cost per ton	$270

	Cracked wheat	Flour
Selling price per ton.	$240	$265
Cost per ton (above).	230	270
Net profit (loss) per ton.	$ 10	$ (5)

The sales manager argues that since the present $265 per ton price for the flour results in a $5 per ton loss, the milling of flour should be discontinued and should not be resumed until the price per ton rises above $270.

The company assigns overhead to the two products on the basis of direct labor-hours. The same amount of time is required to either mill a ton of cracked wheat or to further mill a ton of cracked wheat into flour. Because of the nature of the plant, virtually all overhead costs are fixed. Materials and labor costs are variable.

Required:
1. Do you agree with the sales manager that the company should discontinue milling flour and use the entire milling capacity to mill cracked wheat if the price of flour remains at $265 per ton? Support your answer with appropriate comments and computations.
2. What is the lowest price that the company should accept for a ton of flour? Again support your answer with appropriate comments and computations.

P13–21. **Shutdown versus continue-to-operate decision.** (Note to the student: This type of decision is similar to that of dropping a product line, and the portion of the text dealing with the latter topic should be referred to, if needed.)

Birch Company normally produces and sells 30,000 units of RG–6 each month. RG–6 is a small electrical relay used in the automotive industry as a component part in various products. The selling price is $22 per unit, variable expenses are $14 per unit, fixed overhead costs total $150,000 per month, and fixed selling costs total $30,000 per month.

Employment-contract strikes in the companies that purchase the bulk of the RG–6 units have caused Birch Company's sales to temporarily drop to only 8,000 units per month. Birch Company estimates that the strikes will last for about two months, after which time sales of RG–6 should return to normal. Due to the current low level of sales, however, Birch Company is thinking about closing down its own plant during the two months that the strikes are on. If Birch Company does close down its plant, it is estimated that fixed overhead costs can be reduced to only $105,000 per month and that fixed selling costs can be reduced by 10 percent. Start-up costs at the end of the shutdown period would total $8,000. Since Birch Company normally produces strictly for customer orders, no inventories are on hand.

Required:
1. Assuming that the strikes continue for two months, as estimated, would you recommend that Birch Company close its own plant? Show computations in good form.
2. At what level of sales (in units) for the two-month period would Birch Company be indifferent as between closing the plant or keeping it open? Show computations. (Hint: This is a type of break-even analysis, except that the fixed cost portion of your break-even computation should include only those fixed costs that are relevant [i.e., avoidable] over the two-month period.)

P13–22. **Selected relevant cost questions.** Barker Company has a single product called a Zet. The company normally produces and sells 80,000 Zets each year at a selling price of $40 per unit. The company's unit costs at this level of activity are given below:

Direct materials	$ 9.50
Direct labor	10.00
Variable overhead	2.80
Fixed overhead	5.00 ($400,000 total)
Variable selling expense	1.70
Fixed selling expense	4.50 ($360,000 total)
Total cost per unit	$33.50

A number of questions relating to the production and sale of Zets are given below. Each question is independent.

Required.

1. Assume that Barker Company has sufficient capacity to produce 100,000 Zets each year. The company has an opportunity to sell 20,000 units in an overseas market. Import duties, foreign permits, and other special costs associated with the order would total $14,000. The only selling costs that would be associated with the order would be $1.50 per unit shipping cost. You have been asked by the president to compute the per unit break-even price on this order.

2. One of the materials used in the production of Zets is obtained from a foreign supplier. Civil unrest in the supplier's country has caused a cutoff in material shipments that is expected to last for three months. Barker Company has enough of the material on hand to continue to operate at 25 percent of normal levels for the three-month period. As an alternative, the company could close the plant down entirely for the three months. Closing the plant would reduce fixed overhead costs by 40 percent during the three-month period; the fixed selling costs would continue at two thirds of their normal level while the plant was closed. What would be the dollar advantage or disadvantage of closing the plant for the three-month period?

3. The company has 500 Zets on hand that were produced last month and have small blemishes. Due to the blemishes, it will be impossible to sell these units at the regular price. If the company wishes to sell them through regular distribution channels, what unit cost figure is relevant for setting a minimum selling price?

4. An outside manufacturer has offered to produce Zets for Barker Company and to ship them directly to Barker's customers. If Barker Company accepts this offer, the facilities that it uses to produce Zets would be idle; however, fixed overhead costs would continue at 30 percent of their present level. Since the outside manufacturer would pay for all the costs of shipping, the variable selling costs would be reduced by 60 percent. Compute the unit cost figure that is relevant for comparison against whatever quoted price is received from the outside manufacturer.

P13–23. **Accept or reject special-order business.** Saxon Company produces a single product, Awls. Operating at capacity, the company can produce 50,000 Awls per year. Costs associated with this level of production and sales are given below:

	Unit	Total
Direct materials	$ 6	$ 300,000
Direct labor.	8	400,000
Variable overhead	1	50,000
Fixed overhead	3	150,000
Variable selling expense	2	100,000
Fixed selling expense	4	200,000
Total cost	$24	$1,200,000

The Awls sell for $30 each.

Required:
1. A government agency would like to make a one-time-only purchase of 10,000 Awls. The agency would pay a fixed fee of 40 cents per unit, and in addition it would reimburse Saxon Company for all costs of production associated with the units. There would be no variable selling expenses associated with this order. You may assume that due to a recession, sales of Awls have slumped to only 40,000 units per year. If Saxon Company accepts the agency's business, by how much will profits be increased or decreased from what they would be if only 40,000 units were produced and sold?

2. Assume the same situation as that described in (1) above, except that the company is currently selling 50,000 Awls each year through regular channels. Thus, accepting the agency's business would require giving up regular sales of 10,000 units. If the agency's business is accepted, by how much will profits be increased or decreased from what they would be if the 10,000 units were sold through regular channels?

P13-24. **Make or buy decision.** Rolex Company manufactures a variety of ball-point pens. The company has just received an offer from an outside supplier to provide the ink cartridge for the company's Zippo pen line, at a price of $0.48 per dozen cartridges. The company is interested in this offer, since its own production of cartridges is at capacity.

Rolex Company estimates that if the supplier's offer were accepted, the direct labor and variable overhead costs of the Zippo pen line would be reduced by 10 percent and the direct materials cost would be reduced by 20 percent.

Under present operations, Rolex Company manufactures all of its own pens from start to finish. The Zippo pens are sold through wholesalers at $4 per box. Each box contains one dozen pens. Fixed overhead costs charged to the Zippo pen line total $50,000 each period. (The same equipment and facilities are used to produce several pen lines.) The present cost of producing one dozen Zippo pens (one box) is given below:

Direct materials	$1.50
Direct labor	1.00
Manufacturing overhead	0.80*
Total cost	$3.30

* Includes both variable and fixed overhead, based on capacity production of 100,000 boxes of pens each year.

Required:
1. Should the Rolex Company accept the outside supplier's offer? Show computations.

2. What is the maximum price that Rolex Company would be willing to pay the outside supplier per dozen cartridges?

3. Due to the bankruptcy of a competitor, assume that Rolex Company expects to sell 150,000 boxes of pens next year. In order to produce the extra cartridges, the company would incur added fixed expenses of $20,000 per year. Under these circumstances, should the supplier's offer be accepted? For how many boxes of Zippo cartridges? Show all computations.

4. What nonquantifiable factors should the company consider before accepting the outside supplier's offer?

P13-25. **Special order; relevant costs.** Fred White operates a small machine shop. He manufactures one standard product that is available from many similar businesses, and he also manufactures products to customer order. His accountant prepared the annual income statement shown below:

	Custom sales	Standard sales	Total
Sales	$50,000	$25,000	$75,000
Materials used	9,100	8,400	17,500
Labor	20,000	9,000	29,000
Depreciation.	6,300	3,600	9,900
Power used	2,000	900	2,900
Rent	6,000	1,000	7,000
Heat and light	600	100	700
Total costs	44,000	23,000	67,000
Net profit	$ 6,000	$ 2,000	$ 8,000

The depreciation charges are for machines used in the respective product lines. Mr. White has found that power used consistently equals 10 percent of labor cost. The rent is for the building space, which has been leased for 10 years at $7,000 per year. The rent and heat and light are apportioned to the product lines based on amount of floor space occupied. All other costs are current expenses identified with the product line causing them.

A valued custom-parts customer has asked Mr. White if he would manufacture 5,000 special units for her. Mr. White is working at capacity and would have to give up some other business in order to take this business. He can't renege on custom orders already agreed to, but he could reduce the output of his standard product about one half for one year while producing the specially requested custom part. The customer is willing to pay $7.25 for each part. The material cost will be about $2 per unit, and the labor cost will be $3.60 per unit. Mr. White will have to spend $2,000 for a special device that will be discarded when the job is done.

Required:
1. Calculate the opportunity cost of taking the special order.
2. Would you advise Mr. White to take the order? Show appropriate computations to support your answer.
3. What nonquantitative factors should Mr. White consider before taking the special order?

(CMA, adapted)

P13–26. **Sell or process further decision.** The Cum-Clean Corporation produces a variety of cleaning compounds and solutions for both industrial and household use. While most of its products are processed independently, a few are related, such as the company's Grit 337 and its Sparkle silver polish.

Grit 337 is a coarse cleaning powder with many industrial uses. It costs $1.60 a pound to make, and it has a selling price of $2 a pound. A small portion of the annual production of Grit 337 is retained in the factory for further processing in the mixing department, where it is combined with several other ingredients to form a paste that is marketed as Sparkle silver polish. The silver polish sells for $4 per jar.

This further processing requires one-fourth pound of Grit 337 per jar of silver polish. Other ingredients added and labor costs involved in the processing of a jar of silver polish are:

Other ingredients	$0.65
Direct labor	1.48
Total cost	$2.13

Overhead costs associated with the processing of the silver polish are:

Variable overhead cost	25 percent of direct labor cost

Fixed overhead cost (per month):
Production supervisor	$1,600
Depreciation of mixing equipment	1,400

The production supervisor has no duties other than to oversee production of the silver polish. The mixing equipment is special-purpose equipment acquired specifically to produce the silver polish. It has only a nominal resale value.

Advertising costs for the silver polish total $4,000 per month. Variable selling costs associated with the silver polish are 7.5 percent of sales.

Due to a recent decline in the demand for silver polish, the company is wondering whether its continued production is advisable. The sales manager feels that it would be more profitable to just sell all of the Grit 337 as a cleaning powder.

Required:
1. What is the incremental contribution margin per jar from further processing of Grit 337 into silver polish?
2. What is the minimum number of jars of silver polish that must be sold each month to justify the continued processing of Grit 337 into silver polish? Show all computations in good form. **(CMA, heavily adapted)**

P13–27. **Integrative problem: Relevant costs; pricing.** Jenco, Inc., manufacturers a combination fertilizer–weed killer under the name Fertikil. This is the only product that Jenco produces at present. Fertikil is sold nationwide through normal marketing channels to retail nurseries and garden stores.

Taylor Nursery plans to sell a similar fertilizer–weed killer compound through its regional nursery chain under its own private label. Taylor has asked Jenco to submit a bid for a 25,000-pound order of the private brand compound. While the chemical composition of the Taylor compound differs from that of Fertikil, the manufacturing process is very similar.

The Taylor compound would be produced in 1,000-pound lots. Each lot would require 60 direct labor-hours and the following chemicals:

Chemicals	Quantity in pounds
CW–3	400
JX–6	300
MZ–8	200
BE–7	100

The first three chemicals (CW–3, JX–6, MZ–8) are all used in the production of Fertikil. BE–7 was used in another compound that Jenco discontinued several months ago. The supply of BE–7 that Jenco had on hand when the other compound was discontinued was not discarded because BE–7 does not deteriorate and there have been adequate storage facilities available. Jenco could sell its supply of BE–7 at the prevailing market price less $0.10 per pound selling and handling expenses.

Jenco also has on hand a chemical called CN–5, which was manufactured for use in another product that is no longer produced. CN–5, which cannot be used in Fertikil, can be substituted for CW–3 on a one-for-one basis without affecting the quality of the Taylor compound. The CN–5 in inventory has a salvage value of $500.

Inventory and cost data for the chemicals that can be used to produce the Taylor compound are as shown below:

Raw material	Pounds in inventory	Actual price per pound when purchased	Current market price per pound
CW–3	22,000	$0.80	$0.90
JX–6	5,000	0.55	0.60
MZ–8	8,000	1.40	1.60
BE–7	4,000	0.60	0.65
CN–5	5,500	0.75	(Salvage)

The current direct labor rate is $7 per hour. The manufacturing overhead rate is established at the beginning of the year and is applied consistently throughout the year using direct labor-hours (DLH) as the base. The predetermined overhead rate for the current year, based on a two-shift capacity of 400,000 total DLH with no overtime, is as follows:

Variable manufacturing overhead . . . . . . $2.25 per DLH
Fixed manufacturing overhead . . . . 3.75 per DLH
Combined rate . . . . $6.00 per DHL

Jenco's production manager reports that the present equipment and facilities are adequate to manufacture the Taylor compound. However, Jenco is within 800 hours of its two-shift capacity this month before it must schedule overtime. If need be, the Taylor compound could be produced on regular time by shifting a portion of Fertikil production to overtime. Jenco's rate for overtime hours is 1½ times the regular pay rate, or $10.50 per hour. There is no allowance for any overtime premium in the manufacturing overhead rate.

Jenco's standard markup policy for new products is 40 percent of the full manufacturing cost.

Required:
1. Assume that Jenco, Inc., has decided to submit a bid for a 25,000-pound order of Taylor's new compound. The order must be delivered by the end of the current month. Taylor has indicated that this is a one-time order that will not be repeated. Calculate the lowest price that Jenco could bid for the order without reducing its net income.

2. Refer to the original data. Assume that Taylor Nursery plans to place regular orders for 25,000-pound lots of the new compound during the coming year. Jenco expects the demand for Fertikil to remain strong again in the coming year. Therefore, the recurring orders from Taylor would put Jenco over its two-shift capacity. However, production could be scheduled so that 60 percent of each Taylor order could be completed during regular hours. As another option, some Fertikil production could be shifted temporarily to overtime so that the Taylor orders could be produced on regular time. Jenco's production manager has estimated that the prices of all chemicals will stabilize at the current market rates for the coming

year; also, the variable and fixed overhead costs are expected to continue at the same rates per direct labor-hour.

Calculate the price that Jenco, Inc., should quote Taylor Nursery for each 25,000-pound lot of the new compound, assuming that it is to be treated as a new product and that there will be recurring orders during the coming year.

(CMA, adapted)

P13-28. **Optimum production mix to maximize profits.** (Appendix) Ron Green has just retired and is anxious to open a small pottery business to occupy his time. Mr. Green has decided to produce just two items initially—pots and bowls. The local pottery supply house has indicated that because of shortages in supplies, Mr. Green can be allowed only 80 pounds of high-quality clay and only 11¼ gallons of glazing material each week.

Mr. Green has purchased a used kiln that he feels can be operated about 60 hours per week. His wife will package all finished products; she will have a maximum of 11 hours per week to work for the pottery business. Mr. Green has determined the following additional information:

Operation	Item needed	Per batch	
		Pots	**Bowls**
Molding	Clay	8 lbs.	5 lbs.
Glazing	Glaze	5 qts.	3 qts.
Firing.	—	4 hrs.	6 hrs.
Packaging	—	1 hr.	1 hr.

Mr. Green feels that no more than nine batches of bowls can be sold each week. The pots yield $50 in profits per batch, and the bowls yield $40 per batch. Mr. Green wishes to maximize his profits.

Required:
1. Prepare linear programming equations to express the objective function and each of the constraints. Identify pots as X and bowls as Y.
2. Prepare a linear programming graph to determine how many batches of pots and how many batches of bowls should be produced each week. Place pots on the horizontal *(X)* axis and bowls on the vertical *(Y)* axis.

P13-29. **Basic linear programming.** (Appendix) The Elon Company manufactures two industrial products—X-10, which sells for $90 a unit, and Y-12, which sells for $85 a unit. Each product is processed through both of the company's manufacturing departments. The limited availability of labor, material, and equipment capacity has restricted the ability of the firm to meet the demand for its products. The production department believes that linear programming can be used to routinize the production schedule for the two products.

The following data are available to the production department:

	Amount required per unit	
	X–10	Y–12
Direct material: Weekly supply limited to 1,800 pounds at $12 per pound	4 pounds	2 pounds
Direct labor: Department 1—weekly supply limited to 10 people at 40 hours each at an hourly rate of $6	⅔ hour	1 hour
Department 2—weekly supply limited to 15 people at 40 hours each at an hourly rate of $8	1¼ hours	1 hour
Machine time: Department 1—weekly capacity limited to 250 hours	½ hour	½ hour
Department 2—weekly capacity limited to 300 hours	0 hours	1 hour

The overhead costs for Elon Company are accumulated on a plantwide basis. Overhead is assigned to products on the basis of the number of direct labor-hours required to manufacture them. This base is appropriate for overhead assignment because most of the variable overhead costs vary as a function of labor time. The estimated overhead cost per direct labor-hour is:

Variable overhead cost	$ 6
Fixed overhead cost . , , , , , .	6
Total overhead cost per direct labor-hour	$12

The company wants to produce the mix of the two products that will allow it to maximize total contribution margin.

The production department formulated the following equations for the linear programming statement of the problem:

X = number of units of X–10 to be produced
Y = number of units of Y–12 to be produced

Objective function equation to minimize costs:

$$\text{Minimize:} \quad Z = \$85X + \$62Y$$

Constraint equations:

Material:	$4X + 2Y \leqslant 1{,}800$ pounds
Department 1 labor:	$\tfrac{2}{3}X + Y \leqslant 400$ hours
Department 2 labor:	$1\tfrac{1}{4}X + Y \leqslant 600$ hours

Required:

1. The linear programming equations as prepared by the company's production department contain a number of errors and ommissions. Examine these equations, and explain what errors and omissions have been made.

2. Prepare the proper equations for the linear programming statement of the company's problem.

588

3. Using the equations that you prepared in (2) above, prepare a linear programming graphical solution to determine how many units of X–10 and Y–12 should be produced each week. (Place product X–10 on the horizontal axis and product Y–12 on the vertical axis.)　　　　　　　　　　(CMA, adapted)

P13–30. **Product mix to exhaust remaining stock of materials.** (Appendix) Leastan Company manufactures a line of carpeting that includes a commerical carpeting and a residential carpeting. Two grades of fiber—heavy duty and regular—are used in manufacturing both types of carpeting. The mix of the two grades of fiber differs in each type of carpeting, with the commerical grade using a greater amount of heavy-duty fiber.

In two months, Leastan will introduce a new line of carpeting to replace the current line. The present fiber in stock will not be used in the new line. Management wants to exhaust the present stock of regular and heavy-duty fiber during the last month of production.

Data regarding the current line of commercial and residential carpeting are presented below:

	Commerical	Residential
Selling price per roll of carpet.	$1,000	$800
Production specifications per roll of carpet:		
Heavy-duty fiber.	80 pounds	40 pounds
Regular fiber.	20 pounds	40 pounds
Direct labor-hours	15 hours	15 hours
Standard cost per roll of carpet:		
Heavy-duty fiber ($3/pound)	$240	$120
Regular fiber ($2/pound).	40	80
Direct labor ($10/DLH)	150	150
Variable manufacturing overhead (60% of direct labor cost).	90	90
Fixed manufacturing overhead (120% of direct labor cost)	180	180
Total standard cost per roll of carpet.	$700	$620

Leastan has 42,000 pounds of heavy-duty fiber and 24,000 pounds of regular fiber in stock.

A maximum of 10,500 direct labor-hours are available during the month. The labor force can work on either type of carpeting.

The demand for the present line of carpeting is such that all of the quantities produced can be sold.

Required: 1. A member of Leastan Company's cost accounting staff has stated that linear programming should be used to determine how many rolls of commercial and residential carpeting to manufacture during the last month of production. Explain why linear programming should be used in this situation.
2. Prepare the objective function equation and the constraint equations needed for a linear programming solution to the problem. Use the letter C to denote rolls of commercial carpeting and the letter R to denote rolls of residential carpeting.
3. Using the equations from (2) above, prepare a linear programming graphical solution to the problem, showing how many rolls of commercial carpeting and

how many rolls of residential carpeting should be produced. (Place commercial carpeting on the horizontal axis and residential carpeting on the vertical axis.)

4. Assume that any scrap fiber can be sold for 25 cents per pound. How much revenue would be realized from sale of the scrap? Show computations.

(CMA, adapted)

P13–31. **Optimal candy mixture; cost minimization.** (Appendix) (Based on a situation described by Miller and Starr, *Executive Decisions and Operations Research,* pp. 217–22.) The Sterling Candy Company produces and sells a box of candy made up of caramels and creams. The company would like to find the optimal mixture of the two kinds of candy, in order to meet the specifications per box as outlined in the following table:

	Caramels	Creams	Per box
Weight per piece	1.2 ozs.	0.6 ozs.	18.0 ozs. or more
Number of pieces	?	?	25 or more
Cost per piece	$0.03	$0.02	$0.66 maximum cost

The company wants at least six caramels in each box of candy. The company can produce either caramels or creams in unlimited numbers, so the objective is to minimize the cost of the candy going into each box. The mixture will not affect the selling price per box.

Required: 1. Prepare equations expressing the objective function and the constraints under which the company must operate.

2. Determine the mix of caramels and creams that will minimize the total cost per box of candy. Use a linear programming graph, with caramels on the horizontal axis (X) and creams on the vertical axis (Y).

14 Capital Budgeting Decisions

Learning objectives

After studying Chapter 14, you should be able to:

Explain the concept of present value and make present value computations with and without the present value tables.

Determine the acceptability of an investment project, using the net present value method.

Enumerate the typical cash inflows and cash outflows that might be associated with an investment project and explain how they would be used in a present value analysis.

Determine the acceptability of an investment project, using the time-adjusted rate of return method (with interpolation, if needed).

Explain how the cost of capital is used as a screening tool.

Prepare a net present value analysis of two competing investment projects, using either the incremental-cost approach or the total-cost approach.

Prepare a net present value analysis where a least-cost decision is involved.

Define or explain the key terms listed at the end of the chapter.

The term **capital budgeting** is used to describe actions relating to the planning and financing of capital outlays for such purposes as the purchase of new equipment, the introduction of new product lines, and the modernization of plant facilities. As such, capital budgeting decisions are a key factor in the long-run profitability of a firm. This is particularly true in situations where a firm has only limited investment funds available but has almost unlimited investment opportunities to choose from. The long-run profitability of the firm will depend on the skill of the manager in choosing those uses for limited funds that will provide the greatest return. This selection process is complicated by the fact that most investment opportunities are long term in nature, and the future is often distant and hard to predict.

To make wise investment decisions, managers need tools that will guide them in comparing the relative advantages and disadvantages of various investment alternatives. We are concerned in this chapter with gaining understanding and skill in the use of such tools.

CAPITAL BUDGETING—AN INVESTMENT CONCEPT

Capital budgeting is an *investment* concept, since it involves a commitment of funds now in order to receive some desired return in the future. When speaking of investments, one is inclined to think of a commitment of funds to corporate stocks and bonds. This is just one type of investment, however. The commitment of funds by a business to inventory, equipment, and related uses is *also* an investment in that the commitment is made with the expectation of receiving some return in the future from the funds committed.

Typical capital budgeting decisions

What types of business decisions require capital budgeting analysis? Virtually any decision that involves an outlay now in order to obtain some return (increase in revenue or reduction in costs) in the future. Typical capital budgeting decisions encountered by the business executive are:

1. Cost reduction decisions. Should new equipment be purchased in order to reduce costs?
2. Plant expansion decisions. Should a new plant, warehouse, or other facility be acquired in order to increase capacity and sales?
3. Equipment selection decisions. Would machine A, machine B, or machine C do the job best?
4. Lease or buy decisions. Should new plant facilities be leased or purchased?
5. Equipment replacement decisions. Should old equipment be replaced now or later?

Capital budgeting decisions tend to fall into two broad categories—*screening decisions* and *preference decisions*. **Screening decisions** are those relating to whether a proposed project meets some preset standard of acceptance.

For example, a firm may have a policy of accepting cost reduction projects only if they promise a return of, say, 20 percent before taxes.

Preference decisions, by contrast, relate to selecting from among several *competing* courses of action. To illustrate, a firm may be considering five different machines to replace an existing machine on the assembly line. The choice as to which of the five machines to purchase is a *preference* decision.

In this chapter, we discuss ways of making screening decisions. The matter of preference decisions is reserved until the following chapter.

Characteristics of business investments

Business investments have two key characteristics that must be recognized as we begin our study of capital budgeting methods. These characteristics are (1) that most business investments involve *depreciable assets* and (2) that the returns on most business investments extend over long periods of time.

Depreciable assets   Although most business investments involve depreciable assets, some involve assets that are not depreciable. In those situations where assets are not depreciable, the original sum invested in the assets will still exist at the time the project terminates. For example, if a firm purchases land (a nondepreciable asset) for $5,000 and rents it out at $750 a year for 10 years, at the end of the 10-year term the land will still be intact and should be salable for at least its purchase price. The computation of the rate of return on such an investment is fairly simple. Since the asset (the land) will still be intact at the end of the 10-year period, each year's $750 inflow is a return *on* the original $5,000 investment. The rate of return is therefore a straight 15 percent ($750 ÷ $5,000).

A far more common kind of business investment involves assets that are depreciable in nature. An important characteristic of depreciable assets is that they generally have little or no resale value at the end of their useful lives. Thus, any returns provided by such assets must be sufficient to do two things:

1. Provide a return *on* the original investment.
2. Return the total amount of the *original investment* itself.

To illustrate, assume that the $5,000 investment in the preceding section was made in factory equipment rather than in land. Also assume that the equipment will reduce the firm's operating costs by $750 each year for 10 years. Is the return on the equipment a straight 15 percent, the same as it was on the land? The answer is no. The return being promised by the equipment is much less than the return being promised by the land. The reason is that part of the yearly $750 inflow from the equipment *must go to recoup the original $5,000 investment itself, since the equipment will be worthless at the end of its 10-year life.* Only what remains *after* recovery of this investment can be viewed as a return *on* the investment over the 10-year period.

The time value of money   As stated earlier, another characteristic of business investments is that they promise returns that are likely to extend over fairly long periods of time. Therefore, in approaching capital budgeting decisions, it is necessary to employ techniques that recognize the time value of money. Any business leader would rather receive a dollar today than a year from now. The same concept applies in choosing between investment projects. Those that promise returns earlier in time are preferable to those that promise returns later in time.

The capital budgeting techniques that recognize these two characteristics most fully are those involving *discounted cash flows.* We shall spend the remainder of this chapter illustrating the use of discounted cash flow methods in making capital budgeting decisions. Before discussing these methods, however, it will be helpful to consider the concept of *present value* and the techniques involved in *discounting.*

THE CONCEPT OF PRESENT VALUE

The point was made above that a business leader would rather receive a dollar today than a year from now. There are two reasons why this is true. First, a dollar received today is more valuable than a dollar received a year from now. The dollar received today can be invested immediately, and by the end of a year it will have earned some return, making the total amount in hand at the end of the year *greater* than the investment started with. The person receiving the dollar a year from now will simply have a dollar in hand at that time.

Second, the future involves uncertainty. The longer people have to wait to receive a dollar, the more uncertain it becomes that they will ever get the dollar that they seek. As time passes, conditions change. The changes may be such as to make future payments of the dollar impossible.

Since money has a time value, the manager needs a method of determining whether a cash outlay made now in an investment project can be justified in terms of expected receipts from the project in future years. That is, the manager must have a means of expressing future receipts in present dollar terms so that the future receipts can be compared *on an equivalent basis* with whatever investment is required in the project under consideration. The theory of interest provides managers with the means of making such a comparison.

The theory of interest

If a bank pays $105 one year from now in return for a deposit of $100 now, we would say that the bank is paying interest at an annual rate of 5 percent. The relationships involved in this notion can be expressed in mathematical terms by means of the following equation:

$$F_1 = P(1 + r) \qquad (1)$$

where F_1 = the amount to be received in one year, P = the present outlay to be made, and r = the rate of interest involved.

If the present outlay is $100 deposited in a bank savings account that is to earn interest at 5 percent, then P = $100 and r = 0.05. Under these conditions, F_1 = $105, the amount to be received in one year.

The $100 present outlay can be called the **present value** of the $105 amount to be received in one year. It is also known as the *discounted value* of the future $105 receipt. The $100 figure represents the value in present terms of a receipt of $105 to be received a year from now by an investor who requires a return of 5 percent on his money.

Compounding of interest   What if the investor wants to leave his or her money in the bank for a second year? In that case, by the end of the second year the original $100 deposit will have grown to $110.25:

```
Original deposit .   .   .   .   .   .   .   .   .   .   .   .   $100.00
Interest for the first year:
    $100 × 0.05  .   .   .   .   .   .   .   .   .   .   .   .      5.00
Amount at the end of the first year  .   .   .   .   .   .    105.00
Interest for the second year:
    $105 × 0.05  .   .   .   .   .   .   .   .   .   .   .   .      5.25
Amount at the end of the second year  .   .   .   .   .    $110.25
```

Notice that the interest for the second year is $5.25, as compared to only $5 for the first year. The reason for the greater interest earned during the second year is that during the second year, interest is being paid *on interest.* That is, the $5 interest earned during the first year has been left in the account and has been added to the original $100 deposit in computing interest for the second year. This technique is known as **compounding of interest.** The compounding we have done is annual compounding. Interest can be compounded on a semiannual, quarterly, or even more frequent basis. Many savings institutions are now compounding interest on a daily basis. Of course, the more frequently compounding is done, the more rapidly the invested balance will grow.

How is the concept of compounding of interest expressed in equation form? It is expressed by taking equation (1) and adjusting it to state the number of years, n, that a sum is going to be left deposited in the bank:

$$F_n = P(1 + r)^n \qquad (2)$$

where n = years.

If n = 2 years, then our computation of the value of F in two years will be:

$$F_2 = \$100(1 + 0.05)^2$$
$$F_2 = \$110.25$$

Present value and future value   Exhibit 14–1 shows the relationship between present value and future value as expressed in the theory of interest

EXHIBIT 14–1

The relationship between present value and future value

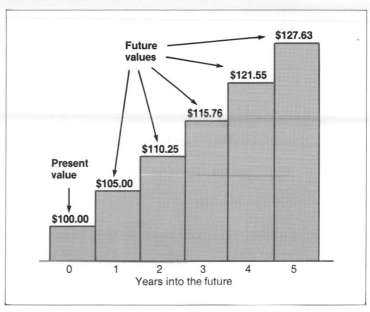

cquations. As shown in the exhibit, if $100 is deposited in a bank at 5 percent interest, it will grow to $127.63 by the end of five years if interest is compounded annually.

Computation of present value

An investment can be viewed in two ways. It can be viewed either in terms of its future value or in terms of its present value. We have seen from our computations above that if we know the present value of a sum (such as our $100 deposit), it is a relatively simple task to compute the sum's future value in n years by using equation (2). But what if the tables are reversed, and we know the *future* value of some amount, but we do not know its present value?

For example, assume that you are to receive $200 two years from now. You know that the future value of this sum is $200, since this is the amount that you will be receiving in two years. But what is the sum's present value—what is it worth *right now*? The present value of any sum to be received in the future can be computed by turning equation (2) around and solving for P:

$$P = \frac{F_n}{(1 + r)^n} \qquad (3)$$

In our example, $F = \$200$ (the amount to be received in the future), $r = 0.05$ (the rate of interest), and $n = 2$ (the number of years in the future that the amount is to be received).

$$P = \frac{\$200}{(1 + 0.05)^2}$$

$$P = \frac{\$200}{1.1025}$$

$$P = \$181.40$$

As shown by the computation above, the present value of a $200 amount to be received two years from now is $181.40 if an interest return of 5 percent is required. In effect, we are saying that $181.40 received *right now* is equivalent to $200 received two years from now, if the investor requires a 5 percent return on his or her money. The $181.40 and the $200 are just two ways of looking at the same item.

The process of finding the present value of a future cash flow, which we have just completed, is called **discounting.** We have *discounted* the $200 to its present value of $181.40. The 5 percent interest figure that we have used to find this present value is called the **discount rate.** Discounting of future sums to their present value is a common practice in business. A knowledge of the present value of a sum to be received in the future can be very useful to the manager, particularly in making capital budgeting decisions. However, we need to find a simpler way of computing present value than using equation (3) every time we need to discount a future sum. The computations involved in using this equation are complex and time-consuming.

Fortunately, tables are available in which most of the mathematical work involved in the discounting process has been done. Table 14A–3 in Appendix B shows the discounted present value of $1 to be received at various periods in the future at various interest rates. The table indicates that the present value of $1 to be received two periods from now at 5 percent is 0.907. Since in our example we want to know the present value of $200 rather than just $1, we need to multiply the factor in the table by $200:

$$\$200 \times 0.907 = \$181.40$$

The answer we obtain is the same answer as we obtained earlier using the formula in equation (3).

Present value of a series of cash flows

Although some business investments involve a single sum to be received (or paid) at a single point in the future, other investments involve a *series* of cash flows. A series (or stream) of cash flows is known as an **annuity.** To provide an example, assume that a firm has just purchased some government bonds in order to temporarily invest funds that are being held for future plant expansion. The bonds will yield interest of $15,000 each year

EXHIBIT 14–2
Present value of a series of cash receipts

Year	Factor at 12 percent (Table 14A–3)	Interest received	Present value
1	0.893	$15,000	$13,395
2	0.797	15,000	11,955
3	0.712	15,000	10,680
4	0.636	15,000	9,540
5	0.567	15,000	8,505
			$54,075

and will be held for five years. What is the present value of the stream of interest receipts from the bonds? As shown in Exhibit 14–2, the present value of this stream is $54,075, if we assume a discount rate of 12 percent compounded annually. The discount factors used in this exhibit were taken from Table 14A–3 in Appendix B.

Two points are important in connection with this exhibit. First, notice that the farther we go forward in time, the smaller is the present value of the $15,000 interest receipt. The present value of $15,000 received a year from now is $13,395, as compared to only $8,505 for the $15,000 interest payment to be received five years from now. This point simply underscores the fact that money has a time value.

The second point is that even though the computations involved in Exhibit 14–2 are accurate, they have involved unnecessary work. The same present value of $54,075 could have been obtained more easily by referring to Table 14A–4 in Appendix B. Table 14A–4 contains the present value of $1 to be received each year over a *series* of years at various interest rates. Table 14A–4 has been derived by simply adding together the factors from Table 14A–3. To illustrate, we used the following factors from Table 14A–3 in the computations in Exhibit 14–2:

Year	Table 14A–3 factors of 12 percent
1	0.893
2	0.797
3	0.712
4	0.636
5	0.567
	3.605

The sum of the five factors above is 3.605. Notice from Table 14A–4 that the factor for $1 to be received each year for five years at 12 percent is also 3.605. If we use this factor and multiply it by the $15,000 to be received each year, then we get the same present value of $54,075 that we obtained earlier in Exhibit 14–2:

$$\$15,000 \times 3.605 = \$54,075$$

Therefore, when computing the present value of a series (or stream) of cash flows, Table 14A–4 should be used.

To summarize, the present value tables in Appendix B should be used as follows:

Table 14A–3: This table should be used to find the present value of a single cash flow (such as a single payment or receipt) occurring in the future.

Table 14A–4: This table should be used to find the present value of a series (or stream) of cash flows occurring in the future.

The use of both of these tables is illustrated in various exhibits on the following pages. *When a present value factor appears in an exhibit, the reader should take the time to trace it back into either Table 14A–3 or Table 14A–4 in order to get acquainted with the tables and how they work.* (Exercise 14–1 at the end of the chapter is designed for those readers who would like some practice in present value analysis before attempting other homework exercises and problems. A solution to Exercise 14–1 is provided immediately following the exercise itself.)

DISCOUNTED CASH FLOWS—THE NET PRESENT VALUE METHOD

Earlier in the chapter, the point was made that business investments have two distinguishing characteristics. The first is that they often involve depreciable assets, and the return that the assets provide must be sufficient to recoup the original investment itself as well as to provide a satisfactory yield on the investment. The second is that business investments are generally long term in nature, often spanning a decade or more. This characteristic lays heavy stress on the necessity to recognize the time value of money in business investment decisions.

If a capital budgeting method is to be fully useful to management, it must be capable of giving full recognition to *both* of the characteristics mentioned above. Although several methods of making capital budgeting decisions are in use, the ones that do the best job are those involving discounted cash flows. The discounted cash flow methods give full recognition to the time value of money and at the same time provide for full recovery of any investment in depreciable assets. No other capital budgeting method is capable of performing *both* of these functions.

There are two approaches to making capital budgeting decisions by means of discounted cash flow. One is known as the *net present value method*, and the other is known as the *time-adjusted rate of return method* (sometimes called the *internal rate of return method*). The net present value method is discussed below; the time-adjusted rate of return method is discussed in a following section.

The net present value method illustrated

Under the net present value method, the present value of all cash inflows is compared against the present value of all cash outflows that are associated with an investment project. The difference between the present value of these cash flows, called the **net present value,** determines whether or not the project is an acceptable investment. To illustrate, let us assume the following data:

Example A

The Harper Company is contemplating the purchase of a machine capable of performing certain operations that are now performed manually. The machine will cost $5,000 new, and it will last for five years. At the end of the five-year period, the machine will have a zero scrap value. Use of the machine will reduce labor costs by $1,800 per year. The Harper Company requires a minimum return of 20 percent before taxes on all investment projects.

Should the machine be purchased? To answer this question, it will be necessary first to isolate the cash inflows and cash outflows associated with the proposed project. In order to keep the example free of unnecessary complications, we have assumed only one cash inflow and one cash outflow. The cash inflow is the $1,800 annual reduction in labor costs. The cash outflow is the $5,000 initial investment in the machine.

The investment decision: The Harper Company must determine whether a cash investment now of $5,000 can be justified if it will result in an $1,800 reduction in cost each year over the next five years, assuming that the company can get a 20 percent return on its money invested elsewhere.

To determine whether the investment is desirable, it will be necessary to discount the stream of annual $1,800 cost reductions to present value and to compare this discounted present value with the cost of the new machine. Since the Harper Company requires a minimum return of 20 percent on all investment projects, we will use this rate in the discounting process. Exhibit 14–3 gives a net present value analysis of the desirability of purchasing the machine.

According to the analysis, the Harper Company should purchase the new machine. The present value of the cost savings is $5,384, as compared to a present value of only $5,000 for the investment required (cost of the machine). Deducting the present value of the investment required from the present value of the cost savings gives a *net present value* of $384. Whenever the *net present value* is positive, as in our example, an investment project is acceptable. Whenever the *net present value* is negative (the present value of the cash outflows exceeds the present value of the cash inflows), an investment project is not acceptable.

A full interpretation of the solution would be as follows: The new machine

EXHIBIT 14–3
Net present value analysis of a proposed project

Initial cost $5,000
Life of the project (years) 5
Annual cost savings $1,800
Salvage value . . . . –0–
Required rate of return 20%

Item	Year(s) having cash flows	Amount of cash flow	20 percent factor	Present value of cash flows
Annual cost savings	1–5	$ 1,800	2.991*	$ 5,384
Initial investment	Now	(5,000)	1.000	(5,000)
Net present value				$ 384

* From Table 14A–4 in Appendix B.

promises slightly more than the required 20 percent rate of return. This is evident from the positive net present value of $384. The Harper Company could spend up to $5,384 for the new machine and still obtain the 20 percent rate of return it desires. The net present value of $384, therefore, shows the amount of "cushion" or "margin of error" that the company has in estimating the cost of the new machine. Alternatively, it also shows the amount of error that can exist in the present value of the cost savings, with the project remaining acceptable. That is, if the present value of the cost savings were only $5,000 rather than $5,384, the project would still promise the required 20 percent rate of return.

Emphasis on cash flows

In organizing data for making capital budgeting decisions, the reader may have noticed that our emphasis has been on cash flows and not on accounting net income. The reason is that accounting net income is based on accrual concepts that ignore the timing of cash flows into and out of an organization. As we stated earlier in the chapter, from a capital budgeting standpoint the timing of cash flows is important, since a dollar received today is more valuable than a dollar received in the future. Therefore, even though the accounting net income figure is useful for many things, it must be ignored in those capital budgeting computations that involve discounted cash flow analysis. Instead of determining accounting net income, the manager must concentrate on identifying the specific cash flows associated with various investment projects and on determining when these cash flows will take place.

In considering an investment project, what kinds of cash flows should the manager look for? Although the specific cash flows will vary from project to project, certain types of cash flows tend to recur and should be looked for, as explained in the following paragraphs.

Typical cash outflows Usually a cash outflow in the form of an initial investment in equipment or other assets will be present. This investment is often computed on an incremental basis, in that any salvage realized from the sale of old equipment is deducted from the cost of the new equipment, leaving only the net difference as a cash outflow for capital budgeting purposes. In addition to this type of investment, some projects require that a firm expand its working capital in order to service the greater volume of business that will be generated. **Working capital** means the amount carried in cash, accounts receivable, and inventory (in excess of current liabilities) which is available to meet day-to-day operating needs. When a firm takes on a new project, the balances in these accounts will often increase. For example, the opening of a new store outlet would require added cash to operate sales registers, increased accounts receivable to carry new customers, and more inventory to stock the shelves. Any such incremental working capital needs should be treated as part of the initial investment in a project. Also, many projects require periodic outlays for repairs and maintenance and for additional operating costs. These should all be treated as cash outflows for capital budgeting purposes.

Typical cash inflows On the cash inflow side, a project will normally either increase revenues or reduce costs. Either way, the amount involved should be treated as a cash inflow for capital budgeting purposes. (In regard to this point, notice that so far as cash flows are concerned, a *reduction in costs is equivalent to an increase in revenues.* Cash inflows are also frequently realized from salvage of equipment when a project is terminated. In addition, upon termination of a project, any working capital that is released for use elsewhere should be treated as a cash inflow. Working capital is released, for example, when a company sells off its inventory, collects its receivables, and uses the resulting funds elsewhere in another investment project.

In summary, the following types of cash flows are common in business investment projects:

Cash outflows:
   Initial investment (including installation costs).
   Increased working capital needs.
   Repairs and maintenance.
   Incremental operating costs.
Cash inflows:
   Incremental revenues.
   Reduction in costs.
   Salvage value.
   Release of working capital.

Recovery of the original investment

When first introduced to present value analysis, students are often surprised by the fact that depreciation is not deducted in computing the profitability of a project. There are two reasons for not deducting depreciation.

First, depreciation is an accounting concept not involving a current cash outflow.[1] As discussed in the preceding section, discounted cash flow methods of making capital budgeting decisions focus on *flows of cash*. Although depreciation is a vital concept in computing accounting net income for financial statement purposes, it is not relevant in an analytical framework that focuses on flows of cash.

A second reason for not deducting depreciation is that discounted cash flow methods *automatically* provide for return of the original investment, thereby making a deduction for depreciation unnecessary. To demonstrate this point, let us assume the following data:

Example B

The Carver Hospital is considering the purchase of an attachment for its X-ray machine that will cost $3,170. The attachment will be usable for four years, after which time it will have no salvage value. It is estimated that the attachment will increase net cash inflows by $1,000 per year in the X-ray department. The hospital's board of directors has instructed that no investments are to be made unless they promise an annual return of at least 10 percent.

A present value analysis of the desirability of purchasing the attachment is presented in Exhibit 14–4. Notice that the attachment promises exactly a 10 percent return on the original investment, since the net present value at a 10 percent discount rate is zero.

EXHIBIT 14–4
Net present value analysis of X-ray machine attachment

Initial cost	$3,170
Life of the project (years)	4
Annual net cash inflow	$1,000
Salvage value	–0–
Required rate of return	10%

Item	Year(s) having cash flows	Amount of cash flow	10 percent factor	Present value of cash flows
Annual net cash inflow.	1–4	$ 1,000	3.170*	$ 3,170
Initial investment	Now	(3,170)	1.000	(3,170)
Net present value				$ –0–

* From Table 14A–4 in Appendix B.

Each annual $1,000 cash inflow arising from use of the attachment is made up of two parts. One part represents a recovery of a portion of the original $3,170 paid for the attachment, and the other part represents a return *on* this investment. The breakdown of each year's $1,000 cash inflow between recovery *of* investment and return *on* investment is shown in Exhibit 14–5.

---

[1] Although depreciation itself does not involve a cash outflow, it does have an effect on cash outflows for income taxes. We shall take a look at this effect in the following chapter, when we discuss the impact of income taxes on management planning.

EXHIBIT 14–5
The Carver Hospital—breakdown of annual cash inflows

Year	(1) Investment outstanding during the year	(2) Cash inflow	(3) Return on investment (1) × 10%	(4) Recovery of investment during the year (2) − (3)	(5) Unrecovered investment at the end of the year (1) − (4)
1	$3,170	$1,000	$317	$ 683	$2,487
2	2,487	1,000	249	751	1,736
3	1,736	1,000	173	827	909
4	909	1,000	91	909	–0–
Total investment recovered . . .				$3,170	

The first year's $1,000 cash inflow consists of a $317 interest return (10 percent) *on* the $3,170 original investment, plus a $683 return *of* that investment. Since the amount of the unrecovered investment decreases over the four years, the dollar amount of the interest return also decreases. By the end of the fourth year, all $3,170 of the original investment has been recovered.

Limiting assumptions

In working with discounted cash flows, at least two limiting assumptions are usually made. The first is that all flows of cash occur at the end of a period. This is somewhat unrealistic in that cash flows typically occur some what uniformly *throughout* a period. The purpose of this assumption is just to simplify computations.

The second assumption is that all cash flows generated by an investment project are immediately reinvested in another project. It is further assumed that the second project will yield a rate of return at least as large as the discount rate used in the first project. Unless these conditions are met, the return computed for the first project will not be accurate. To illustrate, we used a discount rate of 10 percent for the Carver Hospital in Exhibit 14–4. Unless the funds released each period are immediately reinvested in another project yielding at least a 10 percent return, then the return computed for the X-ray attachment will be overstated.

Choosing a discount rate

In using the net present value method, it is necessary to choose some rate of return for discounting cash flows to present value. In example A we used a rate of return of 20 percent before taxes, and in example B we used a rate of return of 10 percent. These rates were chosen somewhat arbitrarily simply for the sake of illustration.

As a practical matter, firms put much time and study into the choice of a discount rate. The rate generally viewed as being most appropriate is a firm's **cost of capital.** A firm's cost of capital is not simply the interest rate that it must pay for long-term debt. Rather, cost of capital is a broad concept, involving a blending of the costs of *all* sources of capital funds, both debt and equity. The mechanics involved in cost of capital computations are covered in finance texts and will not be considered here. The cost of capital is known by various names. It is sometimes called the **hurdle rate,** the **cutoff rate,** or the **required rate of return.**

Most finance people would agree that a before-tax cost of capital of 16 percent to 20 percent would be typical for an average industrial corporation. The appropriate after-tax figure would depend on the corporation's tax circumstances, but it would probably average around 8 to 10 percent.

An extended example of the net present value method

In order to conclude our discussion of the net present value method, we present below an extended example of how it is used in analyzing an investment proposal. This example will also help to tie together (and to reinforce) many of the ideas we have developed thus far.

Example C

Under a special licensing arrangement, the Swinyard Company has an opportunity to market a new product in the western United States for a five-year period. The product would be purchased from the manufacturer, with Swinyard Company responsible for all costs of promotion and distribution. The licensing arrangement could be renewed at the end of the five-year period at the option of the manufacturer. After careful study, Swinyard Company has estimated that the following costs and revenues would be associated with the new product:

Cost of equipment needed	$ 60,000
Working capital needed	100,000
Salvage value of the equipment in five years	10,000
Overhaul of the equipment in four years.	5,000
Annual revenues and costs:	
Sales revenues	200,000
Cost of goods sold	125,000
Out-of-pocket operating costs (for salaries,	
advertising, and other direct costs)	35,000

At the end of the five-year period, the working capital would be released for investment elsewhere if the manufacturer decided not to renew the licensing arrangement. The Swinyard Company's cost of capital is 20 percent. Would you recommend that the new product be introduced? Ignore income taxes.

As shown in the data above, this example involves a variety of cash inflows and cash outflows. The solution is given in Exhibit 14–6.

Notice particularly how the working capital is handled in the exhibit. Also notice how the sales revenues, cost of goods sold, and out-of-pocket costs are handled. **Out-of-pocket costs** mean actual cash outlays made during the period for salaries, advertising, and other operating expenses. Depreciation would not be an out-of-pocket cost, since it involves no current cash outlay.

EXHIBIT 14–6
The net present value method—an extended example

Sales revenues	$200,000
Less cost of goods sold	125,000
Gross margin.	75,000
Less out-of-pocket costs for	
salaries, advertising, etc.	35,000
Annual net cash inflows	$ 40,000

Item	Year(s) having cash flows	Amount of cash flows	20 percent factor	Present value of cash flows
Purchase of equipment	Now	$ (60,000)	1.000	$ (60,000)
Working capital needed	Now	(100,000)	1.000	(100,000)
Overhaul of equipment	4	(5,000)	0.482*	(2,410)
Annual net cash inflows from				
sales of the product line . . .	1–5	40,000	2.991†	119,640
Salvage value of the				
equipment.	5	10,000	0.402*	4,020
Working capital released . . .	5	100,000	0.402*	40,200
Net present value				$ 1,450

* From Table 14A–3 in Appendix B.
† From Table 14A–4 in Appendix B.

Since the overall net present value is positive, the new product should be added, assuming that there is no better use for the investment funds involved.

DISCOUNTED CASH FLOWS—THE TIME-ADJUSTED RATE OF RETURN METHOD

The **time-adjusted rate of return** (or **internal rate of return**) can be defined as the true interest yield promised by an investment project over its useful life. It can be computed by finding the discount rate that will equate the present value of the investment (cash outflows) required by a project with the present value of the returns (cash inflows) that the project promises. In other words, the time-adjusted rate of return is that discount rate which will cause the net present value of a project be equal to zero.

The time-adjusted rate of return method illustrated

Finding a project's time-adjusted rate of return can be very helpful to a manager in making capital budgeting decisions. To illustrate, let us assume the following data:

Example D

The Glendale School District is considering the purchase of a large tractor-pulled lawn mower. If the large mower is purchased, it will replace the hiring of persons to mow with small, individual gas mowers. The large mower will cost $5,650 and will have a life of 10 years. It will have only a negligible scrap value, which can be ignored. It will provide a savings of $1,000 per year in mowing costs because of the labor it will replace.

To compute the time-adjusted rate of return promised by the new mower, it will be necessary to find that discount rate which will cause the net present value of the project to be equal to zero. How do we proceed to do this? The simplest and most direct approach is to divide the investment in the project by the expected annual cash inflow. This computation will give a factor that will be equal to the factor of the time-adjusted rate of return.

$$\frac{\text{Investment in the project}}{\text{Annual cash inflow}} = \text{Factor of the time-adjusted rate of return}$$

The factor can then be located in the present value tables, to see what rate of return it represents. We will now perform these computations for the Glendale School District's proposed project:

$$\frac{\$5,650}{\$1,000} = 5.650$$

The discount factor that will equate a series of $1,000 cash inflows with a present investment of $5,650 is 5.650. We need now to find this factor in Table 14A–4 in Appendix B to see what rate of return it represents. If we refer to Table 14A–4 and scan along the 10-period line, we find that a factor of 5.650 represents a 12 percent rate of return. Therefore, the time-adjusted rate of return promised by the mower project is 12 percent. We can prove this by computing the project's net present value, using a 12 percent discount rate. This computation is made in Exhibit 14–7.

Notice from Exhibit 14–7 that using a 12 percent discount rate equates the present value of the annual cash inflows with the present value of the investment required in the project, leaving a zero net present value. The

EXHIBIT 14–7

Evaluation of the mower purchase using a 12 percent discount rate

Initial cost	$5,650
Life of the project (years)	10
Annual cost savings	$1,000
Salvage value	–0–

Item	Year(s) having cash flows	Amount of cash flow	12 percent factor	Present value of cash flows
Annual cost savings	1–10	$ 1,000	5.650*	$ 5,650
Initial investment	Now	(5,650)	1.000	(5,650)
Net present value				$ –0–

* From Table 14A–4 in Appendix B.

12 percent rate therefore represents the time-adjusted rate of return promised by the project.

The problem of uneven cash flows

The technique just demonstrated works very well if a project's cash flows are even. But what if they are not? For example, what if a project will have some salvage value at the end of its life in addition to the annual cash inflows? Under these circumstances, a trial-and-error process is necessary to find that rate of return which will equate the cash inflows with the cash outflows. The trial-and-error process can be carried out by hand, or it can be carried out by means of canned computer programs that perform the necessary computations in seconds. In short, simply because cash flows are erratic or uneven will not in any way prevent a manager from determining a project's time-adjusted rate of return.

The process of interpolation

Interpolation is the process of finding odd rates of return that do not appear in published interest tables. It is an important concept, since published interest tables are usually printed in terms of whole percentages (10 percent, 12 percent, and so forth), whereas projects often have rates of return that involve fractional amounts. To illustrate the process of interpolation, assume the following data:

Investment required	$6,000
Annual cost savings	1,500
Life of the project	10 years

What is the time-adjusted rate of return promised by this project? We can proceed as before and find that the relevant factor is 4.000.

$$\frac{\text{Investment required}}{\text{Annual cost savings}} = \frac{\$6,000}{\$1,500} = 4.000$$

Looking at Table 14A–4 in Appendix B and scanning along the 10-period line, we find that a factor of 4.000 represents a rate of return somewhere between 20 and 22 percent. To find the rate we are after, we will need to interpolate, as follows:

	Present value factors	
20% factor	4.192	4.192
True factor	4.000	
22% factor		3.923
Difference	0.192	0.269

$$\text{Time-adjusted rate of return} = 20\% + \left(\frac{0.192}{0.269} \times 2\%\right)$$

$$\text{Time-adjusted rate of return} = 21.4\%$$

Using the time-adjusted rate of return

Once the time-adjusted rate of return has been computed, what does the manager do with the information? The time-adjusted rate of return is compared against whatever rate of return (usually the cost of capital) the organization requires on its investment projects. If the time-adjusted rate of return is *greater* that the cost of capital, then the project is acceptable. If it is *less* than the cost of capital, then the project is rejected. A project is not a profitable undertaking if it can't provide a rate of return at least as great as the cost of the funds invested in it.

In the case of the Glendale School District example used earlier, let us assume that the district has set a minimum required rate of return of 10 percent on all projects. Since the large mower promises a rate of return of 12 percent, it clears this hurdle and would therefore be an acceptable investment.

THE COST OF CAPITAL AS A SCREENING TOOL

As we have seen in preceding examples, the cost of capital operates as a *screening* tool, helping the manager to screen out undesirable investment projects. This screening is accomplished in different ways, depending on whether the company is using the time-adjusted rate of return method or the net present value method in its capital budgeting analysis.

When the time-adjusted rate of return method is being used, the cost of capital takes the form of a *hurdle rate* that a project must clear for acceptance. If the time-adjusted rate of return on a project is not great enough to clear the cost of capital hurdle, then the project is rejected. We saw the application of this idea in the Glendale School District example, where the hurdle rate was set at 10 percent.

When the net present value method is being used, the cost of capital becomes the *actual discount rate* used to compute the net present value of

EXHIBIT 14–8
Capital budgeting screening decisions

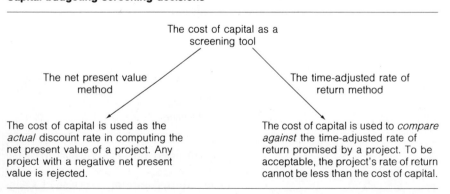

The cost of capital as a screening tool

The net present value method

The cost of capital is used as the *actual* discount rate in computing the net present value of a project. Any project with a negative net present value is rejected.

The time-adjusted rate of return method

The cost of capital is used to *compare against* the time-adjusted rate of return promised by a project. To be acceptable, the project's rate of return cannot be less than the cost of capital.

a proposed project. Any project yielding a negative net present value is screened out and rejected.

The operation of the cost of capital as a screening tool is summarized in Exhibit 14–8.

COMPARISON OF THE NET PRESENT VALUE AND THE TIME-ADJUSTED RATE OF RETURN METHODS

The net present value method has a number of advantages over the time-adjusted rate of return method of making capital budgeting decisions.

First, the net present value method is simpler to use. As explained earlier, the time-adjusted rate of return method often requires a trial-and-error process to find the exact rate of return that will equate a project's cash inflows and outflows. No such trial-and-error process is necessary when working with the net present value method.

Second, using the net present value method makes it easier to adjust for risk. The point was made earlier in the chapter that the longer one has to wait for a cash inflow, the greater is the risk that the cash inflow will never materialize. To show the greater risk connected with cash flows that are projected to occur many years in the future, firms often discount such amounts at higher discount rates than the discount rates used for flows that are projected to occur earlier in time. For example, a firm might anticipate that a project will provide cash inflows of $10,000 per year for 15 years. If the firm's cost of capital is 18 percent before taxes, then it might discount the first five years' inflows at this rate. The discount rate might then be raised to, say, 20 percent for the next five years and then to, say, 25 percent for the last five years. This successive raising of the discount rate would show the greater risk connected with the cash flows that are projected to be received far into the future.

No such selective adjustment of discount rates is possible under the time-adjusted rate of return method. About the only way to adjust for risk is to raise the hurdle rate that the rate of return for a project must clear for acceptance. This is a somewhat crude approach to the risk problem in that it attaches the same degree of increased risk to *all* of the cash flows associated with a project—those that occur earlier in time as well as those that occur later in time.

Third, the net present value method provides more usable information than does the time-adjusted rate of return method. The dollar net present value figure generated by the net present value method is viewed as being particularly useful for decision-making purposes. This point is considered further in the following chapter.

EXPANDING THE NET PRESENT VALUE APPROACH

So far we have confined all of our examples to the consideration of a single investment alternative. We will now expand the net present value approach to include two alternatives. In addition, we will integrate the concept of relevant costs into discounted cash flow analysis.

There are two ways that the net present value method can be used to compare competing investment projects. One is the *total-cost approach,* and the other is the *incremental-cost approach.* Each approach is illustrated below.

The total-cost approach

The total-cost approach is the most flexible and the most widely used method of making a net present value analysis of competing projects. To illustrate the mechanics of the approach, let us assume the following data:

Example E

The Harper Ferry Company provides a ferry service across the Mississippi River. One of its ferryboats is in poor condition. This ferry can be renovated at an immediate cost of $20,000. Further repairs and an overhaul of the motor will be needed five years from now at a cost of $8,000. In all, the ferry will be usable for 10 years if this work is done. At the end of 10 years, the ferry will have to be scrapped at a salvage value of approximately $5,000. The scrap value of the ferry right now is $7,000. It will cost $16,000 each year to operate the ferry, and revenues will total $25,000 annually.

As an alternative, the Harper Ferry Company can purchase a new ferryboat at a cost of $36,000. The new ferry will have a life of 10 years, but it will require some repairs at the end of 5 years. It is estimated that these repairs will amount to $2,500. At the end of ten years, it is estimated that the ferry will have a scrap value of $5,000. It will cost $12,000 each year to operate the ferry, and revenues will total $25,000 annually.

The Harper Ferry Company requires a return of at least 18 percent before taxes on all investment projects.

Should the company purchase the new ferry or renovate the old ferry? The solution is given in Exhibit 14–9.

Two points should be noted from the exhibit. First, observe that *all* cash inflows and *all* cash outflows are included in the solution under each alternative. No effort has been made to isolate those cash flows that are relevant to the decision and those that are not relevant. The inclusion of all cash flows associated with each alternative gives the approach its name—the *total-cost* approach.

Second, notice that a net present value figure is computed for each of the two alternatives. This is a distinct advantage of the total-cost approach in that an unlimited number of alternatives can be compared side by side to determine the most profitable course of action. For example, another alternative for the Harper Ferry Company would be to get out of the ferry business entirely. If management desired, the net present value of this alternative could be computed to compare with the alternatives shown in Exhibit 14–9. Still other alternatives might be open to the company. Once management

EXHIBIT 14–9

The total-cost approach to project selection

	New ferry	Old ferry
Annual revenues	$25,000	$25,000
Annual cash operating costs	12,000	16,000
Net annual cash inflows.	$13,000	$ 9,000

Item	Year(s) having cash flows	Amount of cash flows	18 percent factor*	Present value of cash flows
Buy the new ferry:				
Initial investment	Now	$(36,000)	1.000	$(36,000)
Repairs in five years	5	(2,500)	0.437	(1,093)
Net annual cash inflows	1–10	13,000	4.494	58,422
Salvage of the old ferry	Now	7,000	1.000	7,000
Salvage of the new ferry	10	5,000	0.191	955
Net present value				29,284
Keep the old ferry:				
Initial repairs	Now	$(20,000)	1.000	(20,000)
Repairs in five years	5	(8,000)	0.437	(3,496)
Net annual cash inflows	1–10	9,000	4.494	40,446
Salvage of the old ferry	10	5,000	0.191	955
Net present value				17,905
Net present value in favor of buying the new ferry.				$ 11,379

* All factors are from Tables 14A–3 and 14A–4 in Appendix B.

has determined the net present value of each alternative that it wishes to consider, it can select the course of action that will be most profitable. In the case at hand, given only the two alternatives, the data indicate that the most profitable course is to purchase the new ferry.[2]

The incremental-cost approach

When only two alternatives are being considered, the incremental-cost approach offers a simpler and more direct route to a decision. Unlike the total-cost approach, it focuses only on differential costs.[3] The procedure is to pick out the costs and revenues that differ between the two alternatives being considered and to include only those costs and revenues in the discounted cash flow analysis. To illustrate, refer again to the data in example

---

[2] The alternative with the highest net present value is not always the best choice, although it is the best choice in this case. For further discussion, see the section titled "Preference decisions—the ranking of investment projects" in Chapter 15.

[3] Technically, the incremental-cost approach is misnamed, since it focuses on differential costs (that is, on both cost increases and decreases) rather than just on incremental costs. As used here, the term *incremental costs* should be interpreted broadly to include both cost increases and cost decreases.

E relating to the Harper Ferry Company. The solution using only differential costs is presented in Exhibit 14–10.

Two things should be noted from the data in this exhibit. First, notice that the net present value of $11,379 shown in Exhibit 14–10 agrees exactly with the net present value shown under the total-cost approach in Exhibit 14–9. This agreement should be expected, since the two approaches are just different roads to the same destination.

EXHIBIT 14–10
The incremental-cost approach to project selection

Items	Year(s) having cash flows	Amount of cash flows	18 percent factor*	Present value of cash flows
Incremental investment required to purchase the new ferry	Now	$(16,000)	1.000	$(16,000)
Repairs in five years avoided	5	5,500	0.437	2,403
Increased net annual cash inflows	1–10	4,000	4.494	17,976
Salvage of the old ferry	Now	7,000	1.000	7,000
Difference in salvage value in 10 years.	10	–0–	—	–0–
Net present value in favor of buying the new ferry				$ 11,379

* All factors are from Tables 14A–3 and 14A–4 in Appendix B.

Second, notice that the costs used in Exhibit 14–10 are just mathematical differences between the costs shown for the two alternatives in the prior exhibit. For example, the $16,000 incremental investment required to purchase the new ferry in Exhibit 14–10 is the difference between the $36,000 cost of the new ferry and the $20,000 cost required to renovate the old ferry from Exhibit 14–9. The other figures in Exhibit 14–10 have been computed in the same way.

Least-cost decisions

Revenues are not directly involved in some decisions. For example, a company that makes no charge for delivery service may need to replace an old delivery truck, or a company may be trying to decide whether to lease or to buy its fleet of executive cars. In situations such as these, where no revenues are involved, the most desirable alternative will be the one that promises the *least total cost.* Hence, these are known as least cost decisions. To illustrate a least cost decision, assume the following data:

Example F

The Val-Tek Company is considering the replacement of an old threading machine that is used in the manufacture of a number of products. A new threading machine is available on the market that could substantially reduce annual operating costs. Selected data relating to the old and the new machines are presented below:

	Old machine	New machine
Purchase cost new	$20,000	$25,000
Salvage value now	3,000	—
Annual cash operating costs	15,000	9,000
Overhaul needed immediately.	4,000	—
Salvage value in six years	–0–	5,000
Remaining life	6 years	6 years

The Val-Tek Company's cost of capital is 10 percent.

An analysis of the alternatives, using the total-cost approach, is provided in Exhibit 14–11.

EXHIBIT 14–11

The total-cost approach (least-cost decision)

Items	Year(s) having cash flows	Amount of cash flows	10 percent factor*	Present value of cash flows
Buy the new machine:				
Initial investment	Now	$(25,000)	1.000	$(25,000)†
Salvage of the old machine	Now	3,000	1.000	3,000†
Annual cash operating costs.	1–6	(9,000)	4.355	(39,195)
Salvage of the new machine.	6	5,000	0.564	2,820
Present value of net cash outflows				(58,375)
Keep the old machine:				
Overhaul needed now	Now	$ (4,000)	1.000	(4,000)
Annual cash operating costs.	1–6	(15,000)	4.355	(65,325)
Present value of net cash outflows				(69,325)
Net present value in favor of buying the new machine				$ 10,950

* All factors are from Table 14A–3 and 14A–4 in Appendix B.

† These two items could be netted into a single $22,000 incremental cost figure ($25,000 − $3,000 = $22,000).

As shown in the exhibit, the new machine promises the lowest present value of total costs. An analysis of the two alternatives using the incremental-cost approach is presented in Exhibit 14–12 on the following page. As before, the data going into this exhibit represent the differences between the alternatives as shown under the total-cost approach.

POSTAUDIT OF INVESTMENT PROJECTS

Postaudit of an investment project means a follow-up after the project has been approved to see whether or not expected results are actually realized. This is a key part of the capital budgeting process in that it provides management with an opportunity, over time, to see how realistic the proposals are that are being submitted and approved. It also provides an opportunity to

EXHIBIT 14–12

The incremental-cost approach (least-cost decision)

Items	Year(s) having cash flows	Amount of cash flows	10 percent factor*	Present value of cash flows
Incremental investment required to purchase the new machine	Now	$(21,000)	1.000	$(21,000)†
Salvage of the old machine . . .	Now	3,000	1.000	3,000†
Savings in annual cash operating costs.	1–6	6,000	4.355	26,130
Difference in salvage value in six years	6	5,000	0.564	2,820
Net present value in favor of buying the new machine . . .				$ 10,950

* All factors are from Tables 14A–3 and 14A–4 in Appendix B.

† These two items could be netted into a single $18,000 incremental cost figure ($21,000 − $3,000 = $18,000).

reinforce successful projects as needed, to strengthen or perhaps salvage projects that are encountering difficulty, to terminate unsuccessful projects before losses become too great, and to improve the overall quality of future investment proposals.

In performing a postaudit, the same technique should be used as was used in the original approval process. That is, if a project was approved on a basis of a net present value analysis, then the same procedure should be used in performing the postaudit. However, the data going into the analysis should be *actual data* as observed in the actual operation of the project, rather than estimated data. This affords management with an opportunity to make a side-by-side comparison to see how well the project has worked out. It also helps assure that estimated data received on future proposals will be carefully prepared, since the persons submitting the data will know that their estimates will be given careful scrutiny in the postaudit process. Actual results that are far out of line with original estimates should be carefully reviewed by management, and corrective action taken as necessary. In accordance with the management by exception principle, those managers responsible for the original estimates should be required to provide a full explanation of any major differences between estimated and actual results.

SUMMARY

Decisions relating to the planning and financing of capital outlays are known as capital budgeting decisions. Such decisions are of key importance to the long-run profitability of a firm, since large amounts of money are usually involved and since whatever decisions are made may "lock in" a firm for many years.

A decision to make a particular investment hinges basically on whether the future returns promised by the investment can be justified in terms of the present cost outlay that must be made. A valid comparison between the future returns and the present cost outlay is difficult because of the difference in timing involved. The cost outlay occurs now, and the returns usually come at some future time. This problem is overcome through use of the concept of present value and through employment of the technique of discounting. The future sums are discounted to their present value so that they can be compared on a valid basis with current cost outlays. The discount rate used may be the firm's cost of capital, or it may be some arbitrary rate of return that the firm requires on all investment projects.

There are two ways of using discounted cash flow in making capital budgeting decisions. One is the net present value method, and the other is the time-adjusted rate of return method. The net present value method simply involves the choosing of a discount rate, then the discounting of all cash flows to present value, as described in the preceding paragraph. If the present value of the cash inflows exceeds the present value of the cash outflows, then the net present value is positive and the project is acceptable. The opposite is true if the net present value is negative. The time-adjusted rate of return method finds that discount rate which equates the cash inflows and the cash outflows, leaving a zero net present value.

After an investment proposal has been approved, a postaudit should be performed to see whether expected results are actually being realized. This is a key part of the capital budgeting process, since it tends to strengthen the quality of the estimates going into investment proposals and affords management with an early opportunity to recognize any developing problems.

KEY TERMS FOR REVIEW

Annuity A series, or stream, of cash flows of equal amounts.

Capital budgeting Actions relating to the planning and financing of capital outlays for such purposes as the purchase of new equipment and the introduction of new product lines.

Compound interest The process of paying interest on interest in an investment.

Cost of capital The overall cost to an organization of obtaining investment funds, including the cost of both debt sources and equity sources.

Cutoff rate The minimum rate of return that an investment project must yield in order to be acceptable.

Discount rate The rate of return that is used to find the present value of a future cash flow.

Discounting The process of finding the present value of a future cash flow.

Hurdle rate The minimum rate of return that an investment project must yield in order to be acceptable.

Internal rate of return The discount rate that will cause the net present value of an investment project to be equal to zero; thus, the internal rate of return represents the true interest return promised by a project over its useful life. This term is synonymous with *time-adjusted rate of return*.

Interpolation The process of finding odd rates of return (such as 12.6 percent or 9.4 percent) that do not appear in published interest tables.

Net present value The difference between the present value of the cash inflows and the cash outflows associated with an investment project.

Out-of-pocket costs The actual cash outlays made during a period for salaries, advertising, repairs, and similar costs.

Postaudit The follow-up after a project has been approved and implemented to determine whether expected results are actually realized.

Preference decision A decision as to which of several acceptable investment proposals is best.

Present value The estimated value now of an amount that will be received in some future period.

Required rate of return The minimum rate of return that an investment project must yield in order to be acceptable.

Screening decision A decision as to whether a proposed investment meets some preset standard of acceptance.

Time-adjusted rate of return The discount rate that will cause the net present value of an investment project to be equal to zero; thus, the time-adjusted rate of return represents the true interest return promised by a project over its useful life. This term is synonymous with *internal rate of return*.

Working capital The excess of current assets over current liabilities.

APPENDIX A: INFLATION AND CAPITAL BUDGETING

Students frequently raise the question "What about inflation—doesn't it have an impact in a capital budgeting analysis?" The answer is a qualified yes in that inflation does have an impact on the *numbers* that are used in a capital budgeting analysis, but it does not have an impact on the *results* that are obtained. To show what we mean by this statement, assume the following data:

Example G

Martin Company wants to purchase a new machine that costs $36,000. The machine would provide annual cost savings of $20,000, and it would have a three-year life with no salvage value. For each of the next three years, the company expects a 10 percent inflation rate in cost items associated with its activities. If the company's cost of capital is 16 percent, should the new machine be purchased?

Two solutions to this example are provided in Exhibit 14–13. In the first solution (solution A), inflation is ignored and the net present value of the proposed investment is computed in the same way as we have been computing it throughout the chapter. In the second solution (solution B), inflation is given full consideration.

EXHIBIT 14–13
Capital budgeting and inflation

Solution A: Inflation not considered

Items	Year(s) having cash flows	Amount of cash flows	16 percent factor	Present value of cash flows
Initial investment	Now	$(36,000)	1.000	$(36,000)
Annual cost savings	1–3	20,000	2.246	44,920
Net present value				$ 8,920

Solution B: Inflation considered

Items	Year(s) having cash flows	Amount of cash flows	Price index number	Price-adjusted cash flows	27.6† percent factor	Present value of cash flows
Initial investment	Now	$(36,000)	—	$(36,000)	1.0000	$(36,000)
Annual cost savings . .	1	20,000	1.10	22,000	0.7837‡	17,241
	2	20,000	1.21*	24,200	0.6142‡	14,864
	3	20,000	1.331*	26,620	0.4814‡	12,815
Net present value . . .						$ 8,920

* Computation of the price-index numbers, assuming a 10 percent inflation rate each year: year 2, $(1.10)^2 = 1.21$; year 3, $(1.10)^3 = 1.331$.

† The inflation-adjusted cost of capital consists of three elements:

The basic cost of capital	16.0%
The inflation factor	10.0
The combined effect (16% × 10% = 1.6%)	1.6
Inflation-adjusted cost of capital	27.6%

‡ Discount factors are computed using the formula $1/(1 + r)^n$ where r = discount factor and n = number of years. For year 1, the computations are: $1/1.276 = 0.7837$; for year 2: $1/(1.276)^2 = 0.6142$; for year 3: $1/(1.276)^3 = 0.4814$. Computations have been carried to four decimal places to avoid a rounding error.

Adjustments for inflation

Several points should be noted about solution B. First, note that the annual cost savings are adjusted for the effects of inflation by multiplying each year's savings by a price-index number which reflects a 10 percent inflation rate. (Observe from the footnotes to the exhibit how the index number is computed for each year.)

Second, note that the cost of capital must also be adjusted for the effects of inflation. This is done by adding together three cost elements: the cost of capital itself, the inflation rate, and a combined factor which allows for the reinvestment of inflation-generated earnings. A frequent error in adjusting data for inflation is to omit any adjustment at all to the cost of capital; or, if an adjustment is made, to simply add together the cost of capital and the inflation rate. Both of these procedures are incorrect and will yield errone-ous results.[4]

Finally, note that the net present value obtained in solution B is *identical* to that which was obtained in solution A. It sometimes surprises students

---

[4] The proper way to adjust the discount rate for inflationary effects is widely misunderstood. If the manager omits any adjustment to the cost of capital, or just adds together the cost of capital and the inflation rate, then the result will be to overstate the net present value of an investment project.

to learn that the same net present value will be obtained regardless of whether or not the data are adjusted for the effects of inflation. But if the reader will stop and reflect for a moment, this is a logical result. The reason is that, in adjusting the data for the effects of inflation, we adjust *both* the cash flows and the discount rate, and thus the inflationary effects cancel themselves out. As a result, the net present value is the same as if no adjustments had been made.

How practical are adjustments for inflation?

In actual practice, not all companies make adjustments for inflation when doing a capital budgeting analysis. The reasons are obvious—the computations are very complex, and the same net present value can be obtained by using unadjusted data. The one advantage that is sometimes cited in favor of using inflation-adjusted data is that it may be of more value in the postaudit process. It is argued that using inflation-adjusted data in the original capital budgeting analysis allows the manager to later compare like items in the postaudit, because *both* the estimated data and the actual data will contain the effects of inflation. If unadjusted data are used in the original capital budgeting analysis, then it is argued that the manager is forced to compare *unlike* items in the postaudit. Thus, the manager may be misled in his or her evaluation of how the investment turned out.

Unfortunately, this "advantage" is more illusory than real. For one thing, if inflation-adjusted data are used in the original capital budgeting analysis, then these data and the actual data will be comparable only if the *same rate* of inflation is present in both. The likelihood of having the same rate present in both is small, since inflation is very difficult to predict. Economists rarely agree on the expected rate for the next year, let alone several years into the future. In addition, the use of inflation-adjusted data may conceal sloppy estimates of cash flows by enabling the manager to hide behind the excuse that inflation rates turned out to be different than expected, thus throwing his or her estimates off.

To overcome these problems, a better approach would be to use unadjusted data (because of its simplicity) in the original capital budgeting analysis, and then in the postaudit to adjust the actual data downward for any inflation that has taken place. This would allow for comparison of like items. It would also preclude the manager from hiding behind the excuse that the rate of inflation turned out to be different than expected.

Summary

Although it is possible to make adjustments for inflation in a capital budgeting analysis, it is a very difficult and complex process. Moreover, if the adjustments are properly done, the same net present value will be obtained as if no adjustments had been made. A simpler and more effective approach is to use unadjusted data in capital budgeting computations, as we have done in the chapter, and then to make adjustments to the actual data in the postaudit (when the actual rate of inflation is known), if it is thought that such adjustments are warranted.

APPENDIX B: FUTURE VALUE AND PRESENT VALUE TABLES

TABLE 14A–1

Future value of \$1; $F_n = P(1 + r)^n$

Periods	4%	6%	8%	10%	12%	14%	20%
1	1.040	1.060	1.080	1.100	1.120	1.140	1.200
2	1.082	1.124	1.166	1.210	1.254	1.300	1.440
3	1.125	1.191	1.260	1.331	1.405	1.482	1.728
4	1.170	1.263	1.361	1.464	1.574	1.689	2.074
5	1.217	1.338	1.469	1.611	1.762	1.925	2.488
6	1.265	1.419	1.587	1.772	1.974	2.195	2.986
7	1.316	1.504	1.714	1.949	2.211	2.502	3.583
8	1.369	1.594	1.851	2.144	2.476	2.853	4.300
9	1.423	1.690	1.999	2.359	2.773	3.252	5.160
10	1.480	1.791	2.159	2.594	3.106	3.707	6.192
11	1.540	1.898	2.332	2.853	3.479	4.226	7.430
12	1.601	2.012	2.518	3.139	3.896	4.818	8.916
13	1.665	2.133	2.720	3.452	4.364	5.492	10.699
14	1.732	2.261	2.937	3.798	4.887	6.261	12.839
15	1.801	2.397	3.172	4.177	5.474	7.138	15.407
20	2.191	3.207	4.661	6.728	9.646	13.743	38.338
30	3.243	5.744	10.063	17.450	29.960	50.950	237.380
40	4.801	10.286	21.725	45.260	93.051	188.880	1469.800

TABLE 14A–2

Future value of an annuity of \$1 in arrears; $F_n = \dfrac{(1 + r)^n - 1}{r}$

Periods	4%	6%	8%	10%	12%	14%	20%
1	1.000	1.000	1.000	1.000	1.000	1.000	1.000
2	2.040	2.060	2.080	2.100	2.120	2.140	2.220
3	3.122	3.184	3.246	3.310	3.374	3.440	3.640
4	4.247	4.375	4.506	4.641	4.779	4.921	5.368
5	5.416	5.637	5.867	6.105	6.353	6.610	7.442
6	6.633	6.975	7.336	7.716	8.115	8.536	9.930
7	7.898	8.394	8.923	9.487	10.089	10.730	12.916
8	9.214	9.898	10.637	11.436	12.300	13.233	16.499
9	10.583	11.491	12.488	13.580	14.776	16.085	20.799
10	12.006	13.181	14.487	15.938	17.549	19.337	25.959
11	13.486	14.972	16.646	18.531	20.655	23.045	32.150
12	15.026	16.870	18.977	21.385	24.133	27.271	39.580
13	16.627	18.882	21.495	24.523	28.029	32.089	48.497
14	18.292	21.015	24.215	27.976	32.393	37.581	59.196
15	20.024	23.276	27.152	31.773	37.280	43.842	72.035
20	29.778	36.778	45.762	57.276	75.052	91.025	186.690
30	56.085	79.058	113.283	164.496	241.330	356.790	1181.900
40	95.026	154.762	259.057	442.597	767.090	1342.000	7343.900

TABLE 14A-3

Present value of $1; $P = \dfrac{F_n}{(1+r)^n}$

Periods	4%	5%	6%	8%	10%	12%	14%	16%	18%	20%	22%	24%	26%	28%	30%	40%
1	0.962	0.952	0.943	0.926	0.909	0.893	0.877	0.862	0.847	0.833	0.820	0.806	0.794	0.781	0.769	0.714
2	0.925	0.907	0.890	0.857	0.826	0.797	0.769	0.743	0.718	0.694	0.672	0.650	0.630	0.610	0.592	0.510
3	0.889	0.864	0.840	0.794	0.751	0.712	0.675	0.641	0.609	0.579	0.551	0.524	0.500	0.477	0.455	0.364
4	0.855	0.823	0.792	0.735	0.683	0.636	0.592	0.552	0.516	0.482	0.451	0.423	0.397	0.373	0.350	0.260
5	0.822	0.784	0.747	0.681	0.621	0.567	0.519	0.476	0.437	0.402	0.370	0.341	0.315	0.291	0.269	0.186
6	0.790	0.746	0.705	0.630	0.564	0.507	0.456	0.410	0.370	0.335	0.303	0.275	0.250	0.227	0.207	0.133
7	0.760	0.711	0.665	0.583	0.513	0.452	0.400	0.354	0.314	0.279	0.249	0.222	0.198	0.178	0.159	0.095
8	0.731	0.677	0.627	0.540	0.467	0.404	0.351	0.305	0.266	0.233	0.204	0.179	0.157	0.139	0.123	0.068
9	0.703	0.645	0.592	0.500	0.424	0.361	0.308	0.263	0.225	0.194	0.167	0.144	0.125	0.108	0.094	0.048
10	0.676	0.614	0.558	0.463	0.386	0.322	0.270	0.227	0.191	0.162	0.137	0.116	0.099	0.085	0.073	0.035
11	0.650	0.585	0.527	0.429	0.350	0.287	0.237	0.195	0.162	0.135	0.112	0.094	0.079	0.066	0.056	0.025
12	0.625	0.557	0.497	0.397	0.319	0.257	0.208	0.168	0.137	0.112	0.092	0.076	0.062	0.052	0.043	0.018
13	0.601	0.530	0.469	0.368	0.290	0.229	0.182	0.145	0.116	0.093	0.075	0.061	0.050	0.040	0.033	0.013
14	0.577	0.505	0.442	0.340	0.263	0.205	0.160	0.125	0.099	0.078	0.062	0.049	0.039	0.032	0.025	0.009
15	0.555	0.481	0.417	0.315	0.239	0.183	0.140	0.108	0.084	0.065	0.051	0.040	0.031	0.025	0.020	0.006
16	0.534	0.458	0.394	0.292	0.218	0.163	0.123	0.093	0.071	0.054	0.042	0.032	0.025	0.019	0.015	0.005
17	0.513	0.436	0.371	0.270	0.198	0.146	0.108	0.080	0.060	0.045	0.034	0.026	0.020	0.015	0.012	0.003
18	0.494	0.416	0.350	0.250	0.180	0.130	0.095	0.069	0.051	0.038	0.028	0.021	0.016	0.012	0.009	0.002
19	0.475	0.396	0.331	0.232	0.164	0.116	0.083	0.060	0.043	0.031	0.023	0.017	0.012	0.009	0.007	0.002
20	0.456	0.377	0.312	0.215	0.149	0.104	0.073	0.051	0.037	0.026	0.019	0.014	0.010	0.007	0.005	0.001
21	0.439	0.359	0.294	0.199	0.135	0.093	0.064	0.044	0.031	0.022	0.015	0.011	0.008	0.006	0.004	0.001
22	0.422	0.342	0.278	0.184	0.123	0.083	0.056	0.038	0.026	0.018	0.013	0.009	0.006	0.004	0.003	0.001
23	0.406	0.326	0.262	0.170	0.112	0.074	0.049	0.033	0.022	0.015	0.010	0.007	0.005	0.003	0.002	
24	0.390	0.310	0.247	0.158	0.102	0.066	0.043	0.028	0.019	0.013	0.008	0.006	0.004	0.003	0.002	
25	0.375	0.295	0.233	0.146	0.092	0.059	0.038	0.024	0.016	0.010	0.007	0.005	0.003	0.002	0.001	
26	0.361	0.281	0.220	0.135	0.084	0.053	0.033	0.021	0.014	0.009	0.006	0.004	0.002	0.002	0.001	
27	0.347	0.268	0.207	0.125	0.076	0.047	0.029	0.018	0.011	0.007	0.005	0.003	0.002	0.001	0.001	
28	0.333	0.255	0.196	0.116	0.069	0.042	0.026	0.016	0.010	0.006	0.004	0.002	0.002	0.001	0.001	
29	0.321	0.243	0.185	0.107	0.063	0.037	0.022	0.014	0.008	0.005	0.003	0.002	0.001	0.001	0.001	
30	0.308	0.231	0.174	0.099	0.057	0.033	0.020	0.012	0.007	0.004	0.003	0.002	0.001	0.001	0.001	
40	0.208	0.142	0.097	0.046	0.022	0.011	0.005	0.003	0.001	0.001						

TABLE 14A–4

Present value of an annuity of $1 in arrears; $P_n = \dfrac{1}{r}\left[1 - \dfrac{1}{(1+r)^n}\right]$

Periods	4%	5%	6%	8%	10%	12%	14%	16%	18%	20%	22%	24%	26%	28%	30%	40%
1	0.962	0.952	0.943	0.926	0.909	0.893	0.877	0.862	0.847	0.833	0.820	0.806	0.794	0.781	0.769	0.714
2	1.886	1.859	1.833	1.783	1.736	1.690	1.647	1.605	1.566	1.528	1.492	1.457	1.424	1.392	1.361	1.224
3	2.775	2.723	2.673	2.577	2.487	2.402	2.322	2.246	2.174	2.106	2.042	1.981	1.923	1.868	1.816	1.589
4	3.630	3.546	3.465	3.312	3.170	3.037	2.914	2.798	2.690	2.589	2.494	2.404	2.320	2.241	2.166	1.879
5	4.452	4.330	4.212	3.993	3.791	3.605	3.433	3.274	3.127	2.991	2.864	2.745	2.635	2.532	2.436	2.035
6	5.242	5.076	4.917	4.623	4.355	4.111	3.889	3.685	3.498	3.326	3.167	3.020	2.885	2.759	2.643	2.168
7	6.002	5.786	5.582	5.206	4.868	4.564	4.288	4.039	3.812	3.605	3.416	3.242	3.083	2.937	2.802	2.263
8	6.733	6.463	6.210	5.747	5.335	4.968	4.639	4.344	4.078	3.837	3.619	3.421	3.241	3.076	2.925	2.331
9	7.435	7.108	6.802	6.247	5.759	5.328	4.946	4.607	4.303	4.031	3.786	3.566	3.366	3.184	3.019	2.379
10	8.111	7.722	7.360	6.710	6.145	5.650	5.216	4.833	4.494	4.192	3.923	3.682	3.465	3.269	3.092	2.414
11	8.760	8.306	7.887	7.139	6.495	5.988	5.453	5.029	4.656	4.327	4.035	3.776	3.544	3.335	3.147	2.438
12	9.385	8.863	8.384	7.536	6.814	6.194	5.660	5.197	4.793	4.439	4.127	3.851	3.606	3.387	3.190	2.456
13	9.986	9.394	8.853	7.904	7.103	6.424	5.842	5.342	4.910	4.533	4.203	3.912	3.656	3.427	3.223	2.468
14	10.563	9.899	9.295	8.244	7.367	6.628	6.002	5.468	5.008	4.611	4.265	3.962	3.695	3.459	3.249	2.477
15	11.118	10.380	9.712	8.559	7.606	6.811	6.142	5.575	5.092	4.675	4.315	4.001	3.726	3.483	3.268	2.484
16	11.652	10.838	10.106	8.851	7.824	6.974	6.265	5.669	5.162	4.730	4.357	4.033	3.751	3.503	3.283	2.489
17	12.166	11.274	10.477	9.122	8.022	7.120	6.373	5.749	5.222	4.775	4.391	4.059	3.771	3.518	3.295	2.492
18	12.659	11.690	10.828	9.372	8.201	7.250	6.467	5.813	5.273	4.812	4.419	4.080	3.786	3.529	3.304	2.494
19	13.134	12.085	11.158	9.604	8.365	7.366	6.550	5.877	5.316	4.844	4.442	4.097	3.799	3.539	3.311	2.496
20	13.590	12.462	11.470	9.818	8.514	7.469	6.623	5.929	5.353	4.870	4.460	4.110	3.808	3.546	3.316	2.497
21	14.029	12.821	11.764	10.017	8.649	7.562	6.687	5.973	5.384	4.891	4.476	4.121	3.816	3.551	3.320	2.498
22	14.451	13.163	12.042	10.201	8.772	7.645	6.743	6.011	5.410	4.909	4.488	4.130	3.822	3.556	3.323	2.498
23	14.857	13.489	12.303	10.371	8.883	7.718	6.792	6.044	5.432	4.925	4.499	4.137	3.827	3.559	3.325	2.499
24	15.247	13.799	12.550	10.529	8.985	7.784	6.835	6.073	5.451	4.937	4.507	4.143	3.831	3.562	3.327	2.499
25	15.622	14.094	12.783	10.675	9.077	7.843	6.873	6.097	5.467	4.948	4.514	4.147	3.834	3.564	3.329	2.499
26	15.983	14.375	13.003	10.810	9.161	7.896	6.906	6.118	5.480	4.956	4.520	4.151	3.837	3.566	3.330	2.500
27	16.330	14.643	13.211	10.935	9.237	7.943	6.935	6.136	5.492	4.964	4.525	4.154	3.839	3.567	3.331	2.500
28	16.663	14.898	13.406	11.051	9.307	7.984	6.961	6.152	5.502	4.970	4.528	4.157	3.840	3.568	3.331	2.500
29	16.984	15.141	13.591	11.158	9.370	8.022	6.983	6.166	5.510	4.975	4.531	4.159	3.841	3.569	3.332	2.500
30	17.292	15.373	13.765	11.258	9.427	8.055	7.003	6.177	5.517	4.979	4.534	4.160	3.842	3.569	3.332	2.500
40	19.793	17.159	15.046	11.925	9.779	8.244	7.105	6.234	5.548	4.997	4.544	4.166	3.846	3.571	3.333	2.500

QUESTIONS

14–1. What is meant by the term *capital budgeting?*

14–2. Distinguish between capital budgeting screening decisions and capital budgeting preference decisions.

14–3. What is meant by the term *time value of money?*

14–4. What is meant by the term *discounting,* and why is it important to the business manager?

14–5. Why can't accounting net income figures be used in the net present value and time-adjusted rate of return methods of making capital budgeting decisions?

14–6. Why are discounted cash flow methods of making capital budgeting decisions superior to other methods?

14–7. What is net present value? Can it ever be negative? Explain.

14–8. One real shortcoming of discounted cash flow methods is that they ignore depreciation. Do you agree? Why or why not?

14–9. Identify two limiting assumptions associated with discounted cash flow methods of making capital budgeting decisions.

14–10. If a firm has to pay interest of 14 percent on long-term debt, then its cost of capital is 14 percent. Do you agree? Explain.

14–11. What is meant by an investment project's time-adjusted rate of return? How is the time-adjusted rate of return computed?

14–12. Explain how the cost of capital serves as a screening tool when dealing with *(a)* the net present value method and *(b)* the time-adjusted rate of return method.

14–13. Companies that invest in underdeveloped countries usually require a higher rate of return on their investment than they do when their investment is made in countries that are better developed and that have more stable political and economic conditions. Some people say that the higher rate of return required in the underdeveloped countries is evidence of exploitation. What other explanation can you offer?

14–14. Riskier investment proposals should be discounted at lower rates of return. Do you agree? Why or why not?

14–15. As the discount rate increases, the present value of a given future sum also increases. Do you agree? Explain.

14–16. Refer to Exhibit 14–6 in the text. Is the return promised by this investment proposal exactly 20 percent, slightly more than 20 percent, or slightly less than 20 percent? Explain.

14–17. If an investment project has a zero net present value, then it should be rejected since it will provide no return on funds invested. Do you agree? Why?

14–18. A machine costs $12,000. It will provide a cost savings of $2,000 per year. If the company requires a 14 percent rate of return, how many years will the machine have to be used to provide the desired 14 percent return?

EXERCISES

(Ignore income taxes on all exercises.)

E14–1. (The solution to this exercise is given below). Each of the following situations is independent. Work out your own solution to each situation, and then check it against the solution provided.

1. John has just reached age 58. In 12 years, he plans to retire. Upon retiring, he would like to take an extended vacation, which he expects will cost at least $4,000. What lump-sum amount must he invest now in order to have the needed $4,000 at the end of 12 years if the desired rate of return is:

   a. Eight percent?
   b. Twelve percent?

2. The Morgans would like to send their daughter to an expensive music camp at the end of each of the next five years. The camp costs $1,000 each year. What lump-sum amount would have to be invested now in order to have the $1,000 at the end of each year if the desired rate of return is:

   a. Eight percent?
   b. Twelve percent?

3. You have just received an inheritance from your father's estate. You can invest the money and either receive a $20,000 lump-sum amount at the end of 10 years or receive $1,200 at the end of each year for the next 10 years. If the minimum desired rate of return is 12 percent, which alternative would you prefer?

Solution to Exercise 14–1.

1. a. The amount that must be invested now would be the present value of the $4,000, using a discount rate of 8 percent. From Table 14A–3 in Appendix B, the factor for a discount rate of 8 percent for 12 periods is 0.397. Multiplying this discount factor times the $4,000 needed in 12 years will give the amount of the present investment required: $4,000 × 0.397 = $1,588.

   b. We will proceed as we did in *(a)* above, but this time we will use a discount rate of 12 percent. From Table 14A–3 in Appendix B, the factor for a discount rate of 12 percent for 12 periods is 0.257. Multiplying this discount factor times the $4,000 needed in 12 years will give the amount of the present investment required: $4,000 × 0.257 = $1,028.

   Notice that as the discount rate (desired rate of return) increases, the present value decreases.

2. This part differs from (1) above in that we are now dealing with an annuity rather than with a single future sum. The amount that must be invested now will be the present value of the $1,000 needed at the end of each year for five years. Since we are dealing with an annuity, or a series of cash flows, we must refer to Table 14A–4 in Appendix B for the appropriate discount factor.

   a. From Table 14A–4 in Appendix B, the discount factor for 8 percent for five periods is 3.993. Therefore, the amount that must be invested now in order to have $1,000 available at the end of each year for five years is: $1,000 × 3.993 = $3,993.

   b. From Table 14A–4 in Appendix B, the discount factor for 12 percent for five periods is 3.605. Therefore, the amount that must be invested now in order to have $1,000 available at the end of each year for five years is: $1,000 × 3.605 = $3,605.

Again notice that as the discount rate (desired rate of return) increases, the present value decreases. This is logical, since at a higher rate of return we would expect to have to invest less now than if a lower rate of return were being earned.

3. For this part we will need to refer to both Tables 14A–3 and 14A–4 in Appendix B. From Table 14A–3, we will need to find the discount factor for 12 percent for 10 periods, then apply it to the $20,000 lump sum to be received in 10 years. From Table 14A–4, we will need to find the discount factor for 12 percent for 10 periods, then apply it to the series of $1,200 payments to be received over the 10-year period. Whichever alternative has the highest present value is the one that should be selected.

$$\$20,000 \times 0.322 = \$6,440.$$
$$\$1,200 \times 5.650 = \$6,780.$$

Thus, you would prefer to receive the $1,200 per year for 10 years, rather than the $20,000 lump sum.

E14–2. Consider each of the following cases independently.

1. Annual cash inflows that will arise from two competing investment opportunities are given below. Each investment opportunity will require the same initial investment. You can invest money at a 20 percent rate of return. Compute the present value of the cash inflows for each investment.

Year	Investment X	Investment Y
1	$ 1,000	$ 4,000
2	2,000	3,000
3	3,000	2,000
4	4,000	1,000
	$10,000	$10,000

2. At the end of three years, when you graduate from college, your father has promised to give you a new car that will cost $9,000. What lump sum must he invest now in order to have the $9,000 at the end of three years, if he can invest money at:

   a. Six percent?
   b. Ten percent?

3. Mark has just won the grand prize on the "Hoot 'n' Holler" quiz show. He has a choice between (a) receiving $50,000 immediately and (b) receiving $6,000 per year for eight years plus a lump sum of $20,000 at the end of the eight-year period. If Mark can get a return of 10 percent on his investments, which option would you recommend that he accept? (Use present value analysis, and show all computations.)

E14–3. Each of the following parts is independent.

1. Largo Freightlines plans to build a new garage in three years in order to have more space for repairing its trucks. The garage will cost $400,000. What lump-

sum amount should the company invest now in order to have the $400,000 available at the end of the three-year period? Assume that the company can invest money at:

    a. Eight percent.
    b. Twelve percent.

2. Martell Products, Inc., can purchase a new copier that will save $5,000 per year in copying costs. The copier will last for six years and have no salvage value. What is the maximum purchase price that Martell Products would be willing to pay for the copier if the company's required rate of return is:

    a. Ten percent.
    b. Sixteen percent.

3. Sally has just won the million-dollar Big Slam jackpot at a gambling casino. The casino will pay her $50,000 per year for 20 years as the payoff. If Sally can invest money at a 10 percent rate of return, what is the present value of her winnings? Did she really win a million dollars? Explain.

E14–4.   1. You have just learned that you are a beneficiary in the will of your late Aunt Susan. The executrix of her estate has given you three options as to how you may receive your inheritance:

    a. You may receive $50,000 immediately.
    b. You may receive $75,000 at the end of six years.
    c. You may receive $11,000 at the end of each year for six years.

If your desired rate of return is 8 percent, which option would you prefer?

2. You can purchase an annuity now for $10,000. The annuity will pay you $8,000 per year for the 8th through 10th years in the future, after which it will terminate. If you require a 12 percent rate of return, is the annuity an acceptable investment?

E14–5.   Consider each case below independently.

1. Minden Company requires a minimum return of 18 percent on all investments. The company can purchase a new machine at a cost of $40,350. The new machine would generate cash inflows of $15,000 per year and have a four-year life with no salvage value. Compute the machine's net present value. (Use the format shown in Exhibit 14–3.) Is the machine an acceptable investment? Explain.
2. Leven Products, Inc., is investigating the purchase of a new grinding machine that has a projected life of 15 years. It is estimated that the machine will save $20,000 per year in cash operating costs. What is the machine's time-adjusted rate of return if it costs $93,500 new?
3. Sunset Press has just purchased a new trimming machine that cost $14,125. The machine is expected to save $2,500 per year in cash operating costs and to have a 10-year life. Compute the machine's time-adjusted rate of return. If the company's cost of capital is 16 percent, did it make a wise investment? Explain.

E14–6.   On January 2, 19x2, Bill Davis paid $12,000 for 500 shares of the common stock of Acme Company. Mr. Davis received a $720 dividend on the stock each year for five years. At the end of five years, he sold the stock for $13,500. Mr. Davis would like to earn a minimum return of 12 percent on all of his investments.

Required: Did Mr. Davis earn a 12 percent return on the stock? Use the net present value method and the format shown in Exhibit 14–3 in determining your answer. (Round all computations to the nearest whole dollar.)

E14–7.   Henrie's Drapery Service is investigating the purchase of a new machine for cleaning and blocking drapes. The machine would cost $130,400, including invoice cost, freight, and installation. Henrie's has estimated that the new machine would increase the company's cash inflows, net of expenses, by $25,000 per year. The machine would have a 10-year useful life and no salvage value.

Required: 1.   Compute the machine's time-adjusted rate of return. (Do not round your computations.)
       2.   Compute the machine's net present value. Use a discount rate of 14 percent, and use the format shown in Exhibit 14–7. Why do you have a zero net present value?
       3.   If the company's cost of capital is 10 percent, is this an acceptable investment? Explain.

E14–8.   The Pisa Pizza Parlor is investigating the purchase of a new delivery truck. The truck would cost $10,000 and have a five-year useful life. The truck would save $500 per year over the present method of delivering pizzas. In addition, it would result in delivery of about 1,000 more pizzas each year. The company realizes a contribution margin of $2.50 per pizza.

Required: 1.   What would be the annual net cash inflows associated with the new truck?
       2.   Compute the time-adjusted rate of return promised by the new truck. Interpolate to the nearest tenth of a percent.
       3.   In addition to the data given above, assume that the truck will have a $3,800 salvage value at the end of five years. Under these conditions, compute the time-adjusted rate of return to the nearest *whole* percent. (Hint: You may find it helpful to use the net present value approach; find the discount rate that will cause the net present value to be closest to zero. Use the format shown in Exhibit 14–6.)

E14–9.   Sharp Company has $15,000 to invest. The company is trying to decide between two alternative uses of the funds. The alternatives are:

	Invest in project A	Invest in project B
Investment required	$15,000	$15,000
Annual cash inflows	4,000	—
Single cash inflow at the end of 10 years	—	60,000
Life of the project	10 years	10 years

Sharp Company's cost of capital is 16 percent.

Required: Which investment would you recommend that the company accept? Show all computations using net present value. (Use the format shown in Exhibit 14–6. Prepare a separate computation for each investment.)

E14–10.   Wriston Company has $300,000 to invest. The company is trying to decide between two alternative uses of the funds. The alternatives are:

	Invest in project A	Invest in project B
Cost of equipment required.	$300,000	—
Single cash inflow at the end of five years	500,000	—
Working capital investment required.	—	$300,000
Annual net cash inflows	—	75,000
Life of the project	3 years	3 years

The equipment required for project A will have no salvage value. The working capital needed for project B will be released at the end of three years for investment elsewhere. Wriston Company's cost of capital is 20 percent.

Required: Which investment alternative (if either) would you recommend that the company accept? Show all computations using the net present value format.

PROBLEMS

P14–11. **Basic net present value analysis.** The Doughboy Bakery would like to buy a new machine for putting icing and other toppings on pastries. These are now put on by hand. The machine that the bakery is considering costs $90,000 new. It would last the bakery for eight years but would require a $7,500 overhaul at the end of the fifth year. After eight years, the machine could be sold for $6,000.

The bakery estimates that it will cost $14,000 per year to operate the new machine. The present hand method of putting toppings on the pastries costs $35,000 per year. In addition to reducing operating costs, the new machine will allow the bakery to increase its production of pastries by 5,000 packages per year. The bakery realizes a contribution margin of $0.60 per package. The bakery requires a 16 percent return on all investments in equipment.

Required (ignore income taxes):
1. What are the annual cash inflows that will be provided by the new machine?
2. Compute the new machine's net present value. (Use the incremental-cost approach.) Round all dollar amounts to the nearest whole dollar.

P14–12. **Basic net present value analysis.** Renfree Mines, Inc., owns the mining rights to a large tract of land in a mountainous area. The tract contains a mineral deposit that the company feels might be commercially attractive to mine and sell. An engineering and cost analysis has been made, and it is expected that the following cash flows would be associated with opening and operating a mine in the area:

Cost of equipment required	$500,000
Net annual cash receipts	160,000*
Working capital required.	200,000
Cost of road repairs in three years	90,000
Salvage value of equipment in five years	180,000

* Receipts from sales of ore, less out-of-pocket costs for salaries, utilities, insurance, and so forth.

The company estimates that the mineral deposit would be totally exhausted after five years of operations. The company's cost of capital is 14 percent.

Required (ignore income taxes): Determine the net present value of the proposed mining project. Should the project be undertaken? Explain.

P14–13. **Basic net present value analysis.** Big Byte Computers, Inc., is investigating the purchase of a new etching machine for the production of its circuit boards. The machine would cost $450,000, but it would provide substantial annual reductions in costs, as shown below:

	Annual reduction in costs
Labor costs	$130,000
Material costs.	18,500

The new machine would require considerable maintenance work to keep it in proper adjustment. The company estimates that maintenance costs would increase by $3,750 per month if the machine is purchased. In addition, the machine would require an overhaul at the end of the sixth year that the manufacturer estimates would cost $25,000.

The new etching machine would be usable for 10 years, after which it would be sold for its scrap value of $40,000. It would replace an old etching machine that can be sold now for its scrap value of $18,000. Big Byte Computers, Inc., requires a return of at least 18 percent on investments of this type.

Required (ignore income taxes):

1. Compute the net annual cost savings promised by the new etching machine.
2. Using the data from (1) above and other data from the problem, compute the new machine's net present value. (Use the incremental-cost approach.) Would you recommend purchase? Explain.

P14–14. **Time-adjusted rate of return; sensitivity analysis.** Crescent Fabrics, Inc., is investigating the purchase of an electronic loom to replace a mechanical loom in one of its plants. The electronic loom would cost $450,000, but studies have shown that it would save $80,000 per year in costs (mostly through reduced labor costs). If the new electronic loom is purchased, the old mechanical loom can be sold for its salvage value of $40,000. The manufacturer estimates that the new loom would have a service life of 10 years.

Required (ignore income taxes):

1. What would be the net initial (incremental) cost of the new electronic loom for capital budgeting purposes?
2. Using the investment cost figure computed in (1) above, compute the time-adjusted rate of return on the new loom. Interpolate to the nearest tenth of a percent.
3. Few electronic looms are in use, so the management of Crescent Fabrics, Inc., is unsure about the estimated 10-year life. Compute what the time-adjusted rate of return would be if the useful life of the new loom were *(a)* 8 years and *(b)* 12 years, instead of 10 years. Again interpolate to the nearest tenth of a percent.
4. Refer to the original data. Technology is moving rapidly in the electronics industry, and management may not want to keep the new loom for more than six years. If the new loom is disposed of at the end of six years, it would have a salvage value of $160,000.
   a. Again using the investment figure computed in (1) above, compute the time-adjusted rate of return to the nearest *whole* percent. (Hint: A useful way to proceed is to find the discount rate that will cause the net present value to be equal to, or near, zero.)
   b. If the company's cost of capital is 12 percent, would you recommend purchase? Explain.

P14–15. **Opening a small business; net present value.** Frank White will retire in six years. He has $50,000 to invest, and he wants to open some type of small business operation that can be managed in the free time he has available from his regular occupation, but which can be closed easily when he retires. He is considering several investment alternatives, one of which is to open a laundromat.

After careful study, Mr. White has determined the following:

a. Washers, dryers, and other equipment needed to open the laundromat would cost $48,000. In addition, $2,000 in working capital investment would be required to purchase an inventory of soap, bleaches, and related items and to provide change for change machines. (The soap, bleaches, and related items would be sold to customers basically at cost.)

b. The laundromat would charge 50 cents per use for the washers and 25 cents per use for the dryers. (A regular wash cycle is 20 minutes, and a regular dryer cycle is 15 minutes.) Mr. White expects the laundromat to gross $600 each week from the washers and $375 each week from the dryers.

c. The only variable costs in the laundromat would be 7½ cents per use for water and electricity for the washers and 9 cents per use for gas and electricity for the dryers.

d. Fixed costs would be $1,000 per month for rent, $500 per month for cleaning, and $625 per month for maintenance, insurance, and other items.

e. The equipment would have a 10 percent disposal value in six years.

Mr. White will not open the laundromat unless it provides at least a 12 percent return, since this is the amount that he could earn from an alternative investment opportunity.

Required (ignore income taxes):

1. Assuming that the laundromat would be open 52 weeks a year, compute the expected net annual cash receipts from its operation (gross cash receipts less cash disbursements). (Do not include the cost of the equipment, the working capital, or the salvage values in these computations.)
2. Would you advise Mr. White to open the laundromat? Show computations using the net present value method of investment analysis. Round all dollar amounts to the nearest whole dollar.

P14–16. **Time-adjusted rate of return; sensitivity analysis.** Dr. Karen Black is the managing partner of the Crestwood Dental Clinic. Dr. Black is trying to determine whether or not the clinic should move patient files and other items out of a spare room in the clinic and use the room for dental work. She has determined that it would require an investment of $142,950 for equipment and related costs of getting the room ready for use. Based on receipts being generated from other rooms in the clinic, Dr. Black estimates that the new room would generate a net cash inflow of $37,500 per year. The equipment purchased for the room would have a seven-year estimated useful life.

Required (ignore income taxes):

1. Compute the time-adjusted rate of return on the equipment investment for the new room.
2. Assume that the clinic will not purchase equipment unless it promises at least an 18 percent rate of return. Compute the net present value of the investment in the equipment. (Use an 18 percent discount rate.) Why is your net present value zero?

3. Dr. Black is unsure about the estimated $37,500 annual cash inflow from the room. She thinks that the actual cash inflow could be as much as 20 percent greater or less than this figure.

    a. Assume that the actual cash inflow each year is 20 percent greater than estimated. Recompute the time-adjusted rate of return. Interpolate to the nearest tenth of a percent.

    b. Assume that the actual cash inflow each year is 20 percent less than estimated. Recompute the time-adjusted rate of return. Again interpolate to the nearest tenth of a percent.

4. Refer to the original data. Assume that the equipment is purchased and that the room is opened for dental use. However, due to an increasing number of dentists in the area, the clinic is able to generate only $30,000 per year in net cash receipts from the new room. At the end of five years, the clinic closes the room and sells the equipment to a newly licensed dentist for a cash price of $61,375. Compute the time-adjusted rate of return (to the nearest *whole* percent) that the clinic earned on its investment over the 5-year period. Round all dollar amounts to the nearest whole dollar. (Hint: A useful way to proceed is to find that discount rate which will cause the net present value of the investment to be equal to, or near, zero.)

P14–17. **Net present value analysis; postaudit of a project.** Saxon Products, Inc., is investigating the purchase of a robot for use on the company's assembly line. Selected data relating to the robot are provided below:

Cost of the robot	$375,000
Installation costs	18,000
Annual savings in labor costs	?
Annual increase in power and	
maintenance costs	17,500
Salvage value in 10 years	5,000
Useful life	10 years

A number of workers can be discharged if the robot is purchased, resulting in a reduction of 15,000 hours in labor time worked annually. The labor rate is $8 per hour. The company's cost of capital is 20 percent.

Required (ignore income taxes):

1. Determine the net annual cost savings if the robot is purchased. (Do not include installation costs and salvage value in this computation.)
2. Compute the net present value of the proposed investment in the robot. Would you recommend that the robot be purchased? Explain.
3. Assume that the robot is purchased. At the end of the first year, the cost analyst who prepared the data above tells you that some items haven't worked out as planned. The installation costs were $20,000, due to unforeseen problems; the maintenance and power costs are $500 more per year than the amount planned; and the company has been able to reduce labor time by only 13,500 hours per year, rather than 15,000 hours as planned. Assuming that all the other items of cost data were accurate, did the company make a wise investment? Show computations, using the net present value format as in (2) above. (Hint: It might be helpful to place yourself back at the beginning of the first year, with the new data.)
4. If labor costs increase to $9 per hour, will this make the new robot more or less desirable? Explain. No computations are necessary.

P14–18.   **Investments in securities.**   On January 2, 19x5, Frank Vecci had $100,000 to invest. He used the funds to purchase the following three securities:

a.   Mr. Vecci purchased preferred stock at its par value of $20,000. The stock paid an 8 percent dividend (based on par value) each year for five years. At the end of five years, the stock was sold for $18,000.

b.   Mr. Vecci purchased common stock at a cost of $50,000. The stock paid no dividends, but it was sold for $104,000 at the end of five years.

c.   Mr. Vecci purchased bonds at a cost of $30,000. The bonds paid $1,500 in interest every six months. After five years, the bonds were sold for $36,450. (Note: In discounting a cash flow that occurs semiannually, the procedure is to halve the discount rate and double the number of periods. Use the same procedure in discounting the proceeds from the sale.)

Mr. Vecci's goal is to earn a before-tax rate of return of at least 12 percent on his investments. Round all amounts to the nearest whole dollar.

Required (ignore income taxes):

1.   Compute the net present value of *each* of the three investments. On which investments did Mr. Vecci earn the required 12 percent return?
2.   Considering all three investments together, did Mr. Vecci earn the required 12 percent return?

P14–19.   **Replacement decision.**   Redwing Freightlines, Inc., has a small truck that it uses for intracity deliveries. The truck is in bad repair and must be either overhauled or replaced with a new truck. The company has assembled the following information:

	Present truck	New truck
Purchase cost new	$21,000	$30,000
Remaining book value	11,500	—
Overhaul needed now	7,000	—
Annual cash operating costs	10,000	6,500
Salvage value—now	9,000	—
Salvage value—eight years from now	1,000	4,000

If the company keeps and overhauls its present delivery truck, then the truck will be usable for eight more years. If a new truck is purchased, it will be used for eight years, after which it will be traded in on another truck. The new truck would be diesel-operated, resulting in a substantial reduction in annual operating costs, as shown above.

The company computes depreciation on a straight-line basis. All investment projects are evaluated on a basis of a 16 percent before-tax rate of return.

Required (ignore income taxes):

1.   Should Redwing Freightlines, Inc., keep the old truck or purchase the new one? Use the total-cost approach to net present value in making your decision. Round to the nearest whole dollar.
2.   Redo (1) above, this time using the incremental-cost approach.

P14–20.   **Lease or buy decision.**   Blinko Products wants an airplane available for use by its corporate staff. The airplane that the company wishes to acquire, a Zephyr II, can be either purchased or leased from the manufacturer. The company has made the following evaluation of the two alternatives:

Purchase alternative. If the Zephyr II is purchased, then the costs incurred by the company would be:

Purchase cost of the plane	$850,000
Annual cost of servicing,	
licenses, and taxes	9,000
Repairs:	
First three years, per year	3,000
Fourth year	5,000
Fifth year	10,000

The plane would be sold after five years. Based on current resale values, the company would be able to sell it for about one half of its original cost at the end of the five-year period.

Lease alternative. If the Zephyr II is leased, then the company would have to make an immediate deposit of $50,000 to cover any damage during use. The lease would run for five years, at the end of which time the deposit would be refunded. The lease would require an annual rental payment of $200,000 (payable in installments throughout the year). As part of this lease cost, the manufacturer would provide all servicing and repairs, license the plane, and pay all taxes. At the end of the five-year period, the plane would revert to the manufacturer, as owner.

Blinko Products' cost of capital is 18 percent.

Required (ignore income taxes):

1. Use the total-cost approach to determine the present value of the cash flows associated with each alternative.
2. Which alternative would you recommend that the company accept? Why?

P14–21. **Expansion of facilities; net present value; postaudit of a project.** Quik-Lunch, Inc., operates a number of small sandwich-type food outlets in the downtown area of a large western city. The outlets are open for three hours each day, from 11 A.M. until 2 P.M., and serve a variety of hot and cold sandwiches, as well as salads, ice cream, and drinks. The outlets are open 260 days per year. One outlet is in a particularly favorable location and is now serving an average of 250 customers each hour. The outlet is turning away another 300 customers each day, due to lack of facilities to handle them. A small dress shop next door has just gone out of business, and Quik-Lunch, Inc., is studying two ways in which this space might be used to satisfy the excess demand.

Alternative 1. The wall between the outlet and the dress shop could be torn out and the outlet expanded. Remodeling and equipment would cost $250,000. If this is done, it is expected that all 300 customers now being turned away each day would use the new facilities. Studies show that the average customer takes 20 minutes to eat lunch and spends an average of $2.30. The cost of the food to Quik-Lunch, Inc., is about 70 cents per serving.

Rent for the added space would be $12,000 per year; added salaries would be $45,000 per year; and added insurance, utilities, and other fixed costs would be $26,000 per year. Added working capital of $20,000 would be required for inventories and other working capital needs. The company can obtain a 15-year lease on the dress shop property. At the end of this time, the equipment would have a salvage value of $30,000.

Alternative 2. Vending machines could be placed in the dress shop space. This would entail only minor remodeling at a cost (including equipment) of $80,000. An additional $12,000 would be required for inventories and other working capital needs. It is expected that two thirds of the customers now being turned away each day would use the vending service and purchase an average of $1.50 in food. The food would cost Quik-Lunch, Inc., an average of 45 cents per customer. Rent would still be $12,000 per year, as above, but salaries would be only $10,000 per year, and insurance, utilities, and other fixed costs would be only $15,000 per year. The vending machines would have a salvage value of $5,000 in 15 years.

Required (ignore income taxes):

1. Compute the expected net annual cash inflow from each alternative (cash receipts from sales less related cash expenses). Do *not* include present sales in the computation.

2. Assume that the company has a required rate of return of 12 percent. Compute the net present value of each alternative. (Use the total-cost approach, and round all dollar amounts to the nearest whole dollar.) Which alternative would you recommend?

3. Assume that the company decides to accept alternative 2. At the end of the first year, the company finds that only one half of the customers who were being turned away from the regular outlet have been using the vending service. In light of this new information, did the company make the best choice between the alternatives? Show computations to support your answer. (Hint: It might be helpful to go back to the beginning of the first year under the vending alternative, with the new information.)

P14–22. **Lease or buy decision.** Flamingo Auto Parts, Inc., operates a chain of auto supply stores in the Midwest. The company plans to open a new store soon in a rapidly growing area, and an excellent site has been located for construction of a building. Flamingo Auto Parts has two alternatives as to how the desired site can be acquired, the building constructed, and needed fixtures obtained for use in the store.

Purchase alternative. The company could purchase the building site, construct the building, and purchase store fixtures at a total cost of $750,000. This alternative would require the immediate payment of $300,000 and then a payment of $150,000 each year for the next four years (including interest). Flamingo Auto Parts estimates that the annual costs associated with the property would be:

Property taxes	$ 9,000
Insurance	3,000
Repairs and maintenance	6,000
Total annual costs	$18,000

The company would occupy the property for 15 years. Based on prior experience, it is estimated that the property would have a resale value of about $400,000 at the end of the 15-year period.

Lease alternative. The Worldwide Insurance Company has offered to purchase the site, construct the building, and install fixtures to Flamingo Auto Parts' specifications. The insurance company would then lease the property back to Flamingo Auto Parts under a 15-year lease at an annual lease cost of $100,000. (The first payment would be due now, and the remaining payments would be due in years 1–14.) The insurance company would require a $15,000 security deposit immediately; this would be returned at the termination of the lease. Under the lease agreement, the insurance company would pay for the property taxes and insurance; thus, Flamingo Auto Parts would be required to pay only the repair and maintenance costs associated with the property.

Flamingo Auto Parts' cost of capital is 16 percent.

Using discounted cash flow, determine whether Flamingo Auto Parts, Inc., should lease or buy the desired store facilities. Use the total-cost approach.

P14–23. **Keep or sell rental property.** Wesco Products owns a tract of land on which there is a small factory building. The property was purchased several years ago at a cost of $350,000 with the intention of tearing down the old building and constructing a new building on the land. However, the company decided to construct the new building elsewhere. As a result, the old building is being rented to another company. Consideration is now being given to selling the old building and land, rather than continuing to rent it. Wesco Products' alternatives are:

Keep the property. If Wesco Products keeps the property, it will continue to be rented. Annual revenues and expenses associated with the property follow:

Annual rental revenues.		$90,000
Annual expenses:		
Property taxes.	$16,500	
Insurance	8,900	
Repairs and maintenance	4,600	
Depreciation	20,000	50,000
Net income.		$40,000

Wesco Products makes a $30,000 payment to its bank each year on a loan that was obtained to purchase the property. The loan will be paid off in seven more years. The building can be rented for only about 15 more years, after which the property could be sold for about $500,000.

Sell the property. A realty company has offered to purchase the property now. The realty company would pay $250,000 down on the property and then pay Wesco Products $32,500 per year for the next 15 years. If this option is accepted, Wesco Products would have to pay off its bank loan immediately. The remaining principal balance on the loan is $180,000.

1. Assume that Wesco Products' cost of capital is 14 percent. Compute the present value of the cash flows associated with each alternative. Use the total-cost approach.
2. Would you advise Wesco Products to accept the realty company's offer, or would you advise it to wait for a better offer? Explain.

P14–24. **Net present value; new product line.** Atwood Company has an opportunity to produce and sell a revolutionary new smoke detector for homes. In order to determine whether this would be a profitable venture, the company has gathered the following data on probable costs and market potential:

a. New equipment would have to be acquired in order to produce the smoke detector. The equipment would cost $100,000 and be usable for 12 years. After 12 years, it would have a salvage value equal to 10 percent of the original cost.

b. Production and sales of the smoke detector would require a working capital investment of $40,000 in order to finance accounts receivable, inventories, and day-to-day cash needs.

c. An extensive marketing study projects sales in units over the next 12 years to be:

Year	Sales in units
1	4,000
2	7,000
3	10,000
4–12	12,000

d. The smoke detectors would sell for $45 each; variable costs for production, administration, and sales would be $25 per unit.

e. In order to gain entry into the market, the company would have to advertise heavily in the early years of sales. The advertising program would be:

Year	Amount of advertising
1–2	$70,000
3	50,000
4–12	40,000

f. Other fixed costs for salaries, insurance, maintenance, and straight-line depreciation on equipment would total $127,500 per year. (Depreciation is based on cost less salvage value.)

g. Atwood Company views the smoke detector as a somewhat risky venture; therefore, the company would require a minimum 20 percent rate of return in order to accept it as a new product line.

Required (ignore income taxes):

1. Compute the net cash inflow (cash receipts less yearly cash operating expenses) anticipated from sale of the smoke detectors for each year over the next 12 years.

2. Using the data computed in (1) above and other data provided in the problem, determine the net present value of the proposed investment. Would you recommend that Atwood Company accept the smoke detector as a new product line?

P14–25. Discontinuing a department. You have just been hired as a management trainee by Marley's Department Store. Your first assignment is to determine whether the store should discontinue its housewares department and expand its appliances department. The store's vice president feels that the housewares space could be better utilized selling appliances, since the appliances have a better markup and move more rapidly. The store's most recent income statement is presented below:

MARLEY'S DEPARTMENT STORE
Income Statement
For the Year Ended June 30, 19x1

	Appliances	Housewares	Clothing	Total
Sales	$400,000	$ 50,000	$200,000	$650,000
Cost of goods sold	280,000	40,000	110,000	430,000
Gross margin	120,000	10,000	90,000	220,000
Commissions	40,000	5,000	20,000	65,000
Depreciation.	12,000	8,000	10,000	30,000
Other fixed expenses.	20,000	8,000	15,000	43,000
Total expenses	72,000	21,000	45,000	138,000
Net income	$ 48,000	$(11,000)	$ 45,000	$ 82,000

In the course of your analytical work, you have determined the following:

a. If the housewares department is discontinued, sales of appliances could be expanded by 25 percent. Sales of clothing would be unaffected.

b. The store fixtures being used in the housewares department could not be used in the expanded appliances department. These fixtures would have to be sold for their salvage value of $6,000. (The fixtures could last for eight more years, after which they would have zero sale value.)

c. Since appliances are much more expensive than housewares items, the store would have to expand its working capital investment in inventories and accounts receivable by $30,000.

d. The added level of appliance sales would carry the same proportionate variable expenses (for cost of goods sold and commissions) as are carried by current appliance sales.

e. Expanding the appliances department would require an expenditure of $85,000 for renovation and new fixtures. These fixtures would have an eight-year life and a $4,000 salvage value.

f. The store uses straight-line depreciation. If the fixtures now being used in the housewares department are sold, then all depreciation now being charged to that department would disappear.

g. The "other fixed expenses" in the housewares department represent the salary of a longtime employee who will be retained regardless of whether the housewares department is retained or discontinued.

h. The store has a before-tax required rate of return of 16 percent on all investments.

Required (ignore income taxes):

1. Compute the net annual change in cash flows if the housewares department is discontinued and the appliances department is expanded. (Do not include added investments or salvage values in this computation.)

2. Make a recommendation to the vice president as to whether the housewares department should be discontinued and the appliances department expanded. Use discounted cash flow, covering an eight-year period. Use the incremental-cost approach.

P14–26. **Equipment acquisition; uneven cash flows.** Woolrich Company's market research division has projected a substantial increase in demand over the next several years for one of the company's products. To meet this demand, the company will need to produce units as follows:

Year	Production in units
1	20,000
2	30,000
3	40,000
4–10	45,000

At present, the company is using a single model 2600 machine to manufacture this product. In order to increase its productive capacity, the company is considering two alternatives:

Alternative 1. The company could purchase another model 2600 machine that would operate along with the one it now owns. The following information is available on this alternative:

a. The model 2600 machine now in use cost $165,000 four years ago. Its present book value is $99,000, and its present market value is $90,000.

b. A new model 2600 machine costs $180,000 now. The currently owned model 2600 machine will have to be replaced in six years at a cost of $200,000. The replacement machine will have a market value of about $100,000 when it is four years old.

c. The variable cost required to produce one unit of product using the model 2600 machine is given under the "general information" below.

d. Repairs and maintenance each year on a single model 2600 machine total $3,000.

Alternative 2. The company could purchase a model 5200 machine and use the currently owned model 2600 machine as standby equipment. The model 5200 machine is a high-speed unit with double the capacity of the model 2600 machine. The following information is available on this alternative:

a. The cost of a new model 5200 machine is $250,000.

b. The variable cost required to produce one unit of product using the model 5200 machine is given under the "general information" below.

c. Due to its more complex operation, the model 5200 machine is more costly to maintain than the model 2600 machine. Repairs and maintenance on a model 5200 machine, with a model 2600 machine used as standby, would total $4,600 per year.

The following general information is available on the two alternatives:

a. Both the model 2600 machine and the model 5200 machine have a 10-year life from the time they are first used in production. The scrap value of both machines is nominal and can be ignored. Straight-line depreciation is used by the company.

b. The two machine models are not equally efficient in output. Comparative variable costs per unit of product are:

	Model 2600	Model 5200
Direct materials per unit	$0.36	$0.40
Direct labor per unit	0.50	0.22
Supplies and lubricants per unit	0.04	0.08
Total variable cost per unit	$0.90	$0.70

c. No other factory costs would change as a result of the decision between the two machines.

d. Woolrich Company's cost of capital is 18 percent.

Required (ignore income taxes):
1. Which alternative should the company choose? Show computations using discounted cash flow. (Round to the nearest whole dollar.)
2. Suppose that the cost of materials increases by 50 percent. Would this make the model 5200 machine more or less desirable? Explain. No computations are needed.
3. Suppose that the cost of labor increases by 25 percent. Would this make the model 5200 machine more or less desirable? Explain. No computations are needed.

P14–27. **CVP analysis; discounted cash flow.** Mercury Transit, Inc., has decided to inaugurate express bus service between its headquarters city and a nearby suburb (one-way fare, 50 cents) and is considering the purchase of either 32- or 52-passenger buses, on which pertinent estimates are as follows:

	32-passenger bus	52-passenger bus
Number of each to be purchased	6	4
Useful life	8 years	8 years
Purchase price of each bus (paid on delivery)	$80,000	$110,000
Mileage per gallon	10	7½
Salvage value per bus.	$ 6,000	$ 7,000
Drivers' hourly wage	3.50	4.20
Price per gallon of gasoline	1.50	1.50
Other annual cash expenses.	4,000	3,000

During the four daily rush hours, all buses will be in service and all are expected to operate at full capacity (state law prohibits standees) in both directions of the route, each bus covering the route 12 times (six round trips) during the four-hour period. During the remaining 12 hours of the 16-hour day, 500 passengers would be carried and Mercury Transit would operate only four buses on the route. Part-time drivers would be employed to drive the extra hours during the rush hours. A bus traveling the route all day would go 480 miles each day, and one traveling only during rush hours would go 120 miles each day, during the 260-day year.

Required (ignore income taxes):
1. Prepare a schedule showing the computation of the estimated annual gross revenues from the new route for each alternative.
2. Prepare a schedule showing the computation of the estimated annual drivers' wages for each alternative.
3. Prepare a schedule showing the computation of the estimated annual cost of gasoline for each alternative.
4. Assume that your computations in (1), (2), and (3) above are as follows:

	32-passenger bus	52-passenger bus
Estimated annual revenues.	$365,000	$390,000
Estimated annual drivers' wages.	67,000	68,000
Estimated annual cost of gasoline	85,000	100,000

Assuming that a minimum rate of return of 12 percent before income taxes is desired and that all annual cash flows occur at the end of the year, determine whether the 32-passenger buses or the 52-passenger buses should be purchased. Use discounted cash flow and the total-cost approach. (CPA, adapted)

15 Further Aspects of Investment Decisions

Learning objectives

After studying Chapter 15, you should be able to:

Compute the after-tax cost of a tax-deductible cash expense and the after-tax benefit from a taxable cash receipt.

Explain how depreciation deductions are computed under the Accelerated Cost Recovery System (ACRS).

Compute the tax savings arising from the depreciation tax shield, using both the ACRS tables and the optional straight-line method.

Compute the after-tax net present value of an investment proposal.

Determine the profitability index for an investment proposal.

Rank investment projects in order of preference under both the time-adjusted rate of return and net present value methods.

Determine the payback period for an investment, using the payback formula.

Determine the simple rate of return for an investment, using the simple rate of return formula.

Define or explain the key terms listed at the end of the chapter.

We continue our discussion of capital budgeting in this chapter by focusing on three new topics. First, we focus on income taxes and their impact on the capital budgeting decision. Second, we focus on methods of ranking competing capital investment projects according to their relative desirability. And third, we focus on methods of making capital budgeting decisions, other than discounted cash flow.

INCOME TAXES AND CAPITAL BUDGETING

In our discussion of capital budgeting in the preceding chapter, the matter of income taxes was omitted for two reasons. First, many organizations have no taxes to pay. Such organizations include schools, hospitals, and governmental units on local, state, and national levels. These organizations will always use capital budgeting techniques on a before-tax basis, as illustrated in the preceding chapter. Second, the topic of capital budgeting is somewhat complex and it is best absorbed in small doses. Now that we have laid a solid groundwork in the concepts of present value and discounting, we can explore the effects of income taxes on capital budgeting decisions with little difficulty.

The concept of after-tax cost

If someone were to ask you how much the rent is on your apartment, you would probably answer with the dollar amount that you pay out each month. If someone were to ask a business executive how much the rent is on the factory building, he or she might answer by stating a lesser figure than the dollar amount being paid out each month. The reason is that rent is a tax-deductible expense to a business firm, and expenses such as rent are often looked at on an *after-tax* basis rather than on a before-tax basis. The true cost of a tax-deductible item is not the dollars paid out; rather, it is the amount of payment that will remain *after* taking into consideration any reduction in income taxes that the payment will bring about. An expenditure net of its tax effect is known as **after-tax cost.**

After-tax cost is not a difficult concept. To illustrate the ideas behind it, assume that two firms, A and B, normally have sales of $100,000 each month and cash expenses of $65,000 each month. Firm A is considering an advertising program that will cost $5,000 each month. The tax rate is 40 percent. What will be the after-tax cost to Firm A of the contemplated $5,000 monthly advertising expenditure? The computations needed to compute the after-tax cost figure are shown in Exhibit 15–1.

As shown in the exhibit, the after-tax cost of the advertising program would be only $3,000 per month. This figure must be correct, since it measures the difference in net income between the two companies and since their income statements are identical except for the $5,000 in advertising paid by Firm A. In effect, a $5,000 monthly advertising expenditure would *really* cost Firm A only $3,000 *after taxes*.

EXHIBIT 15–1
The computation of after-tax cost

	Firm A	Firm B
Sales	$100,000	$100,000
Less expenses:		
Salaries, insurance, and other	65,000	65,000
New advertising program.	5,000	—
Total expenses	70,000	65,000
Income before taxes	30,000	35,000
Income taxes (40%)	12,000	14,000
Net income	$ 18,000	$ 21,000
After-tax cost of the new advertising program .		$3,000

A formula can be developed from these data that will give the after-tax cost of *any* tax-deductible cash expense.[1] The formula is:

$$(1 - \text{Tax rate}) \times \text{Cash expense} = \text{After-tax cost} \qquad (1)$$

We can prove the accuracy of this formula by applying it to Firm A's $5,000 advertising expenditure:

$$(1 - 0.40) \times \$5,000 = \$3,000 \text{ after-tax cost of the advertising program}$$

The concept of after-tax cost is very useful to the manager, since it measures the *actual* amount of cash that will be leaving a company as a result of an expenditure decision. As we now integrate income taxes into capital budgeting decisions, it will be necessary to place all cash expense items on an after-tax basis by applying the formula above.

The same reasoning applies to revenues and other *taxable* cash receipts. When a cash receipt occurs, the amount of cash inflow realized by an organization will be the amount that remains after taxes have been paid. The **after-tax benefit,** or net cash inflow, realized from a particular cash receipt can be obtained by applying a simple variation of the cash expenditure formula used above:

$$(1 - \text{Tax rate}) \times \text{Cash receipt} = \text{After-tax benefit (net cash inflow)} \qquad (2)$$

We emphasize the term *taxable cash receipts* in our discussion because not all cash inflows are taxable. For example, the release of working capital at the termination of an investment project would not be a taxable cash inflow, since it simply represents a return of original investment.

The concept of depreciation tax shield

The point was made in the preceding chapter that depreciation deductions in and of themselves do not involve cash flows. For this reason, depreciation

---

[1] This formula assumes that a company is operating at a profit; if it is operating at a loss, then the after-tax cost of an item is simply the amount paid, since no tax benefits will be realized.

deductions were ignored in Chapter 14 in all discounted cash flow computations.

Even though depreciation deductions do not involve cash flows, they do have an impact on the amount of income taxes that a firm will pay, and income taxes *do* involve cash flows. Therefore, as we now integrate income taxes into capital budgeting decisions, it will be necessary to consider depreciation deductions to the extent that they affect tax payments.

A cash flow comparison   To illustrate the effect of depreciation deductions on tax payments, let us compare two firms, X and Y. Both firms have annual sales of $50,000 and cash operating expenses of $40,000. In addition, Firm X has a depreciable asset on which the depreciation deduction is $2,500 per year. The tax rate is 40 percent. A cash flow comparison of the two firms is given at the bottom of Exhibit 15–2.

Notice from the exhibit that Firm X's net cash inflow exceeds Firm Y's by $1,000. Also notice that in order to obtain Firm X's net cash inflow, it is necessary to add the $2,500 depreciation deduction back to the company's net income. This step is necessary since depreciation is a noncash deduction on the income statement.

Exhibit 15–2 presents an interesting paradox. Notice that even though Firm X's net cash inflow is $1,000 *greater* than Firm Y's, its net income is much *lower* than Firm Y's (only $4,500, as compared to Firm Y's $6,000). The explanation for this paradox lies in the concept of the *depreciation tax shield*.

The depreciation tax shield   Firm X's greater net cash inflow comes about as a result of the *shield* against tax payments that is provided by depreciation deductions. Although depreciation deductions involve no out-

EXHIBIT 15–2
The impact of depreciation deductions on tax payments—a comparison of cash flows

Income Statements		
	Firm X	**Firm Y**
Sales	$50,000	$50,000
Expenses:		
Cash operating expenses	40,000	40,000
Depreciation expense	2,500	—
Total	42,500	40,000
Net income before taxes	7,500	10,000
Income taxes (40%)	3,000	4,000
Net income	$ 4,500	$ 6,000

Cash Flow Comparison		
Cash inflow from operations:		
Net income, as above	$ 4,500	$ 6,000
Add: Noncash deduction for depreciation	2,500	—
Net cash inflow	$ 7,000	$ 6,000
Greater amount of cash available to Firm X	$1,000	

flows of cash, they are fully deductible in arriving at taxable income. In effect, depreciation deductions *shield* revenues from taxation and thereby *lower* the amount of taxes that a company must pay.

In the case of Firm X, the $2,500 depreciation deduction taken involved no outflow of cash to the firm. Yet this depreciation was fully deductible on the company's income statement and thereby *shielded* $2,500 in revenues from taxation. Were it not for the depreciation deduction, the company's income taxes would have been $1,000 higher, since the entire $2,500 in shielded revenues would have been taxable at the regular tax rate of 40 percent (40 percent × $2,500 = $1,000). In effect, the depreciation tax shield *has reduced Firm X's taxes by $1,000,* permitting these funds to be retained within the company rather than going to the tax collector. Viewed another way, we can say that Firm X has realized a $1,000 *cash inflow* (through reduced tax payments) as a result of its $2,500 depreciation deduction.

Because they shield revenues from taxation, depreciation deductions are generally referred to as a **depreciation tax shield.** The reduction in tax payments made possible by the depreciation tax shield will always be equal to the amount of the depreciation deduction taken, multiplied by the tax rate. The formula is:

Tax rate × Depreciation deduction

$$= \text{Tax savings from the depreciation tax shield} \qquad (3)$$

We can prove this formula by applying it to the $2,500 depreciation deduction taken by Firm X in our example:

40% × $2,500 = $1,000 reduction in tax payments (shown as "Greater amount of cash available to Firm X" in Exhibit 15–2)

As we now integrate income taxes into capital budgeting computations, it will be necessary to consider the impact of depreciation deductions on tax payments by showing the tax savings provided by the depreciation tax shield.

The concepts that we have introduced in this section and in the preceding section are not complex and can be mastered fairly quickly. In order to

EXHIBIT 15–3

Tax adjustments required in a capital budgeting analysis

Item	Treatment
Cash expense*	Multiply by (1 − Tax rate) to get after-tax cost.
Cash receipt*	Multiply by (1 − Tax rate) to get after-tax cash inflow.
Depreciation deduction	Multiply by the tax rate to get the tax savings from the depreciation tax shield

* Where cash receipts and cash expenses recur *each year,* the expenses should be deducted from the receipts and only the difference should be multiplied by (1 − Tax rate). See the example at the top of Exhibit 15–6.

assist you in your study, a summary of these concepts is given in Exhibit 15–3.

Accelerated Cost Recovery System (ACRS)

Historically, depreciation has been closely tied to the useful life of an asset, with year-by-year depreciation deductions typically computed by the straight-line method, the sum-of-the-years'-digits method, or the double-declining balance method. In computing depreciation deductions, companies have generally given recognition to an asset's expected salvage value by deducting the salvage value from the asset's cost and depreciating only the remainder. Although these concepts can still be used for computing depreciation deductions on financial statements, sweeping changes were made in 1981 in the way that depreciation deductions are computed for tax purposes.

The new approach, called the **Accelerated Cost Recovery System (ACRS)**, accelerates depreciation deductions by abandoning the concept of useful life and placing depreciable assets into one of five property classes. Each class has a prescribed life, as follows:

3-year property: Includes automobiles, light-duty trucks, equipment used in research and development, and certain special tools.

5-year property: Includes all other items of machinery and equipment used in a business that do not fall into the 3-year property class.

10-year property: Includes mostly public utility property (with an 18- to 25-year useful life) and certain limited real property such as theme parks.

15-year property: Includes all public utility property other than that in the 10-year property class.

18-year property: Includes all depreciable real property used in a business, other than that included in the 10-year property class.

Each class of property has a preset table showing allowable depreciation deductions, based on a percentage of the asset's original cost. These tables are presented in Exhibit 15–4. The percentage figures used in the tables are based on the declining-balance method of depreciation, with a 150 percent rate having been used to develop the percentages in the tables dealing with machinery and equipment, and a 175 percent rate having been used to develop the percentages in the tables dealing with depreciable real property. In the case of property in the 5-, 10-, and 15-year classes, the tables automatically switch to straight-line depreciation at the point where depreciation deductions would be greater under that method. The tables in Exhibit 15–4 are effective for assets placed into service after January 1, 1981.

The five property classes outlined above permit depreciation of an asset over a much shorter time period than was allowed previously. As one example, office equipment generally has a useful life of about 10 years, but it would fall into the 5-year property class under the Accelerated Cost Recovery System. Thus, organizations will be able to fully depreciate office equipment over a period equal to about *half* of its actual useful life. Similarly, an office

EXHIBIT 15–4
Accelerated Cost Recovery System tables by property class

Taxable year	3-year	5-year	10-year	15-year utility property	18-year real property*
1	25%	15%	8%	5%	9%
2	38	22	14	10	9
3	37	21	12	9	8
4		21	10	8	7
5		21	10	7	6
6			10	7	6
7			9	6	5
8			9	6	5
9			9	6	5
10			9	6	5
11				6	5
12				6	5
13				6	5
14				6	4
15				6	4
16					4
17					4
18					4

* For real property, depreciation in the year of purchase must be computed according to the number of months that the property is actually owned. The table above assumes a purchase in January (or the first month of a company's fiscal year). Other tables are available and should be referred to if a piece of real property is acquired in a month other than the first month of the year.

building generally has a useful life of about 40 years, but it would be depreciated over an 18-year period since depreciable real property is in the 18-year property class. Under the new system, similar acceleration is provided for all of the depreciable assets used in a trade or business.

A further benefit of ACRS is that under this system it is not necessary to consider the salvage value of an asset in computing depreciation deductions. Thus, the entire cost of an asset can be depreciated without deducting any amount for salvage value, regardless of whether the taxpayer is using the ACRS tables or the optional straight-line method discussed below.

Optional straight-line method ACRS allows flexibility to the extent that a company can elect to compute depreciation deductions by the **optional straight-line method** rather than using the percentages shown in the tables in Exhibit 15–4. If straight-line depreciation is used, taxpayers may elect to use asset lives *greater* than those shown in the five basic classes, as follows:

Class	Optional periods for straight-line depreciation
3-year property	3, 5, or 12 years
5-year property	5, 12, or 25 years
10-year property	10, 25, or 35 years
15-year property	15, 35, or 45 years
18-year property	18, 35, or 45 years

If a company elects to use the straight-line method in lieu of the percentages in the ACRS tables, it must follow what is known as the **half-year convention.** This requires that a half year's depreciation be taken in the first year of the life of an asset, regardless of when the asset is purchased during the year. For example, assume that Emerson Company purchases a new machine at a cost of $10,000 on April 1, 1985. The machine has an $800 salvage value and falls into the five-year property class. Under ACRS, the company would deduct $1,000 depreciation in 1985:

$$\$10,000 \div 5 = \$2,000; \; \$2,000 \times \tfrac{1}{2} = \$1,000$$

For 1986–89 (the next four years) the company would deduct $2,000 depreciation each year, and in 1990 it would deduct the final $1,000 amount, as shown below:

Year	Depreciation deduction
1985 (half year's depreciation)	$1,000
1986	2,000
1987	2,000
1988	2,000
1989	2,000
1990 (half year's depreciation)	1,000

Notice that even though the asset is depreciated over a five-year period, six years are actually involved in the depreciation process, since the first and sixth years each have only one half year's depreciation. Also notice that the asset's salvage value was not considered in computing the depreciation deductions.

As explained earlier, since the asset falls into the 5-year property class, the company could have chosen to depreciate it over either 12 years or 25 years, rather than over the shorter 5-year period. The option of being able to use the straight-line method in lieu of the percentages in the ACRS tables and the option of being able to choose a longer depreciation period, will be of particular value to new firms and to firms experiencing economic difficulties. The reason, of course, is that such firms often have little or no income and thus might prefer to stretch out depreciation deductions rather than to accelerate them.

The choice of a depreciation method

As stated earlier, companies can still elect to use the straight-line, the sum-of-the-years'-digits, and the double-declining-balance methods to compute depreciation for financial statement purposes (and base depreciation deductions on the useful life of the assets), even though they must use the ACRS rules for tax purposes. If a company uses a different depreciation method for financial statement purposes than it does for tax purposes, which method should be used in a capital budgeting analysis? Since capital budgeting is concerned with *actual cash flows,* the answer is that the same depreciation method should be used for capital budgeting purposes as is being used for tax purposes. Under the new law, this will be either the ACRS tables or the optional straight-line method.

For tax purposes, most firms will choose the ACRS tables, since this highly accelerated approach to depreciation will be more advantageous than the optional straight-line method from a present value of tax savings point of view. To illustrate, refer to the data in Exhibit 15–5. This exhibit compares the two depreciation methods in terms of the present value of the tax savings that they provide on a hypothetical asset costing $100,000.

As shown by the exhibit, the ACRS table approach provides a larger present value of tax savings than does the straight-line method. This example goes far to explain why firms often prefer the accelerated method of depreciation over the straight-line method for tax purposes. Since the accelerated method provides more of its tax shield early in the life of an asset, the present value of the resulting tax savings will always be greater than the present value of the tax savings under the straight-line method.

EXHIBIT 15–5
Tax shield effects of depreciation

Cost of the asset	$300,000
Property class life	5 years
Salvage value	–0–
Cost of capital	14% after taxes
Income tax rate	40%

Straight-line depreciation, with half-year convention:

Year*	Depreciation deduction	Tax shield: Income tax savings at 40 percent	14 percent factor	Present value of tax savings
1	$30,000	$12,000	0.877	$10,524
2	60,000	24,000	0.769	18,456
3	60,000	24,000	0.675	16,200
4	60,000	24,000	0.592	14,208
5	60,000	24,000	0.519	12,456
6	30,000	12,000	0.456	5,472
				$77,316

ACRS tables, five-year property class:

Year	Cost	ACRS percentage			
1	$300,000	15%	$45,000	$18,000	0.877	$15,786
2	300,000	22	66,000	26,400	0.769	20,302
3	300,000	21	63,000	25,200	0.675	17,010
4	300,000	21	63,000	25,200	0.592	14,918
5	300,000	21	63,000	25,200	0.519	13,079
						$81,095

* The company could have chosen to depreciate the asset over either 12 years or 25 years, but this would have reduced the present value of the tax savings even further as compared to the present value of the tax savings using the ACRS table.

The investment credit

Depreciable personal property (generally machinery and equipment) used in a trade or business qualifies for the **investment tax credit** in addition to the depreciation deductions allowed under ACRS. The investment tax credit is a direct reduction of income taxes and is taken in the year in which an asset is first placed into service. The amount of the income tax reduction is computed by applying a specified percentage to the cost of the asset acquired. Property in the 3-year class is allowed a 6 percent investment credit; property in the 5-year class is allowed a 10 percent investment credit, as is any machinery and equipment in the 10- and 15-year classes.

The law states, however, that a company must reduce the depreciable cost of an asset (i.e., reduce the amount of cost taken as depreciation expense) by one half of the investment credit taken. Thus, if an asset costs $100,000 and is entitled to a $10,000 investment credit, then only $95,000 of the cost of the asset can be taken as depreciation expense.

In lieu of reducing the depreciable cost of an asset, a company can elect to take a smaller investment tax credit. The smaller investment tax credit is 4 percent for property in the three-year class and 8 percent for property in the five-year class. If the smaller investment credit is taken, then a company is entitled to depreciate the full cost of the property involved. *In this book we will always assume that a company takes the smaller investment credit and thus depreciates the full cost of its property.* There are two reasons why we choose to handle the investment tax credit in this manner. First, this is the way it is handled most frequently on professional examinations. Second, the investment credit is subject to frequent (almost yearly) changes; for teaching purposes, therefore, it seems wisest to use the least complicated approach and to advise the reader to check what rules may be in effect when the investment credit is later used in practice.

To show how the investment credit works, assume that Parkins Company purchased a machine at a cost of $50,000 on August 1, 1985. The machine is in the ACRS five-year property class. The company would be eligible for a $4,000 investment credit for the year ($50,000 × 8% = $4,000). This would be a direct reduction of the income taxes otherwise payable for the year. *The company would still be entitled to depreciate the full $50,000 cost of the machine under the ACRS rules.* On a capital budgeting analysis, the $4,000 investment credit should be shown as a $4,000 cash inflow in year 1 of the life of the investment project (see Exhibit 15–6 for an example of the proper handling of the investment credit figures).

Example of income taxes and capital budgeting

Armed with an understanding of the new ACRS depreciation rules, and with an understanding of the concepts of after-tax cost, after-tax revenue, and depreciation tax shield, we are now prepared to examine a comprehensive example of income taxes and capital budgeting. Assume the following data:

Holland Company owns the mineral rights to land on which there is a deposit of ore. The company is uncertain as to whether it should purchase equipment and open a mine on the property. After careful study, the following data have been assembled by the company:

Cost of new equipment needed	$100,000
Working capital needed	60,000
Estimated annual cash receipts from sales of ore	120,000
Estimated annual cash payments for salaries, insurance, utilities, and other cash expenses of mining the ore	70,000
Cost of road repairs needed in six years	15,000
Salvage value of equipment in eight years.	20,000

The ore in the mine would be exhausted after eight years of mining activity. The equipment needed would fall in the ACRS five-year property class. Holland Company uses the ACRS tables and does not consider salvage value in computing depreciation deductions. The company's after-tax cost of capital is 12 percent, and its tax rate is 40 percent.

Should Holland Company purchase the equipment and open a mine on the property? The solution to the problem is given in Exhibit 15–6. The reader should go through this solution item by item and note the following points:

Cost of new equipment. The initial investment of $100,000 in the new equipment is included in full, with no reductions for taxes. The tax effects of this investment are considered in the depreciation deductions.

Investment credit. The new equipment falls into the ACRS five-year property class, so it is entitled to an 8 percent investment credit. Since this credit is a reduction of income taxes, it is treated as a cash inflow for capital budgeting purposes. Note that the cash inflow occurs during year 1 (rather than "now"). This simply reflects the fact that the investment credit is not an immediate rebate but rather acts as a reduction of income taxes that are due during the first year of the life of an asset.

Working capital. Observe that the working capital needed for the project is included in full, with no reductions for taxes. This represents an *investment,* not an expense, so no tax adjustment is needed. (Only revenues and expenses are placed on an after-tax basis.) Also observe that no tax adjustment is needed when the working capital is released at the end of the project's life. The release of working capital would not be a taxable cash inflow, since it merely represents a return of investment funds back to the company.

Net annual cash receipts. The net annual cash receipts from sales of ore are placed on an after-tax basis, as discussed earlier in the chapter. Note at the top of the exhibit that the annual cash expenses are deducted from the annual cash receipts to obtain a net cash receipts figure. This just simplifies computations. (Many of the exercises and problems that follow already provide a net annual cash receipts figure, thereby eliminating the need to offset the cash receipts and cash expenses.)

EXHIBIT 15–6
Example of income taxes and capital budgeting

	Per year
Cash receipts from sales of ore	$120,000
Less payments for salaries, insurance, utilities, and other cash expenses	70,000
Net cash receipts	$ 50,000

Item and computations		Year(s) having cash flows	Amount of cash flows	12 percent factor	Present value of cash flows
Cost of new equipment		Now	$(100,000)	1.000	$(100,000)
Investment credit (8% × $100,000)		1	8,000	0.893	7,144
Working capital needed		Now	(60,000)	1.000	(60,000)
Net annual cash receipts (above)	$50,000				
Multiply by 1 − 40%	× 60%				
After-tax cash inflow	$30,000	1–8	30,000	4.968	149,040
Road repairs	$15,000				
Multiply by 1 − 40%	× 60%				
After-tax cost	$ 9,000	6	(9,000)	0.507	(4,563)

Depreciation deductions:

Year	Cost	ACRS percentage	Depreciation deduction	Tax shield: Income tax savings at 40 percent	Year(s) having cash flows	Amount of cash flows	12 percent factor	Present value of cash flows
1	$100,000	15%	$15,000	$6,000	1	6,000	0.893	5,358
2	100,000	22	22,000	8,800	2	8,800	0.797	7,014
3	100,000	21	21,000	8,400	3	8,400	0.712	5,981
4	100,000	21	21,000	8,400	4	8,400	0.636	5,342
5	100,000	21	21,000	8,400	5	8,400	0.567	4,763

Item and computations		Year(s) having cash flows	Amount of cash flows	12 percent factor	Present value of cash flows
Salvage value of equipment	$20,000				
Multiply by 1 − 40%	× 60%				
After-tax cash inflow	$12,000	8	12,000	0.404	4,848
Release of working capital		8	60,000	0.404	24,240
Net present value					$ 49,167

Road repairs. Since the road repairs occur just once (in the sixth year), they are treated separately from other expenses. Road repairs would be a tax-deductible cash expense, and therefore they are placed on an after-tax basis, as discussed earlier in the chapter.

Depreciation deductions. The tax savings provided by depreciation deductions under the ACRS rules are included in the present value computations in the same way as was illustrated earlier in the chapter (see Exhibit 15–5). Note that depreciation deductions are kept separate from cash expenses. These are unlike items, and they should be treated separately in a capital budgeting analysis.

Salvage value of equipment. Since under the ACRS rules a company does not consider salvage value in computing depreciation deductions, book value will be zero at the end of the life of an asset. Thus, any salvage value will be fully taxable as income to the company. As discussed earlier, the after-tax benefit to the company from sale of the equipment can be obtained by multiplying the salvage value by (1 − Tax rate).

Since the net present value of the proposed mining project is positive, the equipment should be purchased and the mine opened. The reader should study Exhibit 15–6 until all of its points are thoroughly understood. *Exhibit 15–6 is a key exhibit in the chapter!*

The total-cost approach and income taxes

As stated in the preceding chapter, the total-cost approach is used to compare two or more competing investment proposals. To provide an example of this approach when income taxes are involved, assume the following data:

The *Daily Globe* has an auxiliary press that was purchased two years ago. The newspaper is thinking about replacing this old press with a newer, faster model. The alternatives are:

Buy a new press. A new press could be purchased for $90,000. It would have an economic useful life of eight years, after which time it would be salable for $5,000. The old press could be sold now for $36,000. (The book value of the old press is $56,000.) If the new press is purchased, it would be depreciated using the ACRS tables and would fall into the five-year property class. No salvage value would be recognized in computing depreciation deductions. The new press would cost $45,000 each year to operate and would be fully eligible for the investment credit.

Keep the old press. The old press was purchased two years ago at a cost of $80,000. The press falls into the ACRS five-year property class and is being depreciated by the optional straight-line method. The old press will last for eight more years, but it will need an overhaul in four years that will cost $8,000. Cash operating costs of the old press are $60,000 each year. Although salvage value is not being considered in computing depreciation deductions, the old press will have a salvage value of $4,000 at the end of eight more years.

The tax rate is 40 percent. The *Daily Globe* requires an after-tax return of 10 percent on all investments in equipment.

Should the *Daily Globe* keep its old press or buy the new press? The solution using the total-cost approach is presented in Exhibit 15–7. Most of the items in this exhibit have already been discussed in connection with Exhibit 15–6. Only a couple of points need elaboration:

Annual cash operating costs.   Since there are no revenues identified with the project, we simply place the cash operating costs on an after-tax basis and discount them as we did in Chapter 14.

Disposal of the old press.   The computation of the cash inflow from the disposal of the old press is somewhat more involved than the other items in the exhibit. Note that *two* cash inflows are connected with the disposal of the old press. The first is a $36,000 cash inflow in the form of the sale price. The second is an $8,000 cash inflow in the form of a reduction in income taxes, resulting from the tax shield provided by the loss sustained on the sale. This tax shield functions in the same way as the tax shield provided by depreciation deductions. That is, the $20,000 loss shown in the exhibit on disposal of the old press (the difference between the sale price of $36,000 and the book value of $56,000) is fully deductible from income in the year the loss is sustained. This loss shields income from taxation, thereby causing a reduction in the income taxes that would otherwise be payable. The tax savings resulting from the loss tax shield are computed by multiplying the loss by the tax rate (the same procedure as for depreciation deductions): $20,000 × 40% = $8,000.

A second solution to this problem is presented in Exhibit 15–8, where the incremental-cost approach is used. Notice both from this exhibit and from Exhibit 15–7 that the net present value is $20,281 in favor of buying the new press.

PREFERENCE DECISIONS—THE RANKING OF INVESTMENT PROJECTS

In the preceding chapter, we indicated that there are two types of decisions to make relative to investment opportunities. These are screening decisions and preference decisions. Screening decisions have to do with whether or not some proposed investment is acceptable to a firm. We discussed ways of making screening decisions in the preceding chapter, where we studied the use of the cost of capital as a screening tool. Screening decisions are very important in that many investment proposals come to the attention of management, and those that are not worthwhile must be screened out.

Preference decisions come *after* screening decisions and attempt to answer the following question: "How do the remaining investment proposals, all of which have been screened and provide an acceptable rate of return, rank in terms of preference? That is, which one(s) would be *best* for the firm to accept?" Preference decisions are much more difficult to make than screening decisions. The reason is that investment funds are usually limited, and this often requires that some (perhaps many) otherwise very profitable investment opportunities be forgone.

EXHIBIT 15–7
Income taxes and capital budgeting: Total-cost approach

Item and computations	Year(s) having cash flows	Amount of cash flows	10 percent factor	Present value of cash flows
Buy the new press:				
Initial investment	Now	$(90,000)	1.000	$ (90,000)
Investment credit (8% × $90,000)	1	7,200	0.909	6,545
Annual cash operating costs $45,000				
Multiply by 1 − 40% .... ×60%				
After-tax cost $27,000	1–8	(27,000)	5.335	(144,045)

Depreciation deductions:

Year	Cost	ACRS percentage	Depreciation deduction	Tax shield: Income tax savings at 40 percent
1	$ 90,000	15%	$13,500	$5,400
2	90,000	22	19,800	7,920
3	90,000	21	18,900	7,560
4	90,000	21	18,900	7,560
5	90,000	21	18,900	7,560

Item and computations	Year(s) having cash flows	Amount of cash flows	10 percent factor	Present value of cash flows
(Tax shield) 1	1	$ 5,400	0.909	4,909
2	2	7,920	0.826	6,542
3	3	7,560	0.751	5,678
4	4	7,560	0.683	5,163
5	5	7,560	0.621	4,695
Salvage value, fully taxable since book value will be zero .... $ 5,000				
Multiply by 1 − 40% .... ×60%				
After-tax cash inflow .... $ 3,000	8	3,000	0.467	1,401
Cash flow from disposal of the old press:				
Cash received from sale	Now	36,000	1.000	36,000
Present book value $56,000				
Sale price now 36,000				
Loss on disposal 20,000				
Income tax savings at 40% .... ×40% .... $ 8,000	1	8,000	0.909	7,272
Present value of cash flows				$(155,840)

Keep the old press:

Annual cash operating costs		$60,000			
Multiply by 1 − 40%		× 60%			
After-tax cost		$36,000	1–8	(36,000)	5.335	$(192,060)

Depreciation deductions:

Year	Cost	Depreciation deduction	Tax shield: Income tax savings at 40 percent					
1	$80,000	$16,000*	$ 6,400	1	$ 6,400	0.909	5,818
2	80,000	16,000	6,400	2	6,400	0.826	5,286
3	80,000	16,000	6,400	3	6,400	0.751	4,806
4	80,000	8,000	3,200	4	3,200	0.683	2,186

Salvage value, fully taxable since
  book value will be zero .... $ 4,000
Multiply by 1 − 40% .... × 60%
After-tax cash inflow .... $ 2,400 .... 8 .... 2,400 .... 0.467 1,121

Overhaul at end of year 4 .... $ 8,000
Multiply by 1 − 40% .... × 60%
After-tax cost .... $ 4,800 .... 4 .... (4,800) .... 0.683 .... (3,278)

Present value of cash
  flows. .... $(176,121)

Net present value in favor
of purchasing the
new press. .... $ 20,281

* $80,000 ÷ 5 years = $16,000. Two years' depreciation has already been taken on the old press.

EXHIBIT 15–8
Income taxes and capital budgeting: Incremental-cost approach

Item and computations					Year(s) having cash flows	Amount of cash flows	10 percent factor	Present value of cash flows
Initial investment.					Now	$(90,000)	1.000	$(90,000)
Investment credit (8% × $90,000)					1	7,200	0.909	6,545
Savings in annual cash operating costs.				$15,000				
Multiply by 1 − 40%				×60%				
Net annual savings				$ 9,000	1–8	9,000	5.335	48,015

Difference in depreciation:

Year	New press	Old press	Difference	Tax savings at 40%				
1	$13,500	$16,000	$(2,500)	$(1,000)	1	$ (1,000)	0.909	(909)
2	19,800	16,000	3,800	1,510	2	1,520	0.826	1,256
3	18,900	16,000	2,900	1,160	3	1,160	0.751	871
4	18,900	8,000	10,900	4,360	4	4,360	0.683	2,978
5	18,900	–0–	18,900	7,560	5	7,560	0.621	4,695

Difference in salvage value:

Salvage of the new press				$5,000				
Salvage of the old press				4,000				
				1,000				
Multiply by 1 − 40%				×60%				
After-tax cash inflow				$ 600	8	600	0.467	280

Cash flow from disposal of the old press:

Cash received from sale					Now	36,000	1.000	36,000
Income tax savings from loss (see Exhibit 15–7)					1	8,000	0.909	7,272

Overhaul avoided in four years on the old press				$8,000				
Multiply by 1 − 40%				×60%				
After-tax cash inflow				$4,800	4	4,800	0.683	3,278

Net present value in favor of purchasing the new press								$ 20,281

Note: The figures in this exhibit are derived from the *differences* between the two alternatives given in Exhibit 15–7.

Preference decisions are sometimes called *ranking* decisions, or *rationing* decisions, because they attempt to ration limited investment funds among many competing investment opportunities. The choice may be simply between two competing alternatives, or many alternatives may be involved which must be ranked according to their overall desirability. Either the time-adjusted rate of return method or the net present value method can be used in making preference decisions.

Time-adjusted rate of return method

When using the time-adjusted rate of return method to rank competing investment projects, the preference rule is: *The higher the time-adjusted rate of return, the more desirable the project.* If one investment project promises a time-adjusted rate of return of 18 percent, then it is preferable over another project that promises a time-adjusted rate of return of only 15 percent.

Ranking projects according to time-adjusted rate of return is a widely used means of making preference decisions. The reasons are probably twofold. First, no additional computations are needed beyond those already performed in making the initial screening decisions. The rates of return themselves are used to rank acceptable projects. And second, the ranking data are easily understood by management. Rates of return are very similar to interest rates, which the manager works with every day.

Net present value method

If the net present value method is being used to rank competing investment projects, the net present value of one project cannot be compared directly to the net present value of another project unless the investments in the projects are of equal size. For example, assume that a company is considering two competing investments, as shown below:

	Investment A	Investment B
Investment required	$50,000	$5,000
Present value of cash inflows	51,000	6,000
Net present value	$ 1,000	$1,000

Each project has a net present value of $1,000, but the projects are not equally desirable. A project requiring an investment of only $5,000 that produces cash inflows with a present value of $6,000 is much more desirable than a project requiring an investment of $50,000 that produces cash inflows with a present value of only $51,000. In order to compare the two projects on a valid basis, it is necessary in each case to divide the present value of the cash inflows by the investment required. The ratio that this computation yields is called the **profitability index.** The formula for the profitability index is:

$$\frac{\text{Present value of cash inflows}}{\text{Investment required}} = \text{Profitability index}$$

The profitability indexes for the two investments above would be:

	Investment A	Investment B
Present value of cash inflows	$51,000 *(a)*	$6,000 *(a)*
Investment required	$50,000 *(b)*	$5,000 *(b)*
Profitability index, *(a)* ÷ *(b)*	1.02	1.20

The preference rule to follow when using the profitability index to rank competing investment projects is: *The higher the profitability index, the more desirable the project.* Applying this rule to the two investments above, investment B should be chosen over investment A.

In computing the investment in a project, the cash outlays should be reduced by any salvage recovered from the sale of old equipment being replaced. Investment in a project also includes any working capital that the project may require, as explained in the preceding chapter.

Comparing the preference rules

The profitability index is conceptually superior to the time-adjusted rate of return as a method of making preference decisions. This is because the profitability index will always give the correct signal as to the relative desirability of alternatives, even if the alternatives have different lives and different patterns of earnings. By contrast, if lives are unequal, the time-adjusted rate of return method can lead the manager to make incorrect decisions.

Assume the following situation:

Parker Company is considering two investment proposals, only one of which can be accepted. Project A requires an investment of $5,000 and will provide a single cash inflow of $6,000 in one year. Therefore, it promises a time-adjusted rate of return of 20 percent. Project B also requires an investment of $5,000. It will provide cash inflows of $1,360 each year for six years. Its time-adjusted rate of return is 16 percent. Which project should be accepted?

Although project A promises a time-adjusted rate of return of 20 percent, as compared to only 16 percent for project B, project A is not necessarily preferable over project B. It is preferable *only* if the funds released at the end of the year under project A can be reinvested at a high rate of return in some *other* project for the five remaining years. Otherwise, project B, which promises a return of 16 percent over the *entire* six years, is more desirable.

Let us assume that the company in the example above has a cost of capital of 12 percent. The profitability index approach to ranking competing investment projects would rank the two proposals as follows:

	Project A	Project B
Present value of cash inflows:		
$6,000 received at the end of one year at 12% (factor of 0.893)	$5,358 *(a)*	
$1,360 received at the end of each year for six years at 12% (factor of 4.111)		$5,591 *(a)*
Investment required	$5,000 *(b)*	$5,000 *(b)*
Profitability index, *(a) ÷ (b)*	1.07	1.12

The profitability index indicates that project B is more desirable than project A. This is in fact the case if the funds released from project A at the end of one year can be reinvested at only 12 percent (the cost of capital). Although the computations will not be shown here, in order for project A to be more desirable than project B, the funds released from project A would have to be reinvested at a rate of return *greater* than 14 percent for the remaining five years.

In short, the time-adjusted rate of return method of ranking tends to favor short-term, high-yield projects, whereas the net present value method of ranking (using the profitability index) tends to favor longer-term projects.

OTHER APPROACHES TO CAPITAL BUDGETING DECISIONS

The discounted cash flow methods of making capital budgeting decisions are relatively new. They were first introduced on a widespread basis in the 1950s, although their appearance in business literature predates this period by many years. Discounted cash flow methods have gained widespread acceptance as accurate and dependable decision-making tools. Other methods of making capital budgeting decisions are also available, however, and are preferred by some managers.

The payback method

The payback method centers on a span of time known as the *payback period*. The **payback period** can be defined as the length of time that it takes for an investment project to recoup its own initial cost out of the cash receipts that it generates. In business jargon, this period is sometimes spoken of as "the time that it takes for an investment to pay for itself." The basic premise of the payback method is that the more quickly the cost of an investment can be recovered, the more desirable is the investment.

The payback period is expressed in years. The formula used in computing the payback period is:

$$\text{Payback period} = \frac{\text{Investment required}}{\text{Net annual cash inflow*}} \qquad (4)$$

* If new equipment is replacing old equipment, this becomes *incremental* net annual cash inflow.

To illustrate the mechanics involved in payback computations, assume the following data:

The Concord Company needs a new milling machine. The company is considering two machines, machine A and machine B. Machine A costs $15,000 and will reduce annual operating costs by $5,000. Machine B costs only $12,000 but will also reduce annual operating costs by $5,000.

Required: Which machine should be purchased? Make your calculations by the payback method.

$$\text{Machine A payback period} = \frac{\$15,000}{\$5,000} = 3.0 \text{ years}$$

$$\text{Machine B payback period} = \frac{\$12,000}{\$5,000} = 2.4 \text{ years}$$

According to the payback calculations, the Concord Company should purchase machine B, since it has a shorter payback period than machine A.

Evaluation of the payback method

The payback method is not a measure of how profitable one investment project is as compared to another. Rather, it is a measure of *time* in the sense that it tells the manager how many years will be required to recover the investment in one project as compared to another. This is a major defect in the approach, since a shorter payback period is not always an accurate guide as to whether one investment is more desirable than another. To illustrate this point, consider again the two machines used in the example above. Since machine B has a shorter payback period than machine A, it *appears* that machine B is more desirable than machine A. But if we add one more piece of data, this illusion quickly disappears. Machine A has a projected 10-year life, and machine B has a projected 5-year life. It would take two purchases of machine B to provide the same length of service as would be provided by a single purchase of machine A. Under these circumstances, machine A would be a much better investment than machine B, even though machine B has a shorter payback period. Unfortunately, the payback method has no inherent mechanism for highlighting differences in useful life between investments for the decision maker. Such differences can be very subtle, and relying on payback alone can cause the manager to make incorrect decisions.

A further criticism of the payback method is that it does not consider the time value of money. A cash inflow to be received several years in the future is weighed equally with a cash inflow to be received right now. To illustrate, assume that for an investment of $8,000 you can purchase either of the two following streams of cash inflows:

Year	0	1	2	3	4	5	6	7	8
Stream 1		–0–	–0–	–0–	8,000	2,000	2,000	2,000	2,000
Stream 2		2,000	2,000	2,000	2,000	8,000	–0–	–0–	–0–

Which stream of cash inflows would you prefer to receive in return for your $8,000 investment? Each stream has a payback period of 4.0 years. Therefore, if payback alone were relied on in making the decision, you would be forced to say that the streams are equally desirable. However, from the point of view of the time value of money, stream 2 is much more desirable than stream 1.

On the other hand, under certain conditions the payback method can be very useful to the manager. For one thing, it can help the manager to identify the "ball park" in weeding out investment proposals. That is, it can be used as a screening tool to help answer the question "Should I consider this proposal further?" If a proposal doesn't provide at least some minimum payback period, then there might be no need to consider it further. In addition, the payback period is often of great importance to new firms that are "cash poor." When a firm is cash poor, a project with a short payback period but a low rate of return might be preferred over another project with a high rate of return but a long payback period. The reason is that the company may simply need a faster return of its cash investment.

An extended example of payback

As shown in the formula given earlier, the payback period is computed by dividing the investment in a project by the net annual cash inflows that the project will generate. If new equipment is replacing old equipment, then any salvage to be received on disposal of the old equipment should be deducted from the cost of the new equipment, and only the *incremental* investment should be used in the payback computation. In addition, any depreciation deducted in arriving at the net income promised by an investment project must be added back to obtain the project's expected net annual cash inflow. To illustrate, assume the following data:

Goodtime Fun Centers, Inc., operates many outlets in the eastern states. Some of the vending machines in one of its outlets provide very little revenue, so the company is considering the removal of the machines and the installation of equipment to dispense soft ice cream. The equipment would cost $80,000 and have an eight-year useful life. Incremental annual revenues and costs associated with the sale of ice cream would be:

Sales	$150,000
Less cost of ingredients	90,000
Contribution margin	60,000
Less fixed expenses:	
Salaries	27,000
Maintenance.	3,000
Depreciation.	10,000
Total fixed expenses	40,000
Net income	$ 20,000

The vending machines can be sold for a $5,000 scrap value. The company will not purchase equipment unless it has a payback of three years or less. Should the equipment to dispense ice cream be purchased? (Ignore income taxes.)

An analysis as to whether the proposed equipment meets the company's payback requirements is given in Exhibit 15–9. Several things should be noted from the data in this exhibit. First, notice that depreciation is added back to net income to obtain the net annual cash inflow promised by the new equipment. As stated in the preceding chapter, depreciation does not represent a present cash outlay and thus must be added back to net income in order to adjust it to a cash basis. Second, notice in the payback computation that the salvage value from the old machines has been deducted from the cost of the new equipment, and that only the incremental investment has been used in computing the payback period.

Since the proposed equipment has a payback period of less than three years, the company's payback requirement has been met and the new equipment should be purchased.

EXHIBIT 15–9
Computation of the payback period

Step 1: *Compute the net annual cash inflow.* Since the net annual cash inflow is not given, it must be computed before the payback period can be determined:

Net income (given above)	$20,000
Add: Noncash deduction for depreciation	10,000
Net annual cash inflow	$30,000

Step 2: *Compute the payback period.* Using the net annual cash inflow figure from above, the payback period can be determined as follows:

$$\frac{\text{Cost of the new equipment} - \text{Salvage from the old machines}}{\text{Net annual cash inflow}} = \text{Payback period}$$

$$\frac{\$80,000 - \$5,000}{\$30,000} = 2.5 \text{ years}$$

Payback and uneven cash flows

When the cash inflows associated with an investment project are erratic or uneven, the simple payback formula that we outlined earlier is no longer usable, and the computations involved in deriving the payback period can be fairly complex. Consider the following data:

Year	Investment	Cash inflow
1	$4,000	$1,000
2		–0–
3		2,000
4	2,000	1,000
5		500
6		3,000
7		2,000
8		2,000

What is the payback period on this investment? The answer is 5.5 years, but to obtain this figure it is necessary to balance off the cash inflows against the investment outflows on a *year-by-year* basis. The steps involved in this process are shown in Exhibit 15–10. By the middle of the sixth year, sufficient cash inflows will have been realized to recover the entire investment of $6,000 ($4,000 + $2,000).

EXHIBIT 15–10
Payback and uneven cash flows

	(1) Beginning unrecovered investment	(2) Additional investment	(3) Total unrecovered investment (1) + (2)	(4) Cash inflow	(5) Ending unrecovered investment (3) − (4)
1	$4,000		$4,000	$1,000	$3,000
2	3,000		3,000	–0–	3,000
3	3,000		3,000	2,000	1,000
4	1,000	$2,000	3,000	1,000	2,000
5	2,000		2,000	500	1,500
6	1,500		1,500	3,000	–0–
7	–0–		–0–	2,000	–0–
8	–0–		–0–	2,000	–0–

The simple rate of return method

The **simple rate of return** method is another capital budgeting technique that does not involve discounted cash flows. The method is also known as the accounting method, the unadjusted rate of return method, and the financial statement method. It derives its popularity from the belief that it parallels conventional financial statements in its handling of investment data.

Unlike the other capital budgeting methods that we have discussed, the simple rate of return method does not focus on cash flows. Rather, it focuses on accounting net income. The approach is to estimate the revenues that will be generated by a proposed investment and then to deduct from these revenues all of the projected operating expenses associated with the project. This net income figure is then related to the required investment in the project, as shown in the following formula:

$$\text{Simple rate of return} = \cfrac{\overbrace{\begin{matrix}\text{Incremental} \\ \text{revenue}\end{matrix} - \begin{matrix}\text{Incremental expenses,} \\ \text{including depreciation}\end{matrix}}^{= \text{Net income}}}{\text{Initial investment*}} \quad (5)$$

Or, if the project is a cost reduction project, the formula becomes:

$$\text{Simple rate of return} = \frac{\text{Reduction in costs} - \text{Depreciation}}{\text{Initial investment*}}$$

* The investment should be reduced by any salvage from the sale of old equipment.

Example

Brigham Tea, Inc., is a processor of a nontannic acid tea product. The company is contemplating the purchase of equipment for an additional processing line. The additional processing line would increase revenues by $90,000 per year. Incremental cash operating expenses would be $40,000 per year. The equipment would cost $180,000 and have a 12-year life. No salvage value is projected.

Required:
1. Compute the simple rate of return. (Ignore income taxes.)
2. Compute the time-adjusted rate of return, and compare it to the simple rate of return. (Ignore income taxes.)

Solution:
1. By applying the formula for the simple rate of return found in equation (5), we can compute the simple rate of return to be 16.7 percent:

Simple rate of return

$$= \cfrac{\left[\begin{matrix}\$90,000\text{ incremental} \\ \text{revenues}\end{matrix}\right] - \left[\begin{matrix}\$40,000\text{ cash operating expenses} \\ +\$20,000\text{ depreciation}\end{matrix}\right] = \begin{matrix}\$30,000 \\ \text{net income}\end{matrix}}{\$180,000\text{ initial investment}}$$

Simple rate of return $= 16.7\%$

2. The rate computed in (1) above, however, is far below the time-adjusted rate of return of approximately 24 percent:

$$\text{Time-adjusted rate of return} = \frac{\$180,000}{\$50,000*} = \text{Factor of } 3.600$$

$$\text{Time-adjusted rate of return} = \begin{matrix}\text{Approximately 24\% from Table} \\ \text{14A–4 (in Chapter 14),} \\ \text{scanning across the nine-year line}\end{matrix}$$

* $30,000 net income + $20,000 depreciation = $50,000; or, the annual cash inflow can be computed as: $90,000 increased revenues − $40,000 cash expenses = $50,000.

Criticisms of the simple rate of return

The most damaging criticism of the simple rate of return method is that it does not consider the time value of money. A dollar received 10 years from now is viewed as being just as valuable as a dollar received today. Thus, the manager can be misled in attempting to choose between competing courses of action if the alternatives being considered have different cash flow patterns. For example, assume that project A has a high simple rate of return but yields the bulk of its cash flows many years from now. Another project, B, has a somewhat lower simple rate of return but yields the bulk of its cash flows over the next few years. The manager would probably choose project A over project B because of its higher simple rate of return; however, project B might in fact be a much better investment if the time value of money were considered.

A further criticism of the simple rate of return method is that it often proves to be misleading in its basic approach. The method is supposed to parallel conventional financial statements in its handling of data. Yet studies show that this parallelism is rarely present.[2] The problem is that conventional accounting practice tends to write costs off to expense very quickly. As a result, the net income and asset structure actually reflected on financial statements may differ substantially from comparable items in rate of return computations, where costs tend to be expensed less quickly. This disparity in the handling of data is especially pronounced in those situations where rate of return computations are carried out by nonaccounting personnel.

The choice of an investment base

In our examples, we have defined the investment base for simple rate of return computations to be the entire initial investment in the project under consideration [see formula (5)]. Actual practice varies between using the entire initial investment, as we have done, and using only the *average* investment over the life of a project. As a practical matter, which approach one chooses to follow is unimportant so long as the approach chosen is followed consistently among all projects and followed consistently from year to year. If the average investment is used, rather than the entire initial investment, then the resulting rate of return will be approximately doubled.

SUMMARY

Unless a company is a tax-exempt organization, such as a school or a governmental unit, income taxes should be considered in making capital budgeting computations. When income taxes are a factor in a company, tax-

---

[2] See National Association of Accountants, Research Report No. 35, "Return on Capital as a Guide to Managerial Decisions" (New York, December 1959), p. 64.

deductible cash expenditures must be placed on an after-tax basis by multiplying the expenditure by 1 minus the tax rate. Only the after-tax amount is used in determining the desirability of an investment proposal. Similarly, taxable cash inflows must be placed on an after-tax basis by multiplying the cash inflow by 1 minus the tax rate.

Although depreciation deductions do not involve a present outflow of cash in a company, they are valid expenses for tax purposes and as such affect income tax payments. Depreciation deductions shield income from taxation, resulting in decreased taxes being paid. This shielding of income from taxation is commonly called a depreciation tax shield. The savings in income taxes arising from the depreciation tax shield are computed by multiplying the depreciation deduction by the tax rate itself. Since accelerated methods of depreciation provide the bulk of their tax shield early in the life of an asset, they are superior to the straight-line method of depreciation, from a present value of tax savings point of view.

Preference decisions relate to ranking two or more investment proposals according to their relative desirability. This ranking can be performed using either the time-adjusted rate of return or the profitability index. The profitability index, which is the ratio of the present value of a proposal's cash inflows to the investment required, is generally regarded as the best way of making preference decisions when discounted cash flow is being used.

Instead of using discounted cash flow, some companies prefer to use either payback or the simple rate of return in evaluating investment proposals. Payback is determined by dividing a project's cost by the annual cash inflows that it will generate in order to find out how quickly the original investment can be recovered. The simple rate of return is determined by dividing a project's accounting net income either by the initial investment in the project or by the average investment over the life of the project. Both payback and the simple rate of return can be useful to the manager, so long as they are used with a full understanding of their limitations.

KEY TERMS FOR REVIEW

Accelerated Cost Recovery System (ACRS) A method of depreciation, required for income tax purposes, that abandons the concept of useful life and places all depreciable assets into one of five property classes.

After-tax benefit The amount of net cash inflow realized by an organization from a taxable cash receipt after income tax effects have been considered. The amount is determined by multiplying the cash receipt by the formula (1 − Tax rate).

After-tax cost The amount of net cash outflow resulting from a tax-deductible cash expense after income tax effects have been considered. The amount is determined by multiplying the cash expense by the formula (1 − Tax rate).

Depreciation tax shield The depreciation deductions on the income statement of an organization that result in a reduction of income tax payments. The reduction in tax payments is computed by multiplying the depreciation deduction by the tax rate itself.

Half-year convention A requirement under the Accelerated Cost Recovery System that only a half year's depreciation be taken in the year of purchase of an asset if the optional straight-line method is used in lieu of the ACRS tables.

Investment tax credit A direct reduction of income taxes that is allowed in the year of purchase of depreciable personal property (generally machinery and equipment) used in a trade of business. The reduction of income taxes is based on a percentage of the property's cost.

Optional straight-line method A method of computing depreciation deductions under ACRS that can be used by an organization in lieu of the ACRS tables.

Payback period The length of time that it takes for an investment project to recoup its own initial cost out of the cash receipts that it generates.

Profitability index The ratio of the present value of a project's cash inflows to the investment required.

Simple rate of return The rate of return promised by an investment project when the time value of money is not considered; it is computed by dividing a project's annual net income by the initial investment required.

APPENDIX: INCOME TAX EFFECTS ON PAYBACK AND SIMPLE RATE OF RETURN

As with the discounted cash flow methods of capital budgeting, many managers prefer to deal with the payback and the simple rate of return methods on a before-tax basis rather than on an after-tax basis. For this reason, the discussion of payback and simple rate of return in the chapter did not deal with income tax issues. Other managers do include tax considerations in payback and simple rate of return computations, however, so it is desirable at this point to extend our discussion of these methods to include tax matters.

We will use a single example to demonstrate the tax effects on both payback and simple rate of return. Assume the following data:

Quick-Stop, Inc., operates several convenience-food outlets throughout the West. The company would like to open a new outlet that would require an investment of $180,000 in depreciable equipment. The equipment would fall into the ACRS five-year property class. The company would depreciate the equipment by the optional straight-line method.[3] Quick-Stop, Inc., estimates that the new outlet would generate the following yearly revenues and expenses:

---

[3] For simplicity in computations, we will ignore the half-year convention in this example. In your problems, however, you should always observe the half-year convention unless the problem directs you to do otherwise.

Sales	$800,000
Less cost of merchandise	500,000
Contribution margin	300,000
Less fixed expenses:	
Selling expenses	170,000
Rent.	50,000
Depreciation	36,000*
Other cash expenses	4,000
Total fixed expenses	260,000
Income before taxes	40,000
Less income taxes (40%)	16,000
Net income	$ 24,000

* $180,000 ÷ 5 years = $36,000.

The company requires a payback of 2.5 years or less for a project to be acceptable. The company's cost of capital is 15 percent.

In the following two sections, we compute both the payback and the simple rate of return on this project.

Payback and tax effects

The formula for computing the payback period when taxes are considered is the same as was used earlier in the chapter, except that we must adjust the investment in the project for the investment credit which will be received. The revised formula is:

$$\text{Payback period} = \frac{\text{Investment required} - \text{Investment credit}}{\text{Net annual cash inflow}} \qquad (4a)$$

The payback period for Quick-Stop, Inc.'s new outlet would be:

$$\text{Payback period} = \frac{\$180,000 - \$14,400^*}{\$60,000\dagger}$$

$$= \underline{\underline{2.76 \text{ years}}}$$

* $180,000 × 8% investment credit = $14,400.
† $24,000 net income + $36,000 depreciation = $60,000 net annual cash inflow.

Since the payback period of 2.76 years is greater than the maximum 2.5 years allowed, the company should not open the outlet. Perhaps another location can be found that will generate a larger amount of revenue for the investment required and thus reduce the payback period.

Simple rate of return and tax effects

Only slight modifications are needed to the simple rate of return formulas used earlier in order to adjust the formulas for tax effects. The revised formulas are:

$$\text{Simple rate} \over \text{of return} = \frac{\begin{matrix} \text{Incremental} \\ \text{revenues} \end{matrix} - \begin{matrix} \text{Incremental expenses,} \\ \text{including depreciation} = \text{Net income} \\ \text{and income taxes} \end{matrix}}{\text{Initial investment} - \text{Investment credit}} \quad (5a)$$

Or, if the project is a cost reduction project, the formula becomes:

$$\text{Simple rate of return} = \frac{\text{Reduction in costs} - \text{Depreciation and taxes}}{\text{Initial investment} - \text{Investment credit}}$$

In the case of Quick-Stop, Inc.'s new outlet, the simple rate of return would be [from formula (5a) above]:

$$\text{Simple rate of return} = \frac{\$24,000}{\$180,000 - \$14,400*}$$
$$= 14.5\%$$

* $180,000 \times 8\%$ investment credit = $14,400.

Since the project's 14.5 percent simple rate of return is less than the company's 15 percent cost of capital, the new outlet should not be opened.

QUESTIONS

15–1.   Some organizations will always use capital budgeting techniques on a before-tax basis rather than on an after-tax basis. Name several such organizations.

15–2.   What is meant by after-tax cost, and how is the concept used in capital budgeting decisions?

15–3.   What is a depreciation tax shield, and how does it affect capital budgeting decisions?

15–4.   The three most widely used depreciation methods are straight line, sum-of-the-years' digits, and double-declining balance. Explain why a company might use one or more of these methods, instead of the Accelerated Cost Recovery System, for computing depreciation expense in its published financial statements.

15–5.   Why are accelerated methods of depreciation superior to the straight-line method of depreciation from an income tax point of view?

15–6.   Ludlow Company is considering the introduction of a new product line. Would an increase in the income tax rate tend to make the new investment more or less attractive? Explain.

15–7.   Assume that an old piece of equipment is sold at a loss. From a capital budgeting point of view, what two cash inflows will be associated with the sale?

15–8.   Assume that a new piece of equipment costs $30,000 and that the tax rate is 40 percent. Should the new piece of equipment be shown in the capital budgeting analysis as a cash outflow of $30,000, or should it be shown as a cash outflow of $18,000 [$30,000 $\times$ (1 − 40%)]? Explain.

15–9.   Assume that a company has cash operating expenses of $15,000 and depreciation expense of $10,000. Can these two items be added together and treated as one in a capital budgeting analysis, or should they be kept separate? Explain.

15–10. Distinguish between capital budgeting screening decisions and capital budgeting preference decisions. Why are preference decisions more difficult to make than screening decisions?

15–11. Why are preference decisions sometimes called *rationing* decisions?

15–12. How is the profitability index computed, and what does it measure?

15–13. What is the preference rule for ranking investment projects under the net present value method?

15–14. Can an investment with a profitability index of less than 1.00 be an acceptable investment? Explain.

15–15. What is the preference rule for ranking investment projects under time-adjusted rate of return?

15–16. What is meant by the term *payback period?* How is the payback period determined?

15–17. Sharp Company is considering the purchase of certain new equipment in order to sell a new product line. Expected yearly net income from the new product line is given below. From these data, compute the net annual cash inflow that would be used to determine the payback period on the new equipment.

Sales		$150,000
Less cost of goods sold		45,000
Gross margin		105,000
Less operating expenses:		
Advertising	$35,000	
Salaries and wages	50,000	
Depreciation	12,000	97,000
Net income		$ 8,000

15–18. In what ways can the payback method be useful to the manager?

15–19. What is the formula for computing the simple rate of return?

15–20. What is the major criticism of the payback and simple rate of return methods of making capital budgeting decisions?

EXERCISES

E15–1. a. Stoffer Company has hired a management consulting firm to review and make recommendations concerning Stoffer's organizational structure. The consulting firm's fee will be $100,000. What will be the after-tax cost of the consulting firm's fee if Stoffer's tax rate is 40 percent?

b. The Green Hills Riding Club has redirected its advertising toward a different sector of the market. As a result of this change in advertising, the club's annual revenues have increased by $50,000. If the club's tax rate is 30 percent, what is the after-tax benefit from the increased revenues?

c. The Golden Eagles Basketball Team has just installed an electronic scoreboard in its playing arena at a cost of $300,000. The scoreboard has an estimated eight-year useful life, a salvage value of $20,000, and it is in the ACRS five-year property class. What are the annual cash inflows resulting from the depreciation tax shield? Use the optional straight-line method and ignore salvage value in computing depreciation deductions. The team's tax rate is 40 percent.

d. Repeat (c) above, this time using the ACRS tables.

E15–2. Swick Company would like to purchase equipment that would allow the company to penetrate a new market. The equipment would cost $60,000 and would be in the ACRS three-year property class. The equipment would have a useful life of five years, after which it could be sold for its scrap value of $5,000. The equipment would be depreciated using the ACRS tables. (Remember, salvage value is not considered in computing depreciation deductions under ACRS.)

Use of the equipment would generate before-tax net cash receipts of $25,000 per year. The equipment would require extensive repairs in the fourth year that would cost $20,000. The company's tax rate is 40 percent, and its after-tax cost of capital is 10 percent.

Required: 1. Compute the net present value of the proposed investment in new equipment.
2. Would you recommend that the equipment be purchased? Explain.

E15–3. A company is considering two investment projects. Relevant cost and revenue information on the two projects is given below:

	Project A	Project B
Investment in automobiles	$30,000	—
Investment in working capital	—	$30,000
Net annual revenues or cost savings	7,500	7,500
Life of the project	6 years	6 years

The automobiles will have a $1,000 salvage value in six years. They fall into the ACRS three-year property class. Straight-line depreciation will be used. (Remember, salvage value is not considered in computing depreciation deductions under ACRS.) At the end of six years, the working capital can be released for investment elsewhere. The company requires an after-tax return of 12 percent on all investments. The tax rate is 40 percent.

Required: Compute the net present value of each investment project. (Round all dollar amounts to the nearest whole dollar.)

E15–4. (This exercise should be assigned only if Exercise 15–3 is also assigned.) Refer to the data in Exercise 15–3.

Required: 1. Compute the profitability index for each investment project.
2. Is an investment project with a profitability index of less than 1.0 an acceptable project? Explain.

E15–5. Press Publishing Company hires students from the local university to collate pages on various printing jobs. This collating is all done by hand, at a cost of $46,500 per year. A collating machine has just come on the market that could be used in place of the student help. The machine would cost $85,000 and have a 10-year useful life. It would require an operator at an annual cost of $18,000 and have annual maintenance costs of $3,500. The machine would need an overhaul in five years that would cost at least $10,000. Its salvage value in 10 years would be $7,500.

The company always uses straight-line depreciation for tax purposes and ignores salvage value in computing depreciation deductions. The machine would be in the ACRS five-year property class.

Press Publishing Company requires an after-tax return of 14 percent on all equipment purchases. The company's tax rate is 40 percent.

Required:
1. Determine the before-tax net annual cost savings that the new collating machine will provide.
2. Using the data from (1) and other data from the problem, compute the collating machine's net present value. Would you recommend that it be purchased?

E15–6. Information on four investment proposals is given below:

	Investment proposal			
	A	**B**	**C**	**D**
Investment required	$ (90,000)	$(100,000)	$ (70,000)	$(120,000)
Present value of cash inflows . .	126,000	90,000	105,000	160,000
Net present value	$ 36,000	$ (10,000)	$ 35,000	$ 40,000
Life of the project	5 years	7 years	6 years	6 years

Required:
1. Compute the profitability index for each investment proposal.
2. Rank the proposals in terms of preference.

E15–7. Various assets used by organizations are listed below.

Asset	Economic useful life
a. A printing press used by a newspaper	18 years
b. An office building used by an advertising agency	40 years
c. An automobile driven by a salesperson for a publishing company	6 years
d. A typewriter used by a real estate firm	8 years
e. A warehouse used by a manufacturing company to store raw materials.	35 years
f. Power lines used by an electric utility	25 years
g. Lab equipment used by a pharmaceutical company in cancer research	7 years
h. A pickup truck used by a construction firm	6 years
i. A drill press used in the manufacture of farm equipment.	10 years
j. A frozen food display case used by a food store	15 years

Required: Indicate the ACRS property class into which each of the assets above would fall. Also indicate the percentage investment credit (if any) to which each asset would be entitled.

E15–8. The Heritage Amusement Park would like to construct a new ride called the Sonic Boom, which the park management feels would be very popular. The ride would cost $450,000 to construct, and it would have a 10 percent salvage value at the end of its 15-year useful life. It is estimated that the following annual costs and revenues would be associated with the ride:

Ticket revenues	$250,000

Less operating expenses:

Maintenance	$40,000	
Salaries	90,000	
Depreciation	27,000	
Insurance	30,000	
Total operating expenses		187,000
Net income		$ 63,000

Required:
1. Assume that the Heritage Amusement Park will not construct a new ride unless the ride promises a payback period of six years or less. Would you recommend that the Sonic Boom ride be constructed? (Ignore income taxes.)
2. Compute the simple rate of return promised by the new ride. (Compute investment at initial cost, and ignore income taxes.) If the amusement park's before-tax cost of capital is 12 percent, would you recommend that the new ride be constructed?

E15–9. Martin Company is considering the purchase of a new piece of equipment. Relevant information concerning the equipment follows:

Purchase cost	$180,000
Annual cost savings that will be	
provided by the equipment	37,500
Life of the equipment	12 years
Cost of capital	14%

Required (ignore income taxes):
1. Compute the payback period for the equipment. If the company requires a minimum payback period of four years, would you recommend purchase of the equipment? Explain.
2. Compute the simple rate of return on the equipment. Use straight-line depreciation based on the equipment's useful life. Would you recommend purchase of the equipment? Explain.

E15–10. (Appendix) The Midvale Auto Service would like to install a car wash. The car wash would cost $75,000 and have a 12-year useful life. It would be in the ACRS 5-year property class, but the company would depreciate it by the optional straight-line method over a 12-year period, as allowed by the ACRS rules. The car wash would have no salvage value.

The company estimates that the following annual costs and revenues would be associated with the car wash:

Car wash revenues	$35,000

Less operating expenses:

Utilities	$5,000	
Maintenance	3,750	
Depreciation	6,250	
Total operating expenses		15,000
Income before taxes		20,000
Less income taxes (40%)		8,000
Net income		$12,000

(For simplicity in computations in this exercise, the half-year convention has been ignored in computing straight-line depreciation; you should ignore it, also.)

Required:
1. Compute the payback period on the car wash. Give full consideration to income tax effects. If the company requires a payback of four years, should the car wash be installed?

2. Compute the simple rate of return on the car wash. Again give full consideration to income tax effects.

PROBLEMS

P15–11. **Basic net present value analysis.** The Rapid Parcel Service has been offered a five-year contract to deliver mail and small parcels between army installations. In order to accept the contract, the company would have to purchase new delivery trucks at a cost of $200,000. Other data relating to the contract follow:

Net annual cash receipts (before taxes) from the contract	$65,000
Legal fees and permits (these would be one-time-only costs, incurred and expensed in year 1)	5,000
Salvage value of the trucks in five years	30,000

The trucks will be in the "light-duty truck" category for tax purposes. The company uses the ACRS tables and does not consider salvage value in computing depreciation deductions. The Rapid Parcel Service's after-tax cost of capital is 12 percent. Its tax rate is 40 percent.

Required: Compute the net present value of this investment opportunity. (Be sure that you assign the trucks to the right ACRS property class for tax purposes.) Round all dollar amounts to the nearest whole dollar. Would you recommend that the contract be accepted?

P15–12. **Straightforward net present value analysis.** The Crescent Drilling Company owns the drilling rights to several tracts of land on which natural gas has been found. The amount of gas on some of the tracts is somewhat marginal, and the company is unsure whether it would be profitable to extract and sell the gas which these tracts contain. One such tract is tract 410, on which the following information has been gathered:

Investment in equipment needed for extraction work.	$350,000
Working capital investment needed	90,000
Annual cash receipts from sale of gas, net of related cash operating expenses (before taxes)	100,000
Salvage value of equipment in 10 years	80,000
Cost of restoring land at completion of extraction work	50,000

The natural gas in tract 410 would be exhausted after 10 years of extraction work. The equipment above would be in the ACRS five-year property class. The company uses the ACRS tables and does not consider salvage value in computing depreciation deductions. The tax rate is 40 percent, and the company's after-tax cost of capital is 16 percent.

Required:
1. Compute the net present value of tract 410. (Round all dollar amounts to the nearest whole dollar.)
2. Would you recommend that the investment project be undertaken?

P15–13. **Various depreciation methods; net present value.** Vitro Company has been offered an eight-year contract to produce a key part for a government agency. The following costs and revenues would be associated with the contract:

Cost of special equipment	$200,000
Working capital needed to carry inventories	90,000
Annual revenues under the contract.	180,000
Annual out-of-pocket costs (excluding taxes)	130,000
Salvage value of the equipment in eight years	48,500

The equipment would be in the ACRS five-year property class. Vitro Company's after-tax cost of capital is 10 percent. The tax rate is 40 percent. Ignore salvage value in computing depreciation deductions.

Required:

1. Assume that the company uses the optional straight-line depreciation method. Determine the net present value of the proposed contract. (Round all dollar amounts to the nearest whole dollar.)
2. Assume that the company uses the ACRS tables to compute depreciation. Determine the net present value of the proposed contract. (Round all dollar amounts to the nearest whole dollar.) How do you explain the difference in rate of return between (1) and (2)?

P15–14. **Simple rate of return; payback.** Lugano's Pizza Parlor is considering the purchase of an automobile for delivery of pizza. The auto, fully equipped with racks and a warmer, would cost $12,000; it would have a five-year useful life and a $3,000 salvage value. The following additional information is available:

a. Mr. Lugano estimates that purchase of the auto would allow the pizza parlor to sell 3,000 more pizzas per year. The average price of a pizza is $7.50.
b. The cost of the ingredients in a pizza averages 20 percent of the selling price. Mr. Lugano estimates that incremental annual fixed costs associated with the new business would be: salary of a driver, $9,000; gas and maintenance, $3,600; and insurance, $400.
c. The pizza parlor uses straight-line depreciation on all assets and considers salvage value in computing depreciation deductions.
d. In order to purchase the auto, Mr. Lugano would have to withdraw funds from a savings certificate that yields a before-tax interest rate of 12 percent.

Required (ignore income taxes):

1. Prepare an income statement showing the net income each year from use of the auto. Use the contribution format.
2. Compute the simple rate of return promised by the auto. Should the auto be purchased?
3. Compute the payback period on the auto. If Mr. Lugano wants a two-year payback on any asset, should the auto be purchased?

P15–15. **Various depreciation methods; profitability index.** Stokes Company needs a new machine for use in its research and development program to replace old equipment that is worn out and inefficient. The old equipment has no salvage value. The company is considering two different machines as a replacement, only one of which can be purchased. Cost and other information on the two machines are given below:

	Machine 1	Machine 2
Cost of the machine	$21,000	$30,000
Annual savings in cash operating costs	9,000	12,000
Major repair and adjustment cost required in three years	5,000	7,500
Salvage value	3,000	6,000
Useful life of the machine	5 years	5 years
Depreciation method to be used	*	†

* Straight-line depreciation over the minimum time allowed for tax purposes.
† ACRS tables.

Stokes Company's after-tax cost of capital is 12 percent. The tax rate is 40 percent. Round all dollar amounts to the nearest whole dollar. Do not consider salvage value in computing depreciation deductions.

Required:

1. Compute the net present value of each machine. (Hint: Take care to assign the machines to the right property class for tax purposes.) Based on these data, which machine should be purchased?
2. Compute the profitability index for each machine. Based on these data, which machine should be purchased?

P15–16. Simple rate of return; payback. Regal Machines, Inc., places electronic games and other amusement devices in supermarkets and similar outlets. Regal is investigating the purchase and placement of a new electronic game called Mystic Invaders. The manufacturer will sell Regal 150 games for a total price of $180,000. Regal has determined the following additional information about the game:

a. The game would have a five-year useful life and only a negligible salvage value. The company uses straight-line depreciation.
b. The game would replace other games that are unpopular and generating little revenue. These other games would be sold in bulk for a $30,000 sale price.
c. Regal estimates that Mystic Invaders would generate incremental revenues of $200,000 per year (total for all 150 games). Incremental out-of-pocket costs each year would be (in total): maintenance, $50,000; and insurance, $10,000. In addition, Regal would have to pay a commission of 40 percent of total revenues to the supermarkets and other outlets in which the games were placed.
d. Regal's before-tax cost of capital is 14 percent.

Required (ignore income taxes):

1. Prepare an income statement showing the net income each year from Mystic Invaders. Use the contribution approach.
2. Compute the simple rate of return on Mystic Invaders. Should the game be purchased?
3. Compute the payback period on Mystic Invaders. If the company requires a payback period of three years or less, should the game be purchased?

P15–17. Simple rate of return; payback; time-adjusted rate of return. Honest John's Used Cars, Inc., has always hired students from the local university to wash the cars on the lot. Honest John is considering the purchase of an automatic car wash that would be used in place of the students. The following information has been gathered by Honest John's accountant in order to help Honest John make a decision on the purchase:

a. Payments to students for washing cars totals $15,000 per year at present.

b. The car wash would cost $21,000 installed, and it would have a 15-year useful life. Honest John uses straight-line depreciation on all assets. The car wash would have a negligible salvage value in 15 years.

c. Annual out-of-pocket costs associated with the car wash would be: wages of students to operate the wash, keep the soap bin full, and so forth, $6,300; utilities, $1,800; and insurance and maintenance, $900.

d. Honest John now earns a return of 20 percent before taxes on the funds invested in his inventory of used cars. He feels that he would have to earn an equivalent rate on the car wash in order for the purchase to be attractive.

Required (ignore income taxes):

1. Determine the annual savings that would be realized in cash operating costs if the car wash were purchased.

2. Compute the simple rate of return promised by the car wash. (Hint: Note that this is a cost reduction project.) Based on the simple rate of return, should the car wash be purchased?

3. Compute the payback period on the car wash. Honest John (who has a reputation for being somewhat of a nickel-nurser) will not purchase any equipment unless it has a payback of three years or less. Should the car wash be purchased?

4. Compute (to the nearest whole percent) the time-adjusted rate of return promised by the car wash. Based on this computation, does it appear that the simple rate of return would normally be an accurate guide in investment decisions?

P15–18. Net present value analysis. Fran's Travel Service is located in a large western city. The company, which specializes in recreational travel, is considering the purchase of a large bus to provide sight-seeing tours of the local area. A 40-passenger bus can be purchased for $85,000. The bus would be in the ACRS five-year property class. The company would depreciate the bus by use of the ACRS tables, and it would ignore salvage value in computing depreciation deductions. After ten years of use, the bus could be sold for $10,000.

The out-of-pocket costs of operating the bus for a single season are estimated as follows:

Salaries	$ 7,500
Maintenance	1,200
Fuel	10,000
Promotion	8,000
Licenses and taxes	900
Insurance	2,400
Total	$30,000

Fran's Travel Service estimates that the tours would average two full busloads a day for a 125-day season. The cost for a tour would be $4.50 per person. The company estimates that in six years the bus would require interior repairs and cleaning at a cost of $5,000.

Since bus tours of the area are new, Fran's Travel Service views the project as being somewhat risky. Thus, the company would require an after-tax return of 14 percent for the project to be acceptable. The tax rate is 40 percent.

Required:

1. Compute the net cash receipts (before taxes) each season from operating the bus.

2. By use of the net present value method, determine whether the bus should be purchased. (Round all dollar amounts to the nearest whole dollar.)

P15–19. **Comprehensive problem: Various depreciation methods; net present value.** Sandra Johnson, vice president of Dicer Products, Inc., would like to purchase a new experimental-type kiln for use in the manufacture of one of the company's products. Selected information about the kiln and its operation follows:

Cost of the kiln	$500,000
Annual savings provided by the kiln in cash operating costs (before taxes)	135,000
Cost of relining the kiln in four years	12,500
Salvage value of the kiln.	45,000
Estimated life of the kiln	6 years

The kiln falls into the ACRS three-year property class. An analysis that Ms. Johnson has just received from her staff indicates that the new kiln will not provide the 12 percent after-tax return required by the company. In doing the analysis, Ms. Johnson had instructed her staff to depreciate the kiln by the optional straight-line method and to use the allowable five-year life, since this was closer to the kiln's actual useful life of six years. The company does not consider salvage value in computing depreciation deductions. The tax rate is 40 percent.

Upon seeing the analysis done by Ms. Johnson's staff, the president of Dicer Products suggested that the analysis be redone using the shorter three-year life for the kiln and using the ACRS tables in computing depreciation. Ms. Johnson, surprised by this suggestion, stated, "What difference does it make how we compute depreciation? We have the same total depreciation either way. This new kiln simply doesn't meet our rate of return requirements."

Required:
1. Compute the net present value of the kiln using the optional straight-line method for computing depreciation. Depreciate the kiln over a five-year life, as instructed by Ms. Johnson.
2. Compute the net present value of the kiln using the ACRS tables and the minimum three-year life, as suggested by the president.
3. Explain to Ms. Johnson how the depreciation method used can affect the rate of return generated by an investment project.

P15–20. **Comprehensive problem: Simple rate of return; payback.** Bullrun Meatpackers is considering the purchase of two different items of equipment, as described below.

Machine A. A machine has come onto the market that would allow Bullrun Meatpackers to process and sell an item that was previously a waste product. The following information is available on the machine:

a. The machine would cost $350,000 and would have a 10 percent salvage value at the end of its 12-year useful life. The company uses straight-line depreciation and considers salvage value in computing depreciation deductions.
b. The new product from the machine would generate revenues of $500,000 per year. Variable manufacturing expenses would be 60 percent of sales.
c. Fixed expenses associated with the new product would be (per year): advertising, $36,000; salaries, $90,000; and insurance, $4,000.

Machine B. Another machine has come onto the market that would allow Bullrun Meatpackers to dispose of some antiquated, hand-operated wrapping equipment and replace it with a largely automatic wrapping process. The following information is available:

a. The new wrapping machine would cost $260,000 and would have negligible salvage value at the end of its 13-year useful life. The company would use straight-line depreciation on the new machine.

b. The old hand-operated wrapping equipment could be sold now for $10,000.

c. The new machine would provide substantial annual savings in cash operating costs. It would require an operator at an annual salary of $18,000, and it would require $4,500 in annual maintenance costs. The old hand-operated equipment costs $85,000 per year to operate.

Bullrun Meatpackers requires a return of 16 percent on all equipment purchases. Also, it will not purchase equipment unless the equipment has a payback period of 4.0 years or less.

Required (ignore income taxes):

1. For machine A:
    a. Prepare an income statement showing the expected net income each year from the new product. Use the contribution format.
    b. Compute the simple rate of return.
    c. Compute the payback period.
2. For machine B:
    a. Compute the simple rate of return.
    b. Compute the payback period.
3. Which machine, if either, should the company buy?

P15–21. **Preference ranking of investment projects.** Austin Company is investigating five different investment opportunities. The company's cost of capital is 10 percent. Information on the five investment projects under study is given below:

	Project number				
	1	2	3	4	5
Investment required	$(48,000)	$(36,000)	$(27,000)	$(45,000)	$(40,000)
Present value of cash inflows at a 10 percent discount rate	56,727	43,340	33,614	52,297	37,976
Net present value	$ 8,727	$ 7,340	$ 6,614	$ 7,297	$(2,024)
Life of the project	6 years	12 years	6 years	3 years	5 years
Time-adjusted rate of return	16%	14%	18%	19%	8%

Austin Company has limited funds available for investment and therefore can't accept all of the projects listed above.

Required:

1. Compute the profitability index for each investment project.
2. Rank the five projects according to preference , in terms of:
    a. Net present value.
    b. Profitability index.
    c. Time-adjusted rate of return.
3. Which ranking do you prefer? Why?

P15–22. **Uneven cash flows; net present value.** Emory Mines, Inc., owns the mineral rights to a tract of land that geologists estimate contains 83,750 tons of ore. Fred Mason, vice president in charge of operations, is trying to decide whether the company should purchase equipment and open a mine on the land. He has assembled the following information:

a. It would take eight years to extract all of the ore from the land. Extraction would proceed as follows:

Year	Tons mined and sold
1.	6,250
2.	12,500
3.	15,000
4–8	10,000

b. Equipment costing $750,000 would have to be purchased to extract the ore. The equipment would fall into the ACRS five-year property class and would have a 30 percent sale value in eight years. The company uses the ACRS tables but does not consider salvage value in computing depreciation deductions.

c. A working capital investment of $100,000 would be required in order to carry inventories and accounts receivable and to provide cash operating needs.

d. The selling price of the ore would be $80 per ton. Variable out-of-pocket costs for utilities, supplies, selling expenses, and so forth, would be $20 per ton.

e. Annual out-of-pocket fixed costs for salaries, insurance, and so forth, would be $400,000.

f. After all ore extraction had been completed, the company would have to spend $125,000 to restore the land to its natural condition.

g. Emory Mines' after-tax cost of capital is 14 percent. The tax rate is 40 percent.

Required:
1. Compute the before-tax net cash receipts each year from the mining and sale of the ore. (Do not include the cost to restore the land in this computation.)
2. Using the data from (1) and other data from the problem as needed, prepare a net present value analysis to determine whether the company should purchase the equipment and mine the ore. (Round all dollar amounts to the nearest whole dollar.) You may assume that for the company *as a whole,* there will be a positive taxable income in every year, so that a tax benefit would be realized from any operating losses from this mine.

P15–23. **Preference ranking of investment projects.** Oxford Company has limited funds available for investment and must ration the funds among five competing projects. Selected information on the five projects follows:

Project	Investment required	Net present value	Life of the project (years)	Time-adjusted rate of return (percent)
A	$160,000	$44,323	7	18
B	135,000	42,000	12	16
C	100,000	35,035	7	20
D	175,000	38,136	3	22
E.	150,000	(8,696)	6	8

Oxford Company's cost of capital is 10 percent. (The net present value above has been computed using a 10 percent discount rate.) The company wants your assistance in determining which project to accept first, which to accept second, and so forth.

Required: 1. Compute the profitability index for each project.
2. Rank the five projects in order of preference, in terms of:
   a. Net present value.
   b. Profitability index.
   c. Time-adjusted rate of return.
3. Which ranking do you prefer? Why?

P15–24. Equipment replacement; incremental-cost approach. Coral Lake Resort has recently purchased 40 new motorized golf carts for use on its exclusive golf course. The carts cost the resort considerably more than expected, and the manager of the resort is now wondering whether they will provide the 10 percent after-tax return that the resort's board of directors requires on all equipment purchases. The manager has asked you to make the necessary computations to determine whether the 10 percent return will be realized. You have determined the following information:

a. The new carts cost $150,000; they will have a $25,000 salvage value in 10 years.
b. The carts are in the ACRS five-year property class. The board of directors insists that the optional straight-line method be used to depreciate the carts. (Salvage value is not considered in computing depreciation deductions.)
c. The resort sold 40 old golf carts for a total sale price of $18,000. The old carts had a book value of $30,000 and would have been depreciated at a rate of $5,000 per year over the next six years. (These carts were purchased before the ACRS rules went into effect.)
d. The new carts are expected to generate net cash receipts (before taxes) of $15,000 each year above what the old carts would have generated.
e. According to the manufacturer, the motors in the new carts will have to be rewound in six years at a total cost of $12,500.
f. Coral Lake Resort's tax rate is 40 percent.

Required: Use discounted cash flow to determine whether the new golf carts will provide the required 10 percent rate of return. Use the incremental-cost approach. (Round all dollar amounts to the nearest whole dollar.)

P15–25. Comparison of the total-cost and incremental-cost approaches. Highland Dairies, Inc., is considering the purchase of a new milk separator. The separator would cost $120,000. After five years' use, the separator could be sold for $12,000, but this salvage value would not be considered in computing annual depreciation deductions. The new separator would provide considerable savings in annual operating costs, as shown below:

	Old separator	New separator
Salaries	$34,000	$24,000
Supplies	6,000	5,000
Utilities	8,000	6,000
Cleaning and maintenance	22,000	5,000
Total annual operating costs	$70,000	$40,000

If the new separator is purchased, the old separator will be sold for its present salvage value of $30,000. If the new separator is not purchased, the old separator will be used for five more years, then scrapped for a $2,000 salvage. The old separator's present book value is $50,000. The old separator is being depreciated by the straight-line method, with salvage value ignored for depreciation purposes. (It was purchased before the ACRS rules went into effect.) The new separator would be in the ACRS five-year property class and would be depreciated using the ACRS tables. It would qualify for the investment credit. If kept and used, the old separator would require repairs costing $40,000 in one more year. These repairs would be expensed in full. Highland Dairies, Inc.'s after-tax cost of capital is 18 percent. The tax rate is 40 percent.

Required:
1. Determine whether the new milk separator should be purchased, using the total-cost approach to discounted cash flow. Round to the nearest whole dollar.
2. Repeat (1) above, this time using the incremental approach to discounted cash flow.

P15-26. **Net present value; incremental-cost approach.** The Zeppo Company makes cookies for its chain of snack food stores. On January 2, 19x0, the company purchased a special cookie-cutting machine; this machine has been utilized for two years. Zeppo Company is considering the purchase of a newer, more efficient machine. If purchased, the new machine would be acquired on January 2, 19x2. The company expects to sell 300,000 dozen cookies in each of the next eight years. The selling price of the cookies is expected to average 50 cents per dozen.

Zeppo Company has two options: (1) continue to operate the old machine or (2) sell the old machine and purchase the new machine. The following information has been assembled to help decide which option is more desirable:

	Old machine	New machine
Original cost of machine at acquisition.	$100,000	$150,000
Useful life from date of acquisition	10 years	8 years
Expected annual cash operating expenses:		
Variable cost per dozen cookies	$ 0.20	$ 0.14
Total fixed costs	$ 15,000	$ 14,000
Depreciation method used for tax purposes	Straight line*	ACRS tables
Estimated cash (salvage) value of the machines:		
On January 2, 19x2	$ 35,000	—
On December 31, 19x9	$ 5,000	$ 20,000

* The old machine was purchased before the ACRS rules went into effect. Therefore, it should be depreciated at a uniform rate over the next eight years.

Zeppo Company does not recognize salvage value in computing annual depreciation deductions on equipment. The company is subject to an overall income tax rate of 40 percent. Assume that any gain or loss on the sale of equipment is treated as an ordinary tax item. Zeppo Company requires an after-tax return of 16 percent on all equipment purchases.

Required:
1. Compute the expected savings in cash operating costs (before taxes) each year from use of the new machine.
2. Using the data from (1) above and other data provided in the problem, compute the net present value of purchasing the new machine. Use the incremental-cost approach.
3. Assume that the quantitative differences are so slight between the two alternatives that Zeppo Company is indifferent to the two proposals. Identify and discuss the nonquantitative factors that are important to this decision and that the company should consider.

(CMA, adapted)

P15–27.   **Fast-food operation; effects of write-offs.**   B. Moss and R. Grassley have formed a corporation to franchise a quick food system for shopping malls. They have just completed experiments with the prototype machine that will serve as the basis for the operation, and they feel certain that the food it prepares will be well received by the public. However, because the system is new and has not yet been tried publicly, they have decided to conduct a pilot operation in a nearby mall. If it proves successful, they will aggressively market franchises for the system throughout the nation.

The income statements below represent their best estimates of income from the mall operation for the next four years. At the end of the four-year period, they intend to sell the pilot operation and concentrate on the sale and supervision of franchises for the system. Based on the income stream projected, they believe that the pilot operation can be sold for $120,000; the income tax liability from the sale will be $20,000.

	Year ending December 31			
	19x5	**19x6**	**19x7**	**19x8**
Sales	$140,000	$160,000	$190,000	$220,000
Less:				
Cost of goods sold	70,000	80,000	95,000	110,000
Wages	14,000	20,000	30,000	40,000
Supplies	3,000	3,300	3,400	4,200
Personal property taxes	1,000	1,200	1,600	1,800
Annual rental charge	12,000	12,000	12,000	12,000
Depreciation	10,000	10,000	10,000	10,000
Development costs	20,000	20,000	20,000	20,000
Total expenses	130,000	146,500	172,000	198,000
Net income before taxes	10,000	13,500	18,000	22,000
Income taxes at 40%	4,000	5,400	7,200	8,800
Net income after taxes	$ 6,000	$ 8,100	$ 10,800	$ 13,200

The following additional information is available on the pilot operation:

a.   The shopping mall requires tenants to sign a 10-year lease. Three years' rental is payable at the beginning of the lease period, with annual payments at the end of each of the next seven years (starting with the first year). The advance payment will apply to the last three years under the lease.

b.   The cost of building an operational machine for the pilot operation will be $110,000. The machine will have a salvage value of $10,000 at the end of its 10-year life. Straight-line depreciation will be used for statement purposes, and the ACRS tables will be used for tax purposes. Since the machine is involved in research and development, it falls into the ACRS three-year property class. The machine qualifies for the investment credit. Salvage value will be ignored in computing depreciation deductions.

c.   An earlier prototype machine cost $200,000 to develop and build in 19x3. It is not usable for commercial purposes. However, since it was the early basis for the system, it is being amortized against revenues at $20,000 per year. The same amount will be deducted for tax purposes. (The prototype machine does not qualify for ACRS treatment.)

Required: 1.   Compute the before-tax net cash inflow from operations for each year.
              2.   Moss and Grassley want to employ discounted cash flow techniques to determine

whether the pilot mall operation is a sound investment. Compute the net present value of the contemplated investment, using a minimum desired rate of return of 16 percent after taxes.   (CMA, adapted)

P15–28. (Appendix) **Simple rate of return; payback.** Top-Tone Health Centers is planning to open a new center in a western city. After careful study, Top-Tone's management has determined the following information relating to the new center:

a. Equipment needed to stock the center would cost $360,000. The equipment would be in the ACRS five-year property class, but it would be depreciated by the optional straight-line method over a 12-year period as allowed by the ACRS rules. (For purposes of this problem, ignore the half-year convention in computing depreciation deductions.) The equipment would have negligible salvage value at the end of its 15-year useful life.

b. Membership dues from patrons would total $250,000 per year.

c. Out-of-pocket costs for operating the center each year would be:

Advertising	$15,000
Salaries	90,000
Rent	18,000
Insurance	7,000
Utilities	20,000

d. Top-Tone's tax rate is 40 percent; its after-tax cost of capital is 12 percent; and it requires a payback period of five years or less on all new centers.

Required:

1. Prepare an income statement showing the net income (after taxes) expected each year from the new center.
2. Compute the simple rate of return promised by the new center. Should the new center be opened?
3. Compute the payback period on the new center. Based on this figure, should the new center be opened?

P15–29. (Appendix) **Simple rate of return; payback.** In the past, Marcraft Products has relied heavily on direct labor to manufacture its products. The small amount of equipment that the company has used is now worn out. Marcraft Products is considering the purchase of new, highly efficient equipment that would greatly reduce the company's operating costs. The company's production superintendent has started the following analysis:

Annual cash operating costs—present	$480,000
Annual cash operating costs—new machine	350,000
Reduction in cash operating costs	130,000
Less depreciation on the new machine	?
Income before taxes	?
Less income taxes (40%)	?
Net income from the new machine	$?

The production superintendent is unable to finish the analysis since he is unfamiliar with the ACRS depreciation rules. The new equipment would cost $300,000 and would have a negligible salvage value at the end of its 15-year useful life. It would fall into the ACRS five-year property class. The equipment would be depreciated by the optional straight-line method over a 12-year period as allowed by the ACRS rules. (For purposes of this problem, ignore the half-year convention in computing depreciation deductions.)

Marcraft Products' after-tax cost of capital is 14 percent. The company requires a payback period of four years or less on all investment outlays.

Required:
1. Complete the analysis above that has been started by the production superintendent.
2. Compute the simple rate of return on the new equipment. Should the equipment be purchased?
3. Compute the payback period on the new equipment. Does it meet the company's payback requirement?

P15–30. **(Appendix)** **Payback; simple rate of return; discounted cash flow.** Tune-Ups, Inc., operates a chain of service centers that provide tune-up work and minor repairs for automobiles. The company wants to open a new center and has found what appears to be an acceptable site. After careful study, the following estimates have been made of annual revenues and expenses for the new center:

Service revenue		$300,000
Less cost of parts.		90,000
Contribution margin		210,000
Less fixed expenses:		
Salaries	$85,000	
Rent.	20,000	
Depreciation	45,000*	
Other	10,000	
Total fixed expenses		160,000
Income before taxes		50,000
Less income taxes (40%)		20,000
Net income		$ 30,000

* For simplicity in computations, ignore the half-year convention in answering parts (1) and (2) below.

New equipment costing $225,000 would be purchased for the center. Since the equipment would be electronic in nature and therefore subject to rapid obsolescence, it would have no more than an eight year useful life and only a $37,500 scrap value. The equipment would be in the ACRS five-year property class. The company always uses the optional straight-line depreciation method and ignores salvage value in computing depreciation deductions.

The company's after-tax cost of capital is 16 percent. Also, the company will not open a new center unless the center has a payback period of three years or less.

Required:
1. What is the payback period of the new center? Should the center be opened?
2. What is the simple rate of return on the new center? Is the center an acceptable investment? Explain.
3. The president is uneasy about the results obtained by the simple rate of return and would like some further analysis done.
   a. Compute the net annual cash inflow (before taxes) promised by the new center.
   b. Using the data from (a) and other data from the problem as needed, determine the net present value of the new center. (Round all computations to the nearest whole dollar.) Will the center provide the 16 percent after-tax return required by the company?

PART 3

Selected
Topics for
Further Study

16 Service Department Cost Allocations

Learning objectives

After studying Chapter 16, you should be able to:

Explain what is meant by a service department, and explain why it is necessary to allocate service department costs to producing departments.

Allocate service department costs to other departments, using (1) the step method and (2) the direct method.

Explain why variable service department costs should be allocated separately from fixed service department costs, and give the allocation guidelines for each type of cost.

Explain why fixed service department costs should always be allocated in lump-sum amounts.

Prepare an allocation schedule involving several service departments and several using departments.

Define or explain the key terms listed at the end of the chapter.

As stated in Chapter 1, most organizations have one or more service departments that carry on critical auxiliary services for the entire organization. In this chapter, we look more closely at service departments and consider how their costs are handled for product costing and for other purposes.

THE NEED FOR COST ALLOCATION

Departments within a firm can be divided into two broad classes: (1) producing departments and (2) service departments. **Producing departments** would include those departments where work such as milling, assembly, and painting is done directly on the company's product(s). **Service departments** do not engage directly in production. Rather, they provide services or assistance that facilitate the activities of the producing departments. Examples of such services would include internal auditing, cafeteria, personnel, cost accounting, production planning, and medical facilities.

Although service departments do not engage directly in production, the costs that they incur are generally viewed as being part of the cost of finished units of product, the same as are materials, labor, and overhead.

The predetermined overhead rate revisited

In Chapters 3 and 10, we found that indirect costs such as lubricants, depreciation, and property taxes are allocated to finished products through manufacturing overhead by means of the predetermined overhead rate. Basically, the same procedure is used in the matter of service department costs. That is, before the output of a producing department is charged with overhead costs, the predetermined overhead rate is expanded to include a provision for the cost of services provided by the various service departments throughout the firm. This process, which involves an allocation of service department costs to producing departments and then a subsequent reallocation to finished products by means of the predetermined overhead rate, is illustrated in Exhibit 16–1 on the following page.

Perhaps this allocation process can be seen most clearly by referring to the flexible budget of a producing department. Recall from our discussion in Chapter 10 that the flexible budget forms the basis for computing predetermined overhead rates. Normally, allocated costs from service departments to producing departments are included directly in the flexible budgets of the producing department, as shown in Exhibit 16–2. By this process, producing departments are able to routinely consider service department costs in the computation of predetermined overhead rates. (Notice the computation of the predetermined overhead rate at the bottom of Exhibit 16–2.)

Equity in allocation

The major question that we must consider in this chapter is: How does the manager determine how much service department cost is to be allocated

690

EXHIBIT 16–1
Allocation of service department costs to finished products

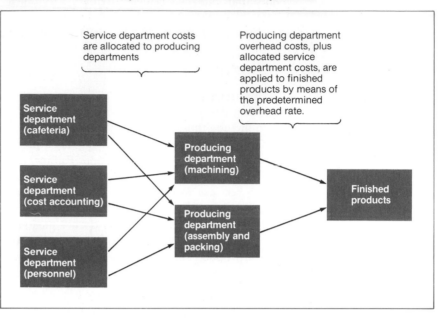

EXHIBIT 16–2
Flexible budget containing allocated service department costs

SUPERIOR COMPANY
Flexible Budget—Milling Department

Budgeted direct labor-hours 5,000

Overhead costs	Cost formula (per direct labor-hour)	Direct labor-hours		
		4,000	5,000	6,000
Variable costs:				
Indirect labor	$0.20	$ 800	$ 1,000	$ 1,200
Indirect material	0.10	400	500	600
Utilities	0.05	200	250	300
Allocation—cafeteria.	*0.15*	*600*	*750*	*900*
Total variable costs	$0.50	2,000	2,500	3,000
Fixed costs:				
Depreciation		4,000	4,000	4,000
Property taxes.		1,000	1,000	1,000
Allocation—cafeteria.		*1,500*	*1,500*	*1,500*
Allocation—personnel department		*2,000*	*2,000*	*2,000*
Total fixed costs		8,500	8,500	8,500
Total overhead costs		$10,500	$11,000	$11,500

Predetermined overhead rate = $\frac{\$11,000}{5,000 \text{ DLH}}$ = $2.20 per direct labor-hour to each of the various producing departments? This is an important question, since the amount of service department cost allocated to a particular department will affect that department's overhead rate and, hence, the amount of overhead cost borne by the products moving through the department. As we shall see, many factors must be considered if allocations are to be equitable between departments.

GUIDELINES FOR COST ALLOCATION

There are several basic guidelines to follow in service department cost allocation. These guidelines relate to (1) selecting the proper allocation base, (2) allocating the costs of interdepartmental services, (3) allocating costs by behavior, and (4) avoiding certain allocation pitfalls. These topics are covered in order in the following four sections.

Selecting allocation bases

Costs of service departments are allocated to producing departments by means of some type of **allocation base.** Allocation bases are selected that reflect as accurately as possible the benefits to be received by the various producing departments from the services involved. A number of such bases may be selected according to the nature of the services. Examples of allocation bases that are frequently used are presented in Exhibit 16–3.

EXHIBIT 16–3
Bases used in allocating service department costs

Service department	Base frequently used
Cafeteria	Number of employees
Medical facilities	Periodic analysis of cases handled; number of employees; hours worked
Materials handling	Hours of service; volume handled
Custodial services (building and grounds)	Measure of square footage occupied
Engineering	Periodic analysis of services rendered; direct labor-hours
Production planning and control	Periodic analysis of services rendered; direct labor-hours
Cost accounting	Labor-hours
Power	Measured usage (in kwh); capacity of machines
Personnel and employment	Number of employees; turnover of labor; periodic analysis of time spent
Receiving, shipping, and stores	Units handled; number of requisition and issue slips; square or cubic footage occupied
Factory administration	Total labor-hours
Maintenance	Machine-hours; total labor-hours (in order of preference)

We should note that the allocation bases being spoken of here are *not* for purposes of computing predetermined overhead rates; rather, they are for allocating service department costs *to* producing departments.

Once allocation bases have been chosen, they tend to remain unchanged for long periods of time. The selection of an allocation base represents a *major policy decision* that is normally reviewed only at very infrequent intervals or when it appears that some major inequity exists.

As we stated earlier, the way in which service department costs are allocated to producing departments will have a heavy influence on the way in which products are costed, so the selection of an allocation base is no minor decision. The criteria for making selections may include: (1) direct, traceable benefits from the service involved, as measured, for example, by the number of service orders handled; and (2) the extent to which space or equipment is made available to a department, as measured, for example, by the number of square feet occupied in a building. In addition to these criteria, the manager must take care to assure that allocations are clear and straightforward, since complex allocation computations run the risk of yielding negative returns. That is, if allocation computations become too complex, the cost of the computations may exceed any benefits that they are trying to bring about. Allocation formulas should be simple and easily understood by all involved, particularly by the managers to whom the costs are being allocated.

Interdepartmental services

Many service departments provide services for each other, as well as for producing departments. The cafeteria, for example, provides food for all employees, including those assigned to other service departments. In turn, the cafeteria may receive services from other service departments, such as from custodial services or from personnel. Services provided between service departments are known as **interdepartmental** or **reciprocal services.**

There are two approaches to handling the costs of services between departments. The first, called the **step method** provides for allocation of a department's costs to other service departments, as well as to producing departments, in a sequential manner. The second, called the **direct method,** ignores the costs of services between departments and allocates all service department costs directly to producing departments.

It is important to note that although most service departments are simply cost centers and thus generate no revenues, a few, such as the cafeteria, may charge employees or other outside parties for the services they perform. If a service department (such as the cafeteria) generates revenues, these revenues should be offset against the department's costs, and only the net amount of cost remaining after this offset should be allocated to other departments within the organization. In this manner, the other departments will not be required to bear costs for which the service department has already been reimbursed.

In the following two sections, we provide examples of both the step method and the direct method of making interdepartmental cost allocations.

Step method   In allocating by the step method, some sequence of allocation must be chosen. The sequence typically begins with the department that provides the greatest amount of service to other departments. After its costs have been allocated, the process continues, step by step, ending with the department providing the least amount of services to other service departments. This step procedure is illustrated graphically in Exhibit 16–4.

To provide a numerical example of the step method, assume the following data:

	Service departments		Producing departments		
	Factory administration	Custodial services	Machining	Assembly	Total
Overhead costs before allocation	$360,000	$84,000	$400,000	$250,000	$1,094,000
Labor-hours	—	10,000	70,000	20,000	100,000
Proportion of labor	—	1/10	7/10	2/10	10/10
Space occupied square feet	5,000	—	10,000	30,000	45,000
Proportion of space	1/9	—	2/9	6/9	9/9

The costs of factory administration are allocated first on a basis of labor-hours in other departments. The costs of custodial services are then allocated on a basis of square footage of space occupied. Allocations by the step method are shown in Exhibit 16–5 on page 695.

Several things should be noted from the data in this exhibit. First, note that the costs of the factory administration department are borne by another service department (custodial services) as well as by the producing departments. Also note that those factory administration costs that have been allocated to custodial services *are included with custodial services costs,* and that the total ($84,000 + $36,000 = $120,000) is allocated only to subsequent departments. That is, no part of custodial services' costs are reallocated back to factory administration, even though custodial services may have provided services to factory administration during the period. This is a key idea associated with the step method: After the allocation of a service department's costs has been completed, costs of other service departments are not reallocated back to it.

Finally, note from the exhibit that after the allocations have been made, all overhead costs are contained in the producing departments. These totals will form the basis for preparing predetermined overhead rates in the production departments for the period.

Direct method   The direct method is much simpler than the step method in that services between departments are ignored and all allocations are made directly to producing departments. Exhibit 16–6 illustrates the direct method, using the data provided earlier.

EXHIBIT 16–4
Graphical illustration—step method

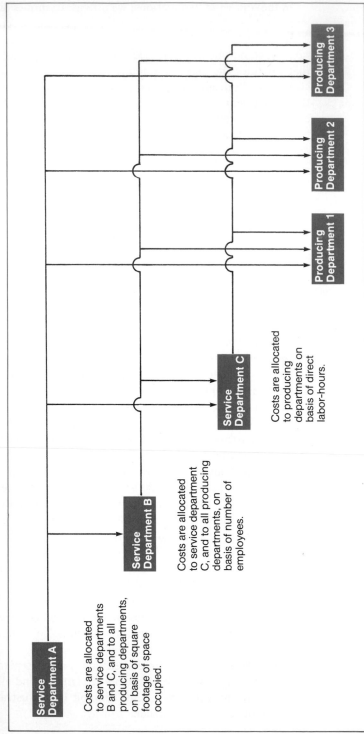

Service
Department A

Costs are allocated
to service departments
B and C, and to all
producing departments,
on basis of square
footage of space
occupied.

Service
Department B

Costs are allocated
to service department
C, and to all producing
departments, on
basis of number of
employees.

Service
Department C

Costs are allocated
to producing
departments on
basis of direct
labor-hours.

Producing
Department 1

Producing
Department 2

Producing
Department 3

EXHIBIT 16–5
Step method of allocation

	Service departments		Producing departments		
	Factory administration	Custodial services	Machining	Assembly	Total
Overhead costs before allocation	$ 360,000	$ 84,000	$400,000	$250,000	$1,094,000
Allocation:					
Factory administration costs (1/10, 7/10, 2/10).	(360,000)	36,000	252,000	72,000	
Custodial services costs (1/4, 3/4)*		(120,000)	30,000	90,000	
Total overhead after allocations	$ –0–	$ –0–	$682,000	$412,000	$1,094,000

* Based on 10,000 + 30,000 = 40,000.

Although simpler than the step method, the direct method is less accurate, since it ignores interdepartmental services. This can be a major defect in that predetermined overhead rates can be affected if the resulting errors in allocation are significant. In turn, incorrect overhead rates can lead to distorted product costs and to ineffective pricing. Even so, many firms use the direct method because of its ease of application.

Allocating costs by behavior

Whenever possible, service department costs should be separated into fixed and variable classifications and allocated separately. This approach is necessary to avoid possible inequities in allocation, as well as to provide more useful data for planning and control of departmental operations.

EXHIBIT 16–6
Direct method of allocation

	Service departments		Producing departments		
	Factory administration	Custodial services	Machining	Assembly	Total
Overhead costs before allocation	$ 360,000	$ 84,000	$400,000	$250,000	$1,094,000
Allocation:					
Factory administration costs (7/9, 2/9)*.	(360,000)		280,000	80,000	
Custodial services costs (1/4, 3/4)†.		(84,000)	21,000	63,000	
Total overhead after allocations	$ –0–	$ –0–	$701,000	$393,000	$1,094,000

* Based on 70,000 + 20,000 = 90,000.
† Based on 10,000 + 30,000 = 40,000.

Variable costs   Variable costs represent direct costs of providing services and will generally vary in total in proportion to fluctuations in the level of service consumed. Food cost in a cafeteria would be a variable cost, for example, and one would expect this cost to vary proportionately with the number of persons using the cafeteria over a given period of time. As a general rule, variable costs should be charged to consuming departments according to whatever activity base controls the incurrence of the cost involved. If, for example, the variable costs of a service department are incurred according to the number of machine-hours worked in producing departments, then they should be allocated to producing departments on that basis. By this means, the departments directly responsible for the incurrence of servicing costs are required to bear them in proportion to their actual usage of the service involved.

Technically, the assigning of variable servicing costs to consuming departments can more accurately be termed *charges* than allocations, since the service department is actually charging the consuming departments at some fixed rate per unit of service provided. In effect, the service department is saying, "I'll charge you X dollars for every unit of my service that you consume. You can consume as much or as little as you desire; the total charge you bear will vary proportionately."

Fixed costs   The fixed costs of service departments represent the cost of having long-run service capacity available. As such, these costs are most equitably allocated to consuming departments on a basis of *predetermined lump-sum amounts*. A **lump-sum allocation** of this type is based either on the peak-period or the long-run average servicing needs of the consuming departments. The logic behind this procedure is as follows:

When a service department is first established, some basic capacity is built into it according to the observed needs of the other departments that it will service. This basic capacity may reflect the peak-level needs of the other departments, or it may reflect their long-run average or "normal" servicing needs. Depending on how much servicing capacity is provided for, it will be necessary to make a commitment of resources to the servicing unit, which will be reflected in its fixed costs. It is generally felt that these fixed costs should be borne by the consuming departments whose servicing needs have made the creation of the service department necessary, and that the costs should be borne in proportion to the individual servicing needs that have been provided for. That is, if available capacity in the service department has been provided to meet the peak-period needs of consuming departments, then the fixed costs of the service department should be allocated in predetermined lump-sum amounts to consuming departments on this basis. If available capacity has been provided only to meet "normal" or long-run average needs, then the fixed costs should be allocated on this basis.

Once set, allocations should not vary from period to period, since they represent each consuming department's "fair share" of having a certain level of service capacity available and on line. The fact that a consuming department does not need a peak level or even a "normal" level of servicing every period is immaterial; if it requires such servicing at certain times, then the capacity to deliver it must be available. It is the responsibility of the consuming department to bear the cost of that availability.

To illustrate this idea, assume that Novak Company has just organized a maintenance department to service all machines in the cutting, assembly, and finishing departments. In determining the capacity that should be built into the newly organized maintenance department, the company recognized that the various producing departments would have the following peak-period needs for maintenance:

Department	Peak-period maintenance needs in terms of number of hours of maintenance work required	Percent of total hours
Cutting.	300	30
Assembly.	600	60
Finishing	100	10
	1,000	100

Therefore, in allocating the maintenance department fixed costs to the producing departments, 30 percent should be allocated to the cutting department, 60 percent to the assembly department, and 10 percent to the finishing department. These lump-sum allocations *will not change* from period to period unless there is some shift in servicing needs due to structural changes in the organization.

Pitfalls in allocating fixed costs

Rather than allocate fixed costs in predetermined lump-sum amounts, some firms allocate them by use of a *variable* allocation base. What's wrong with this practice? The answer is that it can create serious inequities between departments. The inequities will arise from the fact that the fixed costs allocated to one department will be heavily influenced by what happens in *other departments*.

To illustrate, assume that a company has one service department and two producing departments. The service department costs are all fixed. Contrary to good practice, the company allocates these fixed costs to the producing departments on the basis of machine-hours (a variable base). Selected cost data for two years are given below:

	Year 1	Year 2
Service department cost (all fixed)	$30,000 *(a)*	$30,000 *(a)*
Producing Department A machine-hours	15,000	15,000
Producing Department B machine-hours	15,000	5,000
Total machine-hours	30,000 *(b)*	20,000 *(b)*
Allocation rate per machine-hour, *(a) ÷ (b)*	$1.00	$1.50

Notice the Department A maintained a production level of 15,000 machine-hours in both years. On the other hand, Department B allowed its production to drop off from 15,000 hours in year 1 to only 5,000 hours in year 2. The service department costs that would have been allocated to the two departments over the two-year span are as follows:

```
Year 1:
    Department A: 15,000 hours at $1  . . . . . . .  $15,000
    Department B: 15,000 hours at $1  . . . . . . .   15,000
        Total cost allocated  . . . . . . . . . .   $30,000

Year 2:
    Department A: 15,000 hours at $1.50 . . . . . .  $22,500
    Department B: 5,000 hours at $1.50  . . . . . .    7,500
        Total cost allocated  . . . . . . . . . .   $30,000
```

In year 1, the two producing departments share the service department costs equally. In year 2, however, the bulk of the service department costs are allocated to Department A. This is not because of any increase in activity in Department A; rather, it is because of the inefficiency in Department B, which did not maintain its activity level during year 2. Even though Department A maintained the same level of efficiency in both years, the use of a variable allocation base has caused it to be penalized with a heavier cost allocation because of what has happened in *another* department.

This kind of inequity is almost inevitable when a variable allocation base is used to allocate fixed costs. The manager of Department A will be incensed at the inequity forced on his department, but he will feel powerless to do anything about it. The result will be a loss of confidence in the system and the accumulation of a considerable backlog of ill feeling.

Should actual or budgeted costs be allocated?

Should a service department allocate its *actual* costs to producing departments, or should it allocate its *budgeted* costs? The answer is that budgeted costs should be allocated. What's wrong with allocating actual costs? Allocating actual costs burdens the producing departments with the inefficiencies of the service department managers. If actual costs are allocated, then any lack of cost control on the part of the service department manager is simply buried in a routine allocation to other departments.

Any variance over budgeted costs should be retained in the service department and closed out against cost of goods sold along with producing department variances. Producing department managers rarely complain about being allocated a portion of service department costs, but they complain bitterly if they are forced to absorb service department inefficiencies.

Guidelines for allocating service department costs

By way of summary, we can note five key points to remember about allocating service department costs:

1. If possible, the distinction between variable and fixed costs in service departments should be maintained.
2. Variable costs should be allocated at the budgeted rate, according to whatever activity measure (machine-hours, direct labor-hours, number of employees) controls the incurrence of the cost involved.

    a. If the allocations are being made at the beginning of the year, they should be based on the budgeted activity level planned for the consuming departments. The allocation formula would be:

    $$\text{Budgeted rate} \times \text{Budgeted activity} = \text{Cost allocated}$$

    b. If the allocations are being made at the end of the year, they should be based on the actual activity level that has occurred during the year. The allocation formula would be:

    $$\text{Budgeted rate} \times \text{Actual activity} = \text{Cost allocated}$$

    Allocations made at the beginning of the year would be to provide data for computing predetermined overhead rates in the producing departments. Allocations made at the end of the year would be to provide data for comparing actual performance against planned performance.

3. Fixed costs represent the costs of having service capacity available. Where feasible, these costs should be allocated in predetermined lump-sum amounts. The lump-sum amount going to each department should be in proportion to the servicing needs that gave rise to the investment in the service department in the first place. (This might be either peak-period needs for servicing or long-run average needs.) Budgeted fixed costs, rather than actual fixed costs, should always be allocated.
4. If it is not feasible to maintain a distinction between variable and fixed costs in a service department, then the costs of the department should be allocated to consuming departments according to the base that appears to provide the best measure of benefits received.
5. Where possible, reciprocal services between departments should be recognized.

IMPLEMENTING THE ALLOCATION GUIDELINES

We will now show the implementation of these guidelines by the use of specific examples. We will focus first on the allocation of costs for a single department, and then develop a more extended example where multiple departments are involved.

Basic allocation techniques

The Silex Company has a maintenance department that provides maintenance service for two producing departments. Variable servicing costs are budgeted at 10 cents per machine hour. Fixed costs are budgeted at $10,000 per year. Budgeted and peak-period machine-hours are:

	Budgeted hours	Peak-period hours
Producing Department A	12,000	18,000
Producing Department B	10,000	12,000
Total hours	22,000	30,000

The amount of service department cost that would be allocated to each producing department at the beginning of the year would be:

	Producing Department A	Producing Department B
Variable cost allocation:		
$0.10 \times 12,000$ hours	$1,200	
$0.10 \times 10,000$ hours		$1,000
Fixed cost allocation:		
60%* $\times$ $10,000	6,000	
40%* $\times$ $10,000		4,000
Total cost allocated	$7,200	$5,000

* 18,000 hours ÷ 30,000 hours = 60%.
  12,000 hours ÷ 30,000 hours = 40%.

As explained earlier, these allocations would be placed on the flexible budgets of the producing departments, to be included in the computation of predetermined overhead rates.

At the end of the year, the management of Silex Company may want to make a second allocation, this time based on actual activity, in order to compare actual performance for the year against planned performance. Assume that year-end records show that actual service department costs for the year were: variable, $2,760; and fixed, $10,800. We will assume that one producing department worked more hours during the year than planned and that the other one worked less hours than planned.

	Budgeted hours (see above)	Actual hours
Producing Department A	12,000	14,000
Producing Department B	10,000	9,000
Total hours	22,000	23,000

The amount of service department cost chargeable to each producing department would be:

	Producing Department A	Producing Department B
Variable cost allocation:		
$0.10 × 14,000 hours	$1,400	
$0.10 × 9,000 hours		$ 900
Fixed cost allocation:		
60% × $10,000	6,000	
40% × $10,000		4,000
Total cost allocated	$7,400	$4,900

Notice that the variable cost is allocated according to the budgeted rate (10 cents) times the *actual activity,* and that the fixed cost is allocated according to the original budgeted amount. As stated in the guidelines earlier, allocations are always based on budgeted rates and amounts in order to avoid the passing on of inefficiency from one department to another. Thus, a portion of the year-end service department costs will not be allocated, as shown below:

	Variable	Fixed
Total costs incurred	$2,760	$10,800
Costs allocated above	2,300*	10,000
Spending variance—not allocated	$ 460	$ 800

* $0.10 × 23,000 actual hours = $2,300.

These variances will be closed out to cost of goods sold, along with the manufacturing variances for the year.

An extended example

The Proctor Company has three service departments, building maintenance, cafeteria, and inspection. The company also has two producing departments, shaping and assembly. The service departments provide services to each other, as well as to the producing departments. Types of costs in the service departments and bases for allocation are:

Department	Type of cost	Base for allocation
Building maintenance	Fixed costs	Square footage occupied
Cafeteria	Variable costs	Number of employees
	Fixed costs	10% to inspection, 40% to shaping, and 50% to assembly
Inspection	Variable costs	Direct labor-hours
	Fixed costs	70% to shaping and 30% to assembly

The Proctor Company allocates service department costs by the step method in the following order:

1. Building maintenance.
2. Cafeteria.
3. Inspection.

Assume the following budgeted cost and operating data for 19x1:

Department	Variable cost	Fixed cost
Building maintenance	—	$15,000
Cafeteria	$100 per employee	40,000
Inspection	$0.12 per direct labor-hour	20,000

Department	Number of employees	Direct labor-hours	Square footage of space occupied (square feet)
Building maintenance.	6*	—	500
Cafeteria	9*	—	1,000
Inspection	30	—	500
Shaping	240	40,000	4,750
Assembly.	355	56,000	8,750
Total	640	96,000	15,500

* Although there are employees in both of these service departments, under the step method costs are only allocated *forward*—never backward. For this reason, the costs of the cafeteria will be allocated *forward* on the basis of the number of employees in the inspection, shaping, and assembly departments.

Using these data, cost allocations to the producing departments would be as shown in Exhibit 16–7. To save space, we have placed the producing departments' flexible budget overhead costs on the exhibit and computed the predetermined overhead rates there.

No distinction made between fixed and variable costs

As stated in the guidelines given earlier, in some cases it may not be feasible to maintain a distinction between fixed and variable service department costs. We noted there that in such cases the costs should be allocated to producing departments according to the base that appears to provide the best measure of benefits received. An example of such an allocation was given earlier in Exhibit 16–5, where we first illustrated the step method. The reader may wish to turn back and review this example before reading on.

Should all costs be allocated?

For product costing purposes, the general rule is that all service department costs that are incurred as a result of specific services provided to producing departments should be allocated back to these departments and added to product costs via the predetermined overhead rate. The only time when this general rule is not followed is in those situations where, in the view of manage-

EXHIBIT 16-7

THE PROCTOR COMPANY
Beginning-of-Year Cost Allocations for Purposes of
Preparing Predetermined Overhead Rates

	Building maintenance	Cafeteria	Inspection	Shaping	Assembly
Variable costs to be allocated	–0–	$ 62,500	$ 8,520	—	—
Cafeteria allocation at $100 per employee:					
30 employees × $100.	—	(3,000)	3,000	—	—
240 employees × $100.	—	(24,000)	—	$ 24,000	—
355 employees × $100.	—	(35,500)	—	—	$ 35,500
Inspection allocation at $0.12 per direct labor-hour:					
40,000 DLH × $0.12.	—	—	(4,800)	4,800	—
56,000 DLH × $0.12.	—	—	(6,720)	—	6,720
Total	–0–	–0–	–0–	28,800	42,220
Fixed costs to be allocated	$15,000	40,000	20,000		
Building maintenance allocation at $1 per square foot:*					
1,000 square feet × $1.	(1,000)	1,000	—	—	—
500 square feet × $1.	(500)	—	500	—	—
4,750 square feet × $1.	(4,750)	—	—	4,750	—
8,750 square feet × $1.	(8,750)	—	—	—	8,750
Cafeteria allocation:†					
10% × $41,000	—	(4,100)	4,100	—	—
40% × $41,000	—	(16,400)	—	16,400	—
50% × $41,000	—	(20,500)	—	—	20,500
Inspection allocation:‡					
70% × $24,600	—	—	(17,220)	17,220	—
30% × $24,600	—	—	(7,380)	—	7,380
Total	–0–	–0–	–0–	38,370	36,630
Total allocated costs	$ –0–	$ –0–	$ –0–	67,170	78,850
Other flexible budget costs at the planned activity level				220,000	340,000
Total overhead costs				$287,170	$418,850 *(a)*
Budgeted direct labor-hours				40,000	56,000 *(b)*
Predetermined overhead rate, (a) ÷ (b)				$7.18	$7.48

* Square footage of space . . . . 15,500 square feet
  Less building maintenance space . . . . 500 square feet
  Net space for allocation. . . . . 15,000 square feet

$$\frac{\text{Building maintenance fixed costs, \$15,000}}{\text{Net space for allocation, 15,000 square feet}} = \$1 \text{ per square foot}$$

† Cafeteria fixed costs $40,000
  Allocated from building maintenance 1,000
  Total cost to be allocated $41,000

Allocation percentages are given in the problem.

‡ Inspection fixed costs $20,000
  Allocated from building maintenance 500
  Allocated from cafeteria. 4,100
  Total cost to be allocated $24,600

Allocation percentages are given in the problem.

ment, allocation would result in an undesirable behavioral response from producing departments. There are some servicing costs, for example, that are clearly beneficial to producing departments but which these departments may not utilize as fully as they should, particularly in times of cost economizing. Systems design is a good example of such a cost. Utilization of systems design services may be very beneficial to producing departments in terms of improving overall efficiency, reducing waste, and assuring adherence to departmental policies. But if a department knows that it will be charged for the systems design services it uses, it may be less inclined to take advantage of the benefits involved, especially if the department is feeling some pressure to trim costs. In short, the departmental manager may opt for the near-term benefit of avoiding a direct charge, in lieu of the long-term benefit of reduced waste and greater efficiency.

To avoid discouraging use of a service that is helpful to the entire organization, some firms do not charge for the service at all. These managers feel that by making such services a "free" commodity, departments will be more inclined to take full advantage of their benefits.

Other firms take a somewhat different approach. They agree that charging according to usage may discourage utilization of such services as systems design, but they argue that such services should not be free. Instead of providing free services, these firms take what is sometimes called a **retainer fee approach.** Each department is charged a flat amount each year, regardless of how much or how little of the service it utilizes. The thought is that if a department knows that it is going to be charged a certain amount for systems design services, *regardless of usage,* then it will probably utilize the services at least to that extent.

Beware of sales dollars as an allocation base

Over the years, sales dollars have been a favorite allocation base for service department costs. One reason is that sales dollars are simple, straightforward, and easy to work with. Another reason is that people tend to view sales dollars as being a measure of well-being, or "ability to pay," and, hence, as being a measure of how extensively costs can be absorbed from other parts of the organization.

Unfortunately, sales dollars often constitute a very poor allocation base, for the reason that sales dollars vary from period to period, whereas the costs being allocated are often largely *fixed* in nature. As discussed earlier, if a variable base is used to allocate fixed costs, inequities can result between departments since the costs being allocated to one department will depend in large part on what happens in *other* departments. For example, a letup in sales effort in one department will shift allocated costs off that department and onto other, more productive departments. In effect, the departments putting forth the best sales efforts are penalized in the form of higher allocations, simply because of inefficiencies elsewhere that are beyond their control. The result is often bitterness and resentment on the part of the managers of the better departments.

Consider the following situation encountered by the author:

A large men's clothing store has one service department and three sales departments—suits, shoes, and accessories. The service department's costs are allocated to the three sales departments according to sales dollars. A recent period showed the following allocation:

	Suits	Shoes	Accessories	Total
Sales by department.	$78,000	$18,000	$24,000	$120,000
Percentage of total sales	65%	15%	20%	100%
Allocation of service department costs, based on percentage of total sales.	$19,500	$ 4,500	$ 6,000	$ 30,000

In a following period, the manager of the suit department launched a very successful program to expand sales to over $100,000 in his department. Sales in the other two departments remained unchanged. Total service department costs also remained unchanged, but the allocation of these costs changed substantially, as shown below:

	Suits	Shoes	Accessories	Total
Sales by department	$108,000	$18,000	$24,000	$150,000
Percentage of total sales	72%	12%	16%	100%
Allocation of service department costs, based on percentage of total sales	$ 21,600	$ 3,600	$ 4,800	$ 30,000
Increase (or decrease) from prior allocation	2,100	(900)	(1,200)	—

The manager of the suit department complained very bitterly that as a result of his successful effort to expand sales in his department, he was being forced to carry a larger share of the service department costs. On the other hand, the managers of the departments that showed no improvement in sales were being relieved of a portion of the costs that they had been carrying. Yet there had been no change in the amount of services provided for any department.

The manager of the suit department viewed the increased service department cost allocation to his department as a penalty for his outstanding performance, and he wondered whether his efforts had really been worthwhile after all in the eyes of top management.

Sales dollars should be used as an allocation base only in those cases where there is a direct causal relationship between sales dollars and the service department costs being allocated. In those situations where service department costs are fixed in nature, they should be allocated according to the guidelines discussed earlier in the chapter.

SUMMARY

Service departments are organized to provide some needed service in a single, centralized place, rather than to have all units within the organization provide the service for themselves. Although service departments do not engage directly in production, the costs that they incur are vital to the overall productive effort and therefore are properly included as part of the cost of a company's finished products.

Service department costs are charged to producing departments by an allocation process. In turn, the producing departments include the allocated costs within their flexible budgets, from which predetermined overhead rates are computed for product costing purposes.

In order to avoid inequity in allocations, variable and fixed service department costs should be allocated separately. The variable costs should be allocated according to whatever activity measure controls their incurrence. The fixed costs should be allocated in predetermined lump-sum amounts according to either the peak-period or the long-run average servicing needs of the consuming departments. Budgeted costs, rather than actual costs, should always be allocated, in order to avoid the passing on of inefficiency between departments. Any variances between budgeted and actual service department costs should be kept within the service departments for analysis purposes, then written off to cost of goods sold, along with the manufacturing variances.

KEY TERMS FOR REVIEW

Allocation base Any measure of activity (such as labor-hours, number of employees, or square footage of space) that is used to charge service department costs to other departments.

Direct method The allocation of all of a service department's costs straight to producing departments without recognizing services provided to other service departments.

Interdepartmental services Services provided between service departments. See *reciprocal services.*

Lump-sum allocation The charging of fixed service department costs in predetermined amounts based on either the peak-period or the long-run average servicing needs of consuming departments.

Producing department A department engaged directly in the manufacture of units of product.

Reciprocal services Services provided between service departments.

Retainer fee approach A method of allocating service department costs in which other departments are charged a flat amount each period regardless of usage of the service involved.

Service department A department that provides support or assistance to producing departments and which does not engage directly in the production of units of product.

Step method The allocation of a service department's costs to other service departments as well as to producing departments in a sequential manner. The sequence starts with the service department that provides the greatest amount of service to other departments.

QUESTIONS

16–1. What is the difference between a service department and a producing department? Give several examples of service departments.

16–2. In what way are service department costs similar to such costs as lubricants, utilities, and factory supervision?

16–3. "Units of product can be costed equally well with or without allocations of service department costs." Do you agree? Why or why not?

16–4. How do service department costs enter into the final cost of finished products?

16–5. What criteria are relevant to the selection of allocation bases for service department costs?

16–6. What are interdepartmental service costs? How are such costs allocated to other departments under the step method?

16–7. How are service department costs allocated to other departments under the direct method?

16–8. If a service department produces revenues of some type, how do these revenues enter into the allocation of the department's costs to other departments?

16–9. What guidelines should govern the allocation of fixed service department costs to producing and other departments? The allocation of variable service department costs?

16–10. "A variable base should never be used in allocating fixed service department costs to producing departments." Explain.

16–11. Why might it be desirable not to allocate some service department costs to producing departments?

16–12. What is the purpose of the retainer fee approach to cost allocation?

EXERCISES

E16–1. Arbon Manufacturing Company has three service departments and two producing departments. Selected data on the five departments are presented below:

| | Service departments | | | Producing departments | | |
	X	Y	Z	1	2	Total
Overhead costs	$84,000	$67,800	$36,000	$50,000	$90,000	$327,800
Number of employees.	80	60	240	600	300	1,280
Square feet of space occupied	3,000	12,000	10,000	20,000	70,000	115,000
Machine-hours	—	—	—	10,000	30,000	40,000

The company allocates service department costs by the step method in the following order: X (number of employees), Y (space occupied), and Z (machine-hours). The company makes no distinction between fixed and variable service department costs.

Required: Using the step method, make the necessary allocations of service department costs.

E16–2. Refer to the data for Arbon Manufacturing Company in Exercise 16–1. Assume that the company allocates service department costs by the direct method, rather than by the step method.

Required: Assuming that the company uses the direct method, how much overhead cost would be chargeable to each producing department? Show computations in good form.

E16–3. Hannibal Steel Company has a transport services department that provides trucks to haul ore from the company's mine to its two steel mills—the Northern Plant and the Southern Plant. The transport services department has sufficient capacity to handle peak-period needs of 140,000 tons per year for the Northern Plant and 60,000 tons per year for the Southern Plant. At this level of activity, budgeted costs for the transport services department total $350,000 per year, consisting of $0.25 per ton variable cost and $300,000 fixed cost.

During 19x8, the coming year, 120,000 tons of ore are budgeted to be hauled for the Northern Plant and 60,000 tons of ore for the Southern Plant.

Required: Compute the amount of transport services cost that should be allocated to each plant at the beginning of 19x8, for purposes of computing predetermined overhead rates. (The company allocates variable and fixed costs separately.)

E16–4. Refer to the data in Exercise 16–3. Assume that it is now the end of 19x8. During the year, the transport services department actually hauled the following amounts of ore for the two plants: Northern Plant, 130,000 tons; Southern Plant, 50,000 tons. The transport services department incurred $364,000 in cost during the year, of which $54,000 was variable cost and $310,000 was fixed cost.

Management wants end-of-month service department cost allocations in order to compare actual performance against planned performance.

Required:
1. Determine how much of the $54,000 in variable cost should be allocated to each plant.
2. Determine how much of the $310,000 in fixed cost should be allocated to each plant.
3. Will any of the $364,000 in transport services cost not be allocated to the plants? Explain.

E16–5. Reed Company operates a medical services unit for its employees. The variable costs of the medical services unit are allocated to using departments on a basis of the number of employees in each department. Budgeted and actual data for 19x8 are given below:

	Variable costs—19x8	
	Budgeted	**Actual**
Medical services unit	$100 per employee	$105 per employee

	Number of employees			
	Maintenance department	**Producing departments**		
		1	**2**	**3**
Budgeted number of employees.	20	200	700	300
Actual number of employees	21	198	704	295

Required: Determine the amount of medical services cost that should be allocated to each of the four using departments at the end of 19x8, for purposes of comparing actual performance against planned performance.

E16–6. Hofstra Products, Inc., has two service departments, personnel and engineering. All of the costs in these departments are fixed. The company allocates the costs of the service departments to other departments on the following bases:

Department	Basis for allocation	
Personnel.	Number of employees, as follows:	
	Engineering	30 employees
	Cutting department	120 employees
	Assembly department	150 employees
Engineering	Direct-labor hours, as follows:	
	Cutting department	200,000 DLH
	Assembly department	300,000 DLH

Fixed costs in the personnel department total $100,000 per year; fixed costs in the engineering department total $180,000 per year. The company uses the step method in making cost allocations.

Required: 1. Allocate the personnel department costs to other departments.
2. Allocate the engineering department costs to other departments.

E16–7. Lacey's Department Store allocates its fixed administrative expenses to departments on a basis of sales dollars. During 19x1, the fixed administrative expenses totaled $150,000. These expenses were allocated as follows:

	Department				
	1	**2**	**3**	**4**	**Total**
Total sales—19x1	$150,000	$375,000	$525,000	$450,000	$1,500,000
Percentage of total	10%	25%	35%	30%	100%
Allocation (based on above percentages)	$ 15,000	$ 37,500	$ 52,500	$ 45,000	$ 150,000

During 19x2, Department 2 launched a very successful sales campaign to double its sales volume. The sales level in all other departments remained unchanged. As a result, 19x2 sales data appeared as follows:

	Department				
	1	**2**	**3**	**4**	**Total**
Total sales—19x2	$150,000	$750,000	$525,000	$450,000	$1,875,000
Percentage of total	8%	40%	28%	24%	100%

Fixed administrative expenses of the store remained unchanged during 19x2 at $150,000.

Required: 1. Using sales dollars as an allocation base, show the allocation of the fixed administrative expenses among the four departments for 19x2.

2. Compare your allocation from (1) above to the 19x1 allocation found in the main body of the problem. As the sales manager of Department 2, how would you feel about the allocation that has been charged to you for 19x2?

3. Comment on the usefulness of sales dollars as an allocation base.

PROBLEMS

P16–8. **Various allocation methods.** Northstar Company consists of a Machine Tools Division and a Special Products Division. The company has a maintenance department that services the equipment in both divisions. The costs of operating the maintenance department are budgeted at $80,000 per month plus $0.50 per machine-hour. The maintenance department has a capacity to service 200,000 machine-hours per month—based on peak needs of 130,000 machine-hours per month in the Machine Tools Division and 70,000 machine-hours per month in the Special Products Division.

For October, the Machine Tools Division has estimated that it will operate at a 90,000 machine-hours level of activity and the Special Products Division has estimated that it will operate at a 60,000 machine-hours level of activity.

Required:
1. At the beginning of October, how much maintenance department cost should be allocated to each division for flexible budget planning purposes?

2. Assume that it is now the end of October. Cost records in the maintenance department show that actual fixed costs for the month totaled $85,000 and that actual variable costs totaled $78,000. Due to labor unrest and an unexpected strike, the Machine Tools Division worked only 60,000 machine-hours during the month. The Special Products Division also worked 60,000 machine-hours, as planned. How much of the actual maintenance department costs for the month should be allocated to each division? (Management uses these end-of-month allocations to compare actual performance against planned performance.)

3. Refer to the data in (2) above. Assume that the company follows the practice of allocating *all* maintenance department costs each month to the divisions in proportion to the actual machine-hours recorded in each division for the month. On this basis, how much cost would be allocated to each division for October?

4. What criticisms can you make of the allocation method used in (3) above?

5. If managers of producing departments know that fixed service department costs are going to be allocated on a basis of long-run average usage of the service involved, what will be their probable strategy as they report their estimate of this usage to the company's budget committee? As a member of top management, what would you do to neutralize any such strategies?

P16–9. **Beginning- and end-of-year allocations.** Decker Company has only one service department—a cafeteria, in which meals are provided for employees in the company's milling and finishing departments. The costs of the cafeteria are all paid by the company as a fringe benefit to its employees. These costs are allocated to the milling and finishing departments on a basis of meals served in each department. Cost and other data relating to the cafeteria and to the milling and finishing departments for 19x1 are provided below.

Cafeteria:

	19x1	
	Budget	**Actual**
Variable costs for food	$300,000*	$384,000
Fixed costs	200,000	215,000

* Budgeted at $2 per meal served.

Milling and finishing departments:

		Number of meals served	
			19x1	
	Peak-period needs	Budget	Actual
Milling department	140,000	100,000	120,000
Finishing department	60,000	50,000	40,000
Total meals.	200,000	150,000	160,000

The company allocates variable and fixed costs separately.

Required:
1. Assume that it is the beginning of 19x1. An allocation of cafeteria costs must be made to the milling and finishing departments to assist in computing predetermined overhead rates. How much of the budgeted cafeteria cost above would be allocated to each department?
2. Assume that it is now the end of 19x1. Management would like data to assist in comparing actual performance against planned performance in the cafeteria and in the other departments.
   a. How much of the actual cafeteria costs above would be allocated to the milling department and to the finishing department?
   b. Would any portion of the actual cafeteria costs not be allocated to the other departments? If so, compute the amount that would not be allocated, and explain why it would not be allocated.

P16–10. **Cost allocation: Step method versus direct method.** The Ashley Company has budgeted costs in its various departments as follows for the coming year:

Factory administration	$270,000
Custodial services	68,760
Personnel	28,840
Maintenance	45,200
Machining—overhead	376,300
Assembly—overhead	175,900
Total cost	$965,000

The company allocates service department costs to other departments, in the order listed below. Bases for allocation are to be chosen from the following:

	Number of employees	Total labor-hours	Square feet of space occupied	Direct labor-hours	Machine-hours
Factory administration	12	—	5,000	—	—
Custodial services	4	3,000	2,000	—	—
Personnel	5	5,000	3,000	—	—
Maintenance	25	22,000	10,000	—	—
Machining	40	30,000	70,000	20,000	70,000
Assembly	60	90,000	20,000	80,000	10,000
	146	150,000	110,000	100,000	80,000

Machining and assembly are producing departments; the other departments all act in a service capacity. The company does not make a distinction between fixed and variable service department costs; allocations are made to using departments according to the base that appears to provide the best measure of benefits received (as discussed in the text).

Required:

1. Allocate service department costs to using departments by the step method. Then compute predetermined overhead rates in the producing departments, using a machine-hours basis in machining and a direct labor-hours basis in assembly.

2. Repeat (1) above, this time using the direct method. Again compute predetermined overhead rates in machining and assembly.

3. Assume that the company doesn't want to bother with allocating service department costs, but simply wants to compute a single plantwide overhead rate based on total overhead costs (both service department and producing department) divided by total direct labor-hours. Compute the appropriate overhead rate.

4. Suppose that the company wants to bid on a job during the year that will require machine and labor time as follows:

	Machine-hours	Direct labor-hours
Machining department	190	25
Assembly department.	10	75
Total hours	200	100

Using the overhead rates computed in (1), (2), and (3) above, compute the amount of overhead cost that would be assigned to the job if the overhead rates were developed using the step method, the direct method, and the plantwide method.

P16–11. **Cost allocations among divisions.** Precision Plastics maintains its own computer center to service the needs of its three divisions. It has been assigning the costs of the computer center to the three divisions on a basis of the number of lines of print prepared for each division during the month.

In July 19x6, Ms. Benz, manager of Division A, came to the company's controller seeking an explanation as to why her division had been charged a larger amount for computer service in July than in June, although her division had used the computer less in July. During the course of the discussion, the following data were referred to by the controller:

		Division		
	Total	A	B	C
Peak-period needs:				
Lines of print	250,000	100,000	30,000	120,000
Percentage of total	100%	40%	12%	48%
June actual results:				
Lines of print	200,000	80,000	20,000	100,000
Percentage of total	100%	40%	10%	50%
Computer cost assigned	$85,000	$34,000	$8,500	$42,500
July actual results:				
Lines of print	150,000	75,000	30,000	45,000
Percentage of total	100%	50%	20%	30%
Computer cost assigned	$83,750	$41,875	$16,750	$25,125

"You see," said Mr. Hansen, the controller, "the computer center has large amounts of fixed costs that continue regardless of how much the computer is used. We have built into the computer center enough capacity to handle the divisions' peak-period needs, and this cost must be absorbed by someone. I know it hurts, but the fact is that during July your division received a greater share of the computer's output than it did during June; therefore, it has been allocated a greater share of the cost."

Ms. Benz was unhappy with this explanation. "I still don't understand why I would be charged more for the computer, when I used it less," she said. "There has to be a better way to handle all of this."

Required:
1. Is there any merit in Ms. Benz's complaint? Explain.
2. By use of the high-low method, determine the monthly cost of the computer in terms of variable rate per line of print and total fixed cost.
3. Reallocate the computer center costs for June and July in accordance with the cost allocation principles discussed in the chapter. Allocate the variable and fixed costs separately.

P16–12. **Cost allocation in a hospital; step method.** Pleasant View Hospital has three service departments—food services, administrative services, and X-ray services. The costs of these departments are allocated by the step method, using the bases and in the order shown below:

Service department	Costs incurred	Base for allocation
Food services	Variable	Meals served
	Fixed	Full capacity needs—meals
Administrative services	Variable	Files processed
	Fixed	10% X-ray services, 20% Outpatient Clinic, 30% OB Care, and 40% General Hospital
X-ray services	Variable	X rays taken
	Fixed	Analysis of long-term usage

Estimated cost and operating data for all departments in the hospital for the forthcoming month are presented in the following table:

	Food services	Admin. services	X-ray services	Outpatient Clinic	OB Care	General Hospital	Total
Variable costs	$ 73,150	$ 6,800	$38,100	$11,700	$ 14,850	$ 53,400	$198,000
Fixed costs	48,000	33,040	59,520	26,958	99,738	344,744	612,000
Total costs	$121,150	$39,840	$97,620	$38,658	$114,588	$398,144	$810,000
Files processed	—	—	1,500	3,000	900	12,000	17,400
X rays taken	—	—	—	1,200	350	8,400	9,950
Long-term average X-ray needs	—	—	—	1,560	360	10,080	12,000
Meals served	—	1,000	500	—	7,000	30,000	38,500
Peak-period needs—meals	—	1,000	500	—	8,500	40,000	50,000

All billing in the hospital is done through the Outpatient Clinic, OB Care, or General Hospital. The hospital's administrator wants the costs of the three service departments allocated to these three billing centers.

Required: Prepare the cost allocation desired by the hospital administrator. Include under each billing center the direct costs of the center, as well as the costs allocated from the service departments.

P16–13. End-of-year cost allocations. Mangum Products, Inc., operates a power services department that provides electrical power to other departments within the company. Budgeted costs in the power services department for 19x3 total $162,000, of which $150,000 represents fixed costs.

Power consumption in the company is measured in kilowatt-hours (kwh) used. Data relating to budgeted and actual usage of power are given below for 19x3, along with data relating to the peak-period needs in the various departments (in kwh):

	Service departments		Producing departments		
	Engineering	Maintenance	Shaping	Assembly	Total
Budgeted for 19x3	10,000	30,000	252,000	108,000	400,000
Used during 19x3	10,800	21,600	234,000	93,600	360,000
Peak-period needs	20,000	50,000	300,000	130,000	500,000

During 19x3, the power services department incurred $12,600 in variable costs and $153,000 in fixed costs. The department allocates variable and fixed costs separately.

Required:
1. Assume that management makes an allocation of power costs at the end of each year to the four departments listed above in order to compare actual performance against budgeted performance. How much of the power services department's actual costs for 19x3 would be allocated to each department?
2. Will any portion of the year's power costs not be allocated to the four departments? Explain.

P16–14. Step method versus direct method. "I can't understand what's happening here," said Mike Holt, president of Severson Products, Inc. "We always seem to bid too high on jobs that require a lot of labor time in the finishing department, and we always seem to get every job we bid on that requires a lot of machine time in the milling department. Yet we don't seem to be making much money on those milling department jobs. I wonder if the problem is in our overhead rates."

Severson Products manufactures high-quality wood products to customers' specifications. Some jobs take a large amount of machine work in the milling department, and other jobs take a large amount of hand finishing work in the finishing department. In addition to the milling and finishing departments, the company has three service departments. The costs of these service departments are allocated to other departments *in the order listed below*. (For each service department, use the allocation base that provides the best measure of service provided, as discussed in the chapter.)

	Total labor-hours	Square feet of space occupied	Number of employees	Machine-hours	Direct labor-hours
Cafeteria	16,000	12,000	25	—	—
Custodial services . . .	9,000	3,000	40	—	—
Maintenance	15,000	10,000	60	—	—
Milling	30,000	40,000	100	160,000	20,000
Finishing	100,000	20,000	300	40,000	70,000
	170,000	85,000	525	200,000	90,000

Budgeted overhead costs in each department for the current year are as follows (no distinction is made between variable and fixed costs):

Cafeteria	$ 320,000*
Custodial services	65,400
Maintenance	93,600
Milling	416,000
Finishing	166,000
Total budgeted costs	$1,061,000

* This represents the amount of cost subsidized by the company.

The company has always allocated service department costs to the producing departments (milling and finishing) using the direct method of allocation, because of its simplicity.

Required:

1. Allocate service department costs to using departments by the step method. Then compute predetermined overhead rates in the producing departments for the current year, using a machine-hours basis in the milling department and a direct labor-hours basis in the finishing department.

2. Repeat (1) above, this time using the direct method. Again compute predetermined overhead rates in the milling and finishing departments.

3. Assume that during the current year the company bids on a job that requires machine and labor time as follows:

	Machine-hours	Direct labor-hours
Milling department	90	40
Finishing department	30	260
Total hours	120	300

a. Determine the amount of overhead that would be assigned to the job if the company used the overhead rates developed in (1) above. Then determine the amount of overhead that would be assigned to the job if the company used the overhead rates developed in (2) above.

b. Explain to the president why the step method would provide a better basis for computing predetermined overhead rates than the direct method.

P16–15.   **Cost allocation in a hotel; step method.**   The Coral Lake Hotel has three service departments—grounds and maintenance, general administration, and laundry. The costs of these departments are allocated by the step method, using the bases and in the order shown below:

Grounds and maintenance:
  Fixed costs—allocated on a basis of square feet of space occupied.
General administration:
  Variable costs—allocated on a basis of number of actual employees.
  Fixed costs—allocated 20% to laundry, 14% to convention center, 36% to food services, and 30% to lodging.
Laundry: ·
  Variable costs—allocated on a basis of number of items processed.
  Fixed costs—allocated on a basis of peak-period needs for items processed.

Cost and operating data for all departments in the hotel for a recent month are presented in the table below:

	Grounds and main- tenance	General adminis- tration	Laundry	Conven- tion center	Food services	Lodging	Total
Variable costs	–0–	$ 915	$13,725	–0–	$ 48,000	$ 36,450	$ 99,090
Fixed costs	$17,500	12,150	18,975	$28,500	64,000	81,000	222,125
Total overhead costs	$17,500	$13,065	$32,700	$28,500	$112,000	$117,450	$321,215
Square feet of space	2,000	2,500	3,750	15,000	6,250	97,500	127,000
Number of employees.	9	5	10	5	25	21	75
Laundry items processed.	—	—	—	1,000	5,250	40,000	46,250
Peak-period needs—items processed	—	—	—	1,500	6,500	42,000	50,000

All billing in the hotel is done through the convention center, food services, and lodging. The hotel's general manager wants the costs of the three service departments allocated to these three billing centers.

Required: Prepare the cost allocation desired by the hotel's general manager. Include under each billing center the direct costs of the center, as well as the costs allocated from the service departments.

P16–16.   **Service department allocations; predetermined overhead rates; unit costs.**   Apsco Products has two service departments and two producing departments. The service departments are medical services and maintenance. Estimated monthly cost and operating data for the coming year are given below. These data have been prepared for purposes of computing predetermined overhead rates in the producing departments.

	Medical services	Mainte-nance	Producing A	Producing B
Direct labor cost.	—	—	$ 30,000	$ 40,000
Maintenance labor cost	—	$ 5,000	—	—
Direct materials	—	—	50,000	80,000
Maintenance materials.	—	7,536	—	—
Medical supplies.	$ 3,630	—	—	—
Miscellaneous overhead costs	7,500	6,000	104,000	155,000
Total costs	$11,130	$18,536	$184,000	$275,000
Direct labor-hours	—	—	6,000	10,000
Number of employees:				
Currently employed	3	8	38	64
Long-run employee needs	3	10	60	80
Floor space occupied— square feet	800	1,500	8,000	12,000

The Apsco Company allocates service department costs to producing departments for product costing purposes. The step method is used, starting with medical services. Allocation bases for the service departments are:

Department	Cost	Base for allocation
Medical services	Variable	Currently employed workers
	Fixed	Long-run employee needs
Maintenance	Variable	Direct labor-hours
	Fixed	Square footage of floor space occupied

The behavior of various costs is shown below:

	Medical services	Mainte-nance
Maintenance labor cost.	—	V
Maintenance materials	—	V
Medical supplies	V	—
Miscellaneous overhead costs	F	F

V = Variable.
F = Fixed.

Required:
1. Show the allocation of the service department costs for the purpose of computing predetermined overhead rates.
2. Compute the predetermined overhead rate to be used in each of the producing departments (overhead rates are based on direct labor-hours).
3. Assume that production in Department B is planned at 20,000 units for the month. Compute the planned cost of one unit of product in Department B.

P16–17. **Determining allocation base: credit services.** Columbia Company is a regional office supply chain with 26 independent stores. Each store has been responsible for its own credit and collections. The assistant manager in each store is assigned the responsibility for credit activities, including the collection of delinquent accounts, because the stores do not need a full-time employee assigned to credit activities. The company has experienced a sharp rise in uncollectibles during the last two years. Corporate management has decided to establish a collections department in the home office to be responsible for the collection function company-wide. The home office of Columbia Company will hire the necessary full-time personnel. The size of this department will be based on the historical credit activity of all the stores.

The new centralized collections department was discussed at a recent management meeting. Management is having a difficult time deciding what method to use in charging the costs of the new department to the stores, since the type of service involved is somewhat unique. The controller favors using a predetermined or standard rate for charging the costs to the stores. The predetermined rate would be based on budgeted costs. The vice president of sales has a strong preference for an actual cost charging system.

In addition to these two methods of charging costs, possible bases for allocating collection charges to the stores was also discussed. The controller has identified the following four measures of services (allocation bases) that could be used:

a. Total dollar sales.
b. Average number of past-due accounts.
c. Number of uncollectible accounts written off.
d. One twenty-sixth of the cost to each of the stores.

The executive vice president has stated that he would like the accounting department to prepare a detailed analysis of the two charging methods and the four service measures (allocation bases).

Required:
1. Evaluate the two proposed methods—(1) predetermined (standard) rate and (2) actual cost—which could be used to charge the individual stores with the costs of the new collections department. Evaluate each method in terms of *(a)* practicality of application and ease of use, and *(b)* cost control.
2. For each of the four measures of services (allocation bases) identified by the company's controller:
    a. Discuss whether the service measure (allocation base) is appropriate to use in this situation.
    b. Identify the behavioral problems, if any, that could arise as a consequence of adopting the service measure (allocation base).   (CMA, adapted)

17 "How Well Am I Doing?"— Financial Statement Analysis

Learning objectives

After studying Chapter 17, you should be able to:

Explain the need for and limitations of financial statement analysis.

Prepare financial statements in comparative form and explain how such statements are used.

Place the balance sheet and the income statement in common-size form and properly interpret the results.

State what ratios are used to measure the well-being of the common stockholder and give the formula for each ratio.

Tell what is meant by the term *financial leverage* and explain how financial leverage is measured.

Enumerate the ratios used to analyze working capital and the well-being of creditors and give the formula for each ratio.

Define or explain the key terms listed at the end of the chapter.

No matter how carefully prepared, all financial statements are essentially historical documents. They tell what *has happened* during a particular year or series of years. The most valuable information to most users of financial statements, however, concerns what probably *will happen* in the future. The purpose of financial statement analysis is to assist statement users in *predicting the future* by means of comparison, evaluation, and trend analysis.

THE IMPORTANCE OF STATEMENT ANALYSIS

Virtually all users of financial data have concerns that can be resolved to some degree by the predictive ability of statement analysis. The stockholders are concerned, for example, about such matters as whether they should hold or sell their stocks, whether the present management group should remain or be replaced, and whether the company should have their approval to sell a new offering of senior debt. The creditors are concerned about such matters as whether income will be sufficient to cover the interest due on their bonds or notes, and whether prospects are good for their obligations to be paid at maturity. The managers are concerned about such matters as dividend policy, the availability of funds to finance future expansion, and the probable future success of operations under their leadership.

The thing about the future that statement users are most interested in predicting is profits. It is profits, of course, that provide the basis for an increase in the value of the stockholder's stock and that encourage the creditor to risk his or her money in an organization. And it is largely profits that make future expansion possible. The dilemma is that profits are uncertain. For this reason, one must have various analytical tools to assist in interpreting the key relationships and trends that serve as a basis for judgments of potential future success. Without financial statement analysis, the story that key relationships and trends have to tell may remain buried in a sea of statement detail.

In this chapter, we consider some of the more important ratios and other analytical tools that analysts use in attempting to predict the future course of events in business organizations.

Importance of comparisons

Financial statements are not only historical documents, but they are also essentially static documents. They speak only of the events of a single period of time. However, statement users are concerned about more than just the present; they are also concerned about the *trend of events* over time. For this reason, financial statement analysis directed toward a single period is of limited usefulness. The results of financial statement analysis for a particular period are of value only when viewed in *comparison* with the results of other periods and, in some cases, with the results of other firms. It is only through comparison that one can gain insight into trends and make intelligent judgments as to their significance.

Unfortunately, comparisons between firms within an industry are often made difficult by differences in accounting methods in use. For example, if one firm values its inventories by LIFO and another firm values its inventories by average cost, then direct dollar-for-dollar comparisons between the two firms may not be possible. In such cases, comparisons can still be made, but they must focus on data in a broader, more relative sense. Although the analytical work required here may be tougher, it is often necessary if the manager is to have any data available for comparison purposes.

The need to look beyond ratios

There is a tendency for the inexperienced analyst to assume that ratios are sufficient in themselves as a basis for judgments about the future. Nothing could be further from the truth. The experienced analyst realizes that the best-prepared ratio analysis must be regarded as tentative in nature and never as conclusive in itself. Ratios should not be viewed as an end, but rather they should be viewed as a *starting point,* as indicators of what to pursue in greater depth. They raise many questions, but they rarely answer any questions by themselves.

In addition to looking at ratios, the analyst must look at other sources of data in order to make judgments about the future of an organization. The analyst must look, for example, at industry trends, at technological changes that are anticipated or that are in process, at changes in consumer tastes, at regional and national changes in economic factors, and at changes that are taking place within the firm itself. A recent change in a key management position, for example, might rightly serve as a basis for much optimism about the future, even though the past performance of the firm (as shown by its ratios) may have been very mediocre.

STATEMENTS IN COMPARATIVE AND COMMON-SIZE FORM

As stated above, few figures appearing on financial statements have much significance standing by themselves. It is the relationship of one figure to another and the amount and direction of change from one point in time to another that are important in financial statement analysis. How does the analyst key in on significant relationships? How does the analyst dig out the important trends and changes in a company? Three analytical techniques are in wide-spread use:

1. Dollar and percentage changes on statements.
2. Common-size statements.
3. Ratios.

All three techniques are discussed in following sections.

Dollar and percentage changes on statements

A good beginning place in financial statement analysis is to put statements in comparative form. This consists of little more than putting two or more years' data side by side. Statements cast in comparative form will underscore movements and trends and may give the analyst many valuable clues as to what to expect in the way of financial and operating performance in the future.

An example of financial statements placed in comparative form is given in Exhibits 17–1 and 17–2. These are the statements of Brickey Electronics Company, a hypothetical firm. The data on these statements are used as a basis for discussion throughout the remainder of the chapter.

EXHIBIT 17–1

BRICKEY ELECTRONICS COMPANY
Comparative Balance Sheets
December 31, 19x1 and 19x2
(dollars in thousands)

	19x2	19x1	Increase (decrease) Amount	Increase (decrease) Per-cent
Assets				
Current assets:				
Cash	$ 1,000	$ 2,520	$(1,520)	(60.3)
Accounts receivable, net	6,000	4,000	2,000	50.0
Inventory	8,000	10,000	(2,000)	(20.0)
Prepaid expenses	500	200	300	150.0
Total current assets	15,500	16,720	(1,220)	(7.3)
Property and equipment:				
Land	4,000	4,000	–0–	–0–
Buildings and equipment, net.	9,500	6,000	3,500	58.3
Total property and equipment.	13,500	10,000	3,500	35.0
Total assets	$29,000	$26,720	$ 2,280	8.5
Liabilities and Stockholders' Equity				
Current liabilities:				
Accounts payable	$ 5,800	$ 4,000	$ 1,800	45.0
Accrued payables	900	400	500	125.0
Notes payable, short term.	300	600	(300)	(50.0)
Total current liabilities	7,000	5,000	2,000	40.0
Long-term liabilities:				
Bonds payable, 8%	7,500	8,000	(500)	(6.3)
Total liabilities	14,500	13,000	1,500	11.5
Stockholders' equity:				
Preferred stock, $100 par, 6%,				
$100 liquidation value	2,000	2,000	–0–	–0–
Common stock, $10 par	6,000	6,000	–0–	–0–
Additional paid-in capital	1,000	1,000	–0–	–0–
Total paid-in capital	9,000	9,000	–0–	–0–
Retained earnings	5,500	4,720	780	16.5
Total stockholders' equity	14,500	13,720	780	5.7
Total liabilities and stockholders' equity . . .	$29,000	$26,720	$ 2,280	8.5

724

EXHIBIT 17–2

BRICKEY ELECTRONICS COMPANY
Comparative Income Statements and Reconciliation
of Retained Earnings
For the Years Ended December 31, 19x1 and 19x2
(dollars in thousands)

	19x2	19x1	Increase (decrease) Amount	Percent
Sales	$52,000	$48,000	$4,000	8.3
Cost of goods sold	36,000	31,500	4,500	14.3
Gross margin	16,000	16,500	(500)	(3.0)
Operating expenses:				
Selling expenses	7,000	6,500	500	7.7
Administrative expenses	5,875	6,350	(475)	(7.5)
Total operating expenses	12,875	12,850	25	0.2
Net operating income	3,125	3,650	(525)	(14.4)
Interest expense	625	700	(75)	(10.7)
Net income before taxes	2,500	2,950	(450)	(15.3)
Less income taxes (40%)	1,000	1,180	(180)	(15.3)
Net income	1,500	1,770	$ (270)	(15.3)
Dividends to preferred stockholders, $6 per share (see Exhibit 17–1)	120	120		
Net income remaining for common stockholders	1,380	1,650		
Dividends to common stockholders ($1 per share)	600	600		
Net income added to retained earnings	780	1,050		
Retained earnings, beginning of year	4,720	3,670		
Retained earnings, end of year	$ 5,500	$ 4,720		

Horizontal analysis Comparison of two or more years' financial data is known as **horizontal analysis.** Horizontal analysis is greatly facilitated by showing changes between years in both dollar *and* percentage form, as has been done in Exhibits 17–1 and 17–2. Showing changes in dollar form helps the analyst to zero in on key factors that have affected profitability or financial position. For example, observe in Exhibit 17–2 that sales for 19x2 were up $4 million over 19x1, but that this increase in sales was more than negated by a $4.5 million increase in cost of goods sold.

Showing changes between years in percentage form helps the analyst to gain *perspective* and to gain a feel for the *significance* of the changes that are taking place. One would have a different perspective of a $1 million increase in sales if the prior year's sales were $2 million than he would if the prior year's sales were $20 million. In the first situation, the increase would be 50 percent—undoubtedly a significant increase for any firm. In the second situation, the increase would be only 5 percent—perhaps a reflection of just normal growth.

Trend percentages   Horizontal analysis of financial statements can also be carried out by computing *trend percentages*. **Trend percentages** state several years' financial data in terms of a base year. The base year equals 100 percent, with all other years stated as some percentage of this base. To illustrate, assume that Martin Company has reported the following sales and income data for the past five years:

	19x5	19x4	19x3	19x2	19x1
Sales	$725,000	$700,000	$650,000	$575,000	$500,000
Net income	99,000	97,500	93,750	86,250	75,000

By simply looking at these data, one can see that both sales and net income have increased over the five-year period reported. But how rapidly have sales been increasing, and have the increases in net income kept pace with the increases in sales? By looking at the raw data alone, it is difficult to answer these questions. The increases in sales and the increases in net income can be put into proper perspective by stating them in terms of trend percentages, with 19x1 as the base year. These percentages are given below:

	19x5	19x4	19x3	19x2	19x1
Sales	145%	140%	130%	115%*	100%
Net income	132	130	125	115	100

* For 19x2: $575,000 ÷ $500,000 = 115%; for 19x3: $650,000 ÷ $500,000 = 130%; and so forth

Notice that the growth in sales dropped off somewhat between 19x3 and 19x4, and then dropped off even more between 19x4 and 19x5. Also notice that the growth in net income has not kept pace with the growth in sales. In 19x5, sales are 1.45 times greater than in 19x1, the base year; however, in 19x5, net income is only 1.32 times greater than in 19x1.

Common-size statements

Key changes and trends can also be highlighted by the use of *common-size statements*. A **common-size statement** is one that shows the separate items appearing on it in percentage form rather than in dollar form. Each item is stated as a percentage of some total of which that item is a part. The preparation of common-size statements is known as **vertical analysis.**

The balance sheet   One application of the vertical analysis idea is to state the separate assets of a company as percentages of total assets. A common-size statement of this type is shown in Exhibit 17–3 for Brickey Electronics Company.

Notice from Exhibit 17–3 that placing all assets in common-size form clearly shows the relative importance of the current assets as compared to the noncurrent assets. It also shows that significant changes have taken place in the *composition* of the current assets over the last year. Notice, for example, that the receivables have increased in relative importance and that both cash

EXHIBIT 17–3

BRICKEY ELECTRONICS COMPANY
Common-Size Comparative Balance Sheets
December 31, 19x1 and 19x2
(dollars in thousands)

	19x2	19x1	Common-size percentages 19x2	19x1
Assets				
Current assets:				
Cash	$ 1,000	$ 2,520	3.4	9.4
Accounts receivable, net	6,000	4,000	20.7	15.0
Inventory	8,000	10,000	27.6	37.4
Prepaid expenses	500	200	1.7	0.7
Total current assets	15,500	16,720	53.4	62.5
Property and equipment:				
Land	4,000	4,000	13.8	15.0
Buildings and equipment, net	9,500	6,000	32.8	22.5
Total property and equipment	13,500	10,000	46.6	37.5
Total assets	$29,000	$26,720	100.0	100.0
Liabilities and Stockholders' Equity				
Current liabilities:				
Accounts payable	$ 5,800	$ 4,000	20.0	15.0
Accrued payables	900	400	3.1	1.5
Notes payable, short term	300	600	1.0	2.2
Total current liabilities	7,000	5,000	24.1	18.7
Long-term liabilities:				
Bonds payable, 8%	7,500	8,000	25.9	29.9
Total liabilities	14,500	13,000	50.0	48.6
Stockholders' equity:				
Preferred stock, $100 par, 6%, $100 liquidation value	2,000	2,000	6.9	7.5
Common stock, $10 par	6,000	6,000	20.7	22.4
Additional paid-in capital	1,000	1,000	3.4	3.7
Total paid-in capital	9,000	9,000	31.0	33.6
Retained earnings	5,500	4,720	19.0	17.7
Total stockholders' equity	14,500	13,720	50.0	51.3
Total liabilities and stockholders' equity	$29,000	$26,720	100.0	100.0

and inventory have declined in relative importance. Judging from the sharp increase in receivables, the deterioration in the cash position may be a result of inability to collect from customers.

The income statement Another application of the vertical analysis idea is to place all items on the income statement in percentage form in terms of total sales. A common-size statement of this type is shown in Exhibit 17–4.

EXHIBIT 17-4

BRICKEY ELECTRONICS COMPANY
Common-Size Comparative Income Statements
For the Years Ended December 31, 19x1 and 19x2
(dollars in thousands)

			Common-size percentages	
	19x2	19x1	19x2	19x1
Sales	$52,000	$48,000	100.0	100.0
Cost of goods sold	36,000	31,500	69.2	65.7
Gross margin	16,000	16,500	30.8	34.3
Operating expenses:				
Selling expenses	7,000	6,500	13.5	13.5
Administrative expenses	5,875	6,350	11.3	13.2
Total operating expenses	12,875	12,850	24.8	26.7
Net operating income	3,125	3,650	6.0	7.6
Interest expense	625	700	1.2	1.5
Net income before taxes	2,500	2,950	4.8	6.1
Income taxes (40%)	1,000	1,180	1.9	2.4
Net income	$ 1,500	$ 1,770	2.9	3.7

By placing all items on the income statement in common size in terms of sales, it is possible to see at a glance how each dollar of sales is distributed between the various costs, expenses, and profits. For example, notice from Exhibit 17-4 that 69.2 cents out of every dollar of sales was needed to cover cost of goods sold in 19x2, as compared to only 65.7 cents in the prior year; also notice that only 2.9 cents out of every dollar of sales remained for profits in 19x2—down from 3.7 cents in the prior year.

Common-size statements are also very helpful in pointing out efficiencies and inefficiencies that might otherwise go unnoticed. To illustrate, in 19x2, Brickey Electronics Company's selling expenses increased by $500,000 over 19x1. A glance at the common-size income statement shows, however, that on a relative basis selling expenses were no higher in 19x2 than in 19x1. In each year, they represented 13.5 percent of sales.

RATIO ANALYSIS—THE COMMON STOCKHOLDER

The common stockholder has only a residual claim on the profits and assets of a corporation. It is only after all creditor and preferred stockholder claims have been satisfied that the common stockholder can step forward and receive cash dividends or a distribution of assets in liquidation. Therefore, a measure of the common stockholder's well-being provides some perspective of the depth of protection available to others associated with a firm.

Earnings per share

An investor buys and retains a share of stock with the thought in mind of a return coming in the future in the form of either dividends or capital gains. Since earnings form the basis for dividend payments, as well as the basis for any future increases in the value of shares, investors are always extremely interested in a company's reported *earnings per share*. Probably no single statistic is more widely quoted or relied on in investor actions than earnings per share, although it has some inherent dangers, as discussed below.

The computation of **earnings per share** is made by dividing net income remaining for common stockholders by the number of common shares outstanding. "Net income remaining for common stockholders" is equal to the net income of a company, reduced by the dividends due to the preferred stockholders.

$$\frac{\text{Net income} - \text{Preferred dividends}}{\text{Common shares outstanding}} = \text{Earnings per share}$$

Using the data in Exhibits 17–1 and 17–2, we see that the earnings per share for Brickey Electronics Company for 19x2 would be:

$$\frac{\$1,500,000 - \$120,000}{600,000 \text{ shares}} = \$2.30 \tag{1}$$

Two problems can arise in connection with the computation of earnings per share. The first arises whenever an extraordinary gain or loss appears as part of net income. The second arises whenever a company has convertible securities on its balance sheet. These problems are discussed in the following two sections.

Extraordinary items and earnings per share

If a company has extraordinary gains or losses appearing as part of net income, *two* earnings per share figures must be computed—one showing the earnings per share resulting from *normal* operations and one showing the earnings per share impact of the *extraordinary* items. This approach to computing earnings per share accomplishes three things. First, it helps statement users to recognize extraordinary items for what they are—unusual events that probably will not recur. Second, it eliminates the distorting influence of the extraordinary items from the basic earnings per share figure. And third, it helps statement users to properly assess the *trend* of *normal* earnings per share over time. Since one would not expect the extraordinary or unusual items to be repeated year after year, they should be given less weight in judging earnings performance than is given to profits resulting from normal operations.

In addition to reporting extraordinary items separately, the accountant also reports them *net of their tax effect*. By "net of their tax effect," we mean that whatever impact the unusual item has on income taxes is *deducted from* the unusual item on the income statement. Only the net, after-tax gain or loss is used in earnings per share computations.

To illustrate these ideas, let us assume that Amata Company has suffered a fire loss of $4,000, and that management is wondering how the loss should be reported on the company's income statement. The correct and incorrect approaches to reporting the loss are shown in Exhibit 17–5.

As shown under the "correct approach" in the exhibit, the $4,000 loss is reduced to only $2,400 after tax effects are taken into consideration. The reasoning behind this computation is as follows: The fire loss is fully deductible for tax purposes. Therefore, this deduction will reduce the firm's taxable income by $4,000. If taxable income is $4,000 lower, then income taxes will be $1,600 *less* (40% × $4,000) than they *otherwise* would have been. In other words, the fire loss of $4,000 saves the company $1,600 in taxes that otherwise would have been paid. The $1,600 savings in taxes is deducted from the loss that caused it, leaving a net loss of only $2,400. This same $2,400 figure could have been obtained by multiplying the original loss by

EXHIBIT 17–5
Reporting extraordinary items net of their tax effects

Incorrect approach			
Sales.		$50,000	
Cost of goods sold		30,000	Extraordinary gains and losses should not be included with normal items of revenue and expense. This distorts a firm's normal income-producing ability.
Gross margin		20,000	
Operating expenses:			
Selling expenses	$5,000		
Administrative expenses.	8,000		
Fire loss.	4,000	17,000	
Net income before taxes		3,000	
Income taxes (40%)		1,200	
Net income.		$ 1,800	

Correct approach			
Sales.		$50,000	
Cost of goods sold		30,000	
Gross margin		20,000	
Operating expenses:			Reporting the extraordinary item separately and net of its tax effect leaves the normal items of revenue and expense unaffected.
Selling expenses	$5,000		
Administrative expenses	8,000	13,000	
Net operating income		7,000	
Income taxes (40%)		2,800	
Net income before extraordinary item.		4,200	
Extraordinary item:			Original loss. $4,000
Fire loss, net of tax		(2,400)	Less reduction in taxes at a 40% rate. . . . 1,600
Net income.		$ 1,800	Loss, net of tax. $2,400

the formula (1 − Tax rate). [$4,000 × (1 − 0.40) = $2,400]. *Any* before-tax item can be put on an after-tax basis by use of this formula.

This same procedure is used in reporting extraordinary gains. The only difference is that extraordinary gains *increase* taxes; thus, any tax resulting from a gain must be deducted from it, with only the net gain reported on the income statement.

To continue our illustration, assume that the company in Exhibit 17–5 has 2,000 shares of common stock outstanding. Earnings per share would be reported as follows:

Earnings per share on common stock:
On net income before extraordinary item ($4,200 ÷ 2,000 shares)* . . . . $ 2.10
On extraordinary item, net of tax ($2,400 ÷ 2,000 shares) . . . .   (1.20)
Net earnings per share . . . . $ 0.90

* Sometimes called the *primary* earnings per share.

In sum, computation of earnings per share as we have done above is necessary to avoid misunderstanding of a company's normal income-producing ability. Reporting *only* the flat 90 cents per share figure would be misleading and perhaps cause investors to regard the company less favorably than they should.

Fully diluted earnings per share

A problem sometimes arises in trying to determine the number of common shares to use in computing earnings per share. Until recent years, the distinction between common stock, preferred stock, and debt was quite clear. The distinction between these securities has now become somewhat diffused, however, due to a growing tendency to issue convertible securities of various types. Rather than simply issuing common stock, firms today often issue preferred stock or bonds that carry a **conversion feature** allowing the purchaser to convert holdings into common stock at some future time.

When convertible securities are present in the financial structure of a firm, the question arises as to whether these securities should be retained in their unconverted form or treated as common stock in computing earnings per share. The American Institute of Certified Public Accountants has taken the position that convertible securities should be treated *both* in their present and prospective forms. This requires the presentation of *two* earnings per share figures for firms that have convertible securities outstanding, one showing earnings per share assuming no conversion into common stock and the other showing full conversion into common stock. The latter figure is known as the **fully diluted earnings per share.**

To illustrate the computation of a company's fully diluted earnings per share, let us assume that the preferred stock of Brickey Electronics Company in Exhibit 17–1 is convertible into common on basis of five shares of common for each share of preferred. Since 20,000 shares of preferred are outstanding, conversion would require issuing an additional 100,000 shares of common stock. Earnings per share on a fully diluted basis would be:

$$\frac{\text{Net income}}{(600,000 \text{ original shares} + 100,000 \text{ converted shares})}$$

$$= \frac{\$1,500,000}{700,000 \text{ shares}} = \$2.14 \quad (2)$$

In comparing equation (2) with equation (1), we can note that the earnings per share figure has dropped by 16 cents. Although the impact of full dilution is relatively small in this case, it can be very significant in situations where large amounts of convertible securities are present.

Price-earnings ratio

The relationship between the market price of a share of stock and the stock's current earnings per share is often quoted in terms of a **price-earnings ratio.** If we assume that the current market price for Brickey Electronics Company's stock is $25 per share, the company's price-earnings ratio would be computed as follows:

$$\frac{\text{Market price}}{\text{Earnings per share}} = \text{Price-earnings ratio}$$

$$\frac{\$25}{\$2.30 \text{ [see equation (1)]}} = 10.9 \quad (3)$$

The price-earnings ratio is 10.9; that is, the stock is selling for about 10.9 times its current earnings per share.

The price-earnings ratio is widely used by investors as a general guideline in gauging stock values. Investors increase or decrease the price-earnings ratio that they are willing to accept for a share of stock according to how they view its *future prospects.* Companies with ample opportunities for growth generally have high price-earnings ratios, with the opposite being true for companies with limited growth opportunities. If investors decided that Brickey Electronics Company had greater than average growth prospects, then undoubtedly the price of the company's stock would begin to rise. If the price increased to, say, $34.50 per share, then the price-earnings ratio would rise to 15 ($34.50 price ÷ $2.30 EPS = 15.0 P-E ratio).

Dividend payout and yield ratios

Investors hold shares of one stock in preference to shares of another stock because they anticipate that the first stock will provide them with a more attractive return. The return sought isn't always dividends. Many investors prefer not to receive dividends. Instead, they prefer to have the company retain all earnings and reinvest them internally in order to support growth. The stocks of companies that adopt this approach, loosely termed *growth stocks,* often enjoy rapid upward movement in market price. On sale of a growth stock, investors can reap their return in the form of capital gains, which receive very favorable treatment from an income tax point of view. Other investors prefer to have a dependable, current source of income through regular dividend payments and prefer not to gamble on the fortunes of stock prices to provide a return on their investment. Such investors seek out stocks with consistent dividend records and payout ratios.

The dividend payout ratio   The **dividend payout ratio** gauges the portion of current earnings being paid out in dividends. Investors who seek capital gains would like this ratio to be small, whereas investors who seek dividends prefer it to be large. This ratio is computed by relating dividends per share to earnings per share for common stock:

$$\frac{\text{Dividends per share}}{\text{Earnings per share}} = \text{Dividend payout ratio}$$

For Brickey Electronics Company, the dividend payout ratio for 19x2 was:

$$\frac{\$1.00 \text{ (see Exhibit 17–2)}}{\$2.30 \text{ [see equation (1)]}} = 43.5\% \tag{4}$$

There is no such thing as a "right" payout ratio, even though it should be noted that the ratio tends to be somewhat the same for the bulk of firms within a particular industry. Industries with ample opportunities for growth at high rates of return on assets tend to have low payout ratios, and the reverse tends to be true for industries with limited reinvestment opportunities.

The dividend yield ratio   The **dividend yield ratio** is obtained by dividing the current dividends per share by the current market price per share:

$$\frac{\text{Dividends per share}}{\text{Market price per share}} = \text{Dividend yield ratio}$$

If we continue the assumption of a market price of $25 per share for Brickey Electronics Company stock, the dividend yield is:

$$\frac{\$1}{\$25} = 4.0\% \tag{5}$$

In making this computation, note that we used the current market price of the stock rather than the price the investor paid for the stock initially (which might be above or below the current market price). By using current market price, we recognize the opportunity cost[1] of the investment in terms of its yield. That is, this is the yield that would be lost or sacrificed if the investor sold the stock for $25 and bought a new security in its place.

---

[1] Opportunity cost can be defined as the potential benefit that is lost or sacrificed when the choice of one course of action requires the giving up of an alternative course of action.

Return on total assets

Managers have two basic responsibilities in managing a firm—*financing* responsibilities and *operating* responsibilities. Financing responsibilities relate to how one *obtains* the funds needed to provide for the assets in an organization. Operating responsibilities relate to how one *uses* the assets once they have been obtained. Proper discharge of both responsibilities is vital to a well-managed firm. However, care must be taken not to confuse or mix the two in assessing the performance of a manager. That is, whether funds have been obtained partly from creditors and partly from stockholders or entirely from stockholders should not be allowed to influence one's assessment of *how well* the assets have been employed since being received by the firm.

The **return on total assets** is a measure of how well assets have been employed; that is, it is a measure of operating performance. The formula is:

$$\frac{\text{Net income} + [\text{Interest expense} \times (1 - \text{Tax rate})]}{\text{Average total assets}} = \text{Return on total assets}$$

By adding interest expense back to net income, we derive a figure that shows earnings before any distributions have been made to either creditors or stockholders. Thus, we eliminate the matter of how the assets were financed from influencing the measurement of how well the assets have been employed. Notice that before being added back to net income, the interest expense must be placed on an after-tax basis by multiplying the interest figure by the formula (1 − Tax rate).

The return on total assets for Brickey Electronics Company for 19x2 would be (from Exhibits 17–1 and 17–2):

Net income		$ 1,500,000
Add back interest expense: $625,000 × (1 − 0.40)		375,000
Total		$ 1,875,000 *(a)*
Assets, beginning of year		$26,720,000
Assets, end of year		29,000,000
Total		$55,720,000
Average total assets: $55,720,000 ÷ 2		$27,860,000 *(b)*
Return on total assets, *(a) ÷ (b)*		6.7% (6)

Brickey Electronics Company has earned a return of 6.7 percent on average assets employed over the last year.

Return on common stockholders' equity

One of the primary reasons for operating a corporation is to generate income for the benefit of the common stockholders. One measure of a company's success in this regard is the rate of **return on common stockholders' equity** that it is able to generate. The formula is:

$$\frac{\text{Net income} - \text{Preferred dividends}}{\text{Average common stockholders' equity (Average total stockholders' equity} - \text{Preferred stock)}}$$

$$= \text{Return on common stockholders' equity}$$

For Brickey Electronics Company, the return on common stockholders' equity is 11.4 percent for 19x2, as shown below:

Net income	$ 1,500,000	
Deduct preferred dividends	120,000	
Net income remaining for common stockholders. . . .	$ 1,380,000	*(a)*
Average stockholders' equity	$14,110,000*	
Deduct preferred stock	2,000,000	
Average common stockholders' equity	$12,110,000	*(b)*
Return on common stockholders' equity, *(a) ÷ (b)* . . .	11.4%	(7)

* $13,720,000 + $14,500,000 = $28,220,000; $28,220,000 ÷ 2 = $14,110,000.

Compare the return on common stockholders' equity above (11.4 percent) with the return on total assets computed in the preceding section (6.7 percent). Why is the return on common stockholders' equity so much higher? The answer lies in the principle of *financial leverage* (sometimes called "trading on the equity").

The concept of financial leverage   Financial leverage (often called "leverage" for short) involves the financing of assets in a company with funds that have been acquired from creditors or from preferred stockholders at a fixed rate of return. If the assets in which the funds are invested are able to earn a rate of return *greater* than the fixed rate of return required by the suppliers of the funds, then financial leverage is **positive** and the common stockholders benefit.

For example, assume that a firm is able to earn an after-tax return of 12 percent on its assets. If that firm can borrow from creditors at a 10 percent interest rate in order to expand its assets, then the common stockholders can benefit from positive leverage. The borrowed funds invested in the business will earn an after-tax return of 12 percent, but the after-tax interest cost of the borrowed funds will be only 6 percent [10% interest rate × (1 − 0.40) = 6%]. The difference will go to the common stockholders.

We can see this concept in operation in the case of Brickey Electronics Company. Notice from Exhibit 17–1 that the company's bonds payable bear a fixed interest rate of 8 percent. The after-tax interest cost of these bonds is only 4.8 percent [8% interest rate × (1 − 0.40) = 4.8%]. The company's assets (which would contain the proceeds from the original sale of these bonds) are generating an after-tax return of 6.7 percent, as we computed earlier. Since this return on assets is greater than the after-tax interest cost of the bonds, leverage is positive, and the difference accrues to the benefit of the common stockholders. This explains in part why the return on common stockholders' equity (11.4 percent) is greater than the return on total assets (6.7 percent).

Sources of financial leverage   Financial leverage can be obtained from several sources. One source is long-term debt, such as bonds payable or notes payable. Two additional sources are current liabilities and preferred stock. Current liabilities are always a source of positive leverage in that funds are provided for use in a company with no interest return required by the short-term creditors involved. For example, when a company acquires inventory from a supplier on account, the inventory is available for use in the business, yet the supplier requires no interest return on the amount owed to him.

Preferred stock can also be a source of positive leverage so long as the dividend payable to the preferred stockholders is less than the rate of return being earned on the total assets employed. In the case of Brickey Electronics Company, positive leverage is being realized on the preferred stock. Notice from Exhibit 17–1 that the preferred dividend rate is only 6 percent, whereas the assets in the company are earning at a rate of 6.7 percent, as computed earlier. Again, the difference goes to the common stockholders, thereby helping to bolster their return to the 11.4 percent computed earlier.

Unfortunately, leverage is a two-edged sword. If assets are unable to earn a high enough rate to cover the interest costs of debt, or to cover the preferred dividend due to the preferred stockholders, *then the common stockholder suffers.* The reason is that part of the earnings from the assets that the common stockholder has provided to the company will have to go to make up the deficiency to the long-term creditors or to the preferred stockholders, and the common stockholder will be left with a smaller return than would otherwise have been earned. Under these circumstances, financial leverage is said to be **negative.**

The impact of income taxes   Long-term debt and preferred stock are not equally efficient in generating positive leverage. The reason is that interest on long-term debt is tax deductible, whereas preferred dividends are not. This makes long-term debt a much more effective source of positive leverage than preferred stock.

To illustrate this point, assume that a company is considering three ways of financing a $100,000 expansion of its assets:

1. $100,000 from an issue of common stock.
2. $50,000 from an issue of common stock, and $50,000 from an issue of preferred stock bearing a dividend rate of 8 percent.
3. $50,000 from an issue of common stock, and $50,000 from an issue of bonds bearing an interest rate of 8 percent.

Assuming that the company can earn an additional $15,000 each year before interest and taxes as a result of the expansion, the operating results under each of the three alternatives are shown in Exhibit 17–6.

If the entire $100,000 is raised from an issue of common stock, then the return to the common stockholders will be only 9 percent, as shown under alternative 1 in the exhibit. If half of the funds are raised from an issue of preferred stock, then the return to the common stockholders increases to

EXHIBIT 17–6
Leverage from preferred stock and long-term debt

	Alternatives: $100,000 issue of securities		
	Alternative 1: $100,000 common stock	Alternative 2: $50,000 common stock; $50,000 preferred stock	Alternative 3: $50,000 common stock; $50,000 bonds
Earnings before interest and taxes	$ 15,000	$15,000	$15,000
Deduct interest expense (8% × $50,000)	—	—	4,000
Net income before taxes	15,000	15,000	11,000
Deduct income taxes (40%)	6,000	6,000	4,400
Net income	9,000	9,000	6,600
Deduct preferred dividends (8% × $50,000)	—	4,000	—
Net income remaining for common (a)	$ 9,000	$ 5,000	$ 6,600
Common stockholders' equity (b)	$100,000	$50,000	$50,000
Return on common stockholders' equity, (a) ÷ (b)	9%	10%	13.2%

10 percent, due to the positive effects of leverage. However, if half of the funds are raised from an issue of bonds, then the return to the common stockholders jumps to 13.2 percent, as shown under alternative 3. Thus, long-term debt is much more efficient in generating positive leverage than is preferred stock. The reason is that the interest expense on long-term debt is tax deductible, whereas the dividends on preferred stock are not.

The desirability of leverage The leverage principle amply illustrates that having some debt in the capital structure can substantially benefit the common stockholder. For this reason, most companies today try to keep a certain level of debt within the organization—a level at least equal to that which is considered to be "normal" within the industry. Occasionally one comes across a company that boasts of having no debt outstanding. Although there may be good reasons for a company to have no debt, in view of the benefits that can be gained from positive leverage the possibility always exists that such a company is shortchanging its stockholders. As a practical matter, many companies, such as commercial banks and other financial institutions, rely heavily on leverage to provide an attractive return on their common shares.

Book value per share

Another statistic frequently used in attempting to assess the well-being of the common stockholder is **book value per share:**

$$\frac{\text{Common stockholders' equity (Total stockholders' equity − Preferred stock)}}{\text{Number of common shares outstanding}} = \text{Book value per share}$$

The book value of Brickey Electronics Company common stock is:

$$\frac{\$14,500,000 - \$2,000,000}{600,000 \text{ shares}} = \$20.83 \tag{8}$$

If this book value is compared with the $25 market value that we have assumed in connection with the Brickey Electronics Company stock, then the stock appears to be somewhat overpriced. It is not necessarily true, however, that a market value in excess of book value is an indication of overpricing. As we discussed earlier, market prices are geared toward future earnings and dividends. Book value, by contrast, purports to reflect nothing about the future earnings potential of a firm. As a practical matter, it is actually geared to the *past* in that it reflects the balance sheet carrying value of already completed transactions.

Of what use, then, is book value? Unfortunately, the answer must be that it is of limited use so far as being a dynamic tool of analysis is concerned. It probably finds its greatest application in situations where large amounts of liquid assets are being held in anticipation of liquidation. Occasionally some use is also made of book value per share in attempting to set a price on the shares of closely held corporations.

RATIO ANALYSIS—THE SHORT-TERM CREDITOR

Although the short-term creditor is always well advised to keep an eye on the fortunes of the common stockholder, as expressed in the ratios of the preceding section, the short-term creditor's focus of attention is normally channeled in another direction. The short-term creditor is concerned with the near-term prospects of having obligations paid on time. As such, he or she is much more interested in cash flows and in working capital management than in how much accounting net income a company is reporting.

Working capital

The excess of current assets over current liabilities is known as **working capital.** The working capital for Brickey Electronics Company is given below:

	19x2	19x1
Current assets.	$15,500,000	$16,720,000
Current liabilities	7,000,000	5,000,000
Working capital	$ 8,500,000	$11,720,000	(9)

The amount of working capital available to a firm is of considerable interest to short-term creditors, *since it represents assets financed from long-term capital sources that do not require near-term repayment.* Therefore, the greater the working capital, the greater is the cushion of protection available to short-term creditors and the greater is the assurance that short-term debts will be paid when due.

Although it is always comforting to short-term creditors to see a large working capital balance, their joy becomes full only after they have been satisfied that the working capital is turning over at an acceptable rate of speed, and that their obligations could be paid even under stringent operating conditions. The reason is that a large working capital balance standing by itself is no assurance that debts will be paid when due. Rather than being a sign of strength, a large working capital balance may simply mean that stagnant or obsolete inventory is building up. Therefore, to put the working capital figure into proper perspective, it must be supplemented with other analytical work. The following four ratios (the current ratio, the acid-test ratio, the accounts receivable turnover, and the inventory turnover) should all be used in connection with an analysis of working capital.

Current ratio

The elements involved in the computation of working capital are frequently expressed in ratio form. A company's current assets divided by its current liabilities is known as the **current ratio:**

$$\frac{\text{Current assets}}{\text{Current liabilities}} = \text{Current ratio}$$

For Brickey Electronics Company, the current ratio for 19x1 and 19x2 would be:

19x2	19x1	
$\dfrac{\$15,500,000}{\$7,000,000} = 2.21$ to 1	$\dfrac{\$16,720,000}{\$5,000,000} = 3.34$ to 1	(10)

Although widely regarded as a measure of short-term debt-paying ability, the current ratio must be interpreted with a great deal of care. A *declining* ratio, as above, might be a sign of a deteriorating financial condition. On the other hand, it might be the result of a paring out of obsolete inventories or other stagnant assets. An *improving* ratio might be the result of an unwise stockpiling of inventory, or it might point up an improving financial situation. In short, the current ratio is useful, but tricky to interpret. To avoid a blunder, the analyst must take a hard look at the individual items of assets and liabilities involved.

The general rule of thumb calls for a current ratio of 2 to 1. This rule, of course, is subject to many exceptions, depending on the industry and the firm involved. Some industries can operate quite successfully on a current ratio of slightly over 1 to 1. The adequacy of a current ratio depends heavily on the *composition* of the assets involved. For example, although Company X and Company Y below both have current ratios of 2 to 1, one could hardly say that they are in comparable financial condition. Company Y most certainly will have difficulty in meeting its obligations as they come due.

	Company X	Company Y
Current assets:		
Cash.	$ 25,000	$ 2,000
Accounts receivable	60,000	8,000
Inventory	85,000	160,000
Prepaid expenses	5,000	5,000
Total current assets	$175,000	$175,000
Current liabilities.	$ 87,500	$ 87,500
Current ratio	2 to 1	2 to 1

Acid-test ratio

A much more rigorous test of a company's ability to meet its short-term debts can be found in the **acid-test,** or **quick, ratio.** Merchandise inventory and prepaid expenses are excluded from the total of current assets, leaving only the more liquid (or "quick") assets to be divided by current liabilities.

$$\frac{\text{Cash} + \text{Marketable securities} + \text{Current receivables*}}{\text{Current liabilities}} = \text{Acid-test ratio}$$

* This would include both accounts receivable and any short-term notes receivable.

The acid-test ratio is designed to measure how well a company can meet its obligations without having to liquidate or depend too heavily on its inventory. Since inventory is not an immediate source of cash and may not even be salable in times of economic stress, it is generally felt that to be properly protected each dollar of liabilities should be backed by at least $1 of quick assets. Thus, an acid-test ratio of 1 to 1 is broadly viewed as being adequate in many firms.

The acid-test ratios for Brickey Electronics Company for 19x1 and 19x2 are given below:

	19x2	19x1
Cash	$1,000,000	$2,520,000
Accounts receivable . .	6,000,000	4,000,000
Total quick assets . . .	$7,000,000	$6,520,000
Current liabilities . . .	$7,000,000	$5,000,000
Acid-test ratio	1 to 1	1.3 to 1

(11)

Although Brickey Electronics Company has an acid-test ratio for 19x2 that is within the acceptable range, an analyst might be concerned about several disquieting trends revealed in the company's balance sheet. Notice that short-term debts are rising, while the cash position seems to be deteriorating. Perhaps the weakened cash position is a result of the greatly expanded volume of accounts receivable. One wonders why the accounts receivable have been allowed to increase so rapidly in so brief a time.

In short, as with the current ratio, to be used intelligently the acid-test ratio must be interpreted with one eye on its basic components.

Accounts receivable turnover

The *accounts receivable turnover* ratio is frequently used in conjunction with an analysis of working capital, since it provides at least a rough gauge as to how well receivables are turning into cash. The **accounts receivable turnover** is computed by dividing sales on account by the average accounts receivable balance during a period:

$$\frac{\text{Sales on account}}{\text{Average accounts receivable balance}} = \text{Accounts receivable turnover}$$

The accounts receivable turnover for Brickey Electronics Company for 19x2 is:

$$\frac{\text{Sales on account}}{\text{Average accounts receivable balance}} = \frac{\$52,000,000}{\$5,000,000*} = 10.4 \text{ times} \quad (12)$$

* $4,000,000 + \$6,000,000 = \$10,000,000;$ $\$10,000,000 \div 2 = \$5,000,000$ average.

The turnover figure can then be divided into 365 to determine the average number of days being taken to collect an account (known as the **average collection period**).

$$\frac{365 \text{ days}}{\text{Accounts receivable turnover}} = \frac{365}{10.4 \text{ times}}$$

$$= 35 \text{ days average collection period} \quad (13)$$

Whether the average of 35 days taken to collect an account is good or bad depends on the credit terms Brickey Electronics Company is offering its customers. If the credit terms are 30 days, then a 35-day average collection period would be viewed as being very good. Most customers will tend to withhold payment for as long as the credit terms will allow and may even go over a few days. This factor, added to the ever-present few slow accounts, can cause the average collection period to exceed normal credit terms by a week to 10 days and should not be a matter for too much alarm.

On the other hand, if the company's credit terms are 10 days, then a 35-day average collection period may be a cause for some concern. The long collection period may be a result of the presence of many old accounts of doubtful collectibility, or it may be a result of poor day-to-day credit management. The firm may be making sales with inadequate credit checks on the companies to which the sales are being made, or perhaps no follow-ups are being made on slow accounts.

Inventory turnover

The **inventory turnover** ratio measures how many times a company's inventory has been sold during the year. It is computed by dividing the cost of goods sold by the average level of inventory on hand:

$$\frac{\text{Cost of goods sold}}{\text{Average inventory balance}} = \text{Inventory turnover}$$

The average inventory figure is usually computed by taking the average of the beginning and ending inventory figures. Since Brickey Electronics Company has a beginning inventory figure of $10,000,000 and an ending inventory figure of $8,000,000, its average inventory for the year would be $9,000,000. The company's inventory turnover for 19x2 would be:

$$\frac{\text{Cost of goods sold}}{\text{Average inventory balance}} = \frac{\$36,000,000}{\$9,000,000} = 4 \text{ times} \tag{14}$$

The number of days being taken to sell the entire inventory one time (called the **average sale period**) can be computed by dividing 365 by the inventory turnover figure:

$$\frac{365 \text{ days}}{\text{Inventory turnover}} = \frac{365}{4 \text{ times}} = 91\tfrac{1}{4} \text{ days} \tag{15}$$

Grocery stores tend to turn their inventory over very quickly, perhaps as often as every 12 to 15 days. On the other hand, jewelry stores tend to turn their inventory over very slowly, perhaps only a couple of times each year.

If a firm has a turnover that is much slower than the average for its industry, then there may be obsolete goods on hand, or inventory stocks may be needlessly high. Excessive inventories simply tie up funds that could be used elsewhere in operations. Managers often argue that they must buy in very large quantities in order to take advantage of the best discounts being offered. But these discounts must be carefully weighed against the added costs of insurance, taxes, financing, and risks of obsolescence and deterioration that result from carrying added inventories.

An inventory turnover that is substantially faster than the average is usually an indication that inventory levels are inadequate.

RATIO ANALYSIS—THE LONG-TERM CREDITOR

The position of long-term creditors differs from that of short-term creditors in that they are concerned with both the near-term *and* the long-term ability of a firm to meet its commitments. They are concerned with the near term since whatever interest they may be entitled to is normally paid on a current basis. They are concerned with the long term from the point of view of the eventual retirement of their holdings.

Since the long-term creditor is usually faced with somewhat greater risks than the short-term creditor, firms are often required to make various restrictive covenants for the long-term creditor's protection. Examples of such restrictive covenants would include the maintenance of minimum working capital levels and restrictions on payment of dividends to common stockholders. Although these restrictive covenants are in widespread use, they must be viewed as being a poor second to *prospective earnings* from the point of view of assessing protection and safety. Creditors do not want to go to court to collect their claims; they would much prefer staking the safety of their claims for interest and eventual repayment of principal on an orderly and consistent flow of funds from operations.

Times interest earned

The most common measure of the ability of a firm's operations to provide protection to the long-term creditor is the **times interest earned** ratio. It is computed by dividing earnings *before* interest expense and income taxes by the yearly interest charges that must be met:

$$\frac{\text{Earnings before interest expense and income taxes*}}{\text{Interest expense}} = \text{Times interest earned}$$

*This amount is the same as *net operating income* on many financial statements.

For Brickey Electronics Company, the times interest earned ratio for 19x2 would be:

$$\frac{\$3,125,000}{\$625,000} = 5.0 \text{ times} \tag{16}$$

Earnings before income taxes must be used in the computation since interest expense deductions come *before* income taxes are computed. Income taxes are secondary to interest payments in that the latter have first claim on earnings. Only those earnings remaining after all interest charges have been provided for are subject to income taxes.

Various rules of thumb exist to gauge the adequacy of a firm's times interest earned ratio. Generally, earnings are viewed as adequate to protect long-term creditors if the times interest earned ratio is 2 or more. Before making a final judgment, however, it would be necessary to look at a firm's long-run *trend* of earnings, then decide how vulnerable the firm is to cyclical changes in the economy.

Debt-to-equity ratio

Although long-term creditors look primarily to prospective earnings and budgeted cash flows in attempting to gauge the risk of their position, they cannot ignore the importance of keeping a reasonable balance between the portion of assets being provided by creditors and the portion of assets being provided by the stockholders of a firm. This balance is measured by the **debt-to-equity ratio:**

$$\frac{\text{Total liabilities}}{\text{Stockholders' equity}} = \text{Debt-to-equity ratio}$$

	19x2	19x1	
Total liabilities	$14,500,000	$13,000,000 *(a)*	
Stockholders' equity	14,500,000	13,720,000 *(b)*	
Debt-to-equity ratio, *(a) ÷ (b)*	1 to 1	0.95 to 1	(17)

The debt-to-equity ratio indicates the amount of assets being provided by creditors for each dollar of assets being provided by the owners of a company. In 19x1, creditors of Brickey Electronics Company were providing 95 cents of assets for each $1 of assets being provided by stockholders. By 19x2, however, creditors were providing just as much in assets to the company as were its owners.

It should come as no surprise that creditors would like the debt-to-equity ratio to be relatively low. The lower the ratio, the larger is the amount of assets being provided by the owners of a company and the greater is the buffer of protection to creditors. By contrast, common stockholders would like the ratio to be relatively high, since through leverage common stockholders can benefit from the assets being provided by creditors.

In most industries, norms have developed over the years that serve as guides to firms in their decisions as to the "right" amount of debt to include in the capital structure. Different industries face different risks. For this reason, the level of debt that is appropriate for firms in one industry is not necessarily a guide to the level of debt that is appropriate for firms in a different industry.

Summary of ratios and sources of comparative ratio data

As an aid to the reader, Exhibit 17–7 contains a summary of the ratios discussed in this chapter. Included in the exhibit are the formula for each ratio and a summary comment on each ratio's significance to the manager.

EXHIBIT 17–7
Summary of ratios

Ratio	Formula	Significance
Earnings per share (of common stock)	Net income less preferred dividends ÷ Number of common shares outstanding	Tends to have an effect on the market price per share, as reflected in the price-earnings ratio
Fully diluted earnings per share	Net income ÷ (Number of common shares outstanding + Common stock equivalent of convertible securities)	Shows the potential effect on earnings per share of converting convertible securities into common stock
Price-earnings ratio	Current market price per share ÷ Earnings per share	An index of whether a stock is relatively cheap or relatively expensive
Dividend payout ratio	Dividends per share ÷ Earnings per share	An index showing whether a company pays out most of its earnings in dividends or reinvests the earnings internally

EXHIBIT 17–7 *(concluded)*

Ratio	Formula	Significance
Dividend yield ratio	Dividends per share ÷ Market price per share	Shows the dividend return being provided by a stock, which can be compared to the return being provided by other stocks
Return on total assets	Net income + [Interest expense × (1 − Tax rate)]÷ Average total assets	Measure of how well assets have been employed by management
Return on common stockholders' equity	(Net income − Preferred dividends) ÷ Average common stockholders' equity	When compared to the return on total assets, measures the extent to which leverage is being employed for or against the common stockholders
Book value per share	Common stockholders' equity ÷ Number of common shares outstanding	Measures the amount that would be distributed to each share of common stock if assets were liquidated at their balance sheet amounts; based entirely on historical costs
Working capital	Current assets − Current liabilities	Represents current assets financed from long-term sources that do not require near-term repayment
Current ratio	Current assets ÷ Current liabilities	Test of short-term debt-paying ability
Acid-test (quick) ratio	(Cash + Marketable securities + Current receivables) ÷ Current liabilities	Test of short-term debt-paying ability without having to rely on inventory
Accounts receivable turnover	Sales on account ÷ Average accounts receivable balance	Measure of how many times a company's accounts receivable have been turned into cash during the year
Average collection period (age of receivables)	365 ÷ Accounts receivable turnover	Measure of the average number of days taken to collect an account receivable
Inventory turnover	Cost of goods sold ÷ Average inventory balance	Measure of how many times a company's inventory has been sold during the year
Average sale period (turnover in days)	365 ÷ Inventory turnover	Measure of the average number of days taken to sell the inventory one time
Times interest earned	Earnings before interest expense and income taxes ÷ Interest expense	Measure of the likelihood that creditors will continue to receive their interest payments
Debt-to-equity ratio	Total liabilities ÷ Stockholders' equity	Measure of the amount of assets being provided by creditors for each dollar of assets being provided by the stockholders

Exhibit 17–8 contains a listing of published sources that provide comparative ratio data organized by industry. These sources are used extensively by managers, investors, and analysts in doing comparative analyses and in attempting to assess the well-being of companies.

EXHIBIT 17–8
Published sources of financial ratios

Source	Content
Almanac of Business and Industrial Financial Ratios. Prentice-Hall. Published annually.	An exhaustive source that contains common-size income statements and financial ratios by industry and by size of companies within each industry.
Annual Statement Studies. Robert Morris Associates. Published annually.	A widely used publication that contains common-size statements and financial ratios on individual companies. The companies are arranged by industry.
Business Week. "Scoreboard Special Issue." McGraw-Hill. Published annually in March.	A special issue of *Business Week* that provides numerous financial ratios on the 1,200 largest companies in the United States. Data are organized by quarter for the preceding year's activity.
Dow Jones-Irwin Business and Investment Almanac. Dow Jones-Irwin. Published annually.	This source contains mostly industry financial ratios and common-size income statements. Some information is given on very large companies.
Key Business Ratios. Dun & Bradstreet. Published annually.	Fourteen commonly used financial ratios are computed for major industry groupings. This source contains data on over 800 lines of business.
Standard & Poor's Industry Survey. Standard & Poor's. Published annually.	Various statistics, including some financial ratios, are provided by industry and on leading companies within each industry grouping.

SUMMARY

The data contained in financial statements represent a quantitative summary of a firm's operations and activities. If a manager is skillful at taking these statements apart, he or she can learn much about a company's strengths, its weaknesses, its developing problems, its operating efficiency, its profitability, and so forth.

Many analytical techniques are available to assist managers in taking financial statements apart and in assessing the direction and importance of trends and changes. In this chapter, we have discussed three such analytical techniques—dollar and percentage changes in statements, common-size statements, and ratio analysis. In the following chapter, we continue our discussion of statement analysis by focusing on two new topics, funds flow and cash flow, and on their usefulness to the manager in his or her attempts to assess how well the firm is doing.

KEY TERMS FOR REVIEW

(Note: Definitions and formulas for all financial ratios are given in Exhibit 17–7. These definitions and formulas are not repeated here.)

Common-size statements A statement that shows the items appearing on it in percentage form rather than in dollar form. On the income statement, the percentages are based on total sales; on the balance sheet, the percentages are based on total assets or total equities.

Conversion feature The ability to exchange either bonds or preferred stock for common stock.

Financial leverage The financing of assets in a company with funds that have been acquired from creditors or from preferred stockholders at a fixed rate of return.

Horizontal analysis A comparison of two or more years' financial statements.

Negative financial leverage A situation in which the fixed return to a company's creditors and preferred stockholders is greater than the return on total assets. In this situation, the return to common stockholders' equity will be *less* than the return on total assets.

Positive financial leverage A situation in which the fixed return to a company's creditors and preferred stockholders is less than the return on total assets. In this situation, the return on common stockholders' equity will be *greater* than the return on total assets.

Trend percentages The expression of several years' financial data in percentage form in terms of a base year.

Vertical analysis The presentation of financial statements in common-size form.

QUESTIONS

17–1. What three analytical techniques are used in financial statement analysis?

17–2. Distinguish between horizontal and vertical analysis of financial statement data.

17–3. What is the basic objective in looking at trends in financial ratios and other data? Rather than looking at trends, to what other standard of comparison might a statement user turn?

17–4. In financial analysis, why does the analyst compute financial ratios rather than simply studying raw financial data? What dangers are there in the use of ratios?

17–5. What pitfalls are involved in computing earnings per share? How can these pitfalls be avoided?

17–6. What is meant by reporting an extraordinary item on the income statement net of its tax effect? Give an example of both an extraordinary gain and an extraordinary loss net of its tax effect. Assume a tax rate of 40 percent.

17–7. Assume that two companies in the same industry have equal earnings. Why might these companies have different price-earnings ratios? If a company has a price-earnings ratio of 20 and reports earnings per share for the current year of $4, at what price would you expect to find the stock selling on the market?

17-8. Armcor, Inc., is in a rapidly growing technological industry. Would you expect the company to have a high or a low dividend payout ratio?

17-9. Distinguish between a manager's *financing* and *operating* responsibilities. Which of these responsibilities is the return on total assets ratio designed to measure?

17-10. What is meant by the dividend yield on a common stock investment? In computing dividend yield, why do you use current market value rather than original purchase price?

17-11. What is meant by the term *financial leverage?*

17-12. The president of a medium-sized plastics company was recently quoted in a business journal as stating, "We haven't had a dollar of interest-paying debt in over 10 years. Not many companies can say that." As a stockholder in this firm, how would you feel about its policy of not taking on interest-paying debt?

17-13. Why is it more difficult to obtain positive financial leverage from preferred stock than from long-term debt?

17-14. If a stock's market value exceeds its book value, then the stock is overpriced. Do you agree? Explain.

17-15. Weaver Company experiences a great deal of seasonal variation in its business activities. The company's high point in business activity is in June; its low point is in January. During which month would you expect the current ratio to be highest? At what point would you advise the company to end its fiscal year? Why?

17-16. A company seeking a line of credit at a bank was turned down. Among other things, the bank stated that the company's 2 to 1 current ratio was not adequate. Give reasons why a 2 to 1 current ratio might not be adequate.

17-17. If you were a long-term creditor of a firm, would you be more interested in the firm's long-term or short-term debt-paying ability? Why?

17-18. A young college student once complained to the author, "The reason that corporations are such big spenders is that Uncle Sam always picks up part of the tab." What did he mean by this statement?

EXERCISES

E17-1. Comparative income statements are given below for Ryder Company:

RYDER COMPANY
Comparative Income Statements
For the Years Ended June 30, 19x1 and 19x2

	19x2	19x1
Sales.	$5,000,000	$4,000,000
Less cost of goods sold	3,160,000	2,400,000
Gross margin	1,840,000	1,600,000
Selling expenses.	900,000	700,000
Administrative expenses	680,000	584,000
Total expenses	1,580,000	1,284,000
Net operating income	260,000	316,000
Interest expense	60,000	40,000
Net income before taxes	$ 200,000	$ 276,000

The president is concerned that net income is down in 19x2 even though sales have increased during the year. The president is also concerned that administrative expenses have increased, since the company made a concerted effort during 19x2 to pare "fat" out of the organization.

Required:
1. Express each year's income statement in common-size percentages. Carry computations to one decimal place.
2. Comment briefly on the changes between the two years.

E17–2. Noble Company's current assets, current liabilities, and sales have been reported as follows over the last five years:

	19x5	19x4	19x3	19x2	19x1
Sales	$2,250,000	$2,160,000	$2,070,000	$1,980,000	$1,800,000
Cash	$ 30,000	$ 40,000	$ 48,000	$ 65,000	$ 50,000
Accounts receivable	570,000	510,000	405,000	345,000	300,000
Inventory	750,000	720,000	690,000	660,000	600,000
Total	$1,350,000	$1,270,000	$1,143,000	$1,070,000	$ 950,000
Current liabilities	$ 640,000	$ 580,000	$ 520,000	$ 440,000	$ 400,000

Required:
1. Express the asset, liability, and sales data in trend percentages. (Show percentages for each item.) Use 19x1 as the base year, and carry computations to one decimal place.
2. Comment on the results of your analysis.

E17–3. Recent financial statements for Madison Company are given below:

MADISON COMPANY
Balance Sheet
June 30, 19x4
Assets

Current assets:	
Cash	$ 21,000
Accounts receivable, net	160,000
Merchandise inventory	300,000
Prepaid expenses	9,000
Total current assets	490,000
Property and equipment, net	810,000
Total assets	$1,300,000

Liabilities and Stockholders' Equity

Liabilities:		
Current liabilities		$ 200,000
Bonds payable, 10%		300,000
Total liabilities		500,000
Stockholders' equity:		
Common stock, $5 par value	$100,000	
Retained earnings	700,000	
Total stockholders' equity		800,000
Total liabilities and stockholders' equity		$1,300,000

MADISON COMPANY
Income Statement
For the Year Ended June 30, 19x4

Sales	$2,100,000
Less cost of goods sold	1,260,000
Gross margin	840,000
Less operating expenses	635,000
Net operating income	205,000
Less interest expense	30,000
Net income before taxes	175,000
Less income taxes (40%)	70,000
Net income	$ 105,000

Account balances at the beginning of the company's fiscal year (July 1, 19x3) were: accounts receivable, $140,000; and inventory, $260,000. All sales were on account.

Required: Compute financial ratios as follows:
1. Current ratio. (Industry average: 2.3 to 1.)
2. Acid-test ratio. (Industry average: 1.2 to 1.)
3. Accounts receivable turnover in days. (Terms: 2/10, n/30.)
4. Inventory turnover in days. (Industry average: 72 days.)
5. Debt-to-equity ratio.
6. Times interest earned.
7. Book value per share. (Market price: $63.)

E17–4. Refer to the financial statements for Madison Company in Exercise 17–3. In addition to the data in these statements, assume that Madison Company paid dividends of $3.15 per share during the year ended June 30, 19x4. Also assume that the company's common stock had a market price of $63 per share on June 30.

Required: Compute the following:
1. Earnings per share.
2. Dividend payout ratio.
3. Dividend yield ratio.
4. Price-earnings ratio. (Industry average: 10.)

E17–5. Refer to the financial statements for Madison Company in Exercise 17–3. Assets at the beginning of the year totaled $1,100,000, and the stockholders' equity totaled $725,000.

Required: Compute the following:
1. Return on total assets.
2. Return on common stockholders' equity. (Industry average: 12.5 percent.)
3. Was financial leverage positive or negative for the year? Explain.

E17–6. Rightway Products had a current ratio of 2.5 to 1 on December 31 of the current year. On that date, the company's assets were:

Cash		$ 60,000
Accounts receivable	$150,000	
Less allowance for uncollectible accounts	15,000	135,000
Inventory		250,000
Prepaid expenses		5,000
Plant and equipment, net		350,000
Total assets		$800,000

Required:
1. What was the company's working capital on December 31?
2. What was the company's acid-test ratio on December 31?
3. The company paid an account payable of $30,000 immediately after December 31.
    a. What effect did this transaction have on the current ratio? Show computations.
    b. What effect did this transaction have on working capital? Show computations.

E17–7. Selected financial data from the June 30, 19x8, year-end statements of Safford Company are given below:

Total assets	$3,600,000
Long-term debt (12% interest rate)	500,000
Preferred stock, $100 par, 8%	900,000
Total stockholders' equity	2,400,000
Interest paid on long-term debt	60,000
Net income	280,000

Total assets at the beginning of the year were $3,000,000; total stockholders' equity was $2,200,000. There has been no change in the preferred stock during the year. The company's tax rate is 40 percent.

Required:
1. Compute the return on total assets.
2. Compute the return on common stockholders' equity.
3. Is leverage positive or negative? Explain.

E17–8. Midwest Products, Inc., reported income as follows for the past year:

MIDWEST PRODUCTS, INC.
Income Statement
For the Year Ended May 31, 19x9

Sales	$800,000
Cost of goods sold	500,000
Gross margin	300,000
Operating expenses	210,000
Net income before taxes	90,000
Income taxes (40%)	36,000
Net income	$ 54,000

Included in the operating expenses above is a $30,000 loss resulting from a fire in the company's warehouse.

Required:
1. Redo the company's income statement by showing the loss net of tax.
2. Assume that the company has 20,000 shares of common stock outstanding. Compute the earnings per share as it should appear in the company's annual report to its stockholders.

PROBLEMS

P17–9. Ratio analysis and common-size statements. Modern Building Supply sells various building materials to retail outlets. The company has just approached Linden State Bank requesting a $300,000 loan to strengthen the cash account and to pay certain pressing short-term obligations. The company's financial statements for the most recent two years follow:

MODERN BUILDING SUPPLY
Comparative Balance Sheets

	This year	Last year
Assets		
Current assets:		
Cash	$ 90,000	$ 200,000
Marketable securities	—	50,000
Accounts receivable, net	650,000	400,000
Inventory	1,300,000	800,000
Prepaid expenses	20,000	20,000
Total current assets	2,060,000	1,470,000
Plant and equipment, net	1,940,000	1,830,000
Total assets	$4,000,000	$3,300,000
Liabilities and Stockholders' Equity		
Liabilities:		
Current liabilities	$1,100,000	$ 600,000
Bonds payable, 12%	750,000	750,000
Total liabilities	1,850,000	1,350,000
Stockholders' equity:		
Preferred stock, $50 par, 8%	200,000	200,000
Common stock, $10 par	500,000	500,000
Retained earnings	1,450,000	1,250,000
Total stockholders' equity	2,150,000	1,950,000
Total liabilities and stockholders' equity	$4,000,000	$3,300,000

MODERN BUILDING SUPPLY
Comparative Income Statements

	This year	Last year
Sales	$7,000,000	$6,000,000
Less cost of goods sold	5,400,000	4,800,000
Gross margin	1,600,000	1,200,000
Less operating expenses	970,000	710,000
Net operating income	630,000	490,000
Less interest expense	90,000	90,000
Net income before taxes	540,000	400,000
Less income taxes (40%)	216,000	160,000
Net income	324,000	240,000
Dividends paid:		
Preferred dividends	16,000	16,000
Common dividends	108,000	90,000
Total dividends paid	124,000	106,000
Net income retained	200,000	164,000
Retained earnings, beginning of year	1,250,000	1,086,000
Retained earnings, end of year	$1,450,000	$1,250,000

During the past year, the company has expanded the number of lines that it carries in order to stimulate sales and increase profits. It has also moved aggressively to acquire new customers. Sales terms are 2/10, n/30. All sales are on account.

Assume that the following ratios are typical of firms in the building supply industry:

Current ratio	2.5 to 1
Acid-test ratio	1.2 to 1
Average age of receivables	18 days
Inventory turnover in days	50 days
Debt-to-equity ratio	0.75 to 1
Times interest earned	6.0 times
Return on total assets	10%
Price-earnings ratio	9
Net income as a percentage	
of sales	4%

Required: 1. The Linden State Bank is uncertain whether the loan should be made. To assist it in making a decision, you have been asked to compute the following ratios for both this year and last year:

  a. The amount of working capital.
  b. The current ratio.
  c. The acid-test ratio.
  d. The average age of receivables. (The accounts receivable at the beginning of last year totaled $350,000.)
  e. The inventory turnover in days. (The inventory at the beginning of last year totaled $720,000.)
  f. The debt-to-equity ratio.
  g. The number of times interest was earned.

2. For both this year and last year (carry computations to one decimal place):

  a. Present the balance sheet in common-size form.
  b. Present the income statement in common-size form down through net income.

3. From your analysis in (1) and (2) above, what problems or strengths do you see existing in Modern Building Supply? Make a recommendation as to whether the loan should be approved.

P17–10. Investor ratios; consideration of stock sale. Refer to the financial statements and other data in Problem 17–9. Assume that you have just inherited several hundred shares of Modern Building Supply stock. Not being acquainted with the company, you decide to do some analytical work before making a decision about whether to retain or sell the stock you have inherited.

Required: 1. You decide first to assess the well-being of the common stockholders. For both this year and last year, compute:

  a. The earnings per share.
  b. The fully diluted earnings per share. The preferred stock is convertible into common stock at the rate of 2.5 shares of common for each share of preferred. The bonds are not convertible.
  c. The dividend yield ratio for common. The company's common stock is currently selling for $45 per share; last year it sold for $36 per share.
  d. The dividend payout ratio for common.
  e. The price-earnings ratio. How do investors regard Modern Building Supply as compared to other firms in the industry? Explain.
  f. The book value per share of common. Does the difference between market value and book value suggest that the stock at its current price is too high? Explain.

2. You decide next to assess the rate of return that the company is generating. Compute the following for both this year and last year:

a. The return on total assets. (Total assets at the beginning of last year were $2,700,000.)

b. The return on common equity. (Stockholders' equity at the beginning of last year was $1,786,000.)

c. Is the company's financial leverage positive or negative? Explain.

3. Based on your analytical work (and assuming that you have no immediate need for cash), would you retain or sell the stock you have inherited? Explain.

P17–11. **Effect of transactions on various ratios.** Selected amounts from Reingold Company's December 31, 19x1, balance sheet are given below:

Cash	$ 70,000
Marketable securities	12,000
Accounts receivable, net	350,000
Inventory	460,000
Prepaid expenses	8,000
Plant and equipment, net	950,000
Accounts payable	200,000
Accrued liabilities	60,000
Notes due within one year	100,000
Bonds payable in five years	140,000

During the next year (19x2), the company completed the following transactions:

x. Purchased inventory on account, $50,000.
a. Declared a cash dividend, $30,000.
b. Paid accounts payable, $100,000.
c. Collected cash on accounts receivable, $80,000.
d. Purchased equipment for cash, $75,000.
e. Paid a cash dividend previously declared, $30,000.
f. Borrowed cash on a short-term note with the bank, $60,000.
g. Sold inventory costing $70,000 for $100,000, on account.
h. Wrote off uncollectible accounts in the amount of $10,000.
i. Sold marketable securities costing $12,000 for cash, $9,000.
j. Issued additional shares of capital stock for cash, $200,000.
k. Paid off all short-term notes due, $160,000.

Required:

1. Compute the following amounts and ratios as of December 31, 19x1:
   a. Working capital.
   b. Current ratio.
   c. Acid-test ratio.

2. For 19x2, indicate the effect of each of the transactions given above on working capital, the current ratio, and the acid-test ratio. Give the effect in terms of increase, decrease, or none. Item (x) is given below as an example of the format to use:

	The effect on		
Transaction	**Working capital**	**Current ratio**	**Acid-test ratio**
(x) Purchased inventory on account	None	Decrease	Decrease

P17–12. **Comprehensive ratio analysis; industry comparisons.** Company A and Company B are in the same industry. The current year-end balance sheets for the two companies are given below:

Comparative Balance Sheets
December 31, 19x5

	Company A	Company B
Cash	$ 15,000	$ 10,000
Accounts receivable.	49,500	89,500
Inventory	55,000	117,000
Plant and equipment, net	150,000	240,000
Total assets.	$269,500	$456,500
Current liabilities	$ 56,900	$101,000
Bonds payable	100,000	100,000
Preferred stock, 6%, $100 par	35,000	40,000
Common stock, $10 par	50,000	100,000
Retained earnings	27,600	115,500
Total liabilities and capital	$269,500	$456,500

Selected data from the companies' current year-end income statements and other selected data follow:

Data from the Current Year-End Income Statements

	Company A	Company B
Sales.	$500,000	$700,000
Cost of goods sold	325,000	455,000
Interest expense	7,500	8,000
Net income before taxes	30,000	45,000
Net income.	18,000	27,000
Tax rate	40%	40%

Beginning-of-the-Year Data

	Company A	Company B
Accounts receivable	$ 45,500	$ 85,500
Inventory	51,000	113,000
Total assets	250,000	425,000
Common stockholders' equity	71,300	206,900

Industry Averages

Current ratio	2.1 to 1
Acid-test ratio	1.1 to 1
Accounts receivable turnover	10.0 times
Inventory turnover	5.7 times
Times interest earned.	6 times
Debt-to-equity ratio	0.9 to 1

Required: 1. Compute the following amounts and ratios for each company:
a. Working capital.
b. Current ratio.
c. Acid-test ratio.
d. Accounts receivable turnover. (All sales are on account.)
e. Average collection period for receivables. (Terms: n/30.)
f. Inventory turnover.

g. By use of these ratios, explain which company is the better short-term credit risk.

2. Compute the following ratios for each company:
 a. Times interest earned.
 b. Debt-to-equity ratio.
 c. By use of these ratios and any ratios from (1) above, explain which company could better take on *additional* long-term debt.

P17–13. **Stockholder ratio analysis; comparison with industry averages.** Refer to the financial statement data for Company A and Company B in Problem 17–12. Assume the following additional data for these two companies for the current year:

	Company A	Company B
Dividends paid:		
On preferred stock	$2,100	$ 2,400
On common stock	9,600	16,000
Market price per share (common)	48	45
Industry Ratios (averages)		
Dividend yield.	4%	
Price-earnings ratio	15	
Dividend payout ratio	60%	
Return on total assets	8%	
Return on common equity.	12%	

Required: 1. Compute the following ratios for each company for the current year:
 a. Earnings per share.
 b. Dividend yield ratio.
 c. Price-earnings ratio.
 d. Dividend payout ratio.
 e. Return on total assets.
 f. Return on common equity.

2. Is financial leverage positive or negative in the two companies? Explain.

3. By use of the ratios in (1) above, explain which company's stock is the better buy.

P17–14. **Common-size statements; trend analysis; selected ratios.** Comparative financial statements for the last three years are shown below for Palomar Company:

PALOMAR COMPANY
Comparative Income Statements
For the Years Ended May 31, 19x3, 19x4, and 19x5
(in thousands)

	19x5	19x4	19x3
Sales	$15,000	$12,000	$10,000
Less cost of goods sold	9,600	7,260	6,000
Gross margin	5,400	4,740	4,000
Less operating expenses	4,000	3,540	3,000
Net income before taxes.	1,400	1,200	1,000
Less income taxes (40%)	560	480	400
Net income	$ 840	$ 720	$ 600

PALOMAR COMPANY
Comparative Balance Sheets
May 31, 19x3, 19x4, and 19x5
(in thousands)

	19x5	19x4	19x3
Assets			
Current assets:			
Cash	$ 80	$ 100	$ 90
Accounts receivable, net	720	500	400
Inventory.	1,800	900	750
Total current assets	2,600	1,500	1,240
Plant and equipment, net	3,400	3,000	2,760
Total assets	$6,000	$4,500	$4,000
Liabilities and Stockholders' Equity			
Liabilities:			
Current liabilities	$1,250	$ 700	$ 500
Long-term debt	750	300	300
Total liabilities	2,000	1,000	800
Stockholders' equity:			
Common stock.	1,000	1,000	1,000
Retained earnings	3,000	2,500	2,200
Total stockholders' equity	4,000	3,500	3,200
Total liabilities and stockholders' equity	$6,000	$4,500	$4,000

At the end of 19x4, Mr. John Pushard became president of Palomar Company. Mr. Pushard had become president after serving for many years as a district sales manager and then as vice president, sales. He knew that 19x5 (his first year as president) had been the best year in the company's history as a result of a 25 percent increase in sales and an extensive cost-cutting effort that he initiated. For this reason, he was staggered when he received the statements above and noticed the sharp drop in cash and the dramatic increase in current liabilities. He muttered to himself, "With $15,000,000 coming in from sales, how could our cash account show a balance of only $80,000? These statements must be goofy."

Required:
1. Prepare the income statement and the balance sheet in common-size form for all three years. (Round computatons to one decimal place.)
2. Prepare trend percentages covering the three years for both the income statements and the balance sheets. (Round computations to one decimal place, e.g., 115.6 percent.)
3. For all three years, compute the following:
   a. The working capital.
   b. The current ratio. (Industry average: 2.5 to 1.)
   c. The acid-test ratio. (Industry average: 1.0 to 1.)
   d. The accounts receivable turnover in days. (Industry average: 13.0 days.) All sales are on account. The accounts receivable balance at the beginning of 19x3 was $360,000.
   e. The inventory turnover in days. (Industry average: 40.0 days.) The inventory balance at the beginning of 19x3 was $650,000.
4. Comment on the results of your analytical work above. What strengths, weaknesses, or developing problems do you see in the company?

P17–15. **Effect of leverage on the return on common equity.** Mr. J. R. Riddle and several other investors are in the process of organizing a new company to produce and distribute a household cleaning product. Mr. Riddle and his associates feel that $500,000 would be adequate to finance the new company's operations, and the group is studying three methods of raising this amount of money. The three methods are:

Method A: All $500,000 obtained through issue of common stock.

Method B: $250,000 obtained through issue of common stock and the other $250,000 obtained through issue of $100 par value, 10 percent preferred stock.

Method C: $250,000 obtained through issue of common stock and the other $250,000 obtained through issue of bonds carrying an interest rate of 10 percent.

Mr. Riddle and his associates are confident that the company can earn $100,000 each year before interest and taxes. The tax rate is 40 percent.

Required: 1. Assuming that Mr. Riddle and his associates are correct in their earnings estimate, compute the net income that would go to the common stockholders under each of the three financing methods listed above.

2. Using the income data computed in (1) above, compute the return on common equity under each of the three methods.

3. Why do methods B and C provide a greater return on common equity than does method A? Why does method C provide a greater return on common equity than method B?

P17–16. **Extraordinary gains and losses; earnings per share.** Rusco Products, Inc., has 10,000 shares of no-par common stock outstanding. The company's income statement for 19x7 as prepared by the company's accountant is given below:

Sales		$200,000
Cost of goods sold.		120,000
Gross margin.		80,000
Less operating expenses:		
Selling expenses.	$15,000	
Administrative expenses	30,000	
Loss from flood damage.	20,000	65,000
Income before taxes		15,000
Income taxes (40%)		6,000
Net income		$ 9,000

The earnings per share for Rusco Products, Inc.'s common stock over the past three years is given below:

	19x6	19x5	19x4
Earnings per share—common	$1.80	$1.50	$1.20

Required: 1. Consider the income statement as prepared by the company's accountant. Why might an investor have difficulty in interpreting this statement so far as determining Rusco Products, Inc.'s ability to generate normal after-tax earnings is concerned?

2. Recast the company's income statement in better form, showing the loss from flood damage net of tax.

3. Assume that rather than having a $20,000 loss from flood damage, the company has a $20,000 gain from sale of unused plant. Redo the income statement, showing the gain net of tax.

4. Using the income statements that you prepared in (2) and (3) above, compute the earnings per share of common stock.

5. Explain how your computation of earnings per share would be helpful to an investor trying to evaluate the trend of Rusco Products, Inc.'s earnings over the past few years.

P17–17. **Comprehensive problem—Part 1: Investor ratios.** (Problems 17–18 and 17–19 delve more deeply into the data presented below. Each problem is independent.) Empire Labs, Inc., was organized several years ago to produce and market several new "miracle drugs." The company is small but growing, and you are considering the purchase of some of its common stock as an investment. The following data on the company are available for the past two years:

EMPIRE LABS, INC.
Comparative Income Statements
For the Years Ended December 31, 19x1 and 19x2

	19x2	19x1
Sales	$20,000,000	$15,000,000
Less cost of goods sold	13,000,000	9,000,000
Gross margin	7,000,000	6,000,000
Less operating expenses	4,960,000	4,260,000
Net operating income	2,040,000	1,740,000
Less interest expense	240,000	240,000
Net income before taxes	1,800,000	1,500,000
Less income taxes (40%)	720,000	600,000
Net income	$ 1,080,000	$ 900,000

EMPIRE LABS, INC.
Statements of Changes in Retained Earnings
For the Years Ended December 31, 19x1 and 19x2

	19x2	19x1
Retained earnings, January 1	$2,400,000	$1,900,000
Add net income (above)	1,080,000	900,000
Total	3,480,000	2,800,000
Deduct cash dividends paid:		
Preferred dividends	120,000	120,000
Common dividends	360,000	280,000
Total dividends paid	480,000	400,000
Retained earnings, December 31	$3,000,000	$2,400,000

EMPIRE LABS, INC.
Comparative Balance Sheets
December 31, 19x1 and 19x2

	19x2	19x1
Assets		
Current assets:		
Cash	$ 200,000	$ 400,000
Accounts receivable, net	1,500,000	800,000
Inventory	3,000,000	1,200,000
Prepaid expenses	100,000	100,000
Total current assets	4,800,000	2,500,000
Plant and equipment, net	5,200,000	5,400,000
Total assets	$10,000,000	$7,900,000
Liabilities and Stockholders' Equity		
Liabilities:		
Current liabilities	$ 2,500,000	$1,000,000
Bonds payable, 12%	2,000,000	2,000,000
Total liabilities	4,500,000	3,000,000
Stockholders' equity:		
Preferred stock, 8%, $10 par	1,500,000	1,500,000
Common stock, $5 par	1,000,000	1,000,000
Retained earnings	3,000,000	2,400,000
Total stockholders' equity	5,500,000	4,900,000
Total liabilities and stockholders' equity	$10,000,000	$7,900,000

After some research, you have determined that the following ratios are typical of firms in the pharmaceutical industry:

Dividend yield ratio	3%
Dividend payout ratio	40%
Price-earnings ratio	16
Return on total assets	13.5%
Return on common equity	20%

The company's common stock is currently selling for $60 per share. During 19x1, the stock sold for $45 per share.

Required:
1. In analyzing the company, you decide first to compute the earnings per share and related ratios. For both 19x1 and 19x2, compute:
   a. The earnings per share.
   b. The fully diluted earnings per share. Assume that each share of the preferred stock is convertible into two shares of common stock. The bonds are not convertible.
   c. The dividend yield ratio.
   d. The dividend payout ratio.
   e. The price-earnings ratio.
   f. The book value per share of common stock.
2. You decide next to determine the rate of return which the company is generating. For both 19x1 and 19x2 compute:
   a. The return on total assets. (Total assets were $6,500,000 on January 1, 19x1.)

  b. The return on common stockholders' equity. (Common stockholders' equity was $2,900,000 on January 1, 19x1.)
  c. Is financial leverage positive or negative? Explain.
3. Based on your work in (1) and (2), does the company's common stock seem to be an attractive investment? Explain.

P17–18. **Comprehensive problem—Part 2: Creditor ratios.** Refer to the data in Problem 17–17. Although Empire Labs, Inc., has been very profitable since it was organized several years ago, the company is beginning to experience some difficulty in paying its bills as they come due. Management has approached Security National Bank requesting a two-year, $500,000 loan to bolster the cash account.

Security National Bank has assigned you to evaluate the loan request. You have gathered the following data relating to firms in the pharmaceutical industry:

Current ratio	2.4 to 1
Acid-test ratio	1.2 to 1
Average age of receivables	16 days
Inventory turnover in days	40 days
Times interest earned	7 times
Debt-to-equity ratio	0.70 to 1

The following additional information is available on Empire Labs, Inc.:

a. All sales are on account.
b. On January 1, 19x1, the accounts receivable balance was $600,000 and the inventory balance was $1,000,000.

Required:
1. Compute the following amounts and ratios for both 19x1 and 19x2:
    a. The working capital.
    b. The current ratio.
    c. The acid-test ratio.
    d. The accounts receivable turnover in days.
    e. The inventory turnover in days.
    f. The times interest earned.
    g. The debt-to-equity ratio.
2. Comment on the results of your analysis in (1) above.
3. Would you recommend that the loan be approved? Explain.

P17–19. **Comprehensive problem—Part 3: Common-size statements.** Refer to the data in Problem 17–17. The president of Empire Labs, Inc., is very concerned. Sales increased by $5 million in 19x2, yet the company's net income increased by only a small amount. Also, the company's operating expenses went up in 19x2, even though a major effort was launched during the year to cut costs.

Required:
1. For both 19x1 and 19x2, prepare the income statement and the balance sheet in common-size form. (Round computations to one decimal place.)
2. From your work in (1), explain to the president why the increase in profits was so small in 19x2. Were any benefits realized from the company's cost-cutting efforts? Explain.

P17–20. **Determining the effect of transactions on various financial ratios.** In the right-hand column below, certain financial ratios are listed. To the left of each ratio is a business transaction or event relating to the operating activities of Halver Company.

Business transaction or event	Ratio
1. Issued a common stock dividend to common stockholders.	Earnings per share
2. Paid accounts payable.	Debt-to-equity ratio
3. Purchased inventory on open account.	Acid-test ratio
4. Wrote off an uncollectible account against the Allowance for Bad Debts.	Current ratio
5. The market price of the company's common stock increased from 24½ to 30. Earnings per share remained unchanged.	Price-earnings ratio
6. The market price of the company's common stock increased from 24½ to 30. The dividend paid per share remained unchanged.	Dividend yield ratio
7. The company declared a cash dividend.	Current ratio
8. Sold inventory on account at cost.	Acid-test ratio
9. The company issued bonds with an interest rate of 8%. The company's return on assets is 10%.	Return on common stockholders' equity
10. The company's net income decreased by 10% between last year and this year. Long-term debt remained unchanged.	Times interest earned
11. A previously declared cash dividend was paid.	Current ratio
12. The market price of the company's common stock dropped from 24½ to 20. The dividend paid per share remained unchanged.	Dividend payout ratio
13. Obsolete inventory totaling $100,000 was written off as a loss.	Inventory turnover ratio
14. Sold inventory for cash at a profit.	Debt-to-equity ratio
15. Changed customer credit terms from 2/10, n/30 to 2/15, n/30 to comply with a change in industry practice.	Accounts receivable turnover ratio
16. Issued a common stock dividend on common stock.	Book value per share
17. The market price of the company's common stock increased from 24½ to 30.	Book value per share
18. The company paid $40,000 on accounts payable.	Working capital

Required: Indicate the effect that each business transaction or event would have on the ratio listed opposite to it. State the effect in terms of increase, decrease, or no effect on the ratio involved, and give the reason for your choice of answer. In all cases, assume that the current assets exceed the current liabilities both before and after the event or transaction. Use the following format for your answers:

Effect on ratio	Reason for increase, decrease, or no effect
1.	
Etc.	

P17–21. **Interpretation of already completed ratios.**   Being a prudent investor, Sally Perkins always investigates a company thoroughly before purchasing shares of its stock for investment. At present, Ms. Perkins is interested in the common stock of Plunge Enterprises. All she has available on the company is a copy of its annual report for the current year (19x3), which contains the 19x3 financial statements and the summary of ratios given below:

	19x3	19x2	19x1
Current ratio.	2.8 to 1	2.5 to 1	2.0 to 1
Acid-test ratio	0.7 to 1	0.9 to 1	1.2 to 1
Accounts receivable turnover.	8.6 times	9.5 times	10.4 times
Inventory turnover.	5.0 times	5.7 times	6.8 times
Sales trend	130.0	118.0	100.0
Dividends paid per share*	$2.50	$2.50	$2.50
Dividend yield ratio	5%	4%	3%
Dividend payout ratio.	40%	50%	60%
Return on total assets	13.0%	11.8%	10.4%
Return on common equity	16.2%	14.5%	9.0%

* There were no issues or retirements of common stock over the three-year period.

Ms. Perkins would like answers to a number of questions about the trend of events over the last three years in Plunge Enterprises. Her questions are:

a. Is the market price of the company's stock going up or down?

b. Is the amount of the earnings per share increasing or decreasing?

c. Is the price-earnings ratio going up or down?

d. Is the company employing financial leverage to the advantage of the common stockholders?

e. Is it becoming easier for the company to pay its bills as they come due?

f. Are customers paying their bills at least as fast now as they did in 19x1?

g. Is the total of the accounts receivable increasing, decreasing, or remaining constant?

h. Is the level of inventory increasing, decreasing, or remaining constant?

Required:
Answer each of Ms. Perkins' questions, using the data given above. In each case, explain how you arrived at your answer.

P17–22. **Incomplete statements; analysis of ratios.** Incomplete financial statements for Tanner Company are given below:

TANNER COMPANY
Income Statement
For the Year Ended December 31, 19x4

Sales	$2,700,000
Less cost of goods sold	?
Gross margin	?
Less operating expenses	?
Net operating income	?
Less interest expense.	45,000
Net income before taxes.	?
Less income taxes (40%)	?
Net income	$?

TANNER COMPANY
Balance Sheet
December 31, 19x4

Current assets:
Cash . . . . $?
Accounts receivable, net . . . .   ?
Inventory . . . .   ?
    Total current assets . . . .   ?
Plant and equipment, net . . . .   ?
Total assets . . . . $?

Current liabilities $250,000
Bonds payable, 10% . . . .   ?
    Total liabilities . . . .   ?

Stockholders' equity:
Common stock, $2.50 par value . . . .   ?
Retained earnings . . . .   ?
    Total stockholders' equity . . . .   ?
Total liabilities and stockholders' equity . . . . $?

The following additional information is available about the company:

a.   Selected financial ratios computed from the statements above are:

Current ratio . . . . 2.40 to 1
Acid-test ratio . . . . 1.12 to 1
Accounts receivable turnover . . . . 15.0 times
Inventory turnover . . . . 0.0 times
Debt-to-equity ratio . . . . 0.875 to 1
Times interest earned . . . . 7.0 times
Earnings per share $4.05
Return on total assets 14%

b.   All sales during the year were on account.
c.   The interest expense on the income statement relates to the bonds payable; the amount of bonds outstanding did not change throughout the year.
d.   There were no issues or retirements of common stock during the year.
e.   Selected balances at the *beginning* of the current year (January 1, 19x4) were:

Accounts receivable . . . . . . $ 160,000
Inventory   280,000
Total assets 1,200,000

Required: Compute the missing amounts on the company's financial statements. (Hint: You may find it helpful to think about the difference between the current ratio and the acid-test ratio.)

18 "How Well Am I Doing?"— Statement of Changes in Financial Position

Learning objectives

After studying Chapter 18, you should be able to:

Describe the purpose of the statement of changes in financial position.

Enumerate the major sources and uses of working capital in an organization.

Explain what is meant by a direct exchange transaction, and explain how it is handled on a funds statement.

Prepare an analysis of changes in working capital.

Prepare a funds statement in good form to show why working capital increased or decreased during a period.

State how a cash flow statement differs from a funds statement and prepare a cash flow statement.

Adjust the income statement to a cash basis.

Define or explain the key terms listed at the end of the chapter.

Three major statements are prepared annually by most companies—an income statement, a balance sheet, and a statement of changes in financial position. The statement of changes in financial position is less well known than the income statement or the balance sheet, but many view it as being equal in importance. In this chapter, our focus is on the development of the statement and on its use as a tool for assessing the well-being of a company.

THE PURPOSE OF THE STATEMENT

The purpose of the **statement of changes in financial position** is to show the sources and uses of either working capital or cash during an accounting period. The statement is used by managers, investors, and creditors alike to answer such questions as: Why has working capital increased (or decreased)? Is the company managing its cash well? What use was made of net income during the year? How was the company's plant expansion financed? Is the company's dividend policy in balance with its operating policies?

As we have indicated, the statement of changes in financial position can be made to focus either on working capital or on cash. In this section, we look at the statement from the point of view of an analysis of working capital. Later in the chapter, we look at it from the point of view of an analysis of cash.

An example of the statement

An example of a well-prepared statement of changes in financial position (with a focus on working capital) is presented in Exhibit 18–1. This statement has been prepared for Imperial Corporation, a highly diversified, international company dealing in high-quality food products.

Notice that the statement format differs considerably from the format of either the income statement or the balance sheet, although key elements from both the income statement and the balance sheet are represented in it. Three things in particular should be noted about the construction of the statement.

First, notice that the statement deals with *changes* in working capital. Second, notice that net income is a key item on the statement and that it is adjusted for "expenses not requiring the use of working capital," such as depreciation. Third, notice that a major part of the statement consists of changes that have taken place in various noncurrent balance sheet accounts, such as Plant and Equipment, Long-Term Debt, and Common Stock.

More is said in later sections about the construction of the statement. For the moment, let's look at the statement from the point of view of what it tells us about the policies and management of Imperial Corporation. First, observe that dividends are well balanced with net income in that the company has a payout ratio of about 30 percent in both 1984 and 1985 (dividends ÷ net income). Second, observe that in both years the bulk of the company's "Sources of working capital" came from operations. This shows that most

EXHIBIT 18–1

IMPERIAL CORPORATION
Statement of Changes in Financial Position
(In millions of dollars)

	Year ended June 30	
	1985	**1984**
Sources of working capital:		
Operations:		
Net income	$102.6	$ 87.4
Add back expenses not requiring the use of working capital:		
Depreciation expense	70.3	56.9
Increase in deferred income taxes	11.4	8.2
Total from operations	184.3	152.5
Disposals of property, plant, and equipment	16.7	13.1
Sale of investments and other assets	9.8	1.5
Increase in long-term debt	79.1	154.8
Issue of common stock	15.9	81.8
Total sources of working capital	305.8	403.7
Uses of working capital:		
Additions to property, plant, and equipment	254.1	230.6
Investments in stock of other companies	21.0	40.6
Retirements of long-term debt	14.0	35.2
Cash dividends	33.5	26.4
Purchase of treasury stock	1.3	12.8
Total uses of working capital	323.9	345.6
Increase (decrease) in working capital	$ (18.1)	$ 58.1

of the funds needed to support the company's growth are being generated internally, rather than being obtained primarily from outside sources.

Looking at specific years, observe that in addition to generating a substantial amount of working capital from operations in 1984 ($152.5 million), the company obtained additional working capital in that year from an issue of long-term debt ($154.8 million), a sale of common stock ($81.8 million), and two other miscellaneous activities. These funds were then used in 1984 to make substantial additions to property, plant, and equipment ($230.6 million); to acquire stock of other companies ($40.6 million); to retire long-term debt ($35.2 million); and to pay cash dividends ($26.4 million). Even after these needs were met, the company was still able to add $58.1 million to its working capital in 1984.

This buildup of working capital in 1984 was undoubtedly in anticipation of even greater acquisitions of property, plant, and equipment in 1985, which totaled $254.1 million. In that year, the company also retired more debt ($14.0 million) and increased its cash dividends ($33.5 million). These uses of funds in 1985 were financed primarily by operations ($184.3 million), by an additional issue of long-term debt ($79.1 million), and by drawing down some of the increase in working capital from the prior year ($18.1 million).

Notice that over the two-year period, working capital increased by a net amount of $40 million ($58.1 − $18.1 = $40.0), even though during this time the company expended nearly $500 million on additions to property, plant, and equipment. Moreover, this expansion was accomplished while maintaining a consistent and reasonable dividend policy.

In short, this statement provides every indication that Imperial Corporation is a stable, growing, well-managed organization. This is the purpose of the statement of changes in financial position—to draw out those key changes from the income statement and the balance sheet that will provide clues as to an organization's policies and financial management.

Alternative titles of the statement

In published corporate reports, the statement of changes in financial position is occasionally labeled as a *statement of sources and uses of working capital,* as a *statement of sources and application of funds,* or simply as a *funds statement.* The term *statement of changes in financial position* is preferred and should be used in published reports. For convenience in writing, however, the term **funds statement** has the advantage of brevity, and so it will be used to some extent in the remaining pages where we deal with working capital.

SOURCES AND USES OF WORKING CAPITAL

Now that we have an understanding of what the funds statement looks like and what it is designed to accomplish, we are prepared to analyze its construction. Exhibit 18–1 shows that the funds statement has two major sections, one titled "Sources of working capital" and the other titled "Uses of working capital." Several sources and several uses can be identified, as discussed in the two following sections.

Sources of working capital

There are three major sources of working capital in an organization. They are:

1. Profitable operations.
2. Long-term financing (sales of capital stock or issues of long-term debt).
3. Sales of plant, equipment, or other noncurrent assets.

These three sources are discussed below.

Profitable operations   Operations represents by far the most significant continuing source of working capital in most firms. If a company is not able to generate significant amounts of funds from its operations over time, then difficulties in maintaining an adequate working capital balance almost invariably develop. This is because there are limits to the amount of funds that can be obtained through long-term financing or by other means. Thus, operations must generally be depended on as the key source of additions to working capital from year to year. For this reason, many managers feel that the funds provided by operations represents the best leading indicator as to the economic health and well-being of an organization.

In this regard, we can see that Imperial Corporation generated $336.8 million in working capital from operations ($184.3 in 1985 plus $152.5 in 1984) over the two-year period reported in Exhibit 18–1. This is a healthy sign in that the funds generated by operations far exceeded the company's borrowing during this period. Thus, most of the company's growth is being financed by internal sources of funds, as stated earlier.

Long-term financing From time to time, it becomes necessary for a company to bolster its working capital position by turning to external sources of funds, such as Imperial Corporation did in 1984 and 1985. The two chief sources of long-term investment funds are sales of capital stock and issues of long-term debt. Notice from Exhibit 18–1 that Imperial Corporation sold small amounts of common stock in both 1984 and 1985, in addition to a large issue of long-term debt in 1984 ($154.8 million) and a smaller issue in 1985 ($79.1 million). These issues all represented sources of working capital to the company to supplement funds generated by operations.

Sales of assets Although sales of plant, equipment, and various other noncurrent assets (such as patents, leaseholds, and franchises) also constitute sources of working capital, these kinds of transactions are fairly infrequent and cannot be relied on as a significant or continuing source of funds to an organization. The reason is obvious—if an organization sells off its assets, it will cease to exist. Thus, the "Sources of working capital" section from Exhibit 18–1 contains only a nominal amount of funds provided from disposition or retirement of property.

Uses of working capital

The major uses of working capital in an organization are basically the opposite of its sources, with one additional item. The uses are:

1. Unprofitable operations.
2. Retirement of long-term financing (capital stock or long-term debt).
3. Purchase of plant, equipment, or other noncurrent assets.
4. Declaration of dividends.

These four uses are discussed below.

Unprofitable operations If operations are unprofitable, then a firm will suffer a net outflow of resources, resulting in a depletion of working capital for the period. Note, however, that even if the income statement shows a net loss for the year, the amount of working capital provided by operations can still be positive. This can happen, for example, if the depreciation charge deducted on the income statement is greater than the net loss reported for the period. To illustrate, assume that the depreciation deduction for the year is $50,000 and that the net loss shown on the income statement is $35,000. Under the "Sources of working capital" section of the funds statement, we would find:

Net income (loss)	$(35,000)
Add: depreciation	50,000
Total working capital from operations	$ 15,000

Thus, the company would show a positive amount of working capital provided by operations, even though a loss was sustained for the year. As this example suggests, the *composition* of the working capital provided by operations is just as important as the amount provided.

Retirement of long-term financing If a firm decides to retire capital stock or long-term debt, then working capital is drained out of the organization and must be entered under the "Uses of working capital" section of the funds statement. Although Imperial Corporation did not retire any capital stock during 1984 or 1985, we have already noted that the company did retire some of its long-term debt. These retirements appear as "Uses of working capital" on the company's funds statement for the reason just stated. Generally, any decision to retire capital stock or to retire long-term debt will be made only after much advance planning. This is to ensure that the retirement will not impair the company's working capital position.

Purchase of assets A much more common drain on working capital comes in the form of acquisitions of property, plant, and equipment. Investment in these areas is more or less continuous in most firms, and can represent a major use of funds if purchases in a particular year are especially large. The danger comes from expanding more rapidly than operations and long-term financing will permit, with a resulting drain on working capital. We have already noted that Imperial Corporation made major acquisitions of property, plant, and equipment during 1984 and 1985. However, these acquisitions appear to have created no major problems in the company, since they were covered adequately by funds provided by operations and through new issues of long-term debt.

Declaration of dividends Finally, the declaration of dividends represents a major use of working capital. A company's dividend policy must be an integral part of its overall financial planning, since a dividend policy that is poorly coordinated with plant expansion and with other uses of funds can be disastrous even to a profitable firm. Notice that we emphasize the "declaration" of dividends—not the payment of dividends—as having an effect on working capital. This is because the declaration of dividends increases current liabilities and thus reduces working capital. The later payment of the dividend so declared will have no effect on the working capital balance, as explained in a following section.

Summary of sources and uses

To summarize, those transactions that will result in either a source or a use of working capital have a common identifying characteristic: they involve a change in a noncurrent balance sheet account that also affects a current asset or a current liability account in some way. *Reread the preceding sentence before going on.* Refer again to the funds statement in Exhibit 18–1. Run your finger down the sources and uses of working capital shown there. Notice in each case that the item involved represents a change in a noncurrent balance sheet account (asset, liability, or equity) that has affected the company's current assets or current liabilities in some way.

With this thought in mind, we can summarize below the major sources and uses of working capital discussed in this section:

Sources of working capital

1. Profitable operations.
2. Long-term financing (sales of capital stock or issues of long-term debt).
3. Sales of plant, equipment, or other noncurrent assets.

Uses of working capital

1. Unprofitable operations.
2. Retirement of long-term financing (capital stock or long-term debt).
3. Purchase of plant, equipment, or other noncurrent assets.
4. Declaration of dividends.

In order to prepare a funds statement, therefore, one simply analyzes the noncurrent asset, liability, and equity accounts above to see what effect the changes in them had on the company's working capital during the period.

No effect on working capital

There are certain transactions that have no effect on working capital and therefore do not appear on the funds statement. These are transactions affecting only current asset and current liability accounts. For example, the collection of an account receivable will have no effect on the total amount of working capital in an organization. This is because the amount involved is simply transferred from one current asset account (Accounts Receivable) into another current asset account (Cash), with the total amount of working capital left unchanged.

Likewise, the payment of a current liability (such as dividends payable) has no effect on working capital, since both current assets and current liabilities are reduced by an equal amount. In short, if a transaction affects *only* current asset or current liability accounts, it will not change the total amount of working capital available and therefore will not appear on the funds statement.

Direct exchange transactions

Current practice requires that an *all-resources concept* be followed in preparing the funds statement.[1] An **all-resources concept** means that the funds

---

[1] See AICPA, *APB Opinion No. 19,* "Reporting Changes in Financial Position" (New York, March 1971), p. 373.

statement must be broad enough to include all significant financing and investing activities that may have occurred during a period, including any *direct exchange transactions.* Examples of **direct exchange transactions** would be the issue of capital stock in exchange for property or equipment, the conversion of long-term debt or preferred stock into common stock, and the acquisition of property and equipment under a long-term lease arrangement.

Such exchanges have a common identifying characteristic in that they affect only noncurrent balance sheet accounts, with no effect on Cash or other working capital accounts. Even though direct exchange transactions have no effect on working capital, they must still be included on the funds statement because they represent significant financing and investing activities, the existence of which should be made known to statement users. The purpose of the funds statement, as stated earlier, is to identify the sources of a company's financing and to show how the resulting funds were used. To omit direct exchange transactions from the funds statement would be misleading to statement users in that important sources and uses of financing would be concealed from view.

To illustrate how a direct exchange transaction is handled on the funds statement, assume the following situation:

Delsey Company acquired a building and paid for it in full by issuing 5,000 shares of its own common stock, which had a par value of $100 per share. Since the stock was selling for $120 per share at the time the building was acquired, the exchange was recorded as follows:

Building (5,000 shares × $120)	000,000	
Common Stock, $100 Par (5,000 shares × $100) . .		500,000
Paid-In Capital in Excess of Par (5,000 shares × $20) . .		100,000

This transaction had no effect on current assets or current liabilities, but it did involve both a financing activity (the issue of common stock) and an investing activity (the acquisition of the building). Thus, under the all-resources concept, it should be included on the funds statement. In preparing its funds statement for the period, Delsey Company would treat the exchange *as if* two transactions had taken place—first, *as if* 5,000 shares of common stock had been sold at its current market value of $120 per share ($600,000 total), and second, *as if* the proceeds from the sale had been used to acquire the building. By treating the exchange *as if* these two transactions had taken place, it becomes possible to present the following elements on the company's funds statement for the period:

Sources of working capital:
    Issue of common stock $600,000

Uses of working capital:
    Acquisition of building $600,000

All direct exchanges involving noncurrent asset, liability, and owners' equity accounts should be treated on the funds statement as shown above, with the exception of stock dividends and stock splits. The latter two items are not reported on the funds statement, since they are not considered to be financing activities.

THE FUNDS STATEMENT—AN ILLUSTRATION

In order to pull together the ideas considered thus far, we will turn to the financial statements of Example Company presented in Exhibits 18–2, 18–3, and 18–4 and prepare a funds statement. The numbers in these exhibits have been simplified for ease of computation and discussion.

Three basic steps to the funds statement

There are three basic steps to follow in preparing a funds statement:

1. Find the change that has taken place in working capital during the year.
2. Analyze each *noncurrent* balance sheet account to determine whether the change in the account resulted in a source or a use of working capital.
3. Total the sources and the uses of working capital obtained in step 2. The difference between the total sources and the total uses should equal the change in working capital obtained in step 1.

EXHIBIT 18–2

EXAMPLE COMPANY
Balance Sheets
December 31, 19x1 and 19x2

	19x2	19x1
Assets		
Current assets:		
Cash	$ 90	$ 50
Accounts receivable	610	300
Inventory	700	800
Total current assets	1,400	1,150
Long-term investments	300	500
Plant and equipment	3,200	2,500
Less accumulated depreciation	900	650
Net plant and equipment	2,300	1,850
Total assets	$4,000	$3,500
Liabilities and Stockholders' Equity		
Current liabilities:		
Accounts payable	$ 800	$ 400
Taxes payable	50	100
Total current liabilities	850	500
Bonds payable	550	900
Stockholders' equity:		
Capital stock	800	700
Retained earnings	1,800	1,400
Total stockholders' equity	2,600	2,100
Total liabilities and stockholders' equity	$4,000	$3,500

EXHIBIT 18–3

EXAMPLE COMPANY
Income Statement
For the Year Ended December 31, 19x2

Sales		$7,000
Cost of goods sold		4,000
Gross margin		3,000
Operating expenses:		
Selling expense	$1,200	
Administrative expense	950	
Depreciation expense	250	
Total operating expenses		2,400
Net income		$ 600

EXHIBIT 18–4

EXAMPLE COMPANY
Statement of Retained Earnings
For the Year Ended December 31, 19x2

Retained earnings, December 31, 19x1	$1,400
Add: Net income	600
	2,000
Deduct: Dividends declared	200
Retained earnings, December 31, 19x2	$1,800

Analysis of changes in working capital

The starting point in a funds statement is to see what change has taken place in the working capital balance during the year. This change is determined by preparing an **analysis of changes in working capital.** Such an analysis for Example Company is presented in Exhibit 18–5.

The analysis of Example Company's working capital shows that the amount of working capital decreased by $100 during 19x2. Having determined this decrease, we must now determine what caused it to happen. As explained earlier, the cause of a change in working capital can be determined by analyzing the company's *noncurrent* balance sheet accounts.

Changes in noncurrent balance sheet accounts

So far as the end result is concerned, it makes no difference which noncurrent account we analyze first, nor does it matter in which order we proceed. This is simply a matter of choice. Since operations usually represents the most significant source of funds, most analysts prefer to start with an analysis of the Retained Earnings account (which contains the period's net income).

Retained earnings From the balance sheet in Exhibit 18–2, we can see that retained earnings increased by $400 during 19x2 (going from $1,400

EXHIBIT 18–5

EXAMPLE COMPANY
Analysis of Changes in Working Capital
For the Year Ended December 31, 19x2

	19x2	19x1	Working capital increase (decrease)
Current assets:			
Cash	$ 90	$ 50	$ 40
Accounts receivable	610	300	310
Inventory	700	800	(100)
Total current assets	1,400	1,150	250
Current liabilities:			
Accounts payable	800	400	(400)
Taxes payable	50	100	50
Total current liabilities	850	500	(350)
Working capital	$ 550	$ 650	$(100)

at the end of 19x1 to $1,800 at the end of 19x2). To determine the cause of this change, we need to look at another exhibit—Exhibit 18–4—that contains an analysis of the Retained Earnings account. We can see from this exhibit that the $400 increase in retained earnings is a net result of $600 in net income for the year and $200 in dividends declared and paid during the year. From our earlier discussion on sources and uses of working capital, we know that these two items would be classified as a source and as a use, respectively, on the funds statement:

Sources of working capital:
Operations:
Net income $600

Uses of working capital:
Cash dividends $200

Plant and equipment We can now proceed through the other noncurrent balance sheet accounts to determine the impact of their changes on the company's working capital position. Plant and equipment has increased by $700 during the year (going from $2,500 in 19x1 to $3,200 in 19x2). From our earlier discussion, we know that a purchase of property, plant, and equipment represents a use of funds:

Sources of working capital:
Operations:
Net income $600

Uses of working capital:
Cash dividends $200
Purchase of plant and equipment 700

Accumulated depreciation The accumulated depreciation account has increased by $250 during 19x2. Looking at the income statement for Example Company in Exhibit 18–3, we can see that this $250 is a result of a $250 charge for depreciation expense. Since depreciation is an expense that does not require a present outflow of funds, any depreciation charges on the income statement must be added back to net income. This permits the company to see the total amount of funds provided by operations during the period. The computation on the funds statement would be:

Sources of working capital:
Operations:
Net income $600
Add back expenses not requiring
the use of working capital:
Depreciation expense 250
Total from operations 850

Uses of working capital:
Cash dividends $200
Purchase of plant and equipment 700

The mechanics of adding depreciation back to net income on the funds statement often leads people to the hasty conclusion that depreciation is a source of funds. We must state emphatically that depreciation is not a source of funds. We add it back to net income for the reason that it required no funds outlay during the period, yet it was deducted as an expense in arriving at net income. Thus, by adding it back, we are able to cancel out its effect, thereby leaving as part of net income only those items of revenue and expense that did affect the funds position during the period.

Certain other deductions on the income statement also reduce net income without involving an outflow of funds. These deductions include deferred income taxes,[2] depletion of natural resources, and amortization of goodwill, patents, and similar items. Like depreciation, these deductions must be added back to net income in determining the amount of funds provided by operations during a period.

Long-term investments Example Company's balance sheet in Exhibit 18-2 shows a $200 decrease in long-term investments during 19x2. Long-term investments would generally consist of securities (stocks and bonds) of other companies that are being held for some reason or other. If the amount of these investments decreases during a period, the most likely conclusion is that they were sold. From our earlier discussion of sources and uses of working capital, we know that the sale of a noncurrent asset is a source of funds:

Sources of working capital:
Operations:
Net income $600
Add back expenses not requiring
the use of working capital:
Depreciation expense 250
Total from operations 850
Sale of long-term investments 200

Uses of working capital:
Cash dividends $200
Purchase of plant and equipment 700

---

[2] Deferred income taxes represent income taxes deducted currently on the income statement but not remitted to the Internal Revenue Service until a later period (perhaps several years later). Such taxes are carried as a long-term liability on the balance sheet. It is the *increase* in the Deferred Income Taxes account during a particular period that represents the amount that should be added back to net income. See Exhibit 18–1.

Bonds payable Bonds payable decreased by $350 during 19x2 (going from $900 in 19x1 to $550 in 19x2). From our earlier discussion, we know that a retirement of long-term debt represents a use of funds:

```
Sources of working capital:
  Operations:
    Net income . . . . . . . . . . . . . . . .   $600
    Add back expenses not requiring
      the use of working capital:
    Depreciation expense . . . . . . . . . .     250
        Total from operations . . . . . . . .    850
  Sale of long-term investments . . . . . . .    200

Uses of working capital:
  Cash dividends . . . . . . . . . . . . . .   $200
  Purchase of plant and equipment . . . . . .    700
  Retirement of bonds payable . . . . . . . .    350
```

Capital stock Exhibit 18–2 shows that the capital stock account increased by $100 during 19x2. The most likely explanation of this increase is that the company issued more shares of stock during the year. An issue of stock represents a source of funds:

```
Sources of working capital:
  Operations:
    Net income . . . . . . . . . . . . . . . .   $600
    Add back expenses not requiring
      the use of working capital:
    Depreciation expense . . . . . . . . . .     250
        Total from operations . . . . . . . .    850
  Sale of long-term investments . . . . . . .    200
  Issue of capital stock . . . . . . . . . .     100

Uses of working capital:
  Cash dividends . . . . . . . . . . . . . .   $200
  Purchase of plant and equipment . . . . . .    700
  Retirement of bonds payable . . . . . . . .    350
```

The completed funds statement

We can now organize the results of our analytical work into statement form. Using the data that we have developed, a completed funds statement for Example Company is presented in Exhibit 18–6.

Notice from the exhibit that we have computed a total for both the sources of working capital and the uses of working capital. Also notice that the difference between these two totals ($100) equals the change in working capital derived earlier in Exhibit 18–5. Thus, by analyzing the company's noncurrent balance sheet accounts, we have been able to determine why working capital decreased during the year.

Uses of the funds statement

The funds statement is highly regarded as a management planning tool. Although it deals in historical costs, any lack of forward planning, coordina-

EXHIBIT 18–6

EXAMPLE COMPANY
Statement of Changes in Financial Position
For the Year Ended December 31, 19x2

Sources of working capital:
Operations:
    Net income . . . . $ 600
    Add back expenses not requiring
      the use of working capital:
      Depreciation expense. 250
        Total from operations 850
  Sale of long-term investments 200
  Issue of capital stock 100
      Total sources of working capital 1,150

Uses of working capital:
  Cash dividends 200
  Purchase of plant and equipment 700
  Retirement of bonds payable. 350
      Total uses of working captial. 1,250
Decrease in working capital . . . . $ (100)

tion, or balance in working toward long-run objectives becomes quickly evident in the story it has to tell. For example, a company may have as its stated objective to double plant capacity in five years using only funds provided through operations. If the company at the same time is paying dividends equal to earnings and is retiring large amounts of long-term debt, the discrepancy between long-run plans and current actions will be highlighted very quickly on the funds statement.

Some of the more significant ways in which managers use the funds statement include:

1. To coordinate dividend policy with other actions of the company.
2. To plan the financing of additional plant and equipment, the financing of new product lines, and the financing of new marketing outlets.
3. To find ways of strengthening a weak working capital position and thereby strengthening credit lines
4. To check the implementation of plans and policies.

A WORKING PAPER APPROACH TO THE FUNDS STATEMENT

The procedure relied on to this point of simply developing a funds statement through logic has allowed us to concentrate our efforts on learning basic concepts, with a minimum of effort expended on mechanics. For many firms, this simple logic procedure is completely adequate as a means of developing a funds statement.

The balance sheets of some companies, however, are so complex that working papers are needed to help organize the changes in noncurrent accounts into statement form. A number of working paper approaches to the funds statement are available. The one we have chosen to illustrate relies on the use of T-accounts to assist in the analysis and organization of data. In order to illustrate the T-account approach to working paper preparation, we will use the financial statements of Universal Company found in Exhibits 18–7 and 18–8.

Analysis of changes in working capital

The starting point of our analytical work will again be the preparation of an analysis of changes in working capital. This is done in Exhibit 18–9.

Universal Company has suffered a $2,000 decrease in its working capital during 19x2. As before, our objective will be to determine the *causes* of

EXHIBIT 18–7

UNIVERSAL COMPANY
Balance Sheets
December 31, 19x1 and 19x2

	19x2	19x1
Assets		
Current assets:		
Cash	$ 1,000	$ 2,000
Accounts receivable, net	9,000	4,000
Inventory	10,000	12,000
Total current assets	20,000	18,000
Plant and equipment (note 1)	38,500	30,000
Less accumulated depreciation	10,500	9,000
Net plant and equipment	28,000	21,000
Intangible assets:		
Patents	2,000	2,500
Total assets	$50,000	$41,500
Liabilities and Stockholders' Equity		
Current liabilities:		
Accounts payable	$ 7,000	$ 4,000
Accrued liabilities	4,000	2,500
Taxes payable	1,000	1,500
Total current liabilities	12,000	8,000
Mortgage payable	7,500	4,000
Stockholders' equity:		
Preferred stock	4,500	7,500
Common stock	11,000	10,000
Retained earnings	15,000	12,000
Total stockholders' equity	30,500	29,500
Total liabilities and stockholders' equity	$50,000	$41,500

Note 1: Equipment that had cost $1,500 new, and on which there was accumulated depreciation of $1,000, was sold during the year for its book value of $500.

EXHIBIT 18–8

UNIVERSAL COMPANY
Statement of Income and Reconciliation of Retained Earnings
For the Year Ended December 31, 19x2

Sales	$85,000
Cost of goods sold	62,500
Gross margin	22,500
Less operating expenses (note 2)	15,250
Income before taxes.	7,250
Income tax expense.	3,000
Net income.	4,250
Retained earnings, beginning.	12,000
Total	16,250

Less dividends distributed:		
Cash dividends, preferred	$ 250	
Stock dividends, common	1,000	1,250
Retained earnings, ending.		$15,000

Note 2: Operating expenses contain $2,500 of depreciation expense and $500 of patent amortization expense.

EXHIBIT 18–9

UNIVERSAL COMPANY
Analysis of Changes in Working Capital
For the Year Ended December 31, 19x2

	19x2	19x1	Working capital—increase or (decrease)
Current assets:			
Cash	$ 1,000	$ 2,000	$(1,000)
Accounts receivable.	9,000	4,000	5,000
Inventory	10,000	12,000	(2,000)
Total	20,000	18,000	2,000
Current liabilities:			
Accounts payable	7,000	4,000	(3,000)
Accrued liabilities.	4,000	2,500	(1,500)
Taxes payable.	1,000	1,500	500
Total	12,000	8,000	(4,000)
Working capital	$ 8,000	$10,000	$(2,000)

this change in the working capital balance. Also as before, our basic analytical approach will be to review the changes in noncurrent accounts. The only function that the T-accounts will serve will be to assist us in the mechanical process of *organizing* our information as it develops.

The T-account approach

In Exhibit 18–10, we have prepared a T-account for each of the noncurrent accounts found on Universal Company's balance sheet. In these T-accounts,

EXHIBIT 18–10

T-accounts showing changes in noncurrent account balances—Universal Company

	Working Capital	
Sources		Uses

Plant and Equipment		Accumulated Depreciation	
Bal.	30,000	Bal.	9,000
Bal.	38,500	Bal.	10,500

Patents		Mortgage Payable	
Bal.	2,500	Bal.	4,000
Bal.	2,000	Bal.	7,500

Common Stock		Preferred Stock	
Bal.	10,000	Bal.	7,500
Bal.	11,000	Bal.	4,500

Retained Earnings	
Bal.	12,000
Bal.	15,000

we have entered the beginning and ending balances of the noncurrent accounts. The exhibit also contains a T-account titled "Working Capital," which we will use to accumulate the sources and uses of working capital as they develop through our analysis of the noncurrent account changes.

The procedure is to make entries directly in the T-accounts to explain the actions that have caused the changes in the various noncurrent account balances. To the extent that changes in the noncurrent accounts have affected working capital, appropriate entries are made in the T-account representing working capital.

Retained earnings As we mentioned earlier in the chapter, the Retained Earnings account is generally the most useful starting point in developing a funds statement. Exhibit 18–8 presents a detail of the change in the Retained Earnings account of Universal Company. We can note from the exhibit that net income of $4,250 was added to retained earnings during 19x2 and that dividends of $1,250 were charged against retained earnings.

The dividends consisted of $250 in cash dividends and $1,000 in stock dividends.

Entries have been made in the T-accounts in Exhibit 18–11 to show the effect of these activities on the company's working capital, as follows: Entry (1) shows the increase in retained earnings that resulted from the net income reported for 19x2 and the corresponding increase that would have come about in working capital:

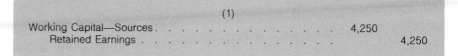

	(1)	
Working Capital—Sources.	4,250	
Retained Earnings		4,250

Entry (2) records the payment of cash dividends on preferred stock and the corresponding drain on working capital:

	(2)	
Retained Earnings	250	
Working Capital—Uses		250

Entry (3) records the distribution of a stock dividend to common stockholders. A stock dividend has no effect on working capital. It simply capitalizes a portion of retained earnings and results in no outflow of assets:

	(3)	
Retained Earnings	1,000	
Common Stock		1,000

The reader should trace these three entries into the T-accounts in Exhibit 18–11.

Notice from the exhibit that these three entries fully explain the change that has taken place in the Retained Earnings account during the period. We can now proceed through the remainder of the noncurrent accounts, analyzing the change between beginning and ending balances in each one, and recording the appropriate entries in the T-accounts.

Plant and equipment   Notice from the T-accounts that the Plant and Equipment account has increased by $8,500 during the year. This increase could simply represent $8,500 in plant and equipment purchases. On the other hand, there may have been retirements or sales during the year that are concealed in this net change.

From the footnote to the balance sheet, we find that certain items of equipment were, indeed, sold during 19x2 at a sale price of $500. The entry to record this sale and its effect on working capital would be:

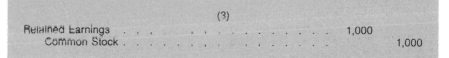

	(4)	
Working Capital—Sources.	500	
Accumulated Depreciation	1,000	
Plant and Equipment		1,500

EXHIBIT 18–11
T-accounts after completion of all noncurrent accounts analysis—Universal Company

Working Capital

Sources			Uses		
(1)	4,250	From operations: Net income	(2)	250	To pay cash dividends
(4)	500	From sale of equipment	(5)	10,000	To purchase equipment
(6)	2,500	From operations: Depreciation	(9)	3,000	To retire preferred stock
(7)	500	From operations: Patent amortization			
(8)	3,500	From issue of mortgage note			

Plant and Equipment

Bal.	30,000		(4)	1,500
(5)	10,000			
Bal.	38,500			

Accumulated Depreciation

(4)	1,000		Bal.	9,000
			(6)	2,500
			Bal.	10,500

Patents

Bal.	2,500		(7)	500
Bal.	2,000			

Common Stock

			Bal.	10,000
			(3)	1,000
			Bal.	11,000

Preferred Stock

(9)	3,000		Bal.	7,500
			Bal.	4,500

Retained Earnings

(2)	250		Bal.	12,000
(3)	1,000		(1)	4,250
			Bal.	15,000

Mortgage Payable

			Bal.	4,000
			(8)	3,500
			Bal.	7,500

Explanation of entries:

(1) To record net income for the year.
(2) To record payment of a cash dividend.
(3) To record a stock dividend.
(4) To record the sale of equipment.
(5) To record the purchase of equipment.
(6) To record the depreciation expense for the year.
(7) To record patent amortization expense for the year.
(8) To record the issue of a mortgage note.
(9) To record retirement of preferred stock.

How much did the company expend on plant and equipment purchases during the year? Overall, we know that the Plant and Equipment account increased by $8,500. Since this $8,500 increase is what remains *after* the $1,500 retirement of equipment recorded above, then purchases during the year must have amounted to $10,000 ($10,000 − $1,500 = $8,500 net increase). Entry (5) records these purchases in the T-accounts:

(5)		
Plant and Equipment.	10,000	
Working Capital—Uses		10,000

Accumulated depreciation Footnote 2 on Universal Company's income statement indicates that depreciation expense totaled $2,500 for the year. The entry in the T-accounts would be:

(6)		
Working Capital—Sources (Operations)	2,500	
Accumulated Depreciation		2,500

This entry, along with entry (4) above, explains the change in the accumulated depreciation account for the year.

Patents Note 2 on Universal Company's income statement indicates that $500 of patent amortization expense was charged against earnings for the year. As stated earlier, amortization expense is similar to depreciation expense and is handled in the same way on the funds statement. The entry would be:

(7)		
Working Capital—Sources (Operations)	500	
Patents		500

Mortgage payable The company obtained funds during the year by increasing the amount of its mortgage debt. The entry in the T-accounts would be:

(8)		
Working Capital—Sources	3,500	
Mortgage Payable		3,500

Preferred Stock Since we have no contrary information, we will have to assume that the $3,000 decrease in the Preferred Stock account is a result of repurchase and retirement of shares. Entry (9) records the repurchase:

(9)		
Preferred Stock	3,000	
Working Capital—Uses		3,000

Common stock   The increase in the Common Stock account is explainable in this example by the $1,000 in stock dividends issued to common stockholders. This issue was recorded in the T-accounts earlier in entry (3). (Although not true in this case, an increase in the Common Stock account will frequently be the result of an issue of additional shares of stock, which will be a source of working capital.)

With this analysis of the Common Stock account, our analysis of the noncurrent accounts on Universal Company's balance sheet is complete.

The completed funds statement

The T-accounts in Exhibit 18–11 now contain the final results of our analysis of Universal Company's noncurrent balance sheet accounts. All that now remains is to organize these data into statement form, which is done in Exhibit 18–12. The reader should review this statement carefully, and as an exercise state in his or her own words what caused working capital in Universal Company to decrease by $2,000 during the year.

EXHIBIT 18–12

UNIVERSAL COMPANY
Statement of Changes in Financial Position
For the Year Ended December 31, 19x2

Sources of working capital:	
Operations:	
Net income	$ 4,250
Add back expenses not requiring	
the use of working capital:	
Depreciation expense	2,500
Patent amortization expense	500
Total from operations	7,250
Sale of equipment	500
Issue of a mortgage note	3,500
Total sources of working capital	11,250
Uses of working capital:	
Cash dividends	250
Purchase of equipment	10,000
Retirement of preferred stock	3,000
Total uses of working capital	13,250
Decrease in working capital	$ (2,000)

FOCUSING ON CHANGES IN CASH

In preparing a statement of changes in financial position, some firms prefer to focus on cash rather than on working capital. The purpose of the statement then becomes to explain what has caused cash to increase or to decrease during a period. A statement with its emphasis on changes in cash (often called a **cash flow statement**) can be particularly useful to a firm that is experiencing cash problems, although that certainly is not a requisite for using cash rather than working capital as the point of focus. With cash as the point of focus, the manager can see what his or her sources of cash were during the period and see how this cash was used. Thus, management is in a better position to monitor the Cash account and to ensure that the company's liquidity position is not impaired by unwise financing or operating decisions.

An Example of a statement of changes in financial position that has a focus on cash flows is presented in Exhibit 18–13. The data on this statement are the same as those used earlier in Exhibit 18–1 (where we first introduced the statement of changes in financial position). Comparison of the data in these two exhibits will show that there is only one difference between a cash flow statement and a funds statement. The difference is that the cash flow statement contains changes in current asset and current liability accounts (such as Accounts Receivable, Inventory, and Accounts Payable), as well

EXHIBIT 18–13

IMPERIAL CORPORATION
Statement of Changes in Financial Position (Cash Basis)
(In millions of dollars)

	Year ended June 30	
	1985	1984
Sources of cash:		
Operations:		
Net income	$102.6	$ 87.4
Add back expenses not requiring the use of cash:		
Depreciation on plant and equipment	70.3	56.9
Deferred income taxes	11.4	8.2
Total from operations	184.3	152.5
Decrease in inventory	2.7	9.6
Increase in accounts payable	80.1	23.4
Disposals of property, plant, and equipment	16.7	13.1
Sale of investments and other assets	9.8	1.5
Increase in long-term debt	79.1	154.8
Issue of common stock	15.9	81.8
Total sources of cash	388.6	436.7
Uses of cash:		
Increase in accounts receivable	54.3	37.5
Decrease in accrued liabilities	16.0	14.1
Additions to property, plant, and equipment	254.1	230.6
Investments in stock of other companies	21.0	40.6
Retirements of long-term debt	14.0	35.2
Cash dividends	33.5	26.4
Purchase of treasury stock	1.3	12.8
Total uses of cash	394.2	397.2
Increase (decrease) in cash	$ (5.6)	$ 39.5

as changes in the noncurrent balance sheet accounts. Thus, our approach to preparing a cash flow statement will differ somewhat from the approach used earlier in preparing a funds statement. We discuss this difference in approach in the following sections.

What activities have an impact on cash?

In our earlier discussion, when we focused on working capital, we found that changes in the noncurrent balance sheet accounts contained the key to why working capital changed during a period. As we now focus on cash, we will again analyze changes in the noncurrent accounts. But, as suggested by the items included on Imperial Corporation's statement in Exhibit 18–13, we must go a step further. We must also analyze changes in the current asset and current liability accounts and include them on the statement as well. The reason is that changes in the current asset and current liability accounts have just as much effect on cash as do changes in the noncurrent accounts. The major sources and uses of cash, as reflected on the cash flow statement, are discussed in the following two sections.

Sources of cash

Sources of cash in an organization include:

1. Profitable operations.
2. Long-term financing (sales of capital stock or issues of long-term debt).
3. Sales of plant, equipment, or other noncurrent assets.
4. An increase in any current liability account.
5. A decrease in any current asset account.

The reader may wish to compare these sources of cash against the sources of working capital listed earlier on page 767. As may be seen from page 767, the first three sources are the same; thus, only items (4) and (5) require any further explanation.

Increase in any current liability. In the normal course of events, short-term creditors extend credit to a firm, are paid off, re-extend credit, and are paid off again, on a continuing basis period after period. Most firms depend on these short-term creditors as a major source of financing and for this reason try to keep the turnover going smoothly. If management should make a decision, however, to defer paying short-term creditors, then the volume of accounts due would expand. The result would be that cash that would otherwise have gone to pay creditors would be kept in the organization and would be available to use internally. By this line of reasoning, one can see that *increases* in amounts due to short-term creditors represent a *source* of cash to a firm.

Decrease in any current asset. Current assets such as inventory and accounts receivable represent an investment of cash. If the level of investment in any current asset is reduced, then cash is freed to flow back into the Cash account. Therefore, a decrease in a current asset (such as inventory or accounts receivable) should be entered on the cash flow statement in the "Sources of cash" section.

Uses of cash

Uses of cash in an organization include:

1. Unprofitable operations.
2. Retirement of long-term financing (capital stock or long-term debt).
3. Purchase of plant, equipment, or other noncurrent assets.
4. Payment of dividends.
5. A decrease in any current liability account.
6. An increase in any current asset account.

Again, the reader may wish to compare these uses of cash against the uses of working capital listed earlier on page 768. As may be seen from page 768, the first four uses are the same, with the exception that we now list the payment of dividends, rather than the declaration of dividends, as a use. Therefore, only items (5) and (6) require any further explanation.

Decrease in any current liability. We stated in the preceding section that if payments to creditors are deferred, the resulting increase in current liabilities represents a source of cash to an organization. By this same line of reasoning, if payments to creditors are accelerated so that overall current liabilities *decrease,* the result will be a net outflow of cash. Therefore, in preparing a cash flow statement, a reduction in a current liability account should be treated as a use of cash.

Increase in any current asset. An increase in a current asset account also represents a use of cash on the cash flow statement. A decision on the part of management, for example, to expand the volume of inventory being carried will cause a drain on the Cash account, as cash is tied up in investment in inventory. In like manner, a decision to liberalize credit terms will result in an expanded volume of receivables as customers take longer to pay. The buildup of receivables will result in decreased cash being available internally.

Managers often fail to recognize that an expansion of inventory or receivables represents just as much of an investment decision as a decision to expand the size of the plant and equipment. As a practical matter, an investment in inventories or in receivables can be just as illiquid as an investment in plant and equipment. Once inventories have been built up, there is always a reluctance to trim them back down, particularly if customers have become used to the greater variety of selection available. And once customers have become used to taking longer to pay, it is an extremely difficult task to speed collections up again.

The cash flow statement—an illustration

To illustrate the preparation of a cash flow statement, we return to the balance sheet and the income statement of Universal Company in Exhibits 18–7 and 18–8. Data from these exhibits have been assembled in working paper form in Exhibit 18–14 as a basis for preparing a cash flow statement

EXHIBIT 18–14
T-account working papers—cash flow statement

Cash

Sources			Uses	
(1)	4,250	(2)	250	
(5)	2,000	(4)	5,000	
(6)	500	(7)	10,000	
(8)	2,500	(12)	3,000	
(9)	500			
(10)	4,000			
(11)	3,500			

From operations: Net income
From decrease in inventory
From sale of equipment
From operations: Depreciation
From operations: Patent amortization
From increase in current liabilities
From issue of mortgage note

To pay cash dividends
To increase accounts receivable
To purchase equipment
To retire preferred stock

Accounts Receivable

Bal.	4,000		
(4)	5,000		
Bal.	9,000		

Inventory

Bal.	12,000	(5)	2,000
Bal.	10,000		

Patents

Bal.	2,500	(9)	500
Bal.	2,000		

Mortgage Payable

		Bal.	4,000
		(11)	3,500
		Bal.	7,500

Plant and Equipment

Bal.	30,000	(6)	1,500
(7)	10,000		
Bal.	38,500		

Accounts Payable

		Bal.	4,000
		(10)	3,000
		Bal.	7,000

Common Stock

		Bal.	10,000
		(3)	1,000
		Bal.	11,000

Accumulated Depreciation

(6)	1,000	Bal.	9,000
		(8)	2,500
		Bal.	10,500

Accrued Liabilities

		Bal.	2,500
		(10)	1,500
		Bal.	4,000

Preferred Stock

(12)	3,000	Bal.	7,500
		Bal.	4,500

Taxes Payable

(10)	500	Bal.	1,500
		Bal.	1,000

Retained Earnings

(2)	250	Bal.	12,000
(3)	1,000	(1)	4,250
		Bal.	15,000

EXHIBIT 18–15

UNIVERSAL COMPANY
Statement of Changes in Financial Position
For the Year Ended December 31, 19x2

Sources of cash:	
Operations:	
Net income.	$ 4,250
Add back expenses not requiring	
the use of cash:	
Depreciation expense	2,500
Patent amortization expense	500
Total from operations.	7,250
Decrease in inventory	2,000
Sale of equipment	500
Increase in current liabilities.	4,000
Issue of mortgage note	3,500
Total sources of cash.	17,250
Uses of cash:	
Cash dividends	250
Increase in accounts receivable	5,000
Purchase of equipment	10,000
Retirement of preferred stock	3,000
Total uses of cash	18,250
Decrease in cash . . . . ,	$ (1,000)

for the company. The only difference between these working papers and the ones prepared earlier is that these contain changes in current asset and current liability accounts as well as changes in the noncurrent accounts. Otherwise, the working papers are set up and analyzed in the same way as was done earlier for the funds statement.

Using the data from the working papers, a cash flow statement for Universal Company is presented in Exhibit 18–15. Observe that the $1,000 decrease in cash shown on the statement agrees with the decrease in cash shown on Universal Company's balance sheet in Exhibit 18–7.

We can summarize the cause of this $1,000 decrease in cash as follows: During 19x2, Universal Company's major sources of cash were from operations, $7,250; from reduction of inventories, $2,000; from expansion of current liabilities, $4,000; and from issue of long-term debt, $3,500. The total of these sources of cash was insufficient to cover all of the uses of cash during the year. The major uses of cash were to expand accounts receivable, $5,000; to purchase equipment, $10,000; and to retire preferred stock, $3,000. The result was an overall reduction of $1,000 in cash available to the firm.

SUMMARY

The statement of changes in financial position is one of the three major statements prepared by business firms. Its purpose is analytical in that it attempts to explain how working capital has been provided and how it has been used during an accounting period. As such, the statement is a very useful tool in attempting to assess how well a firm is doing and how well its management is performing.

If management feels that the information would be more useful, the statement of changes in financial position can be made to focus on changes in cash, rather than on changes in working capital. If working capital is the focus of the statement, then any change in working capital can be explained by an analysis of the noncurrent accounts. If cash is the focus of the statement, then any change in cash can be explained by an analysis of *all* other accounts, current as well as noncurrent.

KEY TERMS FOR REVIEW

All-resources concept The inclusion on the statement of changes in financial position of all significant financing and investing activities that may have taken place during a period, including any direct exchanges. See *Direct exchange transactions.*

Analysis of changes in working capital A schedule showing the effect of increases and decreases in current asset and current liability accounts on working capital during a period.

Cash flow statement A statement of changes in financial position that has its focus on changes in cash.

Direct exchange transaction A transaction involving only noncurrent accounts, such as the issue of capital stock in exchange for property or equipment, the conversion of long-term debt or preferred stock into common stock, and the acquisition of property under a long-term lease agreement.

Funds statement A statement of changes in financial position that has its focus on changes in working capital.

Statement of changes in financial position A statement designed to show the major sources and uses of either working capital or cash during a period.

APPENDIX: MODIFIED CASH FLOW STATEMENT

When preparing a cash flow statement for use internally, some managers prefer a format that adjusts all changes in current asset and current liability accounts through the income statement, rather than setting these changes out on the cash flow statement itself. If changes in the current asset and current liability accounts are adjusted through the income statement, then the resulting cash flow statement will be identical to the funds statement, except for the "funds from operations" figure. Although a cash flow statement prepared in this way is rarely used in published annual reports, it can be useful to the manager internally for analysis purposes.

An illustration

To illustrate how a cash flow statement is prepared using this modified format, refer again to the statements for Universal Company in Exhibits

18–7 and 18–8. The procedure required for adjusting changes in the current asset and current liability accounts through the income statement is presented in Exhibit 18–16. Notice that through this adjustment process the income statement is changed to a cash basis.

Using the "net cash flow from operations" figure derived in Exhibit 18–16, we present a cash flow statement for Universal Company in Exhibit 18–17.

Observe that once the "net cash flow from operations" figure is obtained, the noncurrent balance sheet accounts are analyzed in the same way as was done earlier in the chapter.

EXHIBIT 18–16
Income statement adjusted to a cash basis

Revenue or expense item	Plus or minus adjustments to derive cash basis	Illustration— Universal Company
Revenue (as reported on the income statement)		$85,000
Adjustments to cash basis:		
1. Increase in accounts receivable	−	−5,000
2. Decrease in accounts receivable.	+	
Revenue adjusted to cash basis		$80,000
Cost of goods sold (as reported on the income statement)		$62,500
Adjustments to cash basis:		
3. Increase in inventory	+	
4. Decrease in inventory	−	−2,000
5. Increase in accounts payable	−	−3,000
6. Decrease in accounts payable	+	
Cost of goods sold adjusted to cash basis		57,500
Operating expenses (as reported on the income statement)		$15,250
Adjustments to cash basis:		
7. Increase in accrued liabilities	−	−1,500
8. Decrease in accrued liabilities.	+	
9. Increase in prepaid expenses	+	
10. Decrease in prepaid expenses	−	
11. Period's depreciation, amortization, and depletion ($2,500 + $500)	−	−3,000
Operating expenses adjusted to cash basis		10,750
Income tax expense (as reported on the income statement)		$ 3,000
Adjustments to cash basis:		
12. Increase in accrued taxes payable	−	
13. Decrease in accrued taxes payable.	+	+ 500
14. Increase in deferred income taxes	−	
15. Decrease in deferred income taxes	+	
Income taxes adjusted to cash basis		3,500
Net cash flow from operations		$ 8,250

EXHIBIT 18–17

UNIVERSAL COMPANY
Statement of Changes in Financial Position
For the Year Ended December 31, 19x2

Sources of cash:
Net cash flow from operations.	$ 8,250
Sale of equipment.	500
Issue of mortgage note	3,500
Total sources of cash.	12,250

Uses of cash:
Payment of cash dividends.	250
Purchase of equipment	10,000
Retirement of preferred stock.	3,000
Total uses of cash.	13,250
Decrease in cash.	$ (1,000)

Working paper procedure

Adjustment of the income statement to a cash basis is not necessary if working papers are prepared, since the working papers will make this adjustment automatically. To illustrate, working papers are presented in Exhibit 18–18 from which the modified cash flow statement in Exhibit 18–17 could have been prepared. Notice that these working papers automatically compute the $8,250 "net cash flow from operations" figure needed for the statement. Thus, the adjustment of the income statement to a cash basis, such as illustrated in Exhibit 18–16, is needed only if working papers are *not* prepared.

QUESTIONS

18–1. What is the purpose of the funds statement?

18–2. To the layperson, "funds" means cash. Yet when business executives speak of funds, they generally have working capital in mind. Why do you suppose business executives think of funds in terms of working capital rather than in terms of cash?

18–3. What are the major sources of working capital, and what are the major uses of working capital?

18–4. In determining the amount of funds (working capital or cash) provided by operations, why is it necessary to add depreciation back to net income? What other income statement items must also be added back to net income in determining the amount of funds provided by operations?

18–5. Appleby Company had a net loss for the year, yet its funds statement shows a *positive* amount of funds provided by operations. How is this possible?

18–6. A business executive once stated, "Depreciation is one of our biggest sources of funds." Do you agree that depreciation is a source of funds? Explain.

EXHIBIT 18–18
T-account working papers—modified cash flow statement

Cash

	Sources		Uses
From operations:			
Net income	(1) 4,250	Increase in accounts receivable	(4) 5,000
Decrease in inventory	(5) 2,000		
Depreciation	(8) 2,500		
Patent amortization	(9) 500		
Increase in current liabilities	(10) 4,000		
Net cash flow from operations	8,250		
From sale of equipment	(6) 500	To pay cash dividends	(2) 250
From issue of mortgage note	(11) 3,500	To purchase equipment	(7) 10,000
		To retire preferred stock	(12) 3,000

Accounts Receivable

Bal. 4,000	
(4) 5,000	
Bal. 9,000	

Inventory

Bal. 12,000	(5) 2,000
Bal. 10,000	

Plant and Equipment

Bal. 30,000	(6) 1,500
(7) 10,000	
Bal. 38,500	

Accumulated Depreciation

(6) 1,000	Bal. 9,000
	(8) 2,500
	Bal. 10,500

Patents

Bal. 2,500	(9) 500
Bal. 2,000	

Accounts Payable

	Bal. 4,000
	(10) 3,000
	Bal. 7,000

Accrued Liabilities

	Bal. 2,500
	(10) 1,500
	Bal. 4,000

Taxes Payable

(10) 500	Bal. 1,500
	Bal. 1,000

Mortgage Payable

	Bal. 4,000
	(11) 3,500
	Bal. 7,500

Common Stock

	Bal. 10,000
	(3) 1,000
	Bal. 11,000

Preferred Stock

(12) 3,000	Bal. 7,500
	Bal. 4,500

Retained Earnings

(2) 250	Bal. 12,000
(3) 1,000	(1) 4,250
	Bal. 15,000

18-7. Certain transactions have no effect on working capital and do not appear on the funds statement. Give an example of such a transaction.

18-8. What is meant by the "all-resources concept" of preparing a funds statement?

18-9. Give an example of a direct exchange, and explain how such exchanges are treated on the funds statement.

18-10. During the current year, a company declared, but did not pay, a cash dividend of $50,000 and a 5 percent stock dividend. How will these two items be treated on the current year's funds statement?

18-11. Able Company started the year with $100,000 in accounts receivable. The company ended the year with only $80,000 in accounts receivable. Was this decrease in accounts receivable a source of funds to the company on the funds statement? Explain.

18-12. How does a funds statement differ from a cash flow statement?

18-13. Under what conditions would the cash flow statement be more useful to a firm than the funds statement? Under what conditions would the funds statement be more useful?

18-14. What are the major sources of cash in an organization? What are the major uses of cash?

18-15. An outside member of the board of directors of a small but rapidly growing manufacturing company is puzzled by the fact that the company is very profitable, yet never seems to have enough cash to pay its bills on time. Explain to the director how a company can be profitable, yet experience shortages of cash. The company pays no dividends.

18-16. (Appendix) A merchandising company showed $250,000 cost of goods sold on its income statement. Its beginning inventory was $75,000, and its ending inventory was $60,000. Accounts payable were $50,000 at the beginning of the year and $40,000 at the end of the year. Compute the cost of goods sold adjusted to a cash basis.

18-17. (Appendix) Company X shows operating expenses of $150,000 on its income statement. Depreciation for the period totaled $30,000. Accrued liabilities totaled $16,000 at the beginning of the year and $25,000 at the end of the year. Prepaid expenses totaled $10,000 at the beginning of the year and $15,000 at the end of the year. Compute the operating expenses adjusted to a cash basis.

EXERCISES

E18-1. Strident Company's current asset and current liability accounts for the last two years are given below:

	December 31	
	19x2	19x1
Current assets:		
Cash	$ 21,000	$ 15,000
Accounts receivable, net	40,000	48,000
Inventory	130,000	120,000
Prepaid expenses	2,000	3,000
Total current assets	$193,000	$186,000

Current liabilities:		
Accounts payable	$ 70,000	$ 65,000
Accrued liabilities.	4,000	7,000
Current portion of long-term debt	6,000	5,000
Total current liabilities	$ 80,000	$ 77,000

Required: Prepare an analysis of changes in working capital in good form for 19x2.

E18–2. Comparative financial statement data for Merrill Company are presented below:

	December 31	
	19x5	**19x4**
Current assets	$ 30	$ 20
Long-term investments	10	13
Property and equipment	120	105
Accumulated depreciation	(45)	(36)
Total assets	$115	$102
Current liabilities.	$ 15	$ 9
Long-term debt	6	10
Common stock, no par	30	25
Retained earnings	64	58
Total liabilities and stockholders' equity	$115	$102

Other selected data relating to 19x5 follow:

Net income	$10
Cash dividends declared and paid	4
Depreciation expense	9

Required: 1. Prepare an analysis of changes in working capital.

2. Prepare a funds statement for 19x5.

E18–3. The following selected transactions occurred in Weston Company during the past year:

a. Collected $60,000 in accounts receivable from customers.

b. Sold long-term investments for $120,000 that had cost $100,000.

c. Declared a cash dividend, $18,000.

d. Reported net income, $75,000.

e. Sold 1,000 shares of $50 par common stock for $90 per share.

f. Purchased $80,000 in inventory on account.

g. Purchased equipment at a cost of $40,000.

h. Declared and issued a 10 percent stock dividend in common on common.

i. Reclassified $30,000 in long-term debt (due within the next year) from a long-term liability status to a current liability status.

j. Deducted $20,000 in depreciation expense on the income statement.

k. Paid the cash dividend in *(c)*.

l. Sold for $150,000 a building that had an original cost of $210,000 and on which there was accumulated depreciation of $60,000.

m. Retired fully depreciated equipment that had an original cost of $25,000. (The equipment had no resale value.)

796

n. Issued 800 shares of $50 par value common stock in exchange for land.

o. Repurchased and retired $45,000 in bonds payable that were not due for three years.

The company is in the process of preparing a funds statement for the year and needs help in classifying the items above.

Required: Prepare an answer sheet with the following column headings:

	Working capital		
Transaction	Source	Use	No effect

List transactions *(a)* through *(o)* in the "Transaction" column on your answer sheet. For each transaction, place an *X* in the appropriate column to indicate whether the transaction resulted in a source of working capital, a use of working capital, or had no effect on working capital.

E18–4. Comparative financial statement data for Holly Company are given below:

	December 31	
	19x8	19x7
Cash.	$ 4	$ 10
Accounts receivable, net.	36	30
Inventory	70	61
Plant and equipment	200	179
Accumulated depreciation	(40)	(30)
Total assets	$270	$250
Accounts payable	$ 45	$ 42
Common stock	75	70
Retained earnings	150	138
Total liabilities and stockholders' equity	$270	$250

For 19x8, the company reported net income as follows:

Sales.	$300
Cost of goods sold	200
Gross margin	100
Less operating expenses	80
Net income.	$ 20

Dividends of $8 were declared and paid during 19x8. Depreciation expense for the year was $10.

Required: Prepare a cash flow statement for 19x8, showing the reason(s) for the decrease in cash for the year.

E18–5. The following information has been extracted from the annual reports of Trident Company:

	December 31	
	19x2	**19x1**
Plant and equipment.	$50,000	$38,000
Accumulated depreciation—plant and equipment	21,000	20,000
Net income (loss).	(5,000)	6,000
Depreciation expense	6,000	4,500
Goodwill amortization	2,000	2,000

During 19x2, the company sold equipment that had an original cost of $8,000 for its book value of $3,000.

Required:
1. For 19x2, compute the funds provided by operations. Define funds as working capital.
2. For 19x2, compute the plant and equipment purchases.

E18–6. The following transactions occurred during the past year in Gable Company:

a. Net income reported, $80,000.
b. Accounts receivable collected, $200,000.
c. Common stock issued for cash, $50,000.
d. Equipment purchased for cash, $90,000.
e. Payments made to suppliers on account, $150,000.
f. Preferred stock converted into common stock, $100,000.
g. Marketable securities sold for cash, $35,000.

Required: Put the following column headings on your answer sheet:

	Working capital			Cash		
Transaction	**Source**	**Use**	**No effect**	**Source**	**Use**	**No effect**

List the transactions above in the "Transaction" column. Then, for each transaction, place an *X* in the appropriate column to indicate the effect of the transaction on *both* working capital and cash.

E18–7. Below are selected accounts from Texon Company's general ledger:

Equipment		Debit	Credit	Balance
19x3				
Jan. 1	Balance brought forward			800,000
July 6	Purchase of new machine.	175,000		975,000
Oct. 8	Retirement of fully depreciated			
	equipment		50,000	925,000

Accumulated Depreciation— Equipment		Debit	Credit	Balance
19x3				
Jan. 1	Balance brought forward			450,000
Oct. 8	Retirement of fully depreciated			
	equipment	50,000		400,000
Dec.31	Depreciation expense for the year . .		80,000	480,000

Common Stock

19x3			
Jan. 1	Balance brought forward		250,000
May 12	Sale of 2,000 shares	100,000	350,000
Nov. 4	Stock dividend distributed	40,000	390,000

Retained Earnings

19x3			
Jan. 1	Balance brought forward		600,000
July 1	Cash dividends declared—preferred stock	60,000	540,000
Nov. 4	Stock dividends declared—common stock	40,000	500,000
Dec. 31	Net income for 19x3.	135,000	635,000

The following additional information is available:

a. There were no other changes in noncurrent balance sheet accounts during the year.

b. Working capital increased by $80,000 during 19x3.

Required: Prepare a funds statement for the company for 19x3 by analyzing the changes in the noncurrent accounts given above.

E18–8. (Appendix)   Refer to the data for Holly Company in Exercise 18–4.

Required: 1. Adjust the company's income statement to a cash basis. Use the format shown in Exhibit 18–16 in the text.

2. Prepare a cash flow statement for 19x8. Use the format shown in Exhibit 18–17 in the text.

E18–9. (Appendix)   Hardy Company's income statement for the current year is given below:

HARDY COMPANY
Income Statement
For the Year Ended December 31, 19x8

Sales	$1,000,000
Less cost of goods sold	600,000
Gross margin.	400,000
Less operating expenses.	250,000*
Income before taxes	150,000
Less income taxes	60,000
Net income	$ 90,000

* Includes $40,000 depreciation.

Amounts from selected balance sheet accounts follow:

	January 1, 19x8	December 31, 19x8
Accounts Receivable.	$100,000	$150,000
Inventory	200,000	300,000
Prepaid Expenses.	9,000	18,000
Accounts Payable.	180,000	250,000
Accrued Liabilities.	40,000	30,000
Income Taxes Payable	21,000	16,000
Deferred Income Taxes	36,000	50,000

Required: Adjust the company's income statement to a cash basis. (Use the format shown in Exhibit 18–16.) Show all computations.

PROBLEMS

P18–10.   **Funds statement without working papers.**   Comparative financial statements for Eaton Company follow:

EATON COMPANY
Balance Sheets
December 31, 19x4 and 19x5

	19x5	19x4
Assets		
Cash.	$ 3	$ 1
Accounts receivable	6	3
Inventory	10	14
Long-term investments.	7	5
Equipment	15	10
Accumulated depreciation	(5)	(3)
Land	9	10
Total assets	$45	$40
Equities		
Accounts payable	$ 7	$ 4
Accrued liabilities	2	3
Bonds payable	8	11
Common stock	12	9
Retained earnings	16	13
Total equities	$45	$40

EATON COMPANY
Income Statements
For the Years Ended December 31, 19x4 and 19x5

	19x5	19x4
Sales	$150	$100
Cost of goods sold	90	60
Gross margin	60	40
Operating expenses*	53	35
Net income	$ 7	$ 5

* Includes $2 depreciation expense each year.

The company paid $4 in cash dividends during the year.

Required: 1. Prepare an analysis of working capital for 19x5.
           2. Prepare a funds statement for 19x5.

P18–11.   **Cash flow statement without working papers.**   Refer to the financial statement data for Eaton Company in Problem 18–10.

Required: Prepare a cash flow statement for Eaton Company for 19x5.

P18–12. **Cash flow statement without working papers.** (Appendix) Refer to the financial statement data for Eaton Company in Problem 18–10.

Required:
1. Adjust the income statement for 19x5 to a cash basis. (Use the format shown in Exhibit 18–16 in the Appendix.)
2. Using the data from (1) and other data from the problem as needed, prepare a cash flow statement for the company for 19x5. (Use the format shown in Exhibit 18–17 in the Appendix.)

P18–13. **Funds statement without working papers.** Foxboro Company's bond indenture agreement requires that the company maintain a working capital balance at least equal to the amount of bonds outstanding at any point in time. Accordingly, the company monitors its working capital position with considerable care. Selected information on the company is given below:

a. Balance sheet accounts at the end of the current and preceding year:

	Current year	Preceding year
Cash	$ 4,500	$ 12,000
Accounts receivable	17,000	9,500
Inventory	36,500	25,000
Prepaid expenses	1,500	3,500
Long-term investments	10,000	15,000
Plant and equipment	185,000	160,000
Total	$254,500	$225,000
Accumulated depreciation	$ 50,000	$ 38,000
Accounts payable	26,500	22,000
Accrued liabilities	3,000	4,500
Bonds payable, 10%.	30,000	15,000
Deferred income taxes	14,000	10,000
Common stock, $5 par	100,000	112,500
Retained earnings	31,000	23,000
Total	$254,500	$225,000

b. The company's income statement for the current year:

FOXBORO COMPANY
Income Statement
For the Current Year

Sales	$250,000
Cost of goods sold	180,000
Gross margin	70,000
Operating expenses	45,000
Income before taxes	25,000
Income tax expense	10,000
Net income	$ 15,000

c. The company paid $7,000 in cash dividends during the current year.
d. There were no sales or retirements of plant and equipment during the current year.

Required: 1. Prepare an analysis of changes in working capital for the current year.
2. Prepare a funds statement for the current year.
3. By how much (if any) can the company's working capital decline over the next year without violating the terms of the bond agreement?

P18–14. **Cash flow statement without working papers.**   Refer to the data for Foxboro Company contained in Problem 18–13. M. J. Perry, president of Foxboro Company, considers $8,000 to be a minimum cash balance for operating purposes. As can be seen from the balance sheet data, only $4,500 in cash was available at the end of the current year. The sharp decline in cash is puzzling to Mr. Perry, particularly in view of the fact that working capital is up and the company had a good net income showing for the year.

Required: 1. Prepare a cash flow statement for the current year.
2. Explain to the president the chief cause(s) for the decline in the company's cash position.

P18–15. **Cash flow statement without working papers.**   (Appendix)   Refer to the data for Foxboro Company contained in Problem 18–13. The company's executive committee is pleased that working capital has increased over the last year and that profits are strong. Considerable uneasiness has been expressed about the company's cash position, however, since the Cash account has declined by some $7,500 over the past year.

Required: 1. Adjust the current year's income statement to a cash basis. (Use the format shown in Exhibit 18–16 in the Appendix.)
2. Using the data from (1) and other data from the problem as needed, prepare a cash flow statement for the current year. (Use the format shown in Exhibit 18–17 in the Appendix.)
3. Explain to the executive committee the chief reasons for the sharp decline in cash during the year.

P18–16. **Funds statement without working papers.**   Comparative balance sheets for Allied Company for the two preceding years and the company's income statement for 19x2 are presented below:

ALLIED COMPANY
Balance Sheets
December 31, 19x1 and 19x2

	19x2	19x1
Assets		
Current assets:		
Cash	$ 61,000	$ 70,000
Accounts receivable	184,000	163,000
Inventory.	230,000	248,000
Total current assets	475,000	481,000
Long-term investments	30,000	49,000
Property and equipment	615,000	510,000
Less accumulated depreciation	270,000	240,000
Net property and equipment	345,000	270,000
Total assets	$850,000	$800,000

Liabilities and Stockholders' Equity

Current liabilities:		
Accounts payable.	$200,000	$190,000
Accrued liabilities.	16,000	21,000
Total current liabilities	216,000	211,000
Bonds payable, 12%	90,000	50,000
Total liabilities	306,000	261,000
Stockholders' equity:		
Common stock.	300,000	350,000
Retained earnings	244,000	189,000
Total stockholders' equity	544,000	539,000
Total liabilities and stockholders' equity	$850,000	$800,000

ALLIED COMPANY
Income Statement
For the Year Ended December 31, 19x2

Sales	$1,000,000
Cost of goods sold	600,000
Gross margin	400,000
Operating expenses	320,000
Net income	$ 80,000

The following additional information is available for 19x2:

a. There were no retirements or sales of property and equipment during the year.
b. The company paid cash dividends of $25,000 during the year.

Required: 1. Prepare an analysis of changes in working capital for 19x2.
2. Prepare a funds statement for 19x2.

P18–17. **Cash flow statement without working papers.** Refer to the data for Allied Company in Problem 18–16. As shown by the comparative balance sheets, the company's cash account declined somewhat during 19x2. The president doesn't understand why the cash account declined, since the company issued a large amount of bonds during the year and also sold some long-term investments in order to strengthen the cash position.

Required: 1. Prepare a cash flow statement for 19x2.
2. Explain to the president why the cash account declined during 19x2.

P18–18. **Cash flow statement without working papers.** (Appendix) Refer to the data for Allied Company in Problem 18–16. The president would like to know how much cash was generated by operations during 19x2, and he would also like to know the impact on the Cash account of the financing and investing activities in which the company was involved during 19x2.

Required: 1. Adjust the 19x2 income statement to a cash basis. (Use the format shown in Exhibit 18–16 in the Appendix.)
2. Prepare a cash flow statement for 19x2. (Use the format shown in Exhibit 18–17 in the Appendix.)

P18–19. **Funds statement.** Aquatech, Inc., is a supplier of water purification equipment for home and commercial use. The company is in an aggressive expansion program and will continue to expand if adequate financing can be obtained from its bank.

The company's balance sheets for the last two years follow:

AQUATECH, INC.
Balance Sheets
December 31, 19x5 and 19x6

	19x6	19x5
Assets		
Current assets:		
Cash	$ (9,000)	$ 21,000
Accounts receivable, net	140,000	100,000
Inventory	300,000	250,000
Prepaid expenses	7,000	9,000
Total current assets	438,000	380,000
Plant and equipment	700,000	620,000
Less accumulated depreciation	180,000	150,000
Net plant and equipment	520,000	470,000
Goodwill	42,000	50,000
Total assets	$1,000,000	$900,000
Liabilities and Stockholders' Equity		
Current liabilities:		
Accounts payable	$ 190,000	$163,000
Accrued liabilities	10,000	17,000
Total current liabilities	200,000	180,000
Long term debt	100,000	90,000
Stockholders' equity:		
Common stock	300,000	285,000
Retained earnings	400,000	345,000
Total stockholders' equity	700,000	630,000
Total liabilities and stockholders' equity	$1,000,000	$900,000

The company's income statement for 19x6 is given below:

AQUATECH, INC.
Income Statement
For the Year Ended December 31, 19x6

Sales	$1,500,000
Cost of goods sold	900,000
Gross margin	600,000
Operating expenses	510,000
Net income	$ 90,000

The following additional information is available for 19x6:

a. Equipment that had cost $60,000 new and on which there was accumulated depreciation of $42,000 was sold for its book value of $18,000.
b. The goodwill is being amortized against earnings.
c. The company declared and paid $35,000 in cash dividends.

The company's bank has requested that it be provided with a balance sheet, an income statement, and a funds statement in support of the company's request for additional long-term financing.

Required:
1. Prepare an analysis of changes in working capital for 19x6.
2. Prepare T-account working papers for a funds statement.
3. Prepare a funds statement for 19x6.
4. As the company's banker, what additional information would you want relating to the company's activities during 19x6?

P18–20. **Cash flow statement.** Refer to the data for Aquatech, Inc., in Problem 18–19. After seeing the overdraft in Aquatech's cash account, the company's bank asked for a cash flow statement in order to determine why cash dropped so sharply during the year.

Required:
1. Prepare T-account working papers for a cash flow statement.
2. Prepare a cash flow statement for 19x6.
3. Write a brief memo to the bank explaining the chief causes of the decrease in cash during the year.

P18–21. **Cash flow statement.** (Appendix) Refer to the data for Aquatech, Inc., in Problem 18–19. Rafael Sanchez, president of Aquatech, was surprised to see that the company's Cash account was overdrawn. After studying the statements for a while, he said, "There's obviously something wrong here. We reported a healthy profit for the year, and our working capital position has improved. That Cash account couldn't be overdrawn unless someone has his hand in the till."

Assume that you are the chief financial officer of Aquatech, Inc., and that it is your responsibility to explain to Mr. Sanchez what happened to the company's cash during 19x6.

Required:
1. Prepare T-account working papers for a cash flow statement. (Use the working paper format illustrated in Exhibit 18–18 in the Appendix.)
2. Prepare a cash flow statement for 19x6. (Use the format shown in Exhibit 18–17 in the Appendix.)
3. Write a brief memo to Mr. Sanchez explaining the chief causes of the decrease in cash during the year.

P18–22. **Funds statement.** Marcroft Company had a poor year during 19x5. The company suffered a net loss for the year and saw its current ratio slip from 2.5 to only 1.9. The drop in the current ratio is of particular concern to management, since substantial long-term financing was obtained during the year to bolster the company's working capital position. With the low current ratio, the company may have difficulty in obtaining additional financing if it should be needed during the current year.

Comparative balance sheets for the last two years are given below:

MARCROFT COMPANY
Balance Sheets
December 31, 19x4 and 19x5

	19x5	19x4
Assets		
Current assets:		
Cash	$ 108,000	$ 60,000
Accounts receivable	310,000	270,000
Inventory	530,000	525,000
Prepaid expenses.	12,000	15,000
Total current assets	960,000	870,000
Long-term investments	72,000	45,000
Plant and equipment	1,840,000	1,710,000
Less accumulated depreciation	432,000	395,000
Net plant and equipment	1,408,000	1,315,000
Goodwill.	60,000	70,000
Total assets	$2,500,000	$2,300,000
Liabilities and Stockholders' Equity		
Current liabilities:		
Accounts payable.	$ 470,000	$ 300,000
Accrued liabilities	30,000	50,000
Total current liabilities	500,000	350,000
Bonds payable	650,000	400,000
Stockholders' equity:		
Common stock, $100 par	350,000	370,000
Retained earnings	1,000,000	1,100,000
Total stockholders' equity	1,350,000	1,550,000
Total liabilities and stockholders' equity	$2,500,000	$2,300,000
Current ratio	1.9 to 1	2.5 to 1

The company's income statement for 19x5 follows:

MARCROFT COMPANY
Income Statement
For the Year Ended December 31, 19x5

Sales.	$4,500,000
Cost of goods sold	2,630,000
Gross margin	1,870,000
Operating expenses.	1,950,000
Net loss	$ (80,000)

The following additional information is available for the year:

a. The company has the longest unbroken dividend record in its industry. To maintain this record, cash dividends of $90,000 were declared and paid during the year.

b. Equipment with an original cost of $170,000, and on which there was accumulated depreciation of $163,000, was sold during the year for its book value.

c. During the year, the company repurchased the stock of a dissident stockholder. The stockholder was paid $30,000 for 200 shares of $100 par value stock. The excess over par value was charged to the Retained Earnings account.

d. The goodwill is being amortized against earnings.

Management would like a complete analysis of working capital in order to determine the reason for the drop in the current ratio.

Required:
1. Prepare an analysis of changes in working capital.
2. Prepare T-account working papers for a funds statement.
3. Prepare a funds statement for 19x5 in good form.
4. Explain to management the chief causes of the decrease in working capital during 19x5.

P18–23. **Cash flow statement.** Refer to the financial statements for Marcroft company in Problem 18–22. Linda Allen, president of Marcroft Company, is elated that the company's cash position improved during the year, although she is puzzled as to why it happened. Ms. Allen observed, "With our $80,000 operating loss, our continued payment of dividends, and our large equipment purchases, I was sure we would end the year with almost nothing in the bank. But I find our cash position stronger than it has ever been. I would like a detailed analysis of exactly what happened in the Cash account during the year."

Required:
1. Prepare T-account working papers for a cash flow statement.
2. Prepare a cash flow statement for 19x5 in good form.
3. Write a brief memo to Ms. Allen explaining the chief causes of the increase in cash during the year.

P18–24. **Cash flow statement.** (Appendix)   See the data for Marcroft Company in Problem 18–22. Frank Shaw, a stockholder, has just received a copy of Marcroft Company's 19x5 annual report. After studying the statements in the report for a few moments, he commented, "There's something wrong here. The company lost $80,000 during 19x5, and it paid $90,000 in cash dividends. Yet the Cash account increased by $48,000 during the year. It seems to me that the Cash account should have decreased."

Required:
1. Prepare T-account working papers for a cash flow statement. (Use the working paper format illustrated in Exhibit 18–18 in the Appendix.)
2. Prepare a cash flow statement for 19x6. (Use the format shown in Exhibit 18–17 in the Appendix.)
3. Write a brief explanation as to why the Cash account increased during the year.

P18–25. **Funds statement.** "What could have happened?" asked Erik Lamar, president of Lamar Industries. "Our current ratio is below 2.0 to 1 for the first time in our history."

"I'm baffled," replied Shari Smith, executive vice president. "We did construct that new West Coast plant, but profits and our $450,000 sale of common stock should have covered that easily. We also acquired another block of stock in our chemical subsidiary, but that didn't cost us a dime of cash, since we exchanged $200,000 of our own preferred stock for it."

"Well, *something* happened," replied Mr. Lamar. "And we had better correct it quickly, or we'll put that new bond offering in jeopardy that we have planned for next summer."

"I agree," said Ms. Smith. "I'll have accounting do a complete analysis of working capital to see if we can pinpoint the problem, and then I'll bring the analysis to the next executive committee meeting."

In order to perform the analysis of working capital, accounting has gathered the following information:

a. Balances from the company's general ledger for the current and preceding year are given below:

	November 30	
	19x8	19x7
Debits		
Cash.	$ 340,000	$ 800,000
Accounts receivable	875,000	850,000
Inventory	1,750,000	1,100,000
Prepaid expenses	25,000	45,000
Investments in subsidiaries	650,000	450,000
Property and equipment	3,250,000	2,100,000
Goodwill	410,000	480,000
Total	$7,300,000	$5,825,000
Credits		
Accumulated depreciation	$ 850,000	$ 720,000
Accounts payable	1,340,000	825,000
Accrued liabilities	110,000	130,000
Dividends payable—preferred stock	100,000	–0–
Notes payable—long term	400,000	750,000
Deferred income taxes	350,000	300,000
Preferred stock	850,000	650,000
Common stock	1,500,000	1,000,000
Retained earnings	1,800,000	1,450,000
Total	$7,300,000	$5,825,000
Current ratio	1.9 to 1	2.9 to 1

b. The company's income statement for the current year follows:

LAMAR INDUSTRIES
Income Statement
For the Year Ended November 30, 19x8

Sales		$10,000,000
Less cost of goods sold.		6,000,000
Gross margin		4,000,000
Less operating expenses:		
Salaries.	$ 800,000	
Advertising	1,250,000	
Depreciation	200,000	
Amortization of goodwill	70,000	
Other expenses	230,000	2,550,000
Net operating income.		1,450,000
Less income taxes:		
Current	600,000	
Deferred	50,000	650,000
Net income		$ 800,000

c. During the year, $400,000 in cash dividends were declared.

d. Equipment that had cost $80,000 new, and on which there was accumulated depreciation of $50,000, was sold for its book value.

e. Fully depreciated equipment that had cost $20,000 new was scrapped during the year.

f. A $50,000 stock dividend in common stock was declared and distributed to common stockholders.

Required:
1. Prepare an analysis of changes in working capital for the year ended November 30, 19x8.
2. Prepare T-account working papers for a funds statement.
3. Prepare a funds statement for the year ended November 30, 19x8.
4. Prepare a brief explanation as to why working capital declined during the year.

P18–26. **Funds statement.** During the most recent year, 19x2, Alcorn Products reported a net income in excess of $1,000,000 for the first time in its history. The company's board of directors is especially pleased, since losses had been reported in some earlier years. Comparative income statements for the last two years are given below:

ALCORN PRODUCTS
Income Statements
For the Years Ended June 30, 19x1 and 19x2

	19x2	19x1
Sales	$12,000,000	$9,000,000
Cost of goods sold	7,200,000	5,400,000
Gross margin	4,800,000	3,600,000
Operating expenses	3,000,000	2,600,000
Net income before taxes	1,800,000	1,000,000
Income taxes (40%)	720,000	400,000
Net income	$ 1,080,000	$ 600,000

During the past year, the president of Alcorn Products initiated an aggressive expansion program that allowed the company to enter several new markets. In order to continue this expansion program, the company intends to issue a large amount of bonded debt. The cash received from the sale of these bonds will be used to retire all of the long-term notes currently outstanding, as well as provide for construction of additional facilities. Comparative balance sheet data for the last two years are shown on the next page.

Although the company's board of directors agrees with the expansion program, it believes that the company is expanding too rapidly, as evidenced by the sharp drop in the current ratio during the last year (see the company's balance sheets). As one director stated, "Our working capital situation must be precarious to have a current ratio of only 1.8 to 1."

The following additional information is available for 19x2:

a. Cash dividends declared and paid during the year totaled $100,000.

b. A stock dividend totaling $350,000 was declared and issued during the year.

c. Equipment that had an original cost of $180,000, and on which there was accumulated depreciation of $100,000, was sold during the year for its book value. This was the only sale or retirement of property during the year.

ALCORN PRODUCTS
Balance Sheets
June 30, 19x1 and 19x2

	19x2	19x1
Assets		
Current assets:		
Cash	$ 380,000	$ 410,000
Accounts receivable	950,000	680,000
Inventory.	1,860,000	1,240,000
Prepaid expenses.	50,000	70,000
Total current assets	3,240,000	2,400,000
Investment in affiliated companies	470,000	300,000
Property and equipment	6,500,000	5,200,000
Less accumulated depreciation	2,300,000	2,000,000
Net property and equipment	4,200,000	3,200,000
Goodwill.	90,000	100,000
Total assets	$8,000,000	$6,000,000
Liabilities and Stockholders' Equity		
Current liabilities:		
Accounts payable.	$1,040,000	$ 680,000
Accrued liabilities	260,000	320,000
Current portion—long-term notes	500,000	—
Total current liabilities	1,800,000	1,000,000
Long-term notes	250,000	750,000
Deferred income taxes.	600,000	530,000
Stockholders' equity:		
Common stock, no par	3,000,000	2,000,000
Retained earnings	2,350,000	1,720,000
Total stockholders' equity	5,350,000	3,720,000
Total liabilities and stockholders' equity . . .	$8,000,000	$6,000,000
Current ratio	1.8 to 1	2.4 to 1

d. A warehouse was acquired during the year in exchange for some of the company's common stock. The stock was valued at $650,000.

e. The goodwill is being amortized against earnings.

f. Some $500,000 in long-term notes were reclassified during the year to a current liability status since these notes will fall due during 19x3.

The chairman of the board of directors has asked you to prepare an analysis showing what happened to the company's working capital during the year.

Required: 1. Prepare an analysis of changes in working capital for 19x2.
2. Prepare T-account working papers for a funds statement.
3. Prepare a funds statement for 19x2 in good form.
4. Based on your work above, do you agree that the company's working capital situation is "precarious"? Explain.

Index

This book has been set VideoComp in 10 and 9 point Times Roman, leaded 2 points. Part and chapter numbers are 48 point Times Roman, part titles are 36 point Times Roman, and chapter titles are 24 point Times Roman. The size of the type page is 36 by 48 picas.